Lesikar's Business Communication

CONNECTING IN A DIGITAL WORLD

TWELFTH EDITION

Kathryn Rentz

UNIVERSITY OF CINCINNATI

Marie E. Flatley

SAN DIEGO STATE UNIVERSITY

Paula Lentz

UNIVERSITY OF WISCONSIN–EAU CLAIRE

McGraw-Hill
Irwin

LESIKAR'S BUSINESS COMMUNICATION: CONNECTING IN A DIGITAL WORLD
Published by McGraw-Hill/Irwin, a business unit of The McGraw-Hill Companies, Inc., 1221 Avenue of the Americas, New York, NY, 10020. Copyright © 2011, 2008, 2005, 2002, 1999, 1996, 1993, 1991, 1989, 1984, 1980, 1976 by The McGraw-Hill Companies, Inc. All rights reserved. No part of this publication may be reproduced or distributed in any form or by any means, or stored in a database or retrieval system, without the prior written consent of The McGraw-Hill Companies, Inc., including, but not limited to, in any network or other electronic storage or transmission, or broadcast for distance learning.

Some ancillaries, including electronic and print components, may not be available to customers outside the United States.

This book is printed on acid-free paper.

1 2 3 4 5 6 7 8 9 0 WVR/WVR 1 0 9 8 7 6 5 4 3 2 1 0

ISBN: 978-0-07-337779-7
MHID: 0-07-337779-1

Vice president and editor-in-chief: *Brent Gordon*
Publisher: *Paul Ducham*
Director of development: *Ann Torbert*
Executive editor: *John Weimeister*
Development editor: *Kelly I. Pekelder*
Vice president and director of marketing: *Robin J. Zwettler*
Marketing manager: *Katie Mergen*
Vice president of editing, design and production: *Sesha Bolisetty*
Senior project manager: *Harvey Yep*
Lead production supervisor: *Michael R. McCormick*
Designer: *Cara Hawthorne, Cara David DESIGN*
Senior photo research coordinator: *Lori Kramer*
Photo researcher: *PoYee Oster*
Media project manager: *Cathy L. Tepper*
Cover images: *(clockwise, from top left) DAL, DAL, DAL, Veer, DAL, Veer, Getty, Getty*
Typeface: *10.5/12 Times Roman*
Compositor: *MPS Limited, A Macmillan Company*
Printer: *Worldcolor*

Library of Congress Cataloging-in-Publication Data

Rentz, Kathryn.
    Lesikar's business communication : connecting in a digital world / Kathryn Rentz, Marie
E. Flatley, Paula Lentz.—12th ed.
        p. cm.
    Rev. ed. of: Business communication : making connections in a digital world / Raymond
V. Lesikar, Marie E. Flatley, Kathryn Rentz. 11th ed.
    Includes index.
    ISBN-13: 978-0-07-337779-7 (alk. paper)
    ISBN-10: 0-07-337779-1 (alk. paper)
    1. Commercial correspondence. 2. English language—Business English. 3. Business
communication. I. Flatley, Marie Elizabeth. II. Lentz, Paula. III. Lesikar, Raymond Vincent.
Business communication. IV. Title.
    HF5721.L37 2011
    651.7—dc22   2009047275

www.mhhe.com

We gratefully dedicate this book to Ray Lesikar.

From the first edition in 1976 through the 11th edition in 2008, *Business Communication* has helped students learn the elements of effective business communication. All editions have remained true to Ray's core principles: to be current, to be clear, and to be courteous. All editions have used real-world examples that emphasize the importance of adapting the message to the audience. And all have emphasized the importance of communicating ethically.

Ray brought a wealth of business experience to the book. He consulted for and trained business executives in over 40 companies, including Exxon, Kaiser Aluminum, Dow Chemical, Ford, Sears, and many more. He also worked in China with Chinese scholars on business communication and conducted numerous training programs for the U.S. Department of Agriculture and the Veterans Administration.

In addition, he has mentored many other scholars during his teaching and administrative work at The University of Texas at Austin, Louisiana State University, Texas Christian University, and the University of North Texas. During these years he served as the major professor for 23 recipients of the Ph.D. degree, repeatedly receiving high teaching evaluations including one class that rated him a perfect 4.0 (on a scale of 1 to 4).

Ray's professional leadership also extends to the Association for Business Communication (ABC), the foremost professional society for business communication teachers. Ever since attending his first meeting of the Association in 1948, he has helped shape the field. He has served in many leadership roles, including president and numerous other capacities, as well as publishing in journals. He has been named both a Fellow and Distinguished Member of the Association, and he continues to support the field's scholarly activities by sponsoring the award for best article in the *Journal of Business Communication*.

But while Ray has shown he is the ultimate professional, he is also deeply respected for his personal qualities. A group of his doctoral students once honored him at a meeting, luring him to a suite and then surprising him with applause, singing, testimonials, and expressions of gratitude. Similarly, McGraw-Hill/Irwin honored him by bringing together many of the people he had worked with in different capacities on some of his six titles, which have had over 35 editions. The testimonials heard that night, too, supported him as a truly great man both personally and professionally.

We are honored to continue Ray's work with this 12th edition of *Business Communication*, and we join many, many others in saying "Thank you."

—Kathryn Rentz
Marie Flatley
Paula Lentz

Dr. Kathryn Rentz

Dr. Kathryn Rentz is a Professor of English at the University of Cincinnati. She taught her first business writing class as a doctoral student at the University of Illinois at Urbana–Champaign in the early 1980s and has been teaching workplace writing ever since. She helped establish the University of Cincinnati's professional writing program and has served as its coordinator. She has also won the English Department's teaching award, directed the department's graduate program, and helped direct the composition program.

Dr. Rentz's affiliation with the Association for Business Communication goes back to her beginnings as a business writing teacher. She has performed many roles for the ABC, including serving on the board of directors and chairing the publications board. She served two terms as an Associate Editor of the *Journal of Business Communication* and was Interim Editor from 2000–2001, for which she won the Francis W. Weeks Award of Merit. In 2008 she won the ABC's Meada Gibbs Outstanding Teacher Award.

Dr. Rentz has published articles on business communication pedagogy and research in such journals as *Business Communication Quarterly,* the *Journal of Business Communication, Technical Communication Quarterly,* and the *Journal of Business and Technical Communication.* She has participated in many professional meetings and seminars over the years and is always learning from her colleagues and her students.

Dr. Marie E. Flatley

Dr. Marie E. Flatley is a Professor Emerita at San Diego State University in the Management Information Systems Department where she still teaches various courses in business communication. Additionally, she has served as a Fellow at the university's Center for Teaching and Learning and as a Qualcomm Fellow in the pICT (people, Information, Communication, and Technology) program. She received her B.B.A., M.A., and Ph.D. from the University of Iowa.

Dr. Flatley is active in numerous professional organizations, including the Association for Business Communication, the California Business Education Association, Delta Pi Epsilon, and the National Business Education Association. She has served as president of the Association for Business Communication and is a Distinguished Member and Fellow of the Association. The California Business Education Association recently named her Business Educator of the Year for the senior college/university level. Additionally, she has served as an editorial board member for the *Delta Pi Epsilon Journal,* associate editor for the *Journal of Business Communication,* and editor for the *NABTE Review.* She has also served as a reviewer and member of the editorial review board for the *Journal of Education for Business.*

Her current research interests involve using technology to assist with the communication process. Her research investigates the effective use of new technologies for improved communication. These technologies include cloud computing and web services such as blogging and micro-blogging as well as writing and presenting tools.

Dr. Paula Lentz

Dr. Paula Lentz is a Senior Lecturer in the Department of Business Communication at the University of Wisconsin–Eau Claire. She teaches Business Writing, Business Writing II, and Advanced Business Writing. She is also a developer and coordinator of the department's Business Writing Fundamentals Program, which ensures that students have basic writing skills essential for success in their first business writing course. In addition, she chaired the College of Business's Writing Task Force, which developed a college-wide policy for assessing students' writing skills as part of their grade on any writing assignment in any business class. Extracurricular activities include serving as the faculty advisor for UW–Eau Claire's student chapter of the International Association of Business Communicators.

Dr. Lentz is particularly interested in qualitative research that explores narratives and organizational cultures, genre theory, and writing pedagogy in online environments. She has published in such journals as *Academy of Educational Leadership Journal, Wisconsin Business Education Association Journal, Equal Opportunities International,* and *Qualitative Research in Organizations and Management.* She has also presented her research at several national and regional conferences, including those of the Association for Business Communication and Academy of Management.

Prior to becoming a full-time academic, she worked as a technical writer and publications editor. She continues to do freelance editing and provides consulting and writing services for several organizations. She received a B.A. from Coe College, an M.A. from UW–Eau Claire, and a Ph.D. in Rhetoric and Scientific and Technical Communication from the University of Minnesota.

This revision of Ray Lesikar's classic textbook takes the solid foundational principles of the previous 11 editions and applies them to business contexts in the 21st century. While continuing to focus on careful problem analysis, adaptation of the message to the audience, and the development of positive human relations, this edition discusses current challenges for business communicators and gives students practice meeting those challenges. Toward this end, the book maintains the realism, technological currency, and pedagogical effectiveness for which it has become well known and respected.

REALISTIC

The authors are an interdisciplinary team with diverse training and experience who have worked to bring you the subject matter authoritatively from a thorough review of the field. In addition to being teachers, scholars, and leaders themselves, they have integrated their ideas with information from other researchers and practitioners in the mainstream of business communication, providing the enhanced value of multiple perspectives.

Throughout the text are realistic examples of current business problems and practices. You will find that business information is integrated into examples, message models, reports, text boxes, and end-of-chapter questions, problems, and cases. The extensive range of cases covers both internal and external communication as well as a wide variety of business environments. Furthermore, the cases cover a broad spectrum of challenges that students are likely to find in the workplace—from routine, everyday cases to complex scenarios requiring research and extensive analysis.

TECHNOLOGICALLY CURRENT

The Internet and other communication technologies continue to change the way business does business. From email and text messages to social networking and online collaboration, students need to know their options for communicating, whether across the office or around the globe. The text discusses all these forms and more. In addition, boxed material introduces students to a wide range of helpful electronic tools, from automatic table-of-contents generators to online translation programs and search engines. Additionally, communication technologies appear in both the textbook cases and the Web cases. We believe these efforts will enable students to get up to speed more quickly and communicate more effectively once they're on the job.

THOROUGH

This textbook is the result of extensive consultation with business communication teachers, dialog with business professionals, and research. It includes sound advice on both writing and speaking, covering the main forms of business communication that students are likely to encounter. It also includes special chapters on cross-cultural communication, correctness, communication-related technologies, and research methods. There is an extensive chapter on using graphics to communicate, and other visual components are discussed throughout the book. Whatever level of students you teach or whatever topics you wish to emphasize, you will find reliable advice, illustrations, and exercises here.

LEARNABLE

As in earlier editions, we worked hard to make the book serve the student in every practical way. Our goal was to make the learning experience easy and interesting. The book's structured problem-solving approach guides students through the analytical process for various kinds of business messages, blending concrete advice with a focus on critical thinking, judgment, and creativity. To support this approach we include the following features, all of which have proved to be highly successful in preceding editions:

Readable writing. The writing is in plain, everyday English—the kind the book instructs the students to use.

Learning objectives. Placed at the beginning of all chapters, clearly worded objectives emphasize the learning goals and are tied in to the chapter summaries and exercises.

Introductory situations. A realistic description of a business scenario introduces the student to each type of business communication, providing context for discussion and examples.

Outlines of messages. To summarize and clarify the instructions for writing the basic message types, an outline of each type follows the discussion.

Margin notes. Summaries of content appear in the margins to help students identify the main points and review text highlights.

Full document illustrations. Well-written models with detailed margin comments are provided for all kinds of documents—text messages, emails, letters, memos, proposals, and short and long reports.

Expert advice and commentary. Communication Matters boxes containing anecdotal and authoritative communication messages add interest and make points throughout the book.

Abundant real business illustrations. Both good and bad examples with explanatory criticisms show the student how to apply the text instructions.

Cartoons. Carefully selected cartoons emphasize key points and add interest.

Photographs. Full-color photographs throughout the text emphasize key points and add interest to content. Teaching captions enhance the textual material.

Computer and Web-based applications. Computer and Web-based applications have been integrated throughout the book wherever appropriate—into such topics as the writing process, collaboration, use of graphics, and research methods.

Computer use suggestions. For students who want to know more about how useful computers can be in business communication, pertinent suggestions appear in Technology in Brief boxes and on the text website.

Chapter summaries by learning objectives. Ending summaries in fast reading outline form and by learning objectives enable students to recall text highlights.

Critical thinking questions. End-of-chapter questions emphasize text concepts and provide material for classroom discussion.

Critical thinking exercises. Challenging exercises test the student's understanding of text content.

Problem-solving cases. Over 130 contemporary, in-depth business cases, for all message and report types, teach students about business contexts and provide a wide range of practice opportunities.

Specialized report topics. A list of research topics by major business discipline is available for teachers who prefer to assign reports in the students' areas of specialization.

Student Resource portion of the Online Learning Center <www.mhhe.com/lesikar12e>. Additional resources are provided on a comprehensive, up-to-date website. Included are online quizzes, PowerPoint slides, Web cases, video cases, an extensive collection of annotated links to relevant websites organized by topic, and more.

TEACHABLE

Perhaps more valuable than anything we can do to help the teacher teach is to help the student learn. The features designed to provide such help are listed above.

But we have developed the following additional materials to help both new and experienced teachers make the most of this book:

Instructor's Resource Manual. The following support material is available for easy use with each lecture:

Sample syllabi and grading systems (rubrics).

Summary teaching notes.

Teaching suggestions with notes for each kind of message.

Discussion guides for the slides.

Answers to end-of-chapter critical thinking questions.

Answers to end-of-chapter critical thinking exercises.

Sample solutions to selected problem-solving cases.

PowerPoint slides. Complete full-chapter slide shows are available for the entire text. These colorful slides provide summaries of key points, additional examples, and examples to critique.

Online videos to accompany Business Communication. These video cases are presented by real businesspeople, focusing on the importance of communication in the workplace. Each segment presents a real business problem for student interpretation and classroom discussions. In addition to being motivational and informative, these video cases give the students practice developing their listening skills. (Contact your McGraw-Hill/Irwin representative for more information.)

Test bank. This comprehensive collection of objective questions covers all chapters.

Computerized testing software. This advanced test generator enables the teacher to build and restructure tests to meet specific preferences.

Instructor resources portion of the Online Learning Center <www.mhhe.com/lesikar12e>. An up-to-date website fully supports the text. It includes a database of cases, cases that entail using Web resources to write solutions, an author-selected collection of annotated links to relevant websites organized by topic, enhanced links for the technology chapter, and other active learning material.

NEW CourseSmart ebook. With CourseSmart, your students can have instant online access to this text as a digital eTextbook. In addition to saving money, they can use online tools like search, highlighting, and note taking. You can use these features as well to emphasize key material and enhance student learning.

Tools and Teaching Tips Blog. This blog, accessible on the instructor's website, will include up-to-date material for lectures and assignments as well as a place to communicate with the authors.

ORGANIZATION OF THE BOOK

Because the reviewers and adopters generally approve of the organization of the book, the structure that has characterized this book through 11 successful editions remains as follows:

Part I is an introduction to business communication. It describes the role of communication in the organization, current challenges for business communicators, and the business communication process.

Part II provides a review of the basic techniques of writing, an analysis of the writing process, and an introduction to business messages. Here the emphasis is on clear writing, the effect of words, and special considerations for each written medium in business communication.

Part III covers the patterns of common message types—positive or neutral, negative, and persuasive—and direct versus indirect structure.

Part IV concentrates on report writing. Although the emphasis is on the shorter reports, the long, analytical report also receives complete coverage.

Part V reviews the oral forms of business communication. Included here are such communication activities as giving presentations as well as participating in meetings, telephoning, dictating, and listening.

Part VI consists of special topic chapters for use in particular classes. The part includes chapters on cross-cultural communication, correctness, technology-assisted communication, and business-research methods.

- Ethical issues are integrated throughout, with particular focus on ethical treatment of the reader and on ethical persuasion.

SPECIAL FEATURES OF THE 12TH EDITION

As with previous editions, we have thoroughly updated this edition for currency and greater usefulness. We expanded coverage wherever we and our reviewers thought it would improve content, and we have also made a few organizational changes. Here are the most significant enhancements:

- Chapter 1 now contextualizes business communication by discussing the main challenges facing business people in the 21st century: explosive growth of communication technologies, increasing globalization, growing diversity in the workplace, and an increased focus on social responsibility.

- In Chapter 5, an audience-analysis checklist has been added to a more detailed discussion of the writing process, and social computing has been added to the discussion of the main forms of business writing.

- In Chapter 6, the section on order acknowledgments now covers other thank-you messages as well, complete with sample messages to illustrate and new problem-solving cases for practice.

- Proposals have been moved to the discussion of persuasive messages and claims have been moved to the discussion of negative messages, making a more logical organization.

- Discussion of short and long reports has been streamlined, now covering the topic in two rather than three chapters. In Chapter 10, the discussion of collaborative report writing has been expanded. In Chapter 11, the sample short report and long report have been replaced with more current real-world illustrations.

- The chapter on formal oral communications now foregrounds oral reports rather than speeches and includes an expanded discussion of PowerPoint slide design and use.

- The cross-cultural communication chapter has been revised to include analytical frameworks from cross-cultural experts, more examples and resources, and more thorough, up-to-date advice.

- Chapter 17, on communication-related technologies, focuses more on electronic tools that can assist students with their authoring efforts. It now includes extensive advice on features in today's word processing programs and on the considerations to take into account when preparing documents for print versus online formats.

- The Businesss Research Methods chapter now features qualitative as well as quantitative methods.

- Appendix E has been thoroughly updated in accordance with the latest edition of the MLA Handbook. It also includes a flowchart to help students identify what kind of source they're trying to cite and what format to use.

Finally, the website has updated online quizzes and new Web-based and video cases.

ACKNOWLEDGMENTS

Any comprehensive work such as this must owe credit to a multitude of people. Certainly, we should acknowledge the contributions of all those in the business communication field who came before us, especially those whose teachings have become a part of our thinking. We are especially indebted to those business communication scholars who have served as reviewers for this and past editions. They truly deserve much of the credit for improvements in this book. It is with a sincere expression of gratitude that we recognize them:

Reviewers of the 11th edition:

Laura Alderson, *University of Memphis*

Carolyn Ashe, *University of Houston—Downtown*

Jean Baird, *Bringham Young University—Idaho*

Jill M. Batson, *Henderson State University*

Kenneth R. Bellinder, *National–Louis University*

Audrey Cohen, *Kingsborough Community College*

Brenda A. Cornelius, *University of Arkansas Community College at Hope*

Linda Di Desidero, *University of Maryland University College*

Michael E. Durkee, *Miramar Community College*

Sean J. Glassberg, *Horry–Georgetown Technical College*

Guillermo A. Hernandez, *De Anza College*

Jean Kapinsky, *Northcentral Technical College*

Jeanette A. Karjala, *Winona State University*

Brian Keliher, *Grossmont College*

Anita Leffel, *The University of Texas at San Antonio*

Nancy K. Legrand, *Southeast Missouri State University*

Jere Littlejohn, *University of Mississippi*

Jeanette S. Martin, *University of Mississippi*

Kenneth R. Mayer, *Cleveland State University*

Andrea Muldoon, *University of Wisconsin—Stout*

Rebecca Pope-Ruark, *Elon University*

Windy Rachal, *Nicholls State University*

Evette W. Richardson, *Norfolk State University*

Heidi Schultz, *University of North Carolina—Chapel Hill*

Mageya R. Sharp, *Cerritos College*

Karen J. Smith, *Columbia Southern University*

Jessica Stoudenmire, *El Camino College*

Traci Thompson, *Kilgore College—Longview*

David A. Victor, *Eastern Michigan University*

Kelly Warren, *Wayland Baptist University*

Bennie J. Wilson, III, *University of Texas at San Antonio*

Robert Zackowski, *Horry Georgetown Technical College*

Reviewers of previous editions:

James J. Balakier, *University of South Dakota*

Lecia Barker, *University of Colorado*

Melissa Barth, *Appalachian State University*

Rathin Basu, *Ferrum College*

Linda Bell, *Reading Area Community College*

Sandra K. Christianson, *National American University*

Sara Cushing, *Piedmont Technical College*

Mary Beth Debs, *University of Cincinnati*

Norma J. Dexter, *Florida State University—Panama City*

Gloria Diemer, *Suffolk County Community College*

Carolyn Embree, *The University of Akron*

Donna Everett, *Morehead State University*

Lu Ann Farrell, *Clinton Community College*

Dale Fike, *Redlands Community College*

Alicen Fiosi, *Lamar University*

Sheryl Fitzpatrick, *Waldorf College*

Fernando Ganivet, *Florida International University*

Glenn Good, *Front Range Community College*

Katherine Gotthardt, *National American University*

Diana Green, *Weber State University*

Frances K. Griffin, *Oklahoma State University*

Susan A. Heller, *Reading Area Community College*

Deborah Holder, *Piedmont Technical College*

Robert Insley, *University of North Texas*

Jane Johansen, *University of Southern Indiana*

Susan King, *Union County College*

Melinda Knight, *University of Rochester*

Marianna Larsen, *Utah State University*

John La Lone, *Tarleton State University—Central Texas*

Robert J. McMahon, *National American University*

Elizabeth Metzger, *University of South Florida*

Richard R. Meza, *Columbia College of Missouri*

R. Wayne Preslar, *Methodist College*

Zane Quible, *Oklahoma State University*

Pamela L. Ramey, *Kent State University*

Lillie A. Robinson, *North Carolina AT&T University*

Janet Sebesy, *Cuyahoga Community College*

Stacey Short, *Northern Illinois University*

Julie Simon, *Clarkson College*

Lisa Gueldenzoph Snyder, *North Carolina AT&T University*

Eric Soares, *California State University, East Bay*

Sandy Thomas, *Kansas City Kansas Community College*

David Ward, *University of Wisconsin—Madison*

Gary T. Ward, *Reedley College*

Karen Schelter Williams, *San Diego Mesa College*

Laura Williams, *Lipscomb University*

In addition, over the life of this book many of our professional colleagues have made a variety of inputs, especially at professional meetings. While we cannot acknowledge these colleagues individually, we are grateful to all of them.

Finally, on our respective home fronts, we acknowledge the support of our loved ones. Kathy acknowledges the support of Dave, Caroline, and Michael Rentz; her sister, Rebecca Horn; and friends in the English Department at the University of Cincinnati. Marie acknowledges her immediate family, friends, and San Diego State University colleagues. Paula acknowledges her husband John and other family members, colleagues at the University of Wisconsin–Eau Claire, and Charles Russell, the high-school English teacher who propelled her toward a writing career. Your support has made this book possible.

Kathryn Rentz
Marie E. Flatley
Paula Lentz

A Quick Look

LESIKAR'S BUSINESS COMMUNICATION by Kathryn Rentz and Marie Flatley (with Paula Lentz) attends to the dynamic, fast-paced, and ever-changing means by which business communication occurs by being the most technologically current and pedagogically effective book in the field. The 12th edition continues to set the standard by incorporating a multitude of real business examples and a thorough treatment of technology-driven business communication.

PART OPENERS

Each section in the book begins with part openers featuring quotes from distinguished business leaders from recognized companies such as Dell Computer and ABC Television. These illustrate for students the importance of business communication skills in the real world.

part two

Fundamentals of Business Writing

2 Adaptation and the Selection of Words

3 Construction of Clear Sentences and Paragraphs

4 Writing for a Positive Effect

With a net worth of around $42 billion, Warren Buffett is ranked by *Forbes* magazine as the second-richest person in the world, after Microsoft cofounder and chairman Bill Gates. Buffett made his first stock purchase at the age of 11, but sold before the stock skyrocketed. This early lesson taught him to study hard and carefully analyze potential investments. The result was the development of one of the world's largest holding companies, Berkshire Hathaway, Inc.

Although best known for his ability to pick stocks, Buffett was honored in 2006 by the National Commission on Writing for America's Families, Schools, and Colleges for writing Berkshire Hathaway's annual report. Buffett writes, "One way or another, you have to project your ideas to other people. Writing isn't necessarily easy. . . . But you get better and better at it, and I encourage everybody to do that."

Warren E. Buffett, CEO of Berkshire Hathaway, Inc.

part four

Fundamentals of Report Writing

10 Basics of Report Writing

11 Types of Business Reports

12 Graphics in Reports and Other Documents

Anne Sweeney, President of Disney Channel Worldwide and President of ABC Cable Networks Group, began her television career at age 19 as a network page and as a researcher studying children who liked *Sesame Street* magazine. The research led her to enroll in Harvard's School of Education, where she learned the benefits of investigation for shaping both television programming and business strategy. Named by *Fortune* magazine as one of the most powerful women in business in 2005, Sweeney considers curiosity to be the most important factor in her success. Research of "tween" viewers helped Disney add one million new subscribers per month for five years.

"We had been hearing from kids from the research we were conducting that there was an age group of kids that felt too old for Nickelodeon and too young for MTV. I'm always really interested in what's missing, so we probed deeper. We looked at a lot of lifestyle information, we looked at how kids spent their days, and at what time they came home from school. We took a very hard look at who they are and what was going on in their lives. [That research] really launched our live-action programming strategy."

Anne Sweeney, President of Disney Channel Worldwide and President of ABC Cable Networks Group

at the 12th Edition

GOOD AND BAD EXAMPLES

Numerous good and bad examples of various business documents—from messages to memos to reports—are featured throughout the text. These writing samples allow students to learn by example. For easy reference, good examples are highlighted with a checkmark and bad examples are denoted by a crossout sign.

THEMATIC BOXES

Each chapter features thematic boxes to highlight and reinforce important topics.

INTRODUCTORY SITUATION

Choosing Words That Communicate

As a means of introducing yourself to business communication, place yourself in a hypothetical situation. You are the entrepreneurial manager of a struggling small business. You work very hard to make certain that all aspects of your business function effectively and efficiently. At the moment your attention is focused generally on the communicating done by your subordinates. Specifically, you are concerned about the communicating of Max Elliott, your assistant manager.

You have before you an email report from Max. Following your instructions, he investigated your company's use of available space. He has summarized his findings in this report. At first glance you are impressed with Max's work. But after reading further, you are not sure just what his investigation has uncovered. Here is a typical paragraph:

In the interest of ensuring maximum utilization of the subterranean components of the building currently not apportioned to operations departments, it is recommended that an evaluation of requisites for storage space be initiated. Subject review should be initiated at the earliest practicable opportunity and should be conducted by administrative personnel not affiliated with operative departments.

Max's problem is altogether too commonplace in business. His words, though properly used, do not communicate quickly and easily. This and the following chapter show you what you can do about writing like this.

INTRODUCTORY SITUATION

Each box presents a realistic business scenario and provides students with a context for the topics discussed in the text.

TECHNOLOGY IN BRIEF

Visuals Help Business Writers Add Interest to Sales Messages

Sales messages—both print and rich email—often include art and animation to increase the visual appeal as well as attract attention to the message. In one recent experiment comparing two types of visual email messages, an HTML and a video message, Holland America found that the video message resulted in a 33 percent higher click-through rate than the HTML mailing. Furthermore, once readers got to the site, the average stay was nine minutes compared to five minutes for the HTML message. Additionally, the video message was cost effective, costing only 20 percent more than the HTML message.*

Today's business writers need not be artists or professional photographers to use good visuals in their documents. Major software programs include bundled art, animation, photographs, and sounds; and scanners and easy-to-use programs are readily available to help writers create customized visuals. Additionally, on the web, writers can find a vast assortment of specialists with products and services to help enhance their sales messages.

Here is a short list of a few websites. You'll find more on the textbook website as well.

- <http://webclipart.about.com/> A rich collection of links to websites for clip art, tutorials, hardware, and software.
- <http://www.fotosearch.com/> A meta search tool for finding professional photographs, illustrations, and videos.
- <http://www.animationfactory.com/en/> A subscription website for a variety of professionally prepared media.
- <http://www.freeaudioclips.com/> A site for free audio clips and links to software tools as well as a good search tool.

*Heidi Anderson, "Cruising to E-Mail Results," ClickZ, Incisive Interactive Marketing, 10 July 2003, Web, 15 May 2009.

TECHNOLOGY IN BRIEF

These boxes reflect how current technologies affect business communication, covering topics such as text messaging, email etiquette, and tools and technologies that students will encounter in the workplace.

COMMUNICATION MATTERS

And the Most Overused Marketing Cliché Is . . .

Business author and speaker David Meerman Scott recently conducted a study to identify the most overused marketing expressions. After consulting with other PR professionals to create a list of candidates, he used Factiva's text-mining tools to look for these words and phrases in news releases issued by North American businesses between January and September, 2006.

Here were some of the most overused words and phrases in the 388,000 news releases studied:

Flexible	World class	
Robust	Scalable	
Easy to use	Industry standard	
Cutting edge	Turnkey	
Mission critical	Groundbreaking	
Market leading		

And the winning (or losing) expression? "Next generation."

Instead of using this "gobbledygook," Scott advises, just explain in simple terms how your products "solve customer problems."

Source: "The Gobbledygook Manifesto," David Meerman Scott, David Meerman Scott, 8 August 2007, Web, 7 April 2009.

COMMUNICATION MATTERS

Communication Matters boxes contain authoritative and anecdotal commentary to emphasize communication concepts from each chapter.

MARGIN NOTES

Extensive, running margin notes highlight important key concepts for student review and study.

REAL BUSINESS CASE ILLUSTRATIONS

Numerous examples feature real companies, with notes explaining how concepts discussed in the text are being applied.

RELEVANT AND CHALLENGING CASES

An extensive collection of scenario-based cases gives students practice solving communication problems on a wide range of business topics, from Internet use to customer service to marketing research.

A Wealth

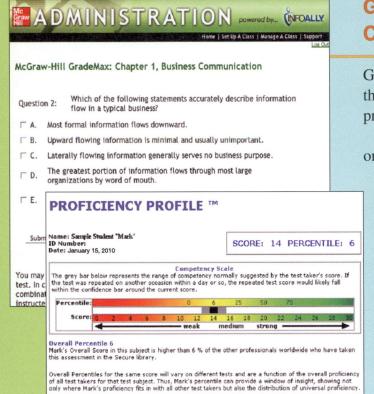

GRADEMAX FOR BUSINESS COMMUNICATION

GradeMax is a testing and remediation program that helps instructors assess student skill levels and provides students with customized assistance.

This adaptive testing engine tests students on the core concepts in each chapter or unit of *Lesikar's Business Communication: Connecting in a Digital World*. As students answer each question, GradeMax alters the difficulty level of successive questions based on the student's response. The result is a unique, detailed view of each student's mastery of each chapter's core concepts. Following the tests, GradeMax provides proficiency reports of each student's comprehension. This allows instructors to adjust their teaching accordingly and also guide students on where to apply their study time. GradeMax offers topic-specific review modules for students to work on areas of weakness.

# of Supplements

ONLINE LEARNING CENTER

Numerous resources are available for both instructors and students online at **www.mhhe.com/lesikar12e**. Downloadable supplements for the instructor include an Instructor's Manual, Test Bank, and PowerPoint slides. Students can access self-grading quizzes, review material, or work through interactive exercises.

BRIEF CONTENTS

CONTENTS

part three

Basic Patterns of Business Messages 85

Contents　　**xxi**

part four

Fundamentals of Report Writing 305

chapter ten

Basics of Report Writing 306

part five

Oral Forms of Business Communication 443

part six

Cross-Cultural Communication, Correctness, Technology, Research 495

Contents   **xxv**

1 Communication in the Workplace

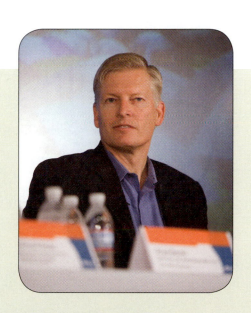

Norm Fjeldheim credits much of the success in his career to learning and developing his business writing and reporting skills. As a leader in a leading company in the digital wireless communications industry, he relies heavily on these well-honed skills. In overseeing all aspects of Qualcomm's information technology, he interacts with people in a wide variety of positions including Qualcomm senior executives and board members, senior executives of customers and suppliers, and occasionally even the Department of Justice and the FBI on security issues. He also keeps his direct reports and customers informed and on track. By far the most important tools he uses daily for the majority of his work are Eudora, PowerPoint, and Word.

When asked about the most important class to take, he definitively answers "Business Communication." He says, "Even if you have great technical skills, your career will get stalled without good communication skills. In fact, the better your communication skills, the further you will go. While technology changes over time, being able to communicate well will always be valuable."

Norm Fjeldheim, Senior Vice President and CIO
Qualcomm

chapter one

Communication in the Workplace

LEARNING OBJECTIVES

Upon completing this chapter, you will understand the role and nature of communication in business. To achieve this goal, you should be able to

1 Explain the importance of communication to you and to business.

2 Describe the main challenges facing business communicators today.

3 Describe the three main categories of business communication.

4 Describe the formal and informal communication networks of the business organization.

5 Describe factors that affect the types and amount of communicating that a business does.

6 Explain why business communication is a form of problem solving.

7 Describe the various contexts for each act of business communication.

8 Describe the business communication process.

THE ROLE OF COMMUNICATION IN BUSINESS

Your work in business will involve communication—a lot of it—because communication is a major and essential part of the work of business.

The Importance of Communication Skills to You

Because communication is so important in business, businesses want and need people with good communication skills. Evidence of the importance of communication in business is found in numerous surveys of executives, recruiters, and academicians. Without exception, these surveys have found that communication (especially written communication) ranks at or near the top of the business skills needed for success.

For example, NFI Research, a private organization that regularly surveys over 2,000 executives and senior managers, recently found that 94 percent of the members "rank 'communicating well' as the most important skill for them to succeed today and tomorrow."[1] A study of skills and competencies needed by accountants strongly supports the value of writing, speaking, and listening,[2] and Deloitte & Touche, rated by *BusinessWeek* in 2007 as the best place to launch a career, cited communication skills as the "most desirable trait" in a job candidate.[3] Employers surveyed for the National Association of Colleges and Employers' *Job Outlook 2009* also cited "communication skills" and the related traits of "a strong work ethic, ability to work in a team, and initiative" as highly prized qualities in job applicants.[4] Recruiters who participated in *The Wall Street Journal*'s latest ranking of MBA programs agreed. They rated "interpersonal and communication skills, a teamwork orientation, personal ethics and integrity, analytical and problem-solving abilities, and a strong work ethic" as most important.[5]

Unfortunately, business's need for employees with good communication skills is all too often not fulfilled. Most employees, even the college trained, do not communicate well. In fact, surveys show that, in the opinion of their employees, even managers and executives who think they communicate well actually fall short.[6] Effective communicators are, therefore, in high demand. Not surprisingly, there is a high correlation between communication skills and income. Even among college graduates, those with higher scores in literacy (use of printed and written information) earn significantly more than lower scoring graduates earn.[7] A study by Office Team revealed that technology magnifies the exposure of one's communications skills, forcing workers to communicate more effectively and articulately because these skills will be showcased more. Email often results in a sender's language skills being placed in front of different people simultaneously, while audio and video will reveal the caliber of one's verbal and diplomacy strengths as well.[8]

The communication shortcomings of employees and the importance of communication in business explain why you should work to improve your communication skills. Whatever position you have in business, your performance will be judged largely by your ability to communicate. If you perform and communicate well, you are likely to be rewarded with advancement. And the higher you advance, the more you will need your communication ability. The evidence is clear: Improving your communication skills improves your chances for success in business.

---

[1] Chuck Martin, *Tough Management: The 7 Winning Ways to Make Tough Decisions Easier, Deliver the Numbers, and Grow the Business in Good Times and Bad* (New York: McGraw-Hill, 2005) 1, print.

[2] *Keying In: Newsletter of the National Business Education Association* 10.3 (2000): 4, print.

[3] Lindsey Gerdes, "The Best Place to Launch a Career," *BusinessWeek* 24 Sept. 2007: 50–51, print.

[4] National Association of Colleges and Employers (NACE), "Employers Cite Qualities, Attributes of 'Perfect' Job Candidate," *NACE*, National Association of Colleges and Employers, 29 Jan. 2009, Web, 3 Apr. 2009.

[5] Ronald Alsop, "Business Schools: The Recruiters' Picks (a Special Report)," *The Wall Street Journal* 17 Sept. 2007, Eastern ed.: R5, print.

[6] "Study Offers Insights on Effective Communication from the Perspective of Employees," *Towers Perrin Monitor*, Towers Perrin HR Services, 7 Jan. 2005, Web, 8 Jan. 2006.

[7] Paul T. Decker et al., *Education and the Economy: An Indicators Report* (Washington, DC: Government Printing Office, 1997) 131, print.

[8] "The Challenge Facing Workers in the Future," *HR Focus* Aug. 1999: 6 ff, print.

What Business Professionals Say about Communication

Communication is the most used skill in almost every job. How you communicate your accomplishments to others is a reflection of the quality of your work. Sure, you must know how to do your tasks to accomplish great results, but that is only a portion of professional success. Good communication skills are required to report your results to others, persuade colleagues to take action, and (most importantly at review time) sell your successes to management.

—Don Zatyko, Lead Project Manager
Kaiser Permanente

Communication is essential to building trust and teamwork among employees. To become a successful leader, you must have a great team. Just look at Michelangelo. He didn't paint the Sistine Chapel by himself, but with the help of his team. It is considered one of the best works in history. It's all about the team.

—Mark Federighi, National Account Director
Skyy Spirits

Your message will get lost if it's not clear, concise and high impact! Get to the point quickly, let the recipient know exactly what you want, and use attention-grabbing techniques whenever possible.

—Amy Betterton, IT Manager
San Diego Hospice and Palliative Care

Whenever I see a business document that has uncorrected typos and other grammatical mistakes, I wonder whether the author is (a) not very bright or (b) sloppy.

—Glenda K. Moehlenpah, CPA, CFP®
Financial Bridges

Why Business Depends upon Communication

● Communication is vital to every part of business.

Every business, even a one-person business, is actually an economic and social system. To produce and sell goods and services, any business must coordinate the activities of many groups of people: employees, suppliers, customers, legal advisors, community representatives, government agencies that might be involved, and others. These connections are achieved through communication.

Consider, for example, the communications of a pharmaceutical manufacturer. Throughout the company, employees send and receive information about all aspects of the company's business, from sales to business strategy to manufacturing. They process information with computers, write messages, complete forms, give and receive orders, talk over the phone, and meet face to face.

Salespeople receive instructions and information from the home office and submit orders and regular reports of their contact with customers. Executives use written and oral messages to conduct business with customers and other companies, manage company operations, and perform strategic planning. Production supervisors receive work orders, issue instructions, receive status reports, and submit production summaries. Shop floor supervisors deliver orders to the employees on the production line, communicate and enforce guidelines for safety and efficiency, troubleshoot problems that arise, and bring any concerns or suggestions to management. Marketing professionals gather market information, propose new directions for company production and sales efforts, coordinate with the research and development staff, and receive direction from the company's executives. Research specialists receive or propose problems to investigate, make detailed records of their research, monitor lab operations for compliance with government regulations, and communicate their findings to management. Public relations professionals use various media to maintain the public's trust. Numerous communication-related activities occur in every other niche of the company as well: finance and accounting, human resources,

Peter Drucker, recipient of the Presidential Medal of Freedom and one of the most respected management consultants, educators, speakers, and writers of our time, made these observations about communication:

> Colleges teach the one thing that is perhaps most valuable for the future employee to know. But very few students bother to learn it. This one basic skill is the ability to organize and express ideas in writing and speaking.

As soon as you move one step from the bottom, your effectiveness depends on your ability to reach others through the spoken or the written word. And the further away your job is from manual work, the larger the organization of which you are an employee, the more important it will be that you know how to convey your thoughts in writing or speaking. In the very large organization . . . this ability to express oneself is perhaps the most important of all the skills a person can possess.

legal, information systems, and others. Everywhere, employees receive and send information as they conduct their work, and they may be doing so across or between continents as well as between buildings or offices.

Oral communication is a major part of this information flow. So, too, are various types of forms and records, as well as the storage and retrieval facilities provided by computers. Yet another major part consists of various forms of written communication—Web postings, instant messaging, text messaging, email, letters, and reports.

- Information is managed and exchanged through many oral, written, and electronic forms.

All of this communicating goes on in business because communication is essential to the organized effort involved in business. Simply put, communication enables human beings to work together.

Current Challenges for Business Communicators

While communication has always been central to business, the nature of work in the 21st century presents special communication challenges. A recent study prepared for the U.S. Department of Labor by the RAND Corporation, a nonprofit research group, discusses trends that are likely to have a huge impact on your communication practices and purposes.[9] Here we highlight three of them.

- The nature of work in the 21st century presents special communication challenges:

The Ongoing Development of New Information Technologies. You have probably heard that we live in "the information age." What does this mean exactly, and how might it affect your future work? According to sociologists and business experts, it means that information has become the hottest commodity there is. Those who can generate, harness, and share information the most quickly and effectively are those who will create the most profitable innovations (think Amazon and Google), tap the best markets, provide the best service, and take advantage of the next great opportunity.

Information technologies—from microchips, nanotechnologies, and the Internet to software, personal computers, and hand-held communication devices—are fueling this competition. And as more and more means of acquiring, storing, retrieving, transmitting, and using information develop, what people do on the job becomes more and more information related. To use the term coined by renowned management thinker Peter Drucker, "knowledge workers" are the employees who are now most in demand. What kinds of abilities does knowledge work require? According to the RAND study,

---

[9] Lynn A. Karoly and Constantijn W. A. Panis, *The 21st Century at Work: Forces Shaping the Future Workforce and Workplace in the United States* (Santa Monica, CA: RAND Corporation, 2004), *RAND Corporation*, Web, 17 January 2008.

the answer is "strong nonroutine cognitive skills, such as abstract reasoning, problem solving, communication, and collaboration."[10]

• making smart use of communication technologies, which requires several kinds of "literacy,"

You will need several kinds of literacy to do knowledge work. Of course you will need *verbal literacy*—the ability to use words to get things done. But you will also need *information literacy*—the ability to find, evaluate, select, and use information. You will need *technological literacy*—the ability to learn and use computer applications, as well as to understand their strengths and limitations. And more and more, you will need *visual literacy*—the ability to interpret and assess visuals and to create visual components for your messages that convey information meaningfully, accurately, and efficiently. There has never been a more demanding—or exciting—time for business communication.

The Increasingly Global Nature of Business. With the information revolution has come rapid globalizaition. E-commerce, communication technologies, and the expansion of business-based economies throughout the world have forged new connections among countries. A purchase at a U.S. store, for example, can trigger an electronic message to a supplier in China who is meeting the demand for that product. The outsourcing of core business functions, such as manufacturing and customer service, to other countries is on the rise, and customers can come from all over the world. No doubt about it—working with those from other cultures is likely to be in your future.

• developing cross-cultural communication skills,

For this reason, you will need to be keenly aware that your assumptions about business and communication are not shared by everyone everywhere. As Chapter 15 points out, businesspeople from other countries may have distinctly different attitudes about *punctuality* and *efficiency*. They can also differ from you in their preference—or lack thereof—for *directness* and the *show of emotion*. And, of course, the core features of their culture, such as their preference for *individualism* or *collectivism,* their *religious beliefs,* their *political environment*, their ideas about *social hierarchy,* and their *attitudes toward work itself* can make their view of how to do business quite different from yours.

On the other hand, global business is possible because businesspeople, from whatever country, generally do share certain goals and values. Your job as a cross-cultural communicator will be to learn about and honor others' cultural orientations in such a way that you and your communication partners can work together for mutual benefit.

• learning to work with many different types of people, and

Growing Diversity in the Workplace and in Types of Workplaces. An awareness of others' preferences and values is crucial not just for cross-cultural communication but also for communication within one's own country and one's own organization. According to the RAND study, we can expect to see more diverse workplaces, with employees of both sexes, various cultures, and all ages likely to be working together. The globalization of business, immigration, the aging of the so-called Baby Boomers, the increasing entry of women into the workforce, and better access to education are all fueling this trend.

In addition, the 20th century model of the vertical organization is now giving way to myriad organizational structures. Because they need to be nimble enough to respond to new information quickly, companies are less hierarchical, with front-line employees having a level of authority and problem-solving responsibility once afforded only to managers. In addition, the breakdown of the old hierarchical model is generating new kinds of employment relationships, such as self-employment, contract work, and temporary help. The challenge for the business communicator is to be able to adapt to quickly changing responsibilities and work relationships.

One more widespread trend underway in business will likely affect the goals of the organization you work for. It is an *increased focus on ethics and social responsibility*.

While ethical scandals have plagued businesses throughout history, the Enron and WorldCom scandals of 2002, in which false reports of financial health cheated employees and shareholders alike, seemed to usher in a new era of concern. Recent

---

[10] Karoly and Panis xiv.

A Chief Marketing Officer on the Importance of Building Trust

The biggest thing going on with U.S. consumers is that they want to trust something. They want to be understood, they want to be respected, they want to be listened to. They don't want to be talked to. It's trust in the largest sense of the word. People really do care what's behind the brand, what's behind the business. They care about the values of a brand and the values of a company. We can never forget that. We can never be complacent about that.

—James Stengel, CMO
Procter & Gamble

Source: Geoff Colvin, "Selling P&G" *Fortune, CNNMoney.com*, Cable News Network, 5 Sept. 2007, Web, 8 Sept. 2009.

accounts of predatory lending, business espionage, and exploitative labor practices have further shaken the public's confidence in business. On a moral level, doing business in a way that harms others is wrong. On a practical level, doing so undermines trust, which is critical to the success of business. The more an organization builds trust among its employees, its shareholders, its business partners, and its community, the better for the business and for economic prosperity overall. A key way to build trust is through respectful, honest communication, backed up by quality goods and services.

Lately, another important dimension of business ethics has developed: corporate social responsibility. The Internet has brought a new transparency to companies' business practices, with negative information traveling quickly and widely. And nongovernmental organizations (NGOs) such as CorpWatch, Consumer Federation of America, and Greenpeace can exert a powerful influence on public opinion and even on governments. Businesses now operate in an age of social accountability, and their response has been the development of corporate social responsibility (CSR) departments and initiatives. As businesses come to be regarded more and more as part of an interdependent web, you may well find that social issues will influence how you do business and communicate in business.

• becoming more attuned to social and ethical issues.

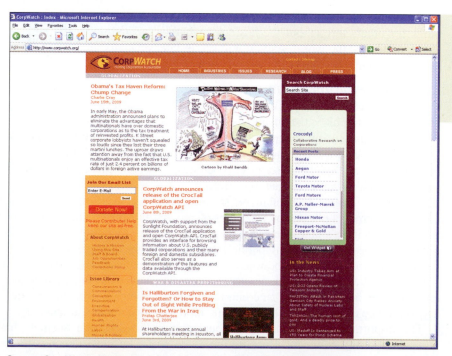

Source: CorpWatch, Home page, *CorpWatch,* n.d., Web, 15 June 2009.

Nongovermental organizations (NGOs) like CorpWatch attest to the growing importance of social responsibility in business.

"The shipment will be delayed. We were supposed to order
the trucks to get loaded at 9:00 AM, but we accidentally
ordered the truckers to get loaded at 9:00 AM."

Main Categories of Business Communication

- There are three categories of communication in business.

As you prepare yourself for all the communicating you will do on the job, it can help to think about business communication as falling into three main categories: internal operational, external operational, and personal.

Internal-Operational Communication. All the communication that occurs in conducting work within a business is internal operational. This is the communication among the business's employees that is done to create, implement, and track the success of the business's operating plan. By *operating plan* we mean the procedure that the business has developed to do whatever it was formed to do—for example, to manufacture products, provide a service, or sell goods.

- (1) Internal-operational communication is the communicating done in conducting work within a business,

- such as giving orders, assembling reports, and writing email.

Internal-operational communication takes many forms. It includes the ongoing discussions that senior management undertakes to determine the goals and processes of the business. It includes the orders and instructions that supervisors give employees, as well as oral exchanges among employees about work matters. It includes reports that employees prepare concerning sales, production, inventories, finance, maintenance, and so on. It includes the email messages that they write in carrying out their assignments and contributing their ideas to the business.

Much of this internal-operational communication is performed on computer networks. Employees send electronic mail and post information on company portals and blogs for others throughout the business, whether located down the hall, across the street, or around the world. As you will see in later chapters, the computer assists the business writer and speaker in many other aspects of communication as well.

External-Operational Communication. The work-related communicating that a business does with people and groups outside the business is external-operational communication. This is the business's communication with its publics—suppliers, service companies, customers, government agencies, the general public, and others.

- (2) External-operational communication is work-related communication with people outside the business,

- such as personal selling, telephoning, advertising, and writing messages.

External-operational communication includes all of the business's efforts at direct selling: salespeople's "spiels," descriptive brochures, telephone callbacks, follow-up service calls, and the like. It also includes the advertising the business does to generate and retain customers. Radio and television messages, newspaper and magazine advertising, website advertising, product placement, and point-of-purchase display material obviously play a role in the business's plan to achieve its work objective. Also in this category is all that a business does to improve its public relations, whether through planned publicity or formal and informal contacts between company representatives and the outside world. In fact, every act of communication with an external audience can be regarded as a public-relations message, conveying a certain image of the company. For this reason, all such acts should be undertaken with careful attention to both content and tone.

- Every external message conveys an image of the company.

The importance of external-operational communication to a business hardly requires supporting comment. Because the success of a business depends on its ability to satisfy customers' needs, it must communicate effectively with those customers.

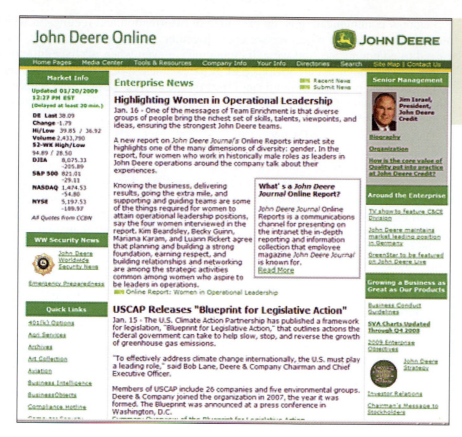

But businesses also depend on each other in the production and distribution of goods and services. Coordinating with contractors, consultants, and suppliers requires skillful communication. In addition, every business must communicate to some extent with a variety of other external parties, such as government agencies and public-interest groups. Some external audiences for today's businesses are illustrated in Figure 1–1. Like internal communication, external communication is vital to business success.

Personal Communication. Not all the communication that occurs in business is operational. In fact, much of it is without apparent purpose as far as the operating plan of the business is concerned. This type of communication is personal. Do not make the mistake of underestimating its importance. Personal communication helps make and sustain the relationships upon which business depends.

- Both internal and external communications are vital to business success.

- (3) Personal communication consists of non-business-related exchanges of information and feelings among people.

Figure 1–1

Likely External Audiences for Today's Businesses

Core Business Partners
(suppliers, contract workers, manufacturers, shippers, distributors ...)

Customers
(consumers, business customers, the government ...)

Your company

Public Groups
(community groups, citizen groups, nongovernmental organizations, schools and foundations ...)

Regulatory Agents
(the government, trade alliances, union officials, national and international legal experts ...)

Industry Partners
(competitors, similar businesses, lobbyists ...)

- Personal communication affects employee attitudes.

Personal communication is the exchange of information and feelings in which we human beings engage whenever we come together. We are social animals. We have a need to communicate, and we will communicate even when we have little or nothing to say. Although not an obvious part of the business's plan of operation, personal communication can have a significant effect on the success of that plan. This effect is a result of the influence that personal communication can have on the attitudes of the employees and those with whom they communicate.

- And attitudes affect employee performance.

- The kinds of personal communication allowed and encouraged in the company affect employee attitudes.

The employees' attitudes toward the business, each other, and their assignments directly affect their productivity. And the nature of conversation in a work situation affects attitudes. In an environment where heated words and flaming tempers are often present, the employees are not likely to give their best efforts to their jobs. Likewise, a rollicking, jovial workplace can undermine business goals. Wise managers cultivate the optimum balance between employees' focus on job-related tasks and their freedom to bring their personal selves to work. They also know that chat around the water cooler or in the break room encourages a team attitude and can often be the medium in which actual business issues get discussed.

- Personal communication elements can enhance internal and external business communication.

Even communication that is largely internal-operational will often include personal elements that relieve the tedium of daily routine and enable employees to build personal relationships. Similarly, communication with external parties will naturally include personal remarks at some point. Sometimes you may find yourself writing a wholly personal message to a client, as when he or she has won a major award or experienced a loss of some kind. Other times, you may compose an external-operational message that also includes a brief personal note, perhaps thanking a client for a pleasant lunch or referring to a personal matter that came up in the course of a business meeting. Personal communication on the job is inevitable. When wisely undertaken, it makes business more successful, pleasant, and fulfilling.

Communication Networks of the Organization

Looking over all of a business's communication (internal, external, and personal), we see an extremely complex system of information flow and human interaction. We see dozens, hundreds, or even thousands of individuals engaging in untold numbers of communication events throughout each workday.

- Information flow in a business can be said to form two complex networks, one formal and one informal.

In fact, as Figure 1–2 shows, there are two complex networks of information in virtually any organization—one formal and one informal. Both are critically important to the success of the business.

The Formal Network. In simplified form, information flow in a modern business is much like the network of arteries and veins in the body. Just as the body

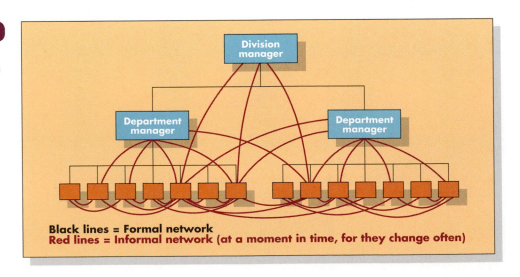

Figure 1–2

Formal and Informal Communication Networks in a Division of a Small Business

Black lines = Formal network
Red lines = Informal network (at a moment in time, for they change often)

has blood vessels, the business has major, well-established channels for information exchange. These are the formal channels—the main lines of operational communication. Through these channels flows the bulk of the communication that the business needs to operate. Specifically, the flow includes the upward, lateral, and downward movement of information in the form of reports, memos, email, and other media within the organization; the downward movement of orders, instructions, advisories, and announcements; and the broad dissemination of company information through the organization's newsletter, bulletin boards, email, intranet, or blogs.

As we have seen, information routinely flows outward as well. Order acknowledgments, invoices, receipts, correspondence with suppliers and consultants, and other standard external-operational communications can make external audiences part of the formal communication network.

These officially sanctioned lines of communication cause certain forms of communication, or *genres,* to exist within the organization. For example, it may be customary in one company for project leaders to require a weekly report from team members. Or the executives in another company may hold monthly staff meetings. Whatever the established form, it will bring with it certain expectations about what can and cannot be said, who may and may not say it, and how the messages should be structured and worded. This means that the favored forms will advance certain practices in the organization and discourage others. It is, therefore, important that the main channels in the formal communication network be carefully thought out and changed as the needs of the business change.

The Informal Network. Operating alongside the formal network is the informal network. It comprises the thousands upon thousands of personal communications that may or may not support the formal communication network of a business. Such communications follow no set pattern; they form an ever-changing and infinitely complex structure linking the members of the organization.

The complexity of this informal network, especially in larger organizations, cannot be overemphasized. Typically, it is really not a single network but a complex relationship of smaller networks consisting of certain groups of people. The relationship is made even more complex by the fact that these people may belong to more than one group and that group memberships and the links between and among groups are continually changing. The department you belong to, the other employees whom you see in the course of your

- The formal network consists of the official, more stable lines of communication.

- Each company has its preferred communication forms, or *genres,* for conducting its business.

- The informal network, consisting largely of personal communications, is highly complex and ever changing.

In large businesses, much of the work done involves internal-operational communication.

workday, and even random personal connections, such as having the same hometown or having kids the same age, can cause links in this network to form.

Known as the *grapevine* in management literature, this communication network is more valuable to the company's operations than a first impression might indicate. Certainly, it carries much gossip and rumor. Even so, the grapevine usually carries far more information than the formal communication system, and on many matters it is more effective in determining the course of an organization. Skillful managers recognize the presence of the grapevine, and they know that the powerful people in this network are often not those at the top of the formal organizational hierarchy. They find out who the talk leaders are and give them the information that will do the most good for the organization. They also make management decisions that will cultivate positive talk.

Employees' personal relations with external audiences add another dimension to a company's informal network. To give just one example, it is likely that someone who leaves a company will maintain personal relations with at least a few employees in that company. As with the grapevine, such relations can either help or hurt the company. Here again, wise managers will be sensitive to the informal network and manage in such a way as to encourage talk that is beneficial to the company.

● Managers cannot control the informal network, but they can influence it.

Variation in Communication Activity by Business

Just how much and what kind of communicating a business does depends on several factors. The nature of the business is one. For example, insurance companies have a great need to communicate with their customers, especially through letters and other mailings, whereas housecleaning service companies have little such need. Another factor is the business's operating plan. Relatively simple businesses, such as repair services, require far less communication than complex businesses, such as automobile manufacturers.

The business's relation to its environment also influences its communication practices. Businesses in a comparatively stable environment, such as textile manufacturing or commercial food processing, will tend to depend on established types of formal communication in a set organizational hierarchy, whereas those in a volatile environment,

● How much and what kinds of communicating a business does depends on the nature of the business, its operating plan, its environment, its geographic dispersion, and the people involved.

such as software development or telecommunications, will tend to improvise more in terms of their communications and company structure.

Yet another factor is the geographic dispersion of the operations of a business. Obviously, internal communication in a business with multiple locations differs from that of a one-location business. Also, the people who make up a business affect its volume of communication. Every human being is unique. Each has unique communication needs and abilities. Thus, varying combinations of people will produce varying needs for communication.

Each business can also be said to possess a certain organizational *culture,* which has a strong effect upon, and is strongly affected by, the company's communication. The concept of organizational or corporate culture was popularized in the early 1980s, and it continues to be a central focus of management consultants and theorists.[11] You can think of a given company's culture as its customary, often unexpressed, ways of perceiving and doing things. It is the medium of preferred values and practices in which the company's members do their work.

- Each business has its own particular *culture,* which profoundly affects, and is affected by, its communication.

Recall places you've worked or businesses you've patronized. In some, the employees' demeanor suggests a coherent, healthy culture in which people seem to know what to do and be happy doing it. At the other extreme are companies where employees exhibit little affiliation with the business and may even be sabotaging it through poor customer service or lack of knowledge about their jobs. The content and quality of the company's communication have a great deal to do with employees' attitudes and behavior.

Take care to note that the official culture and the actual culture in a company are not necessarily the same thing. Officially, the company management may announce and try to promote a certain culture through formal communications such as mission statements and mottoes. But the actual culture of a company is a dynamic, living realm of meaning constructed daily through infinite behaviors and communications at all levels of the company. Having your antennae out for the assumptions that actually drive people's conduct in your or your client's workplace will help you become a more effective communicator.

- The officially publicized and the real company culture may not be the same.

THE BUSINESS COMMUNICATION PROCESS

Although we may view the communication of a business as a network of information flow, we must keep in mind that a business organization consists of people and that communication with those inside and outside the organization occurs among people. It is also helpful to bear in mind that, by and large, each act of business communication is designed to achieve particular goals. The following discussion highlights the main steps in tackling business communication problems.

- The following discussion describes business communication as an interpersonal, goal-directed process.

Business Communication as Problem Solving

Virtually every significant communication task that you will face will involve analyzing a unique configuration of factors that requires at least a somewhat unique solution. For this reason, it makes sense to think of business communication as a problem-solving activity.

- Business communication is a problem-solving activity.

Researchers in many fields—management, medicine, writing, psychology, and others—have studied problem solving. In general, they define *problem* as simply "a gap between where you are now and where you want to be."[12] Within this framework, a problem isn't always something negative; it can also be an opportunity to improve a situation or do things in a better way. As a goal-focused enterprise, business is all about solving problems, and so, therefore, is business communication.

- A problem, as defined here, is not only a negative situation that needs to be remedied; it can also be an opportunity to gain something positive.

[11] See Edgar H. Schein, *Organizational Culture and Leadership,* 3rd ed. (San Francisco: Jossey-Bass, 2004), print, which reviews the literature on this important concept.

[12] For discussions of problem solving, see the following print resources: John R. Hayes, *The Complete Problem Solver,* 2nd ed. (Hillsdale, NJ: Lawrence Erlbaum, 1989); Janet E. Davidson and Robert J. Sternberg, eds., *The Psychology of Problem Solving* (Cambridge, UK: Cambridge University Press, 2003); Rosemary J. Stevenson, *Language, Thought, and Representation* (Chichester, UK: John Wiley, 1993); and Arthur B. VanGundy, *Techniques of Structured Problem Solving* (New York: Van Nostrand Reinhold, 1988).

- There are well-defined and ill-defined problems. Most business communication situations can be categorized as ill-defined problems, requiring analysis, creativity, and judgment.

The problem-solving literature divides problems into two main types: well defined and ill defined. The former can be solved by following a formula, such as when you are computing how much money is left in your department's budget. But most real-world problems, including business communication problems, cannot be solved this way. They do not come to us in neat packages with the path to the best solution clearly implied. Instead, they require research, analysis, creativity, and judgment. One reason why this is the case in business communication is that, as in any communication situation, people are involved—and people are both complex and unique. But the business context itself is often complex, presenting you with multiple options for handling any given situation. For example, if a customer has complained, what will you do about it? Nothing? Apologize? Imply that the customer was at fault? Give a conciliatory discount? Refuse to adjust the bill? Even a "simple" problem like this one requires thinking through the likely short- and long-term effects of several possible solutions.

- *Heuristics* (problem-solving aids such as prior examples, analytical processes, or established communication plans) can help you solve business communication problems more efficiently, but they must be adapted to each unique situation.

Solving ill-defined problems involves combining existing resources with innovation and good judgment. Although this book presents basic plans for several common types of business communication messages, you will not be able to solve particular communication problems by just filling in the blanks of these plans. The plans can be thought of as *heuristics*—"rules of thumb" that keep you from reinventing the wheel with each new problem. But the plans do not tell you all you need to do to solve each unique communication problem. You must decide how to adapt each plan to the given situation.

What this means is that successful business communication is both more challenging and more exciting than you may have thought. You will need to draw on your own powers of interpretation and decision making to succeed with your human communication partners.

- While there is no one perfect solution, a poorly prepared one is likely to fail.

Of course, different people will handle different cases somewhat differently, depending on who they are, how they interpret the situation, and who they imagine their recipients to be. Does this mean that all communication solutions are equally valid? Not at all. While there is no perfect solution, there can be many bad ones that have been developed without enough analysis and effort. Focused thinking, research, and planning will not guarantee success in the shifting, complex world of business communication, but they will make your chances of success as high as possible. The next section will help you perform this kind of analysis.

A Model of Business Communication

Figure 1–3 shows the basic elements of a business communication event. Even though people can, and often do, communicate inadvertently, this communication model focuses on what happens when someone deliberately undertakes to communicate with someone else to achieve particular business-related goals.

- Both parties in a communication event influence the outcome of that event.

You'll notice that the two communicators in the figure are labeled simply "Communicator 1" and "Communicator 2," instead of "Sender" and "Receiver" or "Communicator" and "Audience." Certainly any communication event begins with someone deciding that communication is needed and initiating that communication, with an intended "receiver" (a popular term in speech communication) or "audience" (the preferred term in composition) on the other end. But in many situations, especially those involving real-time conversation, the two parties work together to reach a mutual understanding. Even in situations where a communicator is attempting to deliver a complete, carefully prepared message—as in a letter, report, or oral presentation—the intended recipients have in a sense already participated in the construction of the message via the imaginative efforts of the writer or presenter, who has kept them in mind when composing and designing the message. The labels in this model are thus intended to convey the cooperative effort behind every successful communication event.

- Business communication always takes place within certain contexts, including

The Contexts for Communication. Certain features of the communication situation are already in place as the communicators in our model begin to communicate.

The *larger context* includes the general business-economic climate; the language, values, and customs in the surrounding culture; and the historical moment in which the communication is taking place.

Figure 1–3

The Business Communication Process

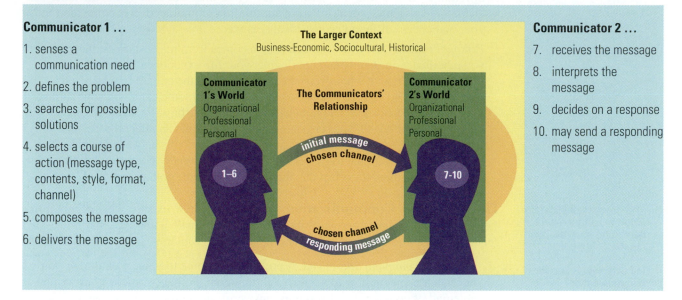

Communicator 1 ...

1. senses a communication need

2. defines the problem

3. searches for possible solutions

4. selects a course of action (message type, contents, style, format, channel)

5. composes the message

6. delivers the message

The Larger Context
Business-Economic, Sociocultural, Historical

Communicator 1's World
Organizational
Professional
Personal

The Communicators' Relationship

Communicator 2's World
Organizational
Professional
Personal

initial message
chosen channel

1–6

7-10

chosen channel
responding message

Communicator 2 ...

7. receives the message

8. interprets the message

9. decides on a response

10. may send a responding message

Think about how these contexts might influence communication. For example, when the country's economy or a particular industry is flourishing, a communicator's message and the recipient's response may well be different from what they would be during an economic slump. The sociocultural context also affects how they communicate. Whether they are communicating in the context of U.S. urban culture, for instance, or the culture of a particular region or another country, or whether they are communicating across cultures, their communication choices will be affected. The particular historical context of their communication can also be a factor. Consider how recent financial scandals in the United States or the increased focus on the environment are influencing the language of business. The skillful communicator is sensitive to these larger contexts, which always exert an influence and, to some extent, are always changing.

- (1) such larger contexts as the general business-economic climate, the surrounding culture, and the historical timing of the communication;

The *relationship of the communicators* also forms an important context for communication. Certainly, communication is about moving information from point A to point B, but it also about interaction between human beings. Your first correspondence with someone begins a relationship between the two of you, whether as individuals, people in certain roles, or both. All future messages between you will need to take this relationship into account.

- (2) the relationship of the communicators; and

The communicators' *particular contexts* exert perhaps the strongest influence on the act of communication. These interrelated contexts can be

- (3) the particular contexts—organizational, professional, and personal—of each communicator.

- *Organizational contexts.* As we've discussed, the type and culture of the organization you represent will shape your communication choices in many ways, and the organizational contexts of your audiences will, in turn, shape their responses. In fact, in every act of business communication, at least one of the parties involved is likely to be representing an organization. What you communicate and how you do so will be strongly shaped by the organization for whom you speak. In turn, the organization to which your audience belongs—its priorities, its current circumstances, even how fast or slow its pace of work—can strongly influence the way your message is received.

- *Professional contexts.* You know from school and experience that different professionals—whether physicians, social workers, managers, accountants, or those involved in other fields—possess different kinds of expertise, speak differently, and tend to focus on different things. What gets communicated and how can be heavily influenced by the communicators' professional roles. Be aware that internal audiences as well as external ones can occupy different professional roles and, therefore, favor different kinds of content and language. Employees in management and engineering, for example, have been demonstrated to have quite different priorities, with the former focusing on financial benefit and the latter on technological achievement.[13] Part of successful communication is being alert to your audiences' different professional contexts.

- *Personal contexts.* Who you are as a person comes from many sources: the genes you inherited, your family and upbringing, your life experiences, your schooling, the many people with whom you've come in contact, the culture in which you were reared. Who you are as a person also depends to some extent on your current circumstances. Successes and failures, current relationships, financial ups and downs, the state of your health, your physical environment—all can affect a particular communicative act. Since much business communication is between individuals occupying organizational roles, personal matters are usually not disclosed. But it is well to keep in mind the effect that these can have on the communicators.

The Process of Communication. No one can know exactly what occurs inside the minds of communicators when they undertake to create a message, but researchers generally agree that the process includes the following activities, generally in this order:

- The process of initiating a communication act can be said to have six basic stages:

- (1) sensing a need for communication,

1. *Sensing a communication need.* A problem has come to your attention, or you have an idea about how to achieve a certain goal. Perhaps someone has written an email of complaint and you must answer it, or perhaps you've noticed that the company could benefit from automating a certain procedure. Whatever the case, you find that an action is in order, and you believe that some form of communication will help you achieve the desired state.

- (2) defining the situation,

2. *Defining the situation.* To create a successful message or plan a communication event, you need to have a well-informed sense of the situation. For example, if you have received a letter of complaint from a customer, what exactly is the problem here? Does the customer have a legitimate point? What further information might you need to acquire in order to understand the situation? In what ways is this problem like or unlike others you have solved? How might your or your organization's goals be hindered or helped depending on your communication choices?

- (3) considering possible communication strategies,

3. *Considering possible communication strategies.* As your definition of the situation takes shape, you will start considering different options for solving it. What kind of communication event will you initiate, and what will you want to achieve with it? What image of yourself, your company, and your communication partners might you project in your message? To generate a good solution, you will need to think about and research your potential audiences and their contexts, your own goals and contexts, your relationship with each audience, and any relevant larger contexts.

- (4) selecting a course of action,

4. *Selecting a course of action.* Considering the situation as you've defined it and looking at your communication options, you will consider the potential costs and benefits of each option and select the optimum one. Your decision will include preliminary choices about the message type, contents, structure, verbal style, and visual format, and about the channel you will use to deliver the message.

- (5) composing the message, and

5. *Composing the message.* Here is where you either craft your message, carefully working out its contents, structure, verbal style, and visual format, or plan your strategy for discussing your solution with your audience. If you have decided to present or initiate your message orally, you will make careful notes or perhaps even write out your whole message or presentation and design any visuals you may need. If you have decided to write your message, you will use your favorite strategies for composing effectively. See the section on "The Process of Writing" in Chapter 5 for the strategies that writing researchers recommend.

---

[13] See research by Dorothy A. Winsor, especially *Writing Power: Communication in an Engineering Center* (Albany: SUNY Press, 2003), print.

COMMUNICATION MATTERS

Channel Choice Affects Message Success

"Its [sic] official, you no longer work for JNI Traffic Control and u [sic] have forfided (sic) any arrangements made." Can you imagine getting such a text message? The Sydney employer was sued over this inappropriate choice of a communication channel for firing an employee. In settling the matter the commissioner went further in stating that email, text messages, and even answering machines were inappropriate for official business communication. Or what about being notified by text message of an overdue bill? While some might think of that as a service, others regard it as invasive and inappropriate.

Historically, the importance of channel choice has been disputed, with some arguing that it is simply a means for transmitting words and others arguing that the chosen channel is, in itself, a message. However, today most people realize that the appropriate choice of communication channel contributes significantly, along with the words, to the success of the message. While early research in media richness provided guidelines for understanding when to use very lean (printed material) to very rich (face-to-face) channels, more recent studies as well as new technologies and laws have added new dimensions to this theory. Not only are there no clear-cut rules or guidelines, but the smallest change in context may lead to different choices.

In selecting a channel, a communicator needs to weigh several factors. Some of these include the message content, the communicators' levels of competency with the channel, the recipient's access to the channel, and the recipient's environment. Appropriate choice of a communication channel helps people communicate clearly, improving both their productivity and personal relationships.

---

6. *Sending the message.* When your message is prepared or carefully planned, you are ready to deliver it to your intended recipients in the channel you have chosen. You choose a good time to deliver it, realizing, for example, that Monday morning may not be the best time to make an important phone call to a busy executive. You also consider sending auxiliary messages, such as a "heads-up" phone call or email, that could increase your main message's chances of success. You want to do all you can to ensure that your message doesn't get lost amidst all the other stimuli competing for your intended audience's attention.

- (6) sending the message.

While these activities tend to form a linear pattern, the communicator often needs to revisit earlier steps while moving through the different activities. In other words, solving a communication problem can be a *recursive* process. This is particularly true for situations that invite many different solutions or heavily involve the audience in the communication process. A communicator may begin a communication event with a certain conception of the situation and then discover, upon further analysis or the discovery of additional facts, that this conception needs to be revised in order to take into account all the involved parties and their goals.

- While the message-creation process tends to be linear, it can also be *recursive,* involving a return to earlier steps.

If all goes as planned, here is what will happen on the recipient's end:

- The recipient of the message will then go through these basic stages:

7. *Receiving the message.* Your chosen channel has delivered your message to each intended recipient, who has perceived and decided to read or listen to your message.

- (7) receiving the message,

8. *Interpreting the message.* Just as you had to interpret the situation that prompted your communication, your recipient now has to interpret the message you sent. This activity will involve not only extracting information from the message but also guessing your communication purpose, forming judgments about you and those you represent, and picking up on cues about the relationship you want to promote between the communicators. If you have anticipated the recipient's particular contexts and interests successfully, he or she will form the impressions that you intended. The recipient may prompt the initiating communicator for help with this interpretive act, especially if the communication is a live conversation.

- (8) interpreting the message,

● (9) deciding on a
response, and

9. *Deciding on a response*. Any time you send a message, you hope for a certain response from your recipient, whether it be increased goodwill, increased knowledge, a specific responding action, or a combination of these. If your message has been carefully adapted to the recipient, it has a good chance of achieving the desired response.

● (10) replying to the
message.

10. *Replying to the message*. The recipient's response to your message will often take the form, at least in part, of replying to your message. When this is the case, the receiver is acting as communicator, following the process that you followed to generate your message.

● Taking an analytical
approach to each
communication situation
will give you the best
chance for success.

Figure 1–4 lists the main questions to consider when developing a communication strategy. Taking this analytical approach will help you think consciously about each stage of the process and give you the best chance of achieving the desired results with your messages.

Figure 1–4

**Planning Your
Communication Strategy:
A Problem-Solving
Approach**

What is the situation?

• What has happened to make you think you need to communicate?

• What background and prior knowledge can you apply to this situation? How is this situation like or unlike others you have encountered?

• What do you need to find out in order to understand every facet of this situation? Where can you get this information?

What are some possible communication strategies?

• To whom might you communicate? Who might be your primary and secondary audiences? What are their different organizational, professional, and personal contexts? What would each care about or want to know? What, if any, is your prior relationship with them?

• What purpose might you want to achieve with each recipient? What are your organizational, professional, and personal contexts?

• What are some communication strategies that might help you achieve your goals?

• How might the larger business/economic, sociocultural, and historical contexts affect the success of different strategies?

Which is the best course of action?

• Which strategies are impractical, incomplete, or potentially dangerous? Why?

• Which of the remaining strategies looks like the optimum one? Why?

• What will be the best message type, contents, structure, style, and format for your message?

• What channel will you use to deliver it?

What is the best way to design the chosen message?

• Given your goals for each recipient, what information should your message include?

• What logical structure (ordering and grouping of information) should you use?

• What kind of style should you use? How formal or informal should you be? What kinds of associations should your language have? What image of yourself and your audience should you try to convey? What kind of relationship with each recipient should your message promote?

• How can you use text formatting, graphics, and/or supporting media to make your message easier to comprehend?

• What are your recipients' expectations for the channel you've chosen?

What is the best way to deliver the message?

• Are there any timing considerations related to delivering your message?

• Should you combine the main message with any other messages?

• How can you best ensure that each intended recipient receives and reads or hears your message?

BUSINESS COMMUNICATION: THE BOTTOM LINE

The theme of this chapter might be summed up this way: The goal of business communication is to create a shared understanding of business situations that will enable people to work successfully together.

Timely and clear transfer of information is critical to business, now more than ever. But figuring out what kind of information to send, whom to send it to, how to send it, and in what form to send it requires good decision making. Since every person has his or her own unique contexts and mental "filters"—preconceptions, frames of reference, and verbal worlds—wording the information so that it will be understood can be a challenge. You and your audience may even attach completely different meanings to the same words (a problem that the communication literature calls "bypassing").

Complicating this picture is the fact that communication is not just about information transfer. The creation and maintenance of positive human relations is also essential to business, and thus to business communication. Every act of communication conveys an image of you and of the way you regard those to whom you're speaking or writing. Successful business communicators pay careful attention to the human-relations dimension of their messages.

Yes, business communication can be challenging. It can also be extremely rewarding because of the results you achieve and the relationships you build. The advice, examples, and exercises in this book will jump-start you toward success. But it will be your ability to analyze and solve specific communication problems that will take you the rest of the way there.

• The goal of business communication is to create a shared understanding of business situations that will enable people to work successfully together.

SUMMARY BY LEARNING OBJECTIVES

1. Business needs and rewards people who can communicate, for communication is vital to business operations.
   • But good communicators are scarce.
   • So, if you can improve your communication skills, you increase your value to business and advance your own career as well.

1 Explain the importance of communication to you and to business.

2. The 21st century presents special challenges to business communicators:
   • The ongoing development of new communication technologies.
   • The increasingly global nature of business.
   • Growing diversity in the workplace and in types of workplaces.
   • An increased focus on ethics and social responsibility.

2 Describe the main challenges facing business communicators today.

3. Communicating in business falls into three categories:
   • *Internal-operational* communication is the communicating a business does to implement its operating plan (its procedure for doing what it was formed to do).
   • *External-operational* communication is the communicating a business does with outsiders (customers, other businesses, the public, government agencies, and others).
   • *Personal* communication consists of informal exchanges of information not formally related to operations but nevertheless important to an organization's success.

3 Describe the three main forms of communication in the business organization.

4. The flow of communication in a business organization forms a complex and ever-changing network. Information continually flows from person to person—upward, downward, and laterally.

4 Describe the formal and informal communication networks in the business organization.

- The communicating that follows the formal structure of the business comprises the *formal* network. Primarily, operational information flows through this network, which is sustained by particular forms of communication (*genres*).
- The flow of personal communication forms the *informal* network, or *grapevine*.

5 Describe factors that affect the types and amount of communicating that a business does.

5. The kind and amount of communicating a business does depend upon such factors as
   - The nature of the business.
   - Its operating plan.
   - Its environment.
   - The geographic dispersion of its members.
   - Its people.
   - Its organizational *culture* (an organization's customary, often unexpressed, ways of perceiving and doing things).

6 Explain why business communication is a form of problem solving.

6. Business communication can be thought of as a problem-solving activity.
   - Finding communication solutions requires analysis, creativity, and judgment.
   - *Heuristics* (problem-solving devices such as common communication plans) can help make your communication problem solving more efficient.
   - The common communication plans must still be adapted to each situation.
   - While there is no one perfect solution, a poorly prepared one is likely to fail.

7 Describe the various contexts for each act of business communication.

7. Business communication takes place in these contexts:
   - The larger business-economic, sociocultural, and historical contexts.
   - The relationship of the communicators.
   - The communicators' own worlds: organizational, professional, and personal.

8 Describe the communication process.

8. The process of communication involves these activities, which tend to be linear in nature but are often *recursive* (revisiting earlier steps):

   The initiator
   - Senses a communication need.
   - Defines the situation.
   - Considers possible communication strategies.
   - Selects a course of action (message type, contents, style, format, channel).
   - Composes the message.
   - Sends the message.

   The intended recipient
   - Receives the message.
   - Interprets the message.
   - Decides on a response.
   - May send a responding message.

CRITICAL THINKING QUESTIONS

1 "If there's no definitive solution, then all ways of handling a business communication problem are equally good." Using the discussion of business communication problem solving in this chapter, explain why this statement is false. **(LO6)**

2 Is communication skill more important to the successful performance of a supervisor than to the successful

performance of a company president? Defend your answer. **(LO1)**

3 To get a feel for how rapidly information technologies are changing and how significant the impact is on business, make a list of all the information technologies (devices and applications) that you've learned to use over the last five years. Now reflect on how your communication, work, and life have changed as a result of these technologies. **(LO2)**

4 "People need to leave their cultures and values at the door when they come to work and just do business." Discuss the possible merits and flaws of this attitude. **(LO2)**

5 List the types of external-operational and internal-operational communication that occur in an organization with which you are familiar (school, fraternity, church, etc.). **(LO3)**

6 "Never mix business with personal matters—it just leads to damaged relationships, poor business decisions, or both." In what ways might this be a fair statement? In what ways is it unwise advice? **(LO3)**

7 Describe the formal network of communication in an organization, division, or department with which you are familiar (preferably a simple one). Discuss why you think the communication network has taken this form and how successfully it seems to meet the business's needs. **(LO4)**

8 Make a list of the types of companies requiring many kinds of communication. Then make a list of types of companies requiring few kinds. What explains the difference between these two groups? **(LO5)**

9 In *Images of Organization,* 2nd ed. (Thousand Oaks, CA: Sage, 1997), management scholar Gareth Morgan has analyzed companies using a variety of metaphors. For example, he has looked at those elements of a company that make it appear to run like a machine (with rigidly organized, specific job roles), an organism (with elements that make it dependent upon and responsive to its environment), a brain (with self-managing teams and employees who can do a variety of jobs as needed), and a political system (with employees vying for power and influence). Think of an organization you know well and decide upon its dominant cultural metaphor. Is it one of Morgan's? Or is it a family? A team? A community? A prison? A mixture of several kinds? Once you settle on your metaphor, be prepared to explain how this organization's culture affects, and is affected by, its communication practices. **(LO5)**

10 As noted in this chapter, companies develop specific forms of communication, or genres, that enable them to get their work done. In a place where you have worked or another organization in which you have been a member, what were the main forms of communication with the employees or members? To what extent were these uniquely adapted to the needs of the organization? **(LO5)**

11 Think of a recent transaction you had with a businessperson or with a staff person at your school. Describe the contexts of your communication, from the larger contexts (business-economic, sociocultural, or historical) to the personal (to the extent you know them). How did these influence the outcome of your communication? **(LO7)**

12 Using this chapter's discussion of communication, explain how people reading or hearing the same message can disagree on its meaning. **(LO7)**

CRITICAL THINKING EXERCISES

1 Watch the video "Did You Know?" at <http://www.youtube.com/watch?v=pMcfrLYDm2U>. Using the content of Chapter 1 to aid you, describe what kinds of skills one will need in order to survive and thrive in this quickly changing world. **(LO2)**

2 Using the Internet, find a company that has a corporate social responsibility program and study what the company's website says about that program. What kind of image as a corporate citizen is the company trying to project, and how? How convincing is this effort, in your opinion, and why? **(LO2)**

3 Choose a certain national or regional culture, ethnicity, or generation—one different from your own—and find out what values the people in this demographic are generally known for. How might working or doing business with a person from one of these groups require you to adapt your own values and communication style? **(LO2)**

4 Find two websites of companies in the same industry— for example, two manufacturers of household products or two wireless service providers. Using the evidence presented on their websites, compare their company cultures. Look at their stated mission (if any), their history (if provided), the gender and qualifications of their personnel (if given), their employee benefits, their information for job applicants, their information for investors, the company image projected by the visual elements on the site—anything that suggests who they are or want you to think they are. Write up your comparison in a well-organized, well-supported message to your instructor. **(LO5)**

5 Megan Cabot is one of 12 workers in Department X. She has strong leadership qualities, and all her co-workers look up to her. She dominates conversations with them and expresses strong viewpoints on most matters. Although she is a good worker, her dominating personality has caused problems for you, the new manager of Department X. Today you directed your subordinates to change a certain work procedure. The change is one that has proven superior in the past whenever it has been tried.

Soon after giving the directive, you noticed the workers talking in a group, with Megan the obvious leader. In a few minutes she appeared in your office. "We've thought it over," she said. "Your production change won't work." Explain what is happening. How will you handle this situation? **(LO4, LO6)**

6 After noticing that some workers were starting work late and finishing early, a department head wrote this message to subordinates:

> It is apparent that many of you are not giving the company a full day's work. Thus, the following procedures are implemented immediately:
>
> a. After you clock in, you will proceed to your workstations and will be ready to begin work promptly at the start of the work period.
>
> b. You will not take a coffee break or consume coffee on the job at the beginning of the work period. You will wait until your designated break times.
>
> c. You will not participate in social gatherings at any time during the workday except during designated break periods.
>
> d. You will terminate work activities no earlier than 10 minutes prior to the end of the work period. You will use the 10 minutes to put up equipment, clean equipment, and police the work area.
>
> e. You will not queue up at the exit prior to the end of the work period.

The message was not well received by the workers. In fact, it led to considerable anger and confusion. Using the discussion of communication planning in this chapter, explain where the department head's problem-solving process went awry. What did he or she fail to take into account? **(LO6–LO8)**

7 Find an article in the business press or general news about a recent incident involving a company—for example, a merger or acquisition, a scandal or crisis, or the launching of a new product. What kind of communication challenges might this event have posed for the company, both internally and externally? What kinds of messages probably needed to be written, and to whom? **(LO1–LO7)**

8 Times are hard for Robo Solutions, a small local company that creates assembly-line robotics. Lately, the clients have been few and far between. But today the sales staff got encouraging news: James Pritchett, president of a nearby tool and die company, has inquired about the possibility of the company's designing a series of computer-run robots for key processes in the plant. There's a hitch, though; it's Sara McCann's turn to try to snare his business (and the commission)—and Pritchett is known to prefer dealing with men. Do you, as Robo Solutions sales manager, send Sarah anyway, or do you send one of your male salespeople to get Pritchett's business, giving Sarah a shot at the next potential client? How would you solve this communication—and ethics—problem? **(LO6)**

With a net worth of around $42 billion, Warren Buffett is ranked by *Forbes* magazine as the second-richest person in the world, after Microsoft cofounder and chairman Bill Gates. Buffett made his first stock purchase at the age of 11, but sold before the stock skyrocketed. This early lesson taught him to study hard and carefully analyze potential investments. The result was the development of one of the world's largest holding companies, Berkshire Hathaway, Inc.

Although best known for his ability to pick stocks, Buffett was honored in 2006 by the National Commission on Writing for America's Families, Schools, and Colleges for writing Berkshire Hathaway's annual report. Buffett writes, "One way or another, you have to project your ideas to other people. Writing isn't necessarily easy. . . . But you get better and better at it, and I encourage everybody to do that."

Warren E. Buffett, CEO of Berkshire Hathaway, Inc.

chapter two

Adaptation and the Selection of Words

Upon completing this chapter, you will be able to adapt your language to specific readers and to select the most effective words for use in business communication. To reach this goal, you should be able to

1 Explain the role of adaptation in selecting words that communicate.

2 Simplify writing by selecting familiar and short words.

3 Use slang and popular clichés with caution.

4 Use technical words and acronyms appropriately.

5 Write concretely and use active verbs.

6 Write with clarity and precision by selecting the right words and by using idioms correctly.

7 Use words that do not discriminate.

Choosing Words That Communicate

As a means of introducing yourself to business communication, place yourself in a hypothetical situation. You are the entrepreneurial manager of a struggling small business. You work very hard to make certain that all aspects of your business function effectively and efficiently. At the moment your attention is focused generally on the communicating done by your subordinates. Specifically, you are concerned about the communicating of Max Elliott, your assistant manager.

You have before you an email report from Max. Following your instructions, he investigated your company's use of available space. He has summarized his findings in this report. At first glance you are impressed with Max's work. But after reading further, you are not sure just what his investigation has uncovered. Here is a typical paragraph:

> In the interest of ensuring maximum utilization of the subterranean components of the building currently not apportioned to operations departments, it is recommended that an evaluation of requisites for storage space be initiated. Subject review should be initiated at the earliest practicable opportunity and should be conducted by administrative personnel not affiliated with operative departments.

Max's problem is altogether too commonplace in business. His words, though properly used, do not communicate quickly and easily. This and the following chapter show you what you can do about writing like this.

THE IMPORTANCE OF ADAPTATION

Clear writing begins with adapting your message to your specific readers. As Chapter 1 explains, readers occupy particular organizational, professional, and personal contexts. They do not all have the same kind or level of vocabulary, knowledge, or values. And you do not have the same relationship with all of them.

To choose words that communicate clearly and with the appropriate tone, you should learn everything possible about those with whom you wish to communicate and take into account any prior correspondence with them. Then you should word your message so that it is easy for them to understand it and respond favorably. Tailoring your message to your readers is not only strategically necessary, it is also a sign of consideration for their time and energy. Everyone benefits when messages are clear and appropriate to the correspondents' situation.

- For writing to be clear, it must be adapted to your readers.

- Use all your knowledge of your readers to adapt your messages to them.

Adaptation Illustrated

The following paragraphs from two company annual reports illustrate the basic principle of adaptation. The writer of the first report apparently viewed the readers as people who were not well informed in finance.

> Last year your company's total sales were $117,400,000, which was slightly higher than the $109,800,000 total for the year before. After deducting for all expenses, we had $4,593,000 left over for profits, compared with $2,830,000 for 2009. Because of these increased profits, we were able to increase your annual dividend payments per share from the 50 cents paid over the last 10 years.

The writer of the second report saw the readers as being well informed in finance. Perhaps this writer believed the typical reader would come from the ranks of stockbrokers, financial managers, financial analysts, and bankers. So this writer adapted the annual report to these readers with language like this:

> The corporation's investments and advances in three unconsolidated subsidiaries (all in the development stage) and in 50 percent–owned companies was $42,200,000 on December 31, 2010, and the excess of the investments in certain companies over net asset value at dates of acquisition was $1,760,000. The corporation's equity in the net

assets as of December 31, 2010, was $41,800,000 and in the results of operations for the years ended December 31, 2009 and 2010, was $1,350,000 and $887,500, respectively. Dividend income was $750,000 and $388,000 for the years 2009 and 2010, respectively.

Which writer was right? Perhaps both. Perhaps neither. The answer depends on what the stockholders of each company were really like. Both examples illustrate the technique of adaptation. They use different words for different audiences, which is what you should try to do.

Adapting to Multiple Readers

Adapting your message to one reader requires considerable care, but what if, as often happens, you need to address your message to several different readers? What if your readers vary widely in education, knowledge of the subject, and so on? How can you write your message in such a way that you communicate to everyone? The solution is to write in such a way that everyone can find and follow the parts of your message that are of value to them.

For example, assume that you are the assistant director of marketing for a telecommunications company and you need to report some complex marketing data to your boss in marketing, to the sales manager, and to the president of the company. How might you design your report so that all three, with their differing levels of familiarity with market research techniques, could understand it?

For the sales manager and the president, the nonexperts, you will need to define any specialized vocabulary you use. You will also spell out the implications of your findings for their domains of interest. For example, the sales manager in our example will need you to say what your findings mean for the sales staff, while the president will want to understand how your findings could enhance the financial health of the company.

Accommodating the nonexperts need not alienate or bore the expert readers. They often can benefit from seeing the bigger picture themselves, and they usually are not bothered when definitions and explanations are provided. Often it is helpful to to provide clearly worded headings in your message so that readers looking for different things can find those parts, read them carefully, and then skim or skip the rest.

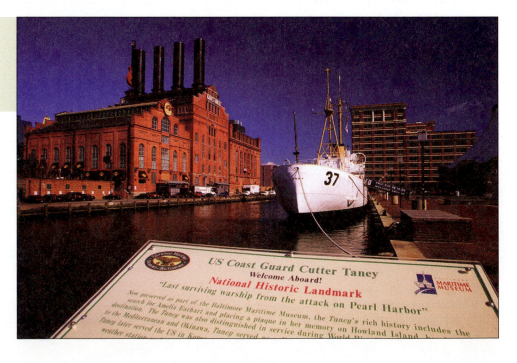

Like good signage at a museum, your writing should be adapted to the skills and interests of your readers.

As with every other element of your messages, your choice of words needs to be guided by your audience and purpose. That is the main "rule" for effective wording. The general guidelines that follow should always be considered in light of this over-arching principle.

• Let your audience and purpose guide your choice of words.

SUGGESTIONS FOR SELECTING WORDS

The advice in the following paragraphs will stand you in good stead in most business communication situations. But, as we say, you should use the words that will communicate best in your particular situation, even if that means ignoring some of this advice.

• Use good judgment when following these suggestions for selecting words.

Use Familiar Words

The foremost suggestion for word selection is to use familiar words. Because words that are familiar to some people may be unfamiliar to others, you will need to decide which ones your readers will understand.

• Familiar words readily communicate. Use your judgment to determine what words are familiar.

In general, using familiar words means using the language that most of us use in everyday conversation. It means avoiding the stiff, more difficult words that do not communicate so precisely or quickly. For example, instead of using the less familiar word *endeavor,* use *try.* Prefer *do* to *perform, begin* to *initiate, find out* to *ascertain, stop* to *discontinue,* and *show* to *demonstrate.*

The suggestion to use familiar words does not rule out some use of more difficult words. You should use them whenever their meanings fit your purpose best and your readers understand them clearly. The mistake that many of us make is to overwork the more difficult words. We use them so much that they interfere with our communication. A good suggestion is to use the simplest words that carry the meaning without offending the readers' intelligence. Perhaps the best suggestion is to write the words you would use in face-to-face communication with your readers.

• Difficult words are not all bad. Use them when they fit your needs and will be understood.

The following contrasting examples illustrate the communication advantages of familiar words over less familiar ones. As you read the examples, consider the effect on communication of an entire message or report written in the styles illustrated.

Unfamiliar Words	Familiar Words
This machine has a tendency to develop excessive and unpleasant audio symptoms when operating at elevated temperatures.	This machine tends to get noisy when it runs hot.
Purchase of a new fleet is not actionable at this juncture.	Buying new trucks is not practical now.
We must leverage our core competencies to maximize our competitiveness.	Relying on what we do best will make us the most competitive.
The most operative assembly-line configuration is a unidirectional flow.	The most efficient assembly-line design is a one-way flow.
The conclusion ascertained from a perusal of pertinent data is that a lucrative market exists for the product.	The data studied show that the product is in high demand.
Company operations for the preceding accounting period terminated with a deficit.	The company lost money last year.

A great resource for business writers—and a great model of the advice it gives—is the U.S. Securities and Exchange Commission's *A Plain English Handbook: How to Create Clear SEC Disclosure Documents* (available at <http:www.sec.gov/pdf/handbook.pdf>).

Here's what the handbook says about using familiar words:

Surround complex ideas with short, common words. For example, use *end* instead of *terminate, explain* rather than *elucidate,* and *use* instead of *utilize.* When a shorter, simpler synonym exists, use it.

Prefer Short Words

● Generally, short words communicate better.

According to studies of readability, short words generally communicate better than long words. Of course, part of the explanation is that short words tend to be familiar words. But there is another explanation: A heavy use of long words—even long words that are understood—leaves an impression of difficulty that hinders communication.

● Some exceptions exist.

The suggestion that short words be chosen does not mean that all short words are easy and all long words are hard. Many exceptions exist. Not everyone knows such one-syllable words as *gybe, verd,* and *id,* whereas even children know such long words as *hippopotamus, automobile*, and *bicycle*. On the whole, however, word length and word difficulty are related. Thus, you should rely mostly on short words and use long ones with caution.

This point is illustrated by many of the examples presented to support the use of familiar words. But the following illustrations give it additional support. In some of them, the long-word versions are likely to be understood by more highly educated readers. Even so, the heavy proportion of hard words clouds the message. Notice how much easier to understand the short-word versions are.

Long Words	Short Words
The *implementation of the proposed enhancement* is *under consideration*.	We are *considering* your *suggestion*.
They *acceded* to the *proposition* to *undertake* a *collaborative venture*.	They agreed to *work with* us.
Prior to *accelerating productive operation*, the supervisor inspected the machinery.	Before *speeding up* production, the supervisor inspected the machinery.
The *unanimity* of current forecasts is not *incontrovertible evidence* of an *impending* business acceleration.	*Agreement* of the forecasts is not *proof* that business *will get better*.
This *antiquated merchandising* strategy is *ineffectual* in *contemporary* business *operations*.	This *old sales* strategy *will not work* in *today's* business.

Use Slang and Popular Clichés with Caution

At any given time in any society, some slang words and clichés are in vogue. In the United States, for example, you might currently hear "voted off the island," "Deal or no deal?," or "Come on down!"—all of which come from U.S. television shows. But other expressions from U.S. television, such as "Where's the beef?" and "That's the $64,000 question," have faded into the past. Business clichés come and go as well. One 2008 television commercial had employees playing business-cliché bingo, listening to a speech and checking off such phrases as "think outside the box" and "push the envelope" as the speaker said them. Perhaps these popular expressions are on their way out.

Slang and clichés may achieve a desired effect in a certain context, but they run the risk of sounding stale and out of date. They can also create problems in cross-cultural communication. Use such expressions sparingly, and only in informal communication with people who will understand and appreciate them.

- Use popular slang and clichés only when appropriate.

- They may make your writing sound stale.

- They may also cause miscommunication.

Use Technical Words and Acronyms with Caution

Every field of business—accounting, information systems, finance, marketing, and management—has its technical language. This language can be so complex that in some cases specialized dictionaries are compiled. Such dictionaries exist for technology, law, finance, and other business specialties. There are even dictionaries for sub-areas such as databases, ecommerce, and real estate.

As you work in your chosen field, you will learn its technical words and acronyms. In time you will use these terms freely in communicating with people in your field, and you should. Frequently, one such word will communicate a concept that would otherwise take dozens of words to describe. Moreover, specialized language can signal to other specialists that you are qualified to communicate on their level.

A problem comes about, however, when you use technical terms with people outside your field. Because these words are everyday words to you, you may forget that not everyone knows them. The result is miscommunication. You can avoid such miscommunication by using technical words only when you are sure your readers know them.

Examples of misuse of technical writing are easy to find. To a worker in the Social Security Administration, the words *covered employment* commonly mean employment covered by social security. To some outsiders, however, they could mean working under a roof. *Annuity* has a clear meaning to someone in insurance. A *contract that guarantees an income for a specified period* would have more meaning to uninformed outsiders. Computer specialists know C++ and Java to be popular programming languages, but these words may have different meanings for others.

Initials (including acronyms) should be used with caution, too. While some initials, such as IBM, are widely recognized, others, such as SOA (service-oriented architecture) are not. If you have any doubt that your reader is familiar with the initials, the best practice is to spell out the words the first time you use them and follow them with the initials. You may also need to go one step further and define what they mean.

- All fields have technical words.

- These words are useful when you communicate with people in your field. But they do not communicate with outsiders. Use them with caution.

- Some examples are *covered employment* and *annuity*. These words are well known to people in special fields, but not to most outsiders.

- Use initials cautiously. Spell out and define as needed.

Source: DILBERT Copyright © 1997 Scott Adams/Dist. by United Feature Syndicate, Inc.

When considering using slang in messages that might go to an international audience, consider this lesson about how even a seemingly straightforward word can go wrong:

> Some interesting problems can arise when attempts are made to reach what are thought to be single-minded markets supposedly speaking a common language. Spanish is probably the most vivid example of a language that, while it has many commonalities throughout its use in different places, also contains certain words that have marked variations in meaning. As a result, the message that's meant to be conveyed isn't necessarily the message that's received.
>
> To illustrate, according to Philip Cateora in his book *International Marketing,* the word *ball* translates in Spanish as *bola. Bola* means ball in several countries and a lie or fabrication in several others, while in yet another, it's a vulgar obscenity. Tropicana brand orange juice, he writes, was advertised as *Jugo de China* in Puerto Rico, but when marketed to the Cuban population of Miami, Florida, it failed to make a dent in the market. To the Puerto Rican, *China* translated into orange, but none of the Cubans in Miami were interested in buying what they perceived to be Chinese juice.

Source: Michael White, *A Short Course in International Marketing Blunders* (Novato, CA: World Trade Press, 2002) 10–11, *Ebrary Online Books,* University of Cincinnati, Web, 22 Apr. 2009.

Your technical language may not be any of the ones illustrated here, but you will have one. You will need to be careful not to use it when you write to people who do not understand it.

Use Concrete Language

- Use concrete words.

Good business communication uses words that tend to form sharp, clear meanings in readers' minds. These are the concrete words.

- Concrete words are specific words.

Concrete is the opposite of abstract. While abstract words are vague, concrete words tend to stand for things the reader can see, feel, taste, or smell. Concrete words are not only more specific; they also generate more interest because readers can relate them to actual experience.

- They stand for things that exist in the real world.

- Abstract nouns have general meanings.

The most concrete words are those that stand for things that exist in the real world, such as *chair, desk, computer, Lance Armstrong,* and the *Empire State Building.* Abstract nouns, on the other hand, cover broad, general meanings as in these examples: *administration, negotiation, wealth, inconsistency, loyalty, compatibility, conservation, discrimination, incompetence,* and *communication.* Note how difficult it is to visualize what these words stand for.

- Concreteness also means exactness.

Concreteness also means being specific. Notice how much clearer the specific words are in the following examples:

Abstract	Concrete
A significant loss	A 53 percent loss
Good attendance record	100 percent attendance record
The leading company	First among 3,212 companies
The majority	62 percent
In the near future	By noon Thursday
A labor-saving robot	A robot that does the work of seven workers
Light in weight	Featherlight
Substantial amount	$3,517,000

Now let us see the difference concreteness makes in the clarity of longer passages. Here is an example of abstract wording:

TECHNOLOGY IN BRIEF

Grammar and Style Checkers Help Writers with Word Selection

Today, word processors will help writers with grammar and style as well as with spelling. By default Word checks spelling and grammar automatically, using red and green underlines to distinguish between them. But as you see in the grammar settings screen shots here, writers can specify whether or not they want help and even which rules are applied to their documents. And they can choose to correct as they go along or to correct on demand. Although grammar and style checkers are not as accurate as spelling checkers, they will identify words, phrases, and sentences that could be improved. In fact, they often suggest a way to fix problems along with an explanation of correct usage.

In the example shown here, the checker found the use of passive voice and suggested a change to active voice. However, the writer must decide whether to accept the suggestion or ignore it. The writer needs to determine whether this passive voice was used intentionally for one of the reasons discussed in this chapter or whether it was used by accident and should be changed.

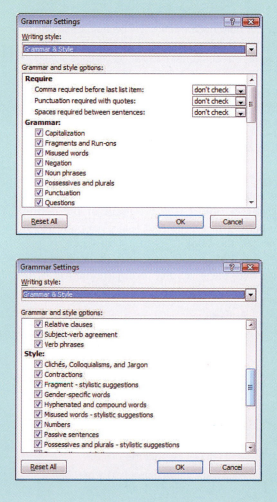

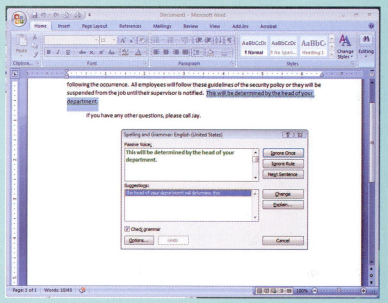

It is imperative that the firm practice extreme conservatism in operating expenditures during the coming biennium. The firm's past operating performance has been ineffectual for the reason that a preponderance of administrative assignments has been delegated to personnel who were ill equipped to perform in these capacities. Recently instituted administrative changes stressing experience in operating economies have rectified this condition.

Written for concreteness, this message might read as follows:

We must reduce operating expenses at least $2 million during 2010–11. Our $1,350,000 deficit for 2008–09 was caused by the inexperience of our two chief administrators, Mr. Sartan and Mr. Ross. We have replaced them with Ms. Pharr and Mr. Kunz, who have had 13 and 17 years, respectively, of successful experience in operations management.

As you can see, specific wording is not only easier to understand; it is also more informative and interesting.

Prefer Active Verbs

• Strong verbs make your writing lively and interesting

• Prefer active verbs to forms of "to be."

Of all parts of speech, verbs do the most to make your writing interesting and lively, for a good reason: they contain the action of the sentence.

But not all verbs add vigor to your writing. Overuse of the verb "to be" and passive voice can sap the energy from your sentences. To see the difference between writing that relies heavily on forms of "to be" and writing that uses active verbs, compare the following two passages (the forms of "to be" and their replacements are italicized):

There *are* over 300 customers served by our help desk each day. The help desk personnel's main tasks *are* to answer questions, solve problems, and educate the callers about the software. Without their expert work, our customer satisfaction ratings *would be* much lower than they *are*.

Our help desk personnel *serve* over 300 customers each day. They *answer* questions, *solve* problems, and *educate* the users about the software. Without their expert work, our customer satisfaction ratings *would drop* significantly.

As these examples show, using active verbs adds impact to your writing, and it usually saves words as well.

• Prefer the active voice to the passive voice.

In addition to minimizing your use of "to be" verbs, you can make your verbs more active by using what grammarians refer to as *active voice*. As you may recall, a sentence with a verb that can take a direct object (the recipient of the action) can be written either in a direct (active) pattern or an indirect (passive) pattern. For example, the sentence "the auditor inspected the books" is in active voice. In passive voice, the sentence would read: "The books were inspected by the auditor." For further support of the advantages of active over passive voice, compare the following sentences:

Passive	Active
The results were reported in our July 9 letter.	We reported the results in our July 9 letter.
This policy has been supported by our union.	Our union supported this policy.
The new process is believed to be superior by the investigators.	The investigators believe that the new process is superior.
The policy was enforced by the committee.	The committee enforced the policy.
The office will be inspected by Mr. Hall.	Mr. Hall will inspect the office.
A gain of 30.1 percent was reported for hardware sales.	Hardware sales gained 30.1 percent.
It is desired by the director that this problem be brought before the board.	The director wants the secretary to bring this problem before the board.
A complete reorganization of the administration was effected by the president.	The president completely reorganized the administration.

• Passive voice is sometimes preferable.

• Passive is better when the doer of the action is not important.

The suggestion that active voice be preferred does not mean passive voice is incorrect or you should never use it. Sometimes passive voice is preferable.

For example, when the doer of the action is unimportant to the message, passive voice properly de-emphasizes the doer.

Everything You Wanted to Know about Active and Passive Voice

Students are often confused by the terms *active voice* and *passive voice*. Here's the lowdown:

Broadly speaking, there are two main categories of verbs in English: those that can take direct objects and those that can't. To illustrate, the verb *repair* can take a direct object (that is, you can repair something), while the verb *happen* cannot (you can't happen anything).

Sentences with verbs that can take direct objects are the ones that can be written in either active or passive voice. When you write in active voice, the sentence is in "who + does/did what + to what/whom" order, as in this for example:

An authorized technician repaired the new laser printer.

   [who]   [did what]   [to what]

When you write the same idea in passive voice, the direct object moves to the start of the sentence and bumps the real subject to a phrase at the end of it (or out of it altogether). With this move, you now have

The new laser printer was repaired by an authorized

   [what]   [had something done to it]

technician.

   [by whom]

Or even just

The new laser printer was repaired.

As you can see, inverting the word order this way makes the sentence less energetic, more roundabout, and sometimes less informative.

You can find instances of passive voice in your own writing by looking for two- and three-word verbs that consist of

- a form of the verb to be (for example, *is, was, has been, will be*) and
- a verb in past-tense form (for example, *installed, reduced, chosen, sent*).

When you find such verbs—*was installed, has been reduced, will be chosen*—see if your meaning would be clearer and sharper if you wrote in the active voice instead.

Advertising is often criticized for its effect on price.

This copier has been repaired.

Passive voice may enable you to avoid accusing your reader of an action:

The damage was caused by exposing the material to sunlight.

The color desired was not specified in your order.

Passive voice also may be preferable when the performer is unknown, as in this example:

During the past year, the equipment has been sabotaged seven times.

- Passive helps you avoid accusing the reader.

- Passive is better when the performer is not known.

Give your writing impact by using strong verbs.

- It is also better when the writer prefers not to name the performer.

Yet another situation in which passive voice may be preferable is one in which the writer does not want to name the performer:

> The interviews were conducted on weekdays between noon and 6 p.m.

> Two complaints have been made about you.

Your writing will be clearest and liveliest, though, when you favor the active voice.

Avoid Overuse of Camouflaged Verbs

- Avoid camouflaged verbs—verbs embedded in nouns.

An awkward construction that should be avoided is the camouflaged verb. When a verb is camouflaged, the verb describing the action in a sentence takes the form of a noun. Then other verbs have to be added. For example, suppose you want to write a sentence in which *eliminate* is the action to be expressed. If you change *eliminate* into its noun form, *elimination,* you must add more words—perhaps *was effected*—to have a sentence. Your sentence might then be: "Elimination of the surplus was effected by the staff." The sentence is indirect and passive. You could have avoided the camouflaged construction with a sentence using the verb *eliminate:* "The staff eliminated the surplus."

- For example, if *cancel* becomes *cancellation*, you must add "to effect a" to have action.

Here are two more examples. If we take the action word *cancel* and make it into a noun, *cancellation,* we would have to say something like "to effect a cancellation" to communicate the action. If we change *consider* to *consideration,* we would have to say "give consideration to." So it would be with the following examples:

Action Verb	Noun Form	Wording of Camouflaged Verb
acquire	acquisition	make an acquisition
appear	appearance	make an appearance
apply	application	make an application
appraise	appraisal	make an appraisal
assist	assistance	give assistance to
cancel	cancellation	make a cancellation
commit	commitment	make a commitment
discuss	discussion	have a discussion
investigate	investigation	make an investigation
judge	judgment	make a judgment
liquidate	liquidation	effect a liquidation
reconcile	reconciliation	make a reconciliation
record	recording	make a recording

Note the differences in overall effect in these contrasting sentences:

Camouflaged Verb	Clear Verb Form
An *arrangement was made* to meet for breakfast.	We *arranged* to meet for breakfast.
Amortization of the account *was effected* by the staff.	The staff *amortized* the account.
Control of the water *was not possible*.	They *could not control* the water.
The new policy *involved the standardization* of the procedures.	The new policy *standardized* the procedures.
Application of the mixture *was accomplished*.	They *applied* the mixture.
We must *bring about a reconciliation of our* differences.	We must *reconcile* our differences.
The *establishment* of a wellness center *has been accomplished* by the company.	The company *has established* a wellness center.

The Trouble with Idioms

Non-native speakers have particular trouble with idiomatic expressions in foreign languages.

Consider the English verbal phrase "put up with." If you're a native English speaker, it makes clear sense to you—but imagine how nonsensical it might sound to a non-native speaker hearing or reading it for the first time.

On the other hand, choosing the appropriate preposition to describe going "to" a certain place can be challenging for a non-native French speaker. The preposition changes depending on whether you are using it with the name of a city or island ("á Paris"), with the feminine name of a country ("au Japon" [Japan]), with the masculine name of a country ("en Belgique" [Belgium]), with the name of a continent ("en Amerique du Sud [South America]"), with the masculine name of a state or region ("dans le Nevada"), or with the feminine name of a state or region ("en Californie" [California])!

When attempting to use the language of another culture, be careful to check your wording against a good phrase dictionary or some other expert source. Likewise, when communicating with an inexperienced user of your language, try to keep idiomatic expressions to a minimum and to be tolerant of errors in idiom that he or she may make.

From these illustrations you can see that our suggestion to avoid camouflaged verbs overlaps with our two preceding suggestions. First, camouflaged verbs are abstract nouns, and we suggested that you prefer concrete words over abstract words. Second, camouflaged verbs frequently require passive voice, and we advised using active voice.

- Avoid camouflaged verbs by (1) writing concretely and (2) preferring active voice.

You can apply with these related suggestions by following two helpful writing hints. The first is to make the subjects of most sentences either persons or things. For example, rather than write "consideration was given to . . . ," you should write "we considered . . . ." The second is to write most sentences in normal order (subject, verb, object), with the doer of the action as the subject. Involved, strained, passive structures often result from attempts at other orders.

- To apply these suggestions, (1) make your subjects persons or things and (2) write sentences in normal order.

Select Words for Precise Meanings

Obviously, writing requires considerable knowledge of the language being used. But beyond basic familiarity with vocabulary, good writers possess a sensitivity to words' shades of meaning. Words, like people, have personalities. Some are forceful and some timid; some are positive and some negative; some are formal and some informal. Any given word can occupy a place on many different scales of tone and meaning. Your task, as a writer attempting to achieve deliberate effects, is to choose the words that will achieve those effects with your intended readers.

- Writing well requires sensitivity to words' meanings.

Consider the differences among *tycoon, industry giant, successful entrepreneur,* and *prominent business executive.* All four terms indicate a person who has acquired wealth and power in business, but you would use these terms in different circumstances. For example, *tycoon* calls to mind the robber barons of the late 19th and early 20th centuries, with their diamond tie pins and ruthless air, whereas *prominent business executive* suggests a less flashy, less greedy person who has achieved success within the constraints of a corporation. Similarly, *fired, dismissed, downsized, separated, terminated,* and *discharged* refer to the same action but have different shades of meaning. So it is with each of the following groups of words:

sell, market, advertise, promote

money, funds, cash, finances

improve, enhance, fix, correct

concern, issue, problem, incident

secretary, administrative assistant, support staff, coordinator

- You should learn the shades of difference in the meanings of similar words.

- You should avoid confusing similar words.

Though the words in each list share the same denotation (barebones meaning), they vary widely in their connotations (their social and emotional associations). Being attentive to how different words are used will make you a more skillful and effective writer.

Knowledge of language also enables you to use words that carry the meanings you want to communicate. For example, *fewer* and *less* mean the same to some people. But careful users select *fewer* to mean "smaller numbers of items" and *less* to mean "reduced value, degree, or quantity." The verbs *affect* and *effect* are often used as synonyms. But *affect* means "to influence" and *effect* means "to bring to pass." Similarly, careful writers use *continual* to mean "repeated but broken succession" and *continuous* to mean "unbroken succession." They write *farther* to express geographic distance and *further* to indicate "more, in addition."

- Use correct idiom. *Idioms* are word combinations that have become standardized.

In your effort to be a precise writer, you should use correct idiom. By *idiom* we mean word combinations that have become standard in a language. Much of our idiom has little rhyme or reason, but if we want to be understood, we should follow it. For example, what is the logic behind the word *up* in the sentence "Look up her name in the directory"? There really is none; this is just the wording we have developed to cover this meaning. "Independent of" is good idiomatic usage; "independent from" is not. Similarly, you "agree to" a proposal, but you "agree with" a person. You are "careful about" a sensitive situation, but you are "careful with" your money. Here are some additional illustrations:

- There is little logical reason for some idioms, but violations are distracting and reflect poorly on you.

Faulty Idiom	Correct Idiom
authority about	authority on
comply to	comply with
different than	different from
enamored with	enamored of
equally as bad	equally bad
in accordance to	in accordance with
in search for	in search of
listen at	listen to
possessed with ability	possessed of ability
seldom or ever	seldom if ever
superior than	superior to

As you can see, some word choices are unwise, some are awkward, and some are just plain wrong. If you are unsure which word you need or would have the best effect, consult a dictionary.

SUGGESTIONS FOR NONDISCRIMINATORY WRITING

- Avoid words that discriminate on the basis of gender, race, nationality, age, sexual orientation, or disability.

Although discriminatory words are not directly related to writing clarity, our review of word selection would not be complete without some mention of them. By discriminatory words we mean words that do not treat all people equally and with respect. More specifically, they are words that refer negatively to groups of people, such as by gender, race, nationality, sexual orientation, age, or disability. Such words run contrary to acceptable views of fair play and human decency. They do not promote good business ethics or good business and thus have no place in business communication.

Many discriminatory words are a part of the vocabularies we have acquired from our environments. We often use them innocently, not realizing how they affect others. We can eliminate discriminatory words from our vocabularies by examining them carefully and placing ourselves in the shoes of those to whom they refer. The following review of the major forms of discriminatory words should help you achieve this goal.

* While we often use discriminatory words without bad intent, they still can have negative effects.

Use Gender-Neutral Words

Take care not to use words that discriminate by gender ("sexist" words). Although this form of discrimination can be directed against men, most instances involve discrimination against women. Our language developed in a society in which it was customary for women to work in the home and for men to be the breadwinners and decision makers. But times have changed, and the language you use in business needs to acknowledge the gender-diverse nature of most workplaces today. Suggestions for doing this follow.

Masculine Pronouns for Both Sexes. Perhaps the most troublesome sexist words are the masculine pronouns (*he, his, him*) when they are used to refer to both sexes, as in this example: "The typical State University student eats *his* lunch at the student center." Assuming that State is coeducational, the use of *his* suggests male supremacy. Historically, of course, the word *his* has been classified as generic—that is, able to refer to both sexes. But many modern-day businesspeople do not agree and are offended by the use of the masculine pronoun in this way.

* Avoid using the masculine pronouns (he, him, his) for both sexes.

You can avoid the use of masculine pronouns in such cases in three ways. First, you can reword the sentence to eliminate the offending word. Thus, the illustration above could be reworded as follows: "The typical State University student eats lunch at the student center." Here are other examples:

* You can do this (1) by rewording the sentence;

Sexist	**Gender-Neutral**
If a customer pays promptly, *he* is placed on our preferred list.	A customer who pays promptly is placed on our preferred list.
When an unauthorized employee enters the security area, *he* is subject to dismissal.	An unauthorized employee who enters the security area is subject to dismissal.
A supervisor is not responsible for such losses if *he* is not negligent.	A supervisor who is not negligent is not responsible for such losses.
When a customer needs service, it is *his* right to ask for it.	A customer who needs service has the right to ask for it.

In today's diverse workplaces, mutual respect between genders and across generations is key.

(2) by making the reference plural,

A second way to avoid sexist use of the masculine pronoun is to make the reference plural. Fortunately, the English language has plural pronouns (*their, them, they*) that refer to both sexes. Making the references plural in the examples given above, we have these nonsexist revisions:

as illustrated here;

If customers pay promptly, *they* are placed on our preferred list.

When unauthorized employees enter the security area, *they* are subject to dismissal.

Supervisors are not responsible for such losses if *they* are not negligent.

When customers need service, *they* have the right to ask for it.

or (3) by substituting neutral expressions,

A third way to avoid sexist use of *he, his,* or *him* is to substitute any of a number of neutral expressions. The most common are *he or she, he/she, s/he, you, one,* and *person*. Using neutral expressions in the problem sentences, we have these revisions:

If a customer pays promptly, *he or she* is placed on our preferred list.

as in these examples.

When an unauthorized employee enters the security area, *he/she* is subject to dismissal.

A supervisor is not responsible for such losses if *s/he* is not negligent.

When *one* needs service, *he/she* has the right to ask for it.

Neutral expressions can be awkward, so use them with caution.

You should use such expressions with caution, however. They tend to be somewhat awkward, particularly if they are used often. For this reason, many skilled writers avoid them. If you use them, you should pay attention to their effect on the flow of your words. Certainly, you should avoid sentences like this one: "To make an employee feel he/she is doing well by complimenting her/him insincerely confuses her/him later when he/she sees his/her co-workers promoted ahead of him/her."

Avoid words suggesting male dominance,

Words Derived from Masculine Words. As we have noted, our culture was male dominated when our language developed. Because of this, many of our words are masculine even though they do not refer exclusively to men. Take *chairman*, for example. This word can refer to both sexes, yet it does not sound that way. More appropriate and less offensive substitutes are *chair, presiding officer, moderator,* and *chairperson*. Similarly, *salesman* suggests a man, but many women work in sales.

How Diverse Is Too Diverse?

Can your employer tell you what to wear, outlaw decorated fingernails, or forbid the display of such body art as tattoos and piercings?

According to EmployeeIssues.com, a website about employee rights, the answer is yes—as long as the appearance policies are clearly stated in writing and are applied fairly to all employees.

Just as employers can require the use of uniforms, they can delineate what kinds of personal clothing will be acceptable on the job. For example, they might define "business casual" in a way that explicitly excludes T-shirts, shorts, flip-flops, and the like. And as long as tattoos and body piercings aren't required by your religion, they can be grounds for being disciplined or even fired—as long as the rules have been clearly laid out and communicated.

Looking professional need not mean selling out your cultural or ethnic heritage, argues Kali Evans-Raoul, founder of an image consultancy for minorities. Everyone must "balance self-expression with workplace realities," she asserts. Just as one doesn't wear a uniform at home, one shouldn't expect to bring one's entire personal look to work.

To avoid conflicts over your on-the-job identity, your best bet is to try to choose an employer whose values align with your own. Then find and abide by that company's appearance policy.

Sources: "Dress Cody Policy," *EmployeeIssues.com,* EmployeeIssues.com, 2003–2008, Web, 8 Apr. 2009, and Dan Woog, "Your Professional Image: Balance Self-Expression with Workplace Expectations," *Monster.com*, Monster.com, 2009, Web, 8 Apr. 2009.

Salesperson, salesclerk, or *sales representative* would be better. Other sexist words and gender-neutral substitutes are as follows:

Sexist	Gender-Neutral	
man-made	manufactured, of human origin	• such as these examples.
manpower	personnel, workers	
congressman	representative, member of Congress	
businessman	business executive, businessperson	
mailman	letter carrier, mail carrier	
policeman	police officer	
fireman	fire fighter	
repairman	repair technician	
cameraman	camera operator	

Many words with *man, his,* and the like in them have nonsexist origins. Among such words are *manufacture, management, history,* and *manipulate.* Also, some sexist words are hard to avoid. *Freshperson,* for example, would not serve as a substitute for *freshman.* And *personhole* is an illogical substitute for *manhole.*

• But not all man-sounding words are sexist.

Words That Lower Status by Gender. Thoughtless writers and speakers use expressions belittling the status of women. You should avoid such expressions. To illustrate, male executives sometimes refer to their female employees by first name only, while using first and last names or titles and last names ("Mr. Cross") for male employees. Then there are the many female forms for words that refer to work roles. In this group are *lady lawyer, authoress, sculptress,* and *poetess.* You should refer to women in these work roles by the same words that you would use for men: *lawyer, author, sculptor, poet.* Using words such as *male nurse* or *male teacher* can be demeaning as well.

• Do not use words that imply a lower status because of gender.

Examples of sexist words could go on and on. In deciding which words to avoid and which to use, you will have to rely on your best judgment. Remember that your goal should be to use words that are fair and that do not offend.

Avoid Words That Stereotype by Race, Nationality, or Sexual Orientation

● Words depicting minorities in a stereotyped way are unfair and untrue.

Words that stereotype all members of a group by race, nationality, or sexual orientation are especially unfair, and frequently they reinforce stereotypical beliefs about this group. Members of any minority vary widely in all characteristics. Thus, it is unfair to suggest that Jews are miserly, that Italians are Mafia members, that Hispanics are lazy, that African Americans can do only menial jobs, that gays are perfectionists, and so on. Unfair references to minorities are sometimes subtle and not intended, as in this example: "We conducted the first marketing tests in the low-income areas of the city. Using a sample of 200 African-American families, we . . . ." These words unfairly suggest that only African Americans live in low-income areas.

● Words that present members of minorities as exceptions to stereotypes are also unfair.

Also unfair are words suggesting that a minority member has struggled to achieve something that is taken for granted in the majority group. Usually well intended, words of this kind can carry subtle discriminatory messages. For example, a reference to a "neatly dressed Hispanic man" may suggest that he is an exception to the rule—that most Hispanics are not neatly dressed, but here is one who is. So can references to "an energetic Puerto Rican," "a Chinese manager," and the like.

● Eliminate such references to minorities by treating all people equally and by being sensitive to the effects of your words.

Eliminating unfair references to minority groups from your communication requires two basic steps. First, you must consciously treat all people equally, without regard to their minority status. You should refer to minority membership only in those rare cases in which it is a vital part of the message to be communicated. Second, you must be sensitive to the effects of your words. Specifically, you should ask yourself how those words would affect you if you were a member of the minorities to which they refer. You should evaluate your word choices from the viewpoints of others.

Avoid Words That Stereotype by Age

● Words that label people as old or young can arouse negative reactions.

Your avoidance of discriminatory wording should be extended to include discriminating by age—against both the old and the young. While those over 55 might be retired from their first jobs, many lead lives that are far from the sedentary roles in which they are sometimes depicted. They also are not necessarily feeble, forgetful, or slow. While some do not mind being called *senior citizens,* others do. Be sensitive with terms such as *mature* and *elderly* as well; perhaps *retired, experienced,* or *veteran* would be better received. Likewise, when tempted to refer to someone as *young* (*young accountant, accomplished young woman*), be sure that calling attention to the person's age is defensible.

Also be careful when using one of the popular generational labels in your writing. While it makes sense for the popular management literature to use such labels as *baby boomer* and *millennial* as short-hand references to different generations, the same labels can seem discriminatory in business messages. Your co-worker Frank probably does not want to be referred to as the "baby boomer in the group," and your manager Courtney probably will not appreciate your saying that she holds the opinions she does because she's a "Generation Xer." As we have suggested, use such labels only when relevant and appropriate.

Avoid Words That Typecast Those with Disabilities

● People with disabilities are sensitive to words that describe their disabilities.

People with disabilities are likely to be sensitive to discriminatory words. Television shows those with disabilities competing in the Special Olympics, often exceeding the performance of average persons, and common sense tells us not to stereotype these people. However, sometimes we do anyway. Just as with age, we need to avoid derogatory labels and apologetic or patronizing behavior. For example, instead of describing one as *deaf and dumb,* use *deaf.* Avoid slang terms such as *fits, spells, attacks;* use *seizures, epilepsy,* or other objective terms. Terms such as *crippled* and *retarded* should be avoided because they degrade in most cases. Work to develop a nonbiased attitude, and show it through carefully chosen words.

The Different Goals of Different Generations

Authors Lynne C. Lancaster and David Stillman propose that the different generations now working together in the United States have the following different motivational goals:

Traditionalists: "The satisfaction of a job well done."

Baby Boomers: "Money, title, recognition, the corner office."

Generation Xers: "Freedom is the ultimate reward."

Millenials: "Work that has meaning for me."

Source: *When Generations Collide: Who They Are, Why They Clash, How to Solve the Generational Puzzle at Work* (New York: HarperCollins, 2002) 77, print.

Some Final Words about Words

There's a lot to keep in mind when selecting the most appropriate words. Under time pressure, it can be tempting to take a shortcut and settle—as Mark Twain once put it—for the best word's "second cousin." But remember: Business and business relationships can be won or lost with one word choice. The effort to say what you mean as clearly, readably, and appropriately as you can is effort well spent.

● The effort to select the best words for the job is effort well spent.

SUMMARY BY LEARNING OBJECTIVES

1. To communicate clearly, you must adapt to your reader.
   - Adapting means using words the reader understands.
   - It therefore involves using all your knowledge of your reader.

1 Explain the role of adaptation in selecting words that communicate.

2. Select words that your reader understands.
   - These are the familiar words (words like *old* instead of *antiquated*).
   - They are also the short words (*agreed to quit* rather than *acceded to the proposition to terminate*).

2 Simplify writing by selecting familiar and short words.

3. Use slang and popular clichés with caution.
   - They may make your writing sound stale.
   - They may also cause miscommunication.

3 Use slang and popular clichés with caution.

4. Use technical words and acronyms with caution.
   - Spell out and define acronyms as needed.
   - However, technical words are appropriate among technical people.

4 Use technical words and acronyms appropriately.

5. Prefer the concrete words and active verbs.
   - Concrete words are the specific ones. For example, *57 percent majority* is more concrete than *majority*.
   - Action verbs are more vigorous and interesting than forms of "to be."
   - In active voice, the subject acts; in passive voice, it receives the action. Prefer the active voice (e.g., *we reported the results* rather than *the results were reported by us*).

5 Write concretely and use active verbs.

- Active voice is stronger, more vigorous, and more interesting. But passive voice can be preferable in some situations.
- Avoid overuse of camouflaged verbs—making a noun of the active verb and then having to add words (e.g., use *appear* rather than *make an appearance*).

6 *Write with clarity and precision by selecting the right words and by using idioms correctly.*

6. Write more clearly and precisely by following these suggestions:
   - Develop a feeling for the personalities of words.
   - Select words for their precise meanings (for example, choose carefully among *concern, issue, problem, incident*).
   - Also, learn the specific ways that combinations of words are used in English and other languages (called *idiom*).

7 *Use words that do not discriminate.*

7. Avoid discriminatory words.
   - Do not use words that discriminate against women (for example, using *he, him,* or *his* to refer to both sexes and words such as *fireman, postman, lady lawyer,* and *authoress*).
   - Do not use words that suggest stereotyped roles of race, nationality, or sexual orientation (African Americans and menial jobs, Italians and the Mafia, gays and perfectionists).
   - Do not use words that discriminate against age or disability.

CRITICAL THINKING QUESTIONS

1 Explain how you would apply the basic principle of adaptation to your choice of words for each of the following writing tasks. **(LO1)**
   a. An editorial in a company newsletter.
   b. A message to Joan Branch, a supervisor of an information systems department, concerning a change in determining project priorities.
   c. A report to the chief engineer on a technical topic in the engineer's field.
   d. A message to employees explaining a change in pension benefits.
   e. A letter to company stockholders explaining a change in company reporting dates.

2 Evaluate this comment: "I'm not going to simplify my writing for my readers. That would be talking down to them. Plus, if they can't understand clear English, that's their problem." **(LO2)**

3 "Some short words are hard, and some long words are easy. Thus, the suggestion to prefer short words doesn't make sense." Discuss. **(LO2)**

4 "It's important to use business clichés like *cutting edge* and *state of the art* to sound professional." Discuss. **(LO3)**

5 "As technical language typically consists of acronyms and long, hard words, it contributes to miscommunication. Thus, it should be avoided in all business communication." Discuss. **(LO4)**

6 Using examples other than those in the book, identify some technical terms that would communicate effectively to others in the field but would need to be clarified for those outside the field. **(LO4)**

7 Define and give examples of active and passive voice. Explain when each should be used. **(LO5)**

8 Style experts advise against monotonous-sounding writing—that is, writing that has a droning, "blah-blah" effect when read aloud. What advice in this chapter might help you avoid a monotonous style? **(LO2, LO5)**

9 Discuss this statement: "When I use *he, him,* or *his* as a generic pronoun, I am not discriminating against women. For many years these words have been accepted as generic. They refer to both sexes, and that's the meaning I have in mind when I use them." **(LO7)**

10 List synonyms (words with similar meanings) for each of the following words. Then explain the differences in shades of meaning as you see them. **(LO6)**

   a. salesperson   g. boss
   b. co-worker   h. misfortune
   c. old   i. inquire
   d. tell   j. stop
   e. happiness   k. lie
   f. customer   l. mistake

CRITICAL THINKING EXERCISES

Using Familiar Words (LO2)

Instructions, Sentences 1–20: Assume that your readers are at about the 10th-grade level in education. Revise these sentences for easy communication to this audience.

1 We must terminate all deficit financing.

2 We must endeavor to correct this problem by expediting delivery.

3 A proportionate tax consumes a determinate apportionment of one's monetary flow.

4 Business has an inordinate influence on governmental operations.

5 It is imperative that consumers be unrestrained in determining their preferences.

6 Mr. Sanchez terminated Kevin's employment as a consequence of his ineffectual performance.

7 Our expectations are that there will be increments in commodity value.

8 Can we ascertain the types of customers that have a predisposition to utilize our instant-credit offer?

9 The preponderance of the businesspeople we consulted envisions signs of improvement from the current siege of economic stagnation.

10 If liquidation becomes mandatory, we shall dispose of these assets first.

11 Recent stock acquisitions have accentuated the company's current financial crisis.

12 Mr. Coward will serve as intermediary in the pending labor–management parley.

13 Ms. Smith's idiosyncrasies supply adequate justification for terminating her employment.

14 Requisites for employment by this company have been enhanced.

15 The unanimity of current forecasts is not incontrovertible evidence of an impending business acceleration.

16 People's propensity to consume is insatiable.

17 The company must desist from its deficit financing immediately.

18 This antiquated merchandising strategy is ineffectual in contemporary business operations.

19 Percentage return on common stockholders' equity averaged 23.1 for the year.

20 The company's retained earnings last year exceeded $2,500,000.

Using Technical Words Appropriately (LO4)

21 From a scholarly business journal, select a paragraph (at least 150 words long) that would be difficult for a student less advanced in the subject than you. Rewrite the paragraph so that this student can understand it easily. (LO4)

Instructions, Sentences 22–48: Revise these sentences to make them conform to the writing suggestions discussed in the book. They are grouped by the suggestion they illustrate.

Selecting Concrete Words (LO5)

22 We have found that young men are best for this work.

23 She makes good grades.

24 John lost a fortune in Las Vegas.

25 If we don't receive the goods soon, we will cancel.

26 Some years ago she made good money.

27 His grade on the aptitude test was not high.

28 Here is a product with very little markup.

29 The cost of the online subscription was reasonable.

30 We will need some new equipment soon.

Limiting Use of Passive Voice (LO5)

31 Our action is based on the assumption that the competition will be taken by surprise.

32 It is believed by the typical union member that his or her welfare is not considered to be important by management.

33 You were directed by your supervisor to complete this assignment by noon.

34 It is believed by the writer that this company policy is wrong.

35 The union was represented by Cecil Chambers.

36 These reports are prepared by the salespeople every Friday.

37 Our decision is based on the belief that the national economy will be improved.

Avoiding Camouflaged Verbs (LO5)

38 It was my duty to make a determination of the damages.

39 Harold made a recommendation that we fire Mr. Schultz.

40 We will ask him to bring about a change in his work routine.

41 This new equipment will result in a savings in maintenance.

42 Will you please make an adjustment on this invoice?

43 Implementation of the plan was effected by the crew.

44 Approval of all orders must be made by the chief.

45 A committee performs the function of determining the award.

46 Adaptation to the new policy was performed easily by the staff.

47 Verification of the amount is made daily by the auditor.

48 The president tried to effect a reconciliation of the two groups.

Selecting Precise Words (LO6)

Instructions, Sentences 49–59: Following is an exercise in word precision. Explain the differences in meaning for the word choices shown. Point out any words that are wrongly used.

49 Performance during the fourth quarter was (average) (mediocre).

50 This merchandise is (old) (antique) (secondhand) (preowned) (used).

51 The machine ran (continually) (continuously).

52 The mechanic is a (woman) (lady) (female).

53 His action (implies) (infers) that he accepts the criticism.

54 Her performance on the job was (good) (top-notch) (excellent) (superior).

55 On July 1 the company will (become bankrupt) (close its door) (go under) (fail).

56 The staff members (think) (understand) (know) the results were satisfactory.

57 I cannot (resist) (oppose) her appointment.

58 Did you (verify) (confirm) these figures?

59 This is an (effective) (effectual) (efficient) plan.

Using Proper Idiom (LO6)

Instructions, Sentences 60–67: These sentences use faulty idioms. Make the changes you think are necessary.

60 The purchasing officer has gone in search for a substitute product.

61 Our office has become independent from the Dallas office.

62 This strike was different than the one in 2000.

63 This letter is equally as bad.

64 She is an authority about mutual funds.

65 When the sale is over with, we will restock.

66 Our truck collided against the wall.

67 We have been in search for a qualified supervisor since August.

Avoiding Discriminatory Language (LO7)

Instructions, Sentences 68–77: Change these sentences to avoid discriminatory language.

68 Any worker who ignores this rule will have his salary reduced.

69 The typical postman rarely makes mistakes in delivering his mail.

70 A good executive plans his daily activities.

71 The committee consisted of a businessman, a banker, and a lady lawyer.

72 A good secretary screens all telephone calls for her boss and arranges his schedule.

73 An efficient salesman organizes his calls and manages his time.

74 Two representatives of our company attended the conference: a Hispanic engineer and one of our younger managers.

75 Three people applied for the job, including two well-educated black women.

76 Handicap parking spaces are strictly for use by the crippled.

77 He is one of the best gay designers in the city.

chapter three

Construction of Clear Sentences and Paragraphs

LEARNING OBJECTIVES

Upon completing this chapter, you will be able to construct clear sentences and paragraphs by emphasizing adaptation, short sentences, and effective paragraph design. To reach this goal, you should be able to

1 Explain the role of adaptation in writing clear sentences.

2 Write short, clear sentences by limiting sentence content and economizing on words.

3 Design sentences that give the right emphasis to content.

4 Employ unity and good logic in writing effective sentences.

5 Compose paragraphs that are short and unified, use topic sentences effectively, and communicate coherently.

Writing Sentences and Paragraphs That Communicate

Introduce yourself to this chapter by continuing in the role of small business manager and immediate superior to Max Elliott (preceding chapter). Max's writing problem would be of concern in any business, but it is especially important in small businesses such as yours. Your company is struggling to survive. It must be more efficient in every aspect of its operations if it is to beat out the competition. Communication is one of these aspects, and this is why you are concerned about what you see in Max's writing.

As you continue your review of Max's writing, you detect more than problems with word choice. Something else

is wrong. His sentences just do not convey sharp, clear meanings. Although grammatically correct, they appear to be needlessly complex and heavy. His long and involved paragraphs also cause you concern.

What you have seen in Max's writing are problems concerning two other determinants of readability: the sentence and the paragraph. As you will learn in the pages ahead, these two writing units play major roles in communicating. This chapter will show you how to construct sentences and paragraphs that produce readable writing.

THE IMPORTANCE OF ADAPTATION

- Sentences should be adapted to readers.

As you have seen, choosing the right words is basic to clear communication. Equally basic is the task of arranging those words into clear sentences and the sentences into clear paragraphs. Like choosing words, constructing clear sentences and paragraphs involves adaptation to the intended readers.

Fitting your writing to your readers requires the reader analysis we discuss in Chapter 1 and Chapter 5. You should study your readers to find out what they are like—what they know, how they think, and what their contexts are. Then write in a way that will communicate with them.

- Use the simpler sentence structures for those less able to understand; use the more complex structures when appropriate.

In general, this procedure involves using the simpler sentence structures to reach people with lower communication abilities and people not knowledgeable about the subject. It involves using the more complex sentence structures only when communicating with more verbal, knowledgeable people. As we will see, even with advanced readers, simplicity is sometimes needed for the best communication effect.

You should aim a little below the level of your reader. Readability research tells us that writing communicates best when it does not tax the reader's comprehension skills. Thus, some simplification is desirable for all readers. Keep this point in mind as you read through the rest of this chapter.

Writing effectively also requires managing the emphasis in your sentences, making each sentence express a main idea, and ordering the sentence elements according to accepted rules of grammar and logic.

The final section of this chapter offers advice about how to turn your well-constructed sentences into well-constructed paragraphs—paragraphs that are united, efficient, forward moving, and coherent. Delivering your contents in easy-to-digest chunks is one of your most powerful strategies for engaging and informing your busy readers.

CARE IN SENTENCE DESIGN

- Writing effective sentences involves grouping and ordering the information.

When you sit down to write a given message, you have many bits of information at hand. How will you turn them into a clear, coherent message?

Your first task will probably be grouping and ordering the information—that is, planning the message's overall pattern of organization or structure. But sooner or later, writing a successful message comes down to figuring out how to stitch your contents together in a series of sentences. How much information will you put into each sentence? And in what order will that information be?

Deciding how to use sentences to group your information is a fundamental challenge for writers. Fortunately, you have a powerful resource at your disposal: your own storehouse of knowledge about the many kinds of clauses, phrases, and types of modifiers that can be used. You may not know the names of all these elements, but you can still use them to good effect. The building blocks for sentences are already part of your competency as an English speaker, whether or not you are conscious of them.

For example, how might we turn the following bits of information about a retiring employee into the opening of an article for a company newsletter?

Bill Jones is a drill press operator. He has been employed by Allied Manufacturing. He has been employed by the company for 15 years. He is retiring. He is retiring on June 15.

Surely we would not report each bit of information separately in this way. It would be too hard for the reader to put the facts together, and the writing would sound childish. Instead, we would combine some of the facts, and we would draw upon our storehouse of possible sentence elements to do it. We might write

Bill Jones, a drill press operator who has been with Allied Manufacturing for 15 years, will be retiring on June 15.

Or we might write

Bill Jones will be retiring on June 15. He has been a drill press operator with Allied Manufacturing for 15 years.

Both ways indicate that "Bill Jones will be retiring" is an important idea because it occupies a main clause, the central statement in any sentence. The first version adds the other facts as modifying phrases, whereas the second version gives certain additional facts a bit more significance by putting them in their own sentence. Which way is better? It depends on the effect you want to achieve and on how much information you think your readers can digest at once.

Of course, you won't start out with all your bits of information as neatly separated as they were in this example. But you will still have to decide how much and what kind of information to put into each sentence, and in what form and order. The more consciously you control the information in your sentences, the more consciously you control your meaning and your reader's response to it. Paying attention to examples of clear, smooth writing and learning more about the different sentence elements will help you with this goal.

So will the advice in the following sections. But remember: adaptation is critical. Your ultimate guide to communicating well is your awareness of your particular readers' skills and likely responses.

Using Short Sentences

Business audiences tend to prefer simple, efficient sentences over long, complex ones. Having too much to do in too little time is a chronic problem in business. A recent study found that 95 percent of executives and managers make a to-do list for each day, but 99 percent of them do not complete the tasks on those lists.[1] Type *time management* or *information overload* into your Web browser's search box and see how many hits you get. No one, whether executive or first-level employee, wants to read writing that wastes time.

- Your familiarity with different sentence elements—whether or not you know their grammatical labels—will help you design sentences that manage the information.

- Cultivating an awareness of the different sentence types and elements will help make you a better writer.

- Your readers are busy. Writing efficient sentences can save them time and effort.

---

[1] Chuck Martin, *Tough Management: The 7 Winning Ways to Make Tough Decisions Easier, Deliver the Numbers, and Grow the Business in Good Times and Bad* (New York: McGraw-Hill, 2005) xiv, print.

Readability Statistics Help Writers Evaluate Document Length and Difficulty

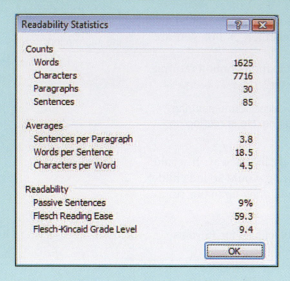

Grammar and style checkers give writers the option of viewing readability statistics. These statistics report the number of words, characters, paragraphs, and sentences in a document along with averages of characters per word, words per sentence, and sentences per paragraph.

The report you see here was generated for a scholarly manuscript. It reports an average of 18.5 words per sentence, a bit high for a business document but probably at an acceptable level for a scholarly document's readers. The Flesch-Kincaid score confirms that the reading grade level is 9.4, too high for business documents but likely appropriate for a scholarly audience. However, the Flesch Reading Ease score should give the writer cause to review the document for accessibility, even for its targeted audience. The 59.3 score is slightly below the 60–70 range Microsoft recommends.

- Short sentences communicate better because of mind limitations.

Favoring short sentences can save your readers time. It can also prevent miscommunication. Readability research tells us that the more words and the more relationships there are in a sentence, the greater is the possibility for misunderstanding. This finding suggests that the mind can hold only so much information at one time. Thus, to give it too much information in your sentences is to risk falling short of your communication purpose.

- Short means about 16–18 words for middle-level readers.

What constitutes a short, readable sentence is related to the reader's ability. Readability studies suggest that writing intended to communicate with the middle-level adult reader should average 16 to 18 words per sentence. For more advanced readers, the average may be higher. For less advanced readers, it should be lower.

- But avoid excessive use of short sentences.

Our emphasis on short sentences does not mean that you should use all short sentences. In fact, you should avoid overusing them. The overuse of short sentences results in a choppy effect and suggests primer simplicity. You should use moderately long sentences occasionally. They are sometimes useful in subordinating information and in increasing interest by adding variety. And sometimes the information needed to convey a thought requires a long sentence. Even so, you should take care not to make the long sentences excessively long.

The following sentence from an employee handbook illustrates the effect of long sentences on communication:

When an employee has changed from one job to another job, the new corresponding coverages will be effective as of the date the change occurs, unless, however, if due to a physical disability or infirmity as a result of advanced age, an employee is changed from one job to another job and such change results in the employee's new job rate coming within a lower hourly job-rate bracket in the table, in which case the employee may, at the discretion of the company, continue the amount of group term life insurance and the amount of accidental death and dismemberment insurance that the employee had prior to such change.

Avoiding Stringy and See-Saw Sentences

If you try to load down a sentence with too much information, you can wind up with a stringy sentence like this:

> While we welcome all applications, we are particularly interested in candidates who have at least three years' experience, although we will consider those with less experience who have a degree in the field or who have earned a certificate from an industry-certified trainer, and we will also consider fluency in Italian a plus.

A see-saw sentence is one that goes back and forth between two points, like this:

> A blog can add visibility to a business, although it can be labor intensive to maintain, but the time spent on the blog could be worthwhile if it generates a buzz among our potential customers.

In these cases, whittle the sentences down to digestible size, use helpful transitional phrases (*in addition*, *on the other hand*) between them, and don't switch directions too often.

Here, for example, are more digestible versions of the problem sentences:

> While we welcome all applications, we are particularly interested in candidates who (1) have at least three years' experience or (2) have less experience but have earned a degree or certificate in the field. Fluency in Italian is also a plus.

> A blog can add visibility to a business. True, maintaining a blog takes time, but if the blog generates a buzz among our potential customers, the time will be well spent.

Chances are that you did not get a clear message from this sentence when you first read it. The explanation is not in the words used; you probably know them all. Neither is it in the ideas presented; they are relatively simple. The problem is the length of the sentence. So many words and relationships are in the sentence that they cause confusion. The result is vague communication at best—complete miscommunication at worst. Now look at the message written in all short sentences. The meanings may be clear, but the choppy effect is distracting and irritating. Imagine reading a long document written in this style.

> An employee may change jobs. The change may result in a lower pay bracket. The new coverage is effective when this happens. The job change should be because of physical disability. It can also be because of infirmity. Old age may be another cause. The company has some discretion in the matter. It can permit continuing the accidental death insurance. It can permit continuing the dismemberment insurance.

The following paragraph takes a course between these two extremes. Clearly, it is an improvement. Generally, it emphasizes short sentences, but it combines content items where appropriate.

> The new insurance coverage becomes effective when because of disability, infirmity, or age an employee's job change results in lower pay. But at its discretion, the company may permit the old insurance coverage to continue.

You can shorten and simplify sentences in two basic ways: (1) by limiting sentence content and (2) by using words economically.

- Short sentences are achieved in two ways.

Limiting Sentence Content

Limiting sentence content is largely a matter of mentally selecting thought units and making separate sentences of most of them. Sometimes, of course, you should combine thoughts into one sentence. You have good reason to do so, for example, when thoughts are closely related or when you want to de-emphasize certain content.

- Limiting content is one way to make short sentences.

The advantage of limiting sentence content is evident in the following contrasting examples:

Long and Hard to Understand	**Short and Clear**
This letter is being distributed with enrollment confirmation sheets, which are to serve as a final check on the correctness of the registration of students and are to be used later when obtaining semester grades from the regline system, which are to be available two weeks after the term officially ends.	This letter is being distributed with enrollment confirmation sheets. These sheets will serve now as a final check on student registration. Later, the codes on them will be used to access course grades through the regline system; the grades will be available two weeks after the term officially ends.
Some authorities in human resources object to expanding normal salary ranges to include a trainee rate because they fear that through oversight or prejudice probationers may be kept at the minimum rate longer than is warranted and because they fear that it would encourage the spread from the minimum to maximum rate range.	Some authorities in human resources object to expanding the normal salary range to include a trainee rate, for two reasons. First, they fear that through oversight or prejudice probationers may be kept at the minimum rate longer than is warranted. Second, they fear that expansion would increase the spread between the minimum and the maximum rate range.
Regardless of their seniority or union affiliation, all employees who hope to be promoted are expected to continue their education either by enrolling in the special courses to be offered by the company, which are scheduled to be given after working hours beginning next Wednesday, or by taking approved online courses selected from a list, which may be seen on the company portal.	Regardless of their seniority or union affiliation, all employees who hope to be promoted are expected to continue their education in either of two ways. (1) They may enroll in special courses to be given by the company. (2) They may take approved online courses selected from the list on the company portal.

When you find yourself writing a sentence that goes on and on, look for a way to divide it into more digestible chunks.

Too many simple sentences create an elementary-sounding style, so combine ideas where appropriate for your adult readers.

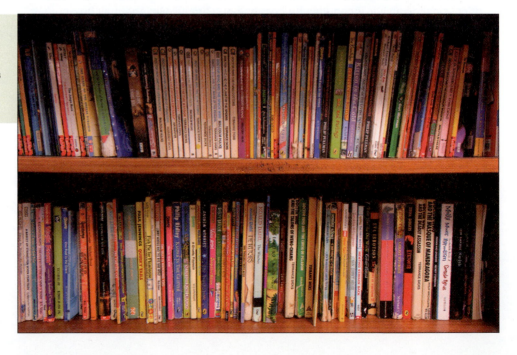

Economizing on Words

A second basic technique of shortening sentences is to use words economically. Anything you write can be expressed in many ways, some shorter than others. In general, the shorter wordings save the reader time and are clearer and more interesting.

Economizing on words generally means seeking shorter ways of saying things. Once you try to economize, you will probably find many ways to trim your writing.

To help you recognize instances of uneconomical wording, we cover the most common types below.

Cluttering Phrases. An often-used uneconomical wording is the cluttering phrase. This is a phrase that can be replaced by shorter wording without loss of meaning. The little savings achieved in this way add up.

Here is an example of a cluttering phrase:

In the event that payment is not made by January, operations will cease.

The phrase *in the event that* is uneconomical. The little word *if* can substitute for it without loss of meaning:

If payment is not made by January, operations will cease.

Similarly, the phrase that begins the following sentence adds unnecessary length:

In spite of the fact that they received help, they failed to exceed the quota.

Although makes an economical substitute:

Although they received help, they failed to exceed their quota.

The following partial list of cluttering phrases (with suggested substitutions) should help you cut down on them:

Cluttering Phrase	Shorter Substitution
Along the lines of	Like
At the present time	Now
For the purpose of	For
For the reason that	Because, since
In accordance with	By
In the amount of	For
In the meantime	Meanwhile
In the near future	Soon
In the neighborhood of	About
In very few cases	Seldom
In view of the fact that	Since, because
With regard to, with reference to	About

Surplus Words. To write economically, eliminate words that add nothing to sentence meaning. As with cluttering phrases, we often use meaningless extra words as a matter of habit. Eliminating these surplus words sometimes requires recasting a sentence, but sometimes they can just be left out.

The following is an example of surplus wording from a business report:

It will be noted that the records for the past years show a steady increase in special appropriations.

The beginning words add nothing to the meaning of the sentence. Notice how dropping them makes the sentence stronger—and without loss of meaning:

The records for the past years show a steady increase in special appropriations.

- Another way to shorten sentences is through word economy.

- Seek shorter ways of saying things.
- Following are some suggestions.

- Avoid cluttering phrases. Substitute shorter expressions.

- Eliminate surplus words.

Is *That* a Surplus Word?

How easy is it to read the following sentence without making a misstep?

> We found the reason for our poor performance was stiff competition from a local supplier.

In such a sentence, adding the word *that* where it is implied would help:

> We found *that* the reason for our poor performance was stiff competition from a local supplier.

In your quest for an economical sentence, do not eliminate *that* when it actually adds clarity.

Here is a second example:

> His performance was good enough *to enable him* to qualify for the promotion.

The words *to enable* add nothing and can be dropped:

> His performance was good enough to qualify him for the promotion.

The following sentences further illustrate the use of surplus words. In each case, the surplus words can be eliminated without changing the meaning.

Contains Surplus Words	Eliminates Surplus Words
He ordered desks *that are of the* executive type.	He ordered executive-type desks.
There are four rules *that* should be observed.	Four rules should be observed.
In addition to these defects, numerous other defects mar the operating procedure.	Numerous other defects mar the operating procedure.
The machines *that were* damaged by the fire were repaired.	The machines damaged by the fire were repaired.

Don't write like a faceless bureaucrat!

The Starbucks Study

Supporting the advice we give in this text is the Starbucks Study conducted by Fugere, Hardaway, and Warshawsky. These researchers selected two actual writing samples. One was written in what they called typical corporate speak—big words and long sentences. The other was written in the straight, clear way stressed in this text. The identities of the companies were hidden. The researchers asked a sample of customers at an Atlanta Starbucks coffee shop to select from a list of 30 common psychological traits (15 good and 15 bad) the ones they would associate with each writing sample. The Starbucks customers did not like the corporate-speak sample, selecting mostly words such as *obnoxious, rude, stubborn,* and *unreliable.* They liked the straight and clear writing sample, selecting words such as *likeable, energetic, friendly, inspiring,* and *enthusiastic.*

Source: Brian Fugere, Cheksea Hardaway, and Jon Warshawsky, *Why Business-people Speak Like Idiots* (New York: The Free Press, 2005) 17, print.

Contains Surplus Words	Eliminates Surplus Words
By *the* examining *of* production records, they found the error.	By examining production records, they found the error.
In the period between April and June, we detected the problem.	Between April and June we detected the problem.
I am prepared to report *to the effect* that sales increased.	I am prepared to report that sales increased.

Roundabout Constructions. As we have noted, you can write anything in many ways. Some of the ways are direct, while some cover the same ground in a roundabout way. Usually the direct ways are shorter and communicate better.

- Avoid roundabout ways of saying things.

This sentence illustrates roundabout construction:

The department budget *can be observed to be decreasing* each *new* year.

Do the words *can be observed to be decreasing* get to the point? Is the idea of *observing* essential? Is *new* needed? A more direct and better sentence is this one:

The department budget decreases each year.

Here is another roundabout sentence:

The union *is involved in the task of reviewing* the seniority provision of the contract.

Now if the union is *involved in the task of reviewing,* it is really *reviewing.* The sentence should be written in these direct words:

The union *is reviewing* the seniority provision of the contract.

The following sentence pairs further illustrate the advantages of short, direct wording over roundabout wording:

Roundabout	Direct
The president *is of the opinion that* the tax was paid.	The president *believes* the tax was paid.
It is essential that the income be used to retire the debt.	The income *must* be used to retire the debt.
Reference is made to your May 10 report *in which you concluded* that the warranty is worthless.	Your May 10 report *concluded* that the warranty is worthless.

Roundabout	Direct
The supervisors *should take appropriate action to determine* whether the absentee reports are being verified.	The supervisors *should determine* whether the absentee reports are being verified.
The price increase *will afford* the company *an opportunity* to retire the debt.	The price *will enable* the company to retire the debt.
During the time she was employed by this company, Ms. Carr was absent once.	*While* employed by this company, Ms. Carr was absent once.
He criticized everyone he *came in contact with*.	He criticized everyone he *met*.

● Repeat words only for effect and emphasis.

Unnecessary Repetition of Words or Ideas. Repeating words obviously adds to sentence length. Such repetition sometimes serves a purpose, as when it is used for emphasis or special effect. But all too often it is without purpose, as this sentence illustrates:

> We have not received your payment covering invoices covering June and July purchases.

It would be better to write the sentence like this:

> We have not received your payment covering invoices for June and July purchases.

Another example is this one:

> He stated that he believes that we are responsible.

The following sentence eliminates one of the *that*s:

> He stated that he believes we are responsible.

● Avoid repetitions of ideas (redundancies).

Repetitions of ideas through the use of different words that mean the same thing (*free gift, true fact, past history*) also add to sentence length. Known as redundancies, such repetitions are illogical and can rarely be justified. Note the redundancy in this sentence:

> The provision of Section 5 provides for a union shop.

By definition, a *provision* provides, so the repetition serves no purpose. The following sentence is better:

> Section 5 provides for a union shop.

Here are other examples of redundancies and ways to eliminate them:

Needless Repetition	Repetition Eliminated
Please *endorse your name on the back* of this check.	Please *endorse* this check.
We must *assemble together* at 10:30 AM *in the morning*.	We must *assemble* at 10:30 AM.
Our new model *is longer in length* than the old one.	Our new model *is longer* than the old one.
If you are not satisfied, *return it back* to us.	If you are not satisfied, *return* it to us.
Tod Wilson is the *present incumbent*.	Tod Wilson is the *incumbent*.
One should know the *basic fundamentals* of clear writing.	One should know the *fundamentals* of clear writing.
The *consensus of opinion* is that the tax is unfair.	The *consensus* is that the tax is unfair.
By acting now, we can finish *sooner than if we wait until a later date*.	By acting now, we can finish *sooner*.
At the present time, we *are* conducting two clinics.	We *are* conducting two clinics.
As a matter of interest, I am interested in learning your procedure.	I am *interested* in learning your procedure.
We should *plan in advance for the future*.	We should *plan*.

Determining Emphasis in Sentence Design

Any written business communication contains a number of items of information, not all of which are equally important. Some are very important, such as a conclusion in a report or the objective in a message. Others are relatively unimportant. One of your tasks as a writer is to form your sentences to communicate the importance of each item.

Sentence length affects emphasis. Short, simple sentences carry more emphasis than long, involved ones. They call attention to their contents by conveying a single message without the interference of related or supporting information.

Longer sentences give less emphasis to their contents. When a sentence contains two or more ideas, the ideas share emphasis. How they share it depends on how the sentence is constructed. If two ideas are presented equally (in independent clauses, for example), they get about equal emphasis. But if they are not presented equally (for example, in an independent and a dependent clause), one gets more emphasis than the other.

To illustrate the varying emphasis you can give information, consider this example. You have two items of information to write. One is that the company lost money last year. The other is that its sales volume reached a record high. You could present the information in at least three ways. First, you could give both items equal emphasis by placing them in separate short sentences:

> The company lost money last year. The loss occurred in spite of record sales.

Second, you could present the two items in the same sentence with emphasis on the lost money.

> Although the company enjoyed record sales last year, it lost money.

Third, you could present the two items in one sentence with emphasis on the sales increase:

> The company enjoyed record sales last year, although it lost money.

Which way would you choose? The answer would depend on what you want to emphasize. You should think the matter through and follow your best judgment. But the point is clear: Your choice makes a difference.

The following paragraphs illustrate the importance of thinking logically to determine emphasis. In the first, each item of information gets the emphasis of a short sentence and none stands out. However, the items are not equally important and do not deserve equal emphasis. Notice, also, the choppy effect that the succession of short sentences produces.

> The main building was inspected on October 1. Mr. George Wills inspected the building. Mr. Wills is a vice president of the company. He found that the building has 6,500 square feet of floor space. He also found that it has 2,400 square feet of storage space. The new store must have a minimum of 6,000 square feet of floor space. It must have 2,000 square feet of storage space. Thus, the main building exceeds the space requirements for the new store. Therefore, Mr. Wills concluded that the main building is adequate for the company's needs.

In the next paragraph, some of the items are subordinated, but not logically. The really important information does not receive the emphasis it deserves. Logically, these two points should stand out: (1) the building is large enough and (2) storage space exceeds minimum requirements. But they do not stand out in this version:

> Mr. George Wills, who inspected the main building on October 1, is a vice president of the company. His inspection, which supports the conclusion that the building is large enough for the proposed store, uncovered these facts. The building has 6,500 square feet of floor space and 2,400 square feet of storage space, which is more than the minimum requirement of 6,000 and 2,000 square feet, respectively, of floor and storage space.

The third paragraph shows good emphasis of the important points. The short beginning sentence emphasizes the conclusion. The supporting facts that the building exceeds the minimum floor and storage space requirements receive main-clause emphasis. The less

- You should give every item its due emphasis.

- Short sentences emphasize contents.

- Long sentences de-emphasize contents.

- Determining emphasis is a matter of good judgment and good logic.

important facts, such as the reference to George Wills, are treated subordinately. Also, the most important facts are placed at the points of emphasis—the beginning and ending.

> The main building is large enough for the new store. This conclusion, reached by Vice President George Wills following his October 1 inspection of the building, is based on these facts. The building's 6,500 square feet of floor space exceed the minimum requirement by 500 square feet. The 2,400 square feet of storage space exceed the minimum requirement by 400 square feet.

The preceding illustrations show how sentence construction can determine emphasis. You can make items stand out, you can treat them equally, or you can deemphasize them. The choices are yours. But what you do must be the result of good, sound thinking and not simply a matter of chance.

Giving Sentences Unity

- All parts of a sentence should concern one thought.

Good sentences have unity. For a sentence to have unity, all of its parts must combine to form one clear thought. In other words, all the things put into a sentence should have a good reason for being together.

- There are two main causes of unity error.

Violations of unity in sentence construction are usually caused by two problems: (1) unrelated ideas and (2) excessive detail.

- First, placing unrelated ideas in a sentence violates unity.

Unrelated Ideas. Placing unrelated ideas in a sentence is the most obvious violation of unity. Putting two or more ideas in a sentence is not grammatically wrong, but the ideas must have a reason for being together. They must combine to complete the single goal of the sentence.

- You can avoid this error by (1) putting unrelated ideas in separate sentences, (2) subordinating an idea, or (3) adding words that show relationship.

You can give unity to sentences that contain unrelated ideas in three basic ways: You can (1) put the ideas in separate sentences, (2) make one of the ideas subordinate to the other, or (3) add words that show how the ideas are related. The first two of these techniques are illustrated by the revisions of the following sentence:

Mr. Jordan is our sales manager, and he has a degree in law.

Perhaps the two ideas are related, but the words do not tell how. A better arrangement is to put each in a separate sentence:

Mr. Jordan is our sales manager. He has a law degree.

Or the two ideas could be kept in one sentence by subordinating one to the other. In this way, the main clause provides the unity of the sentence.

Mr. Jordan, our sales manager, has a law degree.

Adding words to show the relationship of ideas is illustrated in the revision of the following example:

Our production increased in January, and our equipment is wearing out.

The sentence has two ideas that seem unrelated. One way of improving it is to make a separate sentence of each idea. A closer look reveals, however, that the two ideas really are related—the words just do not show how. The sentence could be revised to show the connection:

Even though our equipment is wearing out, our production increased in January.

The following contrasting pairs of sentences further illustrate the technique:

Unrelated	Improved
Our territory is the southern half of the state, and our salespeople cannot cover it thoroughly.	Our territory is the southern half of the state. Our salespeople cannot cover it thoroughly.
Using the cost-of-living calculator is simple, but no tool will work well unless it is explained clearly.	Using the cost-of-living calculator is simple, but, like any tool, it will not work well unless it is explained clearly.
We concentrate on energy-saving products, and 70 percent of our business comes from them.	Because we concentrate on energy-saving products, 70 percent of our business comes from them.

Excessive Detail. Putting too much detail into one sentence tends to hide the central thought. If the detail is important, you should put it in a separate sentence.

This suggestion strengthens another given earlier in the chapter—the suggestion that you prefer short sentences. Obviously, short sentences cannot have much detail. Long sentences—full of detail—can lead to lack of unity, as illustrated in these contrasting examples:

- Excessive detail is another cause of lack of unity. If the detail is important, put it in a separate sentence. This means using short sentences.

Excessive Detail	Improved
Our New York offices, considered plush in the 1990s but now badly in need of renovation, as is the case with most offices that have not been maintained, have been abandoned.	Considered plush in the 1990s, our New York offices have not been maintained properly. As they badly need repair, we have abandoned them.
We have attempted to trace the Plytec insulation you ordered from us October 1, and about which you inquired in your October 10 message, but we have not yet been able to locate it, although we are sending you a rush shipment immediately.	We are sending you a rush shipment of Plytec insulation immediately. Following your October 10 inquiry, we attempted to trace your October 1 order. We were unable to locate it.
In 2006, when I, a small-town girl from a middle-class family, began my studies at Bradley University, which is widely recognized for its business administration program, I set my goal as a career with a large public company.	A small-town girl from a middle-class family, I entered Bradley University in 2006. I selected Bradley because of its widely recognized business administration program. From the beginning, my goal was a career with a large public company.

Wording Sentences Logically

● Often the cause of "awkward" sentences is illogical wording

At some point, you've probably had a teacher write "awkward" beside one or more of your sentences. Often, the cause of such a problem is illogical wording. The paragraphs that follow will help you avoid some of the most common types of illogical sentences. But keep in mind that many awkward sentences defy efforts to label them. The only guards against letting these kinds of sentences slip past you are your own good ear and careful editing.

● Mixing two different patterns of sentences creates an illogical effect.

Mixed Constructions. Sometimes illogical sentences occur when writers mix two different kinds of sentences together.

For example, can you describe what's wrong with the following sentence about cutting costs?

> First we found less expensive material, and then a more economical means of production was developed.

If you said that the first half of the sentence used active voice but the second half switched to passive voice, you're right. Shifts of this kind make a sentence hard to follow. Notice how much easier it is to understand this version:

> First we found less expensive material, and then we developed a more economical means of production.

There's a similar problem in the following sentence:

> The consumer should read the nutrition label, but you often don't take the time to do so.

Did you notice that the point of view changed from third person (*consumer*) to second (*you*) in this sentence? The following revision would be much easier to follow:

> Consumers should read nutrition labels, but they often don't take the time to do so.

Sometimes we start writing one kind of sentence and then change it before we get to the end, illogically fusing parts of two different sentences together. Here's an example:

> Because our salespeople are inexperienced caused us to miss our quota.

Rewriting the sentence in one of the following ways (by either changing the subject or changing the predicate) would eliminate the awkwardness:

> Because our salespeople are inexperienced, we missed our quota.
>
> Our inexperienced salespeople caused us to miss our quota.

These sentences further illustrate the point:

Mixed Construction	Improved
Some activities that the company participates in are affordable housing, conservation of parks, and litter control.	Some causes the company supports are affordable housing, conservation of parks, and litter control.
Job rotation is when you train people by moving them from job to job.	Job rotation is a training method in which people are moved from job to job.
Knowing that she objected to the price was the reason we permitted her to return the goods.	Because we knew she objected to the price, we permitted her to return the goods.
My education was completed in 2006, and then I began work as a manager for Home Depot.	I completed my education in 2006 and then began work as a manager for Home Depot.
The cost of these desks is cheaper.	The cost of these desks is lower. (*or* These desks are cheaper.)

Don't Make Me Laugh

Misplaced modifiers can have unintentionally humorous effects, as these examples show:

The patient was referred to a psychologist with several emotional problems.

Two cars were reported stolen by the Farmingdale police yesterday.

Please take time to look over the brochure that is enclosed with your family.

To keep the joke from being on you, put the modifier next to what it modifies.

Source: Laurie E. Rozakis, *The Complete Idiot's Guide to Grammar and Style*, 2nd ed. (New York: Alpha, 2003) 129, print.

Incomplete Constructions. Certain words used early in a sentence signal that the rest of the sentence will contain a certain kind of content. Be careful to fulfill your reader's expectations.

> For example, the following sentence, while technically a sentence, is incomplete:

She was so happy with the retirement party we gave her.

She was so happy . . . that what? That she sent everyone a thank-you note? That she made a donation to the library in the company's name? In a sentence like this, either complete the construction or leave "so" out.

Or consider the incomplete opening phrase of this sentence:

As far as time management, he is a master of multitasking.

You can rectify the problem in one of two ways:

As far as time management goes [*or* is concerned], he is a master of multitasking.

As for time management, he is a master of multitasking.

● Another kind of illogical sentence is one that starts but does not finish an expected pattern.

Dangling/Misplaced Modifiers. Putting modifiers in the wrong place or giving them nothing to modify in the sentence is another common way that sentence logic can go awry. Consider this sentence:

Believing the price would drop, the purchasing agents were instructed not to buy.

The sentence seems grammatically correct . . . but it doesn't make sense. It looks as though the purchasing agents believed the price would drop—but if they did, why did someone else have to tell them not to buy? The problem is that the people whom the opening phrase is supposed to modify have been left out, making the opening phrase a dangling modifier.

You can correct his problem by putting the right agents after the opening phrase:

Believing the price would drop, we instructed our purchasing agents not to buy.

What makes this sentence hard to follow?

We have compiled a list of likely prospects using the information we gathered at the trade show.

Surely the "prospects" aren't really the ones using the information. The sentence would be clearer if the final phrase were more logically placed, as in

Using the information we gathered at the trade show, we have compiled a list of prospects in the Chicago area.

● Putting modifiers in the wrong place or leaving out what they refer to creates illogical sentences.

Faulty Parallelism. Readers expect the same kinds of things in a sentence to be worded in the same way. Faulty parallelism violates this logical expectation.

● Putting equal things in dissimilar structures creates yet another illogical effect.

How might you make the similar items in this sentence more parallel in wording?

They show their community spirit through yearly donations to the United Way, giving free materials to Habitat for Humanity, and their employees volunteer at local schools.

Here's one way:

They show their community spirit by donating yearly to the United Way, giving free materials to Habitat for Humanity, and volunteering at local schools.

Other rules of grammar besides those mentioned here can help you avoid illogical constructions and write clear sentences. You can review these rules by studying the online material about correctness and completing the diagnostic exercise there to test your understanding of them.

CARE IN PARAGRAPH DESIGN

- Paragraphing shows and emphasizes organization.

- It involves logical thinking and imagination.

Skillful paragraphing is also important to clear communication. Paragraphs show the reader where topics begin and end, thus helping the reader mentally organize the information. Strategic paragraphing also helps make certain ideas stand out.

Designing paragraphs requires the ability to organize and explain information. It also involves anticipating your readers' likely reactions and structuring your content for the desired effect. The following advice will help you use paragraphing to your best advantage.

Giving Paragraphs Unity

- The contents of a paragraph should concern one topic or idea (unity).

Like sentences, paragraphs should have unity. When applied to paragraph structure, unity means that a paragraph sticks to a single topic or idea, with everything in the paragraph developing this topic or idea. When you have finished the paragraph, you should be able to say, "Everything in this paragraph belongs together because every part concerns every other part."

A violation of unity is illustrated in the following paragraph from an application letter. As the goal of the paragraph is to summarize the applicant's coursework, all the sentences should pertain to coursework. By shifting to personal qualities, the third sentence (in italics) violates paragraph unity. Taking this sentence out would correct the problem.

At the university I studied all the basic accounting courses as well as specialized courses in taxation, international accounting, and computer security. I also took specialized coursework in the behavioral areas, with emphasis on human relations. *Realizing the value of human relations in business, I also actively participated in organizations, such as Sigma Nu (social fraternity), Alpha Kappa Psi (professional fraternity), intramural soccer, and A Cappella.* I selected my elective coursework to round out my general business education. Among my electives were courses in investments, advanced business report writing, financial policy, and management information systems. The enclosed résumé provides a complete list of my business-related coursework.

Keeping Paragraphs Short

- Generally, paragraphs should be short.

- Short paragraphs show organization better than long ones and are more inviting.

- About eight lines is a good average length.

- But length can and should vary with need.

As a general rule, you should keep your paragraphs short. This suggestion overlaps with the suggestion about unity, because unified paragraphs tend to be short.

As noted earlier, paragraphs help the reader follow the writer's organization plan. Writing marked by short paragraphs identifies more of the details of that plan. In addition, such writing is inviting to the eye. People simply prefer to read writing with frequent paragraph breaks.

How long a paragraph should be depends on its contents—on what must be included to achieve unity. Readability research has suggested an average length of eight lines for longer papers such as reports. Shorter paragraphs are appropriate for messages.

Keep in mind that these suggestions concern only an average. Some good paragraphs may be quite long—well over the average. Some paragraphs can be very short—as short as one line. One-line paragraphs are an especially appropriate means of emphasizing major points in business messages. A one-line paragraph may be all that is needed for a goodwill closing comment or an attention-grabbing opening.

A good rule to follow is to question the unity of all long paragraphs—say, those longer than 10 lines. If after looking over such a paragraph you conclude that it has unity, leave it as it is. But you will sometimes find more than one topic. When you do, make each topic into a separate paragraph.

- A good practice is to question paragraphs over 10 lines.

Making Good Use of Topic Sentences

One good way of organizing paragraphs is to use topic sentences. The topic sentence expresses the main idea of a paragraph, and the remaining sentences build around and support it. In a sense, the topic sentence serves as a headline for the paragraph, and all the other sentences supply the story.

- Topic sentences can help make good paragraphs. But not every paragraph must have a topic sentence.

Not every paragraph must have a topic sentence. Some paragraphs, for example, introduce ideas, relate succeeding items, or present an assortment of facts that lead to no conclusion. The central thought of such paragraphs is difficult to put into a single sentence. Even so, you should use topic sentences whenever you can. Using topic sentences forces you to find the central idea of each paragraph and helps you check for paragraph unity.

Where the topic sentence should be in the paragraph depends on the subject matter and the writer's plan, but you basically have three choices: the beginning, end, or middle.

- Placement of the topic sentence depends on the content and the writer's plan.

Topic Sentence First.

Topic Sentence First. The most common paragraph arrangement begins with the topic sentence and continues with the supporting material. In fact, the arrangement is so appropriate for business information that one company's writing manual suggests that it be used for virtually all paragraphs.

To illustrate the writing of a paragraph in which the topic sentence comes first, take a paragraph reporting on economists' replies to a survey question asking their view of business activity for the coming year. The facts to be presented are these: 13 percent of the economists expected an increase; 28 percent expected little or no change; 59 percent expected a downturn; 87 percent of those who expected a downturn thought it would come in the first quarter. The obvious conclusion—and the subject for the topic sentence—is that the majority expected a decline in the first quarter. Following this reasoning, we would develop a paragraph like this:

> *A majority of the economists consulted think that business activity will drop during the first quarter of next year.* Of the 185 economists interviewed, 13 percent looked for continued increases in business activity, and 28 percent anticipated little or no change from the present high level. The remaining 59 percent looked for a recession. Of this group, nearly all (87 percent) believed that the downturn would occur during the first quarter of the year.

Topic Sentence at End. The second most common paragraph arrangement places the topic sentence at the end, usually as a conclusion. Paragraphs of this kind usually present the supporting details first, and from these details they lead readers to the conclusion, as in this example:

> The significant role of inventories in the economic picture should not be overlooked. At present, inventories represent 3.8 months' supply. Their dollar value is the highest in history. If considered in relation to increased sales, however, they are not excessive. In fact, they are well within the range generally believed to be safe. *Thus, inventories are not likely to cause a downward swing in the economy.*

Topic Sentence within the Paragraph. A third arrangement places the topic sentence somewhere within the paragraph. This arrangement is rarely used, and for good reason: It does not emphasize the topic sentence, which contains the main point. Still, you can sometimes justify using this arrangement for special effect, as in this example:

> Numerous materials have been used in manufacturing this part. And many have shown quite satisfactory results. *Material 329, however, is superior to them all.* When built with material 329, the part is almost twice as strong as when built with the next best material. It is also three ounces lighter. Most important, it is cheaper than any of the other products.

Leaving Out Unnecessary Detail

You should include in your paragraphs only the information needed to achieve your purpose.

What you need, of course, is a matter of judgment. You can judge best by putting yourself in your reader's place. Ask yourself questions such as these: How will the information be used? What information will be used? What will not be used? Then make your decisions. If you follow this procedure, you will probably leave out much that you originally intended to use.

The following paragraph from a message to an employee presents excessive information.

> In reviewing the personnel records in our company database, I found that several items in your file were incomplete. The section titled "Work History" has blanks for three items of information. The first is for dates employed. The second is for company name. And the third is for type of work performed. On your record only company name was entered, leaving two items blank. Years employed or your duties were not indicated.

This information is important. It is reviewed by your supervisors every time you are considered for promotion or for a pay increase. Therefore, it must be completed. I request that you log into the company portal and update your personnel record at your earliest convenience.

The message says much more than the reader needs to know. The goal is to have the reader update the personnel record, and everything else is of questionable value. This revised message is better:

A recent review of the personnel records showed that yours is incomplete. Please log into the company portal at your earliest convenience to update your personnel record.

Making Paragraphs Coherent

Like well-made sentences, well-made paragraphs move the reader logically and smoothly from point to point. They clearly indicate how the different bits of information are related to each other in terms of logic and the writer's apparent purpose. This quality of enabling readers to proceed easily through your message, without side trips and backward shifts, is called *coherence*.

- Paragraphs should be *coherent*. The relationships of parts should be clear.

The best thing you can do to give your message coherence is to arrange its information in a logical order—an order appropriate for the strategy of the case. So important are such decisions to message writing that we devote whole chapters to different patterns of organization. But logical organization is not enough. Various techniques are needed to tie the information together. These techniques are known as transitional devices. Here we will discuss three major ones: repetition of key words, use of pronouns, and the use of transitional words.

- Presenting information in a logical order is essential for coherence.

Repetition of Key Words. By repeating key words from one sentence to the next, you can smoothly connect successive ideas. The following sentences illustrate this transitional device (key words in italics). The sentences come from a message refusing a request to present a lecture series for an advertising clinic.

- Repetition of key words connects thoughts.

Because your advertising seminar is so well planned, I am confident that it can provide a really *valuable* service to practioners in the community. To be truly *valuable*, I think you will agree, each session must be given the time a thorough preparation requires. As my time for the coming week is heavily committed, may I recommend that you invite Seth Greenley to conduct the ad-writing session?

Use of Pronouns. Because pronouns refer to words previously used, they make good transitions between ideas. So use them from time to time to form idea connections. The demonstrative pronouns, (*this, that, these, those*) can be especially helpful. The following sentences (with the demonstrative pronouns in italics) illustrate this technique.

- Pronouns connect with the words to which they refer.

Ever since the introduction of our Model V nine years ago, consumers have suggested only one possible improvement—voice controls. During all *this* time, making *this* improvement has been the objective of Atkins research personnel. Now we proudly report that *these* efforts have been successful.

One word of caution: When using *this* or another demonstrative pronoun to refer back to an earlier sentence, try to use it with a noun—for example, *this plan*—to make the reference clear.

Transitional Words. When you talk in everyday conversation, you connect many of your thoughts with transitional words. But when you write, you may not use them enough. So be alert for places where providing such words will help move your readers through your paragraphs.

- Use transitional words in your paragraphs.

Among the commonly used transitional words are *in addition, besides, in spite of, in contrast, however, likewise, thus, therefore, for example,* and *also*. A more extensive list appears in Chapter 10, where we review transitions in report writing. These words bridge thoughts by indicating the nature of the connection between what has been said and what will be said next. *In addition,* for example, tells the

- Transitional words reveal the connections between ideas.

reader that what is to be discussed next builds on what has been discussed. *However* clearly shows a contrast in ideas. *Likewise* tells that what has been said resembles what will be said.

Notice how the transitional expressions (in italics) in the following paragraph signal the relations among the parts and move the reader steadily forward through the ideas:

Three reasons justify moving from the Crowton site. *First,* the building rock in the Crowton area is questionable. The failure of recent geologic explorations in the area appears to confirm suspicions that the Crowton deposits are nearly exhausted. *Second,* the distances from the Crowton site to major markets make transportation costs unusually high. Obviously, any savings in transportation costs will add to company profits. *Third,* the obsolescence of much of the equipment at the Crowton plant makes this an ideal time for relocation. The old equipment at the Crowton plant could be scrapped.

The transition words *first, second,* and *third* bring out the paragraph's pattern of organization and make it easy for the reader to follow along.

Keep in mind that transitional devices can also be used between paragraphs—to tie thoughts together, to keep the focus of the message sharp, and to move the reader smoothly from point to point. Strive for coherence on both the paragraph and the document level.

SUMMARY BY LEARNING OBJECTIVES

1 Explain the role of adaptation in writing clear sentences.

1. Writing that communicates uses words that the reader understands and sentence structures that organize the message clearly in the reader's mind. It is writing that is *adapted* to the reader.

2 Write short, clear sentences by limiting sentence content and economizing on words.

2. In general, you should use short sentences, especially when adapting to readers with low reading ability. Do this in two ways:
   * Limit sentence content by breaking up sentences that are too long.
   * Use words economically by following these specific suggestions:
     — Avoid cluttering phrases (*if* rather than *in the event that*).
     — Eliminate surplus words—words that contribute nothing (*It will be noted that*).
     — Avoid roundabout ways of saying things (use *decreases* rather than *can be observed to be decreasing*).
     — Avoid unnecessary repetition (*In my opinion, I think*).

3 Design sentences that give the right emphasis to content.

3. Give every item you communicate the emphasis it deserves by following these suggestions:
   * Use short sentences to emphasize points.
   * Combine points in longer sentences to de-emphasize them.
   * Be aware that how you combine points (by equal treatment, by subordination) determines the emphasis given.

4 Employ unity and good logic in writing effective sentences.

4. Strive for unity and clear logic in your sentences.
   * Make certain all the information in a sentence belongs together—that it forms a unit. These suggestions help:
     — Combine only related thoughts.
     — Eliminate excessive detail.
   * Take care to use logical wording. Watch for these problems:
     — Mixed constructions.
     — Incomplete constructions.
     — Dangling/misplaced modifiers.
     — Faulty parallelism.

5. Design your paragraphs for clear communication by following these standards:
   - Give the paragraphs unity.
   - Keep the paragraphs short.
   - Use topic sentences effectively, usually at the beginning but sometimes within and at the end of the paragraph.
   - Leave out unessential details.
   - Use transitional devices for coherence.

5 Compose paragraphs that are short and unified, use topic sentences effectively, and communicate coherently.

CRITICAL THINKING QUESTIONS

1 How are sentence length and sentence design related to adaptation? **(LO1)**

2 Discuss this comment: "Long, involved sentences tend to be difficult to understand. Therefore, the shorter the sentence, the better." **(LO1, LO2)**

3 Discuss ways to give ideas more or less emphasis in your sentences. Illustrate with an example. **(LO3)**

4 Explain how unity can apply equally well to a sentence, to a paragraph, and to longer units of writing. **(LO4)**

5 What are the principal causes of lack of unity in sentences? **(LO4)**

6 This chapter discusses several kinds of illogical wording in sentences. Give an example, explain the problem, and correct it. **(LO4)**

7 Discuss this comment: "Words carry the message. They would carry the same meanings with or without paragraphing. Therefore, paragraphing has no effect on communication." **(LO5)**

8 Defend the use of short paragraphs in business writing. **(LO5)**

9 "Topic sentences merely repeat what the other sentences in the paragraph say. As they serve only to add length, they should be eliminated." Discuss. **(LO5)**

10 Discuss and illustrate the three main transitional devices.

CRITICAL THINKING EXERCISES

Managing Sentence Content (LO2–LO4)

Instructions, Sentences 1–7: Break up these sentences into shorter, more readable sentences.

1 Records were set by both the New York Stock Exchange Composite Index, which closed at 8,001.40 up 27.08 points, topping its previous high of 7,986.50, set Wednesday, and Standard & Poor's 500 Index, which finished at 1,264.03, up 6.90, moving up significantly and also setting a five-day high.

2 Dealers attributed the rate decline to several factors, including expectations that the U.S. Treasury will choose to pay off rather than refinance some $4 billion of government obligations that fall due next month, an action that would absorb even further the available supplies of short-term government securities, leaving more funds chasing a skimpier number of these securities.

3 The Consumer Education Committee is assigned the duties of keeping informed of the qualities of all consumer goods and services, especially of their strengths and shortcomings, of gathering all pertinent information on dealers' sales practices, with emphasis on practices involving honest and reasonable fairness, and of publicizing any of the information collected that may be helpful in educating the consumer.

4 The upswing in business activity that began in 2009 is expected to continue and possibly accelerate in 2010, and gross domestic product should rise by $664 billion, representing an 8 percent increase over 2009, which is significantly higher than the modest 5 percent increase of 2008.

5 As you will not get this part of Medicare automatically, even if you are covered by Social Security, you must sign up for it and pay $88.50 per month, which the government will match, if you want your physician's bills to be covered.

6 Students with approved excused absences from any of the hour examinations have the option of taking a special makeup examination to be given during dead week or of using their average grade on their examinations in the course as their grade for the work missed.

7 Although we have not definitely determined the causes for the decline in sales volume for the month, we know that during this period construction on the street adjacent to the store severely limited traffic flow and that because of resignations in the advertising department promotion efforts dropped well below normal.

8 Instructions: Assume that you are the assistant manager of a hotel and are describing your hotel's meeting room to a prospective customer who is thinking of holding a seminar there. Turn the following pieces of information into coherent writing, making paragraph breaks where you think appropriate. Be ready to explain why you grouped the information and managed the emphasis the way you did. You may need to add some words or information to make the facts flow smoothly.

We have a meeting room.

It will be available on the date you requested.

It can seat 100 people.

The seating can be arranged to your specifications.

It is quiet.

It is on the ground floor.

It is not near the guest rooms.

The lounge has live music on occasion.

The lounge is at the opposite end of the hotel from the meeting room.

The meeting room has a lectern.

It has a projector.

It has a screen.

It has a laptop hookup.

We can rent additional equipment.

We can rent it at no charge to you.

The charge for the room is $300.

This is the charge for one day.

Making Sentences Economical (LO2)

Instructions, Sentences 9–36: Revise the following sentences for more economical wording.

9 In view of the fact that we financed the experiment, we were entitled to some profit.

10 We should see the prime lending rate increase in the near future.

11 I will talk to him with regard to the new policy.

12 The candidates who had the most money won.

13 There are many obligations that we must meet.

14 We purchased gloves that are lined with wool.

15 Mary is of the conviction that service has improved.

16 Sales can be detected to have improved over last year.

17 It is essential that we take the actions that are necessary to correct the problem.

18 The chairperson is engaged in the activities of preparing the program.

19 Martin is engaged in the process of revising the application.

20 You should study all new innovations in your field.

21 In all probability, we are likely to suffer a loss this quarter.

22 The requirements for the job require a minimum of three years of experience.

23 In spite of the fact that the bill remains unpaid, they placed another order.

24 We expect to deliver the goods in the event that we receive the money.

25 In accordance with their plans, company officials sold the machinery.

26 This policy exists for the purpose of preventing dishonesty.

27 The salespeople who were the most successful received the best rewards.

28 The reader will note that this area ranks in the top 5 percent in per capita income.

29 Our new coats are made of a fabric that is of the wrinkle-resistant variety.

30 Our office is charged with the task of counting supplies not used in production.

31 Losses caused by the strike exceeded the amount of $640,000.

32 This condition can be assumed to be critical.

33 Our goal is to effect a change concerning the overtime pay rate.

34 Mr. Wilson replaced the old antiquated machinery with new machinery.

35 We must keep this confidential information from being shared with others.

36 The consensus of opinion of this group is that Wellington was wrong.

Wording Sentences Logically (LO4)

Instructions, Sentences 37–51: Revise the following to eliminate illogical and awkward wording.

37 Because the Swift Company has a service-oriented culture is the reason it supports all forms of volunteerism.

38 On the night of your party, we experienced a rare occurrence with our seafood supplier canceling at the last minute.

39 Our staff is among the best as we strive for the highest level of customer service.

40 Thank you for your feedback that will help us continue to improve.

41 The meeting room you have reserved has a projector, Internet access, and will enable your attendees to hear the trainer easily.

42 As a five-star hotel, our guests' satisfaction is our top priority.

43 Upon review of the facts, the problem was a short in the wiring.

44 This streamlined process will save us so much money.

45 In order to accommodate your request, please make your reservation by the end of October.

46 On behalf of the management team, I appreciate your extra work on the project.

47 As a member of the marketing staff, the best person to consult on this project is Allal.

48 During tomorrow's staff meeting we will discuss our progress on the new ad campaign and how well the installation of the new software is going.

49 As far as phone call monitoring, I believe we should try other methods first.

50 Through our research of three local charities we feel that each one would make a good sponsor.

51 Each department will now have access to update its section of the website.

Managing Paragraph Focus (LO5)

Instructions, Paragraphs 52–56: Rewrite the following paragraphs in two ways to show different placement of the topic sentence and variations in emphasis of contents. Point out the differences in meaning in each of your paragraphs. (You may change some of the wording as needed.)

52 Jennifer has a good knowledge of office procedures. She works hard. She has performed her job well. She is pleasant most of the time, but she has a bad temper, which has led to many personal problems with the work group. Although I cannot recommend her for promotion, I approve a 5 percent raise for her.

53 Last year our sales increased 7 percent in California and 9 percent in Arizona. Nevada had the highest increase, with 14 percent. Although all states in the western region enjoyed increases, Oregon recorded only a 2 percent gain. Sales in Washington increased 3 percent.

54 I majored in marketing at Darden University and received a B.S. degree in 2009. Among the marketing courses I took were marketing strategy, promotion, marketing research, marketing management, and consumer behavior. These and other courses prepared me specifically for a career in retailing. Included, also, was a one-semester internship in retailing with Macy's Department Stores.

55 Our records show that Penn motors cost more than Oslo motors. The Penns have less breakdown time. They cost more to repair. I recommend that we buy Penn motors the next time we replace worn-out motors. The longer working life offsets Penn's cost disadvantage. So does its better record for breakdown.

56 Recently China ordered a large quantity of wheat from the United States. Likewise, Germany ordered a large quantity. Other countries continued to order heavily, resulting in a dramatic improvement in the outlook for wheat farming. Increased demand by Eastern European countries also contributed to the improved outlook.

chapter four

Writing for a Positive Effect

Affecting Human Relations through Writing

To prepare yourself for this chapter, once again play the role of a small business manager and Max Elliott's superior. As you review Max's writing, you see more evidence of how his communication shortcomings affect your company's effectiveness as it strives to compete. This new evidence appears in the messages Max writes—primarily letters and email. These messages go to the people inside and outside the company. They affect the human relationships that go far toward determining the success of the operation. Poorly written, insensitive messages can produce serious negative reactions. Typical of Max's messages is the following letter:

In this message you detect more than just the readability problem you saw in Max's reports. The words are not polite. Instead of showing concern for the reader, they are blunt, tactless, and unfriendly. Overall, they leave a bad impression—the impression of a writer, and a business, unconcerned about the need for good human relations. This chapter will show you how to avoid such impressions.

Dear Mr. Morley:

Your December 3rd complaint was received and contents noted. After reviewing the facts, I regret to report that I must refuse your claim. If you will read the warranty brochure, you will see that the shelving you bought is designed for light loads—a maximum of 800 pounds. You should have bought the heavy-duty product.

I regret the damage this mistake caused you and trust that you will see our position.

Hoping to be of service to you in the future

THE IMPORTANCE OF A POSITIVE EFFECT

Clarity is the primary goal for most of the writing you will do in business—especially your writing within the organization. Because much of this writing will concern matters that do not involve the readers personally, you will usually be able to communicate in a relatively matter-of-fact way. Your main objective will be to convey information, and you will want to do so quickly and accurately. This is also the kind of writing that your co-workers will want and expect. Even so, you will want to maintain the courtesy and friendliness that is so vital to good working relationships.

When you write messages that tend to be more personal, however, you will be concerned about more than just communicating information. This will especially be the case when you communicate with people outside the organization and a major goal is to gain or maintain favorable relationships. Email messages or letters written for a company to its customers are examples of such communications. The information in these messages will be important, of course. In fact, probably it will be the most important part. But you also will need to achieve certain effects—effects that will contribute to a favorable image of the company.

One effect you should strive for in virtually any message is the goodwill effect. Wise business leaders know that the success of their business is affected by what people think about the business. They know that what people think is influenced by their

- Written communication within a business primarily requires clarity.

- Good business writing, especially to external audiences, requires both clarity and the goodwill effect.

human contact with that business: the services they receive, how they are treated, the professionalism of the employees, and the like. The written word is a major form of human contact and thus a major way to build goodwill.

The goodwill effect in messages is not desirable for business reasons alone. It is, quite simply, the effect most of us want in our relations with people. The things we do and say to create goodwill are the friendly, courteous things that make relations between people enjoyable. Most of us would want to do and say them even if they were not profitable. Such behaviors definitely belong in business; in fact, they are a major and expected part of good business etiquette.

As you read the following chapters, you will see that other effects help ensure the success of written messages. For example, in writing to persuade a reader to accept an unfavorable decision, you can use the techniques of persuasion. In applying for a job, you can use writing techniques that emphasize your qualifications. And in telling bad news, you can use techniques that play down the negative parts. These are but a few ways to manage the effects of your writing.

Getting positive effects with your messages is largely a matter of skillful writing and of understanding how people respond to words. Keeping certain attitudes and techniques can help. The following sections review these attitudes and techniques.

CONVERSATIONAL STYLE

One technique that helps build the goodwill effect is to write in conversational language. Conversational language is warm, natural, and personable. Such language leaves an impression that people like, and it is also the language that is most easily understood. For both reasons, it is courteous to use it.

Resisting the Tendency to Be Formal

Writing conversationally is not as easy as you might think, because business situations can tempt us to write too formally. Instead of writing in friendly, conversational language, we tend to write in stiff, stilted, and difficult words. The result is a cold and

- Most people enjoy building goodwill.

- For their success, letters and some email messages often require achieving other effects.

- Getting the desired effects is a matter of writing skill and of understanding people.

- Writing in conversational language has a favorable effect.

- Writing in conversational language can take conscious effort.

TECHNOLOGY IN BRIEF

Grammar and Style Checkers Help Writers Identify Clichés, Colloquialisms, and Jargon

While not perfect, grammar and style checkers can help writers identify some clichés, colloquialisms, and jargon that creep into their writing. The checker here illustrates that it found a cliché and offers two suggestions for correcting it. By clicking on the explain button, the office assistant will tell the writer what it determines is the case here. Although this software can help, writers still need to be able to identify the trite and overused expressions the software misses. Also, writers need to be able to recast the sentences for clarity and sincerity.

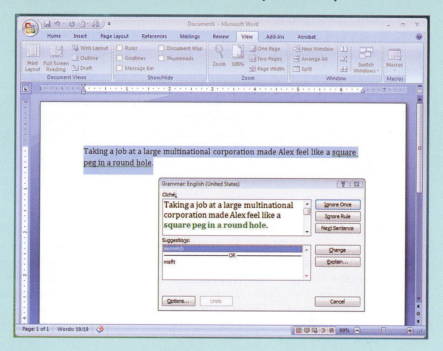

unnatural style—one that doesn't produce the goodwill effect you want your messages to have. The following examples illustrate this problem and how to correct it.

Stiff and Dull	Conversational
Reference is made to your May 7 email, in which you describe the approved procedure for initiating a claim.	Please refer to your May 7 email in which you tell how to file a claim.
Enclosed herewith is the brochure about which you made inquiry.	Enclosed is the brochure you requested.
In reply to your July 11 letter, please be informed that your adherence to instructions outlined therein will greatly facilitate attainment of our objective.	By following the procedures you listed in your July 11 letter, you will help us reach our goal.
This is in reply to your letter of December 1, expressing concern that you do not have a high school diploma and asking if a GED would suffice as prerequisite for the TAA Training Program.	The GED you mention in your December 1 letter qualifies you for the TAA Training Program.
I shall be most pleased to avail myself of your kind suggestion when and if prices decline.	I'll gladly follow your suggestion if the price falls.

Cutting Out "Rubber Stamps"

Rubber stamps (also called *clichés*) are expressions used by habit every time a certain type of situation occurs. They are used without thought and are not adapted to the specific situation. As the term indicates, they are used much as you would use a rubber stamp.

Because they are used routinely, rubber stamps communicate the effect of routine treatment, which is not likely to impress readers favorably. Such treatment tells readers that the writer has no special concern for them—that the present case is being handled in the same way as others. In contrast, words specially selected for this case show the writer's concern for and interest in the readers.

Some examples of rubber stamps you have no doubt heard before are listed below. These phrases, while once quite appropriate, have become stale with overuse.

a blessing in disguise	last but not least
as good as gold	learning the ropes
back against the wall	leave no stone unturned
call the shots	to add insult to injury

Some of the rubber stamps used today are relics from the old language of business—a way of writing that was in vogue over a century ago. In the early days of business writing, a heavily formal, stilted, and unnatural style developed. Messages typically began with such expressions as "your letter of the 7th inst. received . . ." and "your esteemed favor at hand. . . ." They ended with dangling closes such as "trusting to be favored by your response . . ." and "thanking you in advance, I remain. . . ." Messages were filled with such expressions as "deem it advisable," "beg to advise," "this is to inform," and "wherein you state." Fortunately, these awkward and unnatural expressions have faded from use. Even so, a few of the old expressions remain with us, some with modern-day changes in wording. One example is the "thank you for your letter" form of opening sentence. Its intent may be sincere, but its roots in the old language of business and its overuse make it a rubber stamp. Another is the "if I can be of any further assistance, do not hesitate to call on me" type of close. Other examples of rubber stamps in this category are the following:

> Please be advised . . .
>
> I am happy to be able to answer your message.
>
> I have received your message.
>
> This will acknowledge receipt of . . .
>
> Enclosed please find . . .
>
> This is to inform you that . . .
>
> In accordance with your instructions . . .
>
> Thank you in advance for . . .

You do not need to know all the rubber stamps to stop using them. You do not even need to be able to recognize them. You only need to write in the language of good conversation, addressing your comments to a real person.

Six Chix by Kathyrn LeMieux

Source: © Katheryn Lemieu(x). King Features Syndicate.

YOU-VIEWPOINT

Writing from the you-viewpoint (also called *you-attitude*) is another technique for building goodwill in written messages. As you will see in following chapters, it means focusing on the reader's interests, no matter what type of message you are preparing. It is fundamental to the practice of good business communication.

In the broadest sense, you-viewpoint writing emphasizes the reader's perspective. Yes, it emphasizes *you* and *your* and de-emphasizes *we* and *our*, but it is more than a matter of just using second-person pronouns. *You* and *your* can appear prominently in sentences that emphasize the we-viewpoint, as in this example: "If you do not pay by the 15th, you must pay a penalty." Likewise, *we* and *mine* can appear in sentences that emphasize the you-viewpoint, as in this example: "We will do whatever we can to protect your investment." The point is that the you-viewpoint is an attitude of mind that places the reader at the center of things. Sometimes it just involves being friendly and treating people the way they like to be treated. Sometimes it involves skillfully managing people's response with carefully chosen words in a carefully designed order. How you apply it will depend on each situation and your own judgment.

- The you-viewpoint produces goodwill and influences people favorably.

- The you-viewpoint emphasizes the reader's interests. It is an attitude of mind involving more than the use of *you* and *your*.

The You-Viewpoint Illustrated

Although the you-viewpoint involves much more than word selection, examples of contrasting wording help illustrate the principle. First, take the case of a person writing to present good news. This person could write from a self-centered point of view, beginning with such words as "I am happy to report. . . ." Or he or she could begin with news the reader cares about—for example, "Your proposal has been accepted." The messages are much the same, but the effects are likely to be different.

Or consider the case of a writer who must inform the reader that a request for credit has been approved. A we-viewpoint beginning could take this form: "We are pleased

In face-to-face communication, words, voice, facial expressions, and gestures combine to create the desired communication effect. In writing, the printed word alone must do the job.

to have your new account." Some readers might view these words favorably. But some would sense a self-centered writer concerned primarily with making money. A you-viewpoint beginning would go something like this: "Your new charge account is now open for your convenience."

Advertising copywriters know the value of the you-viewpoint perhaps better than any other group. So no advertising copywriter would write anything like this: "We make Kodak digital cameras for three levels: beginner, intermediate, and professional." An advertising copywriter would probably bring the readers into the center of things and write about the product from their point of view: "You can choose the basic, standard, or full-featured model—whichever is right for you."

- Even a bad-news situation can benefit from you-viewpoint wording.

The you-viewpoint can even be used in bad-news messages. For example, take the case of an executive who must say no to a professor's request for help on a research project. The bad news is made especially bad when it is presented in we-viewpoint words: "We cannot comply with your request to use our staff on your project because they are too busy doing their jobs." A skilled writer using the you-viewpoint would look at the situation from the reader's point of view, find an explanation or alternative likely to satisfy this reader, and present the response in you-viewpoint language. The you-viewpoint response might take this form: "While we do not have the available staff to assist you with your project, we would be glad to share sample documents with you. If you will tell me. . . ."

The following contrasting examples demonstrate the different effects that changes in viewpoint are likely to produce.

We-Viewpoint	You-Viewpoint
We are happy to have your order for Hewlett-Packard products, which we are sending today by UPS.	Your selection of Hewlett-Packard products were shipped by UPS today and should reach you by Saturday.
We sell the Chicago Cutlery set for the low price of $24.00 each and suggest a retail price of $36.50.	With a cost of only $24.00, each Chicago Cutlery set you sell at $36.50 will bring you a $12.50 profit.
Our policy prohibits us from permitting outside groups to use our facilities except on a cash-rental basis.	Our policy of renting our facilities to outside groups enables us to make our full range of services available to your guests.
We have been quite tolerant of your past-due account and must now demand payment.	If you are to continue to enjoy the benefits of credit buying, you must clear your account now.
We have received your report of May 1.	Thank you for your report of May 1.
So that we may complete our file records on you, we ask that you submit to us your January report.	So that your file records may be completed, please send us your January report.
We require that you sign the sales slip before we will charge your account.	For your protection, you are charged only after you have signed the sales slip.

A Point of Controversy

- Some say that the you-viewpoint is insincere and manipulative. It can be, but it need not be.

The you-viewpoint has been a matter of some controversy. Its critics point out two major shortcomings: (1) it is insincere and (2) it is manipulative. In either event, they argue, the technique is dishonest; it is better just to "tell it like it is."

These arguments have some merit. Without question, the you-viewpoint can be used to the point of being insincere, and it can be used to pursue unethical goals. But those who favor the technique argue that it need not—in fact, should not—be just a technique. The objective is to treat people courteously, because that is the way we all like to be treated. The you-viewpoint also helps readers see quickly in what ways a given message applies to them. This "translation" work supports both clarity and courtesy.

You do not have to use the you-viewpoint exclusively or overdo it. You can use it when it is friendly and sincere and when your desired effects are ethical. In such cases, using the you-viewpoint is "telling it as it is"—or at least as it should be. With this position in mind, we advocate its use as an important element of good business communication.

ACCENT ON POSITIVE LANGUAGE

As you know, one can say anything in many ways, and each way conveys a different meaning. Whether your written message achieves its goal often will depend on the words you choose. In most cases, positive or neutral wording will succeed better than negative wording.

Effects of Words

As Chapter 2 pointed out, all words have certain emotional associations. Because people generally prefer positive to negative feelings, positive words are usually best for achieving your message goals. This is not to say that negative words have no place in business writing. Such words are powerful, and you will sometimes want to use them. But you will usually need the more positive words. They tend to put the reader in the right frame of mind, and they emphasize the pleasant aspects of the goal. They also create the goodwill that helps build good relations.

Negative words tend to produce the opposite effects. They may stir up your reader's resistance to your goals, and they are likely to be highly destructive of goodwill. Carefully consider the negativeness and positiveness of your words in order to select the ones that are most appropriate in each case.

Be particularly wary of strongly negative words. These words have unhappy and unpleasant associations that usually detract from your goal. They include such words as *mistake, problem, error, damage, loss,* and *failure*. There are also words that deny—words such as *no, do not, refuse,* and *stop*. And there are words whose sounds or meanings have unpleasant effects: *itch, guts, scratch, grime, sloppy,* and *nauseous*. Run these negative words through your mind and think about the meanings they produce. You should find it easy to see that they tend to work against most of the goals you will have for your messages.

Examples of Word Choice

Let's consider the case of a company executive who had to deny a local civic group's request to use the company's meeting facilities. To soften the refusal, the executive

Copyright © 2004 by Randy Glasbergen, www.glasbergen.com

"We're a Limited Partnership. We're limited by Allen's pessimism, Elizabeth's abrasive personality, and Dave's refusal to work weekends."

could let the group use a conference room, which might be somewhat small for its purpose. The executive came up with this totally negative response:

> We *regret* to inform you that we *cannot* permit you to use our auditorium for your meeting, as the Sun City Investment Club asked for it first. We can, however, let you use our conference room, but it seats *only* 60.

The negative words are italicized. First, the positively intended message "We *regret* to inform you" is an unmistakable sign of coming bad news. "*Cannot* permit" contains an unnecessarily harsh meaning. And notice how the good-news part of the message is handicapped by the limiting word *only*.

Had the executive searched for more positive ways of covering the same situation, he or she might have written

> Although the SunCity Investment Club has reserved the auditorium for Saturday, we can offer you our conference room, which seats 60.

Not a single negative word appears in this version. Both approaches achieve the primary objective of denying a request, but their effects on the reader would differ sharply. Clearly the second approach would do a better job of building goodwill.

Or take the case of a writer granting the claim of a woman for cosmetics damaged in transit. Granting the claim, of course, is the most positive outcome that such a situation can have. Even though this customer has had a somewhat unhappy experience, she is receiving what she wants. The negative language of an unskilled writer, however, can so vividly recall the unhappy aspects of the problem that the happy solution is moved to the background. As this negative version of the message illustrates, the effect is to damage the reader's goodwill:

> We received your claim in which you contend that we were responsible for *damage* to three cases of Estée Lauder lotion. We assure you that we sincerely *regret* the *problems* this has caused you. Even though we feel in all sincerity that your receiving clerks may have been *negligent,* we will assume the *blame* and replace the *damaged* merchandise.

Obviously, this version grants the claim grudgingly, and the company would profit from such an approach only if there were extenuating circumstances. The phrase "in which you contend" clearly implies some doubt about the legitimacy of the claim. Even the sincerely intended expression of regret only recalls to the reader's mind the event that caused all the trouble. And the negatives *blame* and *damage* only strengthen the recollection. Certainly, this approach is not conducive to goodwill.

In the following version of the same message, the writer refers only to positive aspects of the situation—what can be done to settle the problem. The job is done without using a negative word and without mentioning the situation being corrected or suspicions concerning the honesty of the claim. The goodwill effect of this approach is likely to maintain business relations with the reader:

> Three cases of Estée Lauder lotion are on their way to you by FedEx and should be on your sales floor by Saturday.

For additional illustrations, compare the differing effects of these contrasting negative-positive versions of messages (the negative words are in italics):

Negative	**Positive**
You *failed* to give us the fabric specifications of the chair you ordered.	To complete your order, please check your choice of fabric on the enclosed card.
Smoking is *not* permitted anywhere except in the lobby.	Smoking is permitted in the lobby only.
We *cannot* deliver until Friday.	We can deliver the goods on Friday.
Chock-O-Nuts do not have that *gummy*, *runny* coating that makes some candies *stick* together when they get hot.	The rich chocolate coating of Chock-O-Nuts stays crispy good throughout the summer months.

COMMUNICATION MATTERS

Parent, Child, or Adult?

In the 1950s, psychologist Eric Berne developed a model of people and relationships that he called "Transactional Analysis." It has proven to be so useful that it is still popular today.

At the core of this model is the idea that, in all our transactions with others (and even within ourselves), people occupy one of three positions: parent, child, or adult.

- A *parent* is patronizing, spoiling, nurturing, blaming, criticizing, and/or punishing.

- A *child* is uninhibited, freely emotional, obedient, whining, irresponsible, and/or selfish.

- An *adult* is reasonable, responsible, considerate, and flexible.

Significantly, the "self" that one projects invites others to occupy the complementary position. Thus, acting "parental" leads others to act "childish" and vice versa, while acting "adult" invites others to be adults.

In both internal and external business messages, strive for "adult–adult" interactions. Your courtesy and professionalism will be likely to elicit the same from your readers.

Negative	Positive
You were *wrong* in your conclusion, for paragraph 3 of our agreement clearly states . . .	Please read paragraph 3 of our agreement, which explains . . .
We *regret* that we *overlooked* your coverage on this equipment and apologize for the *trouble* and *concern* it must have caused you.	You were quite right in believing that you have coverage on the equipment. We appreciate your calling the matter to our attention.
We *regret* to inform you that we must deny your request for credit.	For the time being, we can serve you on a cash basis only.
You should have known that the camera lens *cannot* be cleaned with tissue, for it is clearly explained in the instructions.	The instructions explain why the camera lens should be cleaned only with a nonscratch cloth.
Your May 7 *complaint* about our remote control is *not* supported by the evidence.	Review of the situation described in your May 7 email revealed what happened when you used the remote control.

COURTESY

A major contributor to goodwill in business documents is courtesy. By courtesy we mean treating people with respect and consideration. Courtesy produces friendly relations between people, and the result is a better human climate for solving business problems and doing business.

- Courtesy is a major contributor to goodwill in business documents.

As with every other facet of your communications, how to be courteous ultimately depends on the given situation. Including "please," "thank you," "we're sorry," and other standard expressions of politeness do not necessarily make a message courteous. Rather than focusing on stock phrases, consider what will make your reader feel most comfortable, understood, and appreciated. A message with no overtly polite expressions whatsoever can still demonstrate great courtesy by being easy to read, focusing on the writer's interests, and conveying the writer's feelings of goodwill.

- Courtesy involves the preceding goodwill techniques.

Still, courtesy generally is enhanced by using certain techniques. We have already discussed three of them: writing in conversational language, employing the you-viewpoint, and choosing positive words. More follow.

Tailoring Your Message to Your Reader

One of the additional techniques is to write directly to your specific reader. Messages that appear routine have a cold, impersonal effect. On the other hand, messages

- It also involves writing directly for the one reader.

that appear to be written for one reader tend to make the reader feel important and appreciated.

To design your message for the specific reader, you should write for the one situation. What you say throughout the document should make it clear that the reader is getting individual treatment. For example, a message granting a professor permission to quote company material in the professor's book could end with "We wish you the best of success on the book." This specially adapted comment is better than one that fits any similar case: "If we can be of further assistance, please let us know." Using the reader's name in the message text is another good way to show that the reader is being given special treatment. We can gain the reader's favor by occasionally making such references as "You are correct, Ms. Brock" or "As you know, Bob."

- This means writing for the one situation.

Refraining from Preaching

- The effect of courtesy is helped by not preaching (lecturing).

You can help give your documents a courteous effect by not preaching—that is, by avoiding the tone of a lecture or a sermon. Except in the rare cases in which the reader looks up to the writer, a preaching tone hurts goodwill. Most people like to be treated as equals; they do not want to be bossed or talked down to. Writing that suggests unequal writer-reader relations is likely to hinder your goals.

- Usually preaching is not intended. It often results from efforts to persuade.

Preaching is usually not intended. It often occurs when the writer is trying to convince the reader of something, as in this example:

> You must take advantage of savings like this if you are to be successful. The pennies you save pile up. In time they will turn into dollars.

It is insulting to tell the reader something quite elementary as if it were not known. Such obvious information should be omitted.

- Elementary, flat, and obvious statements often sound preachy.

Likewise, flat statements of the obvious fall into the preachy category. Statements like "Rapid inventory turnover means greater profits" are obvious to the experienced retailer and would probably produce negative reactions. So would most statements that include such phrases as "you need," "you want," "you should," and "you must."

Another form of preachiness is to tell the reader how to react, as in this example: "Would you like to make a deal that would make you a 38 percent profit? Of course you would!" This parental-sounding language would surely offend. Less extreme examples, such as "You'll be happy to know," can have a similar negative effect.

The first step toward creating goodwill with your readers is to put yourself in their shoes.

Doing More Than Is Expected

One sure way to gain goodwill is to do a little bit more than you have to do for your reader. We are all aware of how helpful little extra acts are in other areas of our personal relationships. Too many of us, however, do not use them in our messages. Perhaps in the mistaken belief that we are being concise, we include only the barest essentials in our messages. The result is brusque, hurried treatment, which is inconsistent with the effort to build goodwill.

The writer of a message refusing a request for use of company equipment, for example, needs only to say "no" to accomplish the primary goal. This answer, of course, is blunt and totally without courtesy. A goodwill-conscious writer would explain and justify the refusal, perhaps suggesting alternative steps that the reader might take. A wholesaler's brief extra sentence to wish a retailer good luck on a coming promotion is worth the effort. So are an insurance agent's few words of congratulations in a message to a policyholder who has earned some distinction.

Likewise, a writer uses good judgment in an acknowledgment message that includes helpful suggestions about using the goods ordered. And in messages to customers a writer for a sales organization can justifiably include a few words about new merchandise received, new services provided, price reductions, or any other topic likely to be of interest.

To those who say that these suggestions are inconsistent with the need for conciseness, we would answer that such information is needed to build goodwill. Conciseness concerns the number of words needed to achieve what you want to achieve. Remember that your goal is both to communicate *and* to build positive human relations, and go the extra mile for your readers.

Avoiding Anger

Expressing anger in messages—letting off steam—may sometimes help you emotionally. But anger helps achieve the goal of a message only when that goal is to anger the reader—and that is usually a very unwise goal. With both writer and reader angry, the two are not likely to get together on whatever the message is about.

To illustrate the effect of anger, take the case of an insurance company employee who must write a message telling a policyholder that he or she has made a mistake in interpreting the policy and is not covered on the matter in question. The writer, feeling that any fool should be able to read the policy, might use these angry words:

> If you had read Section IV of your policy, you would know that you are not covered on accidents that occur on water.

One might argue that these words "tell it as it is"—that what they say is true. Even so, they show anger and lack tact. Their obvious effect is to make the reader angry. A more tactful writer would refer courteously to the point of misunderstanding:

> As a review of Section IV of your policy indicates, you are covered on accidents that occur on the grounds of your residence only.

Most of the comments made in anger do not provide needed information but merely serve to let the writer blow off steam. Such comments take many forms: sarcasm, insults, exclamations. You can see from the following examples that you should not use them in your writing:

> No doubt, you expect us to hold your hand.
>
> I cannot understand your negligence.
>
> This is the third time you have permitted your account to be delinquent.
>
> We will not tolerate this condition.
>
> Your careless attitude has caused us a loss in sales.
>
> We have had it!
>
> We have no intention of permitting this condition to continue.

A good rule of thumb is never to send a message written in anger. Tempting as it can be to do so, you will almost always regret it. Take the time to calm down and write

---

- Doing more than necessary builds goodwill.

- As the extras add length, they appear not to be concise. But conciseness means word economy— not falling short of your goals.

- Rarely is anger justified in messages. It destroys goodwill.

in a reasonable tone. A good relationship with your reader is worth much more than a moment's self-indulgence.

Being Sincere

Courteous treatment is sincere treatment. If your messages are to be effective, people must believe you. You must convince them that you mean what you say and that your efforts to be courteous and friendly are well intended. That is, your messages must have the quality of sincerity.

The best way of getting sincerity into your writing is to be sincere. If you honestly want to be courteous, if you honestly believe that you-viewpoint treatment leads to harmonious relations, and if you honestly think that tactful treatment spares your reader's sensitive feelings, you are likely to apply these techniques sincerely. Your sincerity will show in your writing.

Overdoing the Goodwill Techniques. Being sincere will help you avoid two problems. The first is the overdoing of your goodwill techniques. The effort to be positive and to display the you-viewpoint can be taken to such an extreme that readers will be put off. For example, referring too often to your reader by name can seem manipulative, as in this example:

> If you will help these children, Ms. Collins, you will become a heroine in their eyes.

The following example, included in a form letter from the company president to a new charge customer, has a touch of unbelievability:

> I was delighted today to see your name listed among Macy's new charge customers.

Or how about this one, taken from an adjustment message of a large department store?

> We are extremely pleased to be able to help you and want you to know that your satisfaction means more than anything to us.

Exaggerating. The second danger that you should avoid is exaggerating the positive. It is easy to see through most exaggerated statements, and when that happens, you have damaged the reader's trust in you. Exaggerations are overstatements of facts. Although some puffery is conventional in sales writing, even here boundaries exist. The following examples clearly overstep these boundaries:

> Already thousands of new customers are beating paths to the doors of Martin dealers.
> Never has there been, nor will there be, a fan as smooth running and whispering quiet as the North Wind.
> Everywhere coffee drinkers meet, they are talking about the amazing whiteness Rembrandt gives their teeth.

Many exaggerated statements involve the use of superlatives. All of us use them, but only rarely do they fit the reality about which we communicate. Words like *greatest, most amazing, finest, healthiest,* and *strongest* are seldom appropriate. Other strong words may have similar effects—for example, *extraordinary, incredible, delicious, more than happy, sensational, terrific, revolutionary, world-class,* and *perfection.* Such words cause us to question; we rarely believe them.

THE ROLE OF EMPHASIS

Getting desired effects in writing often involves giving proper emphasis to the items in the message. Every message contains a number of facts, ideas, and so on that must be presented. Some of these items are more important than others, and some will be received more positively than others. A part of your job as a writer is to determine which items to emphasize in your message.

The four most useful emphasis techniques are position, space, sentence structure, and mechanical devices. The following paragraphs explain each.

Margin notes:

- Efforts to be courteous must be sincere.

- The effect of sincerity results from being sincere.

- The goodwill effort can be overdone. Too much you-viewpoint sounds insincere.

- Exaggerated statements are obviously insincere.

- Superlatives (*greatest, finest, strongest*) often suggest exaggeration.

- Emphasis also determines a message's effects. Every item communicated should get the proper emphasis.

- There are four basic emphasis techniques.

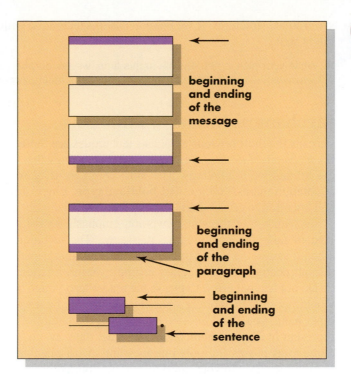

Figure 4–1

Emphasis by Position

beginning
and ending
of the
message

beginning
and ending
of the
paragraph

beginning
and ending
of the
sentence

Emphasis by Position

The beginnings and endings of a writing unit carry more emphasis than the center parts. This rule of emphasis applies whether the unit is the message, a paragraph of the message, or a sentence within the paragraph (see Figure 4–1). We do not know why this is so. Some authorities think that the reader's fresh mental energy explains beginning emphasis. Some say that the last parts stand out because they are the most recent in the reader's mind. Whatever the explanation, research has suggested that this emphasis technique works.

• Position determines emphasis. Beginnings and endings carry emphasis.

If we were to use this technique in a paragraph turning down a suggestion, we might write it like this (the key point is in italics):

> In light of the current budget crunch, we approved those suggestions that would save money while not costing much to implement. While *your plan is not feasible at this time,* we hope you will submit it again next year when we should have more resources for implementing it.

As you can see, putting information in the middle tends to de-emphasize it. Consider position carefully when organizing your message.

Space and Emphasis

The more you say about something, the more emphasis you give it; and the less you say about a topic, the less emphasis you give it. If your message devotes a full paragraph to one point and a scant sentence to another, the first point receives more emphasis. To give the desired effect in your message, you will need to say just enough about each item of information you present.

• The more space a topic is given, the more emphasis the topic receives.

Sentence Structure and Emphasis

As we noted in Chapter 3, short, simple sentences call attention to their content and long, involved ones do not. In applying this emphasis technique to your writing, carefully consider the possible arrangements of your information. Place the more important information in short, simple sentences so that it will not have to compete with other information for the reader's attention. Combine the less important information, taking care that the relationships are logical. In your combination sentences, place the more important material in independent clauses and the less important information in

• Sentence structure determines emphasis. Short, simple sentences emphasize content; long, involved ones do not.

subordinate structures. If we were to use this technique with the previous example, we might write:

> While your plan is not feasible at this time, we encourage you to submit it again next year when we are likely to have more resources for implementing it.

Mechanical Means of Emphasis

- Mechanical devices (underscore, color, diagrams, and the like) also give emphasis to content.

- Do not use emphasis or any other positive-effect technique unethically.

Perhaps the most obvious emphasis techniques are those that use mechanical devices. By *mechanical devices* we mean any of the things that we can do physically to give the printed word emphasis. The most common of these devices are the <u>underscore</u>, "quotation marks," *italics,* and **boldface type.** Lines, arrows, and diagrams also can call attention to certain parts. So can color, special type, and drawings.

As with use of the you-viewpoint, emphasis on the positive, when overdone, can lead to fake and manipulative messages. The technique is especially questionable when it causes the reader to overlook an important negative point in the message—the discontinuation of a service, for example, or information about an unsafe product.

Do not let your effort to please the reader lead you to be dishonest or insincere. That would not only be morally wrong; it would also be a bad way to do business. On the other hand, you should not be naïve about the nature of reality, either. The things we represent in our communication—whether data, events, people, or situations—do not come to us possessing only one meaning. Most phenomena can be rightly perceived in multiple ways. In your quest to achieve your communication purposes, think before you let negative feelings make their way into your messages. You will often be able to depict the glass as half full rather than as half empty, and you will probably find that your own perspective has improved in the process.

SUMMARY BY LEARNING OBJECTIVES

1 Explain the need for a positive effect in business messages.

1. Although clarity is a major concern in all business writing, you should also strive to create positive effects.
   - Specifically, you will need to communicate goodwill, for it creates the good human relations on which business depends.
   - Sometimes you will need to communicate effects that help you persuade, sell, or the like.
   - To achieve these effects, you will need to heed the following advice.

2 Use a conversational style that eliminates the old language of business and "rubber stamps."

2. Write messages in a conversational style (language that sounds like people talking).
   - Such a style requires that you resist the tendency to be formal.
   - It requires that you avoid words from the old language of business (*thanking you in advance, please be advised*).
   - It requires that you avoid the so-called rubber stamps—words used routinely and without thought (*this is to inform, in accordance with*).

3 Use the you-viewpoint to build goodwill.

3. In your messages, you will need to emphasize the you-viewpoint (*your refund is enclosed . . .* rather than *I am happy to report . . .*).
   - But be careful not to be or appear to be insincere.
   - And do not use the you-viewpoint to manipulate the reader.

4 Employ positive language to achieve goodwill and other desired effects.

4. You should understand the negative and positive meanings of words.
   - Negative words have unpleasant meanings (*We cannot deliver until Friday*).
   - Positive words have pleasant meanings (*We can deliver Friday*).
   - Select those negative and positive words that achieve the best effects for your goal.

5. You should strive for courtesy in your messages by doing the following:
   - Practice the goodwill techniques discussed in the chapter.
   - Tailor your message to your reader (write for the one person).
   - Avoid preaching or talking down.
   - Avoid displays of anger.
   - Be sincere (avoiding exaggeration and overdoing the goodwill techniques).
6. Use the four major techniques for emphasis in writing.
   - Determine the items of information the message will contain.
   - Give each item the emphasis it deserves.
   - Show emphasis in these ways:
     — By position (beginnings and endings receive prime emphasis).
     — By space (the greater the space devoted to a topic, the greater the emphasis).
     — By sentence structure (short sentences emphasize more than longer ones).
     — By mechanical means (e.g., color, underscore, boldface).

5 Explain the techniques of achieving courtesy.

6 Use the four major techniques for emphasis in writing.

CRITICAL THINKING QUESTIONS

1 Discuss this comment: "Getting the goodwill effect requires extra effort. It takes extra time, and time costs money." **(LO1)**

2 "Our normal conversation is filled with error. Typically, it is crude and awkward. So why make our writing sound conversational?" Discuss. **(LO2)**

3 "If a company really wants to impress the readers of its messages, the messages should be formal and should include common business expressions." Discuss. **(LO2)**

4 "If you can find words, sentences, or phrases that cover a general situation, why not use them every time that general situation comes about? Using such rubber stamps would save time, and in business time is money." Discuss. **(LO2)**

5 Discuss this comment: "The you-viewpoint is insincere and deceitful." **(LO3)**

6 Evaluate this comment: "It's hard to argue against courtesy. But businesspeople don't have time to spend extra effort on it. Anyway, they want their documents to go straight to the point—without wasting words and without sugar coating." **(LO5)**

7 "I like writers who shoot straight. When they are happy, you know it. When they are angry, they let you know." Discuss. **(LO3–LO5)**

8 A writer wants to include a certain negative point in a message and to give it little emphasis. Discuss each of the four basic emphasis techniques as they relate to what can be done. **(LO6)**

9 Imagine that a customer has written to complain about the lack of attention that she received when visiting a paint store. The manager's responding letter explains why the sales staff were so busy, offers to make a special appointment with the customer to discuss her decorating needs, and then ends with the following paragraph: "We do apologize again for any inconvenience that this situation caused you. We thank you for your understanding. Please do not hesitate to contact us again if we ever fall short of the superior service that you have come to expect from us." If the manager asked for your feedback on this letter, what would you say? It's full of polite expressions. Is it a good concluding paragraph? Discuss. **(LO2–LO6)**

CRITICAL THINKING EXERCISES

Using a Conversational Style (LO2)

Instructions, Rewrite Sentences 1–11 in conversational style.

1 I hereby acknowledge receipt of your July 7 letter.

2 Anticipating your reply by return mail, I remain . . .

3 Attached please find the receipt requested in your May 1st inquiry.

4 You are hereby advised to endorse the enclosed proposal and return same to the undersigned.

5 This is to advise that henceforth all invoices will be submitted in duplicate.

6 Kindly be advised that permission is hereby granted to delay remittance until the 12th.

7 Replying to your letter of the 3rd, we deem it a great pleasure to accept your kind offer to serve on the committee.

8 Please be advised that, with regard to above invoice, this office finds that partial payment of $312 was submitted on delivery date.

9 I am submitting under separate cover the report you requested.

10 In reply to your letter of May 10, please be informed that this office heretofore has generously supported funding activities of your organization.

11 Kindly advise the undersigned as to your availability for participation in the program.

Using the You-Viewpoint (LO3)

Instructions, Sentences 12–26: Rewrite the following using you-viewpoint. You may need to add additional material.

12 Company policy requires that you submit the warranty agreement within two weeks of sale.

13 We will be pleased to deliver your order by the 12th.

14 We have worked for 37 years to build the best lawn mowers for our customers.

15 Today we are shipping the goods you ordered February 3.

16 (From an application letter) I have seven years of successful experience selling office supplies.

17 (From an email to employees) We take pleasure in announcing that, effective today, the Company will give a 20 percent discount on all purchases made by employees.

18 We are happy to report approval of your application for membership.

19 Items desired should be checked on the enclosed order form.

20 Our long experience in the book business has enabled us to provide the best customer service possible.

21 So that we can sell at discount prices, we cannot permit returns of sale merchandise.

22 We invite you to buy from the enclosed catalog.

23 Tony's Red Beans have an exciting spicy taste.

24 We give a 2 percent discount when payment is made within 10 days.

25 I am pleased to inform you that I can grant your request for payment of travel expenses.

26 We cannot permit you to attend classes on company time unless the course is related to your work assignment.

Accentuating the Positive (LO4)

Instructions, Sentences 27–41: Underscore all negative words in these sentences. Then rewrite the sentences for a more positive effect. Use your imagination to envision the situation for each.

27 Your misunderstanding of our January 7 email caused you to make this mistake.

28 We hope this delay has not inconvenienced you. If you will be patient, we will get the order to you as soon as our supply is replenished.

29 We regret that we must call your attention to our policy of prohibiting refunds for merchandise bought at discount.

30 Your negligence in this matter caused the damage to the equipment.

31 You cannot visit the plant except on Saturdays.

32 We are disappointed to learn from your July 7 email that you are having trouble with our Model 7 motor.

33 Tuff-Boy work clothing is not made from cloth that shrinks or fades.

34 Our Stone-skin material won't do the job unless it is reinforced.

35 Even though you were late in paying the bill, we did not disallow the discount.

36 We were sorry to learn of the disappointing service you have had from our sales force, but we feel we have corrected all mistakes with recent personnel changes.

37 We have received your complaint of the 7th in which you claim that our product was defective and have thoroughly investigated the matter.

38 I regret the necessity of calling your attention to our letter of May 1.

39 We have received your undated letter, which you sent to the wrong office.

40 I regret to have to say that I will be unable to speak at your conference, as I have a prior commitment.

41 Do not walk on the grass.

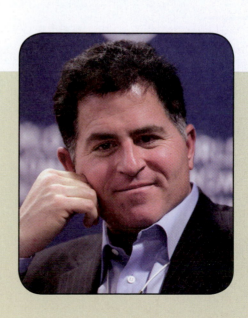

In 1992, Michael Dell was the youngest CEO ever to be listed in the Fortune 500 ranks. His continued success comes from thinking about how Dell products and services can bring value to customers.

"Whenever we're having our discussions with product teams or teams that are focused on unique kinds of customers, we talk about market trends and operating trends—'What are you seeing?' 'What are customers asking for?' 'What are customers buying?' And when I'm out in the field talking to customers, I spend a fair amount of time understanding what our customers are doing, why they're doing it, and where they're going."

Michael Dell, Chairman and CEO, Dell Computer

chapter five

The Writing Process and the Main Forms of Business Messages

LEARNING OBJECTIVES

Upon completing this chapter, you will understand the role of messages in business and the process of writing them. To reach this goal, you should be able to

1 Describe the writing process and effective writing strategies.

2 Explain the importance of readable formatting.

3 Describe the development and current usage of the business letter.

4 Describe the purpose and form of memorandums.

5 Understand the phenomenal growth and nature of email.

6 Follow email conventions and organize and write clear email messages.

7 Understand the nature and business uses of text messaging and instant messaging.

8 Understand the nature and business uses of social networking.

The Nature of Business Messages

Introduce yourself to this chapter by shifting to the role of Max Elliott (your subordinate in the preceding chapters). As Max, you are grateful to your boss for deftly instructing you in readable and sensitive writing. You have been convinced of the importance of good communication to the success of a struggling small business. You are especially grateful because most of the work you do involves communicating with fellow employees, customers, and suppliers. Every day you process dozens of internal email messages. Occasionally you write and receive memorandums. Then there are the more formal communications you exchange with people outside the company—both email and hard copy. And lately you've started using other media on your mobile device. This chapter analyzes these messages and the process of writing them.

THE IMPORTANCE OF SKILLFUL WRITING

Much of this book focuses on writing in business. Is skillful oral communication important? Absolutely. How about skillful use of graphics? It's critical. Then why the extra emphasis on writing?

There are two primary reasons. First, experienced businesspeople themselves tend to place writing skills ahead of other communication skills when asked what they seek in job applicants. And they seek strong writing skills in particular when considering whom to promote. For example, in one study, a majority of the 305 executives surveyed commented that fewer than half their job applicants were well-versed enough in "global knowledge, self-direction, and writing skills" to be able to advance in their companies.[1] As people move up, they do more and more knowledge work, and this work often requires the written forms of communication.

Another reason for our strong focus on writing is that writing is in some ways more difficult to do well than other kinds of communication. Writing is what researchers call a "lean medium," which means that it does not offer the multiple information cues, feedback, and intense personal focus that face-to-face or even phone conversations offer.[2] Writers essentially have no safety net; they can't rely on their facial expressions, body language, or tone of voice to make up for wording that isn't quite what they mean. The symbols on the page or screen must do the whole communication job. Plus, the symbols used in writing—the alphabet, words, punctuation, and so forth—share no characteristics with the thing they represent (unless you count words that sound like the sounds they name, such as "buzz"). Representing something with a photograph is relatively easy. Representing that same thing in words is much harder. Capturing a complex reality by putting one word after another requires ingenuity, discipline, and the ability to anticipate how readers will be likely to react as they read.

The first major section of this chapter will help you achieve this impressive but commonplace feat in the workplace by showing you how to break the writing process down into parts and skillfully manage each part. The remainder of the chapter will discuss the main forms of business messages, which bring with them certain features and conventions of use. These discussions provide the foundation for subsequent chapters on writing different kinds of messages.

---

[1] Paula Wasley, "Tests Aren't Best Way to Evaluate Graduates' Skills, Business Leaders Say in Survey," *The Chronicle of Higher Education,* The Chronicle of Higher Education, January 2008, Web, 23 January 2008.
[2] Robert H. Lengel and Richard L. Daft, "The Selection of Communication Media as an Executive Skill," *The Academy of Management Executive* 2.3 (1988): 226, print.

Figure 5–1

A Model of the Writing Process

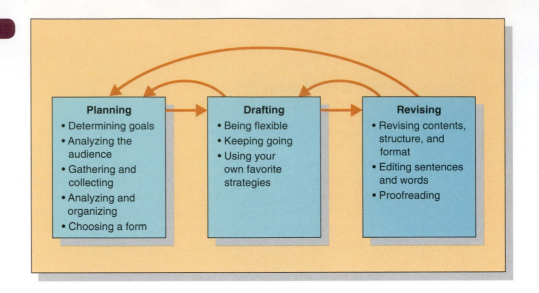

Planning	**Drafting**	**Revising**
• Determining goals • Analyzing the audience • Gathering and collecting • Analyzing and organizing • Choosing a form	• Being flexible • Keeping going • Using your own favorite strategies	• Revising contents, structure, and format • Editing sentences and words • Proofreading

THE PROCESS OF WRITING

- Taking charge of your writing process will make you a more effective writer.

Writing researchers have been studying the composing process since the 1970s. They have found, not surprisingly, that each person's way of developing a piece of writing for a given situation is unique. On the other hand, they have also drawn several conclusions about the nature of the process and about strategies that can help it. Familiarizing yourself with these findings will help make you a more deliberate, effective writer.

- The writing process consists of three main stages: planning, drafting, and revising.

- These stages are *recursive,* not strictly linear.

As Figure 5–1 shows, preparing any piece of writing involves three stages: planning, drafting, and revising. These stages can be defined roughly as figuring out what you want to say, saying it, and then saying it better. Each of these stages can be divided into various specific activities, which the rest of this section describes. But as the arrows in the figure suggest, it is important not to think of the three stages as strictly chronological or separate. In practice, the stages are interrelated. Like the steps for solving business communication problems described in Chapter 1, they are *recursive.* For example, a writer in the planning stage may start writing pieces of the draft. Or, he or she may find when drafting that gathering more information is necessary. Or, he or she may decide that it's necessary to revise a piece of the document carefully before continuing with the drafting. An undue emphasis on keeping the stages separate and chronological will hinder the success of your messages. Allow yourself to blend these stages as necessary.

- Student writers should spend roughly a third of their writing time in each stage.

A good rule of thumb for student writers is to spend roughly a third of their writing time in each of the three stages. A common mistake that such writers make is to spend too much time on drafting and too little on the other two stages, planning and revising. Preparing to write and improving what you have written are as critical to success as the drafting stage, and careful attention to all three stages can actually make your writing process more efficient. Once you have become an experienced business writer, you will be able to write many routine messages without as much planning and revising. Even so, some planning and revising will still be essential to getting the best results with your messages.

Planning the Message

- The problem-solving guide in Chapter 1 is a good guide for the planning stage of writing.

Chapter 1 presents a problem-solving approach to business communication. As Figure 1–4 indicates, you need to develop a definition of the problem that you are trying to solve. Once you have defined your problem, you can plan your message by answering several questions regarding your context and audience. As you plan written documents in particular, you can make the planning process more manageable by thinking about it in five smaller steps: determining goals; analyzing your audience; gathering and collecting information; analyzing and organizing the information; and choosing the form, channel, and format the document will take.

   Planning a good message takes time. The reason is that you have a lot to consider when writing to an audience you may not know all that well. The investment of your time pays dividends when you are able not only to achieve the goal of your message but also enhance your professional image by writing a coherent, concise, and thorough document.

● Planning consists of five general activities:

Determining Goals.

Determining Goals. Because business writing is largely performed in response to a certain situation, one of your main planning tasks is to figure out what you want to do about that situation. Bear in mind that, in business communication, "what to do" means not only what you want your communication to achieve but also any action related to the larger business problem. For example, if you manage a hotel where the air conditioning has stopped functioning, you will need to decide what, if anything, to communicate to your guests about this problem. But this decision is related to other decisions. How and when will you get the air conditioning problem solved? In the meantime, will you simply apologize? Make arrangements for each guest to have a free continental breakfast or complimentary beverages? Rent fans for meeting rooms and any guest rooms occupied by people with health problems? As Figure 5–2 shows, solving the business problem and solving the communication problem are closely related. You will need to bring your business goals to bear on your writing goals—though sometimes, clarifying your writing goals will help you generate business solutions.

● determining goals,

Analyzing Your Audience.

Analyzing Your Audience. Once you know your purpose—what you want your message to do—you need to think about the audience who will read your message. Who will be affected by what you write? What organizational, professional, and personal issues or qualities will affect the audience's response to your message? What organizational, professional, and personal issues or qualities do you have that affect how you will write your message? What is your relationship with your reader? Are you writing to your superior? Your colleagues? Your subordinates? Clients? Answers to these questions and others (see Figure 5–3) will influence your channel of communication, tone, style, content, organization, and format.

   In the hotel manager scenario we discussed, for instance, how might your approach in an announcement to guests who are currently at the hotel differ from your approach in a response to a guest's complaint letter a week after the incident? Though you should take time to analyze your audience early in the planning process, you should continue

● analyzing your audience,

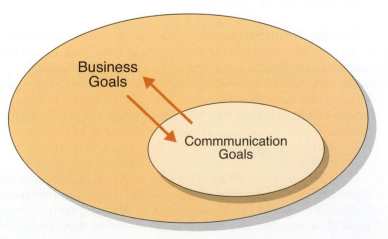

Figure 5–2

The Interrelated Nature of Business Goals and Communication Goals

Figure 5–3

**Audience Analysis
Checklist**

What is my relationship *to* my audience?

☐ Subordinate

☐ Colleague

☐ Superior

☐ Client/Customer

☐ Other: _____

What is my relationship *with* my audience?

☐ Friendly and informal. I know my audience well. We communicate often and have a social business relationship.

☐ Friendly and formal. We've met and have a cordial, business-like relationship.

☐ Neutral or no relationship. I don't know my audience personally.

☐ Unfriendly or hostile.

☐ Other: _____

What will my audience's reaction to my message be?

☐ Positive

☐ Negative

☐ Neutral

What factors in my company culture or other background information should I take into account?

☐ _____

☐ _____

☐ _____

What factors in my audience's culture or background should I take into account?

☐ _____

☐ _____

☐ _____

to think of your audience as you proceed through the rest of the planning stage and through the drafting and revising stages, too. Always be thinking about what kind of information will matter most to your audience and adapt your message accordingly. If you fail to meet your audience's needs, your message fails as well, and your professional image is compromised.

● gathering information,

Gathering Information. Once you have a sense of what you want your message to achieve, you will probably want to do at least some research. In many cases this research can be informal—finding past correspondence; consulting with other employees or with outside advisors; getting sales records, warranties, and product descriptions; and so forth. In other cases you will do formal research such as conducting surveys or reviewing the literature on a certain subject. Chapters 10 and 18 discuss various methods and sources at your disposal for this kind of research. In general, you will collect any information that can help you decide what to do and what to say in your message.

Collecting information by using your memory, imagination, and creativity is also important. Visualizing your readers and bearing their interests in mind is an excellent planning technique. Making a list of pertinent facts is helpful. Brainstorming (generating possible solutions without censoring them) will allow you to develop creative solutions. Drawing a diagram of your ideas can also enable you to collect your thoughts. Let yourself use any strategy that shows promise of contributing to a solution.

Analyzing and Organizing the Information. Once you have a number of ideas, you can start to assess them. If your data are numerical, you will do the calculations that will enable you to see patterns and meaning in the numbers. You will put other kinds of data together as well to see what course of action they might indicate, weighing what the parties involved stand to gain or lose from each possible solution.

As you ponder what to do and say with your message, you will, of course, keep your readers in mind. What kind of information will most matter to them? In the scenario described above, will the hotel guests most likely want information about what caused the air conditioning problem or about when it will be fixed and what they can do to stay comfortable in the meantime? As always, your intended readers are your best guide to what information to include.

They are also your guide for organizing the information. Whatever order will draw the most positive reaction from your readers is the best order to use. If you have information that your readers will want, put it first. This plan, called using the *direct order,* is discussed in the next chapter. On the other hand, if you think your information could run the risk of evoking a negative response, you will use an *indirect order,* using your message's opening to prepare the reader to receive the news as positively as possible. As you will see in Chapter 7, such a message usually requires a more skillful use of organization and word choice than one written in direct order. Regardless of the situation, all readers appreciate a logical pattern for the information. Chapter 10 will discuss different logical plans that you might use to put your thoughts in order and present them in an easy-to-follow way.

- analyzing and organizing the information,

Choosing a Form, Channel, and Format. Writers in school typically produce writing of two types: essays or research papers. But on the job you have a wide range of established forms of communication (genres) to choose from. Which one you think you will use has a huge impact on your planning. For instance, if you want to advertise your company's services, how will you do it? Write potential customers a letter? Email them? Include a brochure? Create a website? Use some combination of these? Each form has its own formatting and stylistic conventions and even conventions about content. Business writers do not launch into writing a document without some sense of what kind of document it will be. The medium itself helps them know what to say and how to say it. On the job, choosing the type of document to be written is an important part of planning.

Specific decisions about a document's format or visual design can be made at any point in the writing process, but usually the planning stage involves preliminary decisions along these lines. Will you be dividing up the contents with headings? How about with a bulleted or numbered list? How long or short will the paragraphs be? Will there be any visual elements, such as a logo or picture or diagram? Anticipating the format can help you plan an inviting and readable message.

Formatting devices have such a large impact on readers' reactions that we will discuss them separately in the next section. But decisions about formatting are an integral part of the business writer's writing process, even in the planning stage.

- and choosing the form, channel, and format for the message.

Drafting

Writing experts' main advice about drafting boils down to these words: "Be flexible." Writers often hinder themselves by thinking that they have to write a finished document on the first attempt with the parts in their correct order and with perfect results. Writing is such a cognitively difficult task that it is better to concentrate only on one thing at a time. The following suggestions can help you draft your messages as painlessly and effectively as possible.

- The best advice about drafting is to be flexible.

Avoid Perfectionism When Drafting. Trying to make your first draft a perfect draft causes two problems. First, spending too much energy perfecting the early parts can make you forget important pieces and purposes of the later parts. Second, premature perfectionism can make drafting frustrating and slow and thus keep you from wanting to revise your message when you're done. You will be much more inclined to go back over your message and improve it if you have not agonized over your first draft.

- Avoiding perfectionism helps you include all important information and makes you more willing to revise.

Keep Going. When turning your planning into a draft, don't let minor problems with wording or grammar distract you from your main goal—to generate your first version of the document. Have an understanding with yourself that you will draft relatively quickly to get the ideas down on paper or onto the screen and then go back and carefully revise. Expressing your points in a somewhat coherent, complete, and orderly fashion is hard enough. Allow yourself to save close reexamination and evaluation of what you've written for the revision stage.

- Keep going, making each statement just good enough to let you move on.

Use Any Other Strategies That Will Keep You Working Productively. The idea with drafting is to keep moving forward at a reasonably steady pace with as little stalling as possible. Do anything you can think of that will make your drafting relatively free and easy. For example, write at your most productive time of day, write in chunks, start with a favorite part, talk aloud or write to yourself to clarify your thoughts, take breaks, let the project sit for a while, create a setting conducive to writing—even promise yourself a little reward for getting a certain amount accomplished. Your goal is to get the first orderly expression of your planned contents written just well enough so that you can go back and work with it.

- Use any other strategies that help you to keep making progress.

Revising

Getting your draft ready for your reader requires going back over it carefully—again and again. Do you say what you mean? Could someone misunderstand or take offense at what you have written? Is your organization best for the situation? Is each word the right one for your goals? Are there better, more concise ways of structuring your sentences? Can you move the reader more smoothly from point to point? Does each element of format enhance readability and highlight the structure of the contents? When revising, you turn into your own critic. You challenge what you have written and look for possibly better alternatives.

- Revision requires going back over your message carefully—several times.

Any given message has so many facets that using what professional writers call "levels of edit" may be helpful: *revision, editing,* and *proofreading.*

- Professional writers recommend editing in levels.

With *revision,* you look at top-level concerns: whether or not you included all necessary information, if the pattern of organization is logical and as effective as possible, if the overall meaning of the message comes through, and if the formatting is appropriate and helpful.

- The three main levels are *revision* of contents, organization, and format;

You then move to the *editing* level, focusing on your style. You examine your sentences to see if they pace the information in such a way that the reader can easily follow it, if they emphasize the right things, and if they combine pieces of information coherently. You also look at your word choices to see if they best serve your purpose.

- *editing* of sentences and words; and

Finally, you *proofread,* looking at mechanical and grammatical elements—spelling, typography, punctuation, and any particular grammar problems that tend to give you trouble. Editing functions in your word-processing program can help you with this task. Careful attention to each level will result in a polished, effective message.

- *proofreading* your document for typos, spelling errors, and other mechanical or grammatical problems.

One last word about revision: Get feedback from others. As you may well know, it is difficult to find weaknesses or errors in your own work. Seek assistance from willing colleagues, and if they give you criticism, receive it with an open mind. It is better to hear this feedback from your intended readers, when costly mistakes may have already been made.

- Get others' opinions on your message.

THE IMPORTANCE OF READABLE FORMATTING

Have you ever opened up a letter or a reading for a class, seen long, unbroken blocks of text, and dreaded jumping into the piece? Business readers are even more likely to have this reaction. They are far too bombarded with messages to have patience with this kind of document. If you want your readers actually to read what you wrote and get your ideas and information, you must pay attention to an important element of any message: its physical format.

Decades ago, you might well have been able to rely on a secretary or typist to format your documents for you. But widespread use of the personal computer, with its full-featured publishing capabilities, has placed the responsibility for readable formatting much more on the writer. Except for projects that will involve a graphic designer, you will make the key formatting decisions for your messages. What kind and size of type will you use? What kind of headings? Will you use any means of typographical emphasis? How about numbered or bulleted lists? Should the document include such visual elements as logos, textboxes, pictures, or diagrams? Smart decisions on such matters will not only increase your readers' motivation to read but also enable them quickly to comprehend the main points and structure of the message.

For example, below is the starting text of a memo (sent by email) from a university registrar to the faculty, with the subject line "'X' and 'WX' Grades Effective for Autumn '10 Grading." How inviting do you find the format, and how easy is it to extract the information about the two new grades?

- Do not put off your readers with a daunting physical format.

- The writer is responsible for making the important formatting decisions.

At its October 20, 2010, meeting, the Faculty Senate, having received a favorable recommendation from the Academic Affairs Committee, voted to approve the creation and Autumn Quarter implementation of two new grades: "X" and "WX." Instructors will record an "X" on the final grade roster for students who never attended any classes and did not submit any assigned work. The "X" will appear on the transcript and will carry zero (0.00) quality points, thus computed into the GPA like the grades of "F" and "UW." Instructors will record a "WX" for those students who officially withdrew from the class (as denoted on the grade roster by either EW or W) but who never attended any classes and did not submit any assigned work. The "WX" may be entered to overwrite a "W" appearing on the grade roster. An assignment of "WX" has no impact on the student's GPA. A "W" will appear on the student's online grade report and on the transcript. The "WX" recognizes the student's official withdrawal from the class and only records the fact of nonparticipation. The need to record nonparticipation is defined in "Rationale" below. With the introduction of the "X" and "WX" grades to denote nonparticipation, by definition all other grades can only be awarded to students who had participated in the class in some way. Instructors will record a "UW" (unofficial withdrawal) only for students who cease to attend a class following some participation. Previously, instructors utilized the "UW" both for those students who had never attended classes and for those who had attended and participated initially but had ceased to attend at some point during the term. In cases of official withdrawal, instructors have three options available at the time of grading: "W," "WX," and "F." If the student has officially withdrawn from the class, a "W" (withdrawal) or "EW" (electronic withdrawal) will appear on the grade roster. If the student participated in the class and the withdrawal was in accordance with the instructor's withdrawal policy as communicated by the syllabus, the instructor may retain the student's "W" grade by making no alteration to the grade roster . . . .

Now look at the first part of the actual message that was sent out. What formatting decisions on the part of the writer made this document much more readable?

At its October 20, 2010, meeting, the Faculty Senate, having received a favorable recommendation from the Academic Affairs Committee, voted to approve the creation and Autumn Quarter implementation of two new grades: "X" and "WX."

Definition of "X" and "WX" Grades, Effective Autumn Quarter 2010

- "X" (nonattendance):

  Instructors will record an "X" on the final grade roster for students who never attended any classes and did not submit any assigned work.

  The "X" will appear on the transcript and will carry zero (0.00) quality points, thus computed into the GPA like the grades of "F" and "UW."

- "WX" (official withdrawal, nonattending):

  Instructors will record a "WX" for those students who officially withdrew from the class (as denoted on the grade roster by either EW or W) but who never attended any classes and did not submit any assigned work.

  The "WX" may be entered to overwrite a "W" appearing on the grade roster. An assignment of "WX" has no impact on the student's GPA. A "W" will appear on the student's online grade report and on the transcript. The "WX" recognizes the student's official withdrawal from the class and only records the fact of nonparticipation. The need to record nonparticipation is defined in "Rationale" below.

Participation and Nonparticipation Grades

With the introduction of the "X" and "WX" grades to denote nonparticipation, by definition all other grades can only be awarded to students who had participated in the class in some way.

Instructors will record a "UW" (unofficial withdrawal) only for students who cease to attend a class following some participation. Previously, instructors utilized the "UW" both for those students who had never attended classes and for those who had attended and participated initially but had ceased to attend at some point during the term.

Official Withdrawals

In cases of official withdrawal, instructors have three options available at the time of grading: "W," "WX," and "F."

1. *If the student has officially withdrawn from the class,* a "W" (withdrawal) or "EW" (electronic withdrawal) will appear on the grade roster. If the student participated in the class and the withdrawal was in accordance with the instructor's withdrawal policy as communicated by the syllabus, the instructor may retain the student's "W" grade by making no alteration to the grade roster. . . .

Reprinted with permission from Dr. Douglas Burgess, Registrar, University of Cincinnati.

- An attractive, readable format is critical to any message's success.

The remaining sections of this chapter describe specific purposes and traits of different message types. Appendix B provides in-depth advice about their physical design. No matter what you're writing, taking time to make careful formatting decisions during your writing process will significantly enhance your chances of achieving your communication goals.

LETTERS

- Letters are the oldest form of business communication.

Letters are the oldest form of business messages. In fact, they have existed since the early days of civilization. Research has documented that the ancient Chinese wrote letters, as did the early Egyptians, Romans, and Greeks. Although many of these early letters pertained to military and personal matters, some clearly concerned business.

From these early days letters have continued to be used in business. Although their use has declined as other forms have developed, they are still the best choice for many communication tasks.

- They are still an important form of business communication.

Letters Defined

The general purpose of a letter is to represent the writer and his or her topic rather formally to the recipient. For this reason, letters are used primarily for corresponding with people outside your organization. When you write to internal readers, they are often familiar to you—and even if they are not, you all share the connection of being in the same company. Your messages to such audiences tend to use less formal media. But when you write to customers, to suppliers, to citizens and community leaders, and to other external audiences, you will often want to put your company's best foot forward by choosing the letter format, complete with an attractive company letterhead and the elements of courtesy built into this traditional format. And your readers will expect this gesture of respect. Once you have established friendly relations with them, you may well conduct your business through emails and phone calls. But especially when corresponding with an external party whom you do not know well, a letter is often the most appropriate form to use.

- Letters are primarily for external audiences.

Letter Form

The format of the business letter is probably already familiar to you. Although some variations in format are generally acceptable, typically these information items are included: date, inside address, salutation (Dear Ms. Smith), body, and complimentary close (Sincerely yours). Other items sometimes needed are attention line, subject line, return address (when letterhead paper is not used), and enclosure information. Figure 5–4 presents one option for formatting a letter. More options are presented in Appendix B.

- Letter format is described in Appendix B.

Figure 5–4

Illustration of a Letter in Full Block Format (Mixed Punctuation)

Doing it right . . . the first time

Ralston's Plumbing and Heating
2424 Medville Road
Urbana, OH 45702
(515) 555-5555
Fax: (515) 555-5544

February 28, 2009

Ms. Diane Taylor
747 Gateway Avenue
Urbana, OH 45702

Dear Ms. Taylor:

Thank you for allowing one of our certified technicians to serve you recently.

Enclosed is a coupon for $25 toward your next purchase or service call from Ralston. It's just our way of saying that we appreciate your business.

Sincerely yours,

Jack Ralston

Jack Ralston
Owner and President

Enclosure

Letter Formality

- Until the latter part of the 20th century, letters used stilted language, especially to express courtesy.

- Today's letters are more strategic and more conversational.

As formal as letters can be, they are not nearly as formal as they used to be. Even as late as the 1950s, the emphasis was on word choice, especially on use of a stiff and stilted manner of expressing courtesy. We referred to this manner of expression in Chapter 4 as "the old language of business."

In more recent times the emphasis has shifted from formal politeness to structure and strategy of content and a more conversational style of wording. As the preceding chapters explain, unduly formal, impersonal writing has now fallen out of favor, and the communication strategy for any business message, including the letter, needs as careful attention as the wording. Despite its heightened formality, the letter should always be regarded as an exchange between real people as well as a strategic means for accomplishing business goals.

MEMORANDUMS (MEMOS)

Memorandums Defined

- Memos are internal letters. Email has largely taken over their function, but they are still the best medium in some situations.

Memorandums, or memos, are a form of letter written inside the business. Though in rare cases they may be used in communicating outside the business, they are usually exchanged internally by employees in the conduct of their work. Originally, they were used only in hard copy, but with the advent of computers they are now often processed electronically. In fact, their function of communicating within the business has been

Businesses with multiple locations send many of their internal messages by email as well as instant and text messaging.

largely taken over by email. Even so, they still are a part of many companies' communications. They are especially useful in communicating with employees who do not use computers in their work.

Memos can be used for a wide range of communication tasks. For example, as we shall see in Chapter 11, some memos communicate factual, problem-related information and can be classified as reports. It is important to be familiar with this traditional workhorse in business.

- Memos can be used for a wide range of tasks, even for reports.

Memorandum Form

Memorandums can be distinguished from other messages primarily by their form. Some companies have stationery printed especially for memos, while many used standard or customized templates in word processors. Sometimes the word *memorandum* appears at the top in large, heavy type. But some companies prefer other titles, such as *Interoffice Memo* or *Interoffice Communication*. Below this main heading come the specific headings common to all memos: *Date, To, From, Subject* (though not necessarily in this order). This simple arrangement is displayed in Figure 5–5. Because memos are often short, some companies use 5 × 8½-inch stationery for them as well as the conventional 8½ × 11-inch size. Hard-copy memos are usually initialed by the writer rather than signed.

- Most large companies use standard memo templates or printed memorandum stationery with *Date, To, From,* and *Subject* headings.

Large organizations, especially those with a number of locations and departments, often include additional information on their memorandum stationery. *Department, Plant, Location, Territory, Store Number,* and *Copies to* are examples (see Figure 5–6). Since in some companies memos are often addressed to more than one reader, the heading *To* may be followed by enough space to list a number of names.

- Some larger companies have additional headings (*Department, Plant, Territory, Store Number, Copies to*).

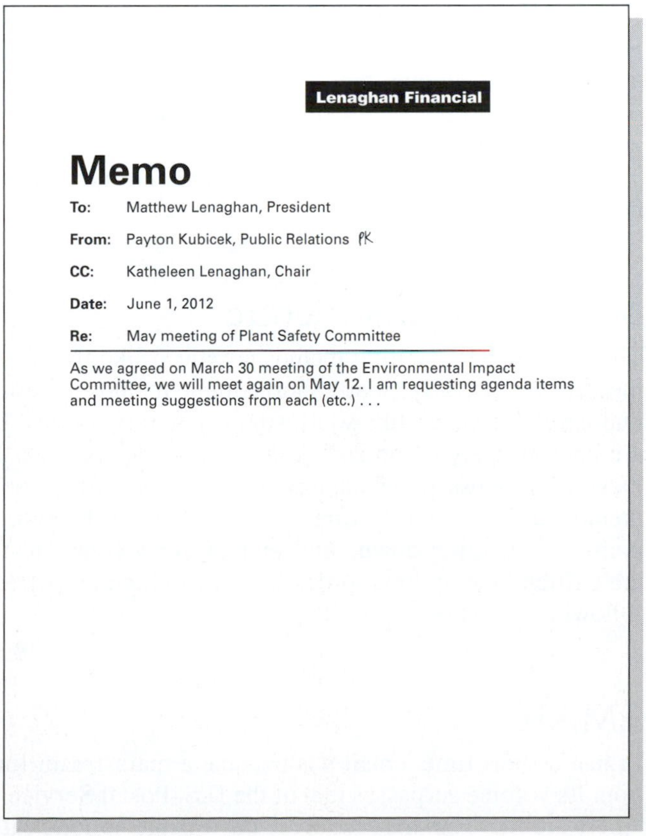

Lenaghan Financial

Memo

To: Matthew Lenaghan, President

From: Payton Kubicek, Public Relations *PK*

CC: Katheleen Lenaghan, Chair

Date: June 1, 2012

Re: May meeting of Plant Safety Committee

As we agreed on March 30 meeting of the Environmental Impact Committee, we will meet again on May 12. I am requesting agenda items and meeting suggestions from each (etc.) . . .

Figure 5–5

Illustration of Memo Form Using the MS Word Professional Template

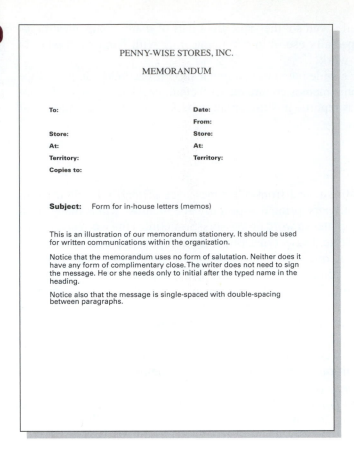

Memorandum Formality

● Memos vary widely in formality.

Because memos usually are messages sent and received by people who work with and know one another, they tend to use casual or informal language. Even so, their degree of formality ranges from one extreme to the other. At one end are the casual notes that workers exchange. At the other are the formal messages written by lower-ranking workers to their top administrators. The typical memorandum falls somewhere between these extremes.

Memorandum Structure

● Because the situations involved are similar, the strategies for writing memos and email are similar.

The strategies for writing memos are much like those for writing the other business messages, especially email. Short, simple memos are often written in casual or informal language, much like short, simple email messages. Longer, more formal memos are appropriately organized in the patterns appropriate for the longer, more formal messages discussed in Chapters 6–8. Like most of the other business messages, most memos are written in a direct pattern, usually beginning with the most important point and working down. And memos conveying sensitive or negative information are written in an indirect order. Direct and indirect patterns are discussed in detail in following chapters.

EMAIL

● The use of email has become widespread.

In just a short time, email has become a mainstream form of business communication. Its volume surpasses that of the U.S. Postal Service. According to one authority, "there are more emails sent every day than telephone calls." It has become so widely used in both small and large organizations that it deserves careful attention.

Many business people use their phones to send and receive emails and text messages. With such a small display screen, conciseness and clarity are especially important.

Email Pros and Cons

The reasons for email's rapid growth are the advantages it has over other communication forms, especially over its principal competitor, the telephone. Among the reasons, the following are most significant:

- Email eliminates "telephone tag"—the problem of trying to contact busy people who are not always available for telephone calls. Messages sent to them can be stored in their electronic mailboxes until they are ready to read them.
- Conversely, email saves the time of these busy people. They are spared the interruptions of telephone calls.
- Email can speed up the process of making business decisions because it permits rapid exchanges from all involved in the decisions.
- Email is cheap. It permits unlimited use at no more than the cost of an Internet connection.
- It provides a written record.

  Email also has its disadvantages. The following stand out:

- Email is not confidential. Any message may be forwarded or shared without the writer's knowledge. In addition, employers have the right to monitor employees' email use.
- Email doesn't communicate the sender's emotions well. Voice intonations, facial expressions, and body movements are not a part of the message as they are in telephone, video, and face-to-face communication.
- Email may be ignored or delayed. The volume of email often makes it difficult for some respondents to read and act on all of their messages quickly. Messages may also be sent to a junk mailbox and not immediately seen by the receiver, or the receiver can simply delete messages without responding.

- Email use has grown because it
- eliminates "telephone tag,"
- saves time,
- facilitates fast decisions,
- is cheap,
- and provides a written record.
- It has disadvantages, too.
- It is not confidential,
- doesn't show emotions, and
- may be ignored or delayed.

The Prefatory Elements

The mechanical parts of the email message are generally standardized and are a part of the template of the software you use in constructing the message. But the second part of your effort, writing the message, is far from standardized. It is here that you will need to use your problem-solving skills.

Although the various email systems differ somewhat, the elements are standardized. They include the following parts:

- **To:** Here the sender places the email address of the recipients. It must be perfect, for any error will result in failure to reach the recipient.

- **Cc:** If someone other than the primary recipient is to receive a *courtesy copy,* his or her address goes here.

- **Bcc:** This line stands for *blind courtesy copy.* The recipient's message will not show this information; that is, he or she will not know who else is receiving a copy of the message.

- **Subject:** This line describes the message as precisely as the situation permits. The reader should get from it a clear idea of what the message is about. Always include a subject line to get your reader's attention and preview the message. In the absence of a subject line, an unfamiliar reader may think your message is junk mail and delete it.

- **Attachments:** In this area you can enter a file that you desire to send along with the message. As will be emphasized later, you should make certain that what you attach is really needed.

- **The message:** The information you are sending goes here. How to write it is the subject of much of the following discussion.

The Message Beginning

Typically, email messages begin with the recipient's name. If writer and reader are acquainted, first name only is the rule. If you would normally address the reader by using a title (Ms., Dr., Mr.), address him or her this way in an initial email. But you can change the salutation in subsequent messages if the person indicates that informality is desired. The salutations commonly used in letters (Dear Mr., Dear Jane) are sometimes used, but something less formal ("Hi, Ron") or no salutation at all is more common. A friendly generic greeting such as "Greetings" is appropriate for a group of people with whom you communicate.

When writing to someone or a group you do not know, it is appropriate to identify yourself early in the message. This identification may include your purpose and your company. Your title and position also may be helpful.

The Message Structure

Even though email messages are often written under time pressure, you would do well to organize them carefully. For most short, informative messages, a "top-down" order is appropriate. This plan, used in newspaper writing, involves presenting the most important material first. The remaining information follows in descending order of importance. Such an arrangement permits a busy reader to get the essential facts first, and the reader accessing email on a smartphone or other small screen to get the essential facts more easily. Many writers routinely follow this practice.

Longer, more complex, and formal email messages frequently follow more involved and strategic organization patterns. The most common of these are reviewed in Chapters 6, 7, 8, and 9. As you will see, these patterns vary depending on how the reader will likely perceive the writer's objective. In general, those messages that are likely to be received positively or neutrally are written in a direct pattern. That is, they get to the goal right away and then present their contents systematically and quickly. Those messages that are likely to be received negatively are appropriately written in an indirect pattern. Their negative content is preceded by conditioning and explanatory words that prepare the reader to receive the bad news.

Some long email messages may resemble business reports. To prepare these messages, can you follow the organization and writing instructions for business reports (Chapters 10–11). In fact, any type of business document can be sent as or by email. The variety of email messages covers the entire spectrum of written business communication.

Email Formality

A discussion of email formality is complicated by the fact that email messages are extremely diverse. They run the range from highly informal to formal. The informal messages often resemble face-to-face oral communication; some even sound like chit-chat that occurs between acquaintances and friends. Others, as we have noted, have the increased formality of reports.

A helpful approach is to view email language in terms of three general classifications: casual, informal, and formal.[3] Your audience should determine which type of language you choose, regardless of your personal style or preference.

Casual. By casual language we mean the language we use in talking with close friends in everyday situations. It includes slang, colloquialisms, contractions, and personal pronouns. Its sentences are short—sometimes incomplete—and it may use mechanical emphasis devices and initialisms freely. Casual language is best limited to your communications with close friends. Following is an example of casual language:

> Hi Cindy:
>
> High-five me! Just back from confab with pinheads. They're high on our marketing plan. But as you crystal balled it, they want a special for the jumbos. ASAP, they said. Let's meet, my cell, 10 AM, Wed.?
>
> TTFN
>
> Brandon

Most of your personal emails (messages to friends) are likely to be casually written. This is the way friends talk, and their email should be no different. Probably some of the email you will write in business will also fall in this category. Much of it will be with your fellow employees and friends in business. But you would be wise to use casual language only when you know your readers well—when you know they expect and prefer casual communication. You should never use slang, initialisms, emphasis devices, or other elements that are not certain to communicate clearly and quickly.

Informal. Informal language retains some of the qualities of casual writing. It makes some use of personal pronouns and contractions. It occasionally may use colloquialisms but more selectively than in casual writing. It has the effect of conversation, but it is polished conversation—not chitchat. Its sentences are short, but they are well structured and organized. They have varied patterns that produce an interesting style. In general, it is the writing that you will find in most of the illustrations in Chapters 6–9, and it is the language that this book uses. You should use it in most of your business email messages, especially when writing to people you know only on a business basis. An example of an email message in informal language is the following:

> Cindy:
>
> The management team has heartily approved our marketing plan. They were most complimentary. But as you predicted, they want a special plan for the large accounts. As they want it as soon as possible, let's get together to work on it. Can we meet Wednesday, 10 A.M., my office?
>
> Brandon

Formal. A formal style of writing maintains a greater distance between writer and reader than informal style. It avoids personal references and contractions, and its sentences are well structured and organized. Formal style is well illustrated in the

- Email messages range from highly informal to formal.

- The language may be casual, informal, or formal.

- Casual language uses slang, colloquialisms, contractions, short sentences.

- Use casual language when writing to friends.

- Informal language resembles polished conversation.

- Formal language keeps a certain distance between writer and reader.

---

[3] Heidi Schultz, *The Elements of Electronic Communication* (Boston: Allyn and Bacon, 2000) 43–47, print.

examples of the more formal reports in Chapter 11. It is appropriate to use in email messages resembling formal reports, in messages to people of higher status, and to people not known to the writer.

Traits of Effective Email

- Follow the writing instructions in preceding chapters.

Instructions for writing email messages are much the same as those given in Chapters 2, 3, and 4 for other types of messages. For the purpose of email writing, we may group the more important of these instructions under three heads: conciseness, clarity, and courtesy. A fourth, correctness (covered in Chapter 17), is equally vital. Each of these important qualities for email writing is briefly reviewed in the following paragraphs.

- Cut nonessentials and write concisely.

Conciseness. Email is often written by busy people for busy people. In the best interests of all concerned, email messages should be as short as complete coverage of the subject matter will permit. This means culling out the extra information and using only that which is essential. It means also that the information remaining should be worded concisely. One rule of thumb is that if a routine message takes more than 10–20 seconds to read, it's too long.[4] If your message is not concise, you may need a different communication channel.

- Minimize references to previous communications.

Frequently in email communication, writers need to refer to previous email messages. The easiest way, of course, is to include the entire message. Unless the entire message is needed, however, this practice adds length. It is better either to paraphrase the essentials from the original or to quote the selected parts that cover the essentials. All quoted material should be distinguished from your own words by the sign > at the beginning and the sign < at the end of the quoted part. Another technique is to place three of these signs (>>>) at the beginning of all parts you write and three of these signs (<<<) at the beginning of all parts you are quoting from previous messages.

- Use the techniques of clear writing.

Clarity. Especially important in email writing is clarity of wording. As suggested in Chapters 2 and 3, you should know and practice the techniques of readable writing. You should select words that quickly create clear meanings. Typically, these are the short, familiar ones. You should strive for concreteness, vigor, and precision. Your sentences should be short, and so should your paragraphs. In fact, all of the advice given in Chapters 2 and 3 is applicable to the writing of clear email messages.

- Be courteous, as suggested in preceding chapters.

Courtesy. It should go without saying that courtesy should be practiced in all business relations. We all want to receive courteous and fair treatment. Even so, the current literature has much to say about anger among email participants. "Flaming," as the practice of sending abusive or offensive language is called, has no place in business. Resist the temptation to destroy goodwill with this practice. As you will recall, Chapter 4 emphasizes using courteous language. The skillful use of positive language and you-viewpoint also can be effective in email, as can the use of conversational language. Nondiscriminatory language also helps, as does sincerity. In fact, virtually all the instructions given on goodwill building apply here.

- Correctness matters even in quick, informal messages. Edit and proofread carefully.

Correctness. Because email messages are frequently written quickly and because their tone is frequently (though not always) informal, writers may be tempted to let speed affect their level of professionalism in terms of proofreading and editing. However, "email is a serious business communications tool, and you should treat it with the

---

[4] Cheri Kerr, *The Bliss or "Diss" Connection?: Email Etiquette for the Business Professional* (Santa Ana, CA: ExecuProv Press, 2007) 63, print.

TECHNOLOGY IN BRIEF

Using Good Email Etiquette Helps Writers Achieve Their Goals

Using proper email etiquette is as easy as applying a bit of empathy to your messages: send only what you would want to receive. The following additional etiquette guides will help you consider a variety of issues when using email.

- Is your message really needed by the recipient(s)?

- Is your message for routine rather than sensitive messages?

- Are you sure your message is not spam (an annoying message sent repeatedly) or a chain letter?

- Have you carefully checked that your message is going where you want it to go?

- Has your wording avoided defamatory or libelous language?

- Have you complied with copyright laws and cited sources accurately?

- Have you avoided humor and sarcasm that your reader may not understand as intended?

- Have you proofread your message carefully?

- Is this a message you would not mind having distributed widely?

- Does your signature avoid offensive quotes or illustrations, especially those that are religious, political, or sexual?

- Is your recipient willing or able to accept attached files?

- Are attached files a size that your recipient's system can handle?

- Are the files you are attaching virus free?

---

same respect as any other business document you write."[5] In other words, though the tone of your writing may be informal, the style of your writing must still be professional, which means you must proofread and edit carefully for grammar, mechanics, spelling, and punctuation.

How one communicates is very much a part of the message. In commenting on the importance of correctness to a writer's professional image, one expert says, "The email you write says a lot about you. It tells the readers that you are thorough, accurate, and attentive—or not. It indicates that your message is to be taken seriously—or not. It implies that you know what you're talking about—or not."[6] Bad spelling, illogical punctuation, and awkward wording stand out. Such errors reflect poorly on the writer, and they can reflect poorly on the credibility of the message. You do not want to make yourself or your company appear incompetent.

- Correctness is a part of the message.

To avoid any suggestion of ignorance or carelessness, you should follow the grammatical and punctuation instructions presented in Chapter 16. And you should follow the basic instructions for using words, constructing sentences, and designing paragraphs presented in the writing chapters. Before pressing the Send button, proofread your message carefully.

The Close of the Message

Most email messages end with just the writer's name—the first name alone if the recipient knows the writer well. But in some messages, especially the more formal ones, a closing statement, complimentary close, or both may be appropriate. "Thanks" and "Regards" are popular. In casual messages, acronyms such as THX (thanks) and

- End with your name and perhaps a closing statement.

---

[5] Sheryl Lindsell-Roberts, *135 Tips on Email and Instant Messages: Plus Blogs, Chatrooms, and Texting* (Boston: Houghton Mifflin Harcourt, 2008) 18, print.

[6] Janis Fisher Chan, *E-Mail: A Write It Well Guide—How to Write and Manage E-Mail in the Workplace.* (Oakland, CA: Write It Well, 2008) 198, print.

Be Careful with "Reply All"

The "Reply All" button may not your friend.

According to management consultant Tracy Peterson Turner, hitting "Reply All" to email messages contributes to information overload at work. It can also be destructive if used to show off or to show up previous commenters. Her advice? "Use 'Reply All' only when all those people on the recipient list need the information. . . . otherwise, respond only to the initiator of the message and let the others do their jobs better."

Source: "Use the 'Reply All' Function in Email Judiciously," *SEO Copywriting*, SEO Copywriting, 2009, Web, 8 oct. 2009.

TTFN (ta-ta for now) are often used. The more formal complimentary closes used in traditional letters (sincerely, cordially) are not widely used, but they are appropriate in messages that involve formal business relationships.

In messages to other businesses, including your company and position is important. Today most email software has a signature feature that will automatically attach a signature file to a message. Most programs even allow the writer to set up an alternative signature, giving users the flexibility to choose a standard or alternate signature or to attach no signature at all. Writers sometimes set up a formal full signature in one file and an informal signature in another. The important point to remember is to close with a signature that gives the reader the information he or she needs about you.

Emphasis Devices in Email

- Some email programs have a limited number of emphasis devices. These substitutes have been developed.

When you write email messages, you may find that certain elements of style are missing either on your system or on your readers' systems. While most of the current versions of Windows and Macintosh email programs support mechanical devices such as underscoring, font variations, italics, bold, color, and even graphics, some older or mainframe-based systems do not. Email writers have attempted to overcome the limitations of these older systems by developing alternative means of showing emphasis.

To show underscoring, they use the sign _ at the beginning of the words needing underscoring. They use asterisks (*) before and after words to show boldface. Solid capital letters are another means of emphasis. Some experts advise that these be avoided because they indicate shouting and make reading difficult. On the other hand a writer may want to capitalize "HOORAY" or "CONGRATULATIONS" to express positive emotion.[7] In addition, in certain cases capitalizing words such as "IMPORTANT" may draw a reader's attention to something he or she may have otherwise missed. Another sign writers use to emphasize items in a list is the bullet. Since there is no standardized bullet character that will display on all computers, many writers of email use substitute characters. One is the asterisk (*) followed by a tab space. Another is the dash (—) followed by a tab space.

Generally these devices are best used in the email messages written in casual or informal language.

Initialisms in Email

- Initialisms have been developed to save time. But use them cautiously.

Probably as a result of the early informal development of email, a somewhat standardized system of initialisms has developed. Their purpose has been to cut message length

---

[7] David Shipley, and Will Schwalbe, *Send: Why People Email So Badly and How To Do It Better* (New York: Knopf, 2008) 134, print.

and to save the writer's time. In spite of these apparent advantages, you would be wise to use them primarily in casual messages and only with readers who you are sure will understand them. Even so, you should be acquainted with the more widely used ones, such as those below.

BTW	by the way
FAQ	frequently asked question
FWIW	for what it's worth
FYI	for your information
IMHO	in my humble opinion
LOL	laughing out loud
TIA	thanks in advance
TTFN	ta-ta for now

Such initialisms are even more common in text messaging and other online communication, as we discuss later in this chapter.

Inappropriate Use of Email

In spite of its popularity and ease of use, email is not always a good medium for your communications. As summarized by two authorities, it should not be used when:

- The message is long, complicated, or requires negotiation.
- Questions or information need clarification and discussion.
- The information is confidential or sensitive, requires security, or could be misinterpreted.
- The message is emotionally charged and really requires tone of voice or conversational feedback to soften the words or negotiate meaning.
- The message is sent to *avoid* direct contact with a person, especially if the message is unpleasant and uncomfortable or seems too difficult to say face-to-face.
- The message contains sensitive issues, relays feelings, or attempts to resolve conflict. Email can make conflict worse.[8]

- Don't use email when
- the message involves these aspects.

> PS. Dear Boss. I know you are reading this
> email as I type so I am writing to you to say
> STOP SPYING ON ME AND GET BACK
> TO WORK THIS MINUTE!

---

[8] Vera Terminello, and Marcia G. Reed, *Email: Communicate Effectively* (Upper Saddle River, NJ: Pearson Education, 2003) 13, print.

THE NEWER MEDIA IN BUSINESS WRITING

Sometimes writers in today's fast-paced, global business world need to communicate more immediately and quickly than a letter, a memo, or an email will allow. Technology provides business writers with many more channels for immediate, quick communication including text messaging, instant messaging, and social networking.

Though many people already use these media in more informal social contexts, these media can also be used effectively in business settings. For example, Microsoft's Office Communicator provides business writers with an instant messaging tool. In addition, a recent survey of the Society for Human Resource Management finds that "nearly 20 percent of employees use professional networking sites such as LinkedIn and Plaxo, while 16 percent use social networking sites such as Facebook, MySpace, and Friendster."[9] However, as with more traditional business writing media such as letters, memos, and emails, the use of these channels should be driven by audience needs and expectations as well as the writer's goals and purposes.

Text Messaging

- Text messaging is widely used in business today.

- Messages are short—160 characters.

- The writing involved stresses brevity and uses abbreviations.

Text messaging, also called short message service (SMS), is, as its name suggests, used for sending short messages (160 characters or less) generally from a mobile phone. Because the purpose of a text message is to convey a quick message, the writing of text messages is quite different from that of other messages. As the message generally is limited to 160 characters, the emphasis is on brevity. You include only the essentials.

The need for brevity has led to the use of many abbreviations. So many of these abbreviations have developed that one might say a new language has developed In fact, a dictionary of over 1,100 text messaging abbreviations has been compiled at Webopedia, an online computer technology encyclopedia (<http://www.webopedia.com/quick_ref/textmessageabbreviations.asp>). Some examples are the following:

b4 (before)	u (you)
gr8 (great)	BTW (by the way)
CU (see you)	NP (no problem)
FBM (fine by me)	HRY (how are you)
TC (take care)	TYT (take your time)

In addition to abbreviations, writers use typed symbols to convey emotions (emoticons), which can also be found at Webopedia:

:-) standard smiley	:-! foot in mouth
;) winking smile	:-(sad or frown
:-0 yell	(((H))) hugs

Whether and when these abbreviations and emoticons are used depends on the writer's relationship with the audience.

---

[9] Marcia Heroux Pounds, "Social Networking Is Key to Business, Worker Success," *SunSentinel.com* 20 May 2009, Web, 21 May 2009.

**"...and I'm proficient in two languages
— English and text messaging."**

Source: © Chris Wildt, www.artizans.com

Good business writers will compose text messages that not only convey the writer's message but also allow for brief responses from the receiver. Let's say, for example, that you've learned that an important visiting customer is a vegetarian and you have reservations for lunch at Ruth's Chris Steakhouse. You might need to let your boss know—before the lunch meeting. However, the boss is leading an important meeting in which a phone call would be disruptive and inappropriate, so you decide to send a text message.

Your immediate thought might be to send the following: *Marina Smith is a vegetarian. Where should we take her for lunch today? Zeke.*

Although your message does convey the major fact and is only 77 characters counting spaces, it forces the recipient to enter a long response—the name of another place. It might also result in more message exchanges about availability and time.

A better version might be this: *Marina Smith is a vegetarian. Shall we go to 1) Fish House, 2) Souplantation, 3) Mandarin House? All are available at noon. Zeke*

This version conveys the major fact in 130 characters and allows the recipient to respond simply with 1, 2, or 3. As the writer, you took the initiative to anticipate your reader's needs, identify appropriate alternatives, and then gather information—steps that are as important with text messaging as they are with other messages. If your text messages are clear, complete, and concise and have a professional and pleasant tone, you will find them a valuable tool for business use.

- Text messages should convey ideas completely with minimal need for response.

Instant Messaging

Instant messaging, commonly referred to as IM-ing or online chatting, is much like telephone conversation in that parties communicate in real time (instantly). It differs primarily in that it is text-based (typed) rather than voice-based communication, though recent developments have made voice-based instant messaging possible. Many writers will use the same abbreviations and emoticons in instant messages that they use in text messages. Here again the use of these devices depends on your audience and purpose.

- Instant messaging is like a telephone conversation, but it uses type rather than voice.

Figure 5–7

An Enterprise Instant-Messaging Platform

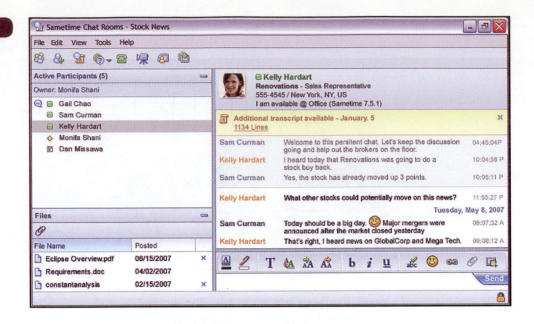

- Write instant messages as you would talk to the other person.

Because instant messages are similar to phone conversations, you should write instant messages much as you would talk in conversation with another person. If the person is a personal friend, your language should reflect this friendship. If the person is the president of your company, a business associate, or fellow worker, the relationship should guide you. The message bits presented in instant messaging are determined largely by the flow of information. Responses often are impromptu. Even so, in business situations you should consciously direct the flow toward your objective.

Some companies have their own instant-messaging platforms that are tailored to their needs and offer security and record-keeping benefits (see Figure 5–7). Whether using these or other IM-ing programs, be sure to keep your language and contents professional.

Social Networking

- Social networking is increasingly popular.

You may already be familiar with such social networking sites as Facebook, MySpace, Twitter, or LinkedIn. Perhaps you have a blog (a "Web log") where you keep an online diary or journal that you share publicly. These social networking sites are increasingly popular—so much so, says *The New York Times,* that in February 2009 people actually spent more time on social networks than they did on their email. The author suggests that this represents "a paradigm shift in consumer engagement with the Internet."[10] Although you may use these sites to connect with friends, family, or classmates, many business writers also use them to connect with clients, customers, colleagues, and supervisors, as they answer questions, promote products, network with other professionals, or interact briefly with co-workers. Many companies have found that these networks promote personal and corporate success. One survey of 1,600 executives "found that firms that rely heavily on external social networks scored 24 percent higher on a measure of radical innovation than companies that

- Business writers use social networking to people both within and outside their companies.

---

[10] Teddy Wayne, "Drilling Down: Social Networks Eclipse E-Mail," *The New York Times* 18 May 2009: B3, Web, 21 May 2009.

Figure 5–8

Example of a Corporate Blog

Source: <http://en.community.dell .com/blogs/direct2dell>, accessed 22 May 2009.

don't."[11] Business professionals, then, are using social networking sites for purposes that are likely very different from your purpose in using them (see the corporate blog in Figure 5–8, for example).

Generally, the messages on social networking sites are brief, with some sites, such as Twitter, restricting messages to 140 characters. Therefore, as with text messaging, messages must not only be brief but concise and clear. In addition, because the messages on these sites are public, you would never want to use language or a tone or writing style that you would be embarrassed to have your boss see, that may have legal implications, or that might get you fired. In fact, if you currently have a page on a social networking site where family and friends are your audience, you will want to remove any pictures or language that you wouldn't want a prospective employer, current employer, co-worker, customer, or client to see. No matter how private you believe your page to be, you can never know what your friends and family are sharing with other people. One expert advises that even though employers may not be within their rights to use information on social networking sites in their hiring decisions (e.g., age, race, or health history), 40 percent of employers indicate that they check social networking sites when hiring new employees, and 80 percent of these employers say the content of these sites influences their hiring decisions.[12]

Regardless of the type of business messages you send, remember that on the job, companies often monitor employees' computer activity. In doing this, companies can detect excessive use, inappropriate or unethical behavior, disclosure of proprietary information, use of sexually explicit language, and attachments with viruses. Companies' monitoring systems also have features that protect the company from legal liabilities. As a business professional, you must know your company's computer use policy and avoid writing anything that would reflect poorly on you or your company or put you or your company at risk.

- Messages on social networking sites are short.

- Be sure the content you post on any social networking site reflects a positive professional image.

- Employers may monitor your computer use at work.

---

[11] Jake Swearingen, "Four Ways Social Networking Can Build Business," *bnet.com*, CBS Interactive, 2009, Web, 8 May 2009.
[12] Jackie Ford, "Why Employers Should Reconsider Facebook Fishing." *MarketWatch.com, The Wall Street Journal* Digital Network, 11 Feb. 2009, Web, 8 May 2009.

1. The writing process consists of five main stages:
   - Planning includes the following activities:
     — Determining goals.
     — Analyzing the audience.
     — Gathering and collecting information.
     — Analyzing and organizing the information.
     — Choosing a form, channel, and format.
   - Drafting needs to be flexible.
     — Avoid perfectionism when drafting.
     — Keep going—don't stop for excessive tinkering.
     — Pursue any strategy that will help you make progress on the draft.
   - Revising involves three main levels of edit:
     — Revising for content, organization, and format.
     — Editing sentences and words.
     — Proofreading to catch mechanical and grammatical errors.
   - The five stages are *recursive*—you can revisit earlier stages at any time.

   1 Describe the writing process and effective writing strategies.

2. Making good formatting decisions is critical to your messages' success.
   - Good formatting makes your messages inviting.
   - Good formatting makes your information easier to find and follow.

   2 Explain the importance of readable formatting.

3. These are the highlights of the development of business letters:
   - The early civilizations (Chinese, Greek, Roman, Egyptian) used them.
   - They are now used largely in more formal situations, especially with external audiences.
   - Letter formats are standardized (see Appendix B).
   - Early business letters used a stilted language.
   - Strategic organization and humanized language characterize today's letters.

   3 Describe the development and current usage of the business letter.

4. The memorandum (memo) is a form of letter written inside the business.
   - Hard-copy memorandums usually are processed on special stationery (*Memorandum* at the top; *Date, To, From,* and *Subject* follow).
   - Large organizations often include more information (*Department, Plant, Location, Copies to, Store Number,* etc.)
   - Memos vary widely in formality, but most are relatively informal.
   - Most memos are written in the direct order, though sometimes strategic indirectness is needed.

   4 Describe the purpose and form of memorandums (memos).

5. Today, email is a mainstream form of business communication.
   - It has grown because it
     — Eliminates "telephone tag."
     — Saves time.
     — Speeds up decision making.
     — Is cheap.
     — Provides a written record.
   - But it has disadvantages:
     — It is not confidential.
     — It doesn't show emotions.
     — It may be ignored or delayed.

   5 Understand the phenomenal growth and nature of email.

- Email should be avoided when
  — The message is long, complicated, or needs negotiating.
  — Content needs discussion.
  — Content needs softening in tone, voice, or words.
  — The message is used to avoid unpleasant and uncomfortable personal contact.
  — The message contains sensitive issues.

6. The way to write good email messages is as follows:
   - Use standardized prefatory parts, paying careful attention to the subject line.
   - Begin with the recipient's name, a greeting, or no salutation as appropriate.
   - Organize logically.
     — For short messages, present the information in descending order of importance.
     — For long messages, use the organization that best presents the information.
   - Use the appropriate level of formality (casual, informal, formal) for your messages.
   - Make the message concise, clear, courteous, and correct.
   - Close with your name or a closing statement.
   - Use asterisks, dashes, solid caps, and other emphasis devices as needed.
   - Sometimes initialisms are useful, but use them cautiously.

6 Follow email conventions and organize and write clear email messages.

7. Text messaging and instant messaging (IM-ing) are important newer types of business messages.
   - Text messaging is widely used today.
   - The writing stresses brevity and uses shortcuts—but never at the expense of clarity.
   - Instant messaging is like a telephone conversation, but it uses type rather than voice.
   - Write your instant messages as though you were talking to the other person.

7 Understand the nature and business uses of text messaging and instant messaging.

8. Social networking sites are becoming increasingly popular.
   - Business writers use them to connect with co-workers, clients, and customers.
   - Be sure that content for any social networking site presents a positive professional image.

8 Understand the nature and business uses of social networking.

CRITICAL THINKING QUESTIONS

1 Identify and explain the steps in the writing process. **(LO1)**

2 Think about a writing project that you recently completed. Using the terminology in this chapter, describe the process that you used. How might using different strategies have made the project more pleasant and productive? What helpful strategies did you use, if any, that were not mentioned in this chapter? **(LO1)**

3 Think about a letter you received or wrote recently, and explain why it was appropriate to use a letter in this situation. **(LO3)**

4 Will hard-copy letters diminish in importance as email continues to grow? Become obsolete? Vanish? **(LO3)**

5 a. Discuss the reasons for social networking's phenomenal growth.

   b. Is this growth likely to continue? **(LO8)**

6 Some authorities say that concerns about correctness inhibit a person's email communication. Does this view have merit? Discuss. **(LO6)**

7 Some authorities say that shortcuts in text messaging and instant messaging will lead to users' inability to spell properly in more formal contexts. Discuss. **(LO7)**

8 Memorandums and email messages can differ more than letters in their physical makeup. Explain and discuss. **(LO4, LO5, LO6)**

9 Explain the logic of using negative words in email and memos to fellow employees that you would not use in letters carrying similar messages. **(LO4, LO5, LO6)**

10 Discuss and justify the wide range of formality used in memos and email messages. **(LO4, LO5)**

11 What factors might determine whether or not instant messaging would be an appropriate medium to use in a given situation? **(LO7)**

CRITICAL THINKING EXERCISES

1 Interview a working professional about his or her writing process. In addition to asking about general strategies for different kinds of writing, ask how he or she tackled a particularly difficult writing situation. Write up the results of your findings in a brief memo report to your instructor. **(LO1)**

2 Find a sample of business writing and evaluate its use of formatting elements. If they are effective, say why; if not, explain what you would do differently. **(LO2)**

3 Using various formatting devices, turn the following contents into a readable, attractive flyer or email announcing a health club's new rates for employees of a nearby hospital. (You may want to consult Appendix B's advice on formatting.) **(LO2)**

New Special Rates for Metropolitan Hospital Staff! The Health Club is now offering special rates for all Metropolitan Hospital employees. The Club is a full-service exercise club located at 42 Adams Street, just across from the hospital. Our facilities may be a good option for Metropolitan employees to explore. We offer the following membership types for Metropolitan employees or retirees: Single Standard, 1 year prepaid ($200/year); Single Standard, by the month ($15/month plus a one-time $50 enrollment fee); Single Deluxe, 1 year prepaid ($300/year). Single Deluxe includes your personal locker and a towel service. Metropolitan employees' spouses or domestic partners are eligible for a 20 percent discount on the Club's normal rates. You can take a tour, join the Club, or ask any questions by calling 555-5555. We have a large free-weight room; new Cybex (Nautilus-style) machines; ellipticals, treadmills, bikes, steppers, and rowers; an Olympic-size swimming pool; aerobics, Pilates, and yoga classes; racquetball and handball courts; a large gym/basketball court; a whirlpool; a steam room and saunas; shower and locker room facilities; and free parking. A small fee for some classes may apply. Our hours are Monday through Friday, 5 AM to 10 PM; Saturday, 7 AM to 8 PM; and Sunday, 7 AM to 6 PM. Our website address is www.healthclubin.org.

4 Instructions: Write a text message shorter than 160 characters for each of the cases below. Be sure your message is both clear and complete. **(LO7)**

a. You own three coffee shops around your area. Although you have a loyal base of regular customers, you realize that there is both room to grow this base and a real need to compete with the growing presence of Starbucks and other competitors. Your coffee is good and reasonably priced, but seasonal fruit and muffins have long been your specialties. In fact, since the local television station included your shop in a healthy eating segment, your low-fat muffins are selling out every day even though you have been increasing production. When some of your loyal customers started grumbling about not always being able to get them, you knew you wanted to serve them better.

Because most of them have mobile phones, text messaging seems like an obvious solution. You have decided to offer an opt-in polling service that would ask their preference for a particular low-fat muffin or fresh fruit. Your customers could select the days of the week they would be interested in getting the poll. Although they would not be placing an order, they would be helping you plan. You'll also be spending well-targeted promotion dollars while creating goodwill with your loyal customers. Now you need to write this poll question.

b. You are on your way to the airport for a trip to a week-long conference when you remember a file you were supposed to send to a customer. So many last-minute details came up that you really don't remember if you sent it. Unfortunately, you cannot access your work computer from outside the company firewall, but you have a colleague, Chris VanLerBerghe, who would be able to check your email outbox to confirm whether or not you sent it. Chris could also send the file, if necessary. However, you cannot reach her by phone now because she is in an important planning meeting, so you decide to send a text message with the exact information she will need to help you out. Be sure your message is both clear and complete.

c. As you are in the morning sales meeting, your mobile phone vibrates, indicating that you have an incoming call. You recognize the source—Yesaya Chan, the high school student you are mentoring/tutoring in math. When you are finally able to listen to the call, you learn that Yesaya needs your help tonight because his teacher moved a test up a couple of days. He wants to know if you can meet him at the local library at 5 PM, noting that it will be open late tonight. You will say yes, but the earliest you can be there on such short notice is 6 PM. Suggest that he still go to the library at 5 PM and work as many of the review problems on his own as he can. You will help him with the others when you get there. Because he is probably in class now, you will send your response as a text message so it won't interrupt his class.

5 Assume the role of the hotel manager we discussed in the "Planning the Message" section of this chapter. The air conditioning has stopped functioning on one of the busiest and hottest weekends of the year. You need to explain the situation and what you are going to do (or have done) about it to three audiences: your guests, your co-workers who will be helping you solve the problem, and your boss, who will not be at the hotel until Monday. Develop a plan for the message you will send to each of these audiences in which you follow the five steps discussed in this chapter for planning a message. (You may find Figure 1–4 useful as well.) Be sure you consider your goal in communicating with each audience, the format/channel your communication will take, the content each audience will need, and the tone and style that will be appropriate for each audience. (LO1)

chapter six

Directness in Good-News and Neutral Messages

Upon completing this chapter, you will be able to write direct-order messages effectively. To reach this goal, you should be able to

1 Properly assess the reader's likely reaction to your message.

2 Describe the general plan for direct-order messages.

3 Write clear, well-structured routine requests for information.

4 Write direct, orderly, and friendly answers to inquiries.

5 Compose adjustment grants that regain any lost confidence.

6 Write order acknowledgments and other thank-you messages that build goodwill.

7 Write clear and effective operational communications.

THE PREVALENCE OF DIRECTNESS IN BUSINESS

Most business messages use a direct organizational pattern. That is, the message leads with its most important point and then moves to additional or supporting information. If you recall what Chapter 1 observed about the nature of business, you will understand why. Communication is central to organized human activity. Especially in business, people need to know what to do, why, and how. They undertake any job understanding that they have a certain function to perform, and they need information to be able to perform it well. When external audiences interact with companies, they also expect and need certain kinds of information presented as expeditiously as possible. It is fair to say that direct messages are the lifeblood of virtually any business activity.

There are, of course, unlimited kinds of direct messages. Each business is unique in some ways, and each, therefore, will have developed its own direct-message types—its preferred purposes, patterns, styles, and formats for these messages. Still, one can identify a certain basic plan for the direct message. Moreover, certain situations calling for a direct approach have occurred so often that we can identify several common types of these messages.

This chapter first describes a general plan for writing all messages of this type. Then we adapt this general plan to some of the more common business situations where it is appropriate. We show why each of these situations requires somewhat special treatment. Although our coverage is not complete, we believe that this review of common direct plans will enable you to adapt them to any related situation.

- Direct order is used in most business messages.

- A general direct plan is presented and then adapted to specific situations.

PRELIMINARY ASSESSMENT

As discussed in Chapter 1, writing any messages other than those for the most mechanical, routine circumstances requires careful thinking about the situation, your readers, and your goals. When determining your message's basic plan, a good beginning is to assess your reader's probable reaction to what you have to say. If the reaction is likely to be positive or even neutral, your best approach is likely to be a direct one—that is, one that gets to the objective right away without delay. If your reader's reaction is likely to be negative, you may need to use the indirect plan, discussed in Chapter 7. The general plan for the direct approach follows.

- Begin by assessing the reader's probable reaction. A positive or neutral reaction calls for directness; a negative reaction, indirectness.

THE GENERAL DIRECT PLAN

Beginning with the Objective

Begin with your objective. If you are seeking information, start by asking for it. If you are giving information, start giving it. Whatever your key point is, lead with it.

In some cases, you might need to open with a brief orienting phrase, clause, or even sentence. Especially if your reader is not expecting to hear from you or is not familiar with you or your company, you may need to preface your main point with a few words of background. But get to the point as soon as possible. For example, the sentence "We have received your May 7 inquiry" does nothing but state the obvious. Keep any prefatory remarks brief and get to the real message. Then stop the first paragraph. Let the rest of the message fill in the details.

- Put the key point up front.

- But you may need to lead with brief orienting information.

Covering the Remaining Part of the Objective

Whatever else must be covered to complete the objective makes up the bulk of the remainder of the message. If you cover all of your objective in the beginning (as in an inquiry in which a single question is asked), nothing else is needed. If

- Complete the objective systematically—perhaps by listing or paragraphing.

additional questions, answers, or information are needed, you cover them. And you cover them systematically—perhaps listing them or arranging them by paragraphs. If these parts have their own explanations or commentary, you include them. In short, you cover everything else that needs to be covered.

Ending with Goodwill

- End with a goodwill comment
- specifically adapted to the message.

End this message with some appropriate friendly comment as you would end a face-to-face communication with the reader.

These final goodwill words will receive the best reader reaction if they are selected to fit the one case. Such general closes as "A prompt reply will be appreciated" and "Thank you for your time and consideration" are positive, for they express a friendly thank-you. And there is nothing wrong with a thank-you sincerely expressed here or elsewhere. The problem is in the routine, rubber-stamp nature of many of these expressions. A more positive reaction results from an individually tailored expression that fits the one case—for example: "If you will answer these questions about Ms. Hill right away, she and I will be most grateful."

Be aware, though, that phrases such as "as soon as possible" or "at your convenience" may have very different meanings for you and your reader. If you need your response by a specific date or time, give your reader that information as well as a reason for the deadline so that your reader understands the importance of a timely response. You may say, for example, "Your answers to these questions by July 1 will help Ms. Hill and us as we meet our deadline for filling the accounting position."

Now let us see how you can adapt this general plan to fit the more common direct message situations.

ROUTINE INQUIRIES

Routine Inquiries

Introduce yourself to routine inquiries by assuming you are the assistant to the vice president for administration of Pinnacle Manufacturing Company. Pinnacle is the manufacturer and distributor of an assortment of high-quality products. Your duties involve helping your boss cover a variety of activities. Many of these activities involve writing messages.

At the moment, your boss is working with a group of Pinnacle executives to select offices for a new regional headquarters. They have chosen the city. Now they must find the best possible offices in this city. As chair of this committee, your boss has accepted responsibility for finding office locations from which to choose. Of course, your boss has delegated much of the work to you.

Already you have found three possible office suites in the chosen city. Now you must get the pertinent information about each so that the executives can make their selection. The first of these you found in the classified advertisements of the local newspaper. It is a 3,200-square-foot office suite, but the ad tells little more. So now you must write the advertiser a routine inquiry seeking the information the management team needs.

Answering inquiries that do not include adequate explanation can be frustrating.

Choosing from Two Types of Beginnings

The opening of the routine inquiry should focus on the main objective, as recommended in the preceding section. Since your objective is to ask for information, begin with a question. This opening question can be either of two types: specific or general.

First, it can be one of the specific questions to be asked (assuming that more than one question needs to be asked). Preferably it should be a question that sets up the other questions. For example, if your objective is to get information about the office suites described in the Introductory Situation, you might begin with these words:

> Can you please send me additional information about the floor plan of the office suite that you advertised in Monday's *Sentinel Times*?

In the body of the message you would include additional specific questions concerning the suite.

Or, the opening question could be a general request for information. The specific questions would follow. This beginning sentence illustrates a general request:

> Will you please send me a description of the features of the 3,200-square-foot office suite advertised in Monday's *Daily Journal*?

Whether you open with a specific or a general question, be sure your reader has a clear sense of your message's purpose.

Informing and Explaining Adequately

To help your reader answer your questions, you may need to include explanation or information. If you do not explain enough or if you misjudge the reader's knowledge, you make the reader's task difficult. For example, answers to your questions about office space for Pinnacle Manufacturing may depend on characteristics or specific needs of the company. Without knowing how Pinnacle Manufacturing will

- Routine inquiries appropriately begin by asking either of two types of questions:

- (1) a specific question that sets up the information wanted or

- (2) a general request for information.

- Somewhere in the message, explain enough to enable the reader to answer.

use the space, even the best realtor or property manager may not know how to answer your questions or perhaps direct you to other office space that better meets your needs.

Where and how you include the necessary explanatory information depend on the nature of your message. Usually, a good place for general explanatory material is before or after the direct request in the opening paragraph. This information helps reduce any startling effect that a direct opening question might have. It often fits logically into this place, serving as a qualifying or justifying sentence for the message.

In messages that ask more than one question, include any necessary explanatory material with the questions. If this is the case, the explanation fits best with the questions to which it pertains. Such messages may alternate questions and explanations in the body of the message.

● Place the explanation anywhere it fits logically.

Structuring the Questions

● If the inquiry involves just one question, begin with it.

After you ask your initial question and provide any relevant background information, your message will take one of two directions. If your inquiry involves only one question, you have achieved your objective, and you may move to a goodwill ending to finish your message. If you have to ask several questions, develop an organized, logical list in the body of your message.

● If it involves more than one, make each stand out. Do this by (1) placing each question in a separate sentence,

If you have more than one question, make them stand out. You can do this in a number of ways. First, you can make each question a separate sentence with a bullet (for example, ●, ○, ■) to call attention to it. Combining two or more questions in a sentence de-emphasizes each and invites the reader to overlook some.

● (2) structuring the questions in separate paragraphs,

Second, you can give each question a separate paragraph whenever your explanation and other comments about each question justify a paragraph.

● (3) ordering or ranking the questions, and

Third, you can order or rank your questions with numbers. By using words (*first, second, third,* etc.), numerals (*1, 2, 3,* etc.), or letters (*a, b, c,* etc.), you make the questions stand out. Also, you provide the reader with a convenient checklist for answering.

● (4) using the question form of sentence.

Fourth, you can structure your questions in question form. True questions stand out. Sentences that merely hint at a need for information do not attract much attention. The "It would be nice if you would tell me . . ." and "I would like to know . . ." types are really not questions. They do not ask—they merely suggest. The questions that stand out are those written in question form: "Will you please tell me . . . ?" "How much would one be able to save . . . ?" "How many contract problems have you had . . . ?"

● Take care when asking questions that produce yes or no answers.

Avoid questions that can be answered with a simple *yes* or *no* unless you really want a simple *yes* or *no* answer. For example, the question "Is the chair available in blue?" may not be what you really want to know. Better wording might be "In what colors is the chair available?" Often, combining a yes/no question with its explanation yields a better, more concise question. To illustrate, the wording "Does the program run with Windows? We use Windows Vista" could be improved with "Does the program run with Windows Vista?"

Ending with Goodwill

● End with a friendly comment that fits the one case.

The goodwill ending described in the general plan is appropriate here, just as it is in most business messages. And we must emphasize again that the closing words do the most toward creating goodwill when they fit the one case. Remember to include important deadlines and reasons for them as well.

Choosing the Right Font

Of all the issues a writer considers when writing an effective business message, the type of font to use may be at the bottom of the list (if it is on the list at all). However, choosing the right font can make your documents look as professional as they sound.

- *What are my choices?* The main choice is either a serif or sans serif font. Letters in serif fonts such as **Times New Roman** have "tails" (serifs). Letters in sans serif fonts such as **Tahoma** do not. You can see that the "T" in Times New Roman has the "tails" that the "T" in Tahoma does not. What do serifs do? Serifs connect letters, which makes the space between words more distinguishable and the text therefore more readable—at least in printed documents. In electronic documents, the serifs may actually hinder readability depending on the font size and monitor resolution. Sans serif fonts, however, allow for more white space, which makes letters and words stand out. A possible choice, then, is to use a sans serif font for headings and a serif font for body text.

- *How many fonts can I use?* Limit yourself to not more than two fonts. It's fine to use only one font. However, if you use more than two, you will have a document that looks cluttered and visually confusing. Remember that excessive formatting of your fonts (bold, italics, underlining) will also undermine the professional look of your document.

- *How big should my fonts be?* This depends on the font. Start with the body text at 9–12 points. Make your headings two points larger than your body text. Whatever size you choose, be sure the text is readable and looks professional. Fonts that are too small are hard to read. Fonts that are too big look amateurish and visually attack the reader.

- *What style should I choose?* That will depend on what kind of document you're writing and to whom. Look at the sample fonts below. Which would be more appropriate in a print ad for party supplies? In an annual report to investors? In an invitation to a formal event? As you can see, each typeface has its own personality. Choose yours carefully to match your situation. For electronic messages, keep in mind that the font will need to be on the recipient's computer in order to display properly. If you have your doubts, choose a more common font or save and send your message as a pdf file.

This font is 12-point Verdana.

This typeface is 12-point Script MT Bold.

This typeface is 12-point Book Antiqua.

THIS TYPEFACE IS 12-POINT GOUDY STOUT.

Reviewing the Order

In summary, the plan recommended for the routine inquiry message is as follows:

- Focus directly on the objective, with either a specific question that sets up the entire message or a general request for information.
- Include necessary explanation—wherever it fits.
- If a number of questions are involved, make them stand out with bullets, numbering, paragraphing, and question form.
- End with goodwill words adapted to the individual case.

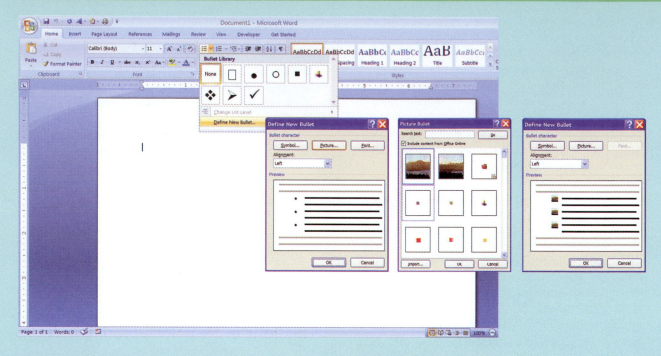

Word processing software allows writers to list items easily with bullets or numbers. Writers generally use numbers to show ordering or ranking and bullets to list unranked or equal items. One way to add interest to lists is to use picture bullets, an easy task today. Rather than selecting one of the six standard bullets, writers can easily customize them with pictures. Microsoft Word includes a nice selection of picture bullets in various colors and styles, some that you see above. However, writers can also select other images to import for use as a bullet. By simply pointing and clicking on the image to import, a writer instantly creates a bullet and resizes it automatically for bullet use.

In a message to its members' meeting in Washington, DC, the executive director of the Association for Business Communication might use one picture bullet to list items members should bring with them for tours of national monuments. The writer might suggest that members bring these items:

 Binoculars for taking in spectacular views.

 All-weather jacket with a hood for protection from sudden showers.

 Cameras with wide lenses for panoramic photos.

The same message might use a different picture bullet for a list of items for a side trip to the Smithsonian. These bullets would add interest through color and convey information about the items as well. Through careful use, picture bullets can help writers present lists that get attention.

Contrasting Examples

- Following are bad and good examples. They could be in email, fax, or letter format.

The following two routine inquiry messages illustrate bad and good approaches to requesting information about office space for a new Pinnacle regional headquarters (recall the introductory situation). The first example follows the indirect pattern that was popular in the past. The second is direct. Here they are presented as letters, as indicated by the "Dear" in the salutation and the "Sincerely" closing, but the points they make apply to inquiries in other media as well. You can also study the Case Illustrations on pages 122 and 123. The margin comments help you see how these sample inquiries follow the advice in this chapter.

As you read the first example below, note that it is marked by a "⊘" icon in the side panel. We use this icon throughout the book wherever we show bad examples. The good examples will be indicated by a "✔" icon.

The Indirect Message. The less effective message begins slowly and gives obvious information. Even if the writer thinks that this information needs to be communicated, it does not deserve the emphasis of the opening sentence. The writer gets to the point of the message in the second paragraph. But there are no questions here—just hints for information. The items of information the writer wants do not stand out but are listed in rapid succession in one sentence. The close is selfish and stiff.

Dear Mr. Piper:

We have seen your advertisement for 3,200 square feet of office space in the *Daily Journal.* As we are interested, we would like additional information.

Specifically, we would like to know the interior layout, annual cost, availability of transportation, length of lease agreement, escalation provisions, and any other information you think pertinent.

If the information you give us is favorable, we will inspect the property. Please send your reply as soon as possible.

Sincerely

This letter's indirect and vague beginning slows reading.

The Direct and Effective Message. The second example begins directly by asking for information. The explanation is brief but complete. The questions, with explanation worked in where needed, are made to stand out; thus, they help to make answering easy. The message closes with a courteous and appropriate request for quick action.

Dear Mr. Piper:

Will you please answer the following questions about the 3,200-square-foot office suite advertised in the June 28 issue of the *Daily Journal*? This space may be suitable for the new regional headquarters we are opening in your city in August.

This direct and orderly letter is better.

- Is the layout of these offices suitable for a work force of two administrators, a receptionist, and seven office employees? (If possible, please send us a diagram of the space.)
- What is the annual rental charge?
- Are housekeeping, maintenance, and utilities included?
- What is the nature of the walls and flooring?
- Does the location provide easy access to mass transportation and the airport?
- What are your requirements for length of lease agreement?
- What escalation provisions are included in the lease agreement?

We look forward to learning more about your property. We hope to secure a space that meets our needs by July 21.

Sincerely,

Routine Inquiries (Getting Information about a Training Program). This email message is from a company training director to the director of a management-training program. The company training director has received literature on the program but needs additional information. The message seeks this information.

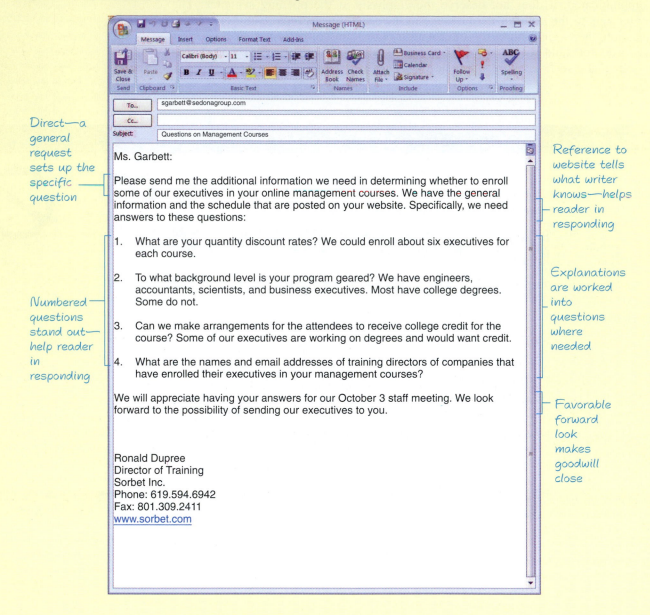

Direct—a general request sets up the specific question

Numbered questions stand out—help reader in responding

Reference to website tells what writer knows—helps reader in responding

Explanations are worked into questions where needed

Favorable forward look makes goodwill close

To... sgarbett@sedonagroup.com

Cc...

Subject: Questions on Management Courses

Ms. Garbett:

Please send me the additional information we need in determining whether to enroll some of our executives in your online management courses. We have the general information and the schedule that are posted on your website. Specifically, we need answers to these questions:

1. What are your quantity discount rates? We could enroll about six executives for each course.

2. To what background level is your program geared? We have engineers, accountants, scientists, and business executives. Most have college degrees. Some do not.

3. Can we make arrangements for the attendees to receive college credit for the course? Some of our executives are working on degrees and would want credit.

4. What are the names and email addresses of training directors of companies that have enrolled their executives in your management courses?

We will appreciate having your answers for our October 3 staff meeting. We look forward to the possibility of sending our executives to you.

Ronald Dupree
Director of Training
Sorbet Inc.
Phone: 619.594.6942
Fax: 801.309.2411
www.sorbet.com

Routine Inquiries (An Inquiry about Hotel Accommodations). This fax message to a hotel inquires about meeting accommodations for a professional association. In selecting a hotel, the company's managers need answers to specific questions. The message covers these questions.

WOMENS media.com™
The Self Improvement Site for Women

Visit us: www.womensmedia.com

TO: Ms. Connie Briggs, Manager
COMPANY: Drake Hotel
FAX: 312.787.1431
DATE: July 17, 2011

FROM: Patti Wolff, Chair of the Site Selection Committee
COMPANY: WomensMedia.com
PHONE: 619.401.9600
FAX: 619.401.9444
EMAIL: pwolff@womensmedia.com

TOTAL PAGES *(including cover):* 1

Direct—a courteous general request sets up the specific question

COMMENTS: Will you please help WomensMedia.com decide whether we can hold our annual meeting at the Drake hotel?

Explanation of situation provides background information

We have selected Chicago for our 2012 meeting, which will be held August 16, 17, and 18. In addition to the Drake, the conference committee is considering the Marriott and the Hilton. In order to decide, we need the following information:

Can you accommodate a group of about 600 employees on these dates? They will need about 400 rooms.

What are your room rates? We need assurance of having available a minimum of 450 rooms, and we could guarantee 400. Would you be willing to set aside this size block of rooms?

Questions stand out— in separate paragraphs

Specific questions— with explanations where needed

What are your charges for conference rooms? We will need eight for each of the three days, and each should have a minimum capacity of 60. On the 18th, for the half-hour business meeting, we will need a large ballroom with a capacity of at least 500.

Also, will you please send me your menu selections and prices for group dinners? On the 17th we plan our presidential dinner. About 500 can be expected for this event.

As meeting plans must be announced by September, may we have your response right away? We look forward to the possibility of being with you in 2012.

Individually tailored goodwill close

TECHNOLOGY IN BRIEF

Shortcut Tools Help Writers Improve Productivity and Quality

Shortcuts help writers save time and improve quality. One of the easiest to use is the AutoCorrect tool in Word (shown here) or the similar QuickCorrect tool in WordPerfect. This tool will automatically replace a word entered with another word set up to replace that particular word. The default setting is generally set up to correct common misspellings and typos. However, it also can be used to expand acronyms or phrases used repeatedly.

If you worked frequently with the Association for Business Communication, you might set up the AutoCorrect tool to replace the acronym ABC with the full name, as you see below. Not only will this shortcut enable you to save time, but it also will improve the quality of your work, by inserting a correctly spelled and typed replacement every time.

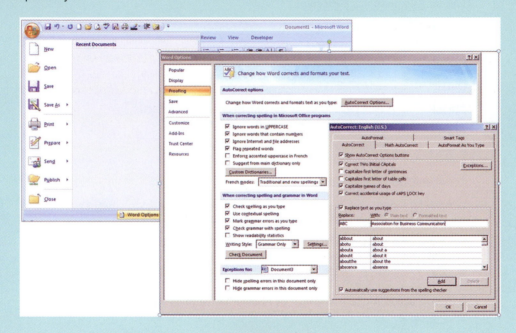

Writing inquiries requires careful wording so that the reader understands clearly what is being asked.

FAVORABLE RESPONSES

INTRODUCTORY SITUATION

Favorable Responses

Continue in your role as assistant to the vice president for operations of Pinnacle Manufacturing Company and answer some of the messages sent to you.

You answer most of the incoming messages favorably. That is, you tell the reader what he or she wants to know. In today's inbox, for example, you have a typical problem of this type. It is a message from a prospective customer for Pinnacle's Chem-Treat paint. In response to an advertisement, this prospective customer asks a number of specific questions about Chem-Treat. Foremost, she wants to know whether the paint is really mildewproof. Do you have supporting evidence? Do you guarantee the results? Is the paint safe? How much does a gallon cost? Will one coat do the job?

You can answer all but one of the questions positively. Of course, you will report this one negative point (that two coats are needed to do most jobs), but you will take care to de-emphasize it. The response will be primarily a good-news message. Because the reader is a good prospect, you will work to create the best goodwill effect.

When you answer inquiries favorably, your primary goal is to tell your readers what they want to know. Because their reactions to your goal will be favorable, directness is in order.

Identifying the Message Being Answered

Because this message is a response to another message, you should identify the message you are answering. Such identification helps the reader recall or find the message being answered. If you are writing an email response, the original message is appended to your message. Hard-copy messages may use a subject line (Subject: Your April 2 Inquiry about Chem-Treat), as illustrated in Appendix B. Or you can refer to the message incidentally in the text ("as requested in your April 2 inquiry"). Preferably you should make this identification early in your message.

Beginning with the Answer

As you can deduce from the preceding examples, directness here means giving the readers what they want at the beginning. Thus you begin by answering. When a response involves answering a single question, you begin by answering that question. When it involves answering two or more questions, one good plan is to begin by answering one of them—preferably the most important. In the Chem-Treat case, this opening would get the response off to a fast start:

- Begin by answering. If there is one question, answer it; if there are more than one, answer the most important.

> Yes, you can use Chem-Treat to prevent mildew.

An alternative possibility is to begin by stating that you are giving the reader what he or she wants—that you are complying with the request. Actually, this approach is really not direct, for it delays giving the information requested. But it is a favorable beginning that does respond to the inquiry, and it does not run the risk of sounding abrupt, which is a criticism of direct beginnings. These examples illustrate this type of beginning:

- Or begin by saying that you are complying with the request.

> The following information should tell you what you need to know about Chem-Treat.

> Here are the answers to your questions about Chem-Treat.

"First the good news—if I cure you, I'll become world famous."

Source: From *The Wall Street Journal*, permission by Cartoon Features Syndicate.

Logically Arranging the Answers

- If one answer is involved, give it directly and completely.

- If more than one answer is involved, arrange the answers so that each stands out.

If you are answering just one question, you have little to do after handling that question in the opening. You answer it as completely as the situation requires, and you present whatever explanation or other information is needed. Then you are ready to close the message.

If, on the other hand, you are answering two or more questions, the body of your message becomes a series of answers. You should order them logically, perhaps answering the questions in the order your reader used in asking them. You may even number your answers, especially if your reader numbered the questions. Or you may decide to arrange your answers by paragraphs so that each stands out clearly.

Skillfully Handling the Negatives

- Emphasize favorable responses; subordinate unfavorable responses.

- Place favorable responses at beginnings and ends. Give them more space. Use words skillfully to emphasize them.

When your response concerns some bad news along with the good news, you will need to handle the bad news with care. Bad news stands out. Unless you are careful, it is likely to receive more emphasis than it deserves. Sometimes you will need to subordinate the bad news and emphasize the good news.

In giving proper emphasis to the good- and bad-news parts, you should use the techniques discussed in Chapter 4, especially positioning. That is, you should place the good news in positions of high emphasis—at paragraph beginnings and endings and at the beginning and ending of the message as a whole. You should place the bad news in secondary positions. In addition, you should use space emphasis to your advantage. This means giving less space to bad-news parts and more space to good-news parts. You also should select words and build sentences that communicate the effect you want. Generally, this means using positive words and avoiding negative words. Your overall goal should be to present the information in your response so that your readers feel good about you and your company.

Considering Extras

- The little extra things you do for the reader will build goodwill.

To create goodwill, as well as future business, you should consider including extras with your answers. These are the things you say and do that are not actually required. Examples are a comment or question showing an interest in the reader's problem, some additional information that may prove valuable, and a suggestion for use of the information supplied. In fact, extras can be anything that does more than skim the surface with hurried, routine answers. Such extras frequently make the difference between success and failure in the goodwill effort.

Illustrations of how extras can be used to strengthen the goodwill effects of a message are as broad as the imagination. A business executive answering a college professor's request for information on company operations could supplement the requested information with suggestions of other sources. A technical writer could amplify highly technical answers with simpler explanations. In the Chem-Treat problem, additional information (e.g., how much surface area a gallon covers) would be helpful. Such extras encourage readers to take the extra step in building a business relationship with you.

Closing Cordially

As in the other direct messages, your ending should be cordial, friendly words that fit the one case. For example, you might close the Chem-Treat message with these words:

> If I can help you further in deciding whether Chem-Treat will meet your needs, please email me again.

Reviewing the Plan

To write a favorable response message, you should use the following plan:

- Identify the message being answered either incidentally or in a subject line.
- Begin with the answer or state that you are complying with the request.
- Continue to respond in a way that is logical and orderly.
- De-emphasize any negative information.
- Consider including extras.
- End with a friendly comment adapted to your reader.

Contrasting Illustrations

Below, the contrasting email messages in answer to the Chem-Treat inquiry illustrate two strategies for answering routine inquiries. The first message violates many of the standards set in this and earlier chapters. The second meets the requirements of a good business message. It accounts for the reader's needs and the writer's business goals.

● Following are bad and good examples of response messages.

An Indirect and Hurried Response. The not-so-good message begins indirectly with an obvious statement referring to receipt of the inquiry. Though well intended, the second sentence continues to delay the answers. The second paragraph begins to respond to the reader's request, but it emphasizes the most negative answer by position and by wording. This answer is followed by hurried and routine answers to the other questions asked. Only the barest information is presented. There is no goodwill close.

Subject: Your inquiry of April 3

Ms. Motley,

I have received your April 3 message, in which you inquire about our Chem-Treat paint. I want you to know that we appreciate your interest and will welcome your business.

In response to your question about how many coats are needed to cover new surfaces, I regret to report that two are usually required. The paint is mildewproof. We do guarantee it. It has been well tested in our laboratories. It is safe to use as directed.

George Moxley

This email is indirect and ineffective.

An Effective Direct Response. The better message begins directly with the most favorable answer. Then it presents the other answers, giving each the emphasis and positive language it deserves. It subordinates the one negative answer by position, volume of treatment, and structure. More pleasant information follows the negative answer. The close is goodwill talk with some subtle selling strategy thrown in. "We know that you'll enjoy the long-lasting beauty of this mildewproof paint" points positively to purchase and successful use of the product.

This direct email does a better job.

Subject: Your April 3 inquiry about Chem-Treat

Ms. Motley,

Yes, Chem-Treat paint will prevent mildew or we will return your money. We know it works because we have tested it under all common conditions. In every case, it proved successful.

When you carefully follow the directions on each can, Chem-Treat paint is guaranteed safe. As the directions state, you should use Chem-Treat only in a well-ventilated room—never in a closed, unvented area.

One gallon of Chem-Treat is usually enough for one-coat coverage of 500 square feet of previously painted surface. For the best results on new surfaces, you will want to apply two coats. For such surfaces, you should figure about 200 square feet per gallon for a long-lasting coating.

We sincerely appreciate your interest in Chem-Treat, Ms. Motley. This mildewproof paint will bring you five years or more of beautiful protection.

George Moxley

ADJUSTMENT GRANTS

INTRODUCTORY SITUATION

Adjustment Grants

Continuing in your role with Pinnacle, this time you find on your computer an email message from an unhappy customer. It seems that Ms. Bernice Watson, owner of Tri-Cities Hardware, is upset because some of the 30 Old London lampposts she ordered from Pinnacle arrived in damaged condition. "The glass is broken in 17 of the units," she writes, "obviously because of poor packing." She had ordered the lights for a special sale. In fact, she notes, she had even featured them in her advertising. The sale begins next Friday. She wants a fast adjustment—either the lamps by sale time or her money back.

Of course, you will grant Ms. Watson's request. You will send her an email message saying that the goods are on the way. And because you want to keep this good customer, you will try to regain any lost confidence with an honest explanation of the problem. This message is classified as an adjustment grant.

● Good news in adjustment grants justifies directness.

When you can grant an adjustment, the situation is a happy one for your customer. You are correcting an error. You are doing what you were asked to do. As in other positive situations, a message written in the direct order is appropriate.

Routine Response Message (Favorable Response to a Professor's Request). This email message responds to a professor's request for production records that will be used in a research project. The writer is giving the information wanted but must restrict its use.

Direct— reports a favorable response

Goodwill— adapted to one cause

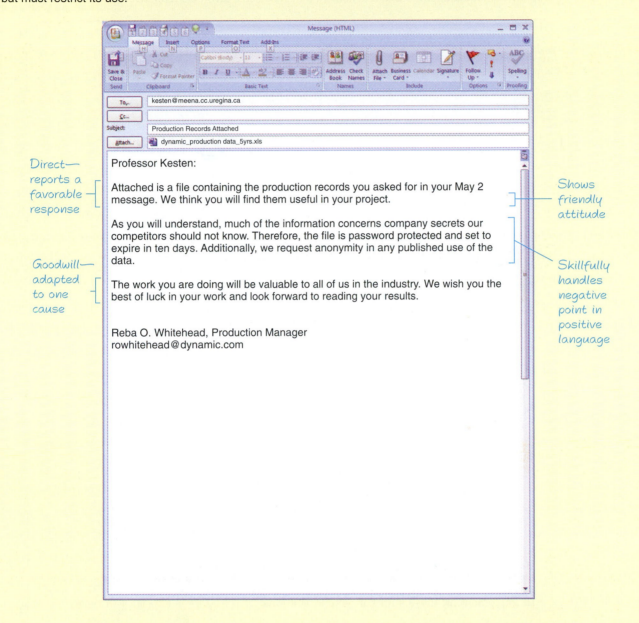

Shows friendly attitude

Skillfully handles negative point in positive language

To... kesten@meena.cc.uregina.ca
Cc...
Subject: Production Records Attached
Attach... dynamic_production data_5yrs.xls

Professor Kesten:

Attached is a file containing the production records you asked for in your May 2 message. We think you will find them useful in your project.

As you will understand, much of the information concerns company secrets our competitors should not know. Therefore, the file is password protected and set to expire in ten days. Additionally, we request anonymity in any published use of the data.

The work you are doing will be valuable to all of us in the industry. We wish you the best of luck in your work and look forward to reading your results.

Reba O. Whitehead, Production Manager
rowhitehead@dynamic.com

Routine Response Message (A Request for Detailed Information). Answering an inquiry about a company's experience with executive suites, this letter numbers the answers as the questions were numbered in the inquiry. The opening appropriately sets up the numbered answers with a statement that indicates a favorable response.

Merck & Co., Inc.
One Merck Drive
P.O. Box 100, WS1A-46
Whitehouse Station NJ 08889

MERCK

August 7, 2012

Ms. Ida Casey, Sales Manager
Liberty Insurance Company
1165 Second Ave.
Des Moines, IA 50318-9631

Dear Ms. Casey:

Direct— tells that writer is complying

Following is the information about our use of temporary executive suites that you requested in your August 3 fax. For your convenience, I have numbered my responses to correspond with the sequence you used.

Sets up listing

Orderly listing of answers

1. Our executives have mixed feelings about the effectiveness of the suites. At the beginning, the majority opinion was negative, but it appears now that most of the antagonism has faded.

2. The suites option definitely has saved us money. Rental costs in the suburbs are much lower than downtown costs; annual savings are estimated at nearly 30 percent.

3. We began using executive suites at the request of several sales representatives who had read about other companies using them. We pilot-tested the program in one territory for a year using volunteers before we implemented it companywide.

4. We are quite willing to share with you the list of facilities we plan to use again. Additionally, I am enclosing a copy of our corporate policy, which describes our guidelines for using executive suites.

Complete yet concise answers

Friendly— adapted to the one case

If after reviewing this information you have any other questions, please write me again. If you want to contact our sales representatives for firsthand information, please do so. I wish you the best of luck in implementing these suites in your operations.

This extra builds goodwill

Sincerely,

David M. Earp

David M. Earp
Office Manager

Enclosure

Considering Special Needs

The adjustment-grant message has much in common with the message types previously discussed. You begin directly with the good-news answer. You refer to the message you are answering, and you close on a friendly note. But because the situation stems from an unhappy experience, you have two special needs. One is the need to overcome the negative impressions that the experience leading to the adjustment has formed in the reader's mind. The other is the need to regain any confidence in your company, its products, or its service that the reader may have lost from the experience.

Need to Overcome Negative Impressions. To understand the first need, just place yourself in the reader's shoes. As the reader sees it, something bad has happened—goods have been damaged, equipment has failed, or sales have been lost. The experience has not been pleasant. Granting the claim will take care of much of the problem, but some negative thoughts may remain. You need to work to overcome any such thoughts.

You can attempt to do this using words that produce positive effects. For example, in the opening you can do more than just give the affirmative answer. You can add goodwill, as in this example:

> The enclosed check for $89.77 is our way of proving to you that we value your satisfaction highly.

Throughout the message you should avoid words that recall unnecessarily the bad situation you are correcting. You especially want to avoid the negative words that could be used to describe what went wrong—words such as *mistake, trouble, damage, broken,* and *loss.* Even general words such as *problem, difficulty,* and *misunderstanding* can create unpleasant effects. Negative language makes the customer's complaint the focus of your message. Your goal is to move the customer beyond the problem and to the solution—that the customer is going to have his or her claim granted. You can only do this if you use positive, reader-centered language.

- Follow the good-news pattern, but consider two special needs.

- One is to overcome negative impressions caused by the problem.

- Overcome them through positive writing.

• Even apologies may be negative.

Also negative are the apologies often included in these messages. Even though well intended, the somewhat conventional "we sincerely regret the inconvenience . . ." type of comment is of questionable value. It emphasizes the negative happenings for which the apology is made. If you sincerely believe that you owe an apology or that one is expected, you can apologize and risk the negative effect. But do it early and move on, and don't repeat it at the end. In most instances, however, your efforts to correct the problem will show adequate concern for your reader's interests.

• Another goal is to regain lost confidence through convincing explanation.

Need to Regain Lost Confidence. Except in cases in which the cause of the difficulty is routine or incidental, you also will need to regain the reader's lost confidence. Just what you must do and how you must do it depend on the facts of the situation. You will need to survey the situation to see what they are. If something can be done to correct a bad procedure or a product defect, you should do it. Then you should tell your reader what has been done as convincingly and positively as you can. If what went wrong was a rare, unavoidable event, you should explain this. Sometimes you will need to explain how a product should be used or cared for. Sometimes you will need to resell the product. Of course, whatever you do must be ethical—supported by truth and integrity.

Reviewing the Plan

To organize a message granting an adjustment, writers should use the following plan:

• Begin directly—with the good news.
• Incidentally identify the correspondence that you are answering.
• Avoid negatives that recall the problem.
• Regain lost confidence through explanation or corrective action.
• End with a friendly, positive comment.

Contrasting Adjustments

• Following are examples of bad and good adjustment messages.

The two messages below illustrate an ineffective and effective way to write adjustment messages. The first, with its indirect order and grudging tone, is ineffective. The directness and positiveness of the second clearly make it the better message.

A Slow and Negative Approach. The ineffective message begins with an obvious comment about receiving the claim. It recalls vividly what went wrong and then painfully explains what happened. As a result, the good news is delayed for an additional paragraph. Finally, after two delaying paragraphs, the message gets to the good news. Though well intended, the close leaves the reader with a reminder of the trouble.

This email is indirect and negative.

Subject: Your broken Old London lights

Ms. Watson,

We have received your May 1 claim reporting that our shipment of Old London lamppost lights reached you with 17 broken units. We regret the inconvenience and can understand your unhappiness.

Following our standard practice, we investigated the situation thoroughly. Apparently the fault is the result of an inexperienced temporary employee's negligence. We have taken corrective measures to assure that future shipments will be packed more carefully.

I am pleased to report that we are sending replacements today. They should reach you before your sale begins. Our driver will pick up the broken units when he makes delivery.

Again, we regret all the trouble caused you.

Stephanie King

The Direct and Positive Technique. The better message uses the subject line to identify the transaction. The opening words tell the reader what she most wants to hear in a positive way that adds to the goodwill tone of the message. With you-viewpoint explanation, the message then reviews what happened. Without a single negative word, it makes clear what caused the problem and what has been done to prevent its recurrence. After handling the essential matter of picking up the broken lamps, the message closes with positive talk removed from the problem.

Subject: Your May 1 Report on Invoice 1248

Ms. Watson:

Seventeen carefully packed Old London lamppost lamps should reach your sales floor in time for your Saturday promotion. Our driver left our warehouse today with instructions to special deliver them to you on Friday.

Because your satisfaction with our service and products is our top priority, we have thoroughly checked our shipping procedures. It appears that the shipment to you was packed by a temporary employee who was filling in for a hospitalized veteran packer. We now have our veteran packer back at work and have taken measures to ensure better performance by our temporary staff.

As you know, the Old London lamppost lights have become one of the hottest products in the lighting field. We are confident they will contribute to the success of your sale.

Stephanie King

This message is direct and positive.

ORDER ACKNOWLEDGMENTS AND OTHER THANK-YOU MESSAGES

INTRODUCTORY SITUATION

Order Acknowledgments and Other Thank-You Messages

The next work you take from your inbox is an order for paints and painting supplies. It is from Mr. Tony Lee of the Central City Paint Company, a new customer whom Pinnacle has been trying to attract for months. You usually acknowledge orders with routine messages, but this case is different. You feel the need to welcome this new customer and to cultivate him for future sales.

After checking your current inventory and making certain that the goods will be on the way to Lee today, you are ready to write him a special acknowledgment and thank him for his business.

In the course of your professional career, you will find yourself in situations where business and social etiquette require thank-you messages. Such messages may be long or short, formal or informal. They may be also combined with other purposes such as confirming an order. In this section we focus on one specific kind of thank-you message—the order acknowledgement—as well as more general thank-you messages for other business occasions.

Adjustment Grant Messages (Explaining a Human Error). This email message grants the action requested in the claim of a customer who received a leather computer case that was monogrammed incorrectly. The writer has no excuse, for human error was to blame. His explanation is positive and convincing.

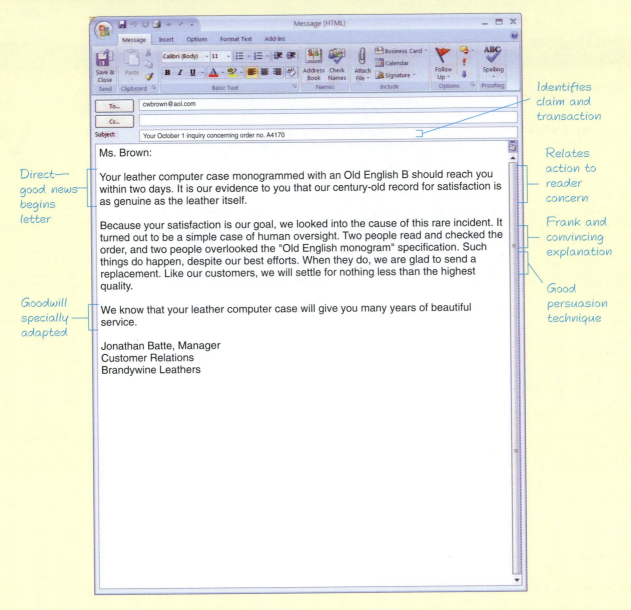

Identifies claim and transaction

Direct—good news begins letter

Relates action to reader concern

Frank and convincing explanation

Good persuasion technique

Goodwill specially adapted

To... cwbrown@aol.com

Subject: Your October 1 inquiry concerning order no. A4170

Ms. Brown:

Your leather computer case monogrammed with an Old English B should reach you within two days. It is our evidence to you that our century-old record for satisfaction is as genuine as the leather itself.

Because your satisfaction is our goal, we looked into the cause of this rare incident. It turned out to be a simple case of human oversight. Two people read and checked the order, and two people overlooked the "Old English monogram" specification. Such things do happen, despite our best efforts. When they do, we are glad to send a replacement. Like our customers, we will settle for nothing less than the highest quality.

We know that your leather computer case will give you many years of beautiful service.

Jonathan Batte, Manager
Customer Relations
Brandywine Leathers

Setting up tables within a document is an easy task. This feature allows writers to create tables as well as import spreadsheet and database files. In both instances, information can be arranged in columns and rows, with detail in the cells. Headings can be formatted and formulas can be entered in the cells. The table you see here could be one the writer created for use in a favorable response to an inquiry about possible locations for a meeting in Chicago.

Organizing information with tables makes it easier for both the writer and the reader. A careful writer will include column and row labels as needed, helping the reader extract information both quickly and accurately.

Hotel Name	Address	Convention Room Rate for Standard Rooms	Guest Rating
Chicago Marriott Downtown	540 North Michigan Avenue, Chicago, IL 60611-3869	$409	4.2
Drake Hotel	140 East Walton Street, Chicago, IL 60611-1545	$309	4.3
Palmer House Hilton	17 East Monroe Street, Chicago, IL 60603-5605	$252	4.4

Order Acknowledgments

Acknowledgments are sent to let people who order goods know the status of their orders. Most acknowledgments are routine. They simply tell when the goods are being shipped. Many companies use form or computer-generated messages for such situations. Some use printed, standard notes with check-off or write-in blanks. But individually written acknowledgments are sometimes justified, especially with new accounts or large orders.

Skillfully composed acknowledgments can do more than acknowledge orders, though this task remains their primary goal. These messages can also build goodwill through their warm, personal, human tone. They can make the reader feel good about doing business with a company that cares and want to continue doing business with that company. To maintain this goodwill for repeat customers, you will want to revise your form acknowledgments regularly.

- Businesses usually acknowledge orders with forms, but they sometimes use written messages.

- Acknowledgments can serve to build goodwill.

Directness and Goodwill Building in Order Acknowledgments

Like the preceding direct message types, the acknowledgment message appropriately begins with its good news—that the goods are being shipped. And it ends on a goodwill note. Except when some of the goods ordered must be delayed, the remainder of the message is devoted to goodwill building. This goodwill building can begin in the opening by emphasizing receipt of the goods rather than merely sending the goods:

> The Protect-O paints and supplies you ordered April 4 should reach you by Wednesday. They are leaving our Walden warehouse today by Arrow Freight.

It can also include a warm expression of thanks for the order, especially when a first order is involved. Anything else you can say that will be helpful to the reader is appropriate in this regard—information about new products, services, or opportunities for the reader. A forward look to continued business relations is an appropriate goodwill gesture in the close.

- Directness and goodwill mark the message.

Tact in Order Acknowledgments

When goods must be delayed, handle this news tactfully.

Sometimes the task of acknowledging is complicated by your inability to send the goods requested right away. You could be out of them, or perhaps the reader did not give you all the information you need to send the goods. In either case, a delay is involved. In some cases, delays are routine and expected and do not pose a serious problem. In these situations, you can use the direct approach. However, you will still want to minimize any negative news so that your routine message does not become a negative-news message. You can do this by using positive language that focuses on what *can* or *will* happen rather than what *didn't* or *won't* happen.

In vague orders, request the needed information positively.

In the case of a vague order, for example, you should handle the information you need without appearing to accuse the reader of giving insufficient information. To illustrate, you gain nothing by writing "You failed to specify the color of phones you want." But you gain goodwill by writing "So that we can send you precisely the phones you want, please check your choice of colors on the space below." This sentence handles the matter positively and makes the action easy to take. It also shows a courteous attitude.

Emphasize receipt of the items in back orders.

Similarly, you can handle back-order information tactfully by emphasizing the positive part of the message. For example, instead of writing "We can't ship the ink jet cartridges until the 9th," you can write "We will rush the ink jet cartridges to you as soon as our stock is replenished by a shipment due May 9." If the back-order period is longer than the customer expects or longer than the 30 days allowed by law, you may choose to give your customer an alternative. You could offer a substitute product or service. Giving the customer a choice builds goodwill.

In some cases delays will lead to major disappointments, which means you will have to write a bad-news message. A more complete discussion of how to handle such negative news is provided in Chapter 7.

Strategies for Other Thank-You Messages

Business and social etiquette require thank-you notes.

One of the first thank-you messages you write will be the one for a job interview, which is discussed in Chapter 9. Once you are employed, you may send thank-you messages after a meeting, when someone does a favor for you or gives you a gift, when you want to acknowledge others' efforts that have somehow benefited you, when you want to thank customers for their business, or perhaps when someone has donated time or money to your organization or a cause it supports. The possibilities for situations when you might send thank-you notes are many, and sending a message of sincere thanks is a great way to promote goodwill and build your and your company's professional image.

Thank-you notes are direct, personal, and often brief.

Thank-you messages are often brief, and because they are positive messages, they are written directly. You can begin with a specific statement of thanks:

Thank you for attending the American Cancer Society fundraiser lunch for Relay for Life last week and for donating money to the cause.

Follow with a personalized comment relevant to the reader:

With your support, the 2012 Relay for Life will be our most successful yet . . . [details follow].

Conclude with a forward-looking statement:

I look forward to joining you on June 12 for this worthy cause.

Your tone should be informal and friendly. If you are on a first-name basis with the reader, you may omit a salutation or use the reader's first name, but if your relationship with the reader is a formal one, do not use the reader's first name to create a contrived sense of closeness.

Margin notes may be sent by email, typed on company stationery, or handwritten.

Whether you hand write the thank-you, send an email, or use company stationery depends on the audience. If you have poor handwriting or believe your handwriting does not convey a professional image, you may choose to type your message. Though you should always check your own spelling, grammar, and punctuation before sending any message, doing so is especially important in handwritten notes when you have no computer software to alert you to possible errors.

Summarizing the Structure of Order Acknowledgments and Other Thank-You Messages

To write an order acknowledgment or thank-you message:

- Use the direct order: begin by thanking the reader for something specific (e.g., an order).
- Continue with your thanks or with further information.
- Use positive, tactful language to address vague or back orders.
- If appropriate, achieve a secondary goal (e.g., reselling or confirming a mutual understanding).
- Close with a goodwill-building comment, adapted to the topic of the message.

Contrasting Acknowledgments

The following two messages show bad and good techniques in acknowledging Mr. Lee's order. As you would expect, the good version follows the plan described in the preceding paragraphs.

- Following are contrasting examples.

Slow Route to a Favorable Message. The bad example begins indirectly, emphasizing receipt of the order. Although intended to produce goodwill, the second sentence further delays what the reader wants most to hear. Moreover, the letter is written from the writer's point of view (note the we-emphasis).

Dear Mr. Lee:

Your April 4 order for $1,743.30 worth of Protect-O paints and supplies has been received. We are pleased to have this nice order and hope that it marks the beginning of a long relationship.

As you instructed, we will bill you for this amount. We are shipping the goods today by Blue Darter Motor Freight.

We look forward to your future orders.

Sincerely,

This one delays the important news.

Fast-Moving Presentation of the Good News. The better message begins directly, telling Mr. Lee that he is getting what he wants. The remainder of the message is a customer welcome and subtle selling. Notice the good use of reader emphasis and positive language. The message closes with a note of appreciation and a friendly, forward look.

Dear Mr. Lee:

Your selection of Protect-O paints and supplies was shipped today by Blue Darter Freight and should reach you by Wednesday. As you requested, we are sending you an invoice for $1,743.30, including sales tax.

Because this is your first order from us, I welcome you to the Protect-O circle of dealers. Our representative, Ms. Cindy Wooley, will call from time to time to offer whatever assistance she can. She is a highly competent technical adviser on paint and painting.

Here in the home plant we also will do what we can to help you profit from Protect-O products. We'll do our best to give you the most efficient service. And we'll continue to develop the best possible paints—like our new Chem-Treat line. As you will see from the enclosed brochure, Chem-Treat is a real breakthrough in mildew protection.

We genuinely appreciate your order, Mr. Lee. We are determined to serve you well in the years ahead.

Sincerely,

This direct message is better.

Online Order Acknowledgement. This email message thanks the reader for her order and invites her to participate in this company's online product review.

From: Gardeners Supply [mailto:gardeners@e-news.gardeners.com]
Sent: Thursday, January 08, 2012 9:08 AM
To: KATHRYN.RENTZ@UC.EDU
Subject: Tell Us What You Think About Our Products

 **GARDENER'S** SUPPLY COMPANY   **New Feature: Customer Reviews**

Dear Kathryn,

Thanks the reader

Thank you for your purchase from Gardener's Supply. We hope you are enjoying your items and that this year's garden will be your best ever!

Moves to another goal of the message

Your satisfaction with our products is important to us, and we want to hear what you have to say about them. We recently added customer reviews to our Web site, which helps us improve our product selection and helps other gardeners find the best products to suit their needs.

Adds a reader benefit and incentive

We're hoping you'll take a moment to rate and review some or all of the items you have purchased from us. Other gardeners will appreciate your opinions and advice, and you may also enjoy reading what fellow gardeners have to say!

Each time you submit a product review to our Web site, your name will be entered in a monthly drawing for a $1000 prize (see information below).

Here are the item(s) you recently purchased. Just click on an item to write a review.

Pictures provide a quick visual confirmation of the order

Men's Waterproof Gloves

⭐ **Rate and review it**

Glove Set, 3 Pairs

⭐ **Rate and review it**

Links make participation easy

Forward-looking ending builds goodwill

Thank you for your time and consideration,

The Employee-Owners at Gardener's Supply

Copyright @2008 America's Gardening Resource, Inc.

Order Acknowledgment (Acknowledgment with a Problem). This email letter concerns an order that cannot be handled exactly as the customer would like. Some items are being sent, but one must be placed on back order and one cannot be shipped because the customer did not give the information needed. The message skillfully handles the negative points.

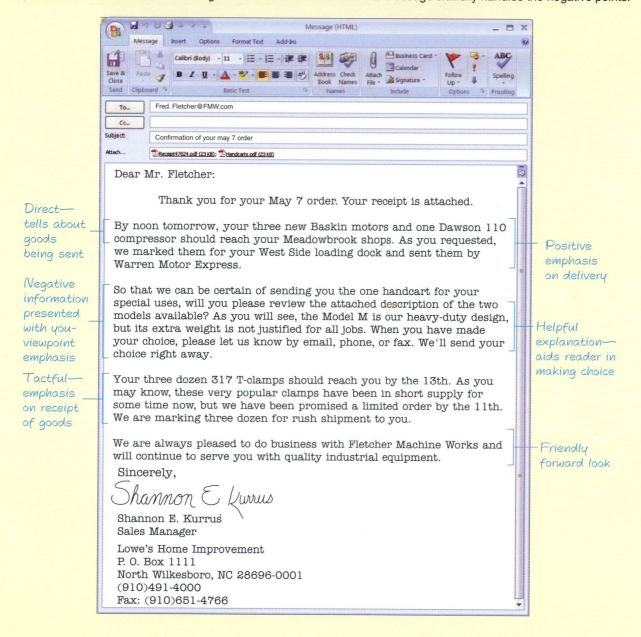

Direct—tells about goods being sent

Negative information presented with you-viewpoint emphasis

Tactful—emphasis on receipt of goods

Positive emphasis on delivery

Helpful explanation—aids reader in making choice

Friendly forward look

To... Fred.Fletcher@FMW.com

Subject: Confirmation of your may 7 order

Attach... Receipt47824.pdf (23 KB); Handcarts.pdf (23 KB)

Dear Mr. Fletcher:

Thank you for your May 7 order. Your receipt is attached.

By noon tomorrow, your three new Baskin motors and one Dawson 110 compressor should reach your Meadowbrook shops. As you requested, we marked them for your West Side loading dock and sent them by Warren Motor Express.

So that we can be certain of sending you the one handcart for your special uses, will you please review the attached description of the two models available? As you will see, the Model M is our heavy-duty design, but its extra weight is not justified for all jobs. When you have made your choice, please let us know by email, phone, or fax. We'll send your choice right away.

Your three dozen 317 T-clamps should reach you by the 13th. As you may know, these very popular clamps have been in short supply for some time now, but we have been promised a limited order by the 11th. We are marking three dozen for rush shipment to you.

We are always pleased to do business with Fletcher Machine Works and will continue to serve you with quality industrial equipment.

Sincerely,

Shannon E. Kurrus

Shannon E. Kurrus
Sales Manager

Lowe's Home Improvement
P. O. Box 1111
North Wilkesboro, NC 28696-0001
(910)491-4000
Fax: (910)651-4766

Thank You from United Plorcon. This email from a representative of a telecommunications equipment company thanks a potential customer in Germany for a recent meeting.

Hello, Herman:

Meeting you and the other members of the product selection team last Friday was a pleasure. We are honored not only that you took the time to explain the current dynamics and structure at General Telekom but also that you gave us your entire day. Thank you for your generosity.

Use of the reader's first name indicates a close business relationship

Specifics add sincerity

I understand that you have graciously offered to share some of United Plorcon's key product qualities with other executives in your company. We are extremely appreciative that you have offered to help in this way. Based on our discussions at the meeting, we will summarize the main points of interest and send them to you.

Politely thanks the reader for something specific (while also reminding him of his promise)

To make the cost-benefit charts more self-explanatory, I will slightly condense the material and add some notes. They will not be confidential, so please share them if you wish. I will send those condensed charts to you before the end of the week. After we send them, I will follow up with you to make sure that you have all the material you need to explain who we are and what we offer.

Prepares for future communications between the two parties

Finally, thank you for your hospitality. Staying in an ideally located hotel, having coffee at a beautiful castle, viewing some of the world's best art, and sharing an exquisite meal made my first visit to Stuttgart a most memorable one. I hope that between our two companies, we can create many opportunities for our United Plorcon team to return to your beautiful city.

Ends on a positive note; looks to the future

I look forward to talking with you again soon.

Respectfully yours,

OPERATIONAL MESSAGES

INTRODUCTORY SITUATION

Operational Messages

As the administrative assistant for the vice president of operations at Pinnacle Manufacturing Company, you have been asked by your boss to send a note to all employees reminding them of the company's shipping policy. Whether customers pay shipping charges depends on the products they order. However, some customers who repeatedly order the same product are sometimes charged for shipping and sometimes are not, which, of course, leads to unhappy customers and is costly for Pinnacle.

As Chapter 1 explained, operational communications are those messages that stay within a business. They are messages to and from employees that get the work of the organization done. The memorandums discussed in Chapter 5 are one form of operational communication. Internal email messages are another, and so are the various documents posted on bulletin boards, mailed to employees, uploaded on intranets, or distributed as handouts.

The formality of operational messages ranges widely. At one extreme are the informal, casual memorandum and email exchanges between employees concerning work matters. At the other are formal documents communicating company policies, directives, and procedures. Then, of course, there are the various stages of formality in between.

- Operational communications are messages to and from employees.

- They range from highly informal to formal.

Casual Operational Messages

The documents at the bottom of the formality range typically resemble conversation. Usually they are quick responses to work needs. Rarely is there time or need for careful

- The highly informal messages are like conversation—frank and casual.

construction and wording. The goal is simply to exchange the information needed in conducting the company's work.

Frankness describes the tone of these highly casual messages as well as many of the messages at more formal levels. The participants exchange information, views, and recommendations forthrightly. They write with the understanding that all participants are working for a common goal—usually what is best for the company—and that people working together in business situations want and need straightforward communication.

Still, remember that being frank doesn't mean being impolite. Even in quick messages, you should build goodwill with a positive, courteous tone.

- Frankness is expected in most internal exchanges.

Moderately Formal Messages

- Most messages of mid-level formality follow a direct pattern.

Moderately formal messages tend to resemble the messages discussed earlier in this chapter. Usually they require more care in construction, and usually they follow a direct pattern. The most common arrangement begins with the most important point and works down. Thus, a typical beginning sentence is a topic (theme) statement. In messages in memorandum form, the opening repeats the subject-line information and includes the additional information needed to identify the situation. The remainder of the message consists of a logical, orderly arrangement of the information covered. When the message consists of items in sequence, the items can be numbered and presented in this sequence.

- The writing should follow the previous advice in this chapter.

Suggestions for writing the somewhat formal internal messages are much the same as those for writing the messages covered previously. Clarity, correctness, and courtesy should guide your efforts. The following example of a hard-copy memorandum illustrates these qualities. It is moderately formal, distinctly above casual writing. Yet it is conversational. It is clearly written and organized in direct order, beginning with the objective and then systematically and clearly covering the vital bits of information. It is straightforward yet courteous.

DATE:	April 1, 2010
TO:	Remigo Ruiz
FROM:	Becky Pharr
SUBJECT:	Request for Cost Information Concerning Meeting at Timber Creek Lodge

- This sample memorandum begins directly—with the objective. The necessary explanation follows.

As we discussed in my office today, please get the necessary cost information for conducting our annual sales meeting at the Timber Creek Lodge, Timber Creek Village, Colorado. Our meeting will begin on the morning of Monday, June 5; we should arrange to arrive on the 4th. We will leave after a brief morning session on June 9.

Specifically, we'll need the following information:

- Then the specific information needed is listed in logical order.

- Travel costs for all 43 participants, including air travel to Denver and ground travel between the airport and the lodge. I have listed the names and home stations of the 43 participants on the attached sheet.
- Room and board costs for the five-day period, including cost with and without dinner at the lodge. As you know, we are considering the possibility of allowing participants to purchase dinners at nearby restaurants.
- Costs for recreational facilities at the lodge.
- Costs for meeting rooms and meeting equipment (e.g., laptops, projectors). We will need a room large enough to accommodate our 43 participants.

- The memorandum ends with courteous words.

I'd like to have the information by April 15. If you need additional information, please contact me at ×3715 or Pharr@yahoo.com.

Highly Formal Messages

- The most formal operational messages are policies, directives, and procedures.

The most formal of the operational messages deserve our special attention. These are the messages presenting policies, directives, and procedures. Usually written by executives for their subordinates, these administrative messages are often compiled in manuals, perhaps kept in loose-leaf form and updated as new material is developed.

Some of these more formal documents are designed to keep employees informed about the company. As we have implied, these higher-level messages are more formally written than most of the internal communications. Their official status explains why. Usually they follow a direct order, although the nature of their contents can require variations. The goal should be to arrange the information in the most logical order for quick understanding. Since the information frequently involves a sequence of information bits, numbering these bits can be helpful. And since these documents must be clearly understood and followed, the writing must be clear to all, including those with low verbal skills. The following example illustrates these qualities:

- Others present company information employees want to know.

- These official documents are more formally written.

DATE: June 10, 2010
TO: All Employees
FROM: Terry Boedeker, President
SUBJECT: Energy Conservation

To help us keep costs low, the following conservation measures are effective immediately:

- Thermostats will be set to maintain temperatures of 78 degrees Fahrenheit throughout the air-conditioning season.
- Air conditioners will be shut off in all buildings at 4 PM Monday through Friday.
- Air conditioners will be started as late as possible each morning so as to have the buildings at the appropriate temperature within 30 minutes after the start of the workday.
- Lighting levels will be reduced to approximately 50- to 60-foot candles in all work areas. Corridor lighting will be reduced to 5- to 10-foot candles.
- Outside lighting levels will be reduced as much as possible without compromising safety and security.

In addition, will each of you help with this conservation effort? Specifically, I ask that you do the following:

- Turn off lights not required in performing work.
- Keep windows closed when the cooling system is operating.
- Turn off all computer monitors and printers at the end of the day.

I am confident that these measures will reduce our energy use significantly. Your efforts to follow them will be greatly appreciated.

- The beginning is direct and immediately identifies the situation.

- Clear writing and listing result in good readability.

- Separate listing of other measures gives order and enchances understanding.

- Closing personal remarks add to effectiveness.

- Sometimes indirectness may be better, as discussed in following chapters.

Even though this message is straightforward, note the writer's courtesy and his use of *us* and *our*. When writing direct messages, skillful managers make use of such strategies for maintaining good relations with employees. Remembering this goal becomes especially important in situations where managers have news to convey or requests to make that employees may not be ready to accept. In fact, in these situations an indirect order will be more appropriate, as Chapters 7 and 8 will discuss. For most operational communication, however, the direct order will be both expected and appreciated.

Summarizing the Structure of Operational Messages

To write an operational message, writers should do the following:

- Organize in the direct order.
- Choose the appropriate tone (formal or informal) and communication medium.
- Be clear and courteous.
- Order the information logically.

Contrasting Examples of Operational Messages

The following two messages show contrasting ways in which the operational message regarding Pinnacle's inconsistent shipping policies (see the introductory situation at the beginning of this section) may be addressed.

A Wordy, Confusing, and Indirect Message. The reader really has to search for the writer's purpose and intent in this message. In addition, it is wordy, long, and disorganized, and lacks visual appeal.

This indirect message wastes time and dwells on the negative.

Subject: Inconsistent Shipping Policies

Pinnacle Manufacturing has been incurring increasing freight expenses and a decline in freight revenue over the last two years, impacting our ability to achieve our financial goals. The warehouse team has done a lot of research into the reasons behind this increase, and it has come to our attention that a very considerable number of shipments are going out of Cedar Rapids (1) as unbillable to the customer, and/or (2) as overnight shipments rather than ground.

Pinnacle Manufacturing only has one product for which shipping is not billed to the customer—the Chem-Treat paint. In all other cases, product shipments are supposed to be billed to the customer. **Therefore, effective immediately, except for Chem-Treat shipments, which by contract provide for free overnight (weekday delivery) shipping, Pinnacle Manufacturing will bill the customer for all shipments of products. Finance will screen all orders to ensure that they indicate billable shipping terms.**

Pinnacle Manufacturing's overnight shipping falls into a few categories, including shipments of products to customers and shipments of marketing materials to prospects and customers. There are no customer programs or marketing programs for which Pinnacle Manufacturing offers overnight shipping (except Chem-Treat). **Therefore, effective immediately, except for Chem-Treat shipments, which by contract provide for overnight (weekday delivery) shipping, Pinnacle Manufacturing will not ship products overnight to customers unless the overnight shipping is billed to the customer. Also effective immediately, shipments of sales/marketing materials are to be shipped ground, not overnight.**

This policy change will impact some of your work processes, requiring you to be more planful in getting products shipped to customers in a businesslike and timely manner, and challenging you to prevent last-minute rush situations. I suspect that much of the freight performance situation, from a financial point of view, is an awareness issue for our Cedar Rapids team. I thank each of you in advance for adherence to this policy. We are fortunate to have an excellent distribution team in Cedar Rapids. That team needs all of our help so that their high quality shipping and inventory control performance becomes matched by strong financial performance.

Exceptions to the billable shipping-only and no overnight shipping policies must be brought to me for approval prior to entering the order.

Dean Yourg

VP, Operations

A Direct, Concise, and Visually Appealing Message. This message is written directly and is more accurate as this message is not a change in policy (as the bad example suggests) but a reminder of the existing policy. This message is also more concise and gives the reader only the information he or she needs to know to comply. In addition, headings and bulleted lists make for much easier reading.

Subject: Refresher on Our Shipping Policy

Please remember that our shipping policy is as follows:

Shipping Charges:

- *Chem-Treat paint* is the only product for which shipping is **not** billed to the customer.
- *All other product shipments* (including sales/marketing materials) **are** billed to the customer.

Overnight Shipping:

- Sales/marketing materials are to be shipped ground, not overnight.
- *Chem-Treat paint* may be shipped overnight at **no charge** to the customer, as provided by contract.
- *All other overnight product shipments* **are billed** to the customer.

Billing our customers accurately and consistently for shipping improves customer satisfaction with our service. In addition, the increased freight revenue will help us achieve our financial goals and control our shipping and inventory costs.

To ensure that your customers receive their products quickly, refer to the shipping and mailing timeline on Pinnacle's intranet.

The Finance Department will be screening all shipment invoices to make sure that shipments are billed accurately. If you have questions regarding the shipping policy or require an exception, please contact me at Ext. 555.

Dean Young

VP, Operations

This direct message will be easy to read and reference. Its tone is straightforward but courteous.

OTHER DIRECT MESSAGE SITUATIONS

In the preceding pages, we have covered the most common direct message situations. Others occur, of course. You should be able to handle them with the techniques that have been explained and illustrated.

In handling such situations, remember that whenever possible, you should get to the goal of the message right away. You should cover any other information needed in good logical order. You should carefully choose words that convey just the right meaning. More specifically, you should consider the value of using the you-viewpoint, and you should weigh carefully the differences in meaning conveyed by the positiveness or negativeness of your words. As in the good examples discussed in this chapter, you should end your message with appropriate and friendly goodwill words.

- Other direct message situations occur.

- You should be able to handle them by applying the techniques covered in this chapter.

SUMMARY BY LEARNING OBJECTIVES

1. Properly assess the reader's likely reaction to your message.
   - If the reaction is likely to be negative, indirect order is your likely choice.
   - If it is likely to be positive or neutral, you probably will want directness.
2. Describe the general plan for direct-order messages.
   - Begin with the objective.
   - Cover any necessary explanation.
   - Systematically present any remaining parts of the objective.
   - End with adapted goodwill.

1 Properly assess the reader's likely reaction to your message.

2 Describe the general plan for direct-order messages.

3. The routine inquiry is a basic direct-order message.

3 Write clear, well-structured routine requests for information.

- Begin it with a request—either (1) a request for specific information wanted or (2) a general request for information.
- Somewhere in the message explain enough to enable the reader to answer.
- If the inquiry involves more than one question, make each stand out—perhaps as separate sentences or separate paragraphs.
- Consider numbering the questions.
- And word them as questions.
- End with an appropriate friendly comment.

4 Write direct, orderly, and friendly answers to inquiries.

4. When responding to inquiries favorably, you should begin directly.

- If the response contains only one answer, begin with it.
- If it contains more than one answer, begin with a major one or a general statement indicating you are answering.
- Identify the message being answered early, perhaps in a subject line.
- Arrange your answers (if more than one) logically.
- And make them stand out.
- If both good- and bad-news answers are involved, give each answer the emphasis it deserves, perhaps by subordinating the negative.
- For extra goodwill effect, consider doing more than was asked.
- End with appropriate cordiality.

5 Compose adjustment grants that regain any lost confidence.

5. As messages granting adjustments are positive responses, write them in the direct order.

- But they differ from other direct-order messages in that they involve a negative situation.
  - Something has gone wrong.
  - You are correcting that wrong.
  - But you also should overcome the negative image in the reader's mind.
- You do this by first telling the good news—what you are doing to correct the wrong.
- In the opening and throughout, emphasize the positive.
- Avoid the negative—words like *trouble, damage,* and *broken.*
- Try to regain the reader's lost confidence, maybe with an explanation or with assurance of corrective measures taken.
- End with a goodwill comment, avoiding words that recall what went wrong.

6 Write order acknowledgments and other thank-you messages that build goodwill.

6. Write order acknowledgments and other thank-you messages in the form of a favorable response.

- Personalized order acknowledgments can build goodwill.
- Good business and social etiquette often require that you write other kinds of thank-you messages.
- Use the direct order: begin by thanking the reader with specific wording.
- Continue with your thanks or with further information.
- Use positive, tactful language to address vague or back orders.
- If appropriate, achieve a secondary goal (e.g., reselling or confirming a mutual understanding).
- Close with a goodwill-building comment adapted to the topic of the message.

7 Write clear and effective operational communications.

7. Operational (internal) communications must also be clear and effective. The following instructions explain how to write operational communications:

- Organize most of them in the direct order.
- Write the casual ones as you would good conversation.

- Make them clear and courteous.
- Give administrative communications (policies, directives, procedures) the careful attention they deserve.
- Organize them logically; strive for clarity.

CRITICAL THINKING QUESTIONS

1 When is the direct order appropriate in inquiries? When would you use the indirect order? Give examples. **(LO1)**

2 "Explanations in inquiries merely add length and should be eliminated." Discuss. **(LO3)**

3 Discuss why just reporting truthfully may not be enough in handling negative information in messages answering inquiries. **(LO4)**

4 Defend a policy of doing more than asked in answering routine inquiries. Can the policy be carried too far? **(LO4)**

5 What can acknowledgment messages do to build goodwill? **(LO6)**

6 Discuss situations where each of the following forms of an order acknowledgment would be preferred: form letter, merged letter, and a special letter. **(LO6)**

7 Discuss how problems (vague orders, back orders) should be handled in messages acknowledging orders. **(LO6)**

8 Why is it usually advisable to do more than just grant the claim in an adjustment-grant message? **(LO5)**

9 Discuss the use of directness in operational communications. Why is it desirable? Can it be overdone? When might indirectness be appropriate? **(LO7)**

CRITICAL THINKING EXERCISES

1 Point out the shortcomings in this email response to an inquiry about a short course in business communication taught by a professor for the company's employees. The inquiry included five questions: (1) How did the professor perform? (2) What was the course format (length, meeting structure)? (3) What was the employee evaluation of the instruction? (4) Was the course adapted to the company and its technical employees? (5) Was homework assigned? **(LO1, LO2, LO4)**

Subject: Course evaluation

Mr. Braden:

Your January 17 inquiry addressed to the Training Director has been referred to me for attention since we have no one with that title. I do have some training responsibilities and was the one who organized the in-house course in clear writing. You asked five questions about our course.

Concerning your question about the instructor, Professor Alonzo Britt, I can report that he did an acceptable job in the classroom. Some of the students, including this writer, felt that the emphasis was too much on grammar and punctuation, however. He did assign homework, but it was not excessive.

We had class two hours a day from 3:00 to 5:00 PM every Thursday for eight weeks. Usually the professor lectured the first hour. He is a good lecturer but sometimes talks over the heads of the students. This was the main complaint in the evaluations the stu-

dents made at the end of the course, but they had many good comments to make also. Some did not like the content, which they said was not adapted to the needs of a technical worker. Overall, the professor got a rating of B– on a scale of A to F.

We think the course was good, but it could have been better adapted to our needs and our people. I also think it was too long—about 10 hours (five meetings) would have been enough. Also, we think the professor spent too much time lecturing and not enough on application work in class.

Please be informed that the information about Professor Britt must be held in confidence.

Casey Webster

2 Point out the shortcomings in this message granting a claim for a fax machine received in damaged condition. Inspection of the package revealed that the damage did not occur in transit. **(LO5)**

Dear Ms. Orsag:

Your May 3 letter in which you claim that the Rigo FAX391 was received in damaged condition has been carefully considered. We inspect all our machines carefully before packing them, and we pack them carefully in strong boxes with Styrofoam supports that hold them snugly. Thus we cannot understand how the damage could have occurred.

Even so, we stand behind our product and will replace any that are damaged. However, we must ask that first you send us the defective one so we can inspect it. After your claim of damage has been verified, we will send you a new one.

We regret any inconvenience this situation may have caused you and assure you that problems like this rarely occur in our shipping department.

Scott Hilderbran

3 List your criticisms of this email message inquiring about a convenience store advertised for sale: **(LO3)**

Subject: Store details needed

Mr. Meeks:

This is in response to your advertisement in the May 17 *Daily Bulletin* in which you describe a convenience store in Clark City that you want to sell. I am very much interested since I would like to relocate in that area. Before I drive down to see the property, I need some preliminary information. Most important is the question of financing. I am wondering whether you would be willing to finance up to $50,000 of the total if I could come up with the rest, and how much interest you would charge and for how long. I also would like to have the figures for your operations for the past two or three years, including gross sales, expenses, and profits. I also need to know the condition of the building, including such information as when built, improvements made, repairs needed, and so on.

Hoping that you can get these answers to me soon so we can do business.

4 Criticize the following thank-you message from a college student to a professor who has sent her a job lead. **(LO6)**

Subject: Thanks

Dear Prof. Smith,

Thanks for the hot tip on the job! I'm interviewing there tomorrow!

Sarah

5 Criticize the following operational message from a hotel manager: **(LO7)**

Housekeeping staff,

It has come to my attention that the cleanliness of our rooms is substandard. We will therefore hold mandatory training sessions over the next three weeks. See your shift supervisor to plan your work schedule so that you can attend.

Management

PROBLEM-SOLVING CASES

Routine Inquiries

1 You recently learned about a service organization on your campus, Mentors for Majors. The Mentors are alumni and other working professionals who have agreed to field student inquiries about the nature of their jobs, about strategies for career success, and so forth.

You've been thinking about a certain kind of career, and you'd like to get more information about it from an experienced professional. Checking over the list, you find that there's a Mentor in your very area. Write an email to him/her in which you ask your questions. Find out the main things you'd like to know about this field of employment in a way that shows consideration for the reader and demonstrates your own serious interest in the type of job he/she does. (If your instructor directs, use either someone you know or someone you've researched on the Internet and through other resources. Turn in a one-paragraph profile of this person along with your email of inquiry.)

2 You're a sales manager in a _____ (you decide what kind of) company, and you just attended a professional meeting where the featured speaker extolled the virtues of a corporate wiki (an online collaboration space for employees). Intrigued, you'd like to learn more about how a wiki might enhance collaboration and "collective intelligence" among your sales staff or in your company in general.

First, do some Internet research on wikis (or example, read the entry on Wikipedia, go to pbworks.com, and listen to the podcast at <http://www.businessweek.com/mediacenter/podcasts/guide_to_tech/guidetotech_03_12_07.htm>). Look at some examples and think about what you'd like to know as you consider setting up a wiki in your workplace.

Then email the speaker you heard—who welcomed follow-up questions—and ask her what you most want to know about setting up and using a corporate wiki in your type of company or department. Whether or not you'll pursue this idea further will depend on her answers, so think carefully about what to ask.

3 You're a new assistant to the marketing director at McGill Medical Publishing, and you've been asked to find a good venue for a focus group that your company wants to conduct. You plan to invite 22 teaching physicians from the United States, Canada, and Europe, where the company's main markets are, to come together for two days and discuss their ideas for improving and updating the textbooks in their fields.

You have held many such focus groups in the past, at various sites in various cities, but your boss has advised you to find a new place this time. The venue you're considering is the Ritz-Carlton in Atlanta (with your instructor's permission, you may select a different hotel). You've studied their website, and now you'd like to submit a detailed inquiry to find out if this location will work for your event. You go to the online form on their website where you are to submit your request for information (<https://www.ritzcarlton.com/en/Properties/Atlanta/Meetings/Request/Default.htm>), and you see that it asks you to attach a file in which you tell them everything you will need.

In consultation with your class and your instructor, come up with sufficient realistic details about the event (dates, number/types of rooms and meeting rooms needed, any computer equipment you'll need, food/beverage requirements, and so forth) to be able to prepare this document. In addition to making it easy for the reader to pick out the essentials, you should also describe your meeting's purpose and the attendees to help the Ritz-Carlton's event staff offer additional information that you might not have thought to ask about. Overall, ask the questions that will enable you to decide if this venue will work, and give enough information so that the reply you get will be as helpful as possible. Save your work as a pdf file so that your nice formatting won't be lost when the hotel staff opens your file.

---

4 Your first assignment as an assistant to the human resources director of Metropolitan Hospital is to find out more about a team-building consulting firm whose services your organization is considering purchasing. You have identified some firms that you think might do a good job and have studied their brochures. But now you want the inside scoop from some of their previous customers. You've decided to write to some of these (whose testimonials were featured in various team-building firms' promotional material) and get more specific information—the kind that will help your boss decide, first, whether to go ahead with such training and, second, which firm to choose if the training seems like a good idea.

As you prepare your email of inquiry, your boss's words play in your head: "We work in a business that can be very stressful. Helping our patients cope with medical and financial issues takes an enormous toll on our front-line staff, and that stress often makes its way up the ladder to our management team. Plus, like everyone else, we're having to do more with less in these tight economic times. With pressures like these, we can lose our patience, our energy, and our focus on our core values. I've gotten approval for a day-long retreat for the department managers and their immediate staff at a nature center outside of town. I'm thinking we should bring in a team-building consultant to help us relax and recharge. We don't have a lot of money to spend on something that our Board of Trustees and the community might view as frivolous, so we need activities that will actually pay off. See if you can find a team-building firm that might be right for us."

You think carefully about what your organization needs and, putting that together with what you've learned so far about team-building consulting, you make a list of questions that you think will elicit the most helpful information. Now write the email that will help you see which firm is likely to warrant the most serious consideration. Fill in additional details as needed to do a good job on this inquiry message.

---

5 You're part of the management team at Castinelli's, a local restaurant chain with five locations in the city. Each month, the management—everyone from the five store managers to the president/owner—has a luncheon meeting in which they discuss any issues that have arisen, the financial health of the business, progress on current initiatives, any ideas for creating new business, and various other topics. You think such meetings are a great idea, and you understand the advantages of face-to-face communication (especially in this company's culture, which is close-knit and family oriented)—but you wonder if these meetings are really worth the time and expense involved.

You recently attended a Restaurant Managers Association meeting where you learned that many of your peers are conducting business meetings online. One online meeting technology you kept hearing about was _____ (WebEx, GoToMeeting, or some other one—you choose). Curious, you checked out the product's website, viewed the demo, and studied the fact sheet. You're thinking that this product just might be a viable alternative to Castinelli's' monthly management meetings.

To gather more facts before sharing your idea with your superiors, you decide to consult a person you met at the RMA meeting who seemed to know a lot about online conferencing and about the particular technology you're interested in. Thinking carefully about what you'd like to learn from this experienced, disinterested party about using this technology for meetings, prepare your questions in the form of an email of inquiry. (Your instructor may choose a different business situation or a different online application.)

6 Parking is tight at your urban university, especially near certain buildings. The campus has two large parking garages, and both of them are far away and downhill from the business building where you have most of your classes as an MBA student. Normally you don't mind since you enjoy the trek from the garage to the business building. But as the president of your local chapter of Delta Pi Epsilon, the national business honor society for graduate students, you find yourself needing to reserve one of the few surface spaces close to the building. You have invited a local businessperson to come speak at the chapter meeting on May 3, from 4:00 to 5:30 PM. This guest will be rushing to the meeting from work and will be carrying a laptop as well as various print materials to distribute. You think it would be impractical as well as rude to force this guest to park in a garage and then trudge up a long hill to get to your building.

The parking services website at your school informs you that any special parking requests must be made in writing and sent via email to Ms. Alvyria Jones. Write Ms. Jones and get permission for the reserved parking space you need. Be sure you make your request at least two weeks in advance as the website directs you to do.

---

7 You've been given an important assignment from your boss, a VP at a small website development firm in Washington, D.C.: to arrange a relax-and-recharge retreat for company employees. The boss wants to hold the retreat in the Luray, Virginia, area in the Shenandoah Valley, about 90 miles from the city. He has specifically instructed you to find a large cabin, not a hotel or resort, because he wants the event to have the feel of a getaway, not a business meeting. But the retreat will serve important business purposes, so employees' families will not be invited.

After a good bit of Internet searching, you think you've found the perfect place: a large, isolated cabin overlooking the valley. You learn a lot about the property from the website—such as how many the cabin will sleep (20), how it is equipped (a large modern kitchen, a deck with a hot tub and 20 chairs, a large-screen TV with cable service, and a game room with an air-hockey table), what it costs ($50 per person per day except on weekends and holidays, when the rate is $75 per day), when it's available, and what kind of linen service is provided. But you need to know more. For example, is there an area inside the cabin where 20 people can comfortably meet and talk? The pictures on the website don't make that clear. Is there Internet access? Cell phone service? A DVD player so that employees can watch movies of their choice? How/when do you pay? When will you need to report an exact headcount? What if some people don't show up—do you still pay for them? And then there are the smaller things. Are charcoal and lighter fluid included with the grill? Are there paper towels? Salt and pepper? Kitchen linens and soap?

You wanted to ask the realtor these and other questions by phone, but you and she have been playing phone tag. Plus, you want a written record of her answers. So you'll craft a well-organized email message asking for the information you need to be sure this important company event will go well—and reflect well on you. Be sure to tell her what she needs to know about your event in order to give you helpful answers. (With your instructor's permission, you may change the venue and other details as appropriate.)

---

8 You work for a large credit union that is upgrading the software it uses to manage and maintain members' account and personal information. Everyone who works with or has access to members' information (tellers, customers service representatives, financial officers, loan representatives, department supervisors and managers, employee trainers, technical writers, marketing specialists, clerical staff, and information systems specialists) will need training on the upgraded software. Your boss has asked you, as the lead corporate trainer, to coordinate training sessions. You discover that the makers of the software (Financial Software Systems, Inc.) can provide training on-site or at its corporate headquarters, which happen to be in your town. You need to know which of these options is not only the most feasible and practical but also which is the most cost effective. You have 500 employees who will need training. You have a corporate training room with 20 computers, an Internet connection that is fairly reliable, and a data projector. The software will be installed in six months. Ideally, you would like to train all of your employees in the two months before the installation. That way they could continue to practice on the software installed in the corporate training room if they like. Although you have thought about calling for the information, you decide to write so that you have a permanent record of the answers to your questions. Write to Ms. Whitley Freeman, training coordinator, to inquire about Financial Software Inc.'s availability to provide training and for information that will help you decide whether to train on site or at company headquarters.

---

9 As Komal Gupta, the person in charge of the opening ceremonies buffet for the university's World Village celebration next month, you need to order food appropriate for the celebration. Your town has a great Middle Eastern restaurant (Zorah's) that you think you want to feature. You visit the restaurant's website and are happy learn that that you would be able to order enough tabouli, hummus and pita bread, rice flavored with almonds and pine nuts, slow-roasted chicken (Zorah's specialty!), and baklava for 120 people.

What you aren't sure of, though, is the cost. In addition, the website says the items can be ordered by the half tray or the whole tray, and you're not sure how many people a half tray or whole tray will serve.

You're hoping that because the event is for a worthy cause and would generate publicity for Zorah's, you might get a bit of a price break on the order. You would even be willing to pick up the order by 11 AM on the Saturday of the event. Using the email address provided on Zorah's website, write a request for the information you need to decide whether you will serve Zorah's food at the World Village celebration.

---

10 You took out your car loan with Community Bank because of its low interest rates. However, your regular checking and savings accounts are at Ocean State Credit Union. You can already tell that sending in a payment coupon and check each month will be neither convenient nor easy to remember. You wonder if you can just have your car payment for Community Bank automatically deducted from your Ocean State account and sent to Community Bank. You go to Community Bank's website and learn that this is possible, but no details are provided regarding the process. So you decide to click the link to "Contact Us" and ask your questions in the text box that appears. Though you'll want to think of more questions, you will at least want to know if there is a fee for this service and how long it would take to set up this payment option.

Favorable Responses

11 A student from your alma mater (either high school or university—you choose, based on your work experience) is considering getting a job like yours, and, having gotten your name from the school's alumni office, he/she has written to ask you what the job entails. (In the case of a high schooler, you suspect that he/she is writing you as part of a class assignment, but what you say could still be very useful; in the case of a college student, the writer is exploring different majors, co-ops, or employment opportunities.)

The writer has asked what your main responsibilities are, what kind of knowledge you need in order to do this job well, and what the working conditions are like. But you can tell that, beyond these basics, what he/she especially wants to know is what it feels like to do this job. Is it fun? Is it meaningful? How'd you get this job? What kind of person would like it?

Using current or past work experience, write the student to give him/her the inside scoop on this kind of employment. Anticipate questions that will come to mind as he/she reads, and offer any valuable tips you may have. Don't forget that this email may become public; anything you say may find its way to your current employer!

---

12 You were delighted today to receive a suggestion from Soledad Lopez, one of your top-notch customer service reps at TuffStuff, that looks like it will not only save you money and lots of work but also improve the quality of your customer communication.

As a small business that specializes in selling a quality line of lawn-maintenance equipment, your company regularly exhibits at trade shows to expose its products to special audiences. You've pretty well mastered coordinating the setup process at these shows with the printers, but the print material you distribute varies from show to show and with the timing of special promotions. As a result, you often end up carting these newly printed documents in extra luggage and boxes with you on flights to various cities. And you've often had to pay extra baggage or overweight charges, since the handouts can be heavy.

For the meeting in Minneapolis next month, Soledad suggested she try using FedEx Kinko's virtual printing program. Unlike FedEx Kinko's older program where documents had to be uploaded to their servers, the new program prints on their printers from your site. Paper and binding can be specified from a large selection and users pay online, so you can pick up the documents at the local FedEx Kinko's in Minneapolis (it's across the street from the meeting site) without having to worry about packing and transporting them. Also, the documents will have up-to-the-minute accuracy, and more can be printed as needed rather than your having to overestimate the need to be on the safe side as you have done in the past.

Soledad's idea is so logical you wish you had thought of it before. As co-owner of Tuff Stuff, you'll give her the approval she needs for this trial. And you'll tell her how much you appreciate her efforts to improve the communication with your customers.

---

13 You're a student worker for the Smithfield College Fund, one of the fundraising offices at Smithfield College. Recently the office sent a mailing to the parents of all graduating seniors announcing the opportunity to purchase an engraved brick to commemorate the achievement of their sons and daughters. The bricks cost $150 each, and, according to the mailing, will be placed in the school's Senior Path. Today your office got an email of inquiry from Jeannie Schlegel, whose daughter, Della Schlegel, is one of the soon-to-be graduates. Here's what Ms. Schlegel's email said:

> I received your mailing about the commemorative bricks and plan to order one for my daughter. But there's a place for only one person on the order form, and I'd like to order a brick as well for her grandmother, Paula Schlegel, who graduated from Smithfield in 1934. (In fact, her two sisters went to Smithfield as well—Maggie Schlegel ['36] and Caroline Schlegel ['38]!) Can I do that? If so, should I just write her name on the order form, too? Should I write one check or two? Also, where will the bricks be placed? Exactly where or what is the Senior Path? If I can order the two bricks, can they be placed side by side? The family would really like to see them together, if possible. Thanks so much.

Respond to Ms. Schlegel. Inform her that she can order two bricks, that the second will cost $150 also, that she can just write the grandmother's name and graduation year on the same form as the daughter's name and year (but she must be careful to write them clearly, and remember—first and last names only), and that she can pay for the two bricks together either by check or by credit card. The Senior Path is the main walkway of the campus that runs between the student center and some of the school's oldest buildings. You do not know whether the two bricks can be put side by side. The plan is to put each year's graduating seniors together. When you ask about this question, your supervisor says, "I'm not sure—just tell her we'll do our best. Even if the two bricks aren't side by side, we'll be sending each family a diagram so they can easily find the bricks they're looking for." So you'll handle this part of the response as skillfully as you can.

---

14 You're an accountant (or manager, or some other title) at Deloitte & Touche (or some other company) in Columbia, South Carolina (or some other city), and you've just received an email from a student at the local university asking if she can shadow you for a day to learn more about what the work in her major will be like. Write the student and tell her she can shadow you; tell her which day of the ones she suggested is best for you and when she should arrive; tell her where to park and enter the building and where/how to meet you; and cover any additional questions she's likely to have. Drawing upon your knowledge of the job you're pretending to have and the kind of company it's in, write a cordial, clear, well-organized, and thorough email that gets the visit set up and prepares the student to have an educational, enjoyable day.

---

15 You are an intern for the director of corporate communications at Wang and Bradley, a financial services firm. She has been asked by the director of sales to lead a seminar for its financial sales representatives about polishing their nonverbal communication skills. Your boss has found several YouTube videos that provide good and bad examples, and she thinks that these will make her presentation more interesting and engaging. The problem is that not all of them are appropriate for a workplace presentation. Your boss has asked you to find four YouTube videos, two that illustrate examples of effective nonverbal communication and two that do not. Before responding, you find four videos that you think will work for her as well as some alternatives. Write a response to her request that contains links to the videos you found as well as a brief summary of what the videos contain and why you think they are appropriate for your boss's presentation.

---

16 As president and owner of a small business that delivers documents and small parcels, you are delighted to respond to an email from Kevin Stamper, director of corporate communications, requesting that the company participate in a cell phone recycling program. In this program, recovered materials can be used to make new products—the cadmium is used to make new batteries, while the nickel and iron are used to make stainless steel products. Cell phones are refurbished and sold when possible, and a portion of the proceeds from the resale of the cell phones would benefit local charities. The program is simple: the company provides prepaid, preaddressed collection boxes, and when they are full, you send them to the recycling company.

Not only do you think Kevin has a great idea, but it is especially timely during this week, April 6–9, National Cell Phone Recycle Week. You may want to suggest that if Kevin heads up the program for your company, he can help identify which charity to choose. He might also want to release a PR blurb on the company's efforts to encourage other small businesses to do the same thing.

Your small business should gain more visibility and goodwill while helping the community. Let Kevin know how much you appreciate his idea.

---

17 Recently, you received a letter from Rick Jenkins, president of Northern University's Beta Upsilon Sigma (BUS) business fraternity. BUS is holding a silent auction to raise money for the local humane association and has contacted you to see if your company, Northern Outfitters, could supply some items for the auction. Your company sells camping gear, hunting and fishing equipment, skis, snowshoes, clothing, nonperishable food and dry goods, canoes, kayaks—anything anyone would need for an outdoor venture no matter how large or how small. In addition, Northern Outfitters offers weekend rental packages that include a tent, canoe, backpacks, and supplies for $200 per weekend. Northern Outfitters also rents canoes, kayaks, skis, snowshoes, and camping gear separately. As the manager for Northern Outfitters, you are happy to grant Rick's request and see this as a great opportunity to advertise your company and do something for the students and community. Respond to Rick's letter, telling him which item or items you will provide for the auction.

Adjustment Grants

18 You're a customer service representative at AutoParts.com, and you recently received a request for an adjustment (see Chapter 7, case #13). The customer makes a good case, and your records verify that he recently bought the coil and resistor in question from you. The records also show that he is a regular customer.

You'll be glad to refund his money, with your apologies for the trouble caused by the error on your website. You will pay the cost difference he requests as long as he sends you the receipt for the parts he purchased locally. (Fortunately, you are authorized to make adjustments up to $400 without having to get prior approval.) Because you'd like a chance to examine the parts to verify his claim, you will also include a shipping label for sending the resistor and damaged coil back to you, postage prepaid of course.

Write the message that will handle the situation to the customer's satisfaction and keep him as a loyal customer.

19 As a co-owner of J&J Plumbing, you're going to have to grant an adjustment on the invoice for a recent job. In the letter Candis Sacchetti included with an unpaid invoice for $230, she claims that the plumber you sent out, Roy O'Dell, failed to fix the clogged drain he worked on for two hours. According to her, he had tried over and over to send a metal snake down the drain—creating an awful noise in the process—but to no avail. He had finally advised Ms. Sacchetti that he would need to correct the problem by knocking a hole in the wall and drilling directly into the pipe. With low confidence in Roy at this point, Ms. Sacchetti had sent him on his way. She had then called in a plumber from another company. After about 30 minutes of using the metal snake, this plumber had fixed the problem. He explained that, after about 10 minutes of trying to send the snake down the drain, he had figured out that the snake was going up the exhaust part of the pipe instead of down to the clog. He had adjusted his technique accordingly and then easily solved the problem.

Ms. Sacchetti refuses to pay for Roy's ineffectual labors. You check with Roy—not one of your better plumbers—and his story of the service call agrees with hers. Thank goodness Ms. Sacchetti called in someone else before she'd taken the drastic measures that Roy had recommended, or else you might have a bigger claim on your hands. This is the last straw—you're going to have to let Roy go. But first write Ms. Sacchetti a letter granting her request and trying to restore her confidence in your company. Create any additional realistic details that will help you keep her as a customer.

20 Play the role of James Logan, director of the Sycamore County Parks Board, and respond to the complaint described in case #11 in Chapter 7 on page 187. You do understand the writer's point of view: The family shouldn't have had to clean up both before and after their event! On the other hand, it wasn't exactly your maintenance crew's fault, either. They had checked all the rental areas the day before and ensured that they were clean. You can't help it that wild creatures roam the parks overnight. True, it would have been better to check each area on the morning of the event, but you simply don't have enough staff to be able to do that in such a short time frame. Plus, the rental agreement advised renters to come early and check over the site, since raccoons and other uninvited guests do sometimes make some cleanup necessary.

Weighing both sides' arguments, you decide to give the writer a partial refund (the claim message left it up to you to decide what adjustment to give). Give what you think is fair and do your best to make the family—and their friends—want to use your facilities again. (It will also be nice to have their votes the next time park funding is on the ballot!)

21 You are a customer service manager for a large sheet music publisher and distributor. You've just received a package from Lisa Thompson of Eau Claire, Wisconsin, containing the books of sheet music your company sent her two weeks ago. Her note to you says that the music you sent was not the music she ordered. As you review the invoices handled by the customer service representative Ms. Thompson worked with on the day the order was placed, you see that Ms. Thompson was simply sent someone else's order. The occasion for which Ms. Thompson needed the music has passed, and she no longer wants the music. She would like the charge for the order removed from her account and a credit to her account for the amount of the postage ($7.95) to return the incorrect order.

Of course her claim is valid. Send Ms. Thompson a response granting her request. Though she did not request it, you may also want to offer some kind of deal on her next purchase.

---

22 As senior customer care representative for Office Depot, you were not too surprised to get a message today reporting that one of your customers, Bao Vang, had trouble with the chair from a desk set you sold her last summer. In fact, due to two injuries suffered from the chair breaking, the Consumer Product Safety Commission has recalled that desk set. While Bao was disappointed that the chair did not hold up, she reported that the acquaintance who had been sitting in the chair when it collapsed was not injured. You are certainly happy that no one was hurt, and you will gladly offer to replace the chair.

You appreciated Bao's thoroughness in including the model number along with a copy of her receipt. It makes it

much easier for you to meet her request quickly. In granting her request, you will need to get the chair back even in its broken condition to reduce any future liability with it. You will offer Bao a gift card for the full value of the $80, but she needs to return the chair to get it.

To help maintain her goodwill and to encourage her to purchase from Office Depot in the future, you may want to remind her that at Office Depot all purchases can be changed or refunded within 30 days with the original receipt. You may even want to offer some promotion that might interest her.

---

23 You are an assistant manager for a Holiday Inn SunSpree Resort, a popular place for family vacations. The good news is that you are completely booked this holiday weekend. The bad news is that your giant heated outdoor pool has had to be closed for the weekend because of a filtration system breakdown. You

decide you must write a message to slip under each guest-room door advising that the pool is closed and offering some kind of adjustment. As you plan this message, you may want to refer to the example in Chapter 5's, "Planning the Message" section regarding the hotel with the faulty air conditioning.

Order Acknowledgments and Other Thank-You Messages

24 As the student who shadowed a professional (see case #3 in Chapter 8), you had a great day with _____ at the _____ company. Sure, there was some downtime when she was answering email and doing paperwork, but she made an effort to tell you what she was doing and why. (Plus, for those downtimes, she'd given you some good

reading material about the company and its industry.) She also included you in a meeting with her team and in chats with other employees on her breaks. She treated you to lunch and had even gone to the trouble to invite a couple of entry-level employees—with jobs like the one you hope to get after you graduate—to join you. All in all, she really outdid herself. Thank her in a way that befits the effort she went to for you.

---

25 You've just been hired as a marketing intern for a large online auto parts dealership, CarWorld.com. Your boss drops by your desk and asks you to take a look at the order-acknowledgment email message that the company currently uses. Here's what it says:

Dear [Customer]:

You have received this message because you have ordered a product from CarWorld.com. If you'd like to be removed from our mailing list, reply with a blank message to sales@CarWorld.com.

Don't forget to keep your [type of car] running smoothly with regular maintenance. We've created a useful guide listing the periodic maintenance items for your car and the schedule for replacing them:

[web link to the maintenance guide].

At CarWorld.com we offer such brand-name replacements as brake parts, steering parts, headlights, wiper parts, all kinds of interior body parts, hubcaps, floor mats, and more. Many of these are at discounted prices. We also sell repair manuals for most cars.

We are also proud to say that we protect the environment by recycling many used parts. You can find many hard-to-find items for older cars and pay less for them here than at other places.

Thanks again for your purchase and we hope you'll choose us again.

The Car World Team

"Think you can do better?" your boss asks. "Absolutely," you answer. Go for it. (If you instructor permits, you may choose another type of business for this case.)

---

26 As vice president and part owner of your parents' restaurant, Zorah's, you responded to Komal Gupta's request for information about serving 120 people at the World Village Celebration (See Routine Inquiry #9). He was thrilled with your response regarding the types of food available. You also said in response to his request for a price break that you would give him a little extra on all the trays and include a full order of olives (priced at $20) at no charge. You also agreed to waive the $100 deposit that is usually required for large orders.

Because each tray serves about 40 people, he placed an order for three trays of each of the following items: tabouli ($60), hummus and pita bread ($50), flavored rice ($60). Because the slow-roasted chicken must cook all day and is only available for dinner customers, he instead ordered grape leaves stuffed with lamb ($.75 each, two per person).

Write a note to Ms. Gupta acknowledging her order and thanking her for his business. Make her feel that she is making a good choice in selecting your cuisine for the event—and be sure that all the details are clear.

---

27 As the assistant to the executive director of the American Society for Training and Development (or the American Management Association, or any professional society of your choice), write the "welcome" message that you will send to new members. The message will include a receipt for their first-year dues, their member number (with which they can access members-only Web pages and get members-only discounts), and of course contact information for the organization. Just as importantly, though, it will make readers feel good about the investment they've just made in their professional development. And the more they take advantage of what the organization has to offer, the more likely they'll be to renew their membership next year. Carefully study the website of the organization you choose and think about which benefits of membership to highlight. Then write about a four-paragraph message to these new members. A fetching "P.S.," in the style of an effective sales message, couldn't hurt.

---

28 Recently, you met with David Williams, marketing manager with Green Living, a major architectural and construction firm. His company released an RFP (request for proposal) for someone to design, host, and maintain his company's website. Your company, Modern Technologies, specializes in Web design and plans to submit a proposal. Fortunately, Mr. Williams was kind enough to meet with you to answer some questions regarding the proposal. He emphasized that Green Living is looking for a creative site that uses modern Web technologies but is user friendly, easily navigated, and visually appealing. Of course, as his company name suggests, Green Living specializes in environmentally friendly design and construction practices; the company's website should reflect this. You also learned that you will need to include a list of all fees you will charge for designing, creating, and hosting the site; if there are fees that Green Living will incur that are not part of the proposal, you must list them, as Green Living wants no surprises. In addition, if you plan to subcontract any of the work (e.g., use freelance designers, artists, writers), you must list the subcontractors in the proposal as well. Furthermore, any work you create would become the property of Green Living, not Modern Technologies. After your talk with Mr. Williams, you are confident that your company's proposal will meet his needs and are excited about submitting it. Write a thank-you note to Mr. Williams for meeting with you and providing you with the information for your proposal.

---

29 You are the community liaison for _____ (you pick the nonprofit organization). Your organization participates in a program in which donors can give to your program through an automatic credit or debit card deduction. Write a letter to these donors, thanking them for their donations and updating them on the organization's accomplishments during the past year and plans for the coming year. *TIP: Think about how you might use technology to help you include a personalized salutation rather than simply "Dear donor."*

Operational Messages

30 You're an owner and vice president of a small software-development firm. Your part time marketing person, Ginny Erikson, has been acting as the company webmaster, but she has simply had too many other duties to be able to do this job well. As a result, you recently purchased several site licenses for a computer program that, when installed on certain employees' computers, will enable these employees to become content editors; that is, they'll be able to edit and update the pages on the company website that pertain to them rather than sending their changes to the busy Ginny and having her upload them. Every page of the site is based on the same template, so the new editors will not be able to alter the essential look of the pages (a good thing, since you don't want your website to turn into an ugly mess). Ginny will also be able to make certain parts of the pages uneditable so that people won't be able to change such important elements as the company logo. However, by using the new program, the people who know the different areas of the company best will be able to keep their information timely and accurate. Ginny will still be the main quality-assurance person for the site and will quickly check over any changes the employees make before their revisions go live, but the new procedure will relieve her of a great deal of busywork and free her up for more important things.

Write an email announcing this change to the department heads in sales, product development, training and support, and other relevant areas, with a copy to Ginny. Advise your readers that each of them will need to attend a one-hour training session on this application. Ginny will conduct the training on two dates so that anyone who has to miss the first session can attend the second one. They'll learn how the tool works and also get to practice using it.

Your company has a positive, teamlike culture, so your readers are not likely, overall, to view this news negatively. You know they've been frustrated with having to pressure Ginny, politely, to get things updated on the website, so they may well be relieved that they can now just do it themselves. On the other hand, nobody really wants extra responsibilities, and some may be terrified at the prospect of editing a Web page (not everyone who works for a software company is familiar with Web authoring!). So anything you can say to get a positive reception for your message would be a good idea. You'll also want to anticipate any questions that these employees may have and give them enough information so that the plan seems well thought out and reasonable. (To gather good technical details for this message, visit the websites for Adobe Contribute, CushyCMS, or similar applications that enable dispersed Web-content editing.)

---

31 While your company has been doing well, you've noticed a sense of detachment of employees from each other that concerns you. In the past, their ability to work well as a team seemed to help them be successful on a variety of projects. But the detachment seemed to start when employees were allowed to bring iPods to work and listen to their own music. Initially, this seemed motivational, and employees seemed to enjoy it, judging from the proliferation of people with earphones. However, you're not sure they are talking with each other as much as they used to do.

When some employees who did not own iPods asked to be able to listen to music of their choice over headphones but streaming from the Internet, you thought it was only fair and permitted it. However, that extended to online news videos

first, then to *Grey's Anatomy,* and sometimes now even movies. Clearly none of these activities are promoting the collaborative environment you once had. As a result, you've decided to limit the amount of time employees can use these technologies to the first and last hours of the workday and the lunch hour unless such use is directly related to the work at hand.

To communicate this new policy, write a message that explains it along with the benefits it is likely to bring both the company and employees. The message will be sent to all employees by mail as well as posted on the company intranet.

To do well on this assignment, you will need to decide what kind of company this is, what kinds of work the employees do, and what your own position/title is.

---

32 As a company that has more than 50 employees living in or near the city where it is located, your company is covered by the U.S. Family Medical Leave Act (FMLA). This means that employees who meet certain criteria, as outlined by the US Department of Labor (<http://www.dol.gov/esa/whd/regs/compliance/whdfs28.pdf>), may take up to 12 weeks of unpaid leave if they have a baby, an extended illness, or an impaired relative to take care of.

Many companies have started "leave donation" programs that enable employees to donate some of their accumulated sick leave or vacation time to fellow employees who have taken unpaid leaves. As office manager for a thriving landscaping company, you periodically remind employees of this opportunity to help their colleagues. You think the time has come around again for this reminder, especially since you're

aware of at least two employees who might need their co-workers' donations.

Write the employees, some of whom have never heard of this program, about the leave donation program. You will direct them to the FMLA website and to your own company's intranet for the full official details, but you will include the basics in your message: how much leave employees need to have accumulated in order to donate, the minimum and maximum amount of hours they can donate, the irreversibility of the donation, what recipients may use it for, how to donate, the fact that donating is strictly voluntary, and/or whatever you think readers need to know in order to decide whether to pursue the matter further. (To generate such details, you can visit FMLA websites and the website at your school or business that describes this kind of policy.)

---

33 Assume that you are an intern in the corporate communications department of the _____ Company (you name it).

You were speaking with Latisha James, your boss, about the business writing course you're taking this term, and when you described the things you were learning, Latisha was particularly interested in the tips about good email practice.

"I think we've fallen into sloppy email practices in this company," she complains. "There's too much emailing going on, for one thing, and it's stealing time away from the real business of our company. This creates a glut of work for our Information Technology (IT) staff, too, who have to figure out how to store and organize the stuff. Plus, I've noticed more and more casual, ungrammatical language in our emails. I worry that this kind of language is creating an unprofessional atmosphere in the company and that this tone could leak into correspondence with clients and other external audiences. And a lot of the email I see is unclear, rambling, and hard to read. It wastes time and miscommunicates. I wonder, too, if people are taking seriously enough the fact that *any* email, addressed to anyone, could find a way of becoming public. We really need a refresher on email communication."

Then she looks at you brightly. "Would you write up what you've learned about good email practice and email it to me so I can send it out? It's about time we nipped this too-casual attitude toward emailing in the bud." "Sure," you say, already thinking about how you can adapt what you've learned to this particular company. Now write a memo for Latisha that she can send out to the employees to help them brush up on their emailing skills. To get them to read the document, you will need to format it carefully and help them see at a glance what's in it (and why they should care). To get them to benefit from the document, you will need to help them see how to apply these words of advice to their work. Sure, Latisha will add her own touches and probably change some of your wording, but the less work she has to do on your memo before sending it out, the better.

Use the information on emailing in Chapter 5 as the basis for your memo (if your instructor directs, find additional material). Obviously you can't cram every detail into your memo; you will need to pick four to six main pieces of advice from the chapter and develop/explain those in such a way that people will understand and apply the advice.

---

34 As president of Jackson Springs, Inc., a members–only swim and tennis club, write an operational message announcing the club's annual meeting to its members. Your mailing should also include a calendar of events for the upcoming summer season, an invoice for this year's fees, and a membership card that each member needs to fill out and return with his/her payment (in the return envelope provided). Include the following information, nicely organized, formatted, and improved in other ways if appropriate.

All members are invited to attend the meeting, as well as to propose agenda items (which needs to be done at least 10 days before the meeting, in writing to the president). The agenda already includes reports from the president, treasurer, and club manager. It also includes election of new members to the club's Board of Trustees. A nominating committee, consisting of Doug Jones, Elizabeth Granada, Melinda Neal, and Ralph Lu, will submit the names of members to be voted on. The new members will serve a three-year term. Other names can be proposed by members not on the nominating committee, but need to be submitted to the president at least 10 days before the meeting.

Members need to send in their fees by May 1. Any payment postmarked after May 15 will incur a $20 late fee. The club will open this year on May 23 at 11:00 AM. Members may not use the club until their fees are paid. Members who wish to change their membership status in any way (for example, from a family to a single membership) should note the change on their payment or call the club.

Members also need to fill out the enclosed membership card so that the club will have an accurate list of member names and accurate emergency contact information for the member or member's family. You particularly want people to be sure to include their email addresses so that you can use that form of communication with them.

Members should visit <www.jacksonsprings.com> during the summer to learn about special events, swim and tennis lessons, changes in the calendar, and so forth. They can also download the membership application form. You want them to spread the good word about the club and encourage their friends to join.

---

35 You are the human resources manager for a company of 200 employees. Your company produces practice management software for hospitals and medical clinics and employs people in many types of positions (e.g., hardware and software development, communication, marketing and sales, accounting, customer service and support, clerical, custodial, training). You were talking with a colleague at a recent Society for Human Resource Management meeting and learned that your colleague's company offers personal development activities for its employees to update or build their skills. The professional development activities are generally workshops where an expert shares his or her knowledge on a particular topic such as conflict resolution or email etiquette. Workshops are held onsite. Most are only an hour or so and are held once a month during the workday. Of course, employees are paid to attend these sessions and are not required to attend all of them—only the ones that interest them. According to your colleague the employees really like this program. Some have even said that because the company invests in their professional development, they feel more loyal to the company. They are also really motivated to attend because of the caliber of the experts who present the programs.

You think this kind of professional development program is just what your company needs. You present your idea to your CEO and receive permission to try the program for six months, so you develop a list of topics, set a schedule, and contact experts who agree to lead the workshops.

Send a message to the employees of your company in which you describe the program and include a brief list of the topics the program will offer in the next six months. Be sure you think about what information might motivate readers to participate in this program. Develop a list of topics you think employees might find interesting.

---

36 It's summer, it's hot, and road construction is everywhere. Your state's Department of Transportation is in the middle of a road construction project that makes your customer parking lot inaccessible from the main road on which your business is located. Your employee parking lot is still accessible from a side street, and because your customers will have to take a three-mile detour to get to your business as it is, you want to at least provide them with convenient parking. As the vice president of operations, you decide that the employee parking lot will become the customer parking lot for the duration of the construction project, which is expected to last for the next four weeks. This means that employees (except those with special needs or accommodations) will have to park on the side streets two blocks from work.

You know that your employees won't necessarily like doing this, but you really don't see this message as bad news for a few reasons: First, you're the only business on the street that actually has the luxury of a second parking lot; the other businesses on your street will have to ask their employees to park at least two blocks away on the side streets. Second, nearly all employees walk on their breaks and during their lunch hours. A two-block walk in the morning and again in the afternoon along a shaded side street would not be that taxing—in fact, depending on where they park in the employee parking lot, some employees may already walk that same distance. Write a message to your employees explaining the new parking requirements. If you feel you need to offer incentives to improve employees' feelings toward the new parking regulation, you may do so.

---

37 Each year your company organizes a team to participate in Relay for Life (for more information visit <http://www.relayforlife.org/relay/>). This year you are the coordinator of your company's Relay for Life team. Your first task is to invite all employees to an informational meeting. Send a message to everyone in the company regarding the meeting and include an agenda for the meeting. A little

research on Relay for Life's website will help you decide what to include in your agenda. Remember to be concise. The website has a lot of information that is specific to team leaders and committee chairs. Your meeting is an initial informational meeting only for those who want to participate in the relay or who may not be sure if they should join the team.

---

38 Your company (you choose the name) requires that an internal proposal be submitted whenever a supervisor needs to hire someone for a new or vacant position. Your company believes that these proposals are important because they help track labor hours and assess which positions are truly necessary. As a department manager (you make up the name of your department), you have several supervisors who work under you and who submit proposals for new or vacant positions. Your job is to review the proposals, approve or deny the positions, and have the supervisors make any revisions to the proposals before you send the approved proposals to human resources for further action.

The requirements for the proposals are very specific. In fact, there's a template on the company's intranet that everyone is supposed to use in completing the proposals. The problem is that you find yourself increasingly spending a lot of time reading the proposals and marking them for revisions. Some supervisors appear to ignore the template. Others seem to make an effort to follow the template but do not provide enough detail. You suspect some are just lazy.

You simply cannot spend so much time revising these proposals and believe that most of the issues would be addressed if employees would pay attention to the template. In fact, one hiring decision was delayed for over a month, resulting in a backlog of work and overtime pay (which the company likes to avoid). The main issues with the proposals submitted are that they are frequently missing headings; sections of the proposal required in the template are missing because supervisors rely on you to fill in the information rather than finding it themselves; writers put information under the wrong headings; writers deviate from the template and combine information under headings that they make up; and the data that they use to justify the position is often inadequate or not calculated correctly. You're stuck. Your success depends on your supervisors' ability to have adequate staffing. They know this. Why should they invest the energy in writing the proposal when you will revise it to what you want and need anyway? What is their incentive to do well?

Write a message to your department supervisors about meeting the requirements for their hiring proposals. You will need to work very hard at cultivating a reader-centered view so that the supervisors are motivated to write better proposals.

39 Revise the following poorly written message so that the message is clear. You may add information if you need to for the message to make sense. Be sure to fix any grammar, mechanics, punctuation, or word choice errors.

From: Reynolds, Sarah
Sent: Tuesday, June 2, 2012
To: All Employees
Subject: Security System

As many of you have noticed the security system is not working at this time, we are aware of this problem and are awaiting repair parts to correct the issue.

In response, the outer doors are unlocked and you will not need to use your badge until we are repaired.

Later this evening we will be falling back to keyed door locks for the evening.

If you are going out the front door, you will need to use the handle to get out the exterior doors after 5 PM.

Thank you for your patients,

Sarah Reynolds
Building Supervisor
Ext. 5555

chapter seven

Indirectness in Bad-News Messages

Upon completing this chapter, you will be able to write indirect responses to convey bad news. To reach this goal, you should be able to

1   Determine which situations require using the indirect order for the most effective response.

2   Write indirect-order messages following the general plan.

3   Use tact and courtesy in refusals of requests.

4   Compose tactful, yet clear, claim messages.

5   Write adjustment refusals that minimize the negative and overcome bad impressions.

6   Write negative announcements that maintain goodwill.

SITUATIONS REQUIRING INDIRECTNESS

As explained in Chapter 6, when a message is primarily bad news, you should probably write in the indirect order. The indirect order is especially effective when you must say "no" or convey other disappointing news. The main reason for this approach is that negative news is received more positively when an explanation precedes it. An explanation may even convince the reader that the writer's position is correct. In addition, an explanation cushions the shock of bad news. Not cushioning the shock makes the message unnecessarily harsh, and harshness destroys goodwill.

You may want to use directness in some bad-news situations. If, for example, you think that your negative answer will be accepted routinely, you might choose directness. For example, in many buyer–seller relationships in business, both parties expect backorders and order errors to occur now and then. Thus, messages reporting this negative information would not really require indirectness. You also might choose directness if you know your reader well and feel that he or she will appreciate frankness. But such instances are less common than those in which indirectness is the preferable strategy.

As in the preceding chapter, we first describe a general plan. Then we adapt this plan to specific business situations—four in this case. First is the refusal of a request, a common task in business. Next we cover two related types of negative messages: claims and adjustment refusals. Finally, we cover negative announcements, which are a form of bad-news messages with unique characteristics.

- Usually bad-news messages should be in the indirect order.

- There are exceptions, as when the bad news is routine or when the reader prefers frankness.

- Following is a general plan for bad-news messages and four applications.

THE GENERAL INDIRECT PLAN

The following five-part plan will be helpful for most negative-news situations.

Using a Strategic Buffer

Indirect messages presenting bad news often begin with a strategic buffer. By *buffer* we mean an opening that identifies the subject of the message but does not indicate overtly that negative news is coming. That is, it raises the topic of the message but does not indicate what the rest of the message will say about it.

A buffer can be neutral or positive. A neutral buffer might simply acknowledge your receipt of the reader's earlier message and indicate your awareness of what it said. A positive buffer might thank the reader for bringing a situation to your attention or for being a valued customer or employee. You do need to use care when opening on a positive note. You do not in any way want to raise the reader's hopes that you are about to deliver the news that he or she may be hoping for. That would only make your task of maintaining good relations more difficult.

Some may argue that not starting with the good news is, for savvy readers, a clear tip-off that bad news is coming. If this is the case, then why not just start with the bad news? True, for some readers in some situations, a direct approach may be the best. For example, if you are writing to tell customers that there is a defective part in a car they have purchased and that they should return the car to the dealership immediately for repairs, it would be almost unethical not to feature this important information in the opening paragraph. Most readers in most situations, however, appreciate a more gradual introduction to the message's main negative point. It gives them a chance to prepare for the news—and even if they suspect that it will be negative, the use of a buffer indicates consideration for their feelings.

- Use a buffer in indirect bad-news messages.
- Begin with a buffer that identifies the subject.
- Use a neutral buffer or a positive one that does not raise readers' hopes.

- Sometimes the direct approach is best, especially if ethical issues are involved.

Setting Up the Negative News

For each case, you will have thought through the facts involved and decided that you will have to say "no" or present some other kind of negative news. You then have to figure out how you will present your reasons in such a way that your reader will accept

- Follow the buffer with an explanatory strategy before presenting the negative news.

the news as positively as possible. Your strategy might be to explain the fairness of a certain action. It might be to present facts that clearly make the decision necessary. Or you might cite the expert opinion of authorities whom both you and your reader respect. It might even be possible to show that your reasons for the negative decision actually will benefit the reader in the long run.

Whatever explanatory strategy you have chosen, these reasons should follow your buffer and precede the negative news itself. In other words, the paragraph after the buffer should start explaining the situation in such a way that by the time the negative news comes, the reader is prepared to receive it in the most favorable light possible. Examples of how to accomplish this follow.

Presenting the Bad News Positively

● Refuse as positively as the situation permits.

Next, you present the bad news. If you have developed your reasoning convincingly, this bad news should appear as a logical outcome. And you should present it as positively as the situation will permit. In doing so, you must make certain that the negative message is clear—that your positive approach has not given the wrong impression.

● Avoid second person to reduce the negative impact.

One useful technique is to present your reasoning in first and third person, avoiding second person. To illustrate, in a message refusing a request for a refund on a returned product, one could write these negative words: "Since you have broken the seal, state law prohibits us from returning the product to stock." Or one could write these more positive words emphasizing first and third person: "State law prohibits us from returning to stock all products with broken seals."

● Link negative news to a reader benefit to lessen the sting.

It is sometimes possible to take the sting out of negative news by linking it to a reader benefit. For example, if you preface a company policy with "in the interest of fairness" or "for the safety of our guests," you are indicating that all of your patrons, including the reader, get an important benefit from your policy.

● Be certain that you are honest and clear.

Your efforts to present this part of the message positively should employ the positive word emphasis described in Chapter 4. In using positive words, however, you must make certain your words truthfully and accurately convey your message. Your goal is to present the facts in a positive way, not to confuse or mislead.

Offering an Alternative Solution

For almost any negative-news situation that you can think of, there is something you can do to help the reader with his or her problem.

● Help solve the reader's problem.

● Show concern to maintain goodwill.

If someone seeks to hold an event on your company grounds and you must say no, you may be able to suggest other sites. If someone wants information that you cannot give, you might know of another way that he or she could get similar information. If you cannot volunteer your time and services, perhaps you know someone who might, or perhaps you could invite the reader to make the request again at a later, better time. If you have to announce a cutback on an employee benefit, you might be able to suggest ways that employees can supplement this benefit on their own. Taking the time to help the reader in this way is a sincere show of concern for the reader's situation. For this reason, it is one of your most powerful strategies for maintaining goodwill.

Ending on a Positive Note

● End with specially adapted goodwill.

Since even a skillfully handled bad-news message can be disappointing to the reader, you should end the message on a forward-looking note. Your goal here is to shift the reader's thoughts to happier things—perhaps what you would say if you were in face-to-face conversation with the person. Preferably your comments should fit the one case, and they should not recall the negative message. They should make clear that you value your relationship with the reader and still regard it as a positive one.

Following are adaptations of this general plan to four of the more common negative business message situations. From these applications you should be able to see how to adapt this general plan to almost any other situation requiring you to convey bad news.

INTRODUCTORY SITUATION

Refused Requests

As in Chapter 6, assume the role of assistant to the Pinnacle vice president. Today your boss assigned you the task of responding to a request from the local chapter of the National Association of Peace Officers. This worthy organization has asked Pinnacle to contribute to a scholarship fund for certain needy children.

The request is persuasive. It points out that the scholarship fund is terribly short. As a result, the association is not able to take care of all the needy children. Many of them are the children of officers who were killed in the line of duty. You have been moved by the persuasion, and you would like to comply, but you cannot.

You cannot contribute now because Pinnacle policy does not permit it. Even though you do not like the effects of the policy in this case, you think the policy is good. Each year Pinnacle earmarks a fixed amount—all it can afford—for contributions. Then it donates this amount to the causes that a committee of its executives considers the most worthy. Unfortunately, all the money earmarked for this year has already been given away. You will have to say no to the request, at least for now. You can offer to consider the association's cause next year.

Your response must report the bad news, though it can hold out hope for the future. Because you like the association and because you want it to like Pinnacle, you will try to handle the situation delicately. The task will require your best strategy and your best writing skills.

The refusal of a request is definitely bad news. Your reader has asked for something, and you must say no. Your primary goal, of course, is to present this bad news. You could do this easily with a direct refusal. But as a courteous and caring businessperson, you have the secondary goal of maintaining goodwill. To achieve this second goal, you must convince your reader that the refusal is fair and reasonable.

- Refusing a request involves both saying no and maintaining goodwill.

Developing the Strategy

Finding a fair and reasonable explanation involves carefully thinking through the facts of the situation. First, consider why you are refusing. Then, assuming that your reasons are just, try to find the best way of explaining them to your reader. In doing this, you might well place yourself in your reader's shoes. Try to imagine how the explanation will be received. What comes out of this thinking is the strategy you should use in your message.

- Think through the situation, looking for a good explanation.

One often-used explanation is that company policy forbids compliance. This explanation may work but only if the company policy is defensible and clearly explained. Often you must refuse simply because the facts of the case justify a refusal—that is, you are right and the reader is wrong. In such cases, your best course is to review the facts, taking care not to accuse or insult and to appeal to the reader's sense of fair play. There are other explanations, of course. You select the one that best fits your situation.

Setting Up the Explanation in the Opening

Having determined the explanation, you begin the message with words that set up discussing it. For example, take the case described at the beginning of this discussion—refusing an association's request for a donation. The following opening meets this case's requirements well:

- Begin with words that set up the explanation.

> Your organization is doing a commendable job of educating needy children. Like many other worthy efforts, it well deserves the support of our community.

This beginning, on-subject comment clearly marks the message as a response to the inquiry. It implies neither a yes nor a no answer. The second statement sets up the explanation, which will point out that the company has already given its allotted donation money to other worthy organizations. Also, it puts the reader in an agreeable or open frame of mind—ready to accept the explanation that follows.

Presenting the Explanation Convincingly

- Then present your explanation.

As with the general plan, you next present your reasoning. To do this you use your best persuasion techniques: positive wording, proper emphasis, convincing logic, and supporting detail. In general, you use all your presentation skills in your effort to convince your reader.

Handling the Refusal Positively

- The refusal should flow logically from the reasoning. Do not emphasize it.

Your handling of the refusal follows logically from your reasoning. If you have built the groundwork of explanation and fact convincingly, the refusal comes as a logical conclusion and as no surprise. If you have done your job well, your reader may even support the refusal. Even so, because the refusal is the most negative part of your message, you should not give it too much emphasis. You should state it quickly, clearly, and positively. You should keep it away from positions of emphasis, such as paragraph endings.

- State the refusal quickly.

To state the refusal quickly, use as few words as possible. Laboring over the refusal for three or four sentences when a single clause would do gives it too much emphasis.

- If you imply the refusal, be sure it's still clear.

You might even be able to make the message clear without stating the negative news explicitly. For example, if you are refusing a community member's request to use your company's retreat facility for a fundraiser, you will convey *no* clearly if you say that you must restrict the use of the facility to employees only and then go on to offer

Telling people news they don't want to hear requires your most careful communication effort.

alternative locations. You must be sure, though, that your message leaves no doubt about your answer. Being unclear the first time will leave you in the position of writing an even more difficult, more negative message.

To state the refusal positively, you should study carefully the effects of your words. Such harsh words as *I refuse, will not*, and *cannot* stand out. So do such time-worn apologies as "I deeply regret to inform you . . ." and "I am sorry to say. . . ." You can usually phrase your refusal in terms of a positive statement of policy. For example, instead of writing "your insurance does not cover damage to buildings not connected to the house," write "your insurance covers damage to the house only." Or instead of writing "We must refuse," a wholesaler could deny a discount by writing "We can grant discounts only when. . . ." In some cases, your job may be to educate the reader. Not only will this be your explanation for the refusal, but it will also build goodwill.

Using a Compromise When Practical

If the situation justifies a compromise, you can use it in making the refusal positive. More specifically, by saying what you can do (the compromise), you can clearly imply what you cannot do. For example, if you write "The best we can do is to (the compromise) . . . ," you clearly imply that you cannot do what the reader requested. Such statements contain no negative words and usually are as positive as the situation will permit.

Closing with Goodwill

Even a skillfully handled refusal is the most negative part of your message. Because the news is disappointing, it is likely to put your reader in an unhappy frame of mind. That frame of mind works against your goodwill goal. To leave your reader with a feeling of goodwill, you must shift his or her thoughts to more pleasant matters.

The best closing subject matter depends on the facts of the case, but it should be positive talk that fits the one situation. For example, if your refusal involves a counterproposal, you could say more about the counterproposal. Or you could make some friendly remark about the subject of the request as long as it does not remind the reader of the bad news. In fact, your closing subject matter could be almost any friendly remark that would be appropriate if you were handling the case face to face. The major requirement is that your ending words have a goodwill effect.

Ruled out are the timeworn, negative apologies. "Again, may I say that I regret that we must refuse" is typical of these. Also ruled out are the equally timeworn appeals for understanding, such as "I sincerely hope that you understand why we must make this decision." Such words sound selfish and emphasize the bad news.

Fitting the General Plan to Refused Requests

Adapting the preceding analysis to the general plan, we arrive at the following outline for the refused request:

- Begin with words that indicate a response to the request, are neutral about the answer, and set up the strategy.
- Present your justification or explanation, using positive language and you-viewpoint.
- Refuse clearly and positively.
- Include a counterproposal or compromise when appropriate.
- End with an adapted goodwill comment.

Contrasting Refusals

The advantage of the indirect order in refusal messages is illustrated by the following contrasting examples. Both refuse clearly. But only the one that uses the indirect order is likely to gain the reader's goodwill.

Harshness in the Direct Refusal. The first example states the bad news right away. This blunt treatment puts the reader in an unreceptive frame of mind. The result is that the reader is less likely to accept the explanation that follows. The explanation is clear, but note the unnecessary use of negative words (*exhausted, regret, cannot consider*). Note also how the closing words leave the reader with a strong reminder of the bad news.

This bad email is harsh because of its directness and negative language.

Subject: Your request for a donation

Ms. Cangelosi:

We regret to inform you that we cannot grant your request for a donation to the association's scholarship fund.

So many requests for contributions are made of us that we have found it necessary to budget a definite amount each year for this purpose. Our budgeted funds for this year have been exhausted, so we simply cannot consider additional requests. However, we will be able to consider your request next year.

We deeply regret our inability to help you now and trust that you understand our position.

Mark Stephens

Tact and Courtesy in an Indirect Refusal. The second example skillfully handles the negative message. Its opening words arc on subject and neutral. They set up the explanation that follows. The clear and logical explanation ties in with the opening. Using no negative words, the explanation leads smoothly to the refusal. Note that the refusal also is handled without negative words and yet is clear. The friendly close fits the one case.

This email using the indirect approach is better.

Subject: Your scholarship fund request

Ms. Cangelosi:

Your efforts to build the scholarship fund for the association's needy children are commendable. We wish you good success in your efforts to further this worthy cause.

We at Pinnacle are always willing to assist worthy causes whenever we can. That is why every January we budget for the year the maximum amount we believe we are able to contribute to such causes. Then we distribute that amount among the various deserving groups as far as it will go. Since our budgeted contributions for this year have already been made, we are placing your organization on our list for consideration next year.

We wish you success in your efforts to improve the lives of the children in our city.

Mark Stephens

Claims

Play the role of Jeff Sutton, owner and president of Sutton Creative Services. You've just received a bill from Regal Banquet Center for the winter-holiday party that your company held there last week. It's for $1,410, which you had agreed to pay for an elegant three-course meal, plus drinks, for your 27 employees.

The food was as good as its reputation, but there were two problems. First, the room for the party was much too warm. You complained to the servers but to no avail. You would have opened windows to correct the problem yourself, but the room you were given did not have any windows (something you weren't happy about either). Second, there was apparently a shortage of servers on the night of your event. Some of your employees had to wait a long time for their food, while those who had their food first either had to start eating before the others or let their food get cold while waiting for all to be served. This ragged timing ruined the dinner, and it also threw off the timing of the program you had planned.

You were embarrassed by these problems. They reflected poorly on you and your efforts to thank your employees for their work. While you understand that unexpected problems can arise, you just don't think you should have to pay the full amount for a subpar experience. You'll need to write a claim message asking for an adjustment to your bill.

When something goes wrong between a business and its customers, usually someone begins an effort to correct the situation. Typically, the offended party calls the matter to the attention of those responsible. This claim can be made in person, by phone, or by written message (email or letter). Our concern here is how to make it in a written message. You would probably choose this more formal medium if you wanted a record of the interchange or if you were not on personal terms with the recipient.

Using Directness versus Indirectness

Some writers organize claim messages directly, arguing that most businesses want to know right away when something has gone wrong. Others argue that blurting out the problem at the beginning puts readers on the defensive. Who is right?

- Some argue for directness in claims; some argue for indirectness.

We believe that the best strategy is usually a mixture of the two approaches. Unlike most other types of negative messages, claim messages should indicate early on that a problem has occurred. Beating around the bush may annoy your readers and make you seem unassertive. But it is risky to make your actual request for an adjustment before you have presented the facts of the case. We thus recommend that you save this part of the message for the last or next-to-last paragraph. As with all messages, however, many variations are possible. You should choose your solution based upon the parties involved and the events that have occurred.

- We suggest getting directly to the problem but delaying the actual request for an adjustment.

Choosing the Right Tone

Your goal in a claim message is to convince your recipient that you deserve some kind of compensation or remedy for a situation that has occurred. But even if you are completely in the right, you will not advance your cause with accusatory, one-sided language. When writing this kind of message, project an image of yourself as a reasonable person. Just as importantly, project an image of the reader as a reasonable person. Give him or her a chance to show that, if presented with the facts, he or she will do the right thing. Do not give in to the temptation to blame or whine. Keep your tone as objective as you can while also making sure that the reader understands the problems caused by the situation. Focus as much as possible on facts, not feelings.

- Focus as much as possible on facts, not feelings.

Leading into the Problem in the Beginning

A claim message needs to identify the transactions involved. This you can do early in the message as a part of the beginning. One way is to put the identification in the subject head in an email message or in the subject line of a letter, as in this example:

Subject: Damaged condition of fire extinguishers on arrival, your invoice C13144

Another way is just to describe the situation in the opening paragraph, as in this example:

Today we received via FedEx Ground the fire extinguishers we ordered on 5 May 2009 (invoice # C13144). Seven of the 35 extinguishers arrived in damaged condition.

- State the problem early—but without triggering defensive reactions.

Whether you use a subject line and your first paragraph or the first paragraph alone to announce the problem, choose your words with care. Such negatively charged words as *complaint* or *disappointment* can put your readers on the defensive before you've even had a chance to make your case.

Describing the Problem Clearly

- Include concrete evidence to support your claim.

In the body of your message, explain what happened. The words describing the problem should be courteous yet firm. And they should cover the problem completely, giving enough information to permit the reader to judge the matter. If there were

Since unanticipated problems routinely occur in business, writing a clear, complete, and fair-minded claim will usually solve them.

consequences of what happened, you may benefit your case by naming them. This beginning sentence illustrates the point:

> The Model H freezer (Serial No. 713129) that we bought from you September 17 suddenly quit working. As a result, $517 of frozen foods were ruined.

Notice that this example uses the passive voice. It says ". . . were ruined" rather than "your freezer ruined. . . ." This sentence type keeps the second person (*you, your*) out of the most negative part of the message, helping you avoid accusations.

Requesting the Correction

The facts you present should prove your claim. So your next step is to follow logically with making the claim. How you handle the claim, however, is a matter for you to decide. You have two choices: You can state what you want (money back, replacement), or you can leave the decision to the reader. You decide which, based on the situation.

● Request what you think is fair—or leave it to your reader to decide.

Overcoming Negativeness with a Fair-Minded Close

Your final friendly words should leave no doubt that you are trying to maintain a positive relationship. For added strength, you could express appreciation for what you seek. This suggestion does not support use of the timeworn "Thanking you in advance." Instead, say something like "I would be grateful if you could get the new merchandise to me in time for my Friday sale." Whatever final words you choose, they should clearly show that yours is a firm yet cordial and fair request.

● Conclude with an even-tempered ending.

Outlining the Claim Message

Summarizing the preceding points, we arrive at this outline for the claim message:

- Identify the situation (invoice number, product information, etc.) and lead into the problem.
- Present enough of the facts to permit a decision.
- Seek corrective action.
- End positively—friendly but firm.

Contrasting Examples of Claim Messages

The following two messages show contrasting ways of handling Jeff Sutton's problem with the Regal Banquet Center. The first is blunt and harsh. The second is courteous, yet clear and firm.

A Blunt and Harsh Message. From the very beginning, the first message—a letter that the reader is returning along with his reduced payment—is insulting. "To whom it may concern" shows that the writer does not regard the reader as a person. The opening paragraph is a further affront, blurting out the writer's stance in angry language. The middle of the message continues in this negative vein, accusing the reader with *you* and *your* and using emotional language. The negative writing continues into the close, leaving a bad final impression. Such wording is more likely to produce resistance than acceptance.

This blunt and accusing letter is unlikely to lead to a cooperative reply or further business with the reader.

Subject: Bill Adjustment

To whom it may concern:

I just received a bill for $1,410 for the winter party that I held for my employees at the Regal Banquet Center. I absolutely refuse to pay this amount for the subpar job you did of hosting this event.

First, you put us in an unpleasant room with no windows even though we had made our reservations weeks in advance. The room was also much too warm. I asked your staff to adjust the temperature, but apparently they never did. Since the room didn't have any windows, we just had to sit there and swelter in our dress clothes. As if this weren't bad enough, it took the servers so long to bring all our food out that some people had finished eating before others were even served. This made a complete mess of the nice dinner and the scheduled program.

I had heard good things about your center but now regret that I chose it for this important company event. The uncomfortable and chaotic experience reflected poorly on me and on my appreciation for my employees. Enclosed is my payment for $1,000, which I feel is more than fair.

Sincerely,

Jeff Sutton, Owner and President

Sutton Creative Services

A Firm Yet Courteous Message. The second message follows the plan suggested in preceding paragraphs. A subject line quickly identifies the situation. The claim message begins with a lead-in to the problem. Next, in a tone that shows firmness without anger, it tells what went wrong. Then it requests a specific remedy. The ending uses subtle persuasion by implying confidence in the reader. The words used here leave no doubt about the writer's interest in a continued relationship.

This more tactful but honest email invites the reader to do what is fair and retains goodwill.

Subject: Invoice #3712 (for Sutton Party on 12/12/10)

Dear Ms. Sanchez,

I held my company's annual holiday party at your facility on the evening of December 12. I have now received the invoice for the event, in the amount of $1,410. While the food was exceptional, I am sorry to say that we did not have a good experience.

The room we were given for the event was Salon C. As you know, the room has no windows and is not one of your more attractive rooms. Because we had made our reservation two months in advance, I had hoped for a more pleasant environment for this special event. The location also had the drawback of making the temperature hard to control. The servers were sympathetic but were apparently unable to keep the room from getting too warm. This made for an uncomfortable evening for my 27 employees.

It also appeared that not enough servers had been scheduled for our party. The fare was elegant, but it was served with such ragged timing that some guests had finished eating before others had even started. We also had to start the after-dinner program in the middle of the meal.

Overall, the event was not a very impressive "thank-you" to my hard-working employees. In light of these circumstances, I am requesting a revised invoice of $1,000. I believe this is a fair amount for an experience that I am sure did not represent the Regal's typical level of customer service.

Sincerely yours,

Jeff Sutton, President and Owner

Sutton Creative Services

Refused Request Message (Turning Down a Speaking Invitation). This example shows good strategy in turning down a request to speak at a convention.

On-subject beginning—compliment gains reader's favor

Offer of alternative—shows concern, builds goodwill

Goodwill close—adapted to this one case

Set-up for explanation

Reasonable, convincing explanation

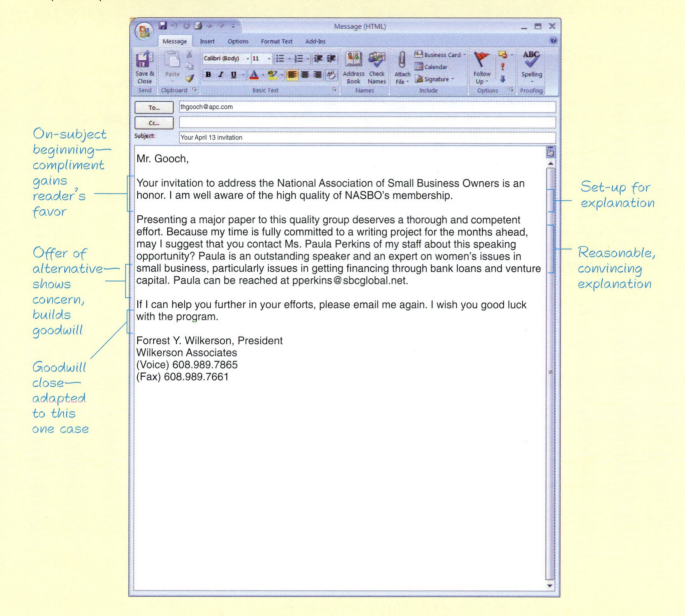

To... thgooch@apc.com
Cc...
Subject: Your April 13 invitation

Mr. Gooch,

Your invitation to address the National Association of Small Business Owners is an honor. I am well aware of the high quality of NASBO's membership.

Presenting a major paper to this quality group deserves a thorough and competent effort. Because my time is fully committed to a writing project for the months ahead, may I suggest that you contact Ms. Paula Perkins of my staff about this speaking opportunity? Paula is an outstanding speaker and an expert on women's issues in small business, particularly issues in getting financing through bank loans and venture capital. Paula can be reached at pperkins@sbcglobal.net.

If I can help you further in your efforts, please email me again. I wish you good luck with the program.

Forrest Y. Wilkerson, President
Wilkerson Associates
(Voice) 608.989.7865
(Fax) 608.989.7661

ADJUSTMENT REFUSALS

INTRODUCTORY SITUATION

Adjustment Refusals

Sometimes your job at Pinnacle involves handling a complaint. Today you have to do that, for the morning email has brought a strong claim for adjustment on an order for Pinnacle's Do-Craft fabrics. The claim writer, Ms. Arlene Sanderson, explains that a Do-Craft fabric her upholstering company used on some outdoor furniture has faded badly in less than 10 months. She even includes photographs of the fabric to prove her point. She contends that the product is defective, and she wants her money back—all $2,517 of it.

Inspection of the photographs reveals that the fabric has been subjected to strong sunlight for long periods. Do-Craft fabrics are for inside use only. Both the Pinnacle brochures on the product and the catalog description stress this point. In fact, you have difficulty understanding how Ms. Sanderson missed it when she ordered from the catalog. Anyway, as you see it, Pinnacle is not responsible and should not refund the money. At the same time, it wants to keep Ms. Sanderson as a repeat customer. Now you must write the message that will do just that. The following discussion tells you how.

Adjustment refusals are a special type of refused request. Your reader has made a claim asking for a remedy. Usually you grant claims. Most are legitimate, and you want to correct any error for which you are responsible. But such is not the case here. The facts require that you say no.

Determining the Strategy

The primary difference between this and other refusal messages is that in these situations, as we are defining them, your company will probably have clear, reasonable guidelines for what should and should not be regarded as legitimate requests for adjustment. You will, therefore, not have to spend much time figuring out why you cannot grant the reader's request. You will have good reasons to refuse. The challenge will be to do so while still making possible an ongoing, positive relationship with the reader.

Setting Up Your Reasoning

- Begin with words that set up your reasoning.

- A point of common agreement is one good possibility.

With your strategy in mind, you begin with words that set it up. Since this message is a response to one the reader has sent, you also acknowledge this message. You can do this by a date reference early in the message. Or you can do it with words that clearly show you are writing about the specific situation.

One good way of setting up your strategy is to begin on a point of common agreement and then to explain how the case at hand is an exception. To illustrate, a case involving a claim for adjustment for failure of an air conditioner to perform properly might begin thus:

You are correct in believing that an 18,000 BTU Whirlpool window unit should cool the ordinary three-room apartment.

The explanation that follows this sentence will show that the apartment in question is not an ordinary apartment.

Email Templates Allow Writers to Reuse and Customize Messages

Templates allow writers to reuse frequently repeated text. Whether your message is a monthly status report for your boss or a refusal message to people wanting to reserve a room in your fully booked hotel, you can create a template that allows you to reuse and customize the basic message. In Outlook 2007, it's an easy task. After you've written the message the first time, save it as an Outlook template. The next time you need it, you can bring it up from the Tools menu by clicking Forms and selecting Choose Form. Then select User Templates to bring up your list of templates and click on one. When the message opens, you can enter text in any of the placeholders you've created for variable information, and you can modify any generic information to customize the message to fit the particular use.

Spending a little extra time creating and polishing your original message will help ensure that you are only reusing well-written messages.

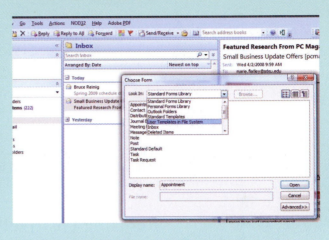

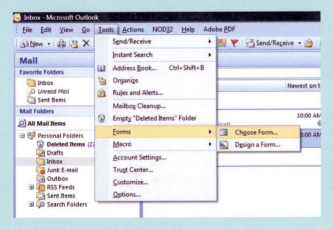

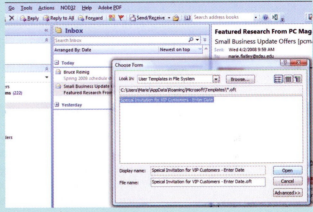

Another strategy is to build the case that the claim for adjustment goes beyond what can reasonably be expected. A beginning such as this one sets it up:

> Assisting families to enjoy beautifully decorated homes at budget prices is one of our most satisfying goals. We do all we reasonably can to reach it.

The explanation that follows this sentence will show that the requested adjustment goes beyond what can be reasonably expected.

- Another is to show that the claim goes beyond what is reasonable.

Making Your Case

In presenting your reasons for refusal, explain your company's relevant policy or practice. Without accusing the reader, call attention to facts that bear on the case—for example, that the item in question has been submerged in water, that the printed material

- Explain your refusal by associating the facts of the case with a policy or practice.

*"I don't know why you're upset
with us. Didn't we provide
you with excellent excuses?"*

warned against certain uses, or that the warranty has expired. Putting together the policy and the facts should lead logically to the conclusion that the adjustment cannot be granted.

Refusing Positively and Closing Courteously

● Refuse positively and end with goodwill.

As in other refusal messages, your refusal derives from your explanation. It is the logical result. You word it clearly, and you make it as positive as the circumstances permit. For example, this one is clear, and it contains no negative words:

> For these reasons, we can pay only when our employees pack the goods.

If a compromise is in order, you might present it in positive language like this:

> In view of these facts, the best we can do is repair the equipment at cost.

As in all bad-news messages, you should end this one with some appropriate, positive comment. You could reinforce the message that you care about the reader's business or the quality of your products. In cases where it would not seem selfish, you could write about new products or services that the reader might be interested in. Neither negative apologies nor words that recall the problem are appropriate here.

Adapting the General Plan

When we apply these special considerations to the general plan, we come up with the following specific plan for adjustment refusals:

* Begin with words that are on subject, are neutral about the decision, and set up your strategy.
* Present the strategy that explains or justifies, being factual and positive.
* Refuse clearly and positively, perhaps including a counterproposal.
* End with off-subject, positive, forward-looking, friendly words.

Contrasting Adjustment Refusal Messages

Bad and good treatment of Pinnacle's refusal to refund the money for the faded fabric are illustrated by the following two messages. The bad one, which is blunt and insulting, destroys goodwill. The good one, which uses the techniques described in the preceding paragraphs, stands a fair chance of keeping goodwill.

Bluntness in a Direct Refusal. The bad email begins bluntly with a direct statement of the refusal. The language is negative (*regret, must reject, claim, refuse, damage, inconvenience*). The explanation is equally blunt. In addition, it is insulting ("It is difficult to understand how you failed . . ."). It uses little tact, little you-viewpoint. Even the close is negative, for it recalls the bad news.

Subject: Your May 3 claim for damages

Ms. Sanderson,

I regret to report that we must reject your request for money back on the faded Do-Craft fabric.

We must refuse because Do-Craft fabrics are not made for outside use. It is difficult for me to understand how you failed to notice this limitation. It was clearly stated in the catalog from which you ordered. It was even stamped on the back of every yard of fabric. Since we have been more than reasonable in trying to inform you, we cannot possibly be responsible.

We trust that you will understand our position. We regret very much having to deny your request.

Marilyn Cox, Customer Relations

The bad email shows little concern for the reader's feelings.

Tact and Indirect Order in a Courteous Refusal. The good message begins with friendly talk on a point of agreement that also sets up the explanation. Without accusations, anger, or negative words, it reviews the facts of the case, which free the company of blame. The refusal is clear, even though it is made by implication rather than by direct words. It is skillfully handled. It uses no negatives, and it does not receive undue emphasis. The close shifts to helpful suggestions that fit the one case—suggestions that may actually result in a future sale. Friendliness and resale are evident throughout the message, but especially in the close.

Subject: Your May 3 message about Do-Craft fabric

Ms. Sanderson,

Certainly, you have a right to expect the best possible service from Do-Craft fabrics. Every Do-Craft product is the result of years of experimentation. And we manufacture each yard under the most careful controls. We are determined that our products will do for you what we say they will do.

Because we do want our fabrics to please, we carefully inspected the photos of Do-Craft Fabric 103 you sent us. It is apparent that each sample has been subjected to long periods in extreme sunlight. Since we know that Do-Craft fabrics cannot withstand exposure to sunlight, we clearly state this in all our advertising, in the catalog from which you ordered, and in a stamped reminder on the back of every yard of the fabric. Under the circumstances, all we can do concerning your request is suggest that you change to one of our outdoor fabrics. As you can see from our catalog, all of the fabrics in the 200 series are recommended for outdoor use.

You may also be interested in the new Duck Back cotton fabrics listed in our 500 series. These plastic-coated cotton fabrics are economical, and they resist sun and rain remarkably well. If we can help you further in your selection, please contact us at service@pinnacle.com.

Marilyn Cox, Consumer Relations

This better email is indirect, tactful, and helpful.

Adjustment Refusal Letter (Refusing a Refund for a Woman's Dress). An out-of-town customer bought an expensive dress from the writer and mailed it back three weeks later, asking for a refund. The customer explained that the dress was not a good fit and that she really did not like it anymore. But perspiration stains on the dress proved that she had worn it. This letter skillfully presents the refusal.

103 BREAKER RD. HOUSTON, TX 77015 713-454-6778 Fax: 713-454-6771

February 19, 2010

On-subject opening—neutral point from claim letter

Ms. Cherie Ranney
117 Kyle Avenue E
College Station, TX 77840-2415

Dear Ms. Ranney:

We understand your concern about the exclusive St. John's dress you returned February 15. As always, we are willing to do as much as we reasonably can to make things right.

Set-up for explanation

Review of facts— supports writer's position

What we can do in each instance is determined by the circumstances. With returned clothing, we generally give refunds. Of course, to meet our obligations to our customers for quality merchandise, all returned clothing must be unquestionably new. As you know, our customers expect only the best from us, and we insist that they get it. Thus, because the perspiration stains on your dress would prevent its resale, we must consider the sale final. We are returning the dress to you. With the proper alterations, it can be an elegant addition to your wardrobe.

Good restraint—no accusations, no anger

Positive language in refusal

Emphasis on what can be done—helps restore goodwill

Please visit us again when you are in the Houston area. It would be our pleasure to serve you.

Friendly goodwill close

Sincerely,

Marie O. Mitchell

Marie O. Mitchell
President

dm

NEGATIVE ANNOUNCEMENTS

Negative Announcements

In your role as assistant to Pinnacle's vice president for administration, you have been given the difficult assignment of writing a bad-news message for your boss. She has just returned from a meeting of the company's top executives in which the decision was made to deduct 25 percent of the employees' medical insurance premiums from their paychecks. Until now, Pinnacle has paid it all. But the rising cost of health coverage is forcing the company to cut back on these benefits, especially since Pinnacle's profits have declined for the past several quarters. Something has to give if Pinnacle is to remain competitive while also avoiding lay-offs. The administrators decided on a number of cost-cutting measures including this reduction in Pinnacle's payment for medical insurance. The message you will write to Pinnacle employees is a negative announcement.

Occasionally, businesses must announce bad news to their customers or employees. For example, a company might need to announce that prices are going up, that a service or product line is being discontinued, or that a branch of the business is closing. Or a company might need to tell its employees that the company is in some kind of trouble, that people will need to be laid off, or, as in the example above, that employee benefits must be reduced. Such announcements generally follow the instructions previously given in this chapter.

● Sometimes negative announcements are necessary.

When making a negative announcement, remember that an indirect, tactful approach is usually better than a blunt "loud" approach.

Determining the Strategy

● First decide whether to use direct or indirect organization.

When faced with the problem of making a negative announcement, your first step should be to determine your overall strategy. Will you use direct or indirect organization?

● Indirect order usually is better.

In most cases the indirect (buffer) arrangement will be better. This route is especially recommended when it is reasonable to expect that the readers would be surprised, particularly disappointed, or even angered by a direct presentation. When planning an indirect announcement, you will need to think about what kind of buffer opening to use, what kind of explanation to give, how to word the news itself, and how to leave your readers feeling that you have considered their interests.

Setting Up the Bad News

● Select a strategy that prepares the reader to accept the bad news.

As with the preceding negative message types, you should plan your indirect (buffer) beginning carefully. You should think through the situation and select a strategy that will set up or begin the explanation that justifies the announcement. Perhaps you will begin by presenting justifying information. Or maybe you will start with complimentary or cordial talk focusing on the good relationship that you and your readers have developed. Whatever you choose should be what will be most likely to prepare your reader to accept the coming bad news.

Positively Presenting the Bad News

● The bad news should follow logically from your opening.

In most cases, the opening paragraph will enable you to continue with background reasons or explanations in the next paragraph, before you present the negative news. Such explaining will help you put the negative news in the middle of the paragraph rather than at the beginning where it would be emphasized.

● Word it positively, and include all necessary details.

As in other negative situations, you should use positive words and avoid unnecessary negative comments when presenting the news itself. Since this is an announcement, however, you must make certain that you cover all the factual details involved. People may not be expecting this news. They will, therefore, want to know the whys and whats of the situation. And if you want them to believe that you have done all you can to prevent the negative situation, you will need to provide evidence that this is true. If there are actions the readers must take, these should be covered clearly as well. All questions that may come to the readers' minds should be anticipated and covered.

Focusing on Next Steps or Remaining Benefits

● Help people solve their problem and focus on any positive aspects.

In many cases negative news will mean that things have changed. Customers may no longer be able to get a product that they have relied upon, or employees may have to find a way to pay for something that they have been getting for free. For this reason, a skillful handling of a negative announcement will often need to include an effort to help people solve the problem that your news just created for them. In situations where you have no further help to offer—for example, when announcing certain price increases—you can still help people feel better about your news by calling attention to the benefits that they will continue to enjoy. You can focus on the good things that have not changed and perhaps even look ahead to something positive or exciting on the horizon.

Closing on a Positive or Encouraging Note

● Close with goodwill.

The ending words should cement your effort to cover the matter positively. They can be whatever is appropriate for this one situation—a positive look forward, a sincere expression of gratitude, or an affirmation of your positive relationship with your readers.

Reviewing the Plan

Applying the preceding instructions to the general plan, we arrive at this specific plan for negative announcements written in indirect order:

• Start with a buffer that begins or sets up justification for the bad news.

• Present the justification material.

Negative Announcement (A Message Reporting a Price Increase). Here a TV cable company informs a customer of a rate increase. The cordial opening makes friendly contact that leads to an explanation of the action. Then the news is presented clearly yet positively. The goodwill close continues the cordiality established earlier in the message.

Heartland Cable TV, Inc.
37411 Jester Road, Kansas City, MO 64106

Ms. Ellen Butler
396 Scott Street
Kansas City, MO 64109
Ph: 815.555.1212
Fax: 815.555.1213
www.heartlandcabletv.com

March 14, 2010

Dear Ms. Butler:

Cordial opening contact

Your cable company has been working extra hard to provide you with the highest-quality TV entertainment. We think we have succeeded. The quantity of programming as well as its quality has continued to improve over the past year.

Explanation sets up bad news

Bad news presented in terms of reader interests

Positive information ends paragraph

We have also been working hard to keep the cost of these services as low as possible and continue to maintain high standards. Last year we were able to do this and pass along savings of up to 20 percent on two of our premium services. As you may have heard in the news, our costs continue to increase. Thus, in order to continue to maintain our goals of high quality at the lowest possible cost, we are announcing a price adjustment effective April 1. The monthly cost of your basic package of 59 stations will increase $1.50 (from $37.99 to $39.49) The cost of all premium services (HBO, Cinemax, Encore, Starz, and Showtime) will remain the same.

Friendly forward look follows bad news

In our continuing efforts to improve your total entertainment value, we are planning a number of exciting new projects. We will announce them before the year's end.

Cordial words end the message

We appreciate your business and assure you that we will continue to bring you the very best in service and entertainment.

Sincerely,

Carlos H. Rodriguez

Carlos H. Rodriguez
President

Balance, Not "Spin," in Negative Announcements

Like all human resources professionals, Joan McCarthy, Director of Human Resources Communication for Comcast Cable, sometimes has to deliver negative news to employees, whether it's about healthcare coverage, organizational change, or other issues. Her advice? "Balance, not spin, is the key. Frequent, candid communication that balances the good with the bad will go much further toward restoring and maintaining employee trust than the most creative 'spin.'"

Sometimes McCarthy will state negative news directly, while other times she takes a more gradual approach. Whichever pattern you use, "it's important to communicate openly and honestly," she advises. But you should also balance out the negative by "reinforcing the positive, putting the news in perspective, and showing what the organization is doing to help." In these ways you can "communicate bad news in a way that preserves your company's credibility and keeps employee trust and morale intact."

- Give the bad news positively but clearly.
- Help solve the problem that the news may have created for the reader.
- End with appropriate goodwill talk.

Contrasting Negative Announcements

Good and bad techniques in negative announcements are shown in the following two messages. The bad one is direct, which in some circumstances may be acceptable but clearly is not in this case. The good one follows the pattern just discussed.

Directness Here Alarms the Readers. This bad example clearly upsets the readers with its abrupt announcement in the beginning. The readers aren't prepared to receive the negative message. They probably don't understand the reasons behind the negative news. The explanation comes later, but the readers are not likely to be in a receptive mood when they see it. The message ends with a repetition of the bad news.

Directness here sends a negative message.

To our employees:

Pinnacle management sincerely regrets that effective February 1 you must begin contributing 25 percent of the cost of your medical insurance. As you know, in the past the company has paid the full amount.

This decision is primarily the result of the rising costs of health insurance, but Pinnacle's profits also have declined the last several quarters. Given this tight financial picture, we needed to find ways to reduce expenses.

We trust that you will understand why we must ask for your help with cutting costs to the company.

Sincerely,

Convincing Explanation Begins a Courteous Message. The better example follows the recommended indirect pattern. Its opening words begin the task of convincing the readers of the appropriateness of the action to be taken. After more convincing explanation, the announcement flows logically. Perhaps it will not be received positively by all recipients, but it is a reasonable deduction from the facts presented. After the announcement comes an offer of assistance to help readers deal with their new situation. The last paragraph reminds readers of remaining benefits and reassures them that management understands their interests. It ends on an appreciative, goodwill note.

To All Employees:

Companies all across the United States, no matter how large or small, are struggling to keep up with the rising cost of health care. Legislators, health care providers, and businesspeople everywhere are struggling to find a solution to the skyrocketing cost of health insurance.

We are feeling this situation here in our own company. The premiums that we pay to cover our health benefits have increased by 34 percent over the last two years, and they now represent a huge percentage of our expenditures. Meanwhile, as you know, our sales have been lower than usual for the past several quarters.

For the short term, it is imperative that we find a way to cut overall costs. Your management has considered many options and rejected such measures as cutting salaries and reducing personnel. Of the solutions that will be implemented, the only change that affects you directly concerns your medical insurance. On **March 1** we will begin deducting 25 percent of the cost of the premium. The other savings measures will be at the corporate level.

Jim Taylor in the Personnel Office will soon be announcing an informational meeting about your insurance options. Switching to spousal coverage, choosing a less expensive plan with lighter deductibles, or setting up a flexible spending account may be right for you. You can also see Jim after the meeting to arrange a personal consultation. He is well versed in the many solutions available and can give you expert advice for your situation.

Our health care benefits are some of the best in our city and in our industry, and those who continue with the current plan will not see any change in their medical coverage or their co-pays. Your management regards a strong benefits program as critical to the company's success, and we will do all we can to maintain these benefits while keeping your company financially viable. We appreciate your cooperation and understanding.

Sincerely,

This indirect example follows the bad-news pattern.

Using Directness in Some Cases

In some cases it is likely that the reader will react favorably to a direct presentation of the bad news. If, for example, the negative news is expected (as when the news media have already revealed it), its impact may be viewed as negligible. There is also a good case for directness when the company's announcement will contain a remedy or

• Directness is appropriate when the news is expected or will have little negative impact,

Dear Ms. Cato:

As a long-time customer, you will be interested in knowing that we are discontinuing our Preferred Customer program so that we may offer several new promotions.

Effective January 1 we will take your accumulated points and convert them to a savings coupon worth as much as or more than your points total. Your new points total is on the coupon enclosed with this letter. You may apply this coupon in these ways:

• When shopping in our stores, present your coupon at the register.
• When shopping from our catalogs, give the coupon number to the telephone service agent, enclose your coupon with your mail order, or enter it with your web order.

In all these cases we will deduct your coupon value from your purchase total. If you have any questions, please call us at 1-800-343-4111.

We thank you very much for your loyalty. You'll soon hear about exciting new opportunities to shop and save with us.

Sincerely,

• as in this example.

announce new benefits that are designed to offset the effects of the bad news. As in all announcements with some negative element, this part must be handled in good positive language. Also, the message should end on a goodwill note. The preceding example of a store's announcement about discontinuing a customer reward program illustrates this situation.

OTHER INDIRECT MESSAGES

- Adapt the techniques of this chapter to other situations where indirectness seems in order.

The types of indirect messages covered in the preceding pages are the most common ones. There are other indirect types, such as persuasive messages and some job applications. They are covered in the following chapters. You should be able to handle all the other indirect types that you encounter by adapting the techniques explained and illustrated in these chapters.

SUMMARY BY LEARNING OBJECTIVES

1 Determine which situations require using the indirect order for the most effective response.

1. When the main point of your message is bad news, use the indirect order.
   - But exceptions exist, as when you believe that the news will be received routinely.
   - Make exceptions also when you think the reader will appreciate directness.

2 Write indirect-order messages following the general plan.

2. In general, bad-news messages follow this general plan.
   - Begin with a buffer that sets up the strategy.
   - Develop the strategy.
   - Present the bad news as a logical result of the strategy and as positively as possible.
   - Try to offer an alternative solution.
   - End on a positive note.

3 Use tact and courtesy in refusals of requests.

3. The refusal of a request is one bad-news situation that you will probably choose to treat indirectly.
   - In such situations, strive to achieve two main goals:
     — to refuse and
     — to maintain goodwill.
   - Begin by thinking through the problem, looking for a logical explanation (or reasoning).
   - Write an opening that sets up this explanation.
   - Then present your explanation (reasoning), taking care to use convincing and positive language.
   - Refuse clearly yet positively.
   - Use a compromise when practical.
   - Close with appropriate, friendly talk that does not recall the bad news.

4 Compose tactful, yet clear, claim messages.

4. Claim messages are somewhat more direct, but it is still usually best to lead up to the request.
   - Decide how direct you want to be.
   - Plan to write neutrally and reasonably.
   - Lead into the problem with your beginning.
   - Then describe the problem clearly, thoroughly, and tactfully.
   - Either ask for what you seek or invite your reader to decide what is fair.
   - End on a positive, but firm, note that leaves open the possibility for future business.

5. Indirectness is usually best for refusals of adjustments.
   - First, determine your explanation (reasoning) for refusing.
   - Begin with neutral words that set up your reasoning and do not give away the refusal.
   - Then present your reasoning, building your case convincingly.
   - Refuse clearly and positively.
   - Close with appropriate friendly talk that does not recall the refusal.

5 Write adjustment refusals that minimize the negative and overcome bad impressions.

6. Sometimes businesses must announce bad news to their customers or employees.
   - Indirect organization usually is better for these announcements.
   - This means that a convincing explanation precedes the bad news.
   - And positive words are used to cover the bad news.
   - Sometimes directness is appropriate.
   - This is the case when the news is expected or will have little negative impact.
   - Even so, handle the negative with positive wording.

6 Write negative announcements that maintain goodwill.

CRITICAL THINKING QUESTIONS

1 Give examples of times (or situations) when directness is appropriate for responses giving negative (bad-news) information. **[LO1]**

2 Writing in the indirect order usually requires more words than does writing in the direct order. Since conciseness is a virtue in writing, how can the indirect order be justified? **[LO1]**

3 What strategy is best in a message refusing a request when the reasons for the refusal are strictly in the writer's best interests? **[LO3]**

4 "Apologies in refusals are negative because they call attention to what you are refusing. Thus, you should avoid using them." Discuss. **[LO3]**

5 Explain how a claim message can be both direct and indirect. **[LO4]**

6 "If I'm not emotional in my claim messages, the readers won't understand how upset I am." Respond to this statement. **[LO4]**

7 Some business writers explain an adjustment refusal simply by saying that company policy did not permit granting claims in such cases. Is this explanation adequate? Discuss. **[LO5]**

8 Negative announcements usually need to include much more than the announcement. Explain. **[LO6]**

9 Give examples of negative announcements that appropriately are written in the direct order. **[LO6]**

CRITICAL THINKING EXERCISES

1 Point out the shortcomings in the following email message from a sports celebrity declining an invitation to speak at the kickoff meeting for workers in a fund-raising campaign for a charity. **[LO3]**

Subject: Your request for free lecture

Ms. Chung:

As much as I would like to, I must decline your request that I give your membership a free lecture next month. I receive many requests to give free lectures. I grant some of them, but I simply cannot do them all. Unfortunately, yours is one that I must decline.

I regret that I cannot serve you this time. If I can be of further service in the future, please call on me.

Sincerely yours,

2 Criticize the following message refusing the claim for a defective riding lawn mower. The mower was purchased 15 months earlier. The purchaser has had difficulties with it for some time and submitted with the claim a statement from a local repair service verifying the difficulties. The writer's reason for refusing is evident from the email. **[LO5]**

Subject: Your May 12 claim

Mr. Skinner:

Your May 12 claim of defective workmanship in your Model 227 Dandy Klipper riding mower has been reviewed. After considering the information received, I regret to report that we cannot refund the purchase price.

You have had the mower for 15 months, which is well beyond our one-year guarantee. Even though your repair person says that you had problems earlier, he is not one of our authorized repair people. If you will read the warranty you refer to in your letter, you will see that we honor the warranty only when our authorized repair people find defects. I think you will understand why we must follow this procedure.

If you will take the machine to the authorized service center in your area (La Rue Lawn and Garden Center), I am confident they can correct the defect at a reasonable charge.

If I can be of additional service, please contact me.

Sincerely,

3 You work for an online mail-order company, Nonsensicals, that sells such novelty items as t-shirts with clever sayings, unique toys and games, and such household accessories as framed posters and retro table lamps. Most of the employees are young, somewhat quirky, and very Internet savvy. Now consider the following email sent to everyone from the company president: **[LO6]**

Subject: No More Social Networking during Work Hours

It has become obvious to me that people are spending too much time doing social networking and not enough time actually working while on the job. From now on, you must do your networking (whether on MySpace, Facebook, LinkedIn, or any other such network) on breaks or during other personal time. Anyone found using these websites on company time will receive an official reprimand.

Considering the advice in this chapter, what would be the main ways to improve this negative announcement?

PROBLEM-SOLVING CASES

Refused Requests

1 As the HR director at Quality Construction, you couldn't be happier with how your efforts to establish an employee-volunteer program have worked out. Thanks to the employees' donations of their time and expertise through the "Quality Construction Cares" program, the community where you live has been improved and QC has gained a more positive public profile. But sometimes there are still bumps in the road, and today you're dealing with one of them.

Part of the program you set up is a database of company-approved schools, foundations, and other nonprofit organizations for which employees may volunteer. In order to get approved time off work for their contributions, employees must choose one of these organizations. There are over 30 organizations on the list, and more are added each month as employees propose new causes for the company to support.

Jeff Saluda, one of the engineers, has just sent you an email requesting that the Peace Collaborative be approved as one of QC's nonprofit partners. This is an organization that goes into schools and teaches students conflict resolution, collaborative problem solving, nonviolent communication, and other skills. You're familiar with this program. In fact, your son participated in it at his school, and you were impressed with what he learned. But you simply cannot grant Jeff's request. For obvious reasons, the guidelines for proposing an addition to the list of supported organizations state that the organization can have no religious or political affiliations. While the Peace Collaborative has no official political ties, it is clearly at the liberal end of the political spectrum. You do not believe it is a neutral enough organization to qualify. In fact, the two founders of QC are political conservatives as well as military veterans. You suspect that adding the Peace Collaborative to the list would sit very poorly with them.

You worked very hard to get the employees behind the new volunteer program, and you don't want Jeff to start any negative talk about it. Refuse his request in such a way that you do not lose his support for the program. And remember that your email can be read at any time by your bosses.

---

2 As a relatively new engineer (or some other employee) for Westin & Smith, a design and manufacturing company specializing in highway construction equipment, you have mixed feelings about the email you just read. It's from President Smith himself, and it asks if you will lead the company's effort to partner with Habitat for Humanity. Specifically, he wants you to create a program in which employees will devote certain weekends throughout the coming year to building a complete Habitat house, which the company will then feature proudly on its website.

Mr. Smith knows that you were instrumental in launching the company's employee volunteer program, and he cites several other examples of leadership that you have shown. He believes you're the perfect person to organize this important project. He promises all the financial and managerial support you will need.

His praise makes you feel great. But it also makes you feel even worse that you have to say no. As the proud dad of a seven-week-old girl, you have been stretched thin. You and your wife, who runs her own accounting services firm, have been getting up two and three times a night to tend the baby, who is not a good sleeper. Both of you are exhausted—and there's no way your wife will support your taking on additional responsibilities that will involve countless meetings, extra hours at the computer, and even weekends away from home. Your boss's recognition and request couldn't have come at a worse time.

Figure out how to say no while also showing that you are the kind of leader and contributor that your boss thinks you are. Maybe some kind of counteroffer will help.

---

3 You stare at yet another solicitation from a well-meaning service organization. This time it's from Help Your Neighbor, a local nonprofit endorsed by various churches in the city. They're inviting your company, St. Bernard Home & Garden, to be a featured sponsor of their annual Help-Out Day. This event, their major fundraiser and publicity effort, has volunteers from all over the city contributing one day's labor to help their less fortunate neighbors with yardwork, home repairs, and other tasks. Your contribution of $5,000 will help pay for the volunteers' t-shirts (on which your company's name will appear), the supplies, and the picnic that will follow the day's work.

While this amount doesn't sound like much for a successful business, you're a comparatively small organization that can afford to make only a limited number of charitable contributions. This year, your company is channeling its support into organizations that are helping those who have lost their jobs or their homes because of the economic slump. Many of your employees know such people, and the general feeling in the company is that donations should go to such organizations as the food bank, the homeless shelter, and nonprofits that assist those looking for work. You've given over $10,000 to such causes this year, and that's all you can afford right now. But these are the types of organizations you will probably continue to choose to support until the economy improves.

Write the Help Your Neighbor chair a letter turning down his or her request for a sponsorship. Write the letter in such a way that you maintain a positive company image while also making clear that you won't become a sponsor now or any time soon. Perhaps you can think of something you can offer that will help soften the "no." (Or, play the role of office manager and assume that your boss has asked you to write the letter for his or her signature.)

---

4 As executive director of the Southeast Realtors Association, you have been gathering information to help the organization's board of directors decide where to hold its annual meeting three years from now. Specifically, the board has asked you to investigate two possible sites: New Orleans and Atlanta. In both cities you received good help from representatives of the chamber of commerce. But Dominique Toussaint of New Orleans was particularly helpful. She went out of her way to show you the city and give you insider information on its jazz clubs and restaurants. She also took you to the hotels with appropriate facilities for your event and introduced you to the managers. Overall, she was a delightful tour guide. You were hoping to send your organization's business her way.

Unfortunately, the board has decided on Atlanta for the meeting. Now it is your job to inform Ms. Toussaint that New Orleans's bid has been turned down. Certainly you will express your thanks for her help. You can also report that the decision was a close one and that New Orleans will be considered for later years. Send your message to Ms. Toussaint via letter. Don't forget that the board will see a copy of it. (If your instructor directs, research the two cities and come up with plausible reasons why Atlanta was chosen.)

---

5 As a new college graduate, you're delighted that not one but two companies have offered you a position in their _____ (you decide which) department. You met representatives of both companies at your university's job fair. From this first contact came an invitation for an on-site job interview with each company. You really enjoyed learning more about the operations of both companies and meeting their friendly employees. Both companies have great employee benefits, and the salaries they're offering are comparable.

After careful thought, you've decided to go with Company B. You sense a little better match between their values and yours, and you think the opportunity for advancement might be better there as well.

Write the recruiter at Company A to reject their offer. Of course you will convey your appreciation for their consideration, and the things you learned on your visit will enable you to give them some well-deserved compliments. What will be stickiest is figuring out how to explain why you're choosing another offer. The explanation won't need to be long, but the company does deserve one. You certainly don't want to close the door on future employment or even business relations with this company, so the time you spend crafting this letter will be time well spent. (If your instructor directs, research two companies to use for this assignment.)

6 You're a clerk in room scheduling at your university. Today you got a room request via the form on your website from a graduate student. He would like to reserve the atrium of the Language Studies building—a nice, open space with comfortable chairs, a skylight, and plants—for a lecture by a visiting business executive. The date he proposes will work, but in his description of the event, he mentions that the lecture will be followed by a wine and cheese reception. This is a problem. Your university has a strict alcohol policy. First, alcohol can be served in designated areas only, and the atrium is not one of these areas. Moreover, even in designated areas, several rules govern the serving of alcohol. (Check the alcohol policy at your school to see what these might be.) He should read the policy on your university's website (in fact, you can't believe he didn't think to read it already).

Send this well-meaning but inexperienced student an email with your response. In dealing with the situation, remember that your university has been trying to change its reputation as an impersonal bureaucracy and see what you can do to cooperate with this effort.

---

7 You landed a coveted marketing internship with the Athletic Department at San Francisco State University where your responsibilities include community relations and local publicity. You count as one of your recent accomplishments a very successful speaking engagement you arranged for an assistant baseball coach with the local Rotary Club.

Three weeks ago, though, things really heated up. Tom King, a pitcher on the surging Aztec baseball team, began receiving unprecedented media attention for his 101 mph fastball and an unbroken string of five no-hitters—just one shy of the NCAA record. Just last week you helped the athletic director set up a live appearance for your star on a prime-time broadcast of ESPN, a huge plus for your résumé.

But today the athletic director hit the roof. She says the constant phone calls from the media and the reporters camped outside her office have become a huge distraction to the team and especially to Tom. The final straw was when she learned that Tom missed a Business Law exam because he was busy signing autographs at the campus bookstore. The AD says Tom has not displayed the necessary maturity to properly handle such exposure. No more media appearances for Tom until the end of the spring term, she declares.

Unfortunately, you had promised T.J. Smith, a local sports reporter, an exclusive in-person interview with Tom when he pitched his record-setting sixth no-hitter. Tom's sixth victory was today. You heard of this directly from Tom through an exchange on Skype. Write a note to the reporter explaining why the in-person interview is cancelled. Consider any and all alternatives that could help make this less upsetting to T.J. since your relationship with her is of great importance to you.

---

8 The professional development program at Affinity Software Solutions has been discontinued (see case #31). However, you, the budget director, have received a proposal from Victor Ramos, one of your four senior sales managers, to attend the annual United Professional Sales Association's annual conference. Mr. Ramos knows the funding for professional development has been discontinued, but he has an idea. As a senior sales manager he (along with *all* employees in the sales department) earns a bonus when the sales department exceeds corporate sales goals. These bonuses have not been cut because Affinity sees these bonuses as an incentive for the sales staff and senior management to work harder to attract new customers, and during these tough economic times, Affinity needs all of the customers it can get. Mr. Ramos proposes, though, that instead of paying him the money for his sales bonus, the company use the money to pay for his trip to the annual sales conference.

Initially, you tell Mr. Ramos that you think this is a great idea. As long as an employee is motivated to do well, you don't think should matter to the company what the incentive is. Granted, the company could just pay Mr. Ramos the bonus money and let him use it as he wishes, but then Mr. Ramos would have to pay income tax on the amount received. It seems like a win-win situation, especially given that Mr. Ramos has agreed to take vacation time to attend the conference.

You take Mr. Ramos's proposal to the others on your executive management team (the president, CEO, and vice president) and are surprised when they reject Mr. Ramos's proposal. How could they? It seems like a no-brainer. But the executive management has some valid reasons. If Mr. Ramos is allowed to do this, then all of the other 25 senior managers will need to be allowed to do so also, which would create an administrative nightmare for the people in accounting. Furthermore, even though Mr. Ramos is willing to take vacation time to attend the conference, the company must pay him if he is on company business—which he seemingly would be if the company paid for him to attend the conference—and there is no way you can just let him have the time off. The other senior managers may be angry and see Mr. Ramos as getting special treatment.

Your job is to write a response to Mr. Ramos on behalf of the executive management team refusing his request. You think his initiative and creative thinking in finding another funding source for professional development are commendable. Be sure you retain his goodwill so that he is motivated to continue doing such a wonderful job for Affinity.

---

9 You are a supervisor in your company's (you pick the company) marketing department. You and four others have been working on a campaign for a company product (you can make up the product) that will be released in three months. Today is Wednesday. Because your boss, the manager of the marketing department, needs a week to prepare the presentation of the campaign to the board of directors, she has asked for the campaign materials by Monday of next week. You and the rest of your team have known about the deadline for three months. As a supervisor, you're the team leader. This morning you received a message from Mary, the graphic artist, saying that there is no way she can finish her portion of the project by Monday. She is requesting an extension of only three days; she estimates that she can have her work done by Thursday of next week. In her message she says she has been swamped with work for two other projects. In addition, her children have been sick this week with colds, so she has had to take time off to care for them, and she is hosting a birthday party for one of her children on Sunday, so she can't work over the weekend to finish her part of the project.

You talk to your boss, who says she cannot wait until Thursday for Mary's work. To be honest, neither can you, as it reflects poorly on your leadership and supervisory abilities if you cannot deliver a team project on time. It's not that your boss is unsympathetic. Her calendar is so busy that she really needs a full week to get her presentation ready for the board, and if her presentation is not excellent, it reflects badly on the entire department. You, though, may be just a bit unsympathetic; Mary has had three months to get her work done, and many times—just yesterday, as a matter of fact—you have seen her on Facebook or on personal phone calls when she should have been working on the project. She was also late with her work for the last project you worked on together, and you are a bit annoyed that this is happening again.

You are thinking that since you have two other graphic artists in the department, you will ask one of them to work with you on future projects. You know for sure that if Mary does not have her material ready by Monday, you will be talking about Mary's inability to meet deadlines in her performance and salary review next month. Though you plan to talk with Mary in person, you also want a permanent record of your decision, so you decide to write a message to Mary denying her request for an extension and offering at least one suggestion for what she might do to meet her deadline.

---

10 You are a grower at a greenhouse. Your policy is that before you sell a new plant variety to the public, you grow it in a test garden for a year to ensure the product is one you can endorse. Last year, Morgan Levine, a salesperson with H&M Horticulture and Nursery, asked you to sell her company's *Buddleia davidii,* "Purple Butterfly" (butterfly bush), at your greenhouse, so you planted it in your trial garden. You've seen the pictures of this variety of buddleia as well as others and were really hoping you would be able to sell it, as you know many of your customers would enjoy the butterflies the bush is known to attract. However, you are in Wisconsin, which is in garden hardiness Zone 4, and though Morgan assured you that this bush can grow in Zone 4, the plants you tried did not survive the winter. You just received an email from Morgan asking if you would like to sell the plant at your greenhouse in the next season. Write an email to her declining to sell the product.

Claims

11 You need to write the Parks Board in your county a request for a refund. You held a family reunion at Whitewater Park on Saturday at the Oak Pavilion, which you had reserved for your group at a cost of $150. When the guests arrived, the picnic site was littered with trash. Your family had to spend the first half hour or so of their reunion cleaning up (and some of the trash wasn't that pleasant to handle!). Plus, since some of the trash had been dragged across the picnic tables, you had to wipe down them down with makeshift cleaning products before the guests could even sit down. These problems reflected poorly on you, the organizer, and also detracted from the guests' experience. You figure you deserve some money back (especially since some of your city tax dollars were spent on maintenance of the parks). Write the director, James Logan, and tell him so.

---

12 Boy, are you mad at BigTime Airlines! Here's what happened.

You booked a round-trip flight from Indianapolis to Chicago to attend a meeting with a client. As you were driving to the Indianapolis airport, you hit a terrible traffic jam. Apparently a truck had taken an exit ramp too fast and flipped over onto the highway leading to the airport. The traffic sat completely still for over an hour as the emergency crew tried to clear a path through the wreckage. Once you got to the airport, you parked as quickly as you could and ran inside, relieved that you still had 20 minutes before your departure time, but when you tried to print your boarding pass, the kiosk displayed a message that you needed to have checked in at least 30 minutes ahead of your flight time to be able to get your pass. You pleaded with the airline staff to let you onto the flight—you had carry-on luggage and could easily have made it—but they said their hands were tied. The best they could do was direct you to another airline's ticketing counter, where you could purchase a later, one-way flight to Chicago. This you did—at a cost of $199.

But it got worse. When you returned to the Chicago airport after your meeting and tried to print your return boarding pass, the kiosk displayed the message that it couldn't find you in the system. You waited in line to get to speak with a ticketing agent and then told him that you were booked on the 9:45 flight but for some reason couldn't get your pass from the kiosk. The agent looked on her computer and then said, "Oh, that's because you canceled your first flight. When you change your itinerary like that, the whole flight is canceled." "But I paid for that return flight!" you argue. "I missed the outbound flight because of a terrible traffic jam." The agent shakes her head. "Did you read the terms and conditions of your ticket when you made your reservation?" she asks. "It's all explained there." You have to admit that you didn't read the fine print. "I can get you a seat on the Indianapolis flight," she offers, "but it'll cost you $149." You sigh and say okay—you have to get home somehow.

Once you get home, you go to BigTime Airlines' website and dig down to the Terms and Conditions link for ticket sales. Nowhere does the text say that if you miss the first part of a round-trip flight, the second part will be canceled. All it says is, "Any change in itinerary will result in a cancellation of this reservation." You doubt anybody would know that missing the first part of a round-trip flight would count as a "change in itinerary"—if they read far enough even to get to this wording.

Altogether, you wound up paying over $600 for this $299 trip, and that just doesn't seem fair. Look online for the best way to submit your claim request and try to get some of your money back.

---

13 You're a do-it-yourselfer when it comes to your 1989 Chrysler, which you bought before cars came equipped with all those computer systems that make it hard for people like you to work on them. Recently you ordered a coil and resistor from AutoParts.com that, according to its website, were right for your year and model of car, but when you installed them, the car started and then, with an ominous noise and smell, quickly died. You took the new parts out and examined them. You figured out that you got the wrong model of resistor, which burned out the coil when you started the car. Aggravated, you called a friend and asked him to drive you to an auto parts store. The service person agreed that the resistor was wrong. Fortunately, the store had the right model of resistor, as well as the right coil for your car—though at higher prices than what you paid for the ones from AutoParts.com.

At least when you got back home and installed them, they worked great.

You're relieved to have your car running again, but now you want your money back in addition to the cost difference between AutoParts.com's parts and their replacements: you paid $240 and $3.20 for the coil and resistor from AutoParts.com, and $282 and $3.80 for the ones from the store. You also need to know if the company wants the parts back. If it does, you definitely will not pay for the shipping. In making your case, you will explain the root of the problem: that AutoParts.com's website brought up the wrong model of resistor when you entered your car's make and model in the search field.

Using the "contact us" link on the company's website, make your request. Whether you do business with this company in the future will probably depend on their reply.

---

14 Today you notice that a crack in the wall of your family room, a crack that the Mr. Fixit Home Repairs company had repaired for $300 three months ago, has returned. And you know why.

Pleased with the repair work the company had done, you had scheduled another job with the same company, this time to install an outdoor electrical outlet. The installation had taken a long time, and the drilling of the hole for the outlet had made a terrible noise and vibration. Afterwards, the repair person had commented that it had been difficult to get through the stucco-like material on the outside of the house.

Thinking nothing of it, you paid the person $160, glad to get that job checked off your to-do list.

This was yesterday. Now you realize that the jarring of the exterior wall must have cracked the plaster on your family-room wall again. The extended vibrating shook the inside wall so badly that the repaired plaster (which you had already carefully painted over) cracked.

You think you're entitled to have someone from Mr. Fixit come out and repair the crack again at no charge. You're going to write them and tell them so, including a photo of the cracked wall.

---

15 When Ultimate Fitness Gym opened in your town, you were thrilled. You took advantage of the grand opening deal of a lifetime membership fee of $25 per month. That was three years ago. The gym is building a new facility. You are a little surprised when you receive a letter four months before the new gym's grand opening offering you a new lifetime membership of $39.99 per month. The letter says that previous lifetime memberships will not be valid at the new facility and encourages you to take advantage of this great deal. You're thinking that $39.99 per month is definitely not as great a deal as your current lifetime membership of $25 per month, and you wonder why you would pay the increased price when you've already bought what is supposed to be a lifetime membership.

You called the gym and were told, "The 'lifetime' in 'lifetime membership' refers only to the life of your membership in this building. A new building means a new membership, and our new lifetime memberships are $39.99 per month." Your brother, who is an attorney, reads the contract and says even though it does not specify that "lifetime" means the life of the membership in a particular building, it is worded in such a way that the gym can change the terms. This seems like a pretty flimsy explanation for raising your membership fee. In fact, it seems as though the gym is desperate for a way to raise revenue to cover the cost of the new building and is targeting lifetime memberships. You also feel you were misled about the terms of your contract when you were told you had purchased a "lifetime" membership for $25 per month.

Write a letter to the gym's owner asking that he reconsider the new lifetime membership fee and allow yours to remain at $25 per month.

16 You are the director of a small regional arts center. Your center has three baby grand pianos that you have tuned several times a year so that they are ready for performances. The piano tuner you used has retired. Based on her recommendation you hired Max Kersten to tune your pianos. Max is just starting out, and you were happy to give him your business, especially given the enthusiastic recommendation from your former tuner. He tuned your pianos yesterday, and the orchestra that is performing in two weeks rehearsed last night. Afterward, the pianist complained that several keys (C1, D3, F5, and G4) on the piano she played were not tuned and that two of the keys (C6 and E6) were sticking.

You're not a pianist, but even you can hear that she is right. The piano player does not like the other two pianos and refuses to play them for the concert, so you need that piano repaired immediately—before the next rehearsal tomorrow night. You call Max, and he quite bluntly and cavalierly tells you that the soonest he can get to you is next week, three days before the performance. He tells you to check your schedule and email him with a time next Wednesday morning that will work and to include in your message a description of what the pianist wants fixed. Your first reaction to Max's unprofessional tone and writing style is to hire a new tuner, but you have no choice. The two other piano tuners in your area are already booked. Email Max and tell him that next Wednesday at 10 a.m. will work fine. However, you are not happy with Max's customer service, piano tuning skills, and attitude and aren't sure you'll use him again. You can't believe that your former tuner, whom you really liked and respected, would recommend someone like him. You would hope that the retuning would be at no cost and that as an act of good faith, Max would offer you a discount on your next service—assuming you're willing to give him another chance.

Adjustment Refusals

17 What a complicated complaint from one Adele Griffith! (See case #12.) You certainly see how the situation must look from her point of view. For reasons beyond her control, she missed the outbound flight that she'd paid for, and then, because of that "change in itinerary," she also forfeited the return flight that she'd paid for! It does seem unfortunate, if not unfair, that her $299 trip wound up costing her over twice that amount, as well as a lot of stress.

Unfortunately, your hands are tied. The ticket receipt does clearly state that passengers must be present at least 30 minutes in advance to be allowed to check in. And the fine print under Terms and Conditions does legally allow the airline to cancel the return flight when a passenger misses the outbound flight (even though, you agree, many readers probably wouldn't understand that missing a flight counts as a "change in itinerary"). But as a lowly customer-service representative, you simply are not allowed to give refunds in such cases. However, you are allowed to give a coupon toward the customer's next flight with you.

Respond to Ms. Griffith's complaint, trying to the best of your ability to restore good relations with her.

18 You're going to have to say no to Seri Paulding's request for a refund.

According to the handwritten note she included with the kitchen blender that she just mailed back to you, she purchased the item almost three months ago. She then stored it and kept it until her husband's birthday last week. When he opened his present and tried the blender, it made a weird sound and electrical smell. So Ms. Paulding has sent the blender back and is asking for a refund to her credit card.

The problem is that Seri has waited too late to make this return. As the packing slip said, any defective products need to be returned within 60 days of purchase. After that, there's nothing you can do except recommend an authorized repair center. Write to Seri to give her the bad news. See if you can figure out how to keep her goodwill and her future business.

19 You're the owner of the Mr. Fixit Home Repair franchise in your area. You've just received a request for an adjustment from Arthur Monfort, for whom you've done two jobs recently (see case #14).

While you empathize with the homeowner, you are not going to give him the free repair that he asks for. You spoke with Alex Lester, the repair person who installed the outdoor electrical outlet, and he said that the material on the outside of the house—some kind of stucco-like polymer—had been nearly impossible to drill through. He felt lucky that he could even complete the job. Plus, he hadn't charged Mr. Monfort for the extra time it took to do it. As for the plaster damage documented in the photo that Mr. Monfort sent, it's unlikely that the drilling alone could have caused the crack. Last summer your city had the worst drought in recent history, causing many foundations to sink as the ground hardened. It's likely that the foundation of the customer's family room has sunk away from the room to some extent, leaving the walls unsupported in places.

You'd be glad to come back and repair the wall, but you'll have to charge a fee. You think a 20 percent discount on the job is fair. But before you come out again, Mr. Monfort may want to have a structural engineer assess the state of his foundation. It could be that no repair job will last until the root problem is addressed.

It looked like you were developing a loyal customer until this problem occurred. See if you can make Mr. Monfort a loyal customer still.

---

20 Snellville & Sons is a family-owned electronics retailer specializing in the sales and installation of home theater systems. Tom Snellville has built a solid reputation in the community through word-of-mouth marketing by highly satisfied customers. You were recently hired by Snellville & Sons to help Mr. Snellville manage customer relations for his growing business. One of your first tasks on the job is to respond to a letter from a long-time customer, Alexander Rogers, who is angry and claims that Snellville & Sons owes him a replacement unit or a full refund for his home theater system.

Mr. Rogers purchased a $2,900 Bose home theater system 13 months ago. At the time of purchase, Mr. Rogers was offered an extended warranty package, but he declined. The standard factory warranty for Mr. Rogers's system expired one month ago. Snellville & Sons will be unable to replace Mr. Rogers's system. Mr. Snellville is willing to offer Alexander Rogers a discount on a new system or on repair costs. Your task is to deny Mr. Rogers's refund request. (Consider visiting the Bose website to learn more about exciting new product features.)

---

21 You work in the customer service department of a pest control company, Gooden Gone, operating in the southeast region of the U.S. Recently, Marjorie Evansville, a client located in Atlanta, encountered a termite infestation in the lower level of her 1940s bungalow in in-town Atlanta. Ms. Evansville will need to replace the entire first floor of her home. She claims that Gooden Gone is responsible for the cost of her repairs. After researching the case you learn that Ms. Evansville has two homes under termite coverage with your company, one in Greenville, South Carolina, and one in Atlanta, Georgia. The Greenville home is protected by the Kitchen Sink protection plan which covers annual treatments and the full costs of repairs should an infestation occur. The Atlanta home, the one with the current infestation, is covered by the Backup protection plan that covers only annual prevention treatments. The Backup plan does not cover the cost of repairs; however, it will cover retreatment once the repairs have been made.

You need to write to Marjorie Evansville and inform her that Gooden Gone is not responsible for the cost of her floor repairs in the Atlanta home. Marjorie has been a client for over 30 years. Maintain her goodwill while making sure she fully understands why the claim is being rejected.

---

22 You are a branch manager for a large bank. On July 1 the bank began assessing a $15 surcharge to all debit cards that had not been used in six months. The $15 fee was deducted from card holders' checking or savings accounts. Eight weeks before the July 1 deadline, the bank's customer service department sent letters to all debit-card holders whose cards had been inactive telling them that if they didn't use their cards by July 1, they would be assessed the $15 fee. Customers were also told that if they no longer wished to have the card, they were to call an 800-number to deactivate it. In addition, all card holders were reminded that after July 1 they had to use their cards at least once every six months to avoid the fee. The notice was also placed on card holders' monthly statements, posted on the bank's website, included in the bank's quarterly newsletter, and advertised in branch office lobbies.

After July 1 the accounts of customers with unused cards were assessed the $15 fee. Many customers who somehow missed the notices of the policy change called customer service to express their anger and disappointment. Once the customer service representatives reminded these customers of the multiple notices regarding the fee, most grudgingly accepted that they should have paid more attention. One particularly angry customer, though, was not satisfied with this explanation. After her phone call to customer service, Laura Nelson wrote a letter to you, the branch manager, saying that the bank had done an insufficient job in informing customers of the fee. She said a phone call would have been the best way to let her and others know, and she wants the $15 fee returned to her account. She says that if you don't give her the $15, she will take her accounts elsewhere.

You believe that the bank did all it could do to inform the customers. Making phone calls to all of them would have been unreasonable and inefficient given the many other ways the bank advertised the fee. Besides, in a society where phone scams and financial fraud are becoming common, would she have thought a voice message about a $15 fee on a debit card was credible? You doubt it. That's why you put the notices in writing. Write a response to Ms. Nelson denying her request to return the $15 to her account. Retain her goodwill so that she does not take her accounts to another bank.

---

23 You are a manager for Jimmy's, a large, upscale sports bar and grill. During the summer months, Jimmy's sponsors a summer co-ed softball league where any company can provide a team of its own or individuals can sign up to be on one of Jimmy's teams. The sports league is very popular. Nearly every night of the week, there is a softball game at Jimmy's, and you actually have a waiting list of companies who want to sponsor a team and individuals who want to play on one of the teams. The rules are simple. Companies pay a $180 fee to sponsor a team. Individuals pay a $20 fee to be on one of Jimmy's teams. The fees are nonrefundable once the playing schedule is announced.

Jimmy's used to refund the fee at any time, but so many people or companies would sign up, be placed on a team, and then change their minds that it was an administrative nightmare to continually update teams and schedules. Furthermore, finding teams and individuals to fill so many vacancies after the schedules were announced was difficult because many of the companies and individuals on the waiting list would already be committed to other teams. The non-refundable fee is meant to encourage people and companies to be more responsible participants in the league.

This year Sullivan Office Products decided to field a team and paid the fee. The team is on the schedule that was announced three weeks ago, and Sullivan's team is scheduled to play its first game next week. Taylor King from Sullivan emailed you today and asked that the company's team be removed from the roster. Three people have quit the team, and several others have scheduling conflicts. Mr. King thinks that for some of the games, only two or three people from Sullivan would be able to attend. He also asked that you refund the fee. Send a reply to Mr. King denying his request. You may be able to think of a way to help Mr. King fill his team.

Negative Announcements

24 You're a regional sales manager for Metropolitan Financial Services, which advises businesses of all types on credit-card use and policies, investments, payroll, debt management, and other money-related issues. Just now you were "called on the carpet" by your boss, the regional manager, for excessive expenditures for wining and dining clients. She says that your seven-person sales force spent over $15,000 last quarter—over $2,000 per person—taking representatives of companies, hospitals, and other organizations out to lunch and dinner, either to thank them for their business or attract them as customers. Sure, landing even one good contract with a large organization can mean thousands of dollars for F&F, and representatives of a financial services company can't afford to look "cheap." But you have to agree that things have gotten out of hand. Your boss says that many of the receipts are for the most expensive restaurants in the area, and for such extravagant purchases as $200 bottles of wine. This has got to stop. There are plenty of perfectly elegant ways to say "thank you" or to appeal to a client besides spending money extravagantly.

Using your good problem-solving skills, think about how to advise your employees. Then write the negative announcement that will change their behavior but also maintain their goodwill and their drive to succeed.

---

25 Assume that you are the _____ (you choose the supervisory position) of a small _____ (you choose the type) company or department. More and more, you've noticed when walking past employees' cubicles and offices that a social networking site such as Facebook, MySpace, or LinkedIn is up on the screen. You've read some articles pointing out that social networking on the job can be quite a drain on employees' productivity, and you worry that this is happening in your company (have you noticed any lapses in performance lately?). You think the time has come to send an email to the employees advising them to limit their use of social networking on the job.

The thing is, you know that social networking does also bring certain company benefits. You don't want to have the IT person block or monitor the use of social-networking sites, nor do you want a strict policy that will actually be counterproductive. So you're going to try to get people to monitor themselves.

Think carefully about what you want the employees to do and why (for example, instead of doing social networking, what should they be doing?). Then write the message that will get them to change their behavior.

26 As customer service supervisor at Medical Billing Services, you've been receiving complaints about your staff's work from some of your clients. These are doctors' offices, imaging centers, hospitals, and other medical-related businesses. They hire your company to collect their fees and resolve any financial issues that come up (their bills instruct the patients to call your company directly with any billing questions they may have). The customer representatives of your clients are getting complaints from their patients about being put on hold for long periods of time and being treated brusquely when they call your company with their questions. So now these representatives have complained to you.

You think the time has come to purchase a call-monitoring system, and your boss, the president of the company, agrees. Now you need to tell your staff what you're going to do, when, and why. Do some online research, perhaps even some interviewing, to gather good material for this message. For example, how common are call-monitoring systems? Do they serve positive purposes as well as exposing the poor performers? How does the company as a whole benefit?

Inform your staff of the new policy and answer their likely questions in clear language. But do so in such a way that you will get as positive a response as possible. You want their attitude and behavior to improve, not get worse.

---

27 Play the role of Julie Schubert, office manager for Whitney Dental Office. (With your instructor's permission, you may choose a different organization that serves its customers through scheduled appointments.) Your office's policy is "three strikes and you're out": If patients break three appointments within 18 months and without notice, they are not allowed to make any further appointments.

Write the form letter that you will send to patients who violate this policy, telling them that they'll need to get their dental care elsewhere. In your form letter, leave blanks where information specific to each case will be included and indicate in brackets what kind of information that will be. Think carefully about the facts you'll need to include in order to justify your position. And do what you can to maintain the patient's goodwill. True, you will never see this patient again, but you do not want to alienate his or her family and friends, some of whom may also be patients at your office.

---

28 The campus branch of the YMCA is going out of business. Now that the new state-of-the-art university recreation center has opened, this YMCA is simply not generating enough income to enable sufficient maintenance of the facilities and the expensive exercise equipment. As director, you need to write your current members—most of them faculty and staff at the university—to let them know that your Y will be closing.

There is another YMCA relatively nearby. If members want to use up the rest of their yearly membership at this Y, they will be allowed to do so. Once it's time to renew, how-ever, they'll pay a somewhat higher fee at this Y than they did at the one that's closing, but they'll still pay less than they would have to pay for using the university's recreation center. (Plus, the other Y is bigger and nicer than yours.) Of course, if your members don't wish to transfer the rest of their membership to the nearby Y, they will be refunded the remainder of their membership fee. You'll tell them how this will happen.

Make them feel good about this decision and about the YMCA organization as a whole.

---

29 You work as an administrative intern for Holden and Baines, a small public accounting firm located in Detroit, Michigan. Traditionally, Holden and Baines replaces employee computers on a rotating schedule every two years. Last year the firm updated its technology for about half the company's employees. These employees were given the option of selecting a laptop or desktop computer. The laptop option was selected by 100 percent of the employees whose machines were replaced. The employees who received laptops last year report a high level of satisfaction with the mobility their new machines allow. Consequently, the employees who were not upgraded last year are looking forward to their chance to upgrade this year.

However, this year Holden and Baines has lost two of its major clients to bankruptcy. With the loss of these clients and the uncertain economic climate in Detroit, the senior partners have had to significantly tighten the company's operating budget. One of the casualties of the tighter budget is the technology upgrade. Instead of purchasing new computers, the company will add memory to existing machines and redistribute the current laptops to employees who are required to travel. While this decision is not ideal, the senior partners feel it is critical to be prudent with the company's budget in order to avoid layoffs or employee furloughs in the coming year.

Your task is to draft a message for Mr. Holden, senior partner, to send to all employees informing them of the decision to forgo the biannual technology upgrade and to redistribute the laptops to select employees who travel often on company business.

---

30 You work for CreekAir, a small regional airlines with daily flights to Las Vegas from the Pacific Northwest. Company policy and FAA regulations mandate that pets over 12 pounds are not allowed to fly in the main cabin of the plane. Consequently, your company does not book pet flights for larger animals during the months of May, June, July, August, and September because the cargo hold can become too hot for the animals. Today is April 15 and the Southwest is experiencing a severe heat wave. Temperatures are well over 90 degrees, an unsafe temperature for animals in the cargo hold when the plane is on the tarmac. Your boss has made the decision that allowing pets to fly into Las Vegas during this heat wave would be unwise for both the health of the pets and the liability of the company. Fortunately, there are only two clients scheduled to fly in the next two days with large pets. Unfortunately, the clients will not be allowed to bring their pets. While the pet-ticketing fees will be refunded, passenger rescheduling or ticket changes will incur the standard change fees.

You must contact the two passengers, Jenny Miles and Fabian Uzcategui, and inform them that they will not be able to bring their pets on their flights. Since you are a small company and Jenny Miles and Fabian Uzcategui are both frequent fliers, you will need to maintain goodwill.

---

31 Your company, Affinity Software Solutions, has a policy that allows your senior management staff to attend one professional development activity a year (e.g., an annual professional conference, a continuing-education course). The senior managers really enjoy this program because it provides a break in their routine and lets them travel, network, and build their skills. The program has been a fabulous morale builder among your senior management staff and has provided assistant managers with motivation to earn senior management status.

However, business has not been good this past year, and to save money, the company has decided to suspend this policy indefinitely. You know the employees are going to be unhappy, but when the alternatives are layoffs, increased employee contributions toward health insurance or switching to an employee plan with less coverage, and eliminating sales performance bonuses, this policy seems to be one of the least necessary expenses for the company. If senior managers want to take vacation time and pay for the professional development activities on their own, they certainly may, but the company will no longer pay for any time off or any costs associated with professional development activities.

As Affinity's budget director, you know senior managers will be upset. They really look forward to professional development activities. The policy has been around so long that some even see this policy as a right rather than a privilege. Some others may wonder how they will maintain their skills or network. They certainly won't want to pay for these activities themselves. Write a message to your senior management staff explaining that the policy is being discontinued. Appeal to their management expertise so that they see this as a good business decision. Encourage them to seek other ways to develop their skills and network without having to travel.

---

32 You own a small new- and used-book store and café with free wireless Internet access. You enjoy the calm, quiet atmosphere of your store and like that your customers choose your store to conduct business, socialize with friends, or just enjoy a good book and a cup of coffee. Increasingly, many customers have been talking on their cell phones—very loudly and in places where they shouldn't be. They hold up the order line by talking on the phone when they should be talking to the cashier. They disrupt others who are enjoying the quiet atmosphere to work or read. Sure, customers who are working on the computer may need to talk on the phone, but must these customers be so loud and disruptive that those across the room who are trying to read can hear their conversations?

Many customers have actually complained. You want to make these customers happy but not at the expense of making your cell phone users unhappy. Write a cell phone use policy for your store. Attach to your solution a cover note explaining where and how the notice will be distributed.

---

33 The company break room is a mess (you may choose the company name). People are not wiping the tables after they eat, used napkins remain on the tables or on the floor, and dirty dishes are left in the sink. People will heat food that overflows or explodes in the microwave and just leave without cleaning it up, and some of the food in the refrigerator is over a month past its due date. Given all the complaining you have heard about the break room, you would think that people would be more diligent in cleaning up after themselves. In fact, someone left the message "CLEAN UP AFTER YOURSELF!!!!!!! YOUR MOTHER DOESN'T WORK HERE!!!!!!!!!!!!!!!!!!!!!!!!!" on the microwave last week. Your recent signs in the break room reminding people to clean up their messes are obviously ineffective. As the office manager, send an email to employees to encourage them to clean up after themselves. Just last week you were giving a tour to a member of your town's chamber of commerce and were thoroughly embarrassed when you took him through the break room.

chapter eight

Indirectness in Persuasive Messages

LEARNING OBJECTIVES

Upon completing this chapter, you will be able to use persuasion effectively, especially when making requests, composing sales messages, and writing proposals. To reach this goal, you should be able to

1   Describe important strategies for writing any persuasive message.

2   Write skillful persuasive requests that begin indirectly, develop convincing reasoning, and close with goodwill and action.

3   Discuss ethical concerns regarding sales messages.

4   Describe the planning steps for direct mail or email sales messages.

5   Compose sales messages that gain attention, persuasively present appeals, and effectively drive for action.

6   Write well-organized and persuasive proposals.

THE RATIONALE FOR INDIRECTNESS

Everything you write on the job will have some kind of persuasive purpose—to convince the reader of your professionalism, convey an appealing company image, promote good relations, and the like. But in some situations, persuasion will be your central goal. In these cases, your readers will hold a certain position, and your task will be to move them from this position to another one that is more favorable to you and/or your company. Meeting this challenge requires careful analysis, strategic thinking, and skillful writing.

Because you will be proposing something that your reader probably does not already agree with or want to do, it is often best to organize persuasive messages in an indirect order. Preparing the reader to accept your idea is a much better strategy than blurting out the idea from the start and then having to argue uphill through the rest of the message. Ideally, you should organize each persuasive message so that, from the title or subject line to the end, your readers will agree with you. If you try to have them on your side from start to finish, you'll have your best chance of success.

Although indirectness works for many kinds of persuasive messages, sometimes you will want to use a direct approach. For example, if you know your reader prefers directness or if you believe your readers will discard your message unless you get to the point early, then directness is in order. As we discuss later in this chapter, proposals in response to specific requests may also use directness.

In the following pages we first provide some general advice for effective persuasion using the indirect approach. We then explain how the indirect order is used in two kinds of persuasive messages: the persuasive request and the sales message. Finally, we cover another important category of persuasive writing: proposals. These, as you will see, can use either the direct or indirect pattern, depending on whether they are invited or uninvited.

- Persuasive messages are appropriately written in indirect order.

- Following are words of advice for persuasion in general and then for three common types of persuasive writing: requests, sales messages, and proposals.

GENERAL ADVICE ABOUT PERSUASION

All our previous advice about adapting your messages to your readers comes into play with persuasive messages—only more so. Moving your reader from an uninterested or even antagonistic position to an interested, cooperative one is a major accomplishment. To achieve it, keep the following advice in mind.

- Adaptation is especially important in persuasive messages.

Know Your Readers

For any kind of persuasive message, thinking about your subject from your readers' point of view is critical. To know what kind of appeals will succeed with your readers, you need to know as much as you can about their values, interests, and needs. Companies specializing in email and direct-mail campaigns spend a great deal of money to acquire this kind of information. Using a variety of research techniques, they gather demographic information (such as age, gender, income, and geographic location) and psychographic information (such as social, political, and personal preferences) on their target audience. They also develop mailing lists based on prior shows of interest from consumers and purchase mailing lists from other organizations that have had success with certain audiences.

But even an individual charged with writing an internal or external persuasive message can increase the chances for success by learning as much as possible about the intended readers. He or she can talk with the customer service people about the kinds of calls they're getting, study the company's customer database, chat with people around the water cooler or online, and run ideas past colleagues. Good persuasion depends on knowledge as well as on imagination and logic.

- Understanding your readers is critical.

Choose and Develop Targeted Reader Benefits

No one is persuaded to do something for no reason. Sometimes their reasons for acting are related to *tangible* or measurable rewards. For example, they will save money, save time, or acquire some kind of desired object. But often, the rewards that persuade are *intangible*. People may want to make their lives easier, gain prestige, or have more freedom. Or perhaps they want to identify with a larger cause, feel that they are helping

- People can be motivated by either *tangible* or *intangible* rewards.

others, or do the right thing. In your quest for the appeals that will win your readers over, do not underestimate the power of intangible benefits, especially when you can pair them with tangible rewards.

- Prefer *intrinsic* benefits over *extrinsic* benefits.

When selecting the reader benefits to feature in your persuasive messages, bear in mind that such benefits can be *intrinsic, extrinsic,* or a combination. Intrinsic benefits are benefits that readers will get automatically by complying with your request. For example, if you are trying to persuade people to attend your company's awards dinner, the pleasure of sharing in their colleagues' successes will be intrinsic to the event. Door prizes would be an extrinsic benefit. We might classify the meal itself as a combination—not really the main feature of the event but definitely central to it. Intrinsic benefits are tightly linked to what you're asking people to do, while extrinsic ones are added on and more short-lived. Let intrinsic benefits do the main work of your persuasive effort. Focusing too much on extrinsic benefits can actually cheapen your main cause in the readers' eyes.

- Turn your product *features* into reader *benefits*.

When presenting your reader benefits, be sure the readers can see exactly how the benefits will help them. The literature on selling makes a useful distinction between product *features* and reader *benefits*. If you say that a wireless service uses a certain kind of technology, you're describing a feature. If you say that the technology results in fewer missed or dropped calls, you're describing a benefit. Benefits persuade by enabling readers to envision the features of the recommended product or action in their own worlds.

- Use *scenario painting* to help readers visualize themselves enjoying the benefits of the product.

One common technique for achieving this goal is to use what we call *scenario painting*—a description that pictures the reader in a sample situation enjoying the promised benefits. Here is an example of scenario painting from the Carnival Cruise Lines website:

> Think your schedule is too tight to take a fun-filled vacation? Our Baja Mexico sailings are just the cruises to change your mind. You can experience the tropical beauty of Baja with a 3-day weekend cruise to Ensenada. Relax in the privacy of Ensenada's private beaches before hitting the fashionable shops of Avenida Primera for new jewelry—duty-free, of course.
>
> Have an extra day to spare? Our 4-day Baja cruises visit Catalina Island. Who knows? You may spot some of Hollywood's elite while sunning on the golden beaches of California's Emerald Island.

Scenario painting is very common in sales messages, but you can also use it to good advantage in other persuasive messages, even internal ones. Whatever your persuasive situation or strategy, be sure to provide enough detail for readers to see how they will benefit from what you are asking them to do.

Make Good Use of Three Kinds of Appeals

- Aristotle identified three kinds of persuasive appeals: *logic* based, *emotion* based, and *character* based.

The first acknowledged expert on persuasion, the Greek philosopher Aristotle, lived almost 2,500 years ago, but many of his core concepts are still widely taught and used. Of particular value is his famous categorizing of persuasive appeals into three kinds: those based on *logic* (logos), those based on *emotion* (pathos), and those based on the *character* of the speaker (ethos). All three kinds come into play in every persuasive message—in fact, one might say, in every kind of message. But as the writer of a persuasive message, you will need to think especially carefully about how to manage these appeals and which ones to emphasize given your intended audience.

In practice, these three kinds of appeals often cannot be neatly separated, but to get a sense of your options, you might benefit from thinking about each in turn. What kind of logical appeals might you use—saved money? Saved time? A more dependable or effective product? How about emotional appeals? Higher status? More sex appeal? Increased popularity? And don't neglect appeals based on character. What kind of image of yourself and your company will resonate with the reader? Should you get a celebrity or expert to endorse your product or to serve as the spokesperson? Not only when planning but also when revising your persuasive message, assess your appeals. Be sure to choose and develop the ones most likely to persuade your audience.

Make It Easy for Your Readers to Comply

Sometimes writers focus so much on creating persuasive appeals that they put insufficient thought into making the requested action as clear and easy to perform as possible. If you want people to give money or buy your product, tell them where and how to do it, and supply a preaddressed mailing envelope or a web address if applicable. If you want employees to give suggestions for improving products or operations, tell them exactly where and how to submit their ideas and make it easy for them to do so. If you want people to remember to work more safely or conserve on supplies, give them specific techniques for achieving these goals and include auxiliary reminders at the actual locations where they need to remember what to do. Making the desired action specific and easy to perform is a key part of moving your readers from resistance to compliance with your request.

With this general advice in mind, we now turn to the three main types of persuasive writing in business: persuasive requests, sales messages, and proposals.

- Be sure to make the requested action clear and easy.

PERSUASIVE REQUESTS

Persuasive Requests

Introduce yourself to the next business message situation by returning to your hypothetical position at Pinnacle. As a potential executive, you spend some time working for the community. Pinnacle wants you to do this volunteer work for the sake of good public relations. You want to do it because it is personally rewarding.

Currently, as chair of the fund-raising committee of the city's Junior Achievement program, you head all efforts to get financial support for the program from local businesspeople. You have a group of workers who will call on businesspeople. But personal calls take time, and there are many people to call on.

At its meeting today, the Junior Achievement board of directors discussed the problem of contacting businesspeople. One director suggested using a letter to sell them on giving money. The board accepted the idea with enthusiasm. With just as much enthusiasm, it gave you the assignment of writing the letter.

As you view the assignment, it is not a routine letter-writing problem. Although the local businesspeople are probably generous, they are not likely to part with money without good reason. In fact, their first reaction to a request for money is likely to be negative. So you will need to overcome their resistance in order to persuade them. Your task is indeed challenging.

There will be many times in your work life when you will need to make persuasive requests. Perhaps, as in the scenario above, you will be asked to write a fund-raising message. Perhaps you will need to ask your management for another staff position or for special equipment. You may need to persuade a potential client to join you in a meeting so that you can demonstrate the benefits of your products. Or maybe you will be trying to persuade your employees to change their behavior in some way.

Whether written to internal or external readers, requests that are likely to be resisted require a slow, deliberate approach. You must persuade the reader that he or she should grant the request before making the request. More specifically, you must present facts and logical reasoning that support your case. And you must do it convincingly. Such a presentation requires that you begin by developing a plan.

Determining the Persuasive Plan

Developing your persuasive plan involves three interrelated tasks: determining what you want, figuring out your readers' likely reactions, and deciding upon a persuasive strategy that will overcome reader objections and evoke a positive response.

- Planning your strategy involves three interrelated tasks:

- considering your own goals for the message,

- considering your readers' needs and interests,

- and deciding upon a persuasive plan.

- A special persuasive plan is the problem-solution strategy, which uses the *common-ground* technique.

Think carefully about your actual goals for your persuasive requests. A request for a one-time-only donation might be written very differently from a request that is intended to create a long-time, multiple donor. If you were convincing employees to leave the parking places next to the building for customers' use, you would write a very different message if you cared about maintaining the employees' goodwill than you would if you simply wanted to order them to comply. Your goals, considered in the context of your organization's goals and your relationship with your readers, are key shapers of your persuasive message.

As we have said, thinking about your readers' needs and interests is paramount when planning any persuasive message. Considering everything you know about your readers, put yourself in their shoes. Look at the request as they are likely to see it. Figure out what's in it for them, and anticipate their likely objections. From this thinking and imagining, your plan should emerge.

The specific plan you develop will depend on the facts of the case. You may be able to show that your reader stands to gain in time, money, or the like. Or you may be able to show that your reader will benefit in goodwill or prestige. In some cases, you may persuade readers by appealing to their love of beauty, excitement, serenity, or other emotions. In different cases, you may be able to persuade readers by appealing to the pleasant feeling that comes from doing a good turn. You decide on the benefits that will be most likely to win over your readers.

A special kind of persuasive request is one that casts the request as a problem–solution message. With this strategy, you first present a problem that you and the readers share—called the *common-ground* persuasion technique—and then show how doing as you propose will solve the problem for all concerned. Many fund-raising letters start with this ploy, giving us striking facts about the current economic climate, the environment, or living conditions in a certain area of the world. But this strategy can also be a powerful one for internal audiences who might not be receptive to a straightforward proposal for action but who share your opinion that something needs to be done.

A persuasive request situation is a special opportunity for analysis, creativity, and judgment. With careful use of all three, you can plan messages that will change your readers' minds and move them to action.

Many persuasive messages arrive uninvited. They have goals that are likely to encounter reader resistance. Unless they gain the reader's attention at the beginning, they are likely to end up in a trash can.

Gaining Attention in the Opening

In the indirect messages discussed in Chapter 7, the goal of the opening is to set up the explanation. The same goal exists in persuasive requests. Your beginning should lead to your central strategy. But the opening of a persuasive request has an additional goal: to gain attention.

You need to draw your reader in with the opening of your persuasive message because you are writing to a person who has not invited your message and may not agree with your goal. An interesting beginning is a good step toward getting this person in a receptive mood.

Determine what your reader will find compelling. It might be some statement that arouses curiosity, or it might be a statement offering or implying a reader benefit. Because questions get people thinking, they are often effective openings. The following examples indicate the possibilities.

From the cover letter of a questionnaire seeking the opinions of medical doctors:

What, in your opinion as a medical doctor, is the future of the private practice of medicine?

From a message requesting contributions for orphaned children:

While you and I dined heartily last night, 31 orphans at San Pablo Mission had only dried beans to eat.

From a message seeking the cooperation of business leaders in promoting a fair:

What would your profits be if 300,000 free-spending visitors came to our town during a single week?

If writing your request in the form of a problem–solution message, you should start with a goal that you and the readers share. For example, let's say that a project manager in your company has retired and that, as one of your company's executive committee, you want a certain member of the office staff to be promoted into the position. The challenge is that no office person in your company has ever broken into the managerial ranks, so any direct proposal to promote your candidate will, you feel sure, be met with this objection. To get readers on your side from the beginning, you could start your message with facts that everyone can agree upon: that someone has retired, that his or her duties are important, that someone capable needs to be found, and fast. Your subject line for an email along these lines might be something like, "Reassigning Jim Martin's Duties" (which everyone supports), not "Promoting Kathy Pearson" (which your readers will resist unless you have prepared them for the idea).

Whatever the case, the form of indirectness that you choose for your opening should engage your readers right away and get them thinking along the lines that will lead to their approval of your request.

Developing the Appeal

Following the opening, you should proceed with your goal of persuading. Your task here is a logical and orderly presentation of the reasoning you have selected.

As with any argument intended to convince, you should do more than merely list points. You should help convey the points with convincing details. Since you are trying to penetrate a neutral or resistant mind, you need to make good use of the you-viewpoint. You need to pay careful attention to the meanings of your words and the clarity of your expression. You need to use logic and emotion appropriately and project an appealing image. And, because your reader may become impatient if you delay your objective, you need to make every word count.

Making the Request Clearly and Positively

After you have done your persuading, move to the action you seek. You have tried to prepare the reader for what you want. If you have done that well, the reader should be ready to accept your request.

- The opening sets up the strategy and gains attention.

- It should make the reader receptive to your message.

- An effective attention-getter is both creative and adapted to your reader.

- The opening of a problem–solution message describes a problem that you and your readers share.

- Your persuasion follows.

- Present the points convincingly (selecting words for a positive effect, using you-viewpoint, and the like).

- Follow the persuasion with the request.

● Word the request for best effect.

As with negative messages, your request requires care in word choice. You should avoid words that detract from the request. You also should avoid words that bring to mind images and ideas that might work against you. Words that bring to mind reasons for refusing are especially harmful, as in this example:

● Do not use a negative tone.

I am aware that businesspeople in your position have little free time to give, but will you please consider accepting an assignment to the board of directors of the Children's Fund?

The following positive tie-in with a major point in the persuasion strategy does a much better job:

● Be positive.

Because your organizing skills are so desperately needed, will you please serve on the board of directors of the Children's Fund?

● The request can end the message or be followed by more persuasion.

Whether your request should end your message will depend on the needs of the case. In some cases, you will profit by following the request with further persuasive words. This procedure is especially effective when a long persuasion effort is needed or when you think your reader will be impatient to hear your objective. In such cases, you simply cannot present all your reasoning before stating your goal. On the other hand, you may end less involved presentations with the request. Even in this case, however, you may want to follow the request with one last appeal. As illustrated in the example messages on pages 203 and 204, this strategy associates the request with the advantage that saying "yes" will give the reader.

● Ending with a reminder of the appeal is also good.

Summarizing the Plan for Requests

● Follow this general plan when writing persuasive requests.

From the preceding discussion, the general plan for persuasive requests can be summarized as follows:

- Open with words that (1) gain attention and (2) set up the strategy.
- Develop the appeal using persuasive language and the you-viewpoint.
- Make the request clearly and without negatives (1) either at the end of the message or (2) followed by words that recall the persuasive appeal.

Contrasting Persuasive Requests

The persuasive request is illustrated by contrasting letters that ask businesspeople to donate to Junior Achievement. The first message is direct and weak in its persuasion; the second is indirect and persuasive. The second message, which follows the approach described above, produced better results.

A Selfish Blunt Approach. The weaker letter begins with the request. Because the request is opposed to the reader's wishes, the direct beginning is likely to get a negative reaction. In addition, the comments about how much to give tend to lecture rather than suggest. Some explanation follows, but it is weak and scant. In general, the letter is poorly written. It makes little use of the you-viewpoint. Perhaps its greatest fault is that the persuasion comes too late. The selfish close is a weak reminder of the action requested.

This direct, bland approach is not likely to persuade.

Dear Mr. Williams:

Will you please donate to the local Junior Achievement program? We have set $50 as a fair minimum for businesses to give. But larger amounts would be appreciated.

The organization badly needs your support. Currently, about 900 young people will not get to participate in Junior Achievement activities unless more money is raised. Junior Achievement is a most worthwhile organization. As a business leader, you should be willing to support it.

If you do not already know about Junior Achievement, let me explain. Junior Achievement is an organization for high school youngsters. They work with local business executives to form small businesses. They operate the businesses. In the process, they learn about our economic system. This is a good thing, and it deserves our help.

Hoping to receive your generous donation,

Skillful Persuasion in An Indirect Order. The next message follows the recommended indirect pattern. Its opening generates interest and sets up the persuasion strategy. Notice the effective use of the you-viewpoint throughout. Not until the reader has been sold on the merits of the request does the message ask the question. It does this clearly and directly. The final words leave the reader thinking about the benefits that a *yes* answer will give.

This indirect, interesting, detailed letter has a much greater chance of success.

Dear Mr. Williams:

Right now—right here in our city—620 teenage youngsters are running 37 corporations. The kids run the whole show; their only adult help comes from business professionals who work with them.

Last September these young people applied for charters and elected officers. They created plans for business operations. For example, one group planned to build websites for local small businesses. Another elected to conduct a rock concert. Yet another planned to publish electronic newsletters for area corporations. After determining their plans, the kids issued stock—and sold it, too. With the proceeds from stock sales, they began their operations. Now they are operating. This May they will liquidate their companies and account to their stockholders for their profits or losses.

What's behind these impressive accomplishments? As you've probably guessed, it's Junior Achievement. Since 1919, this nonprofit organization has been teaching school kids of all ages about business, economics, and entrepreneurship. Thanks to partnerships between volunteers and teachers, these kids gain hands-on experience with real business operations while learning the fundamentals of economics and financial responsibility. They also learn cooperation and problem solving. It's a win–win situation for all involved.

To continue to succeed, Junior Achievement needs all of us behind it. During the 13 years the program has been in our city, it has had enthusiastic support from local business leaders. But with over 900 students on the waiting list, our plans for next year call for expansion. That's why, as a volunteer myself, I ask that you help make the program available to more youngsters by contributing $50 (it's deductible). By helping to cover the cost of materials, special events, and scholarships, you'll be preparing more kids for a bright future in business.

Please make your donation now by completing our online contribution form at <www.juniorachievement.org>. You will be doing a good service—for our kids, for our schools, and for our community.

Sincerely,

A Persuasive External Request (Asking for Information about Employment Applicants). In this letter a trade publication editor seeks information from an executive for an article on desirable traits of job applications. Granting the request will involve time and effort for the executive. Thus, indirect persuasion is appropriate.

FastTrack
Jumpstarting Your Business Career

November 20, 2012

Ms. Adelade O. Romano
Director of Human Resources
Chalmers-DeLouche, Inc.
17117 Proden Road
St. Paul, MN 55108

Dear Ms. Romano:

Question opening gets attention

What clues have you found in employment applications that help you estimate a person's character and desirability to your firm?

Opening topic sets up explanation

Explanation follows logically

Young people entering business are eager for any clue that will put them on the other side of the fence. They want to know what goes on in your mind when you are judging the people behind the letters. In our column, "Applications That Talk," we want to send a message especially to those people. To make the article as practical as possible, we are drawing our information from people in the field who really know.

A mutual friend of ours, Max Mullins, told me of your recent problem of finding the most desirable person behind 250 applications. What specific points did you look for in these applications? What clues distinguished some people from the others? When the going got hard, what fine points enabled you to make your final choice? The young professionals of today are eager for answers to such questions.

Request evolves from presentation of appeal

Explanation is straightforward— appeals subtly to good feeling from helping others

You can help solve their problem if you will jot down your personal comments on a diverse sample of these applications and allow me to interview you about your judgments. All applicant information would of course be kept confidential.

Will you share your insights with me and with hundreds of young professionals? If so, please call or email me to set up an interview time that is convenient for you. It is just possible that, through this article, you will contribute to the success of a future leader in your own company. At the least, you will be of service to the many young people who are trying to get "that" job that is so important to them right now.

Final words recall basic appeal

Clear statement of the request

Sincerely,

Charlotte C. Clayton

enclosures

Charlotte C. Clayton
Associate Editor

405 Perrin Ave.

Austin, TX 78716

512-437-7080

FAX: 512-437-7081

Clayton@fasttrack.com

A Persuasive Internal Request (Using a Central Emotional Appeal Supported by Logical and Character-Based Appeals). The writer wants employees to participate in the company's annual blood drive. He needs to convince them of the importance of the drive and overcome their likely objections. This message will be distributed to employees' mailboxes.

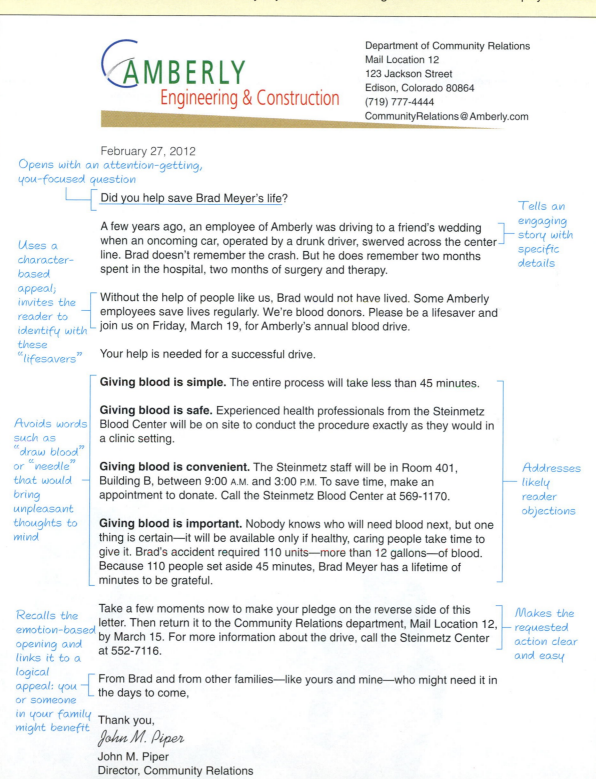

AMBERLY
Engineering & Construction

Department of Community Relations
Mail Location 12
123 Jackson Street
Edison, Colorado 80864
(719) 777-4444
CommunityRelations@Amberly.com

February 27, 2012

Opens with an attention-getting, you-focused question

Did you help save Brad Meyer's life?

Tells an engaging story with specific details

A few years ago, an employee of Amberly was driving to a friend's wedding when an oncoming car, operated by a drunk driver, swerved across the center line. Brad doesn't remember the crash. But he does remember two months spent in the hospital, two months of surgery and therapy.

Uses a character-based appeal; invites the reader to identify with these "lifesavers"

Without the help of people like us, Brad would not have lived. Some Amberly employees save lives regularly. We're blood donors. Please be a lifesaver and join us on Friday, March 19, for Amberly's annual blood drive.

Your help is needed for a successful drive.

Avoids words such as "draw blood" or "needle" that would bring unpleasant thoughts to mind

Giving blood is simple. The entire process will take less than 45 minutes.

Giving blood is safe. Experienced health professionals from the Steinmetz Blood Center will be on site to conduct the procedure exactly as they would in a clinic setting.

Giving blood is convenient. The Steinmetz staff will be in Room 401, Building B, between 9:00 A.M. and 3:00 P.M. To save time, make an appointment to donate. Call the Steinmetz Blood Center at 569-1170.

Addresses likely reader objections

Giving blood is important. Nobody knows who will need blood next, but one thing is certain—it will be available only if healthy, caring people take time to give it. Brad's accident required 110 units—more than 12 gallons—of blood. Because 110 people set aside 45 minutes, Brad Meyer has a lifetime of minutes to be grateful.

Recalls the emotion-based opening and links it to a logical appeal: you or someone in your family might benefit

Take a few moments now to make your pledge on the reverse side of this letter. Then return it to the Community Relations department, Mail Location 12, by March 15. For more information about the drive, call the Steinmetz Center at 552-7116.

Makes the requested action clear and easy

From Brad and from other families—like yours and mine—who might need it in the days to come,

Thank you,

John M. Piper

John M. Piper
Director, Community Relations

203

INTRODUCTORY SITUATION

Sales Messages

Introduce yourself to the next message type by assuming the role of Anthony A. Killshaw, a successful restaurant consultant. Over the past 28 years, you have acquired an expert knowledge of restaurant operations. You have made a science of virtually every area of restaurant activity: menu design, food control, purchasing, kitchen organization, service. You also have perfected a simple system for data gathering and analysis that quickly gets to the heart of most operations' problems. Testimonials from a number of satisfied clients prove that the system works.

Knowing that your system works is one thing. Getting this knowledge to enough prospective clients is another. So you have decided to publicize your work by writing restaurant managers and telling them about what you have to offer.

At the moment your plan for selling your services is hazy. But you think you will do it by email. It's a fast and easy way to reach your potential customers, you think. They will be more likely to read your message than if you used direct mail. Probably you will use a basic message that will invite the readers to look at your website. The website conveys the details—much more than you could get into the message.

Because sales writing requires special skills, you have decided to use the help of a local advertising agency—one with good experience with this type of selling. However, you have a pretty good idea of what you want, so you will not leave the work entirely up to the agency's personnel. You will tell them what you want included, and you will have the final word on what is acceptable.

• Professionals usually do the sales writing, so why study the subject?

One of the most widely disseminated forms of business communication is the sales message. It is such an important component of most businesses' sales strategies that it has become an elaborate, highly professionalized class, backed by extensive consumer research. Think about the typical sales letter that you receive. Careful attention has been paid to the message on the envelope, to the kinds of pieces inside, and to the visual appeal of those pieces, as well as to the text of the letter itself. Clearly, advertising professionals produce many of these mailings, as well as much of the fund-raising literature

Face-to-face selling is only part of the picture. Many sales occur through mail and email.

that we receive. You can also see a professional's hand in many of the sales emails that appear in your in-box. Why, then, you might ask, should you study sales writing?

As a businessperson, you will often find yourself in the position of helping to shape a major sales campaign. You may well have valuable insight into your product's benefits and your potential customers. You need to be familiar with the conventions for sales messages and to be able to offer your own good ideas for their success.

In addition, knowledge of selling techniques can help you in many of your other activities, especially the writing of other kinds of business messages, for in a sense most of them involve selling something—an idea, a line of reasoning, your company, yourself. Sales techniques are more valuable to you than you might think. After you have studied the remainder of this chapter, you should see why.

- You need to be able to share your insider knowledge and judgment with sales-writing professionals.

- Knowing selling techniques helps you write other types of messages.

Questioning the Acceptability of Sales Messages

We begin our discussion of sales messages by noting that they are a controversial area of business communication, for two main reasons: they are often unwanted, and they sometimes use ethically dubious persuasive tactics. You probably know from your own experience that direct-mail sales literature is not always received happily. Called "junk" mail, these mailings often go into the wastebasket without being read. Even so, they must be successful, for the direct-mail business has survived for over a century.

- Direct-mail sales messages are not always well received.

Sales messages sent by email appear to be creating even more hostility among intended customers. Angrily referred to as "spam," unsolicited email sales messages have generated strong resistance among email users. Perhaps it is because these messages clutter up in-boxes. Maybe the rage results from the fact that mass mailings place a heavy burden on Internet providers, driving up costs to the users. Or perhaps the fact that they invade the reader's privacy is to blame. There are the downright unethical practices of some email advertisers who use "misleading subject lines and invalid email addresses to thwart filtering attempts and get respondents to open them."[1] Whatever the explanation, the resistance is real. You will need to consider these objections any time you use this sales medium.

- Email sales messages are even more unpopular, and for good reason.

Fortunately, a more acceptable form of email selling has developed. Called *permission email* or *opt-in email marketing,* it permits potential customers to sign up for email promotions on a company's website or offer their email addresses to a catalog, phone marketer, or other recipient. The potential customers may be asked to indicate the products, services, and specific topics of their interest. Thus the marketers can tailor their messages to the customer, and the customer receives only what he or she wants. According to a recent white paper by eMarketer, building permission-based email distribution lists is one of the most important steps in waging successful emarketing campaigns.[2] Such practices can help address the problem of unwanted sales messages.

- Permission email marketing is emerging.

As for the charge that persuasive messages use unfair persuasive tactics, this is, unfortunately, sometimes the case. The unfair tactics could range from deceptive wording and visuals to the omission of important information to the use of emotional elements that impair good judgment. In a Missouri court case, Publishers Clearing House was found guilty of deception for direct mail stating that the recipients were already winners, when in fact they were not.[3] To consider a different example, one linen supply company sent a letter to parents of first-year students at a university telling them that the students would need to purchase extra-long sheets, offered by this company, to fit the extra-long beds on campus—but omitted

- Some persuasive messages use unethical tactics, such as

- deceptive claims,

- omission of important information,

---

[1] Rich Gray, "Spamitize Your Inbox," *Smart Computing in Plain English* 8.7 (2000): 66, *Smart Computing,* Web, 20 July 2009.

[2] "Effective E-Mail: The Seven Golden Rules You Know (But May Forget to Follow)," *eMarketer,* eMarketer, 10 Mar. 2006, Web, 21 Mar. 2006.

[3] See Helen Rothschild Ewald and Roberta Vann, "'You're a Guranteed Winner': Composing 'You' in a Consumer Culture," *Journal of Business Communication* 40 (2003): 98–117, print.

- and heavy reliance on images that trigger a visceral response.

- Considering the ethical dimension is, therefore, critical for persuasive messages.

the information that only one dorm out of four had such beds. And it is well documented that images, because they work on a visceral level, persuade in ways that tend to bypass the viewers' reasoned judgment, leading some to question the ethics of such elements.[4]

Any persuasive message is, by its very nature, biased. The writer has a favored point of view and wants to persuade the reader to adopt it. Therefore, considering the ethical dimension of your communication, while important for all types of messages, is especially critical for persuasive messages. Let your conscience and your ability to put yourself in the readers' shoes guide you as you consider how to represent your subject and win others to your cause.

Preparing to Write a Sales Message

- Begin work on a sales message by studying the product or service to be sold.

Before you can begin writing a sales message, you must know all you can about the product or service you are selling. You simply cannot sell most goods and services unless you know them and can tell the prospects what they need to know. Before prospects buy a product, they may want to know how it is made, how it works, what it will do, and what it will not do. Clearly, a first step in sales writing is careful study of your product or service.

- Also, study your readers.

In addition, you should know your readers. In particular, you should know about their needs for the product or service. Anything else you know about them can help: their economic status, age, nationality, education, and culture. The more you know about your readers, the better you will be able to adapt your sales message to them.

- Research can help you learn about prospective customers. If research is not possible, use your best logic.

In large businesses, a marketing research department or agency typically gathers information about prospective customers. If you do not have such help, you will need to gather this information on your own. If time does not permit you to do the necessary research, you may have to follow your best logic. For example, the nature of a product can tell you something about its likely buyers. Industrial equipment would probably be bought by people with technical backgrounds. Expensive French perfumes and cosmetics would probably be bought by people in high-income brackets. Burial insurance would appeal to older members of the lower economic strata. If you are purchasing a mailing list, you usually receive basic demographics such as age, sex, race, education, income, and marital status of those on the list. Sometimes you know more—interests, spending range, consumption patterns, and the like.

Determining the Central Appeal

- Next, decide on what appeals and strategies to use, and pick a central selling point.

With your product or service and your prospects in mind, you are ready to create the sales message. This involves selecting and presenting your persuasive appeals, whether emotional, logical, character based, or a combination. But for most sales messages, one appeal should stand out as the main one—mentioned in the beginning, recalled in the middle, and reiterated at the end. While other benefits can be brought in as appropriate, the message should emphasize your central, best appeal.

- Appeals may be emotional (appealing to the feelings),

Emotional appeals—those based on our senses and emotions—can be found in almost any sales message, but they predominate in messages for goods and services that do not perform any discernable rational function. Illustrating emotional appeal is the following example from a message that attempts to sell perfume by linking the romance of faraway places with the product's exotic scent:

> Linger in castle corridors on court nights in London. Dance on a Budapest balcony high above the blue Danube. Seek romance and youth and laughter in charming capitals on five continents. And there you'll find the beguiling perfume that is fragrance Jamais.

---

[4] Charles A. Hill, "The Psychology of Rhetorical Images," *Defining Visual Rhetorics*, ed. Charles A. Hill and Marguerite Helmers (Mahwah, NJ: Lawrence Erlbaum, 2004), 30–38, print.

The Growing Popularity of White Papers

A kind of sales writing that more and more companies are using is the white paper. Originally, it was used to brief government officials on affairs of state, but it is becoming extremely popular as a more indirect form of selling than the obvious sales pitch.

A business white paper typically opens with a description of a situation, usually some kind of problem that the recipient's company faces or soon will face, or a need that it has. Sometimes this section can go on for several paragraphs or pages without even mentioning the seller's product. At some point, though, the white paper will offer the seller's products or services as a solution to the problem or answer to the need. The document thus often appears to serve an educational purpose, only secondarily selling a product.

For example, a recent white paper written by a telecommunications company opened with a description of the competitive forces threatening providers of telecommunications services. It then offered the company's product—which integrated voice, video, and data services—as an answer to piecemeal solutions. Most white papers, like this example, are written business to business, informing one's partners in the industry of new technology or other kinds of products that can benefit all concerned.

Many white papers are beautifully formatted and illustrated, as if produced by the staff of a professional magazine. In fact, they are similar in nature to the subtly promotional articles in trade magazines. For guidelines and examples, visit the website of Michael A. Stelzner, author of the White-PaperSource newsletter, at <www.stelzner.com>.

Logical appeals are more rational. These include strategies based on saving money, making money, doing a job better, and getting better use from a product. Illustrating a rational appeal (saving money) are these words from a message selling magazine subscriptions:

- or they may be rational (appealing to reason),

> We're slashing the regular rate of $36 a year down to only $28, saving you a full 22 percent. That means you get 12 information-filled new issues of *Science Digest* for only $2.33 a copy. You save even more by subscribing for 2 or 3 years.

Appeals based on character persuade by implying such arguments as "I use this product, so you should, too" or "I am an authority, so you should do what I recommend." Ads that employ sports figures, film stars, or experts to sell their products are relying heavily on character-based appeals. Companies themselves can often take on an appealing "character" in their sales campaigns. Note how the following excerpt from a sales letter for *Consumer Reports* magazine uses the company's identity to persuade:

- or they may be based on the projected character of the seller.

> *Consumer Reports* is on your side. We're a nonprofit consumer protection organization with no commercial interests whatsoever. To put it bluntly, we don't sell out to big companies and private interest groups—we're accountable to no one except to consumers. And when you're not beholden to advertisers (like other so-called consumer protection publications), you can tell it like it is.

People may also buy a certain product because they want to identify with, and be identified with, a certain successful, socially responsible, or "cool" company as projected in the company's sales messages.

In any given case, many appeals are available to you. You should consider those that fit your product or service and your readers best. Such products as perfume, style merchandise, candy, and fine food lend themselves to emotional appeals. On the other hand, such products as automobile tires, tools, and industrial equipment are best sold through rational appeals. And almost any product could be promoted through a character-based appeal. Often a combination of appeals is your best strategy, but be sure that they work together to create a coherent effect.

- Select the appeals that fit the product and the prospects.

- The prospects' uses
  of the product often
  determine which appeal
  is best.

How the buyer will use the product may be a major basis for selecting a sales strategy. Cosmetics might well be sold to the final user through emotional appeals. Selling cosmetics to a retailer (who is primarily interested in reselling them) would require rational appeals. A retailer would be interested in their emotional qualities only to the extent that these make customers buy. A retailer's main questions about the product are: Will it sell? What turnover can I expect? How much money will it make for me?

Determining the Makeup of the Mailing

- To know what to say in
  your sales message, you
  will need to decide what
  the auxiliary pieces, if
  any, will be.

When you write a sales message to be sent by mail or email, a part of your effort is in determining the makeup of the mailing. To know what you want to say in your main message, you'll need to decide what kinds of additional pieces will be included and how they will support the main piece.

- Direct mail can contain
  many kinds of creative
  components.

Consider, for example, a recent mailing by Scotts LawnService (see the case illustration on page 212). The mailing comes in a 9-inch by 12-inch white envelope with the words "LAWN ANALYSIS ENCLOSED FOR (the recipient's address)" on the front, as well as the words "(recipient's city) RESIDENTS: PLEASE TAKE NOTICE." Both the kind of envelope used and the wording on it convey the image of an official, personalized document.

Inside are these three 7½-inch by 10½-inch pages:

- A top page that includes the main sales letter on the front, with bold letters in the top right corner advertising a **"FREE No-Obligation Lawn Analysis for (the resident's address)."** On the back are six testimonials under the heading **"Here's what our customers say about Scotts LawnService."**

- A second page, on glossy paper, that has "before" and "after" pictures of a lawn under the heading **"Now you can enjoy a thick, green, beautiful lawn . . . *and Scotts LawnService will do the work!*"** On the back are various character appeals for the company, under the heading **"Here's why you can expect more from Scotts LawnService than any other lawn service."**
- A replica of a "FREE LAWN ANALYSIS" form "TO BE COMPLETED FOR (the recipient's) FAMILY at (the recipient's address)," with "SAMPLE" stamped (or appearing to be stamped) across the form.

The last piece is a return envelope with a detachable form to fill out and return. Both parts advertise again the "FREE No-Obligation Lawn Analysis."

The author of this elaborate mailing determined that the free lawn analysis would be the immediate selling point, with the main reader benefit being the beautiful lawn that the analysis would lead to. With these decisions made, the writer could then decide what to place in the foreground of the letter, what other pieces to include, and how to

coordinate the letter with the other pieces. Even if someone else, such as a graphic artist or desktop publishing expert, will be designing the pieces of your mailing, you will need to plan how all parts of the sales package will work together, especially for a complex mailing like this one.

Email sales messages can use all the publishing features available on the computer. The message can be presented creatively with color, font variations, box arrangements, artwork, and more. It may include links to support material as well as to the ordering procedure. And it may have attachments. Just as with a direct-mail package, the email sales package uses many elements to persuade and to make available all the information a reader needs to complete the sale.

Gaining Attention

The beginnings of all sales messages have one basic requirement: to gain attention. If they do not do so, they fail. Because sales messages are sent without invitation, they are not likely to be received favorably. Unless they gain attention early, the messages will not be read.

With direct mail, the envelope containing the message is the first attention getter. All too often the reader recognizes the mailing as an uninvited sales message and promptly discards it. For this reason many direct-mail writers place an attention getter on the envelope. It may be the offer of a gift ("Your gift is enclosed"). It may present a brief sales message ("12 months of *Time* at 60% off the newsstand price"). It may present a picture and a message (a picture of a cruise ship and "Tahiti and more at 2-for-1 prices"). An official-appearing envelope sometimes is used. So are brief and simple messages such as "Personal," "Sensitive material enclosed," and "May we have the courtesy of a reply." The possibilities are numerous.

With email, of course, there is no envelope. The attention begins with the from, to, and subject fields. As one authority explains, you should clearly tell who you are and identify your company.[5] Many "spam" messages disguise these identities, and you hope your readers will not regard your message as spam. You should also address the reader by name. Though some readers will delete the message even with this clear identification, the honesty conveyed will induce some to read on.

The subject line in email messages is the main place for getting attention. Here honesty and simplicity should be your guide. The subject line should tell clearly what your message is about, and it should be short. It should avoid sensational wording, such as "How to earn $60,000 the first month." In addition, avoiding sensationalism involves limiting the use of solid caps, exclamation points, dollar signs, and "free" offers. In fact, you risk having spam filters block your message or send it to the junk folder of your readers' computers if you use "free" or other words and phrases commonly used in spam. An email with the subject line "Making your restaurant more profitable" that is sent to a researched list of restaurant managers and owners is much more likely to be opened and read than a message with the subject line "You have to read this!" that is sent to thousands of readers indiscriminately.

Holding Attention in the Opening

The first words of your message also have a major need to gain attention. The reader must be moved to read on. What you do here can be creative, but the method you use should help set up your strategy. It should not just gain attention for attention's sake. Attention is easy to gain if nothing else is needed. In a sales letter, a small explosion set off when the reader opens the envelope would gain attention. So would an electric

- Email sales messages can use all the creativity that computers allow.

- The basic requirement of the beginning is to gain attention.

- With direct mail, attention-getting begins with the envelope.

- With email, it begins with the from, to, and subject fields. Be honest.

- Make the subject line clear and short. Avoid sensationalism.

- The opening sentence should hold attention and set up the strategy.

[5] Jim Sterne and Anthony Priore, *Email Marketing: Using Email to Reach Your Target Audience and Build Customer Relationships* (New York: John Wiley & Sons, 2000) 143, print.

shock or a miniature stink bomb. But these methods would not be likely to assist in selling your product or service.

One of the most effective attention-gaining techniques is a statement or question that introduces a need that the product will satisfy. For example, a rational-appeal message to a retailer would clearly tap his or her strong needs with these opening words:

> Here is a proven best-seller—and with a 12 percent greater profit.

Another rational-appeal attention getter is this beginning of an email sales message from eFax.com:

> Never type a fax again!

This paragraph of a message selling a fishing vacation at a lake resort illustrates a need-fulfilling beginning of an emotional-appeal approach:

> Your line hums as it whirs through the air. Your line splashes and dances across the smooth surface of the clear water as you reel. From the depth you see the silver streak of a striking bass. You feel a sharp tug. The battle is on!

As you can see, the paragraph casts an emotional spell, which is what emotional selling should do. A different tack is illustrated by the following example. It attracts interest by telling a story and using character-based appeal:

> In 1984 three enterprising women met to do something about the lack of accessible health information for women.

Whatever opening strategy you choose, it should introduce or lead into your central selling point.

Building a Persuasive Case

With the reader's attention gained, you proceed with the sales strategy that you have developed. In general, you establish a need. Then you present your product or service as fulfilling that need.

The plan of your sales message will vary with each case. But it is likely to follow certain general patterns determined by your choice of appeals. If your main appeal is emotional, for example, your opening has probably established an emotional atmosphere that you will continue to develop. Thus, you will sell your product based on its effects on your reader's senses. You will describe the appearance, texture, aroma, and taste of your product so vividly that your reader will mentally see it, feel it—and want it. In general, you will seek to create an emotional need for your product.

If you select a rational appeal as your central theme, your sales description is likely to be based on factual material. You should describe your product based on what it can do for your reader rather than how it appeals to the senses. You should write matter-of-factly about such qualities as durability, savings, profits, and ease of operation.

When using character-based appeals, you will emphasize comments from a well-known, carefully selected spokesperson. Or, if the character being promoted is that of the company itself, you will provide evidence that your company is expert and dependable, understands customers like "you," and stands behind its service or product.

The writing that carries your sales message can be quite different from your normal business writing. Sales writing usually is highly conversational, fast moving, and aggressive. It even uses techniques that are incorrect or inappropriate in other forms of business writing: sentence fragments, one-sentence paragraphs, folksy language, and the like. As the case illustrations show, it also uses mechanical emphasis devices (underscore, capitalization, boldface, italics, exclamation marks, color) to a high degree. It can use all kinds of graphics and graphic devices as well as a variety of type sizes and fonts. And its paragraphing often appears choppy. Any sales message

- It can use logic,
- emotion,
- or character appeal.
- Plans vary for presenting appeals. Emotional appeals usually involve creating an emotional need.
- Rational appeals stress fact and logic.
- Character-based appeals create trust in or identification with the seller.
- Sales writing is stylistically and visually interesting.

A Direct-Mail Message (Selling a Lawn-Care Service). This sales letter uses all three types of appeals (logical, emotional, and character based). It also comes with several other pieces—including "before" and "after" pictures, customer testimonials, and a sample "free lawn analysis" form with the customer's name and address printed on it.

Scotts LawnService®
271 2nd Street
Saddle Brook, NJ 07663

Announces the immediate benefit that will lead to the main benefit: a beautiful lawn

FREE No-Obligation Lawn Analysis for
14111 Scottslawn Rd-Attn Dan Adams

March 27, 2012

The Adams Family
14111 Scottslawn Rd-Attn Dan Adams
Marysville, OH 43041-0001

YOU'LL BE SEEING OUR TRUCK ON SCOTTSLAWN RD A LOT THIS YEAR!

Makes it seem as though Scotts may have already looked at the customer's lawn

Dear Adams Family,

Do you know what's wrong with your lawn?

What do you need to do now to protect your lawn from unsightly weeds, insects you can't even see, and damaging turfgrass diseases? Call Scotts LawnService®! We have developed NEW Ortho Weed-B-Gon Pro® and Ortho® Max™ Pro Insect Control to handle tough weed and insect lawn problems.

Uses the bandwagon appeal—do what so many of your neighbors are doing

Sign up for Scotts LawnService like so many of your neighbors who had those problems. You'll see us treating their lawns throughout the season.

Now you can have a Scotts LawnService professional inspect your lawn for potential problems.

Uses you-attitude; suggests that you need to call in the experts

Builds Scotts' ethos as a company of knowledgeable professionals

We'll carefully examine your lawn and give you a detailed report on what we find, and what you need to do to keep your lawn thick, green and healthy.

And there's absolutely no cost and no obligation for this FREE Lawn Analysis.

Simply call us Toll Free at 1-800-736-0205 within the next 14 days, and Scotts LawnService will arrange for your FREE Lawn Analysis. It's easy, and you don't have to be home. We'll also include our recommendations for a Scotts LawnService program that's right for your lawn, plus a no-obligation price quote.

Makes several logical appeals

Appeals to emotion and logic and builds trust in the Scotts professionals

If you decide to become a Scotts LawnService customer, we'll put together a program that will give you the beautiful lawn you've always wanted. We use Scotts® slow-release, professional fertilizers on your lawn – and you can really see the difference in the results.

We'll evaluate your lawn during every visit, foreseeing and solving problems that may occur and taking personal responsibility for its progress. That's why Scotts LawnService offers you a Satisfaction Guarantee.

Requested action is clear and easy and linked to the main benefit

Call Scotts LawnService now or mail in the slip enclosed in the postage-paid envelope to request your FREE No-Obligation Lawn Analysis. It's the first step to having a thick, green, healthy lawn you can be proud of.

Sincerely,

Mike Pribanic

Mike Pribanic
North Jersey, Branch Manager

A final reminder of the main benefit and the easy first step

P.S. It's important to start early—to enjoy a beautiful lawn all season long. Please provide your phone number on the request slip, detach, and mail in the enclosed postage-paid envelope. For faster service, call 1-800-736-0205 to receive your FREE No-Obligation Lawn Analysis.

is competing with many other messages for the intended reader's attention. In this environment of information overload, punchy writing and visual effects that enable quick processing of the message's main points have become the norm in professional sales writing.

Stressing the You-Viewpoint

In no area of business communication is the use of the you-viewpoint more important than in sales writing. A successful sales message bases its sales points on reader interest. You should liberally use and imply the pronoun *you* throughout the sales message as you present your well-chosen reader benefits.

● The you-viewpoint is critically important in sales writing.

The techniques of you-viewpoint writing in sales messages are best described through illustration. For example, assume you are writing a sales message to a retailer. One point you want to make is that the manufacturer will help sell the product with an advertising campaign. You could write this information in a matter-of-fact way: "HomeHealth products will be advertised in *Self* magazine for the next three issues." Or you could write it based on what the advertising means to the reader: "Your customers will read about HomeHealth products in the next three issues of *Self* magazine." Viewing things from the reader's perspective will strengthen your persuasiveness. The following examples further illustrate the value of presenting facts as reader benefits:

Facts	You-Viewpoint Statements
We make Aristocrat hosiery in three colors.	You may choose from three lovely shades.
The Regal weighs only a few ounces.	You'll like Regal's featherlight touch.
Lime-Fizz is a lime-flavored carbonated beverage.	You'll enjoy the refreshing citrus taste of Lime-Fizz.
Baker's Dozen is packaged in a rectangular box with a bright bull's-eye design.	Baker's Dozen's new rectangular package fits compactly on your shelf, and its bright bull's-eye design is sure to catch the eyes of your customers.

You may also want to make use of scenario painting, putting the reader in a simulated context that brings out the product's appeal. The J. Peterman clothing company is famous for this technique, exemplified in the following excerpt from an advertisement for a men's silk sweater:

> Your P-38 has lost a wing in a dogfight somewhere over France.
>   You eject seconds before it turns into a fireball.
>   Newton was right—those trees down there are getting close fast.
>   Hard pull on the ripcord, a loud "whump," a bone-jarring shock . . . you look up and hallelujah, there it is:
>   The silk.
>   Can you think of a single good reason why a man shouldn't have a sweater made of this same terrific stuff?

Choosing Words Carefully

In persuasive messages, your attention to word choice is extremely important, for it can influence whether the reader acts on your request. Try putting yourself in your reader's place as you select words for your message. Some words, while closely related in meaning, have clearly different emotional effects. For example, the word *selection* implies a choice while the word *preference* implies a first choice. Consider how changing a single adjective changes the effect of these sentences:

● Carefully consider the effect of each word.

    You'll enjoy our hot salsa.
    You'll enjoy our fiery salsa.
    You'll enjoy our spicy salsa.

Framing your requests in the positive is also a proven persuasive technique. Readers will tend to opt for solutions to problems that avoid negatives. Here are some examples:

Original Wording	Positive Wording
Tastee ice cream has nine grams of fat per serving.	Tastee ice cream is 95 percent fat free.
Our new laser paper keeps the wasted paper from smudged copies to less than 2 percent.	Our new laser paper ensures smudge-free copies over 98 percent of the time.

Including All Necessary Information

- Give enough information to sell. Answer all questions; overcome all objections.

Of course, the information you present and how you present it are matters for your best judgment. But you must make sure that you present enough information to complete the sale. You should leave none of your readers' questions unanswered. Nor should you fail to overcome any likely objections. You must work to include all such basic information in your message, and you should make it clear and convincing.

- Make the letter carry the main sales message. Enclosures should serve as supplements.

As we say, you will also need to decide how to apportion your information across all the pieces in your mailing or the layout of a screen. With direct mail, you should use your letter to do most of the persuading, with any enclosures, attachments, or links providing supplementary information. These supplements might provide in-depth descriptions, price lists, diagrams, and pictures—in short, all the helpful information that does not fit easily into the letter. You may want to direct your readers' attention to these other pieces with such comments as "you'll find comments from your satisfied neighbors in the enclosed brochure," "as shown on page 7 of the enclosed catalog," or "you'll see testimonials of satisfied customers in the blue shaded boxes."

- In email sales messages, the supporting information can be accessed through links or attachments.

When you send the sales message by email, the supporting information must be worked into the message or presented in links or attachments that you invite the reader to view. You must take care to avoid the appearance of too much length or clutter when working this material into the message. By skillfully chunking the message visually (see the case illustration on the next two pages), you can reduce the effect of excessive

An Email Sales Message (Persuading Professionals to Attend a Seminar). This message uses logical and character-based appeals. Note how short paragraphs, bold text, and underlining facilitate quick reading and generate excitement.

From: "Advertising Club of Cincinnati" <jethompson001@msn.com>
To: <Kathryn.Rentz@uc.edu>
Sent: Thursday, April 17, 2011 8:00 AM
Subject: ExactTarget Roadshow Comes to West Chester

Sender's name and subject line are likely to appeal to readers on this organization's mailing list

To view this email as a web page, go here.

We pledge allegiance to great ideas.

Colorful "letterhead" and catchy tagline generate interest

ROUTE 1to1 ExactTarget. **The New eMarketing Essentials** One day seminars sponsored by Omniture and Salesforce.com › Register Now $59 Early Bird Special

Dear ADCLUB Member (or Member-To-Be):

Are you wondering if integrating your CRM and web analytics programs with email can help increase your marketing ROI?

Opening question with professional lingo invites further reading

The answer is YES. And, ExactTarget, one of ADCLUB Cincinnati's longtime trusted business partners, can show you how.

Character appeal adds to the persuasion

ExactTarget is launching a road show—**Route 1 to 1: The New eMarketing Essentials**—and it's coming your way! ExactTarget, Omniture, Salesforce.com, and SLI Systems are joining forces to make sure your CRM, web analytics, and email integrations drive highly-effective marketing return from day one. And thanks to our partnership, there's a special deal just for you!

Spend one day with ExactTarget and learn how to take your email marketing program to new heights.

View Agenda & Register Now!

Link here makes action easy to take

Logical appeals are the core of the message

ExactTarget's one day **Route 1 to 1** seminar series teaches you how to leverage your CRM and web analytics data and:

- Engage prospects
- Maximize marketing ROI
- Drive higher sales
- Increase "return-on customer"
- Build brand loyalty

Register for the Cincinnati Seminar! It's being held at the fabulous Savannah Center in West Chester. (The first 20 people to enter the code **R1T1ADCLUB** receive $20 off registration)

Yet another opportunity to register

A clever act now strategy

(continued)

Yet more reader benefits

In addition to presentations from ExactTarget's email thought leaders, top industry experts and analysts will provide one-to-one marketing technology insight. ExactTarget clients will also be on-site to share real-life examples of their B2B and B2C email marketing success.

Hope to see you there!

Best regards,

Judy

Judy Thompson
Executive Director
ADCLUB Cincinnati

P.S. The first 20 ADCLUB Cincinnati registrants will receive a $20 discount! Just enter the code R1T1ADCLUB while registering.

Reminder to act now

Special thanks to our Sponsors!

Gold Sponsor

red echo post.

Silver Sponsor

GREENEBAUM
GREENEBAUM DOLL & McDONALD PLLC

Bronze Sponsors

CREATIVES ON CALL

STEINHAUSER

These ads further contribute to the organization's credibility

Thanks, also to our ADCLUB Partners:
Cincy, Exact Target, Millcraft Paper, Primax Studio, Radisson Hotel, & Visual Aids Electronics

AAF

ADCLUB Cincinnati is proud to be affiliated with the American Advertising Federation. For more information, go to www.aaf.org.

One final character appeal

This email was sent to: Kathryn.Rentz@uc.edu

This email was sent by: **Advertising Club of Cincinnati**
602 Main Street, Suite 806 Cincinnati, OH, 45202 USA

Go here to leave this mailing list or modify your email profile.
We respect your right to privacy. View our policy.

Powered by
ExactTarget.
Learn more.

Provides reader with opt-out choice

COMMUNICATION MATTERS

Persuasive Strategies Vary across Cultures

When writing persuasive messages, be especially careful to adapt your messages to the culture of the intended readers.

For example, while sales letters in English and Chinese use many of the same core elements, there are also these crucial differences:

- English sales letters often use attention-getting headlines and postscripts that pressure readers to act, while Chinese sales letters do not use these seemingly harsh strategies.

- Both types of letters contain a salutation, but it is more formal in Chinese letters (for example, "Honored Company" instead of "Dear Mr. Smith"). Furthermore, Chinese letters follow the salutation with polite words of greeting, whereas English letters go directly into sales talk.

- English letters tend to describe the product's benefits by using "you," whereas the Chinese, finding the use

of "you" disrespectful, tend to use "we" (as in "Our consistent goal is to produce comfortable luxury cars of high standard and good quality").

- Both types of letters extol the benefits of the product, but Chinese letters use fewer details, especially about price.

- When making the actual request, Chinese letters are less pushy than English letters, favoring such mild language as "If you are interested in our products, please contact us."

- Both types of letters use a complimentary close, but instead of "Sincerely yours," the Chinese attempt to promote cooperation and mutual respect with such closings as "Wishing good health."

Source: Zhu Yunxia, "Building Knowledge Structures in Teaching Cross-Cultural Sales Genres," *Business Communication Quarterly* 63.4 (2000): 49–69, print.

---

length. And by making the boxes attractive with imaginative use of color, font selection, and formatting, you can enhance the effectiveness of the presentation. In either mail or email selling, your goal is to give the readers all they need to know to complete a sale, while allowing them the option of reading only as much as they desire.

Driving for the Sale

After you have developed your reader's interest in your product or service, the next logical step is to drive for the sale. After all, this is what you have been working for all along. It is a natural conclusion to the sales effort you have made.

● End with a drive for the sale.

How to word your drive for the sale depends on your strategy. If your selling effort is strong, your drive for action also may be strong. It may even be worded as a command. ("Order your copy today—while it's on your mind.") If you use a milder selling effort, you could use a direct question ("May we send you your copy today?"). In any event, the drive for action should be specific and clear. For best effect, it should take the reader through the motions of whatever he or she must do. Here are some examples:

● In strong selling efforts, a command is effective. For milder efforts, a request is appropriate. Take the reader through the motions.

> Just check your preferences on the enclosed order form. Then fax it to us today at 888.755.5265!

> Mail the enclosed card today—and see how right *Fast Company* is for you!

Similarly, in email selling you will need to make the action easy. Make it a simple click—a click to an order form or to the first part of the ordering process. Words such as these do the job well: "Just click the button below to order your customized iPhone case now!" and "You can download our free new catalog of business gifts at <http://thankyoutoo.com>." Many sales emails, such as the one shown in Figure 8–1, make the desired action easy by including multiple places for readers to perform it.

Figure 8–1

An Email that Makes the Desired Action Easy

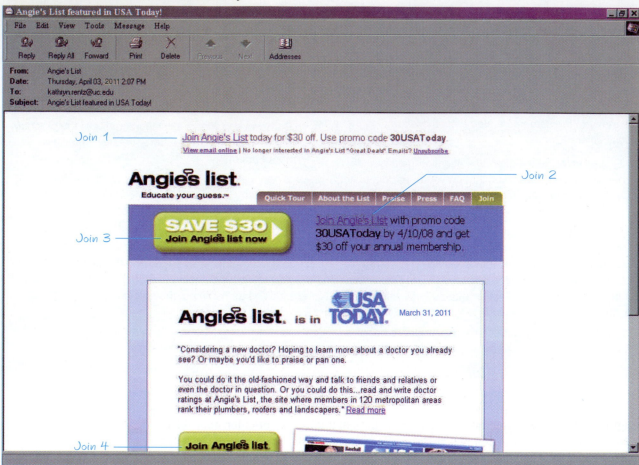

- Urge immediate action.

Because readers who have been persuaded sometimes put things off, you should urge immediate action. "Do it now" and "Act today" are versions of this technique, although some people dislike the commanding tone of such words. Even so, this type of action is widely used. A milder and generally more acceptable way of urging action is to tie it in with a practical reason for doing it now. Here are some examples:

. . . to take advantage of this three-day offer.

. . . so that you can be ready for the Christmas rush.

. . . so that you can immediately begin enjoying . . . .

- Recalling the appeal in the final words is good technique.

Another effective technique for the close of a sales message is to use a few words that recall the main appeal. Associating the action with the benefits that the reader will gain by taking it adds strength to your sales effort. Illustrating this technique is a message selling Maxell DVDs to retailers. After building its sales effort, the message asks for action and then follows the action request with these words:

. . . and start taking your profits from the fast-selling Maxell DVDs.

Another illustration is a message selling a fishing resort vacation that follows its action words with a reminder of the joys described earlier:

It's your reservation for a week of battle with the fightingest bass in the Southland.

Adding a Postscript

Unlike other business messages where a postscript (P.S.) appears to be an afterthought, a sales message can use a postscript as a part of its design. It can be used effectively in a number of ways: to urge the reader to act, to emphasize the major appeal, to invite attention to other enclosures, to suggest that the reader pass along the sales message, and so on. Postscripts effectively used by professionals include the following:

> PS: Remember—if ever you think that *Action* is not for you, we'll give you every cent of your money back. We are that confident that *Action* will become one of your favorite magazines.

> PS: Hurry! Save while this special money-saving offer lasts.

> PS: Our little magazine makes a distinctive and appreciated gift. Know someone who's having a birthday soon?

> PS: Click now to order and automatically enter our contest for a Motorola Q smartphone.

• Postscripts are acceptable and effective.

Offering Name Removal to Email Readers

Until January 1, 2004, it was a courtesy to offer the recipients of commercial email the option of receiving no further emails from the sender. Now, thanks to the so-called CAN-SPAM Act, it is a legal requirement as well.[6] Consider placing this invitation in a prominent place—perhaps even before the main message (see Figure 8–1). According to one authority, "This is the equivalent of asking, 'Is it OK if we come in?' "[7]

• Offer to remove readers from your email list—it's the law.

Reviewing the General Sales Plan

From the preceding discussion, a general plan for the sales message emerges. This plan is similar to the classic AIDA (attention, interest, desire, action) model developed almost a century ago. It should be noted, however, that in actual practice, sales messages vary widely. Creativity and imagination are continually leading to innovative techniques. Even so, the general prevailing plan is the following:

• Sales messages vary in practice, but this plan is used most often.

- Gain favorable attention.
- Create desire by presenting the appeal, emphasizing supporting facts, and emphasizing reader viewpoint.
- Include all necessary information—using a coordinated sales package (brochures, leaflets, links, appended parts, and such).
- Drive for the sale by urging action now and recalling the main appeal.
- Possibly add a postscript.
- In email writing, offer to remove the party contacted from your email list to comply with new legal requirements.

Evaluating Contrasting Examples

The following two email sales messages show bad and good efforts to sell Killshaw's restaurant consulting services.

Weakness in An Illogical Plan. Although the subject line of the amateur's sales message presents the main appeal, it is dull and general. The opening statement is little more than an announcement of what the consultant does. Then, as a continuation of the opening, it offers the services to the reader. Such openings do little to gain attention

---

[6] For further information, visit the Federal Trade Commission's website at <http://www.ftc.gov/spam/>.
[7] Nick Usborne, as quoted in Sterne and Priore, *Email Marketing* 151.

or build desire. Next comes a routine, I-viewpoint review of the consultant's services. The explanation of the specific services offered is little better. Although the message tells what the consultant can do, it is dull. The drive for action is more a hint than a request. The closing words do suggest a benefit for the reader, but the effort is too little too late.

This me-focused message is short on appealing reader benefits.

Subject: A plan to increase profits

Ms. Collins,

You have probably heard in the trade about the services I provide to restaurant management. I am now pleased to be able to offer these services to you.

From 28 years of experience, I have learned the details of restaurant management. I know what food costs should be. I know how to find other cost problems, be they the buying end or the selling end. I know how to design menu offerings for the most profitability. I have studied kitchen operations and organization. And I know how the service must be conducted for best results.

From all this knowledge, I have perfected a simple system for analyzing a restaurant and finding its weaknesses. This I do primarily from guest checks, invoices, and a few other records. As explained on my website (<http://www.restaurantimp.com>), my system finds the trouble spots. It shows exactly where to correct all problems.

I can provide you with the benefits of my system for only $1,500—$700 now and $800 when you receive my final report on your operations. If you will fill out and return by email the information requested below, I will show you how to make more money.

Larry Kopel, Consultant

Skillful Presentation of a Rational Appeal. The better message follows the conventional sales pattern described in the preceding pages. Its main appeal is rational, which is justified in this case. Its subject line gains interest with a claim of the main message presented in you-viewpoint language. The beginning sentence continues this appeal with an attention-holding testimonial. The following sentences explain the service quickly— and interestingly. Then, through good you-viewpoint writing, the reader learns what he or she will get from the service. This part is loaded with reader benefits (profits, efficiency, cost cutting). Next, after the selling has been done, the message drives for action. The last sentence ties in the action with its main benefit—making money. A post note about how to "unsubscribe" is both courteous and in compliance with U.S. federal law.

The you-viewpoint and better details give this message strong appeal.

Subject: A proven plan that guarantees you more profits

Ms. Collins,

"Killshaw is adding $35,000 a year to my restaurant's profits!"

With these words, Bill Summers, owner of Boston's famed Pirate's Cove, joined the hundreds of restaurant owners who will point to proof in dollars in assuring you that I have a plan that can add to your profits.

My time-proven plan to help you increase profits is a product of 28 years of intensive research, study, and consulting work with restaurants all over the nation. I found that where food costs exceed 40 percent, staggering amounts slip through restaurant managers' fingers. Then I tracked down the causes of these losses. I can find these trouble spots in your business—and I'll prove this to you in extra income dollars!

To make these extra profits, all you do is send me, for a 30-day period, your guest checks, bills, and a few other items. After analyzing these items using my proven method, I will write you an eye-opening report that will tell you how much money your restaurant should make and how to make it.

From the report, you will learn in detail just what items are causing your higher food costs. And you will learn how to correct them. Even your menu will receive thorough treatment. You will know what "best-sellers" are paying their way—what "poor movers" are eating into your profits. All in all, you'll get practical suggestions that will show you how to cut costs, build volume, and pocket a net 10 to 20 percent of sales.

For a more detailed explanation of this service, review the information presented at my website (<http://www.restaurantimp.com/>). Then let me prove to you, as I have to so many others, that I can add money to your income this year. This added profit can be yours for the modest investment of $1,500 ($700 now and the other $800 when our profit plan report is submitted). Just email the information requested below and I'll do the rest.

That extra $35,000 or more will make you glad you did!

Larry Kopel, Consultant

You were sent this message because of your interest in the white paper you recently downloaded from our site. If you wish to be removed from our list, please send an email with the word "unsubscribe" in the subject line.

PROPOSALS

INTRODUCTORY SITUATION

Proposals

Play the role of Evan Lockley, vice president of account management at Whitfield Organizational Research. Your company collects internal information for businesses that want to improve their management techniques, their information flow, employee morale, work processes, and so forth. To keep a steady stream of clients coming in, Whitfield must write numerous proposals for performing this kind of research.

As the manager of client accounts and the lead proposal writer at Whitfield, you now sit down to write a proposal for RT Industries. This company is about to implement an enterprise resource planning (ERP) system. This implementation will require employees in every functional area of the business—from purchasing to inventory to design, manufacturing, and shipping—to learn the system and enter the data for their area. If the implementation is successful, the management at RT Industries will be able to tell, with the click of a few buttons, exactly

how every facet of the business is doing. But implementing such a system is a major, and potentially disastrous, organizational change, and RT knows it. That's why they want to pay an organizational research firm to track the implementation and make sure it's as successful as possible. RT has invited Whitfield, along with other firms, to bid on this job.

You and one of your principal researchers have visited with the implementation team at RT Industries to learn more about the system they've chosen and their particular concerns. Whitfield has experience tracking such organizational changes, so you feel your odds of winning this client are good. But now you need to make your case. How can you craft a proposal that will make as positive an impression as possible? How can you make sure the readers at RT Industries will choose you over the competition? Read on to see how to write a persuasive proposal.

Proposals share certain characteristics with reports. Both genres require that information be carefully gathered and presented. Visually, they can seem quite similar; at their most formal, they use the same kinds of prefatory material (title page, letter of transmittal, table of contents, and so forth). And proposals frequently use the direct pattern

● Proposals resemble reports but differ in their fundamental purpose.

Visuals Help Business Writers Add Interest to Sales Messages

Sales messages—both print and rich email—often include art and animation to increase the visual appeal as well as attract attention to the message. In one recent experiment comparing two types of visual email messages, an HTML and a video message, Holland America found that the video message resulted in a 33 percent higher click-through rate than the HTML mailing. Furthermore, once readers got to the site, the average stay was nine minutes compared to five minutes for the HTML message. Additionally, the video message was cost effective, costing only 20 percent more than the HTML message.*

Today's business writers need not be artists or professional photographers to use good visuals in their documents. Major software programs include bundled art, animation, photographs, and sounds; and scanners and easy-to-use programs are readily available to help writers create customized visuals. Additionally, on the web, writers can find a vast assortment of specialists with products and services to help enhance their sales messages.

Here is a short list of a few websites. You'll find more on the textbook website as well.

- <http://webclipart.about.com/> A rich collection of links to websites for clip art, tutorials, hardware, and software.
- <http://www.fotosearch.com/> A meta search tool for finding professional photographs, illustrations, and videos.
- <http://www.animationfactory.com/en/> A subscription website for a variety of professionally prepared media.
- <http://www.freeaudioclips.com/> A site for free audio clips and links to software tools as well as a good search tool.

*Heidi Anderson, "Cruising to E-Mail Results," *ClickZ,* Incisive Interactive Marketing, 10 July 2003, Web, 15 May 2009.

- Proposals are intentionally persuasive.

that most reports use. But proposals differ from reports in one essential way: proposals are intentionally *persuasive*. Proposal writers are not just providing information in an orderly, useful form. They are writing to get a particular result, and they have a vested interest in that result. Whether they use the direct or indirect approach, their purpose is to persuade. The following sections provide an introduction to the main types of proposals and offer guidelines for preparing them.

- There are many kinds of proposals.

Types of Proposals

Proposals can vary widely in purpose, length, and format. Their purpose can be anything from acquiring a major client to getting a new copier for your department. They can range from one page to hundreds of pages. Their physical format can range from an email to a letter to a long, highly structured report. They are usually written, but they can be presented orally or delivered in both oral and written form. As with other kinds of business communication, the context will determine the specific traits of a given proposal. But all proposals can be categorized as either internal or external, and either solicited or unsolicited. It is with the unsolicited type that indirect organization most often comes into play.

- Proposals can be either *internal* or *external*.

- Internal proposals help you get what you need for you or your department to do your work.

Internal or External. Proposals can be either *internal* or *external*. That is, they may be written for others within your organization or for readers outside your organization.

The reasons for internal proposals differ, but you will almost surely find yourself having to write them. They are a major means by which you will get what you need in order to do or enhance your job or to effect an important change in your organization. Whether you want a computer upgrade, an improved physical environment, specialized training, travel money, or additional staff members, you will usually need to make your case to management. Of course, much of what you need as an employee will already be provided by your company. But when resources are tight, as they almost always are, you will have to persuade your superiors to give you the money rather

than allocating it to another employee or department. Even if your idea is to enhance company operations in some way—for example, to make a procedure more efficient or cost effective—you may find yourself having to persuade. Companies tend to be conservative in terms of change. The management wants good evidence that the trouble and expense of making a change will pay off.

In addition, as the practice of outsourcing has grown, many companies have adopted a system in which departments have to compete with external vendors for projects. As the director of technical publications for a company, for example, you may find yourself bidding against a technical-writing consulting firm for the opportunity, and the funding, to write the company's online documentation. If you are not persuasive, you may find yourself with a smaller and smaller staff and, eventually, no job yourself. Clearly, the ability to write a persuasive internal proposal is an important skill.

External proposals are also written for a variety of reasons, but the most common purpose is to acquire business for a company or money from a grant-awarding organization. Every consulting firm—whether in training, financial services, information technology, or virtually any other business specialty—depends upon external proposals for its livelihood. If such firms cannot persuade companies to choose their services, they will not be in business for long. Companies that supply other companies with goods they need, such as uniforms, computers, or raw materials, may also need to prepare proposals to win clients. Business-to-business selling is a major arena for external proposals.

- External proposals acquire business for the company or external funding for a project.

But external proposals are also central to other efforts. A company might propose to merge with another company; a city government might propose that a major department store choose the city for its new location; a university professor might write a proposal to acquire research funding. Many nonprofit and community organizations depend upon proposals for the grant money to support their work. They might write such proposals to philanthropic foundations, to wealthy individuals, to businesses, or to government funding agencies. Depending on the nature of the organization that you work for, proficiency in external proposal writing could be critical.

CHAPTER 8   Indirectness in Persuasive Messages

Solicited or Unsolicited. Another way to categorize proposals is *solicited* versus *unsolicited*. A solicited proposal is written in response to an explicit invitation tendered by a company, foundation, or government agency that has certain needs to meet or goals to fulfill. An unsolicited proposal, as you can probably guess, is one that you submit without an official invitation to do so.

The primary means by which organizations solicit proposals is the request for proposals, or RFP (variations are requests for quotes—RFQs—and invitations for/to bid—IFBs or ITBs—both of which tend to focus only on price). These can range from brief announcements to documents of 50, 100, or more pages, depending upon the scope and complexity of the given project. As you might expect, their contents can also vary. But a lot of thought and research go into a good RFP. In fact, some RFPs—for instance, a company's request for proposals from IT firms to design and implement their technology infrastructure—need to be just as elaborately researched as the proposals being requested. Whatever the originating organization, the RFP needs to include a clear statement of the organization's need, the proposal guidelines (due date and time, submission process, and proposal format and contents), and the approval process, in addition to such helpful information as background about the organization.

When responding to an RFP, you should be careful to heed its guidelines. With some firms, your proposal gets eliminated if it arrives even one minute late or omits a required section. This is particularly true for proposals to the federal government, whose proposal guidelines are notoriously, and perhaps understandably, regimented (see Figure 8–2). On the other hand, most RFPs give you some latitude to craft your proposal in such a way that your organization can put its best foot forward. You will want to take advantage of this maneuvering room to make your proposal the most persuasive of those submitted. Of course, you will decide in the first place to respond only to those RFPs that give your organization (or, if it is an internal RFP, your department) a fighting chance to win.

In business situations, solicited proposals usually follow preliminary meetings between the parties involved. For example, if a business has a need for certain production equipment, its buyers might first identify likely suppliers by considering those they already know, by looking at industry material, or by asking around in their professional networks. Next they would initiate meetings with these potential suppliers to discuss the business's needs. Some or all of these suppliers would then be invited to submit a proposal for filling the need with its particular equipment. As you can see, the more relationships you have with companies that might use your goods or services, the more likely it is that they will invite you to a preliminary meeting and then invite you to bid. One expert, in fact, asserts that the success of a proposal depends even more on the conversations and relationships that led to the proposal than on the proposal itself.[8] Another advises that "proposals can be won (or lost) before the RFP hits the streets."[9]

Even if you are preparing a proposal for a government or foundation grant, it is wise—unless the RFP specifically forbids it—to call the funding source's office and discuss your ideas with a representative.

When writing unsolicited proposals, your job is harder than with solicited proposals. After all, in these scenarios, the intended reader has not asked for your ideas or services. For this reason, your proposal should resemble a sales message. It should quickly get the readers' attention and bring a need of theirs vividly to mind. It should then show how your product or services will answer the need and drive for action. And from beginning to end, it should build your credibility. For example, if you want to provide training for a company's workforce or persuade a company to replace its current insurance provider with your company, you will need to target your readers' need in the opening, use further details to prepare them to receive your plan, lay out the benefits of your proposal quickly and clearly, and get the readers to believe that yours is the best company for the job. Careful and strategic preparation of unsolicited proposals can result in much success.

- Proposals can be either *solicited* or *unsolicited*.
- Organizations use requests for proposals—RFPs—to solicit proposals.
- Writing a good RFP requires considerable research itself.
- When responding to a solicited proposal, carefully follow the RFP guidelines.
- The response to an RFP should be part of a larger business relationship.
- Making contact with the granter can lead to stronger proposals for grants.
- Unsolicited proposals are like sales messages.

---

[8] Alan Weiss, *How to Write a Proposal That's Accepted Every Time,* expanded 2nd ed. (Peterborough, NH: Kennedy Information, Inc., 2003) 13, print.

[9] "What a Private Sector Company Can Learn From Government Proposals," *Captureplanning.com,* CapturePlanning.com, 2007, Web, 18 Aug. 2009.

This "presolicitation" posted on a U.S. government website gave advance notice of a Request for Quote (RFQ). As the links at the bottom show, the RFQ and the specifications for the project were later posted. The RFQ is 37 pages long, and the specifications are 39 pages. Any company that hopes to win this bid must study them carefully.

Figure 8–2

First Announcement of a Request for Quote (RFQ) by the U.S. Small Business Administration

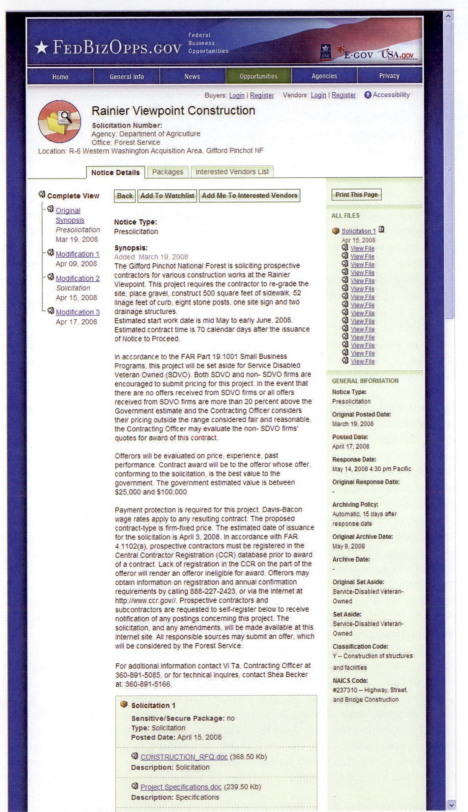

Wise Words from a Professional Proposal Writer

A proposal or grant is the beginning of a relationship. Essentially, the readers are interviewing your company or organization, trying to determine whether a basis for a positive, constructive alliance exists. Your proposal is the face you are presenting to the client or funding source. If they feel comfortable with your proposal, they will feel comfortable with your company or organization.

Source: Richard Johnson-Sheehan, *Writing Proposals*, 2nd ed. (New York: Pearson/Longman, 2008) 232–33, print.

- Prior contact with your recipient, if possible, is desirable for unsolicited proposals as well.

As with solicited proposals, you should try, if at all possible, to make prior contact with a person in the organization who has some power to initiate your plan. All other things being equal, a proposal to someone you know is preferable to a "cold" proposal. It is best to view the unsolicited proposal as part of a larger relationship that you are trying to create or maintain.

Proposal Format and Contents

- As with reports, proposal format and formality can vary.

Every proposal is unique, but some generalizations can be made. To succeed, proposals must be designed with the key decision makers in mind, emphasize the most persuasive elements, and present the contents in a readable format and style.

- Their formats vary from short emails to long, elaborate proposals.

Format and Formality. The physical arrangement and formality of proposals vary widely. The simplest proposals resemble formal email messages. Internal proposals (those written for and by people in the same organization) usually fall into this category, though exceptions exist. The more complex proposals may take the form of full-dress, long reports, including prefatory pages (title pages, letter of transmittal, table of contents, executive summary), text, and an assortment of appended parts. Most proposals have arrangements that fall somewhere between these extremes.

- Select the format appropriate for your one case.

Because of the wide variations in the makeup of proposals, you would be wise to investigate carefully before designing a particular proposal. In your investigation, try to determine what format is conventional among those who will read it. Look to see what others have done in similar situations. In the case of an invited proposal, review the request thoroughly, looking for clues concerning the preferences of the inviting organization. If you are unable to follow any of these courses, design a format based on your analysis of the audience and your knowledge of formatting strategies. Your design should be the one that you think is best for the one situation.

- The formality requirements of proposals vary. Do what is appropriate.

The same advice applies to your decisions about formality. Let your reader and the circumstances be your guide. Internal proposals tend to be less formal than external ones because the parties are often familiar with each other and because internal documents, in general, are less formal than external ones. If you are proposing a major initiative or change, however, using a formal presentation—whether oral, written, or both—may be in order. Likewise, external proposals, while they tend to be formal, can be quite informal if they are short and the two parties know each other well. Many successful business proposals are pitched in letter format. As with every other kind of message, knowledge of and adaptation to your reader are key.

- The primary objective of your content is to make a persuasive argument.

Content. Whether you are writing an external or internal proposal or a solicited or unsolicited one, your primary goal is the same: to make a persuasive argument. Every element of your proposal—from the title to the cover letter to the headings and organization of your content to the way you say things—needs to contribute to your central argument.

COMMUNICATION MATTERS

The Seven Deadly Sins of Proposal Writing

1. Failure to focus on the client's business problems and payoffs—the content sounds generic.

2. No persuasive structure—the proposal is an "information dump."

3. No clear differentiation of this vendor compared to others.

4. Failure to offer a compelling value proposition.

5. Buried key points—no impact, no highlighting.

6. Lack of readability because content is full of jargon, too long, or too technical.

7. Credibility killers—misspellings, grammar and punctuation errors, use of the wrong client's name, inconsistent formats, and similar mistakes.

Source: Tom Sant, *Persuasive Business Proposals* (New York: American Management Association, 2004) 11, print.

To be able to design your proposal according to this principle, you need to know your readers and their needs (which may be represented in an RFP). You also need to know how you can meet those needs. From these two sets of facts, you can develop your central argument. What is your competitive edge? Value for the money? Convenience? Reliability? Fit of your reader's needs or mission with what you have to offer? Some or all of the above? How you frame your argument will depend on how you think your proposal will be evaluated.

- First, review the readers' needs and your own ability to meet them.

- Then develop your central argument.

The reader of a business proposal will bring three basic criteria to the evaluation process:

- Readers of business proposals bring three main criteria to the evaluation process.

- Desirability of the solution (Do we need this? Will it solve our problem?)

- Qualifications of the proposer (Can the author of the proposal, whether an individual or company, really deliver, and on time and on budget?)

- Return on investment (Is the expense, whether time or money, justified?)

If you can answer these three questions affirmatively from the point of view of your intended recipient, you have a good chance of winning the contract or your management's approval.

When you have figured out what to propose and why, you need to figure out how to propose it. If the RFP provides strict guidelines for contents and organization, follow them. Otherwise, you have considerable discretion when determining your proposal's components. Although the number of content possibilities is great, you should consider including the eight topics listed below. They are broad and general, and you can combine or subdivide them as needed to fit the facts of your case. (See page 228 and pages 229–234 for two very different examples.)

- Consider including these eight topics:

1. *Writer's purpose and the reader's need.* An appropriate beginning is a statement of the writer's purpose (to present a proposal) and the reader's need (such as reducing turnover of field representatives). If the report is in response to an invitation, that statement should tie in with the invitation (for example, "as described in your July 10 announcement"). The problem should be stated clearly, in the way described in Chapter 10. This proposal beginning illustrates these recommendations:

- 1. Writer's purpose and the reader's need.

As requested at the July 10 meeting with Alice Burton, Thomas Cheny, and Victor Petrui in your Calgary office, Murchison and Associates present the following proposal for studying the high rate of turnover among your field representatives. We will assess the job satisfaction of the current sales force, analyze exit interview records, and compare company compensation and human resource practices with industry norms to identify the causes of this drain on your resources.

An Internal, Unsolicited Proposal. This email proposal asks a company to sponsor an employee's membership in a professional organization. Starting with the subject line, the writer tries to avoid saying anything that the reader—in this case, the head of a corporate communications department—would disagree with. When enough background and benefits are given, the writer states the request and then describes the cost in the most positive terms. Offering to try the membership for one year helps the proposal seem relatively modest.

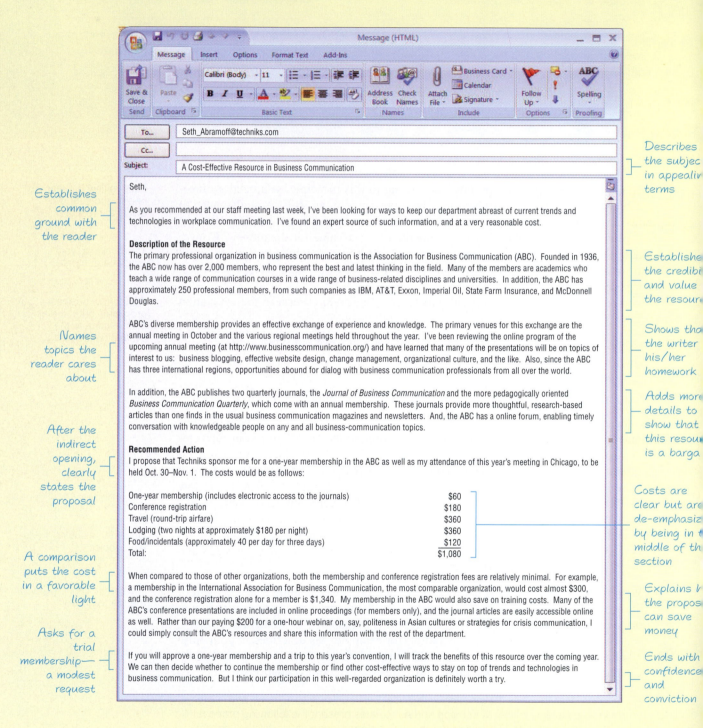

Describes the subject in appealing terms

Establishes common ground with the reader

Names topics the reader cares about

After the indirect opening, clearly states the proposal

A comparison puts the cost in a favorable light

Asks for a trial membership— a modest request

Establishes the credibility and value of the resource

Shows that the writer did his/her homework

Adds more details to show that this resource is a bargain

Costs are clear but are de-emphasized by being in the middle of the section

Explains how the proposal can save money

Ends with confidence and conviction

To... Seth_Abramoff@techniks.com

Cc...

Subject: A Cost-Effective Resource in Business Communication

Seth,

As you recommended at our staff meeting last week, I've been looking for ways to keep our department abreast of current trends and technologies in workplace communication. I've found an expert source of such information, and at a very reasonable cost.

Description of the Resource
The primary professional organization in business communication is the Association for Business Communication (ABC). Founded in 1936, the ABC now has over 2,000 members, who represent the best and latest thinking in the field. Many of the members are academics who teach a wide range of communication courses in a wide range of business-related disciplines and universities. In addition, the ABC has approximately 250 professional members, from such companies as IBM, AT&T, Exxon, Imperial Oil, State Farm Insurance, and McDonnell Douglas.

ABC's diverse membership provides an effective exchange of experience and knowledge. The primary venues for this exchange are the annual meeting in October and the various regional meetings held throughout the year. I've been reviewing the online program of the upcoming annual meeting (at http://www.businesscommunication.org/) and have learned that many of the presentations will be on topics of interest to us: business blogging, effective website design, change management, organizational culture, and the like. Also, since the ABC has three international regions, opportunities abound for dialog with business communication professionals from all over the world.

In addition, the ABC publishes two quarterly journals, the *Journal of Business Communication* and the more pedagogically oriented *Business Communication Quarterly*, which come with an annual membership. These journals provide more thoughtful, research-based articles than one finds in the usual business communication magazines and newsletters. And, the ABC has a online forum, enabling timely conversation with knowledgeable people on any and all business-communication topics.

Recommended Action
I propose that Techniks sponsor me for a one-year membership in the ABC as well as my attendance of this year's meeting in Chicago, to be held Oct. 30–Nov. 1. The costs would be as follows:

One-year membership (includes electronic access to the journals)	$60
Conference registration	$180
Travel (round-trip airfare)	$360
Lodging (two nights at approximately $180 per night)	$360
Food/incidentals (approximately 40 per day for three days)	$120
Total:	$1,080

When compared to those of other organizations, both the membership and conference registration fees are relatively minimal. For example, a membership in the International Association for Business Communication, the most comparable organization, would cost almost $300, and the conference registration alone for a member is $1,340. My membership in the ABC would also save on training costs. Many of the ABC's conference presentations are included in online proceedings (for members only), and the journal articles are easily accessible online as well. Rather than our paying $200 for a one-hour webinar on, say, politeness in Asian cultures or strategies for crisis communication, I could simply consult the ABC's resources and share this information with the rest of the department.

If you will approve a one-year membership and a trip to this year's convention, I will track the benefits of this resource over the coming year. We can then decide whether to continue the membership or find other cost-effective ways to stay on top of trends and technologies in business communication. But I think our participation in this well-regarded organization is definitely worth a try.

A Solicited External Proposal. A design and manufacturing company has invited research firms to propose plans for tracking its implementation of an enterprise resource planning (ERP) system—information technology that integrates all functions of the company, from job orders to delivery and from accounting to customer management. The midlevel formality of this proposal responding to the RFP is appropriate given the proposal's relative brevity and the two parties' prior meeting.

WHITFIELD
Organizational Research

7 Research Parkway, Columbus, OH 45319 614-772-4000 Fax: 614-772-4001

February 3, 2012

Ms. Janice Spears
Chief Operations Officer
RT Industries
200 Midland Highway
Columbus, OH 45327

Dear Janice:

Identifies the context for the proposal and shows appreciation for being invited to submit.

Thank you for inviting Whitfield Organizational Research to bid on RFP 046, "Study of InfoStream Implementation at RT Industries." Attached is our response.

Reminds the reader of the previous, pleasant meeting.

We enjoyed meeting with you to learn about your goals for this research. All expert advice supports the wisdom of your decision to track InfoStream's implementation. As you know, the road of ERP adoption is littered with failed, chaotic, or financially bloated implementations. Accurate and timely research will help make yours a success story.

Reinforces the need for the study.

Whitfield Organizational Research is well qualified to assist you with this project. Our experienced staff can draw upon a variety of minimally invasive, cost-effective research techniques to acquire reliable information on your employees' reception and use of InfoStream. We are also well acquainted with ERP systems and can get a fast start on collecting the data you need. And because Whitfield is a local firm, we will save you travel and lodging costs.

Summarizes the proposing company's advantages.

Compliments the receiving company, shows the writer's knowledge of the company, and states the benefits of choosing the writer's company.

RT's culture of employee involvement has earned you a persistent presence on *Business Ohio's* list of the Best Ohio Workplaces. The research we propose, performed by Whitfield's knowledgeable and respectful researchers, will help you maintain your productive culture through this period of dramatic change. It will also help you reap the full benefits of your investment.

We would welcome the opportunity to work with RT Industries on this exciting initiative.

Indirectly asks the reader for the desired action.

Sincerely yours,

Evan Lockley

Evan Lockley
Vice President, Account Management

enclosure

Response to RFP 046:
Study of InfoStream Implementation at RT Industries

Proposed by
Whitfield Organizational Research
February 3, 2012

Executive Summary

Provides a clear overview of the problem, purpose, and benefits.

RT Industries has begun a major organizational change with its purchase of InfoStream enterprise resource planning (ERP) software. To track the effect of this change on personnel attitudes and work processes in the company, RT seeks the assistance of a research firm with expertise in organizational studies. Whitfield Organizational Research has extensive experience with personnel-based research, as well as familiarity with ERP software. We propose a four-part plan that will take place across the first year of implementation. It will yield three major deliverables: an initial, a midyear, and a year-end report. Our methodology will be multifaceted, minimally disruptive, and cost effective. The results will yield a reliable picture of how InfoStream is being received and used among RT's workforce. Whitfield can also advise RT management on appropriate interventions during the process to enhance the success of this companywide innovation.

Project Goals

RT Industries has so far invested over $1.6 million and over 1,000 employee hours in the purchase of and management's training on InfoStream's ERP system. As RT integrates the system fully into its company of 800+ employees over the next 12 months, it will invest many additional dollars and hours in the project, with the total investment likely to top $2 million. Adopting such a system is one of the most wide-ranging and expensive changes a company can make.

Shows knowledge of the company; reminds readers of the investment they want to protect.

Reinforces the need for the study.

As Jeri Dunn, Chief Information Officer of Nestle USA, commented in *CIO Magazine* about her company's well-publicized troubles with their ERP software, "No major software implementation is really about the software. It's about change management." An ERP system affects the daily work of virtually everyone in the company. The most common theme in ERP-adoption failure stories—of which there are many—is lack of attention to the employees' experience of the transition. Keeping a finger on the pulse of the organization during this profound organizational change is critical to maximizing the return on your investment.

Our research will determine

- How well employees are integrating InfoStream into their jobs.
- How the new system is changing employees' work processes.
- How the system is affecting the general environment or "culture" in the company.

Statement of benefits, supported by clear logic.

Whitfield has designed a four-part, multimethod research plan to gather these data. Through our periodic reports, you will be able to see how InfoStream is being integrated into the working life of the company. As a result, you will be

(continued)

Whitfield Organizational Research   2

able to make, and budget for, such interventions as strategic communications and additional training. You will also find out where employee work processes need to be adjusted to accommodate the new system.

Instituting a change of this magnitude *will* generate feedback, whether it is employee grumbling or constructive criticism. Whitfield associates will gather this feedback in a positive, orderly way and compile it into a usable format. The findings will enable RT's management to address initial problems and ward off future problems. The research itself will also contribute to the change management efforts of the company by giving RT's employee stakeholders a voice in the process and allowing their feedback to contribute to the initiative's success.

Deliverables

The information you need will be delivered as shown below. All dates assume a project start date of July 1, 2012.

Approximate Date:	Deliverable:
October 1, 2012	Written report on **initial** study of 12–14 employees' work processes and attitudes and on companywide survey.
February 1, 2013	Written report at **midyear** on employees' work processes and attitudes and on companywide survey.
June 30, 2013	**Year-end** report (written and oral) on employees' work processes and attitudes and on companywide survey.

Readers can see the products of the proposed research up front.

Anticipated Schedule/Methods

The research will take place from July 1, 2012, the anticipated go-live date for InfoStream at RT, to approximately June 30, 2013, a year later. As shown below, there will be four main components to this research, with Part III forming the major part of the project.

Research Part and Time Frame	Purpose	Methods
Part I (July '12)	Gather background information; recruit research participants	Gather data on RT (history, products/mission, organizational structure/culture, etc.). Interview personnel at RT and at InfoStream about why RT considered adopting an ERP system, why RT bought InfoStream, and how employees at RT have been informed about InfoStream. During this period we will also work with the COO's staff to recruit participants for the main part of the study (Part III).

Gives details of the project in a readable format.

231

(continued)

Whitfield Organizational Research   **3**

Research Part and Time Frame	Purpose	Methods
Part II (July '12):	Obtain the perspective of the launch team on InfoStream	Focus-group interview with RT's launch team for InfoStream, with emphasis on their goals for and concerns about the implementation. Anticipated duration of this interview would be one hour, with participants invited to share any additional feedback afterward in person or by email.
Part III (July–Sept. '12; Nov. '09–Jan. '13; Mar.–June '13):	Assess the impact of InfoStream on employee work processes and attitudes	Conduct three rounds of 1–2 hour interviews with approximately 12–14 RT employees to track their use of InfoStream. Ideally, we will have one or two participants from each main functional area of the company, with multiple levels of the company represented.
Part IV (September '12, January '13, May '13)	Assess companywide reception of InfoStream	Conduct three web-based surveys during the year to track general attitudes about the implementation of InfoStream.

This plan yields the following time line:

	7/12	8/12	9/12	10/12	11/12	12/12	1/13	2/13	3/13	4/13	5/13	6/13
Initial research	■											
Focus group	■											
1st round of interviews	■	■	■									
1st web survey			■									
Initial report				■								
2nd round of interviews					■	■	■					
2nd web survey							■					
Mid-year report								■				
3rd round of interviews									■	■	■	
3rd web survey											■	
Year-end report												■

Timeline makes it easy to see what will happen at each point.

232

(continued)

Interview Structure and Benefits

While Parts I, II, and IV will provide essential information about the project and its reception, the most valuable data will come from Part III, the on-site interviews with selected RT employees. Gathering data in and about the subject's own work context is the only reliable way to learn what is really happening in terms of the employees' daily experience. Following is a description of our methodology for gathering these kinds of data:

Initial interview:

- Gather background information about the participants (how long they have worked at RT, what their jobs consist of, what kind of computer experience they've had, how they were trained on InfoStream).
- Ask them to show us, by walking us through sample tasks, how they use InfoStream.
- Ask them to fill out a questionnaire pertaining to their use of InfoStream.
- Go back over their answers, asking them to explain orally why they chose the answers they did.
- Ask them either to keep notes on or email us about any notable experiences they have with InfoStream.
- Take notes on any interruption, interactions, and other activities that occur during the interview.

From data gained in these interviews, we will assess how well the participants' current work processes are meshing with InfoStream. We will also document how use of InfoStream is affecting the participants' attitudes and their interactions with other employees and departments. We will check our findings with the participants for accuracy before including these data in the initial report.

Midyear interview:

- Ask the participants if they have any notable experiences to relate about InfoStream and/or if any changes have occurred in the tasks they perform using InfoStream.
- Have the participants fill out the same questionnaire as in the first interviews.
- Discuss with participants the reasons for any changes in their answers since the first questionnaire.
- Observe any interactions or other activities that occur during the interview.
- Check our findings with the participants for accuracy before including these data in the midyear report.

Year-end interviews:

- Will be conducted in the same fashion as the second interviews.
- Will also include questions allowing participants to debrief about the project and about InfoStream in general.

Benefits of this interview method:

- Because researchers will be physically present in the employees' work contexts, they **can gather a great deal of information,** whether observed or reported by the employee, **in a short amount of time.**
- Because employees will be asked to elaborate on their written answers, the researcher **can learn the true meaning of the employee's responses.**

Special section elaborates on the company's unique methodology; helps justify the most expensive part of the plan.

(continued)

- Asking employees to verify the researcher's findings **will add another validity check and encourage honest, thorough answers.**

Specific Knowledge Goals

We will design the interviews and the companywide surveys to find out the extent to which

- InfoStream is making participants' jobs easier or harder, or easier in some ways and harder in others.
- InfoStream is making their work more or less efficient.
- InfoStream is making their work more or less effective.
- They believe InfoStream is helping the company overall.
- They are satisfied with the instruction they have received about the system.
- InfoStream is changing their interactions with other employees.
- InfoStream is changing their relations with their supervisors.
- InfoStream is affecting their overall attitude toward their work.

The result will be a detailed, reliable picture of how InfoStream is playing out at multiple levels and in every functional area of RT Industries, enabling timely intervention by RT management.

A tantalizing list of what the readers most want to know whets their desire to hire the proposing company.

Cost

Because we are a local firm, no travel or lodging expenses will be involved.

Research Component	Estimated Hours	Cost
Part I (background fact finding)	6 hours	$300
Part II (focus group with launch team)	3 hours (includes preparation and analysis)	$300
Part III (3 rounds of on-site interviews)	474 hours	$18,960
Part IV (3 rounds of web-based surveys)	48 hours	$1,920
Preparation of Reports	90 hours	$3,600
		Total: $25,080

Cost breakdown justifies the expense but is not so detailed that the readers can nitpick specific items.

Credentials

Whitfield Organizational Research has been recognized by the American Society for Training and Development as a regional leader in organizational consulting. We have extensive education and experience in change management, organizational psychology, quantitative and qualitative research methods, and team building. Our familiarity with ERP software, developed through projects with such clients as Orsys and PRX Manufacturing, makes us well suited to serve RT's needs. Résumés and references will be mailed upon request or can be downloaded from <www.whitfieldorganizationalresearch.com>.

Efficient credentials section focuses only on those qualifications that are relevant to this situation.

If a proposal is submitted without invitation, its beginning has an additional requirement: it must gain attention. As noted previously, uninvited proposals are much like sales messages. Their intended readers are not likely to be eager to read them. Thus, their beginnings must overcome the readers' reluctance. An effective way of doing this is to begin by briefly summarizing the highlights of the proposal with emphasis on its benefits. This technique is illustrated by the beginning of an unsolicited proposal that a restaurant consultant sent to prospective clients:

The following pages present a proven plan for operations review that will (1) reduce food costs, (2) evaluate menu offerings for maximum profitability, (3) increase kitchen efficiency, (4) improve service, and (5) increase profits. Mattox and Associates proposes to achieve these results through its highly successful procedures, which involve analysis of guest checks and invoices and observational studies of kitchen and service work.

Your clear statement of the purpose and problem may be the most important aspect of the proposal. If you do not show right away that you understand what needs to be done and have a good plan for doing it, you may well have written the rest of your proposal in vain.

2. *Background*. A review of background information promotes an understanding of the problem. Thus, a college's proposal for an educational grant might benefit from a review of the college's involvement in the area to which the grant would be applied. A company's proposal of a merger with another company might review industry developments that make the merger desirable. Or a chief executive officer's proposal to the board of directors that a company be reorganized might present the background information that justifies the proposal.

● 2. Background.

3. *Need*. Closely related to the background information is the need for what is being proposed. In fact, background information may well be used to establish need. But because need can be presented without such support, we list it separately. You might wonder if this section applies in situations where an RFP has been issued. In such cases, won't readers already know what they need? In many cases the answer is no, not exactly. They may think they know, but you may see factors that they've overlooked. Plus, recasting their problem in ways that lead to your proposed solution helps your persuasive effort. And whatever the situation, elaborating on the receiving organization's needs enables your readers to see that *you* understand their needs.

● 3. Need.

4. *Description of plan*. The heart of a proposal is the description of what the writer proposes to do. This is the primary message of the proposal. It should be concisely presented in a clear and orderly manner, with headings and subheadings as needed. It should give sufficient detail to convince the reader of the plan's logic, feasibility, and appropriateness. It should also identify the "deliverables," or tangible products, of the proposal.

● 4. Plan description.

5. *Benefits of the proposal*. Your proposal should make it easy for your readers to see how your proposed action will benefit them. A brief statement of the benefits should appear at the front of your proposal, whether in the letter of transmittal, executive summary, opening paragraph, or all of the above. But you should elaborate on those benefits in the body of your proposal. You might do so in the section describing your plan, showing how each part will yield a benefit. Or, you might have a separate section detailing the benefits. As with sales writing, the greater the need to persuade, the more you should stress the benefits.

● 5. Benefits of the proposal (especially if selling is needed).

As an example of benefits logically covered in proposals, a college's request for funding to establish a program for retraining the older worker could point to the profitability that such funding would give local businesses. And a proposal offering a consulting service to restaurants could stress such benefits as improved work efficiency, reduced employee theft, savings in food costs, and increased profits.

6. *Cost and other particulars*. Once you have pitched your plan, you need to state clearly what it will cost. You may also need to cover such other particulars as time schedules, performance standards, means of appraising performance, equipment

● 6. Particulars (costs schedules, time, performance standards, equipment and supplies needed, and anything else that needs to be settled up front).

"We need something to come after this part. Any ideas?"

and supplies needed, guarantees, personnel requirements, and the like. Remember that a proposal is essentially a contract. Anticipate and address any issues that may arise, and present your requirements in the most positive light.

● 7. Ability to deliver.

7. *Evidence of ability to deliver.* The proposing organization must sometimes establish its ability to perform. This means presenting information on such matters as the qualifications of personnel, success in similar cases, the adequacy of equipment and facilities, operating procedures, environmental consciousness, and financial status. Whatever information will serve as evidence of the organization's ability to achieve what it proposes should be used. With an external proposal, resist the temptation to throw long, generic résumés at the readers. The best approach is to select only the most persuasive details about your personnel. If you do include résumés, tailor them to the situation.

● 8. Concluding comments (words directed toward the next step).

8. *Concluding comments.* In most proposals you should urge or suggest the desired action. This statement often occurs in a letter to the readers, but if there is no cover letter or the proposal itself is not a letter, it can form the conclusion of your proposal. You might also include a summary of your proposal's highlights or provide one final persuasive push in a concluding section.

Whatever you're writing—whether a proposal, request, sales message, or some other kind of message—the art of persuasion can be one of your most valuable assets. Adding the tips in this chapter to your general problem-solving approach will help you prepare for all those times in your career when you will need others' cooperation and support.

SUMMARY BY LEARNING OBJECTIVES

1 Describe important strategies for writing any persuasive message.

1. Certain advice applies to all persuasive messages:
   - Know your readers—well.
   - Choose and develop targeted reader benefits.
     — Both tangible and intangible benefits can be persuasive.
     — Prefer intrinsic to extrinsic benefits.
     — Express product features as reader benefits.
     — Use scenario painting to help your readers experience the product's appeal.

- Make good use of three kinds of appeals.
  — Emotional appeals play on our senses (taste, hearing, and so on) and our feelings (love, anger, and the like).
  — Rational appeals appeal to logic (e.g., thrift, durability, efficiency).
  — Character-based appeals use an appealing spokesperson or an attractive image of the company to help sell the product.
- Make it easy for your readers to comply.

2. Requests that are likely to be resisted require an indirect, persuasive approach.
- Such an approach involves developing a strategy—a plan for persuading.
- Your opening words should set up this strategy and gain attention.
- Follow with convincing persuasion.
- Then make the request—clearly yet positively.
- The request can end the message, or more persuasion can follow (whichever you think is appropriate).

2 Write skillful persuasive requests that begin indirectly, use convincing reasoning, and close with goodwill and action.

3. Sales messages are a controversial area of business communication.
- Many sales messages are unwanted.
  — "Junk" mail clutters people's mailboxes.
  — "Spam" clutters their in-boxes.
- Some sales messages use unethical tactics.
  — They may make deceptive claims.
  — They may omit important information.
  — They may rely heavily on visuals that trigger a visceral response.
- Use your conscience and your ability to put yourself in the readers' shoes to create ethical persuasive messages.

3 Discuss ethical concerns regarding sales messages.

4. A sales message requires special planning.
- Learn all you can about your service or product and your intended readers.
- Then select an appropriate central appeal and supporting appeals.
- Determine the makeup of the mailing.
  — Decide what you will include in the letter and what you will put in auxiliary pieces.
  — Consider a creative approach to the letter format itself.
  — Email sales messages can also have auxiliary pieces and innovative format.

4 Describe the planning steps for direct mail or email sales messages.

5. Although innovations are frequently used, the basic sales message generally follows this traditional plan:
- The opening seeks to gain attention and set up the sales presentation.
- The body makes your persuasive case.
  — It develops the appeals you have chosen.
  — It uses punchy writing and techniques for visual emphasis (typography, white space, color, and other visual elements).
- In emotional selling, the words establish an emotional atmosphere and build an emotional need for the product or service.
- Character-based appeals build trust and invite identification with the company.
- In rational selling, the appeal is to the thinking mind, using facts and logical reasoning.
- Throughout the message, emphasis is on good sales language and the you-viewpoint.
- All the information necessary for a sale (prices, terms, choices, and the like) is included in the message, though references are made to supporting information.

5 Compose sales messages that gain attention, persuasively present appeals, and effectively drive for action.

- Next comes a drive for a sale.
  — It may be a strong drive, even a command, if a strong sales effort is used.
  — It may be a direct question if a milder effort is desired.
  — In either case, the action words are specific and clear, frequently urging action *now*.
  — Taking the action may be associated with the benefits to be gained.
  — Postscripts often are included to convey a final sales message.
  — In email messages, opt-out links are often provided as a professional courtesy, and to comply with new laws.

6 Write well-organized and persuasive proposals.

6. Proposals resemble reports but differ in their fundamental purpose.
- They are intentionally persuasive.
- They can be categorized in two ways:
  — Internal or external.
  — Solicited or unsolicited.
- They vary widely in terms of format and formality.
  — As with reports, proposal formats can range from short emails to long, elaborate documents.
  — Their levels of formality vary as well.
- The goal for your content is to make a persuasive argument.
  — Review your readers' needs and your ability to address them.
  — Then develop your central argument.
  — Bear in mind the main criteria that evaluators use.
- The contents of proposals vary with need, but one should consider these topics:
  — Writer's purpose and reader's need.
  — Background.
  — Need.
  — Plan description.
  — Benefits.
  — Particulars (time, schedule, costs, performance standards, and such).
  — Ability to deliver.
  — Concluding comments.

CRITICAL THINKING QUESTIONS

1 Explain why a persuasive request is usually written in the indirect order. Could the direct order ever be used for such messages? Discuss. **[LO2]**

2 What is the role of the you-viewpoint in persuasive requests? **[LO2]**

3 Compare persuasive requests and sales messages. What traits do they share? How are they different? **[LO2, LO5]**

4 Consider ads that you have seen on television. Which ones rely heavily on emotional appeals? Which on logical appeals? Which on character-based appeals? Do the chosen appeals seem appropriate given the product, service, or cause that is being promoted? **[LO1, LO5]**

5 Think of a television, radio, print, email, or Internet sales message or persuasive request that you regard as especially effective. Explain why you think it was well designed. **[LO2, LO5]**

6 What appeals would be appropriate for the following products when they are being sold to consumers? **[LO1, LO4]**

a. Shaving cream
b. Carpenter's tools
c. Fresh vegetables
d. Software
e. Lubricating oil
f. Perfume
g. CD players
h. Women's dresses
i. Fancy candy
j. Hand soap

7 When could you justify addressing sales letters to "occupant"? When to each reader by name? [LO5]

8 "Rarely should a sales letter exceed a page in length." Discuss this statement. [LO5]

9 Should the traditional sales-message organization discussed in the text ever be altered? Discuss. [LO5]

10 Discuss the relationship between the sales message and its accompanying support information in an example you've seen. What was the purpose of each piece? [LO4, LO5]

11 When do you think a strong drive for action is appropriate in a sales message? When do you think a weak drive is appropriate? [LO5]

12 Think of a sample persuasive request or sales message that you regard as ethically questionable. Discuss the nature of the ethical problems. [LO3]

13 "To be successful, a proposal must be persuasive. This quality makes the proposal different from most short reports (which stress objectivity)." Discuss. [LO6]

14 Discuss the differences between solicited and unsolicited proposals. [LO6]

15 For what kinds of situations might you select email format for your proposal? Letter format? A longer, reportlike format? [LO6]

16 "I don't need to discuss my readers' needs in my proposal. They know what their needs are and don't want to waste time reading about them." Discuss. [LO6]

CRITICAL THINKING EXERCISES

1 Assume that, as a volunteer for a nonprofit organization in your town, you have been asked to write the next fundraising letter for the organization. In what ways might you gather enough information about the intended readers to write a successful message? [LO1]

2 List the tangible and intangible benefits that you might describe when promoting the following items or services: [LO1]

   a. Membership in a health club.

   b. High-speed Internet service or digital cable service.

   c. A certain line of clothing.

3 List some extrinsic benefits you might use as an extra push if you were promoting the items in number 2. [LO1]

4 For each item in number 2, list two likely product features and then turn them into reader benefits. [LO1]

5 Choose one of the items in number 2 and write a paragraph that uses scenario painting to promote the item. [LO1]

6 Criticize the persuasive request message below. It was written by the membership chairperson of a chapter of the Service Corps of Retired Executives (SCORE), a service organization consisting of retired executives who donate their managerial talents to small businesses in the area. The recipients of the message are recently retired executives. [LO2]

Dear Ms. Petersen:

As membership chair it is my privilege to invite you to join the Bay City chapter of the Service Corps of Retired Executives. We need you, and you need us.

We are a volunteer, not-for-profit organization. We are retired business executives who give free advice and assistance to struggling small businesses. There is a great demand for our services in Bay City, which is why we are conducting this special membership drive. As I said before, we need you. The work is hard and the hours can be long, but it is satisfying.

Please find enclosed a self-addressed envelope and a membership card. Fill out the card and return it to me in the envelope. We meet the first Monday of every month (8:30 at the Chamber of Commerce office). This is the fun part—strictly social. A lot of nice people belong.

I'll see you there Monday!

Sincerely yours,

7 Evaluate the following sales message. It was written to people on a mailing list of fishing enthusiasts. The writer, a professional game fisher, is selling his book by direct mail. The nature of the book is evident from the letter. [LO5]

Have you ever wondered
why the pros catch fish
and you can't?

They have secrets. I am a pro, and I know these secrets. I have written them and published them in my book, *The Bible of Fishing*.

This 240-page book sells for only $29.95, including shipping costs, and it is worth every penny of the price. It tells where to fish in all kinds of weather and how the seasons affect fishing. It tells about which lures to use under every condition. I describe how to improve casting and how to set the hook and reel them in. There is even a chapter on night fishing.

I have personally fished just about every lake and stream in this area for over forty years and I tell the secrets of each. I have one chapter on how to find fish without expensive fish-finding equipment. In the book I also explain how to determine how deep to fish and how water temperature affects where the fish are. I also have a chapter on selecting the contents of your tackle box.

The book also has an extensive appendix. Included in it is a description of all the game fish in the area—with color photographs. Also in the appendix is a glossary that covers the most common lures, rods, reels, and other fishing equipment.

The book lives up to its name. It is a bible for fishing. You must have it! Fill out the enclosed card and send it to me in the enclosed stamped and addressed envelope. Include your check for $29.95 (no cash or credit cards, please). Do it today!

Sincerely yours,

8 Criticize each of the following parts of sales messages. **[LO5]**

Email Subject Lines

a. Earn BIG profits NOW!!!

b. Reduce expenses with an experienced consultant's help.

c. Free trial offer ends this week!

Openings

Product or Service: A Color Fax Machine

a. Now you can fax in color!

b. Here is a full-color fax that will revolutionize the industry.

c. If you are a manufacturer, ad agency, architect, designer, engineer, or anyone who works with color images, the Statz Color Fax can improve the way you do business.

Product or Service: A Financial Consulting Service

d. Would you hire yourself to manage your portfolio?

e. Are you satisfied with the income your portfolio earned last year?

f. Dimmitt-Hawes Financial Services has helped its clients make money for over a half century.

Parts of Sales Presentations

Product or Service: A Paging Service

a. Span-Comm Messaging is the only paging service that provides service coast to coast.

b. Span-Comm Messaging is the only paging service that gives you the freedom to go coast to coast and still receive text messages.

c. Span-Comm Messaging gives you coast-to-coast service.

Product or Service: A Color Fax Machine

d. The Statz Color Fax is extraordinary. It produces copies that are indistinguishable from the originals.

e. The extraordinary Statz Color Fax produces copies identical to the originals.

f. Every image the Statz Color Fax produces is so extraordinary you may not be able to tell a fax from an original.

Product or Service: Vermont Smoked Ham

g. You won't find a better-tasting ham than the old-fashioned Corncob Smoked Ham we make up here on the farm in Vermont.

h. Our Corncob Smoked Ham is tender and delicious.

i. You'll love this smoky-delicious Corncob Smoked Ham.

Product or Service: A Unique Mattress

j. Control Comfort's unique air support system lets you control the feel and firmness of your bed simply by pushing a button.

k. The button control adjusts the feel and firmness of Control Comfort's air support system.

l. Just by pushing a button you can get your choice of feel and firmness in Control Comfort's air support system.

Action Endings

Product or Service: An Innovative Writing Instrument

a. To receive your personal Airflo pen, just sign the enclosed card and return it to us.

b. You can experience the writing satisfaction of this remarkable writing instrument by just filling out and returning the enclosed card.

c. Don't put it off! Now, while it's on your mind, sign and return the enclosed card.

Product or Service: A News Magazine

d. To begin receiving your copies of *Today's World*, simply fill out and return the enclosed card.

e. For your convenience, a subscription card is enclosed. It is your ticket to receiving *Today's World*.

f. If you agree that *Today's World* is the best of the news magazines, just sign and return the enclosed card.

Postscripts

a. You can also monogram items you order before November 1.

b. If you order before November 1, you can monogram your items.

c. Items ordered before November 1 can be monogrammed.

9 Find and study the online RFP for Rotary Foundation District Simplified Grants. What are the criteria (both explicit and implied) for a successful proposal? When reviewing a set of proposals that all meet these criteria, what kinds of facts might lead the selection committee to fund certain projects and not others? **[LO6]**

10 Pretend you are writing an unsolicited internal proposal requesting funding for traveling to a major professional meeting in your area of expertise. What kinds of information will you need to include? What arguments might your supervisors or management find convincing? What kinds of objections might you need to overcome? **[LO6]**

PROBLEM-SOLVING CASES

Persuasive Requests

1 As a student employee in your school's human resources department, you've attracted positive attention for the ways you've improved the writing on the department's website. As a result, the assistant director has asked you on several occasions to critique other written material, such as news releases and university announcements from this office. That business communication course you took last quarter must have really paid off!

Today your boss drops by your desk with a printout of an email that he's frowning over. "We're not getting the participation we want in our yearly Take Our Daughters and Sons to Work Day," he complains. Handing you the email, he says, "Here's what we sent out this year. I think this invitation may be part of the problem." You read what it says:

> Subject: Take Our Daughters and Sons to Work Day—April 23
>
> In accordance with the national "Take Our Daughters and Sons to Work Day," university faculty and staff are invited to bring their children who are between 8–18 to work with them on April 23. This day will expose children to activities that occur on a typical day while working, learning, and playing at UC. It will include departmental tours, financial awareness workshops, Public Safety fingerprinting and mug shots, visiting a residence hall, athlete autographs, recreation center activities, and dining discounts. Faculty and staff who would like to participate should reply to Amber Bradley at the email address above or call 572-3384 by April 21. Please include the following information:
>
> Your name, department, and phone number
>
> Number of children
>
> Age of each child
>
> To learn more about the national program, please visit <http://www.daughtersandsonstowork.org/wmspage.cfm?parm1=485>. If you would like to provide a different learning activity for the children, please contact me immediately.
>
> Amber Bradley
>
> Human Resources
>
> 572-3382

You agree that the invitation is not very appealing, nor does it answer some of the readers' likely questions. Using your best problem-solving strategies for persuasive requests, rewrite it for your boss. (Your instructor may substitute a different campus event.)

2 As an entry-level employee for a business research firm, Martin & Hobart, you've been assigned the task of recruiting survey participants for a report on practices in companies' customer contact centers. The survey will gather such information as the companies' key performance indicators (KPIs)—that is, such quantitative data as number of customers served, how quickly they were served, their satisfaction ratings, and so forth—as well as information on such additional topics as training provided for center staff, any performance incentives offered, and the types of communication channels used. In short, your company hopes to create a report that companies can use in order to "benchmark" their contact center's practices against those of others in their industry. The report will be sold, along with many other industry reports, on M&H's website.

Write a persuasive email that will get the supervisors of various contact centers to participate in your survey. Your email will contain a link to the web-based survey, so the message you are writing will not need to discuss the contents of the survey in great detail. Instead, use the email to get readers to appreciate the importance of the information they will be helping to generate. You can offer them a free copy of the resulting report, and five of the participants will be selected at random to receive a free flip video camcorder. The individual responses will be shared with no one, and the data will be presented in aggregated form so that no particular companies will be identified in the report. The survey will run from May 6 to May 24, 2010. The report will be finished by June 30, 2010. Add any additional material that you believe is warranted. Remember: the more successful your invitation, the better the report (and the better you and your company will look).

3 Assume that your business communication instructor is requiring you to "shadow" a professional in your field for a half day so that you can use your observations as the basis of a short report. Find someone in your field whose job you want to learn more about and write him/her a persuasive email requesting that you be allowed to tag along for a morning or afternoon. Do not choose someone you know. Think carefully about the reader's possible objections and include the information that will make your request successful.

---

4 As a respected businessperson in your neighborhood, you've been elected to its community council, the group that officially represents the neighborhood to the city council. Like other community councils, yours promotes the economic viability of the community and its quality of life in such ways as organizing community events, raising funds for beautification projects, blocking any development projects that would detract from the community, and addressing crime issues. It's toward this last goal that you think you'll offer your business-writing services to your local police department.

Last year, the officers distributed a flyer to all residents inviting them to volunteer for the Citizens on Patrol crime-prevention program (such as the one described for Irving, Texas, at <http://www.cityofirving.org/police/community-pages/community-programs/citizens-on-patrol.html>). No one did, to the disappointment of the police and the council. At last night's council meeting, the main officer for your neighborhood expressed his disappointment and asked if anyone had any suggestions for improving the flyer, which he is preparing to distribute again. Taking a look at it, you immediately see some problems. There's not enough information about the program, the benefits of volunteering are weak, and it's not clear how to volunteer. You do like the fact that the flyer includes data on police calls received over the last year (1 for murder, 13 for rape, 44 for robbery, 16 for assault, 123 for burglary, 404 for theft, 46 for auto theft, and numerous calls for various other things—totaling 6,132 police responses), though you're not sure you like how these are presented.

After creating a detailed profile of your neighborhood (real or imagined), write the kind of flyer that will recruit some volunteers for this worthy cause.

---

5 As an employee of the _____ Company (you decide what kind), you're in charge of this year's fundraising for the United Performing Arts Fund (UPAF) of southeast Wisconsin (or for the Fine Arts Fund of Cincinnati, or of a comparable fund in another city or region). Your company is a proud contributor to this organization's yearly campaign, and you want to do your best to help the company achieve its goal of $ _____ (you decide how much) for this year.

Employees will make their contributions via the fund's website. They should log in using their company email address and use the password *goodco*. This way, the company's total contribution can be tracked. Depending on the actual organization you choose for this assignment, there may be different payment options available, including automatic payroll deductions. In addition to being eligible for the perks that the fund itself offers donors of various levels, your company will also enter the names of all participating employees into a drawing for prizes (you decide what would be realistic and appealing). But of course it's the intrinsic benefits that you'll use for your main persuasive effort.

---

6 You work as a marketing co-op in the office of Community Relations and Marketing at your school. This office promotes and oversees all university events offered in partnership with nonprofit organizations. One such event is the yearly donation drive on behalf of Dress for Success, a national organization with a chapter in your city. This organization helps disadvantaged women enter the workplace and stay there. An important part of achieving this goal is collecting business-appropriate clothing for them to wear on job interviews. They also get a week's worth of working clothes when they are hired. (You can learn more about the organization at <www.dressforsuccess.org>.)

Your job is to write a persuasive message to send to all campus faculty and staff soliciting their donations of new or nearly new suits (pants or skirts), blouses, shoes, and certain accessories. All items should be clean and stylish, and they should be turned in on hangers or in boxes. Let readers know when and where they can drop off their donations. Tell them that volunteers will be on hand at the collection sites next week during certain hours to accept the donations and give receipts for them. The volunteers will also be happy to accept donations in the form of checks or cash, but if people want to donate by credit card, they'll need to do so via the organization's website.

7 As a representative of the student government organization at your school, you've spearheaded an effort to find out how students might be better served by Blackboard, the school's course management system. (With your instructor's permission, you may substitute a different system and change the details of this case as appropriate.) During two weeks in January, you conducted an online poll of students asking them "On a scale from 1 (not important) to 5 (very important), how important is it to you that your instructors post information about their courses on Blackboard?" Of the 6,452 students responding, nearly 95 percent chose 4 or 5 as their answer.

This is why you are now writing the faculty to persuade them to use the "Course Preview" feature in Blackboard, which they can find listed on the control panel screen along with other tools. When faculty click the link to this feature, they land on a Web form that asks about features such as delivery format (e.g., lecture, discussion, experiential), whether or not a graduate assistant will help teach the course, required and recommended texts, attendance policy, and so forth. These data will then be automatically linked to the course schedule on the registration website so that when a student goes there to register and clicks on a certain course, this information will come up along with the short course description that is already provided for each course.

Write the kind of email message that will encourage faculty to use this feature of Blackboard, in addition to its other features, to give students information about their courses. When planning your appeal, think carefully about any objections that faculty members may have.

---

8 You work at the company headquarters for Luningers, a grocery-store chain with over 20 stores located throughout the northeastern United States. One of your jobs is to recruit customers for your Email Advisory Panel. Customers who join this panel receive approximately eight surveys a year on such topics as product selection, customer service, and the general shopping experience. Essentially, the panel is a group of loyal Luningers customers who make it easy for you to get feedback that helps your stores remain competitive. For each survey they complete, the panel members are automatically entered into a drawing for $1,000. They do need to complete every survey in order to continue to be panel members.

Your first step in recruiting members is to include on customers' receipts an invitation for them to visit the company website, take a survey, and have their names entered into a drawing for $1,000. Anyone who takes this first step then receives an email inviting him or her to join the panel.

Write the email invitation, persuading those who have already shown interest in the store to join the panel and become regular survey respondents.

---

9 GrowHealth is a community health organization that provides behavioral health services. You work in the community relations department and are planning your annual children's health fair. The fair is a large community event where children can receive free medical checkups, dental screening, and well-child immunizations, and also learn about living a healthy life. Last year, the fair drew a crowd of 5,000, mostly low- and moderate-income families with no health insurance coverage for their children. The health fair is the only time that many of the participating children receive any health care each year.

The major sponsor for the annual event has always been Wachovia, which recently merged with WellsFargo. Since the merger, the community support division has been restructured and there are new sponsorship and giving regulations in place for the bank. Your GrowHealth's children's health conference is dependent upon the sponsorship and financial contributions from the bank. You must write to the new community relations director of WellsFargo, Mr. William Padilla, to request the support of WellsFargo for the GrowHealth children's health fair. The fair will need the support of WellsFargo in order to continue.

---

10 You are an intern in the human resources department at a large health care clinic. Your boss has instructed you to send an announcement to all staff letting them know that the staff photo will be at 7:45 AM. next Tuesday before any patients arrive. The office takes a staff photo once a year. Sometimes the pictures are used in promotional material; sometimes they just hang in the hallway of the lobby. Unfortunately, in recent years fewer people have shown up for the picture. Last year only a quarter of the clinic's 200 employees attended. Excuses included "I'm too busy," "I don't photograph well," "That was today?" "I had to take my children to school," "I had a breakfast meeting," "I don't work until 11:00," and "No way." You can't force people to attend the photo shoot, and to be honest, you probably wouldn't want to show up that early either just to have your picture taken. Your boss is counting on you to write a persuasive announcement to the employees requesting that they take the time to show up for the photo; she hopes that everyone will be there. They don't have to do anything special. All they have to do is take five minutes to be part of the picture. As you write, think about why taking such a photo might be important to the clinic, the patients, and the staff.

Sales

11 As a member of the sales team of the Cincinnati Zoo & Botanical Garden, you've just attended a strategizing session in which the sales team generated ideas for increasing zoo memberships. Your boss presented data about current memberships broken down by demographic categories. One group that stood out for its low memberships was the 50-and-over crowd. "We're doing well attracting families with children," your boss says, "but we're not attracting enough senior citizens. In fact, our data show that people with children tend to cancel their memberships once those children are no longer at home."

The team decides that one strategy to remedy this problem will be to send a letter to those 50 and over who have let their zoo membership lapse. You've been assigned the task of creating this mailing. Studying the zoo's website at <www.cincinnatizoo.org> and, using your powers of analysis and imagination, write the letter that will persuade these former members to rejoin. Consider carefully how to turn features of the zoo into benefits for your readers. (Your instructor may require you to create certain additional pieces for this mailing, or may change the organization.) Alternative assignment: Write the letter for those 50 and over who have never been members of the zoo. Assume that you're using a list of AARP (American Association of Retired Persons) members in your area to identify these prospects.

12 You're the secretary of a service organization on campus. To raise money for your activities, your members put together and sell care packages for parents to buy for their kids on their birthdays. When their son's or daughter's special day comes around, your organization delivers the package. It's time to write this year's sales letter for these packages.

Inventing reasonable details about the organization and the packages, considering what would appeal to the parents, and anticipating the information you will need from them, write the letter (and order form) that will get them to purchase a birthday care package. The student needs to live in a residence hall in order to be eligible.

13 You work for Maureen O'Connor, the business manager for the playhouse in your city (you can use a theatre in your city for this case or research one in another city). It's time to sell subscriptions to the playhouse for the coming season, and the job of writing the sales letter falls to you.

From credit-card receipts, you have a record of most people who attended at least one performance last year but were not subscribers. These will be the recipients of your message. Try to get them to purchase a package of seven tickets (for the price of six!). These tickets can be used for any show(s) in any combination; for example, the subscriber could use two or three tickets for two or three shows or use them all at once for a party of seven. There are two subscription plans. With Plan A, the subscriber makes all his or her reservations for the entire season, though these tickets can be changed to another evening later if necessary. With Plan B, the subscriber can simply schedule tickets as the season goes along—though it's possible that a show the subscriber wants will be sold out by the time he/she tries to schedule the tickets for it. With either plan, the subscriber pays up front. If they have questions, subscribers should call the Box office, ext. 1. To purchase subscriptions, they can either return the enclosed form (which lists the prices for adult, seniors, and student subscriptions), call the box office, or go to the theatre's website. Assume that a color brochure about the plays in this year's season will be included in the mailing.

Using fetching details about the upcoming season (which you can gather from websites or generate yourself), see if you can turn a good percentage of infrequent attenders into subscribers.

14 Choose a type of catalog- and online-based company that sells products you're familiar with—for example, home furnishings, medical/herbal products, auto parts/accessories—and write a sales letter to past customers who haven't bought from you in a while. You'll offer them 20 percent off their next order, with no minimum purchase required. (To get the discount, they'll need to use the promotional code 16652A.)

Tell them where/how they can make their purchase, reacquaint them with your appealing products, and give them a reason to act now. (You can assume that legal language about not combining this offer with any other offer, not using the offer to pay for taxes and processing/shipping charges, and a few other caveats will be typed in small print at the bottom of the letter.)

15 Like other large airlines, Global Airlines has a points-based incentive program. Customers who join Global's FreeMiles program earn points by purchasing tickets from Global or by using their member number when purchasing goods and services from Global's business partners (hotels, rental-car companies, florists, even movie-rental companies). The points can then be put toward the purchase of tickets for future flights.

You work in the office that runs this program. Lately, some of Global's business partners have been grumbling that they are not getting enough business through this program. These are companies with big name recognition, and they feel they should be getting more for letting Global use their names to attract frequent flyers. So your boss directs you to design an email for the FreeMiles members announcing a special promotion that will generate more business for your partners. You'll be offering your readers an opportunity to earn up to 25,000 bonus miles if they register for the promotion. Once they've registered, the number of purchases they make from your nonairline partners in a designated two-month period will determine how many bonus miles they will get. They will earn 1,000 extra miles per separate purchase, up to 25,000 miles. (Readers will find out what "separate purchase" means when they go to the registration website.)

Carefully consider the persuasive, logistical, and visual elements to include and then write the message.

16 You are a recent B-school grad and have an entrepreneurial spirit. Before you attended B-school, you didn't know what to expect in your business classes and assumed that your regular English and math classes would prepare you adequately for your upper division business classes. Once you were taking business classes, you realized that although you had the basic skills, you could have used more preparation in statistics and communication—two skills sets that are difficult to master, but critical for professional success. Now that you have graduated, you have decided to start a tutoring business for students who want to get a leg up in their business classes. You and two of your friends are offering online and in-person tutoring sessions in statistics and business writing for $30/session or $300/semester. To solicit customers, you are going to send a sales message to all prebusiness majors at your alma mater. You think that an email message will be most effective.

17 Last semester you worked as a TA for a professor who used Second Life, a 3D virtual environment, as a teaching tool. When helping students learn to use Second Life, you noticed that students with no gaming experience had a hard time learning to navigate their avatars in Second Life. However, with a little training session from you, these students easily mastered the basic skills necessary to participate.

Like most students you are cash strapped, so you hit upon the idea of selling your services as a Second Life trainer. You offered your services to students, but they weren't interested. So you decided to package your training for instructors to adopt as part of their required course materials. You designed your training as a short machinima, a 3-D computer graphic animated film. This animated movie teaches students all they need to know to get oriented in Second Life and begin participating in classes. You have decided to market your product by sending a sales message to all university professors using Second Life at _____ (college or university of your choice).

18 You are a financial planner. Write a brief message to your customers for your firm's next newsletter persuading them that they should still be investing even when the economy and stock market are performing poorly. Also persuade them that the services of a financial planner such as yourself would be necessary for them to make these investments.

19 You work for Mountain View Fitness Center. It's a full-service gym with a pool, group exercise classes, cardio deck, weight room, and basketball/volleyball courts. Summer is a slow time, because many members suspend their memberships and instead enjoy outdoor fitness opportunities. You suspect many other potential new members are doing the same. Who wants to take out a gym membership when summer is so short and there's so much to do outdoors? Mountain View decides to offer special summer individual memberships for just $99 from Memorial Day through Labor Day. At only around $33 per month, that is $15 less than the regular individual monthly fee. You are in charge of writing the content for the flyers you will post around town and the ad that will appear in the paper. Persuade new members to purchase a summer membership.

20 You work in the sales department of the Great Northern Insurance Company, a provider of auto, home, and life insurance. Great Northern also sells identity theft insurance as an add-on policy to any of these basic policies. You recently sold an auto insurance policy to Lindsey Grey, a systems analyst for a local school district. When you sold her the auto insurance policy, you mentioned the identity theft policy, thinking that as an information technology expert, she would appreciate the added security that identity theft insurance would provide. However, she was in a hurry and didn't want to purchase the insurance at your meeting. You were surprised that, given her profession, she really didn't seem all that interested in or knowledgeable about the topic.

You decide to send a follow up message to her in which you thank her for purchasing auto insurance through Great Northern and persuade her to purchase the identity theft add-on policy. You really believe this is a great policy. In fact, you've done a lot of research on identity theft and consider yourself somewhat of an expert. You'll tell her about forms that identity theft can take, how to avoid it, and what to do if she becomes a victim. You let her know that your insurance policy covers any expenses incurred by purchases the thief would make, court costs related to crimes committed in a victim's name, or by the effort to get the victim's credit rating restored. You may need to do a bit of research on identity theft and identity theft insurance policies to have sufficient detail in your message to persuade Lindsey that the cost of this policy is worth the purchase.

Proposals

21 Find the call for nominations for a campuswide faculty award at your school and, thinking of it as a type of RFP, respond with your "proposal": a letter persuading the selection committee to choose your nominee as the winner. Be careful to study the criteria for the award and to provide convincing evidence that your nominee meets these criteria. In addition to collecting your memories of the nominee, be sure to learn all you can about his or her accomplishments—for example, from the school or faculty member's own website, from other Internet resources, or from various news archives.

22 Excitement is in the air at Online Conferencing. Your small company has just been invited to bid on becoming Standard Uniform's teleconferencing service provider. If you beat out the competition for this contract, it will mean over $300,000 a year for the next three years. Your company has never before had an opportunity to bid on this large a contract.

Effective collaboration will be essential to this effort. The marketing people will write the overall narrative for the proposal and put the pieces together, but employees in other departments will also need to contribute. The technology architecture department will need to match up your product's features with Standard Uniform's needs and technological capabilities. The accounting department will need to price the products and work up the proposed budget. Sales and training will need to develop a plan for training Standard Uniform's employees on the system. And the legal department will need to work out the terms and conditions for the contract.

Until now, this kind of collaboration has taken place through email and face-to-face meetings. But as a new member of the marketing team, you think there's a better way: Google Docs. With this hosted application, all members of the proposal-writing team can easily send their contributions to everyone else as well as actually edit documents together online.

After studying and exploring Google Docs at docs. google.com, write a proposal recommending to your boss, the marketing director, that the team use this application to create the proposal for Standard Uniform. Think carefully about what your boss will want to know as well as about how to handle any drawbacks of this idea. (With your instructor's permission, you may substitute another platform for online collaboration.)

23 As director of corporate communications and public relations for Howe's Building Supplies, you think the time has come to create a more formal, robust employee-volunteer program. Your company is a good community citizen; it already gives time, money, and supplies on a random basis to many local charities. But that's the problem: these donations are random, and it's hard to use random acts of kindness as a basis for compelling publicity for your company.

Write a proposal in which you (1) convince the owners of the need for a better-organized corporate volunteer program and (2) request permission to undertake the first phase of creating such a program: conducting an employee survey to find out what employees are already doing along these lines, what kind of program they'd be in favor of, what would motivate them to participate, and so forth. By approving your request, the owners will not be committing themselves to any particular program—but they will be committing themselves to some kind of program. It would be disastrous to invite the employees to contribute their opinions only to have these amount to nothing.

Research the benefits of employee-volunteer programs, think carefully about the logistics of your plan, and do any additional planning that will enable you to decide exactly what you want to ask for and why. Then write the proposal. Send it as an email attachment to VP Amy Sutherland, who is interested in your idea and has agreed to share it with the other executives. Invent any additional details that will not significantly alter the challenge before you.

24 You are working as an intern for the CFO of a mid-sized microbrewery. The brewery currently operates four locations in Missouri and one in Kansas. You are located at the company headquarters in St. Louis. During your first week on the job, you learn that the brewery does not use XBRL reporting and has not looked into any XBRL reporting software or systems.

In one of your accounting classes, you recently learned about the SEC requirements for XBRL reporting. On January 30, 2009, the SEC adopted rules that would require companies to provide financial statements in XBRL format. These new reporting rules became effective April 13, 2009, and apply to domestic and foreign companies using U.S. GAAP. The rules will be implemented in three phases. The first two phases of implementation apply mainly to large corporations.

The final phase requires all remaining filers using U.S. GAAP to comply with XBRL reporting formats by June 15, 2011.

Although the brewery has some time before the third phase of XBRL regulation is implemented, you want to prepare a brief proposal for the adoption of _____ (your recommendation) XBRL financial analysis and reporting software that will allow the brewery to comply with SEC requirements for XBRL. You raise the topic with your boss, who is impressed with your initiative and gives you permission to write up your proposal. Before thoroughly researching the software, you speak to the company's IT director, who informs you that any solution you recommend must be compatible with Microsoft software because the company uses Windows Vista and Microsoft Office 2007 and cannot change software or operating systems.

---

25 You are a store manager at a discount shoe retailer located in the regional Southwest and known for its exceptional customer service. The shoe retailer, MyFoot, has a corporate office in each state where there are satellite retail locations: New Mexico, Arizona, Utah, and Texas. Each month store managers are required to attend a store managers' meeting at the MyFoot's corporate offices in their state. Since cities and towns in the Southwest are not geographically close to one another, most managers drive an average of 175 miles to reach the monthly meetings.

The meetings are important to MyFoot because they allow managers from different stores to interact, share ideas, and build community. Additionally, the monthly meetings allow the corporate team to show store managers new products

and highlight features of the inventory that will be arriving in the next month. Unfortunately, you've noticed that while you are away at the managers' meetings, sales in your store are down an average of 12 percent each day of your absence. You feel that traveling to the meetings not only cuts into your own productivity but also costs the company a significant amount of money.

Since you recognize the importance of meeting with other managers and having a good connection to corporate, you would like the company to implement a monthly managers' video Web conference and biannual meetings at each state's headquarters in place of the monthly face-to-face meetings. You decide to research video Web conferencing and submit a proposal for your idea to your boss in Albuquerque, New Mexico.

---

26 You work in the accounting department of NH Aerospace, a specialized aviation parts manufacturer located in southern California. Your new boss, Jack Draper—who has a background in environmental accounting—understands that the total cost of managing materials and equipment is much more than the initial acquisition cost. In particular, Mr. Draper has noted that the costs related to environmental management at NH Aerospace are often overlooked. For example, the company has not yet conducted an assessment of how to decrease the costs of scrap and material losses or how

by-products of the manufacturing process may be used to increase revenues. Mr. Draper would like to form a company task force to research and monitor environmental accounting projects for the company. Mr. Draper has asked you to prepare a proposal for the CEO that proposes this task force and will persuade the CEO that such a task force is a wise investment of resources. (For more information on Environmental Accounting you might conduct an Internet search or visit the EPA resources website at <http://www.epa.gov/oppt/library/pubs/archive/acct-archive/resources.htm>.)

---

27 You are the assistant manager of a local bead store. Your boss, the manager, is on maternity leave for the next two months, so you are given the task of creating the schedule for all of the sales associates. As you draft the schedule for the upcoming month of May, you look back to sales trends and scheduling for May of the last two years. When reviewing these data you notice that there have been very few sales on Sunday and Monday of Memorial Day weekend.

You do a little more research and find that over the past four years there have only been, on average, five customers on Memorial Day Sunday and Monday combined, and the Memorial Day weekend Saturday sales are 63 percent lower than average Saturday sales in May or June. The average pay for sales associates is $12.00/hr. You estimate that remaining open for Memorial Day weekend with two associates and a manager is costing the company around $300 a day. A typical sale for the store is approximately $36. Since historically there have been few sales on the Sunday or Monday of Memorial Day weekend, you believe that the store could save money by closing for the weekend. On a personal note, you'd certainly like to have the weekend off.

Thinking of any possible objections your boss might have and figuring out how to address them, propose to her that she close the store for the Memorial Day weekend.

---

28 As the supervisor of your company's communications department (you may pick the company), you and your team are becoming tired of the amount of editing you need to do whenever someone submits material to your department for publication in the company newsletter, press releases, annual report, and website. You're pretty sure that the routine correspondence that doesn't come through your department for editing could use some help as well.

Even within your department, there is no consistency in formatting, punctuation, and mechanics. For example, some people use the series comma (see Chapter 17, Cma 2-1) and some don't. Some people use round bullets for lists, and some use square bullets. You've seen as many variations in capitalization, number uses, and abbreviations as there are people in the company. And it's not only the writing that is not consistent. People use several variations of the company's logo in their work—size, color, or incorporation with other graphics.

To employees outside your department, these issues may seem trivial, but with so many variations in style and usage, your publications would look sloppy and thrown together if your team didn't edit everyone's work for uniformity. Furthermore, your clients should see your logo represented consistently and have a reasonable expectation that every document they receive from you, from routine correspondence to material on the website, will look and sound as though it came from the same company. If the look and content of your documents and logo vary, customers may question the legitimacy of your material.

You know that it's your job and your staff's job to edit written materials before publishing them, but you also think that the employees who write them could be more consistent. After all, how hard is it for someone to use a round bullet instead of a square bullet? Furthermore, it is reasonable to expect that everyone in your department have some consistency in their initial drafts so that editing and revising are not so time consuming when your team members edit one another's work before the final publication of a document. Plus, you worry that the documents you don't see (e.g., letters, emails) may not be written or edited as well as they could be.

You think a corporate style guide is your answer and decide to propose to your CEO that the company have one. You and your team will develop it and implement it. Because this is summer, it's your slow time anyway, so you have the time to create it. In your proposal, make the case for creating and using a style guide, include a timeline for developing it, and propose a plan for implementing the style guide at your company. An Internet search for corporate style guides will help you gather information for your proposal.

---

29 You have just returned from a national sales conference where you learned that many of the nation's top companies are establishing a presence through social networking—blogs, Facebook, MySpace, Twitter, LinkedIn. You think social networking would be great for your company, Jean's Specialty Shoppe, which sells wine, cheese, sausage, tea, gourmet chocolate, and novelty gifts. You're telling Jean, your boss, about social networking opportunities, but she doesn't understand. Your business is already very successful. In addition to the customers who visit your store, you have customers from all 50 states and even a few from Canada and Germany who have ordered from your popular website. What would these social networking sites do for the company that your website and local advertising don't already accomplish?

She's not against social networking; she just doesn't quite see the possibilities. So she tells you to put your proposal in writing. Do a little research on social networking and develop a proposal for her. Why might Jean's Specialty Shoppe use social networking? What are the benefits? Are there any drawbacks? What kind of social networking do you propose? Why? Who will be responsible for setting it up and maintaining it? Answer these and any other questions you think Jean might want answers to before she lets you go ahead and create a social networking presence for her business.

---

30 You work for the _____ company (you decide what kind) as a _____ (you decide what position). You want to take an online course on _____ (you decide what topic) and have the company cover the cost. You've run the idea past your supervisor, who is basically supportive but will need to get the OK from the boss. For this you'll need to make your case persuasively and in writing. Write an email proposal to your supervisor requesting that the company cover the cost of the course. Convince the decision maker that the course is worth the money. Be sure to tie it to your current or likely future job responsibilities and explain how the company will benefit. Remember to think of the major objections your boss might have and be sure to account for these as you build your argument. To ensure that your proposal has a sufficient level of detail, you may want to do some research on a few colleges' online course offerings for relevant classes.

chapter nine

Communicating in the Job-Search Process

LEARNING OBJECTIVES

Upon completing this chapter, you will be able to conduct an effective job search; compose effective cover messages, résumés, and follow-ups; and prepare for interviews. To reach these goals, you should be able to

1 Develop and use a network of contacts in your job search.

2 Assemble and evaluate information that will help you select a job.

3 Identify the sources that can lead you to an employer.

4 Compile print and digital résumés that are strong, complete, and organized.

5 Write targeted cover messages that skillfully sell your abilities.

6 Explain how you can participate effectively in an interview.

7 Write application follow-up messages that are appropriate, friendly, and positive.

8 Maintain your job-search activities.

The Job-Search Process

Introduce yourself to this chapter by assuming a role similar to one you are now playing. You are Jason Andrews, a student at Olympia University. In a few months, you will complete your studies for work in marketing.

You believe that it is time to begin seeking the job for which those studies have been preparing you. But how do you do this? Where do you look? What does the search involve? How should you present yourself for the best results? The answers to these and related questions are reviewed in the following pages.

THE JOB SEARCH

- For success in job seeking, use the following procedures.

Of all the things you do in life, one of the most important is getting a job. Whether it involves your first job or one further down your career path, job seeking is directly related to your success and your happiness. It is vital that you conduct the job search properly—that you prepare wisely and carefully and proceed diligently. The following review of job-search strategies should help you succeed.

Building a Network of Contacts

- Begin the job search by building a network of contacts in this way:

- (1) Broaden your circle of friends.

You can begin the job search long before you are ready to find employment. In fact, you can do it now by building a network of contacts. More specifically, you can build relationships with people who can help you find work when you need it. Such people include classmates, professors, and businesspeople.

At present, your classmates are not likely to be holding positions in which they make or influence hiring decisions. But in the future, when you may want to make a career change, they may hold such positions. Right now, some of them may know people who can help you. The wider your circle of friends and acquaintances, the more likely you are to make employment contacts.

- (2) Know your professors.

Knowing your professors and making sure that they know you also can lead to employment contacts. Because professors often consult for business, they may know key executives and be able to help you contact them. Professors sometimes hear of position openings and can refer you to the hiring executives. Demonstrating your work ethic and your ability in the classroom is probably the best way to get your professors to know you and help you. Take advantage of opportunities to meet your professors outside the classroom, especially the professors in your major field.

- (3) Meet businesspeople.

Obviously, meeting business professionals also can lead to employment contacts. You already may know some through family and friends. But broadening your relationships among businesspeople would be helpful. You can do this in various ways, especially through college professional groups such as the Association for Information Technology Professionals, Delta Sigma Pi, and the Society for the Advancement of Management. By taking an active role in the organizations in your field of study, especially by working on program committees and by becoming an officer, you can get to know the executives who serve as guest speakers. You also might meet businesspeople online. If you share a particular interest on a blog or are known as one who contributes valuable comments to others' blogs, you may get some good job leads there.

- (4) Work with community organizations.

In addition to these more common ways of making contacts, you can use some less common ones. By working in community organizations (charities, community improvement groups, fund-raising groups), you can meet community leaders. By attending meetings of professional associations (every field has them), you can meet the leaders in your field. In fact, participation in virtually any activity that provides contacts with businesspeople can be mutually beneficial, both now and in the future.

Obtaining an Internship

Internships are a wonderful way to network with people in your field, gain professional knowledge and experience, or simply learn whether your current field is where you want to build a career. According to one professional, getting an internship is "just one of those things you have to have before employers will even consider looking at your résumé."[1] In fact, according to *BusinessWeek*, "internships are the main pipeline to full-time recruiting. . . . Top companies often rely on their internship programs for as much as 90 percent of their new college hires, so an applicant without an internship is at a big disadvantage."[2]

- Internships are a great way to gain experience in your field.

Internships are provided not only through top companies. Small companies, the government, and nonprofit organizations offer paid or unpaid internships that also provide valuable experience in any field. Though a quick Web search for internships will net several links to internship types, the first step in finding an internship simply may be to contact your school's career services office. You may also want to use many of the networking strategies discussed in the previous section.

- Many companies hire from intern programs.

Identifying Appropriate Jobs

To find the right job (or internship), you need to investigate both internal and external factors. The best fit occurs when you have carefully looked at yourself: your education, personal qualities, experience, and any special qualifications. However, to be realistic, these internal qualities need to be analyzed in light of the external factors. Some of these factors may include the current and projected job market, economic needs, location preferences, and family needs.

- Look at both internal and external factors.

Analyzing Yourself. When you are ready to search for a job, you should begin the effort by analyzing yourself. In a sense, you should look at yourself much as you would look at a product or service that is for sale. After all, when you seek employment, you are really selling your ability to work—to do things for an employer. A job is more than something that brings you money. It is something that gives equal benefits to both parties—you and your employer. Thus, you should think about the qualities you have that enable you to be an accountable and productive worker that an employer needs. This self-analysis should cover the following categories.

- Begin with a self-analysis covering these background areas:

Education. The analysis might well begin with education. Perhaps you have already selected your career area such as accounting, economics, finance, information systems, international business, management, or marketing. If you have, your task is simplified, for your specialized curriculum has prepared you for your goal. Even so, you may be able to note special points—for example, electives that have given you special skills or that show something special about you (such as psychology courses that have improved your human-relations skills, communication courses that have improved your writing and speaking skills, or foreign language courses that have prepared you for international assignments).

- (1) Education. For specialized curricula, the career path is clear.

If you have pursued a more general curriculum, such as one in general business or liberal arts, you will need to look at your studies closely to see what they have prepared you to do. Perhaps you will find an emphasis on computers, written communication,

- For general curricula, a career choice must be made.

[1] Emily Fredix, "An Internship Matchmaker . . . for a Fee: College Students Wanting Internships Can Turn to a Growing Number of Businesses That Promise to Find That Prized Summer Job," *The Seattle Times* 10 June 2007, Web, 31 May 2009.
[2] Lindsey Gerdes, "College Undergrads: No Internship? No Problem. Summer Internships for College Students at Top Employers Are Scarce, But There Are Alternatives That Are Just as Valuable," *BusinessWeek* 7 May 2009, Web, 31 May 2009.

STEIN

THE CHRONICLE OF HIGHER EDUCATION

ELI STEIN

*"Do you have any other references besides
these people in your chat room?"*

Source: © 2000 Eli Stein.

human relations, foreign languages—all of which are highly valued by some businesses. Or perhaps you will conclude that your training has given you a strong general base from which to learn specific business skills.

- Consider the quality of your educational record (grades, honors, courses taken).

In analyzing your education, you should look at the quality of your record—grades, projects honors, special recognitions. If your record is good, you can emphasize it. But what if your work was only mediocre? As we will point out later, you will need to shift the emphasis to your stronger sales points—your willingness to work, your personality, your experience. Or perhaps you can explain—for example, by noting that while working your way through school may have limited your academic performance, it gave you valuable business qualities such as initiative, collaboration, and risk-taking.

- (2) Personal qualities (e.g., people skills, leadership ability).

Personal Qualities. Your self-analysis also should cover your personal qualities. Employers often use personality tests such as the Myers-Briggs to screen new hires, and you can take them online as well as at most campus career centers. Qualities that relate to working with people are especially important. Qualities that show leadership or teamwork ability are also important. And if you express yourself well in writing or speaking, note this, for good communication skills are valuable in most jobs.

Of course, you may not be the best judge of your personal qualities, so you may need to check with friends to see whether they agree with your assessments. You also may need to check your record for concrete evidence supporting your assessments. For example, organization membership and participation in community activities are evidence of people and teamwork skills. Holding office in an organization is evidence of leadership ability. Participation on a debate team, college bowl, or collegiate business policy team is evidence of communication skills.

- (3) Work experience (with interpretations).

Work Experience. If you have work experience, you should analyze it. Of course, work experience in your major field deserves the most emphasis, but work experience not related to the job you seek also can tell something important about you.

Career fairs and job boards are good places to look for announcements of job openings.

Your part-time server job or summer construction job may not seem like a big deal to you, but these jobs provide you with assets that any employer in any company can use, such as attention to detail, initiative, team skills, communication skills, and the ability to work well under pressure. You don't want to under sell this experience.

Special Qualifications. Your self-analysis also should include special qualifications that might be valuable to an employer. The ability to speak a foreign language can be very helpful for certain business environments. Athletic participation, hobbies, and interests also may be helpful. To illustrate, athletic experience might be helpful for work for a sporting goods distributor, a hobby of automobile mechanics might be helpful for work with an automotive service company, and an interest in music might be helpful for work with a piano manufacturer or an online music website. An interest in or skills with computers would be valuable across a broad range of businesses.

- (4) Special qualities (e.g., languages, communication skills).

You also might take an interest inventory such as the Strong Campbell Interest Inventory or the Minnesota Vocational Interest Inventory. These tests help match your interests to those of others successful in their careers. Most college counseling and career centers make these tests available to their students, and some are available online. Getting good help in interpreting the results is critical to providing you with valuable information.

Analyzing Outside Factors. After you have analyzed yourself, you need to combine this information with the work needs of business and other external influences. Your goal in this process is to give realistic direction to your search for employment. Where is the kind of work you are seeking available? Are you willing to move? Is such a move compatible with others in your life—your partner, your children, your parents? Does the location meet with your lifestyle needs? Although the availability of work may drive the answer to some of these questions, you should answer them as well as you can on the basis of what you know now and then conduct your job search accordingly. Finding just the right job should be one of your most important goals.

- Also consider external factors.

Finding Your Employer

You can use a number of sources in your search for an employer with whom you will begin or continue your career. Your choice of sources will probably be influenced by the stage of your career.

- Search for potential employers by using these sources:

- (1) your school's career center,

Career Centers. If you are seeking an internship or just beginning your career, one good possibility is the career center at your school. Most large schools have career centers, and these attract employers who are looking for suitable applicants. Many centers offer excellent job-search counseling and maintain databases on registrants' school records, résumés, and recommendations that prospective employers can review. Most have directories listing major companies with contact names and addresses. And most provide interviewing opportunities. Campus career centers often hold career fairs, which are an excellent place to find employers who are looking for new graduates as well as to gather information about the kinds of jobs different companies offer. By attending them early, you often find out about internships and summer jobs as well as gather ideas for selecting courses that might give you an advantage when you do begin your career search.

- (2) your network of personal contacts,

Network of Personal Contacts. As we have noted, the personal contacts you make can be extremely helpful in your job search. In fact, according to some employment reports, personal contacts are the leading means of finding employees. Obviously, personal contacts are more likely to be a source of employment opportunities later in your career when you may need to change jobs. Business acquaintances may provide job leads outside those known to your friends.

- (3) classified advertisements,

Classified Advertisements. Help-wanted advertisements in newspapers and professional journals, whether online or in print, provide good sources of employment opportunities for many kinds of work. The opportunities they provide for new college graduates, however, may be limited. Classified ads are good sources for experienced workers who want to improve their positions, and they are especially good sources for people who are conducting a major search for high-level positions. Keep in mind that they provide only a partial list of jobs available. Many jobs are snapped up before they reach the classifieds, so be sure yor are part of the professional grapevine in your field.

- (4) online sources,

Online Sources. In addition to finding opportunities in classifieds, you also will find them in online databases. Monster.com, for example, lists jobs available throughout the U.S. and beyond, with new opportunities posted regularly. Many companies even post

The *Occupational Outlook Handbook* is one of the best resources for finding out about a wide variety of jobs, including needed education, expected earnings, job activities and conditions, and more.

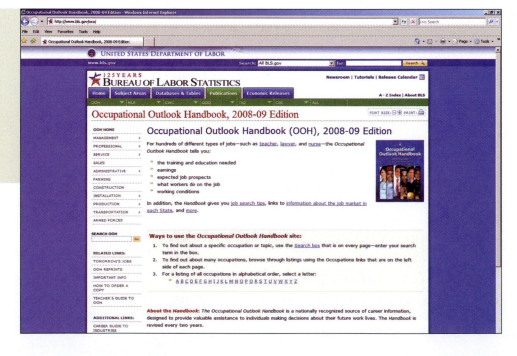

Webpage Profiles Can Work for You

Posting a webpage profile is another way of showcasing yourself and your communication skills. Not only can you add much more detail than on a print résumé, but you can also use colorful photos, videos, and sounds. You can show examples of real projects, documents, and presentations you have created as well as demonstrate your skills and creativity. A webpage profile can range from the simple one you see here, created by completing an online form, to the mailable one you see in Figure 9–6, to a sophisticated one that uses a full range of media and interaction.

Today, creating a simple webpage profile is pretty easy, even for the beginner. In fact, you may already have a webpage authoring tool if you have FrontPage or access to website builders. Some of these Web-based applications let you create for free and for a small fee will host your webpage profile, too. You can find links to some of these sites on your textbook website. And once you have posted your profile, you will want to be sure to include its URL on your print résumé as well as on any business cards you use in the job search.

Technologies such as VisualCV (<http://www.visualcv.com>) also offer an easy, convenient way to create a Web profile or portfolio. Just be sure the information on your page is what you want made public.

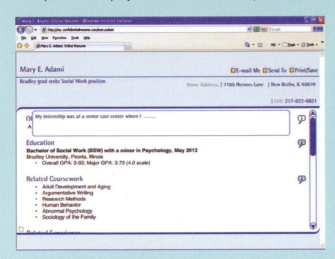

job openings on the Web, some with areas dedicated to new college graduates. If you are working now, you may want to check the company's intranet or portal for positions there, too. And professional associations often maintain job databanks. Furthermore, you could use blogs to post queries about job openings that readers might know of. All these online systems are sources for job opportunities. See the textbook website for links to these and more.

Employment Agencies. Companies that specialize in finding jobs for employees can be useful. Of course, such companies charge for their services. The employer sometimes pays the charges, usually if qualified applicants are scarce. Executive search consultants (headhunters) are commonly used to place experienced people in executive positions.

• (5) employment agencies,

Employment agencies also can help job seekers gain temporary employment. Do not discount the value of such placements. Temping can lead to permanent employment with a good fit. It allows the worker to get a feel for the company and the company to observe the worker before making a job commitment. You can also gain valuable on-the-job training in a temporary assignment.

Personal Search Agents. In addition to searching online sources, you can request that job notices be sent to you automatically by websites. These sites use tools called personal search agents or job agents. Using a filter based on a confidential profile you have completed for the site, these tools find jobs that match your profile and send you email messages about these jobs. Starting with a very precise or narrow profile first is wise. You can always modify your profile to something broader later if you find the number or nature of the job leads isn't what you expected. If you learn of a job listing

• (6) personal search agents,

that interests you for a company recruiting at your school, you should ask the recruiter about it. Not only will it show the employer you have done your homework, but it will also show that you have a sincere interest in working for the company.

- (7) webpage profiles,

Webpage Profiles. To make yourself more visible to potential employers, you may want to consider posting your résumé to the Web. Some employers actively search for new employees on university websites. Posting a Web-based profile is not difficult. Today's word processors let you save your documents in hypertext markup language (HTML), creating a basic webpage for you. Additionally, easy-to-use webpage building and generating tools are available on the Web to help novices create personal web profiles. Once posted, it is a good idea to link your webpage to your major department or to a business student club, allowing more potential employers to find it. With a little extra effort, you can create a webpage that greatly expands and enhances the printed résumé. You will want to put your webpage address on your printed résumé.

- (8) prospecting techniques.

Prospecting. Some job seekers approach prospective employers directly, by either personal visit, mail, or email. Personal visits are effective if the company has an employment office or if a personal contact can set up a visit. Mail contacts typically include a résumé and a cover letter. An email contact can include a variety of documents and be sent in various forms. The construction of these messages is covered later in the chapter.

PREPARING THE APPLICATION DOCUMENTS

INTRODUCTORY SITUATION

Résumés and Applications

In your role as Jason Andrews, you consider yourself well qualified for a career in marketing. You know the field from both personal experience and classroom study. You grew up in a working-class neighborhood. From an early age, you worked at a variety of jobs, the most important of which was a job as a pollster. You were a restaurant host and a food server for two years. Your college studies were especially designed to prepare you for a career in marketing. You studied Olympia University's curriculum in marketing, and you carefully chose the electives that would give you the best possible preparation for this career. As evidenced by your grades, your preparation was good.

Now it is time to begin your career. Over the past weeks you diligently looked for the right kind of job opening in your field. Unfortunately, you had no success. Now you will send written applications to a select group of companies that you think might use a person with your knowledge and skills. You have obtained the names of the executives you should contact at these companies. You will send them the main application documents—the résumé and cover message. The following discussion shows you how to prepare these documents for best results, both in print and digital form.

- Pursue job openings by personal visit, online, mail, email, or fax.

How you pursue the employment opportunities that your research has yielded will depend on your circumstances. When it is convenient and appropriate to do so, you make contact in person. It is convenient when the distance is not great, and it is appropriate when the employer has invited such a contact. When a personal visit is not convenient and appropriate, you apply online or by mail, email, or fax.

Whether or not you apply in person, you are likely to need some written material about yourself. If you apply in person, probably you will take a résumé with you to leave as a record of your qualifications. If you do not apply in person, of course, the application is completely in writing. Typically, it consists of a résumé, a cover message, and a reference sheet. At some point in your employment efforts, you are likely to use each of these documents.

- You are likely to use résumés, cover messages, and reference sheets in your job search.

Approach preparing these documents as you would when preparing a sales campaign. Begin your work by studying what you are selling, and what you are selling is you. Take personal inventory, performing the self-analysis discussed earlier in the chapter, and list all the information about you that you believe an employer would want to know. Then learn as much as you can about the company—its plans, its policies, its operations. You can study the company's website, read its annual report and other publications, find any recent news articles about the company, and consult a variety of business databases. (See Chapter 18 for a more detailed list of resources for company information.) You can also learn the requirements of the work the company wants done. Today, campus career centers and student organizations often invite employers to give information sessions. Reading about various careers in the *Opportunity Outlook Handbook* at <http://www.bls.gov/oco/> will tell you about the nature of the work as well as salary range and demand.

- Prepare them as you would prepare a sales mailing.

- Study the product (you) and the work.

With this preliminary information assembled, you are ready to plan the application. First, you need to decide just what your application will consist of. Will it be just a cover message, a cover message and a résumé (also called a *vita, curriculum vita, qualifications brief,* or *data sheet*), or a cover message, résumé, and reference sheet? Though most select the combination of cover message and résumé, some people prefer to use a detailed cover message alone, while others include all three documents. You should use whatever will best support your case.

- Next, decide on whether to send a message alone, with a résumé, or with a résumé, and a reference sheet.

CONSTRUCTING THE RÉSUMÉ

After you have decided to use the résumé, you must decide whether to use a print or a digital format. Constructing these forms is similar, but they differ in some very important ways.

- Choose the print or digital format.

The traditional print format is used in face-to-face interviews where you know it will be used exclusively there. If you have reason to believe the company will store your résumé digitally, you should use a scannable print format.

A digital (electronic) format, on the other hand, is used when sending your application document by email or submitting or posting it via the Web. Depending on the capabilities of the recipient's system and any forms an employer may specify, the documents can range from ASCII or text form to attached files, to full-featured webpages. In both the print and digital formats, you set up the documents to present your credentials in the most favorable way.

After deciding what your format will be, you construct the parts. In selecting these parts you not only choose how to present them but also tailor the content and order to the specific job you are applying for. While the print résumé you will use as an intern or new graduate may be one page long, after you've worked several years it may grow to a couple of pages. However, the digital version has no physical page limitation, so you should include all information that is relevant to the particular job.

- Select and order the parts to the particular job.

Traditional Print Résumé

Your print résumé should include all the information that your cover letter reviews plus supporting and incidental details. Designed for quick reading, the résumé lists facts that have been arranged for the best possible appearance. Rarely does it use sentences.

The arrangements of résumés differ widely, but the following process generally represents how most are written:

- Logically arrange information on education (institutions, dates, degrees, major field); information on employment (dates, places, firms, job titles, and accomplishments); personal details (memberships, interests, and achievements—but not religion, race, and sex); and skills or specialized knowledge. Add a reference sheet as needed.

- Place your name and contact information at the top of the résumé and create subheadings for the main parts.

- Include other vital information such as objectives and contact information.

- Arrange the data for best visual appeal, making the résumé look balanced—without too much white space or too much text.

> Follow this plan in constructing a résumé.

Selecting the Background Facts. Your first step in preparing the résumé is to review the facts you have assembled about yourself and then to select the ones you think will help your reader evaluate you. You should include all the information covered in the accompanying cover message, bacause this is the most important information. In addition, you should include significant supporting details not covered in the accompanying cover message to avoid making that message too cluttered.

> Begin by reviewing the facts you have assembled. Select the facts that will help the reader evaluate you.

Arranging the Facts into Groups. After selecting the facts you want to include, you should sort them into logical groups. Many grouping arrangements are possible. The most conventional is the three-part grouping of *Education, Experience,* and *Skills* or *Interests.* Another possibility is a grouping by job functions or skills, such as *Selling, Communicating,* and *Managing.* You may be able to work out other logical groups.

> Sort the facts by conventional groups, job functions, time, or a combination.

You also can derive additional groups from the four conventional groups mentioned above. For example, you can have a group of *Achievements.* Such a group would consist of special accomplishments taken from your experience and education information. Another possibility is to have a group consisting of information highlighting your major *Qualifications.* Here you would include information drawn from the areas of experience, education, and skills or personal qualities. Illustrations of and instructions for constructing groups such as these appear later in the chapter.

> Also, consider groups such as *Achievements* and *Qualifications.*

Constructing the Headings. With your information organized, a logical next step is to construct the headings for the résumé. Figure 9–1 provides a list of category headings to consider.

> Write headings for the résumé and its parts.

In a way, your name could be considered the main heading. It should be presented clearly; usually this means using larger and bolder type so that the name stands out from the rest of the résumé. If an employer remembers only one fact from your résumé, that fact should be your name. It can be presented in all caps or caps and lowercase, as in this example:

> Your name should be considered the main heading.

Terrence P. Lenaghan

The next level of headings might be *Objective, Education, Experience,* and *Skills.* These headings can be placed to the left or centered above the text that follows.

Consider using more descriptive headings. This form uses words that tell the nature of what follows. For example, instead of using the head, *Education,* you might use *Specialized Training in Accounting* or *Computer Software Application Skills.* Obviously, these heads add to the information covered. They help the reader interpret the facts that follow.

> Consider using descriptive headings for résumé sections.

As you can see from the illustrations in the chapter, the headings are distinguished from the other information in the résumé by the use of different sizes and styles of

> Use a special font to distinguish the headings from the other information.

Figure 9–1

Résumé Headings & Titles

Academic Achievements	Credentials	Professional Objective
Academic History	Degree(s)	Professional Affiliations
Academic Honors	Designations	Professional Affiliations & Awards
Academic Training	Dissertation	Professional Employment
Accomplishments	Education	Professional Experience
Activities	Education Highlights	Professional Leadership
Additional Professional Training	Education and Training	Professional Memberships
Additional Experience	Educational Background	Professional Organizations
Additional Training	Employment	Professional Qualifications
Affiliations	Employment Objective	Professional Seminars
Appointments	Employment History	Professional Summary
Areas of Expertise	Exhibitions and Awards	Publications
Associations	Experience(s)	Published Works
Athletic Involvement	Experience Highlights	Qualifications
Awards	Extracurricular Involvement	References
Awards and Distinctions	Field Placement	Related Course Work
Background and Interests	Foreign Language	Related Experience
Business Experience	Graduate School	Relevant Course Work
Career Goal	Graduate School Employment	Research Experience
Career Highlights	Graduate School Activities	Seminars
Career History	Hardware/Software	Skill(s) Summary
Career Objective	Highlights of Qualifications	Skills and Attributes
Career Profile	Honors, Activities, & Organizations	Skills and Qualifications
Career Related Fieldwork	Honors	Special Awards and Recognitions
Career Related Workshops	Honors and Awards	Special Training
Career Related Training	International Experience	Special Awards
Career Related Experience	International Travel	Special Abilities
Career Skills and Experience	Internship Experience	Special Skills
Career Summary	Internship(s)	Special Interests
Certificate(s)	Job History	Special Projects or Studies
Certifications	Languages	Special Licenses and Awards
Classroom Experience	Leadership Roles	Special Courses
Coaching Experience	License(s)	Strengths
Coaching Skills	Major Accomplishments	Student Teaching
College Activities	Management Experience	Student Teaching Experience
Communication Experience	Memberships	Study Abroad
Community Involvement	Memberships and Activities	Summary
Computer Background	Military Experience	Summary of Experience
Computer Experience	Military Service	Summary of Qualifications
Computer Knowledge	Military Training	Teaching Experience
Computer Languages	Objective	Teaching and Coaching Experience
Computer Proficiencies	Occupational History	Teaching and Related Experience
Computer Systems	Other Skills	Thesis
Computer Skills	Other Experience	Travel Abroad
Consulting Experience	Overseas Experience	Travel Experience
Cooperative Education Experience	Overseas Employment	Volunteer Experience
Cooperative Education	Planning & Problem Solving	Work Experience
Course Highlights	Portfolio	Work History
Course Work Included	Position Objective	Workshops and Seminars
Courses of Interest	Practicum Experience	

College of Business, *The Job Campaign Workbook* (Eau Claire, WI: University of Wisconsin–Eau Claire, 2009) 17, *Student Professional Development Programs,* Web, 3 June 2009.

type. The main head should appear to be the most important of all (larger and heavier). Headings for the groups of information should appear to be more important than the information under them. Your goal is to choose forms that properly show the relative importance of the information and are pleasing to the eye.

Including Contact Information. Your address, telephone number, and email address are the most likely means of contacting you. Most authorities recommend that you display them prominently somewhere in the résumé. You also may want to display your fax number or webpage address. The most common location for displaying contact information is at the top, under the main head.

When it is likely that your address or telephone number will change before the job search ends, you would be wise to include two addresses and numbers: one current and the other permanent. If you are a student, for example, your address at the time of applying for a job may change before the employer decides to contact you. Therefore, you may want to consider using the voice-mail on your cell phone or an Internet-based voice message service so that you can receive your messages wherever you go. Be sure the language in your outgoing message is professional and appropriate for the employers who call you.

The logic of making the contact information prominent and inclusive is to make it easy for the employer to reach you. However, recently, in the interest of privacy, some schools have begun advising their students to include only their names, phone numbers, and an innocuous email address created specifically for job searches. For business use, a professional email address is always preferable to an informal one such as surferchick@hotmail.com. However, you will likely still need to include complete information on application forms provided by employers.

Including a Statement of Objective. Although not a category of background information, a statement of your objective is appropriate in the résumé. Headings such as *Career Objective, Job Objective,* or just *Objective* usually appear at the beginning.

Not all authorities agree on the value of including the objective, however. Recommending that they be omitted from today's résumés, some authorities suggest that the résumé should concentrate instead on skills, experience, and credentials. They argue that the objective includes only obvious information that is clearly suggested by the remainder of the résumé. Moreover, they point out that an objective limits the applicant to a single position and eliminates consideration for other jobs that may be available.

Those favoring the use of a statement of objective reason that it helps the recruiter see quickly where the applicant might fit into the company. Since this argument appears to have greater support, at least for the moment, probably you should include the objective. When your career goal is unclear, you may use broad, general terms. And when you are considering a variety of employment possibilities, you may want to have different versions of your résumé for each possibility.

Primarily, your statement of objective should describe the work you seek. When you know the exact job title of a position you want at the targeted company, use it.

Objective: Marketing Research Intern

Another technique includes using words that convey a long-term interest in the targeted company, as in this example. However, using this form may limit you if the company does not have the career path you specify.

Objective: Sales Representative for McGraw-Hill leading to sales management.

Also, wording the objective to point out your major strengths can be very effective. It also can help set up the organization of the résumé.

Objective: To apply three years of successful ecommerce accounting experience at a small startup to a larger company with a need for careful attention to transaction management and analysis.

Presenting the Information. After crafting your job objective, you need to determine what information to present under the rest of your headings. Though the order of the headings will largely depend on your organizational strategy (see Organizing for Strength, page 264), the information under each heading generally appears as follows.

Work Experience. The description of your work experience should contain your job title/position, company name, location, and dates of employment. You should also include your job duties and skills you acquired, especially those that relate to the position for which you are applying. Consider the following example:

Marketing and Public Relations Intern

Alliant Health Plans, Incorporated, Boston, MA

Jan. 2012–May 2012

- Created a webpage, brochure, and press release for a community wellness program
- Interviewed and wrote about physicians, customers, and community leaders for newsletter articles
- Worked with a team of interns in other departments to analyze and update the company's website

- When covering work experience, at a minimum include dates, places, firms, and responsibilities.

- When appropriate, show achievements.

Note in the above example that in addition to the basic information regarding the job, the writer lists duties that anyone in a marketing or public relations field would likely use in a related position. The duties are represented with action-oriented, past tense verbs because the position has ended. If the intern were still in the position, he or she would have used simple present tense verbs for duties he or she currently performs (e.g., interview, write). In addition, the writer mentions teamwork, which is a skill necessary in most business settings. The use of these action verbs strengthens a job description because verbs are the strongest of all words. If you choose them well, you will do much to sell your ability to do the jobs you are targeting. A list of the more widely used action verbs appears in Figure 9–2.

- Use action verbs to strengthen the appeal.

Note also that the writer uses both months and dates. This is especially important when you consider that simply saying "2012" doesn't let the reader know how long the internship was. In another example, if a reader sees dates of employment as 2011–2012, he or she does not know if that included a full year of employment or if the writer started on December 31, 2011, and quit on January 1, 2012. Including the months along with the dates is the clearest and most ethical way to represent your employment timeline.

Education. Because your education is likely to be your strongest selling point for your first job after college, you will probably cover it in some detail. (Unless it adds something unique, you usually do not include your high school education once you have finished a college degree. Similarly, you also minimize the emphasis on all your education as you gain experience.) At a minimum, your coverage of education should include institutions, dates, degrees, and areas of study. For some jobs, you may want to list and even describe specific courses, especially if you have little other information to present or if your coursework has uniquely prepared you for those jobs. In particular, if you are applying for an internship, you may want to list your course work as an indication of your current level of academic preparation as it relates to the requirements of the position. If your grade-point average (GPA) is good, you may want to include it. Remember, for your résumé, you can compute your GPA in a way that works best for you as long as you label it accurately. For example, you may want to select just those courses in your major, labeling it Major GPA. Or if your last few years were your best ones, you may want to present your GPA for just that period. In any case, include GPA when it works favorably for you.

- For education, include institutions, dates, degrees, and areas of study.

Personal Information. What personal information to list is a matter for your best judgment. In fact, the trend appears to be toward eliminating such information. If you do include personal information, you should omit race, religion, sex, age, and marital status because current laws prohibit hiring based on them. Interestingly, not everyone agrees on this matter. Some authorities believe that at least some of these items should be included. They argue that the law only prohibits employers from considering such information in hiring—that it does not prohibit applicants from presenting the information. They reason that if such information helps you, you should use it. The illustrations shown in this chapter support both viewpoints.

- For legal reasons, some personal information (on race, religion, sex) should probably not be listed.

Figure 9–2

A List of Action Verbs That Add Strength to Your Résumé

**Communication/
People Skills**

Addressed
Advertised
Arbitrated
Arranged
Articulated
Authored
Clarified
Collaborated
Communicated
Composed
Condensed
Conferred
Consulted
Contacted
Conveyed
Convinced
Corresponded
Debated
Defined
Developed
Directed
Discussed
Drafted
Edited
Elicited
Enlisted
Explained
Expressed
Formulated
Furnished
Incorporated
Influenced
Interacted
Interpreted
Interviewed
Involved
Joined
Judged
Lectured
Listened
Marketed
Mediated
Moderated
Negotiated
Observed
Outlined
Participated

Persuaded
Presented
Promoted
Proposed
Publicized
Reconciled
Recruited
Referred
Reinforced
Reported
Resolved
Responded
Solicited
Specified
Spoke
Suggested
Summarized
Synthesized
Translated
Wrote

Creative Skills

Acted
Adapted
Began
Combined
Composed
Conceptualized
Condensed
Created
Customized
Designed
Developed
Directed
Displayed
Drew
Entertained
Established
Fashioned
Formulated
Founded
Illustrated
Initiated
Instituted
Integrated
Introduced
Invented
Modeled
Modified

Originated
Performed
Photographed
Planned
Revised
Revitalized
Shaped
Solved

**Data/Financial
Skills**

Administered
Adjusted
Allocated
Analyzed
Appraised
Assessed
Audited
Balanced
Budgeted
Calculated
Computed
Conserved
Corrected
Determined
Developed
Estimated
Forecasted
Managed
Marketed
Measured
Netted
Planned
Prepared
Programmed
Projected
Qualified
Reconciled
Reduced
Researched
Retrieved

Helping Skills

Adapted
Advocated
Aided
Answered
Arranged
Assessed
Assisted

Clarified
Coached
Collaborated
Contributed
Cooperated
Counseled
Demonstrated
Diagnosed
Educated
Encouraged
Ensured
Expedited
Facilitated
Familiarized
Furthered
Guided
Helped
Insured
Intervened
Motivated
Prevented
Provided
Referred
Rehabilitated
Represented
Resolved
Simplified
Supplied
Supported
Volunteered

**Management/
Leadership Skills**

Administered
Analyzed
Appointed
Approved
Assigned
Attained
Authorized
Chaired
Considered
Consolidated
Contracted
Controlled
Converted
Coordinated
Decided
Delegated

Developed
Directed
Eliminated
Emphasized
Enforced
Enhanced
Established
Executed
Generated
Handled
Headed
Hired
Hosted
Improved
Incorporated
Increased
Initiated
Inspected
Instituted
Led
Managed
Merged
Motivated
Navigated
Organized
Originated
Overhauled
Oversaw
Planned
Presided
Prioritized
Produced
Recommended
Reorganized
Replaced
Restored
Reviewed
Scheduled
Secured
Selected
Streamlined
Strengthened
Supervised
Terminated

**Organizational
Skills**

Approved
Arranged

Catalogued
Categorized
Charted
Classified
Coded
Collected
Compiled
Corrected
Corresponded
Distributed
Executed
Filed
Generated
Incorporated
Inspected
Logged
Maintained
Monitored
Obtained
Operated
Ordered
Organized
Prepared
Processed
Provided
Purchased
Recorded
Registered
Reserved
Responded
Reviewed
Routed
Scheduled
Screened
Submitted
Supplied
Standardized
Systematized
Updated
Validated
Verified

Research Skills

Analyzed
Clarified
Collected
Compared
Conducted
Critiqued

Figure 9–2

(continued)

Detected	Measured	Communicated	Instructed	Calculated	Overhauled
Determined	Organized	Conducted	Motivated	Computed	Printed
Diagnosed	Researched	Coordinated	Persuaded	Conserved	Programmed
Evaluated	Reviewed	Coordinated	Simulated	Constructed	Rectified
Examined	Searched	Developed	Stimulated	Converted	Regulated
Experimented	Solved	Enabled	Taught	Debugged	Remodeled
Explored	Summarized	Encouraged	Tested	Designed	Repaired
Extracted	Surveyed	Evaluated	Trained	Determined	Replaced
Formulated	Systematized	Explained	Transmitted	Developed	Restored
Gathered	Tested	Facilitated	Tutored	Engineered	Solved
Inspected	**Teaching Skills**	Focused	**Technical Skills**	Fabricated	Specialized
Interviewed	Adapted	Guided	Adapted	Fortified	Standardized
Invented	Advised	Individualized	Applied	Installed	Studied
Investigated	Clarified	Informed	Assembled	Maintained	Upgraded
Located	Coached	Instilled	Built	Operated	Utilized

Source: "Job-Seeker Action Verbs—By Skills Sets," *Quintessential Careers,* Quintessential Careers, 2009, Web, 3 June 2009.

Personal information that is generally appropriate includes all items that tell about your personal assets. Information on your organization memberships, civic involvement, and social activities is evidence of experience and interest in working with people. Hobbies and athletic participation tell of your balance of interests. Such information can be quite useful to some employers, especially when personal qualities are important to the work involved. Figure 9–11 presents a résumé that emphasizes education and experience.

- Information on activities and interests tells about one's personal qualities.

References. Authorities disagree on whether to list references on the résumé. Some think that references should not be contacted until negotiations are further along. Others think that references should be listed because some employers want to check them early in the screening process. One recent study by the Society for Human Resource Management of 2,500 human resource professionals said that 96 percent of their companies always check references.[3] Therefore, including them on the résumé would make it easier for the company to proceed through the background check process. Clearly, both views have substantial support. You will have to make the choice based on your best knowledge of the situation.

- Consider listing references, but know that some authorities favor postponing using them.

Some résumé writers may be tempted to put "references available upon request" at the bottom of their résumés. However, this expression is outdated and serves no purpose. When you think about it, of course you would always make your references available at the employer's request, which means you're stating the obvious. Though some may argue that including this statement shows a willingness to provide the information, you can show your willingness by including a separate references sheet. You may want to use the space you would devote to this statement by adding another line to your job duties or other experience to sell your skills and abilities.

When you do list someone as a reference, good business etiquette requires that you ask for permission first. Although you will use only those who can speak highly of you, sometimes asking for your reference's permission beforehand helps that person prepare better. And, of course, it saves you from unexpected embarrassment such as

- Good etiquette requires that you get permission.

---

[3] Cheryl Soltis, "Eagle-Eyed Employers Scour Résumé for Little White Lies," *The Wall Street Journal* 21 Mar. 2006: B7, print.

a reference not remembering you, being caught by surprise, or, worse yet, not having anything to say.

A commonly used tool is a separate reference sheet. When the reader wants to check references, you give or send her or him this sheet. The type size and style of the main heading of this sheet should match that used in your résumé. It may say something like "References for [*your name*]." Below this heading is a listing of your references, beginning with the strongest one. In addition to solving the reference dilemma, use of this separate reference sheet allows you to change both the references and their order for each job. A sample reference sheet is shown in the example in Figure 9–5 on page 269.

- Consider using a separate sheet for references.

How many and what kinds of references to include will depend on your background. If you have an employment record, you should include one for every major job you have held—at least for recent years. You should include references related to the work you seek. If you base your application heavily on your education or your personal qualities, or both, you should include references who can vouch for these areas: professors, clergy, community leaders, and the like. Your goal is to list those people who can verify the points on which your appeal for the job is based. At a minimum, you should list three references. Five is a good maximum.

- Select references that cover your background.

Your list of references should include accurate mailing addresses, with appropriate job titles. Also useful are telephone and fax numbers as well as email addresses. Job titles (officer, manager, president, supervisor) are helpful because they show what the references are able to tell about you. It is appropriate to include forms of address: Mr., Mrs., Ms., Dr., and so on.

- Include accurate mailing and email addresses and job titles.

Organizing for Strength. After you have identified the information you want to include on your résumé, you will want to organize or group items to present yourself in the best possible light. Three strategies for organizing this information are the *reverse chronological approach,* the *functional* or *skills approach,* and the *accomplishments/ achievements* or *highlights approach.*

- Choose an organizing strategy that best presents your case.

The *reverse chronological* organizational layout (Figures 9–6 and 9–7) presents your education and work experience from the most recent to oldest. It emphasizes the order and time frame in which you have participated in these activities. It is particularly good for those who have progressed in an orderly and timely fashion through school and work.

- The *reverse chronological* approach is orderly.

A *functional* or *skills* layout (Figure 9–8) organizes around three to five areas particularly important to the job you want. Rather than forcing an employer to determine that you developed one skill on one job and another skill on another job, this organizational plan groups related skills together. It is particularly good for those who have had many jobs, for those who have taken nontraditional career paths, and for those who are changing fields. Creating this kind of résumé takes much work and careful analysis of both jobs and skills to show the reader that you are a good match for the position. If you use a functional résumé, be sure that readers can see from the other sections— such as employment and education—where you likely developed the skills that you are emphasizing. Enabling your readers to make these connections lends credibility to your claims to have such skills.

- The *functional* or *skills* approach emphasizes relevant skills.

An *accomplishments/achievements* layout (Figure 9–9) presents a picture of you as a competent worker. It puts hard numbers and precise facts behind skills and traits you have. Refer to Figure 9–2 for some good verb choices to use in describing accomplishments. Here is an example illustrating this arrangement in describing work done at a particular company:

- The accomplishments/ achievements approach shows you can perform.

Successfully managed the Austin store for two years in a period of low unemployment with these results:

- Reduced employee turnover 55 percent.
- Increased profits 37 percent.
- Grew sales volume 12 percent.

Information covered under a *Highlights* or *Summary* heading may include key points from the three conventional information groups: education, experience, and personal qualities. Typically, this layout emphasizes the applicant's most impressive background facts that pertain to the work sought, as in this example:

The highlights or summary approach shows you are a good fit for the position.

Highlights

- **Experienced:** Three years of full-time work as programmer/analyst in designing and developing financial databases for the banking industry.
- **Highly trained:** B.S. degree with honors in management information systems.
- **Self-motivated:** Proven record of successful completion of three online courses.

Although such items will overlap others in the résumé, using them in a separate group emphasizes strengths while showing where they were obtained. See an example of an accomplishments layout in Figure 9–9.

Writing Impersonally and Consistently. Because the résumé is a listing of information, you should write without personal pronouns (no *I*'s, *we*'s, *you*'s). You should also write all equal-level headings and the parts under each heading in the same (parallel) grammatical form. For example, if one major heading in the résumé is a noun phrase, all the other major headings should be noun phrases. The following four job duties illustrate the point. All but the third are verb phrases. The error can be corrected by making the third a noun phrase, as in the examples to the right:

- List the information without use of personal pronouns (I, we, you).
- Use the same (parallel) grammatical form for all equal-level headings and for the parts listed under each heading.

Not Parallel	Parallel
Greeted customers	Greeted customers
Processed transactions	Processed transactions
Data entry in Excel spreadsheets	Entered data in Excel spreadsheets
Balanced a cash drawer	Balanced a cash drawer

The following items illustrate grammatical inconsistency in the parts of a group:

Have fluency in Spanish

Active in sports

Ambitious

Inspection of these items shows that they do not fit the same understood words. The understood word for the first item is *I* and for the second and third, the understood words are *I am*. Any changes that make all three items fit the same understood words would correct the error (e.g., fluent in Spanish).

Making the Form Attractive. The attractiveness of your résumé will say as much about you as the words. The appearance of the information that the reader sees plays a part in forming his or her judgment. While using a template is one solution, it will make you look like many other applicants. A layout designed with your reader and your unique data in mind will probably do a better job for you. Not only will your résumé have a distinctive appearance, but the design should sell you more effectively than one where you must fit your data to the design. A sloppy, poorly designed presentation, on the other hand, may even ruin your chances of getting the job. Thus, an attractive physical arrangement is a must.

- Make the résumé attractive.

There is no one best arrangement, but a good procedure is to approach the task as a graphic designer would. Your objective is to design an arrangement of type and space that appeals to the eye.

- Design it as a graphic designer would. Use balance and space for eye appeal.

Margins look better if at least an inch of space is left at the top of the page and on the left and right sides of the page and if at least 1½ inches of space are left at the bottom of the page. Your listing of items by rows and columns appears best if the items

- Here are some suggestions on form.

are short and if they can be set up in two uncrowded columns, one on the left side of the page and one on the right side. Longer items of information are more appropriately set up in lines extending across the page. In any event, you would do well to avoid long and narrow columns of data with large sections of wasted space on either side. Arrangements that give a heavy crowded effect also offend the eye. Extra spacing between subdivisions and indented patterns for subparts are especially pleasing to the eye.

● Choose fonts carefully.

While layout is important in showing your ability to organize and good spacing increases readability, other design considerations such as font and paper selection affect attractiveness almost as much. Commercial designers say that type size for headings should be at least 12 to 14 points and for body text, 10 to 12 points. They also recommend using no more than two font styles on a page. Some word processing programs have a "shrink to fit" feature that allows the user to fit information on one page. It will automatically adjust font sizes to fit the page. Be sure the resulting type size is both appropriate and readable.

● Conservative paper usually is best.

Another factor affecting the appearance of your application documents is the paper you select. The paper should be appropriate for the job you seek. In business, erring on the conservative side is usually better; you do not want to be eliminated from consideration simply because the reader did not like the quality or color of the paper. The most traditional choice is white, 100 percent cotton, 20- to 28-lb. paper. Of course, reasonable variations can be appropriate.

● Figures 9–3 and 9–4 show bad and good form.

Contrasting Bad and Good Examples. The résumés in Figures 9–3 and 9–4 are at opposing ends of the quality scale. The first one, scant in coverage and poorly arranged, does little to help the applicant. Clearly, the second one is more complete and better arranged.

Weakness in Bad Arrangement and Incompleteness. Shortcomings in the first example (Figure 9–3) are obvious. First, the form is not pleasing to the eye. The weight of the type is heavy on the left side of the page. Failure to indent wrapped lines makes reading difficult.

This résumé also contains numerous errors in wording. Information headings are not parallel in grammatical form. All are in topic form except the first one. The items listed under *Personal* are not parallel either and contain irrelevant and inappropriate personal information. Throughout, the résumé coverage is scant, leaving out many of the details needed to present the best impression of the applicant. Under *Experience,* little is said about specific tasks and skills in each job; and under *Education,* high school work is listed needlessly. The references are incomplete, omitting street addresses and job titles.

Strength through Good Arrangement and Completeness. The next résumé (Figure 9–4) appears better at first glance, and it gets even better as you read it. It is attractively arranged. The information is neither crowded nor strung out. The balance is good. Its content is also superior to that of the other example. Additional words show the quality of Mr. Andrews's work experience and education, and they emphasize points that make him suited for the work he seeks. This résumé excludes inappropriate personal information and has only the facts that tell something about Andrews's personal qualities. A bulleted list of duties under each job describes the skills and qualities Mr. Andrews brings to a marketing position. A separate references sheet with complete contact information permits the reader to contact the references easily. Job titles tell how each is qualified to evaluate the subject. Note that moving the references to a separate page frees space in the résumé for presenting Mr. Andrews's qualifications.

● The scannable résumé should be constructed to be read accurately by a computer and retrieved when an appropriate position is being filled.

Scannable Print Résumé

Although paper résumés are not obsolete, a recent addition to the job-search process is the scannable résumé. This résumé bridges the print-to-digital gap. It is simply one

Figure 9–3

Incompleteness and Bad Arrangement in a Traditional Print Résumé. This résumé presents Jason Andrews ineffectively (see "Introductory Situation" for "Résumés and Applications"). It is scant and poorly arranged.

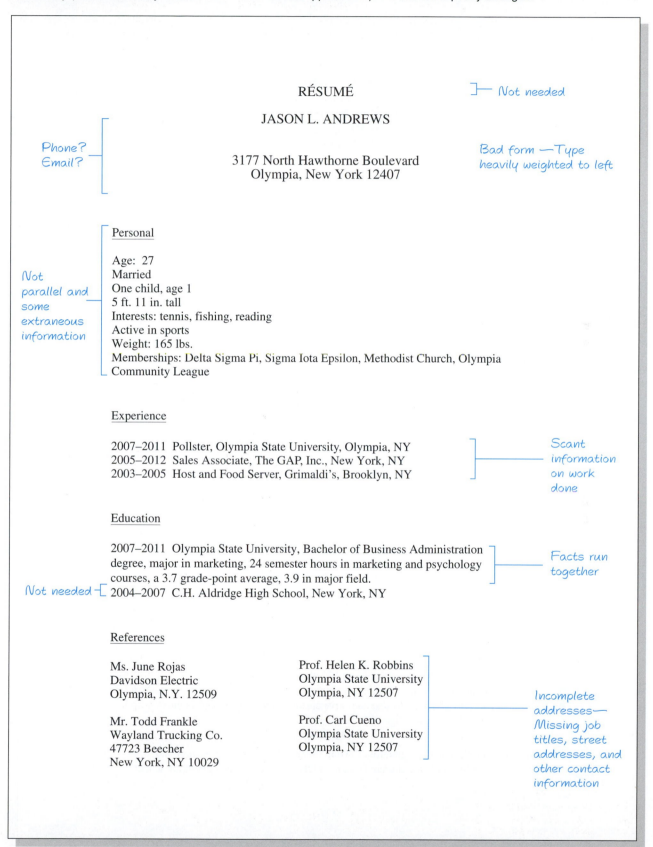

RÉSUMÉ   ⊢ Not needed

JASON L. ANDREWS

Phone?
Email?

3177 North Hawthorne Boulevard
Olympia, New York 12407

Bad form —Type
heavily weighted to left

Personal

Not
parallel and
some
extraneous
information

Age: 27
Married
One child, age 1
5 ft. 11 in. tall
Interests: tennis, fishing, reading
Active in sports
Weight: 165 lbs.
Memberships: Delta Sigma Pi, Sigma Iota Epsilon, Methodist Church, Olympia
Community League

Experience

2007–2011 Pollster, Olympia State University, Olympia, NY
2005–2012 Sales Associate, The GAP, Inc., New York, NY
2003–2005 Host and Food Server, Grimaldi's, Brooklyn, NY

Scant
information
on work
done

Education

2007–2011 Olympia State University, Bachelor of Business Administration
degree, major in marketing, 24 semester hours in marketing and psychology
courses, a 3.7 grade-point average, 3.9 in major field.
2004–2007 C.H. Aldridge High School, New York, NY

Facts run
together

Not needed ⊏

References

Ms. June Rojas
Davidson Electric
Olympia, N.Y. 12509

Prof. Helen K. Robbins
Olympia State University
Olympia, NY 12507

Mr. Todd Frankle
Wayland Trucking Co.
47723 Beecher
New York, NY 10029

Prof. Carl Cueno
Olympia State University
Olympia, NY 12507

Incomplete
addresses—
Missing job
titles, street
addresses, and
other contact
information

Figure 9–4

Thoroughness and Good Arrangement in a Traditional Print Résumé. This complete and reverse chronologically organized résumé presents Jason Andrews's case effectively (see "Introductory Situation" for "Résumés and Applications").

Jason L. Andrews

3177 North Hawthorne Boulevard
Olympia, NY 12407-3278
914.967.3117 (Voice/Message)
jandrews@hotmail.com

Presents contact data clearly

Objective

A position in marketing that will lead to work as a marketing manager for an ebusiness.

Education

Bachelor of Business Administration
Olympia State University—May 2012
GPA: 3.7/4.0

Major: Marketing
Minor: Psychology
Dean's List

Layout emphasizes key educational facts

Highlights most relevant courses and subjects

Related Coursework:
- Strategic Marketing
- Marketing Research
- Marketing Communications & Promotion
- Global Marketing
- Interpersonal Communication
- Statistical Analysis
- Consumer and Buyer Behavior
- Social Psychology

- Research Projects: Cultural Influence on Purchasing, Customer Brand Preference, and Motivating Subordinates with Effective Performance Appraisals.

Experience

Intern-Pollster, Olympia State University, Olympia, NY, May 2011–present
- Survey over 20 students and alumni weekly over the phone and in person
- Compile statistical data and present reports to the Chancellor's Council
- Supervise a team of ten undergraduate pollsters
- Exceeded university goals by 5% last year for the number of surveys completed

Sales Associate, The Gap, Inc., New York, NY, Jan. 2009–April 2011
- Was named top store sales associate four of eight quarters
- Created merchandise displays
- Trained new sales associates

Host and Food Server, Grimaldi's, Brooklyn, NY, Aug. 2007–Dec. 2008
- Provided exceptional customer service
- Worked well as part of a team to seat and serve customers quickly and efficiently

Action verbs portray an image of a hard worker with good interpersonal skills

Activities

Includes only most relevant information

Delta Sigma Pi (professional); Sigma Iota Epsilon (honorary), served as treasurer and president; Board of Stewards for church; League of Olympia, served as registration leader

Figure 9–5

Thoroughness and Good Arrangement for a Reference Sheet. This reference sheet presents Jason Andrews's references completely.

Jason L. Andrews

3177 North Hawthorne Boulevard
Olympia, NY 12407-3278
914.967.3117 (Voice/ Message)
jandrews@hotmail.com

Heading format matches résumé

Ms. June Rojas, Polling Supervisor
Olympia State University
7114 East 71st Street
Olympia, NY 12509-4572
Telephone: 518.342.1171
Fax: 518.342.1200
Email: June.Rojas@osu.edu

Mr. Todd E. Frankle, Store Manager
The Gap, Inc.
Lincoln Square
New York, NY 10023-0007
Telephone: 212.466.9101
Fax: 212.468.9100
Email: tfrankle@gap.com

Professor Helen K. Robbins
Department of Marketing
Olympia State University
Olympia, NY 12507-0182
Telephone: 518.392.6673
Fax: 518.392.3675
Email: Helen.Robbins@osu.edu

Professor Carol A. Cueno
Department of Psychology
Olympia State University
Olympia, NY 12507-0234
Telephone: 518.392.0723
Fax: 518.392.7542
Email: Carol.Cueno@osu.edu

Complete information and balanced arrangement

Figure 9–6

Traditional Print Résumé Organized in Reverse Chronological Format

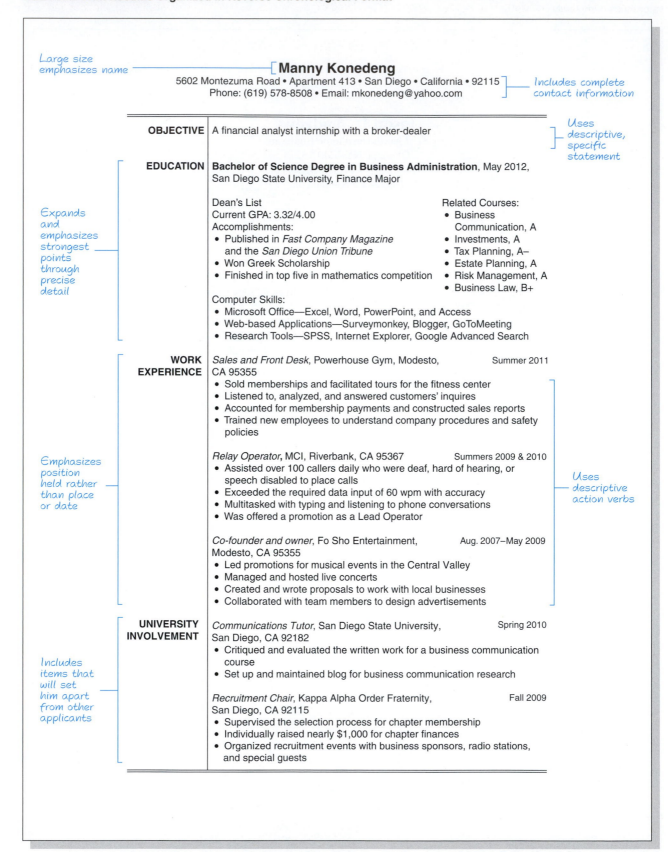

Large size emphasizes name —

Manny Konedeng

5602 Montezuma Road • Apartment 413 • San Diego • California • 92115
Phone: (619) 578-8508 • Email: mkonedeng@yahoo.com

Includes complete contact information

OBJECTIVE A financial analyst internship with a broker-dealer

Uses descriptive, specific statement

EDUCATION **Bachelor of Science Degree in Business Administration**, May 2012, San Diego State University, Finance Major

Expands and emphasizes strongest points through precise detail

Dean's List
Current GPA: 3.32/4.00
Accomplishments:
- Published in *Fast Company Magazine* and the *San Diego Union Tribune*
- Won Greek Scholarship
- Finished in top five in mathematics competition

Related Courses:
- Business Communication, A
- Investments, A
- Tax Planning, A–
- Estate Planning, A
- Risk Management, A
- Business Law, B+

Computer Skills:
- Microsoft Office—Excel, Word, PowerPoint, and Access
- Web-based Applications—Surveymonkey, Blogger, GoToMeeting
- Research Tools—SPSS, Internet Explorer, Google Advanced Search

WORK EXPERIENCE *Sales and Front Desk*, Powerhouse Gym, Modesto, CA 95355 Summer 2011
- Sold memberships and facilitated tours for the fitness center
- Listened to, analyzed, and answered customers' inquires
- Accounted for membership payments and constructed sales reports
- Trained new employees to understand company procedures and safety policies

Emphasizes position held rather than place or date

Relay Operator, MCI, Riverbank, CA 95367 Summers 2009 & 2010
- Assisted over 100 callers daily who were deaf, hard of hearing, or speech disabled to place calls
- Exceeded the required data input of 60 wpm with accuracy
- Multitasked with typing and listening to phone conversations
- Was offered a promotion as a Lead Operator

Uses descriptive action verbs

Co-founder and owner, Fo Sho Entertainment, Modesto, CA 95355 Aug. 2007–May 2009
- Led promotions for musical events in the Central Valley
- Managed and hosted live concerts
- Created and wrote proposals to work with local businesses
- Collaborated with team members to design advertisements

UNIVERSITY INVOLVEMENT *Communications Tutor*, San Diego State University, San Diego, CA 92182 Spring 2010
- Critiqued and evaluated the written work for a business communication course
- Set up and maintained blog for business communication research

Includes items that will set him apart from other applicants

Recruitment Chair, Kappa Alpha Order Fraternity, San Diego, CA 92115 Fall 2009
- Supervised the selection process for chapter membership
- Individually raised nearly $1,000 for chapter finances
- Organized recruitment events with business sponsors, radio stations, and special guests

Figure 9–7

Digital HTML Résumé Organized in Reverse Chronological Format and Sent as Rich Email. This "front page" presents the applicant's education and experience and highlights career-related experience. Links help provide detailed support. See this résumé on the textbook webpage and explore its links.

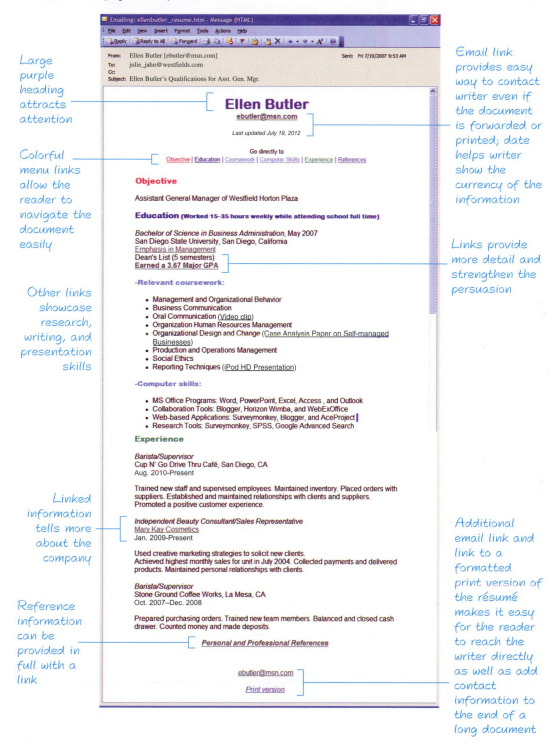

Large purple heading attracts attention

Colorful menu links allow the reader to navigate the document easily

Other links showcase research, writing, and presentation skills

Linked information tells more about the company

Reference information can be provided in full with a link

Email link provides easy way to contact writer even if the document is forwarded or printed; date helps writer show the currency of the information

Links provide more detail and strengthen the persuasion

Additional email link and link to a formatted print version of the résumé makes it easy for the reader to reach the writer directly as well as add contact information to the end of a long document

Figure 9–8

Traditional Print Résumé Using the Functional Organization for the Skills Section

Carolynn W. Workman

12271 69th Terrace North
Seminole, FL 33772
727.399.2569 (Voice/Message)
cworkman@msn.com

Emphasizes tight organization through use of horizontal ruled lines

Objective	An accounting position with a CPA firm

Education

Layout emphasizes degree and GPA

Bachelor of Science: University of South Florida, December 2012
Major: Business Administration
Emphasis: Accounting
GPA: 3.42 with Honors

Uses internal bullets to increase readability

Accounting-Related Course Work:
Financial Accounting ❖ Cost Accounting and Control ❖ Accounting Information Systems ❖
Auditing ❖ Concepts of Federal Income Taxation ❖ Financial Policy ❖ Communications for
Business and Professions

Activities:
Vice-President of Finance, Beta Alpha Psi
Editor, Student Newsletter for Beta Alpha Psi
Member, Golden Key National Honors Society

Emphasizes key skills relevant to objective

Skills
Computer

▶ Assisted in installation of small business computerized accounting system using QuickBooks Pro.
▶ Prepared tax returns for individuals in the VITA program using specialty tax software.
▶ Mastered Excel, designing data input forms, analyzing and interpreting results of most functions, generating graphs, and creating and using macros.

Accounting

▶ Experienced with financial statements and general ledger.
▶ Reconciled accounts for center serving over 1300 clients.
▶ Experienced in preparing income, gift, and estate tax returns.
▶ Processed expense reports for twenty professional staff.
▶ Experienced in using Great Plains and Solomon IV.

Varies use of action verbs

Business
Communication

▶ Conducted client interviews and researched tax issues.
▶ Communicated both in written and verbal form with clients.
▶ Delivered several individual and team presentations on business cases, projects, and reports to business students.

Work History
Administrative
Assistant

Office of Student Disability Services, University of South Florida
Tampa, FL. Spring 2011.

Tax Assistant

Rosemary Lenaghan, Certified Public Accountant. Seminole, FL Jan. 2009–May 2011.

Figure 9–9

Traditional Print Résumé Using Highlights of Qualifications and Accomplishments Sections

Kimberly M. VanLerBerghe

2411 27th Street
Moline, IL 61265
309.764.0017 (Mobile)
kmv@yahoo.com

JOB TARGET	TRAINER/TRANSLATOR for a large, worldwide industrial company

HIGHLIGHTS OF QUALIFICATIONS

Emphasizes those qualifications most relevant to position sought

- Experienced in creating and delivering multimedia PowerPoint presentations.
- Enthusiastic team member/leader whose participation brings out the best in others.
- Proficient in analytical ability.
- Skilled in gathering and interpreting data.
- Bilingual—English/Spanish.

EDUCATION

Presents the most important items here

DEGREE	B.A. English—June 2012—Western Illinois University	
EMPHASIS	Education	MAJOR GPA—3.87/4.00
HONORS	Dean's List, four semesters	
	Chevron Scholarship, Fall 2010	
MEMBER	Mortar Board, Women's Golf Team	

EMPLOYMENT

Identifies most significant places of work and de-emphasizes less important work

DEERE & COMPANY, INC.	CONGRESSMAN J. DENNIS HASTERT
Student Intern, Summer 2011	Volunteer in Computer Services, Fall 2011

Several years' experience in the restaurant business including supervisory positions.

ACCOMPLISHMENTS

Presents only selected accomplishments from various work and volunteer experience that relate to position sought

- ► Trained executives to create effective cross-cultural presentations.
- ► Developed online training program for executive use of GoToMeeting.
- ► Designed and developed a database to keep track of financial donations.
- ► Coded new screens and reports; debugged and revised screen forms for easier data entry.
- ► Provided computer support to virtual volunteers on election committee.

that can be scanned into a database and retrieved when a position is being filled. Since the objective is getting your résumé reviewed in order to be interviewed, you should use the following strategies to improve your chances of having it retrieved by the computer.

- Use keywords that describe precisely what you can do.

Include Keywords. One strategy, using keywords, is often recommended for use with electronic scanning software. These keywords are usually nouns or concrete words that describe skills and accomplishments precisely. Instead of listing a course in comparative programming, you would list the precise languages compared, such as PHP, C++, and Java. Instead of saying you would like a job in information systems, you would name specific job titles such as systems analyst, network specialist, or application specialist. Using industry-specific terminology is highly recommended.

- Use keywords common to those an employer would use to retrieve your résumé.

Some ways to identify the keywords in your field are to read ads, listen to recruiters, and listen to your professors. Start building a list of words you find used repeatedly. From this list, choose those words most appropriate for the kind of work you want to do. Amplify your use of abbreviations, acronyms, and jargon appropriate to the work you want to do.

Some experts recommend using a separate keyword section at the beginning of the résumé, loading it with all the relevant terms. If you use this technique, include the heading "Keywords" before your objective and follow it with six to twelve keywords. However, many résumé writers are well aware of the importance of using keywords and consciously work to integrate them into their résumés. This is especially true of those who use the hybrid résumés to cover both the face-to-face and scanning purposes in one document. Remember, though, to be ethical in your use of keywords from the job posting by using only those key words that actually represent your qualifications.

- Use precise nouns on the scannable résumé.

Choose Words Carefully. Unlike the traditional résumé, the scannable résumé is strengthened not by the use of action verbs but rather by the use of nouns. Informal studies have shown that those retrieving résumés from such databases tend to use precise nouns.

- Use both precise nouns and action verbs in the hybrid résumé.

For the hybrid résumé, one you use in both face-to-face and scanning situations, you can combine the use of precise nouns with strong action verbs. The nouns will help ensure that the résumé gets pulled from the database, and the verbs help the face-to-face recruiter see the link to the kind of work you want to do.

- Be sure the font you use can be read easily by scanners.

Present the Information. Since you want your résumé to be read accurately, you will use a font most scanners can read easily, such as Helvetica, Arial, and Times Roman. Most scanners can easily handle fonts between 10 and 14 points. Although many handle bold, when in doubt use all caps for emphasis rather than bold. Also, because italics often confuse scanners, avoid them. Underlining is best left out as well. It creates trouble with descending letters such as *g* or *y* when the line cuts through the letter. In fact, you should use all lines sparingly. Also, avoid graphics and shading; they just confuse the software. Use white paper to maximize the contrast, and always print in the portrait mode. The Manny Konedeng résumé in Figure 9–10 is a scannable résumé employing these guidelines.

- Send your résumé by the channel that serves you best.

Today companies accept résumés by mail, fax, and email. Be sure to choose the channel that serves you best. Some companies ask for résumés by fax or email; others still prefer to see an applicant's ability to organize and lay out a printed page. Some employers give the option to the sender. Obviously, when speed gives you a competitive advantage, you'll choose the fax or email options. However, you do lose some control over the quality of the document. If you elect to print and send a scannable résumé, do not fold it. Just mail it in a 9 × 12 envelope. For a little extra cost, you will help ensure that your résumé gets scanned accurately rather than wondering if your keywords were on a fold that a scanner might have had difficulty reading.

Figure 9–10

Scannable Résumé for Employers Who Use Scanning Software to Screen Résumés. Notice how the writer has expanded the length through some added text when no longer confined to one physical page.

Manny Konedeng
5602 Montezuma Road
Apartment 413
San Diego, California 92115
Phone: (619) 578-8058
Email: mkonedeng@yahoo.com

Avoids italics and underlines yet is arranged for both scanner and human readability

OBJECTIVE

A financial analyst internship with a broker-dealer where both analytical and interpersonal communication skills and knowledge are valued

Uses all caps and spacing for enhanced human readability

EDUCATION

Bachelor of Science Degree in Business Administration, May 2012
San Diego State University, Finance Major

Dean's List
Current GPA: 3.32/4.00

Related Courses

Business Communication A
Investments A
Tax planning A-
Estate Planning A
Risk Management A
Business Law B+

All items are on one line and tabs avoided for improved comprehension

Computer Skills

Microsoft Office: Excel, Word, PowerPoint, Access
Web-based Applications: Surveymonkey, Blogger, GoToMeeting
Research Tools: SPSS, Internet Explorer

Accomplishments

Published in Fast Company Magazine and the San Diego Union Tribune
Won Greek scholarship
Finished in top five mathematics competition

WORK EXPERIENCE

Powerhouse Gym, Sales and Front Desk, Summer 2011 Modesto,
CA 95355

Sold memberships and facilitated tours for the fitness center
Listened to, analyzed, and answered customers inquires
Accounted for membership payments and constructed sales reports
Trained new employees to understand company procedures and safety policies

Integrates precise nouns and industry-specific jargon as keywords

MCI, Relay Operator, Summer 2009 & 2010, Riverbank, CA 95367

Assisted over 100 callers daily who were deaf, hard of hearing, or speech disabled to place calls
Exceeded the required data input of 60 wpm with accuracy
Multitasked with typing and listening to phone conversations
Was Offered a promotion as a Lead Operator

Figure 9–10

(continued)

Fo Sho Entertainment, Co-founder and Owner, Aug. 2007–May 2009
Modesto, CA 95355

Led promotions for musical events in the Central Valley
Managed and hosted live concerts
Created and wrote proposals to work with local businesses
Collaborated with team members to design advertisements

UNIVERSITY EXPERIENCE

Information Decision Systems, Communications Tutor, Spring 2011,
San Diego, CA 92182
Critiqued and evaluated the written work for a business communica-
tion course
Set up and maintained blog for business communication research

Kappa Alpha Order Fraternity, Recruitment Chairman, Fall 2010,
San Diego, CA 92115

Supervised the selection process for chapter membership
Individually raised nearly $1,000 for chapter finances
Organized recruitment events with business sponsors, radio stations,
and special guests

Avoids graphics and extra lines

ACTIVITIES AND SERVICE

Campus Leadership

Recruitment Chair, Kappa Alpha Order Fraternity
Supervised all new member recruitment
Coordinated fundraisers for chapter finances
Organized recruitment events with business sponsors, radio stations,
and special guests
Advocated Freshmen Summer Orientation and Greek life

Correspondent for External Chapter Affairs, Kappa Alpha Order
Fraternity

Communicated with chapter alumni and National Office to fulfill
chapter obligations

Upsilon Class Treasurer, Kappa Alpha Order Fraternity

Managed chapter budgets and expenditures

Several Interfraternity Council Roles

Member, Fraternity Men against Negative Environments and Rape
Situations
Cochairman, Greek Week Fundraiser
Candidate, IFC Treasurer

Professional and Community Service

Member, Finance & Investment Society
Presenter, Peer Health Education
Marshal, SDSU New Student & Family Convocation
Sponsor, Muscular Dystrophy national philanthropy
Sponsor, Service for Sight philanthropy
Sponsor, Victims of Domestic Violence philanthropy
Sponsor, Camp Able philanthropy
Associated Students' Good Neighbor Program volunteer
Volunteer, Designated Driver Association
Volunteer, Beach Recovery Project

Adds other relevant information since there is no physical page limit

Uses black on white contrast for improved scanning accuracy

Digital Résumé

Transmitting a digital résumé involves making decisions about the receiver's preferences and capabilities for receiving it as well as leveraging the technology to present you in the best possible light. These résumés range from low-end plain text files, to formatted word processor files, to full-blown multimedia documents and webpages.

While much of the content of a digital résumé is similar to that of the print résumé, two important changes should be made. The first is to delete all contact information except your email address. Not only can you lose control over the distribution of the document since digital files can be passed along easily and quickly, but your information could be added to databases and sold. Many experts recommend setting up a Web-based email account that you use solely for your job search. Second, you should date the résumé. That way if an unscrupulous recruiter pulls it from a database and presents it to your boss two years later, you will be able to explain that you are truly happy working there and that the résumé is clearly dated before you went to work for your employer. These content changes should be made to all forms of the digital résumé.

The low-end digital résumé is usually a document saved as a plain (unformatted) ASCII or text file. You will use it when an employer requests that form. Sometimes you will send it as an attached file and other times you will place it inside your email. Since you can create it in your word processor and run a spell checker on it, you will probably want to cut and paste from it when you are completing online applications. It is also a good idea to test it out by sending it to yourself and viewing it with as many different email programs as you can. Then you will know if you need to shorten lines, add spacing, or make other changes to improve its readability.

To help ensure readability, you may want to send your résumé as a formatted attached file. Of course, you would only send it this way when you know the receiver welcomes getting résumés this way. You have a couple of choices of file format with attached files. You could send the résumé in a standard word processing file format, one that is widely read by a variety of programs. Or you could send it as an RTF (rich text format) or PDF (portable document file). All these formats attempt to preserve the layout of your document. You also can help by using standard fonts most readers are likely to have installed or by embedding your font, so that the receiver's view is the one you intended. Note that if you are sending your résumé as a Word document and have aligned your information using your tab key or your space bar, your formatting may not be preserved when the résumé is sent electronically. One way to preserve the alignment is to set up the résumé in a table. In addition, if you are working in Word, unless you know that your reader can open documents in Word 2007 (.docx files), be sure to send your files in an earlier (.doc) format so that the reader can open them.

The multimedia format can be a dramatic extension of the print résumé. Not only can you add links, color, and graphics, but you can also add sound, animation, and even video. If your receiver is like many others today, he or she is likely able to receive HTM files within the email program. You could use the email as a cover message with a link to a webpage profile (an example is shown in the technology box in this chapter), or you could put the HTM résumé file inside the email. An HTM file allows you to display links to supporting files and include color, graphics, photos, and so on in your résumé. If used effectively, it could enhance your strengths and showcase your knowledge, creativity, and skills.

Since length is not the issue it is with the print résumé, the digital résumé should include all the detail needed to support your case. You also should take care to use the terms and keywords on which the document is likely to be searched, including nouns, buzzwords, jargon, and even acronyms commonly used in the field. You want your résumé retrieved when an appropriate position is available. A sample digital résumé is shown in Figure 9–7.

- Digital résumés enable you to leverage the technology.
- Digital résumés are used in three basic file formats.

- (1) ASCII or text files;

- (2) word processor, RTF, and PDF files;

- (3) multimedia HTM files.

- Digital résumés are not constrained in length by a page size.

Figure 9–11

Traditional Print Résumé Emphasizing Education and Relevant Experience

Derek Masters
4321 Oak Street • Eau Claire, WI 54701
Home phone: (715) 555-5555 • Email: dlmasters@gmail.com

OBJECTIVE	A full-time position in the automotive maintenance field	*States type of position and field*

EDUCATION

Chippewa Valley Technical College
Eau Claire, WI
Diploma: Automotive Maintenance Technician program, July 2012

- Received President's list status for the 2010 fall semester and 2011 summer semester
- Obtained All Data certification
- Earned certification to work with Freon
- Completed a basic welding course with arc, oxyacetylene, and wire feed welding

Lists honors and course work other graduates may not have

RELEVANT EXPERIENCE

Intern - Cooperative Education Capstone
January 2012 – May 2012
River Valley Motors
5555 Highway 93, Eau Claire, WI 54701 Phone: (715) 832-3859

- Provided excellent customer service
- Learned and then trained coworkers how to use newly purchased tire balancer
- Performed many fluid flushes and changes

Uses a separate category heading to highlight internship

EMPLOYMENT HISTORY

Shift Supervisor
February 2010 – Present
McDonald's Restaurant
4321 Hastings Way, Eau Claire, WI 54701
Phone: (715) 839-4444

As do many vocational resumes, this lists employers' contact information

- Train new employees
- Motivate employees to be positive and friendly
- Multi-task well in stressful situations
- Trusted to work alone on many different projects

Uses action verbs to portray dependability, trustworthiness, and work ethic

Night Stocker
Sam's Club
4001 Gateway Avenue, Eau Claire, WI 54701
Phone: (715) 835-3333
December 2007 – January 2010

- Worked alone and in teams to stock shelves
- Took charge of my area to maintain and increase standards
- Assembled and created displays to sell products

ACTIVITIES

- Meals on Wheels volunteer: Deliver 20 meals per week to the elderly and homebound
- Church choir member

Activities show a well rounded individual

WRITING THE COVER MESSAGE

You should begin work on the cover message by fitting the facts from your background to the work you seek and arranging those facts in a logical order. Then you present them in much the same way that a sales writer would present the features of a product or service, carefully managing the appeal. Wherever possible, you adapt the points you make to the reader's needs. Like those of sales messages, the organizational plans of cover messages vary depending on whether the print or digital channel is chosen.

- Writing the cover message involves matching your qualifications with the job.

Print Cover Letters

Cover letters come in two types: solicited (invited) and unsolicited (prospecting). As their names suggest, a solicited letter is written in response to an actual job opening, and unsolicited letter is written when you don't know whether a job exists but would like to investigate the possibility of employment with a company. Generally, a cover letter is organized according to the following plan:

- An introduction that gets the reader's attention and provides just a brief summary of why you are interested or qualified or previews the information in the body of the letter. If you are writing a solicited letter, you will also mention where you learned of the position.
- A body that matches your qualifications to the reader's needs. You should also use good sales strategy, especially the you-viewpoint and positive language.
- A conclusion that requests action such as an interview and provides contact information that makes a response easy.

    Figures 9–12 through 9–15 provide examples of effective cover letters.

- This plan for writing the letter has proven to be effective.

Gaining Attention in the Opening. As in sales writing, the opening of the cover message has two requirements: It must gain attention and it must set up the review of information that follows.

Gaining attention is especially important in prospecting messages (cover messages that are not invited). Such letters are likely to reach busy executives who have many things to do other than read cover messages. Unless the writing gains favorable attention right away, the executives probably will not read them. Even invited messages must gain attention because they will compete with other invited messages. Invited messages that stand out favorably from the beginning have a competitive advantage.

- Gain attention and set up the information review in the opening.
- Gaining attention in the opening makes the letter stand out.

Figure 9–12

Sample Prospecting Letter. Using a company executive's name to gain attention, this message is conservative in style and tone.

Mildred E. Culpepper

2707 Green Street
Lincoln, NE 68505
Voice/Message: 402-786-2575
Fax: 402-594-3675
Email: mculpepper@credighton.edu

April 22, 2012

Ms. Marlene O'Daniel
Vice President for Administration
Continental Insurance Company
3717 Saylor Road
Des Moines, IA 50313-5033

Dear Ms. O'Daniel:

One of your employees, Victor Krause, suggested that I apply for the communications specialist position you have open. Here are a summary of my qualifications and a résumé for your review.

Gains attention with associate's name— opens door

Presently, I am in my fifth year as a communications specialist for Atlas Insurance. My work consists primarily of writing a wide variety of documents for Atlas policyholders. This work has made me a convert of business communication, and it has sharpened my writing skills. And, more importantly, it has taught me how to get and keep customers for my company through writing well.

Employs conservative style and tone

Additional experience working with businesspeople has given me an insight into the communication needs of business. This experience includes planning and presenting a communication improvement course for local civil service workers, a course in business writing for area executives, and an online course in financial communication for employees of Columbia National Bank.

Shows the writer knows the skills needed for the job

Uses subtle you-viewpoint— implied from writer's understanding of work

My college training provided a solid foundation for work in business communication. Advertising and public relations were my areas of concentration for my B.S. degree from Creighton University. As you will see on the enclosed résumé, I studied all available writing courses in my degree plan. I also studied writing through English and journalism.

References résumé

In summary, Ms. O'Daniel, both my education and experience have prepared me for work as your communication specialist. I know business writing, and I know how it can be used to your company's advantage. May we discuss this in an interview? You can reach me at 402-786-2575 to arrange a convenient time and place to meet.

Brings review to a conclusion— fits qualifications presented to the job

Moves appropriately for action

Sincerely,

Mildred Culpepper

Mildred E. Culpepper

Enc.

Figure 9–13

Cover Letter (Interest and Good Organization in a Response to an Advertisement). Three job requirements listed in an advertisement determined the plan used in this letter.

4407 Sunland Avenue
Phoenix, AZ 85040-9321
July 8, 2012

Ms. Anita O. Alderson, Manager
Tompkins-Oderson Agency, Inc.
3901 Tampico Avenue
Los Angeles, CA 90032-1614

Dear Ms. Alderson:

Uses reader's words for good attention gainer

Sound background in advertising … well trained … works well with others….

Demonstrates ability to write advertising copy through writing style used

These key words in your July 6 advertisement in the *Times* describe the person you want, and I believe I am that person.

Shows clearly what the writer can do on the job

I have gained experience in every area of retail advertising while working for the *Lancer*, our college newspaper. I sold advertising, planned layouts, and wrote copy. During the last two summers, I gained firsthand experience working in the advertising department of Wunder & Son. I wrote a lot of copy, some of which I am enclosing for your inspection; you will find numerous other examples on my blog at <http://janekbits.blogspot.com>. This experience clearly will help me contribute to the work in your office.

Shows strong determination through good interpretation

In my major, I studied marketing with a specialization in advertising and integrated marketing communications. My honor grades show that I worked hard, especially on a project using a variety of media raising money for schools in Louisiana, Texas, and Mississippi's hurricane damaged areas. Understanding the importance of being able to get along well with people, I actively participated in Sigma Chi (social fraternity), the Race for the Cure (breast cancer), and Pi Tau Pi (honorary business fraternity). From the experience gained in these associations, I am confident that I can fit in well at Tompkins-Oderson.

Provides good evidence of social skills

Leads smoothly to action

As you can see from this description and the enclosed résumé, I am well qualified for your position in advertising. You can email me at janek@hotmail.com or call and text message me at 602-713-2199 to arrange a convenient time to talk about my joining your team.

Sincerely,

Michael S. Janek

Michael S. Janek

enclosures

12712 Sanchez Drive
San Bernadino, CA 92405
April 9, 2012

Mr. Conrad W. Butler
Office Manager
Darden, Inc.
14326 Butterfield Road
San Francisco, CA 94129

Dear Mr. Butler:

Gains attention with question

Can Darden, Inc., use a hardworking Grossmont College business administration major who wants a career in today's technology-intensive office? My experience, education, and personal qualities qualify me well for this work.

Sets up rest of letter

My five years of work experience (see the attached résumé) have taught me the major aspects of office work. For the past two years I have been in charge of payroll at Gynes Manufacturing Company. As the administrator of payroll, I have had to handle all types of office operations, including records management and general communication. Although I am happy at this job, I am excited about the career opportunity I see at Darden.

Justifies job search

Brings out highlights with review of experience

Complementing my work experience are my studies at Grossmont College. In addition to studying the prescribed courses in my major field of business office technology, I selected electives in Dreamweaver, QuickBooks, and professional speaking to help me in my career objective. And I believe I have succeeded. In spite of full-time employment through most of my time in college, I was awarded the Associate of Arts degree last May with a 3.3 grade point average (4.0 basis). But most important of all, I learned from my studies how office work should be done efficiently.

Interprets education facts for the reader

In addition, I have the personal qualities that would enable me to fit smoothly into your organization. I like people, and through work and academic experiences, I have learned how to work with them as both a team player and a leader.

Sets up action and uses adaptation in concluding statement

I am well prepared for work in office administration, Mr. Butler. May I meet with you to talk about working for Darden? Please call me at 714-399-2569 or email me at jgoetz@gmail.com to arrange an interview.

Requests action clearly and appropriately

Sincerely,

Jimmy I. Goetz

Jimmy I. Goetz

Enc.

Figure 9–15

A Form Prospecting Letter. Written by a recent college graduate seeking her first job, this letter was prepared for use with a number of different types of companies.

MARY O. MAHONEY

May 17, 2012

Mr. Nevil S. Shannon
Director of Personnel
Snowdon Industries, Inc.
1103 Boswell Circle
Baltimore, MD 21202

Dear Mr. Shannon:

Effective attention-getting question

Will you please review my qualifications for work in your management trainee program? My education, work attitude, and personal skills qualify me for this program.

Good organization plan setup

Good interpretation of education

My education for administration consists primarily of four years of business administration study at State University. The Bachelor of Business Administration degree I will receive in June has given me a broad foundation of business knowledge. As a general business major, I studied all the functional fields (management, marketing, information systems, finance, accounting) as well as the other core business subjects (communications, statistics, law, economics, production, and human resources). I have the knowledge base that will enable me to be productive now, and I can build upon this base through practical experience.

My grade point record at State is evidence that I took my studies seriously and that I worked hard. My 3.8 overall average (4.0 basis) placed me in the top 10 percent of the graduating class. I also worked diligently in student associations. My efforts were recognized by the special assignments and leadership roles you see listed in the enclosed résumé. I assure you that I would bring these work habits with me to Snowdon Industries.

Links qualifications to the company

Good use of fact to back up personal qualities

Throughout college, I devoted time to the development of my personal skills. As an active member of the student chapter of the Society for the Advancement of Management, I served as treasurer and program chairperson. I participated in intramural golf and volleyball, and I was an active worker in the Young Republicans, serving as publicity chairperson for three years. All this experience has helped me to have the balance you seek in your administrative trainees.

Good ending message

These highlights and the additional evidence presented in the enclosed résumé present my case for a career in management. May I have an interview to continue my presentation? You can reach me at 301.594.6942 or marymahoney@yahoo.com. I could be in your office at your convenience to talk about working for Snowdon.

Clear request for action — flows logically from preceding presentation

Sincerely,

Mary O Mahoney

Mary O. Mahoney

Enclosure

1718 CRANFORD AVENUE • ROCKWELL, MD • 20854
VOICE/MESSAGE/FAX: 301.594.6942 • EMAIL: MARYMAHONEY@YAHOO.COM

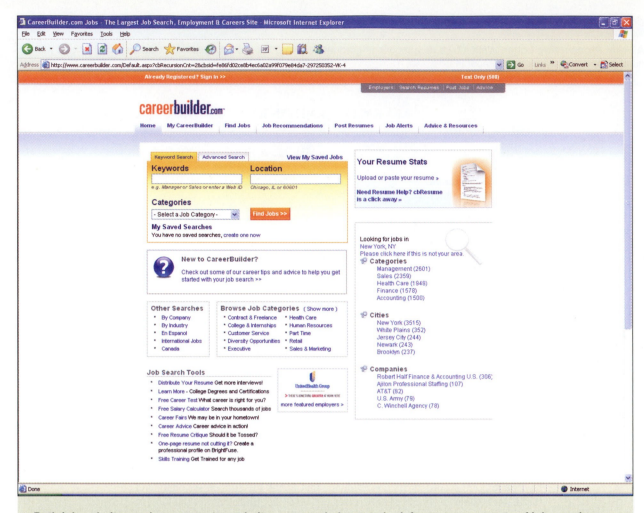

Both job websites and career center websites are good places to look for announcements of job openings.

Source: <http://www.careerbuilder.com>.

- Use your imagination in writing the opening. Make the opening fit the job.

As the cover message is a creative effort, you should use your imagination in writing the opening. But the work you seek should guide your imagination. Take, for example, work that requires an outgoing personality and a vivid imagination such as sales or public relations. In such cases, you would do well to show these qualities in your opening words. At the opposite extreme is work of a conservative nature, such as accounting or banking. Openings in such cases should normally be more restrained.

- An invited application should refer to the job and the source of the invitation.

In choosing the best opening for your case, you should consider whether you are writing a prospecting or an invited message. If the message has been invited, your opening words should refer to the job posting, and begin qualifying you for the advertised work, as in these examples:

> Will an honors graduate in accounting, with experience in tax accounting, qualify for the work you listed in today's *Times*?

> Because of my specialized training in accounting at State University and my practical experience in cost-based accounting, I believe I have the qualifications you described in your *Journal* advertisement.

- You can gain attention by showing an understanding of the reader's operations.

You can gain attention in the opening of an unsolicited letter in many ways. One way is to use a topic that shows understanding of the reader's operation or of the work

Developing a Professional Portfolio

Imagine yourself in an interview. The interviewer says, "This position requires you to use PowerPoint extensively. How are your presentation and PowerPoint skills?" What do you say? Of course you say your skills are excellent. And so does everyone else who interviews.

One way you can set yourself apart from other applicants is to take a professional portfolio to an interview to demonstrate your qualifications. A portfolio may contain a title page, your résumé, references list, cover letter, a transcript, a program description, copies of licenses and certifications, work samples, letters of recommendation, personal mission statements—whatever creates your best professional image. All you need to do is put your documents in sheet protectors in a professional looking three-ring binder for easy editing and updating and create tab dividers for the sections of the portfolio, and you're on your way. One note of advice, though: Protect your information by including a confidentiality statement; removing any student ID numbers, SSN numbers, or other private information from your documents; and using copies rather than originals of any licenses or certificates.

Source: "Portfolios," *University of Wisconsin–Eau Claire Career Services*, University of Wisconsin–Eau Claire, 9 Mar. 2008, Web, 5 June 2009.

to be done. Employers are likely to be impressed by applicants who have made the effort to learn something about the company, as in this example:

> Now that Taggart, Inc., has expanded operations to Central America, can you use a broadly trained international business major who knows the language and culture of the region?

Another way is to make a statement or ask a question that focuses attention on a need of the reader that the writer seeks to fill. The following opening illustrates this approach:

> How would you like to hire a University of Cincinnati business major to fill in for your vacationing summer employees?

- You can stress a need of the reader that you can fill.

Sometimes one learns of a job possibility through a company employee. Mentioning the employee's name can gain attention, as in this opening sentence:

> At the suggestion of Mr. Michael McLaughlin of your staff, I am sending the following summary of my qualifications for work as your loan supervisor.

- Using an employee's name gains attention.

Many other possibilities exist. In the final analysis, you will have to use what you think will be best for the one case. But try to avoid the overworked beginnings that were popular a generation or two ago such as "This is to apply for . . ." or writer-centered beginnings such as "I am writing to apply for . . ." or the tentative "I would like to apply for. . . ."

- Many opening possibilities exist, but avoid the old-style ones.

Selecting Content. Following the opening, you should present the information about your qualifications for the work. Begin this task by reviewing the job requirements. Then select the facts about you that qualify you for the job.

If your application has been invited, you may learn about the job requirements from the source of the invitation. If you are answering an advertisement, study it for the employer's requirements. If you are following up on an interview, review the interview for information about job requirements. If you are prospecting, your research and your logical analysis should guide you.

- Present your qualifications. Fit them to the job.
- You do this by studying the job. Use all available information sources.

- Include education, experience, and personal qualities.

In any event, you are likely to present facts from three background areas: education, experience, and skills and/or personal details.

- The emphasis each of these areas deserves varies by job. So consider the job in determining emphasis.

How much you include from each of these areas and how much you emphasize each area should depend on the job and on your background. Most of the jobs you will seek as a new college graduate will have strong educational requirements, and your education is likely to be your strongest selling point at this stage of your career. Thus, you should stress your education. When you apply for work after you have accumulated experience, you will probably need to stress experience. As the years go by, experience becomes more and more important—education, less and less important. Your personal characteristics are of some importance for some jobs, especially jobs that involve working with people.

- Do not rely too heavily on the résumé. The cover message should carry all the major selling points.

If a résumé accompanies the cover message, do not rely on it too much. Remember that the message does the selling, and the résumé summarizes the significant details. Thus, the message should contain the major points around which you build your case, and the résumé should include these points plus supporting details. As the two are parts of a team effort, somewhere in the message you should refer the reader to the résumé.

- In organizing the background facts, select the best of these orders: logical grouping, time, job requirements.

Organizing for Persuasion. You will want to present the information about yourself in the order that is best for you. In general, the plan you select is likely to follow one of three general orders. The most common order is a logical grouping of the information, such as education, experience, and skills and/or personal details. A second possibility is a time order. For example, you could present the information to show a year-by-year preparation for the work. A third possibility is an order based on the job requirements. For example, selling, communicating, and managing might be the requirements listed in an advertised job.

- Use words that present your qualifications convincingly.

Merely presenting facts does not ensure conviction. You also will need to present the facts in words that make the most of your assets. Think of this as the difference between showing and telling. You could tell the reader for example, that you "held a position" as sales manager, but it is much more convincing to say that you "supervised a sales force of 14," which actually shows your ability. Likewise, you do more for yourself by writing that you "earned a degree in business administration" than by writing that you "spent four years in college." And it is more effective to say that you "learned tax accounting" than to say that you "took a course in tax accounting."

- Use the you-viewpoint wherever practical.

You also can help your case by presenting your facts in reader-viewpoint language wherever this is practical. More specifically, you should work to interpret the facts based on their meaning for your reader. For example, you could present a cold recital like this one:

I am 21 years old and have an interest in mechanical operations and processes. Last summer I worked in the production department of a container plant.

Or you could interpret the facts, fitting them to the one job:

The interest I have held in things mechanical over most of my 21 years would help me fit into one of your technical manufacturing operations. Last summer's experience in the production department of Miller Container Company is evidence that I can and will work hard.

- Avoid the tendency to overuse *I* 's, but use some.

Since you will be writing about yourself, you may find it difficult to avoid overusing I-references. But you should try. An overuse of *I*'s sounds egotistical and places too much attention on the often repeated word. This creates the impression that you are more focused on yourself than you are on the reader's needs. Some *I*'s, however, should be used. The message is personal. Stripping it of all I-references would rob it of its personal warmth.

Overall, you are presenting your professional image, not only as a prospective employee but also as a person. Carefully shaping the character you are projecting

Websites Offer Valuable Interview Advice

The Web is a rich resource for help with interviewing. Your school's career center may have a website with interview schedules. Sites such as Monster.com and many of the other online job database sites offer tips on all aspects of interviewing. You can get ideas for questions to ask interviewers, techniques for staying calm, and methods of handling the telephone screening interview. They even include practice interactive virtual interviews with immediate feedback on your answers to questions as well as suggestions and strategies for handling difficult questions. The Monster site includes a planner listing a host of good commonsense tips from polishing your shoes to keeping an interview folder to keeping track of all written and oral communication. Using these sites to help you prepare for interviews not only will help you feel more confident and interview more effectively, but also can help you evaluate the company as well.

Source: <http://www.monster.com>, by permission.

is arguably just as important to the success of your cover message as using convincing logic.

Driving for Action in the Close. The presentation of your qualifications should lead logically to the action that the close proposes. You should drive for whatever action is appropriate in your case. It could be a request for an interview or an invitation to engage in further communication (perhaps to answer the reader's questions). Rarely would you want to ask for the job in a first message. You are concerned mainly with opening the door to further negotiations.

• In the close, drive for whatever action is appropriate.

Your action words should be clear and direct. As in the sales message, the request for action may be made more effective if it is followed by words recalling a benefit

• Make the action words clear and direct.

that the reader will get from taking the action. The following closes illustrate this technique, although the second may be overly aggressive in some circumstances:

> The highlights of my education and experience show that I have been preparing for a career in human resources. May I now discuss beginning this career with you? You can reach me at 727-921-4113 or by email at owensmith@att.com to talk about how I can help in your human resource work.

> I am very much interested in discussing with you how my skills will contribute to your company's mission. If I do not hear from you by Friday, April 22, I'll call on Monday to arrange a time for a mutually convenient meeting.

Contrasting Cover Messages. Illustrating bad and good techniques, the following two prospecting messages present the qualifications of Jason L. Andrews, the job seeker described in the introductory situation at the beginning of the chapter. The first message follows few of the suggestions given in the preceding pages, whereas the second message is in general accord with these suggestions.

A Bland and Artless Presentation of Information. The bad message begins with an old-style opening. The first words are of little interest. The following presentation of qualifications is a matter-of-fact, uninterpreted review of information. Little you-viewpoint is evident. In fact, most of the message emphasizes the writer (note the *I*'s), who comes across as bored and selfish. The information presented is scant. The closing action is little more than an I-viewpoint statement of the writer's availability.

This prospecting message is dull and poorly written.

Dear Mr. Stark:

This is to apply for a position in marketing with your company.

At present, I am completing my studies in marketing at Olympia State University and will graduate with a Bachelor of Business Administration degree with an emphasis in marketing this May. I have taken all the courses in marketing available to me as well as other helpful courses such as statistics, organizational psychology, and ecommerce.

I have had good working experience as a host and food server, sales associate, and pollster. Please see details on the enclosed résumé. I believe that I am well qualified for a position in marketing and am considering working for a company of your size and description.

Because I must make a decision on my career soon, I request that you write me soon. For your information, I will be available for an interview on March 17 and 18.

Sincerely,

Skillful Selling of One's Ability to Work. The better message begins with an interesting question that sets the stage for the rest of the contents. The review of experience is interpreted, showing how the experience would help in performing the job sought. The review of education is similarly covered. Notice how the interpretations show that the writer knows what the job requires. Notice also that reader-viewpoint is stressed throughout. Even so, a moderate use of *I*'s gives the letter a personal quality, and the details show the writer to be a thoughtful, engaged person. The closing request for action is a clear, direct, and courteous question. The final words recall a main appeal of the letter.

Dear Mr. Stark:

Is there a place in your marketing department for someone who is well trained in the field and can talk easily and competently with clients? My background, experience, and education have given me these qualifications.

My studies at Olympia State University were specially planned to prepare me for a career in marketing. I studied courses in advertising, marketing communication, marketing research, and ecommerce. In addition, I studied a wide assortment of supporting subjects: economics, business communication, information systems, psychology, interpersonal communication, and operations management. My studies have given me the foundation to learn an even more challenging practical side of marketing work. I plan to begin working in June after I receive the Bachelor of Business Administration degree with honors (3.7 grade point average on a basis of 4.0).

My work experiences have also prepared me for a marketing career. While in high school, I worked mornings and evenings in New York's garment district, primarily as a host and food server. For two years, between high school and college, I worked full time as a pollster for Olympia State University. Throughout my four years of college, I worked half time as a sales associate for The Gap, where I was the top seller for four of eight quarters. From these experiences, I have learned to understand marketing. I speak marketing's language and listen carefully to people.

These brief facts and the information in my résumé describe my diligent efforts to prepare for a position in marketing. May I now talk with you about beginning that position? You can reach me at 917.938.4449 to arrange an interview to talk about how I could help in your marketing department.

Sincerely,

Email Cover Messages

Like other email messages, an email cover message it needs a clear subject line; like print cover messages, it needs a formal salutation and closing. And its purpose is still to highlight your qualifications for the particular job you are applying for. While it could be identical to one you might create for print, most readers prefer shorter documents onscreen. The primary job of the email cover message is to identify the job, highlight the applicant's strengths, and invite the reader to review the résumé.

Notice how the solicited cover message below quickly gains the reader's attention in the opening, highlights the skills in the body, and calls for action in the close.

To: Kate Troy <kate_troy@thankyoutoo.com>
From: Megan Adami <mmadami@msn.com>
Date: October 1, 2012
Subject: Web Design Intern Position
Dear Ms. Troy:

Yesterday my advisor here at Brown University, Dr. Payton Kubicek, suggested that I contact you about the summer intern position in Web design you recently announced.

At Brown I have taken courses that have given me a good understanding of both the design aspects as well as the marketing functions that a good website needs. Additionally, several of my course projects involved working with successful Web-based businesses, analyzing the strengths and weaknesses of their business models.

I would enjoy applying some of these skills in a successful site targeted at the high-end retail customers that Thankyoutoo.com attracts. You will see from my webpage profile at <http://www.meganadami.com/> that my design skills complement those on your company's website, allowing me to contribute almost immediately. I can be available for an interview at any time the rest of this month.

Sincerely,

Megan Adami
mmadami@msn.com

HANDLING THE INTERVIEW

- A successful application will eventually involve an *interview*.

Your initial contact with a prospective employer can be by mail, email, phone, or a personal (face-to-face) visit. If all goes well, your application will eventually involve a personal visit—or an *interview*. Sometimes, before inviting candidates to a formal interview session, recruiters use phone interviews for preliminary screening.

- The interview is essential. For it, follow these procedures:

In a sense, the interview is the key to the success of the application—the "final examination." You should carefully prepare for the interview, as the job may be lost or won in it. The following review of employment interview highlights should help you understand how to deal with the interview in your job search. You will find additional information about interviewing in the resource links on the textbook website.

Investigating the Company

- (1) Find out what you can about the employer.

Before arriving for an interview, you should learn what you can about the company: its products or services, its personnel, its business practices, its current activities, its management. Such knowledge will help you talk knowingly with the interviewer. And perhaps more important, the interviewer is likely to be impressed by the fact that you took the time to investigate the company. That effort might even give you an advantage.

Making a Good Appearance

- (2) Make a good appearance (conservative dress and grooming).

How you look to the interviewer is a part of your message. Thus, you should work to present just the right image. Interviewers differ to some extent on what that image is, but you would be wise to present a conservative appearance. This means avoiding faddish, offbeat styles, preferring the conservative, conventional business colors such as black, brown, navy, and gray. Remember that the interviewer wants to know whether you fit into the role you are seeking. You should appear to look like you want the job.

Some may argue that such an insistence on conformity in dress and grooming infringes on one's personal freedom. Perhaps it does. We will even concede that employers should not force such biases on you, but you will have to be realistic if you want a successful career. If the people who can determine your future have fixed views on matters of dress and grooming, it is good business sense to respect those views.

Anticipating Questions and Preparing Answers

You should be able to anticipate some of the questions the interviewer will ask. Questions about your education (courses, grades, honors) are usually asked. So are questions about work experience, interests, career goals, location preferences, and activities in organizations. You should prepare answers to these questions in advance. Your answers will then be thorough and correct, and your words will display poise and confidence. Your preparation will also reflect your interest.

● (3) Anticipate the questions; plan the answers.

"You walk the walk and talk the talk. We need

- Be prepared to handle standard questions,

In addition to general questions, interviewers often ask more complicated ones. Some of these are designed to test you—to learn your views, your interests, and your ability to deal with difficult problems. Others seek more specific information about your ability to handle the job in question. Although such questions are difficult to anticipate, you should be aware that they are likely to be asked. Following are questions of this kind that one experienced interviewer asks:

What can you do for us?

Would you be willing to relocate? To travel?

Do you prefer to work with people or alone?

How well has your performance in the classroom prepared you for this job?

What do you expect to be doing in 10 years? In 20 years?

What income goals do you have for those years (10 and 20 years ahead)?

Why should I rank you above the others I am interviewing?

Why did you choose _____ for your career?

How do you feel about working overtime? Nights? Weekends?

Did you do the best work you are capable of in college?

Is your college record a good measure of how you will perform on the job?

What are the qualities of the ideal boss?

What have you done that shows leadership potential? Teamwork potential?

What are your beginning salary expectations?

Sometimes interviewers will throw in tough questions to test your poise. These are naturally stressful, but being prepared for these kinds of questions will keep you cool and collected.[4] Here are some examples:

- tough questions,

What is your greatest weakness?

With hindsight, how could you have enhanced your achievements?

What kind of decisions are most difficult for you?

What is the worst thing you have heard about this company?

See this pen I'm holding? Sell it to me.

Tell me about a time when you put your foot in your mouth.

What kinds of people do you find it difficult to deal with?

Some questions, though, may not be legal regardless of the interviewer's intent, whether the interviewer is making small talk, is unaware the questions are illegal, plans to discriminate against you, or just wants to test whether you respond. How you respond is up to you; before you respond, you may want to ask how the question is relevant to the position, or you may politely decline to answer.

- illegal questions,

What religion do you practice?

How old are you?

Are you married?

Do you plan to have children?

- brainteaser or critical thinking questions,

If you get through these types of questions, some brainteasers or puzzles may be thrown your way. Microsoft often gets credit for starting this trend because the company used it extensively in attempting to hire only the best and brightest employees. Other companies soon followed, often creating their own versions of some of these questions or creating some tougher ones of their own. Many of these questions do not have a right answer; rather, they are designed to elicit an applicant's thinking, logic, and creativity skills. In answering them, be sure that you reason aloud rather than

---

[4] Martin Yate, *Knock'em Dead 2006* (Avon, MA: Adams Media Corp., 2006) 205–32, print.

sitting there silently so that you can show you are thinking. You may make assumptions as well as to supply needed information. Giving a good answer the interviewer has not heard before is often a good strategy. Here are some real questions that have been asked in interviews by Microsoft and other companies:[5]

Why are manhole covers round?

Why do mirrors reverse right and left instead of up and down?

How many piano tuners are there in the world?

How many times a day do a clock's hands overlap?

Design a spice rack for a blind person.

Why are beer cans tapered at the top and bottom?

You have eight coins, and one of them is lighter than the others. Find the light coin in two weighings of a pan balance.

Recently, the behavioral interview style has become popular with campus recruiters. Rather than just determining your qualifications for the job, interviewers are attempting to verify if you can do the work. They ask questions about what you would do in certain situations because how you behave now is likely to transfer to similar situations in another job. Here are a few examples of behavioral questions:

What major problem have you faced in group projects and how have you dealt with it?

Do you tend more toward following the rules or toward stretching them?

Describe a conflict you had with someone and how you resolved it.

For more practice preparing for questions, check the resource links on the textbook website.

- and behavioral questions.

Putting Yourself at Ease

Perhaps it is easier to say than to do, but you should be at ease throughout the interview. Remember that you are being inspected and that the interviewer should see a calm and collected person. How to appear calm and collected is not easy to explain. Certainly, it involves talking in a clear and strong voice. It also involves controlling your facial expressions and body movements. Developing such controls requires self-discipline—working at it. You may find it helpful to convince yourself that the stress experienced during an interview is normal. Or you may find it helpful to look at the situation realistically—as merely a conversation between two human beings. Practicing your answers to common interview questions out loud may be helpful. You may even want to record one of these practice sessions and analyze your performance. Your school's career services office may be able to help with this. Other approaches may work better for you. Use whatever approaches work. Your goal is to control your emotions so that you present the best possible appearance to the interviewer.

- (4) Be at ease—calm, collected, confident.

Helping to Control the Dialogue

Just answering the questions asked is often not enough. Not only are you being evaluated, but you are evaluating others as well. The questions you ask and the comments you play off them should bring up what you want the interviewer to know about you. Your self-analysis revealed the strong points in your background. Now you should make certain that those points come out in the interview.

How to bring up points about you that the interviewer does not ask is a matter for your imagination. For example, a student seeking a job in advertising believed that her teamwork skills should be brought to the interviewer's attention. So at an appropriate

- (5) Help bring out the questions that show your qualifications.

- Here are some examples of how to do it.

---

[5] William Poundstone, *How Would You Move Mount Fuji?: Microsoft's Cult of the Puzzle: How the World's Smartest Companies Select the Most Creative Thinkers* (Boston, MA: Little, Brown and Company, 2003) 80–6, 118–20, print.

time in the interview, she asked, "How important is the ability to collaborate in this company?" The anticipated answer—"very important"—allowed her to discuss her skills. To take another example, a student who wanted to bring out his knowledge of the prospective employer's operations did so with this question: "Will your company's expansion in the Bakersfield area create new job opportunities there?" How many questions of this sort you should ask will depend on your need to supplement your interviewer's questioning. You might also want to ask questions to determine if the company is a good fit for you such as "How would you describe the work environment here?" Your goal should be to make certain that both the interviewer and you get all the information you consider important.

FOLLOWING UP AND ENDING THE APPLICATION

- Follow up the interview with thank-you, status-inquiry, job-acceptance, and job-rejection messages.

The interview is only an early step in the application process. A variety of other steps can follow. Conveying a brief thank-you message by letter, email, or telephone is an appropriate follow-up step. It not only shows courtesy but also it can give you an advantage because some of your competitors will not do it. If you do not hear from the prospective employer within a reasonable time, it is appropriate to inquire by telephone, email, or letter about the status of your application. You should certainly do this if you are under a time limit on another employer's offer. The application process may end with no offer (frequently with no notification at all—a most discourteous way of handling applicants), with a rejection notice, or with an offer. How to handle these situations is reviewed in the following paragraphs.

Other Job-Search Messages

Writing a Thank-you Message. After an interview it is courteous to write a thank-you message, whether or not you are interested in the job. If you are interested, the message can help your case. It singles you out from the competition and shows your interest in the job.

Such messages are usually short. They begin with an expression of gratefulness. They say something about the interview, the job, or such. They take care of any additional business (such as submitting information requested). And they end on a goodwill note—perhaps a hopeful look to the next step in the negotiations. The following message does these things:

> Dear Mr. Woods:
>
> Thank you for talking with me yesterday. You were most helpful, and you did a great job of selling me on Sony Corporation of America.
>
> As you requested, I have enclosed samples of the financial analysis I developed as a class project. If you need anything more, please let me know.
>
> I look forward to the possibility of discussing employment with you soon.
>
> Sincerely,

- Common courtesy requires that you write a thank-you message following an interview.

- The typical order for such a message is as follows: (1) expression of gratefulness, (2) appropriate comments fitting the situation, (3) any additional information needed, and (4) a goodwill close.

Constructing a Follow-up to an Application. When a prospective employer is late in responding or you receive another offer with a time deadline, you may need to write a follow-up message. Employers are often just slow, but sometimes they lose the application. Whatever the explanation, a follow-up message may help to produce action.

Such a message is a form of routine inquiry. As a reason for writing, it can use the need to make a job decision or some other good explanation. The following message is an example:

> Dear Ms. Yang:
>
> Because the time is approaching when I must make a job decision, could you please tell me the status of my application with you?
>
> You may recall that you interviewed me in your office November 7. You wrote me November 12 indicating that I was among those you had selected for further consideration.
>
> SAIC remains one of the organizations I would like to consider in making my career decision. I will very much appreciate hearing from you by December 3.
>
> Sincerely,

- When employers do not respond, you may write a follow-up message. It is ordered like the routine inquiry.

Planning the Job Acceptance. Job acceptances in writing are merely favorable response messages with an extra amount of goodwill. Because the message should begin directly, a "yes" answer in the beginning is appropriate. The remainder of the message should contain a confirmation of the starting date and place and comments about the work, the company, the interview—whatever you would say if you were face to face with the reader. The message need not be long. This one does the job well:

> Dear Ms. Garcia:
>
> Yes, I accept your offer of employment. After my first interview with you, I was convinced that Allison-Caldwell was the organization for me. I am delighted that you think I am right for Allison-Caldwell.
>
> Following your instructions, I will be in your Toronto headquarters on May 28 at 8:30 AM ready to work for you.
>
> Sincerely,

- You may need to write to accept a job. Write it as you would a favorable response.

Writing a Message Refusing a Job. Messages refusing a job offer follow the indirect refusal pattern. One good technique is to begin with a friendly comment—perhaps

- To refuse a job offer, use the normal refusal pattern (indirect).

something about past relations with the company. Next, explain and present the refusal in clear yet positive words. Then end with a more friendly comment. This example illustrates the plan:

Dear Mr. Chen:

Meeting you and the other people at Northern was a genuine pleasure. Thank you for sharing so much information with me and for the generous job offer.

In considering the offer, I reflected on the many topics we discussed, particularly on the opportunity to work abroad. While I have accepted an offer with a firm that has extensive opportunities along these lines, I was very impressed with all I learned about Northern.

I appreciate the time and the courteous treatment you gave me.

Writing a Resignation.   At some point in your career you are likely to resign from one job to take another. When this happens, you will probably inform your employer of your resignation orally. But when you find it more practical or comfortable, you may choose to resign in writing. In some cases, you may do it both ways. As a matter of policy, some companies require a written resignation even after an oral resignation has been made. You also may prefer to give a written resignation following your oral announcement of it.

Your resignation should be as positive as the circumstances permit. Even if your work experiences have not been pleasant, you will be wise to depart without a final display of anger. As an anonymous philosopher once explained, "When you write a resignation in anger, you write the best letter you will ever regret."

The indirect order is usually the best strategy for negative messages like a resignation. But many are written in the direct order. They present the resignation right away, following it with expressions of gratitude, favorable comments about past working experiences, and the like. Either approach is acceptable. Even so, you would do well to use the indirect order, for it is more likely to build the goodwill and favorable thinking you want to leave behind you.

The example below shows the indirect order, which is well known to you. It begins with a positive point—one that sets up the negative message. The negative message follows, clearly yet positively stated. The ending returns to positive words chosen to build goodwill and fit the case.

Dear Ms. Shuster:

Working as your assistant for the past five years has been a genuinely rewarding experience. Under your direction I have grown as an administrator, and I know you have given me a practical education in retailing.

As you may recall from our past discussions, I have been pursuing the same career goals that you held early in your career, so you will understand why I am now resigning to accept a store management position with Lawson's in Belle River. I would like my employment to end on the 31st, but I could stay a week or two longer if needed to help train my replacement.

I leave with only good memories of you and the other people with whom I worked. Thanks to all of you for a valuable contribution to my career.

Sincerely,

Continuing Job-Search Activities

Continuously keeping your finger on the pulse of the job market is a good idea. Not only does it provide you with information about changes occurring in your field, but it also keeps you alert to better job opportunities as soon as they are announced.

Maintaining Your Résumé.   While many people intend to keep their résumés up to date, they just do not make it a priority. Some others make it easy by updating as changes occur. And a few update their résumés at regularly designated times such as a birthday, New Year's Day, or even the anniversary of their employment. No matter

Marginal notes:

- Job resignations are made in person, by letter, or both.

- Make the letter as positive as circumstances permit.

- Preferably use the indirect order for this negative situation.

- This illustration begins and ends positively.

- Keeping your attention on the job market alerts you to changes and opportunities in the field.

- Update your résumé regularly to reflect new accomplishments and skills.

what works best for you, updating your résumé as you gain new accomplishments and skills is important. Otherwise, you will be surprised to find how easily you can lose track of important details.

Reading Job Ads/Professional Journals. Nearly as important as keeping your résumé updated is keeping up on your professional reading. Most trade or professional journals have job notices or bulletin boards you should check regularly. These ads give you insight into what skills are in demand, perhaps helping you choose assignments where you get the opportunity to develop new skills. Staying up to date in your field can be stimulating; it can provide both challenges and opportunities.

● Keeping current in your professional reading brings many benefits.

SUMMARY BY LEARNING OBJECTIVES

1. A good first step in your job search is to build a network of contacts.
   - Get to know people who might help you later: classmates, professors, and businesspeople.
   - Use their knowledge to help you find a job.
   - Obtain an internship to develop your skills and build your network.

1 Develop and use a network of contacts in your job search.

2. When you are ready to find work, analyze yourself and outside factors.
   - Look at your education, personal qualities, and work experience.
   - From this review, determine what work you are qualified to do.
   - Then select the career that is right for you.

2 Assemble and evaluate information that will help you select a job.

3. When you are ready to find a job, use the contact sources available to you.
   - Check university career centers, personal contacts, advertisements, online sources, employment agencies, personal search agents, and webpage profiles.
   - If these do not produce results, prospect by mail.

3 Identify the sources that can lead you to an employer.

4. In your application efforts, you are likely to use résumés and cover messages. Prepare them as you would written sales material.
   - First, study your product—you.
   - Then study your prospect—the employer.
   - From the information gained, construct the résumé, cover message, and reference sheet.

4 Compile print and electronic résumés that are strong, complete, and organized.

   In writing the résumé (a listing of your major background facts), you can choose from two types.
   - The *print résumé*—traditional and scannable.
   - The *digital résumé*—ASCII, attached file, and HTM file.

   In preparing the traditional résumé, follow this procedure:
   - List all the facts about you that an employer might want to know.
   - Sort these facts into logical groups: *experience, education, personal qualities, references, achievements, highlights.*
   - Present the facts. As a minimum, include job experience (dates, places, firms, duties) and education (degrees, dates, fields of study). Use some personal information, but omit race, religion, sex, marital status, and age.
   - List your references on a separate page. Use complete mailing addresses, and have a reference for each major job held.
   - Include other helpful information: address, telephone number, email address, webpage address, and career objective.

- Write headings for the résumé and for each group of information; prefer descriptive headings.
- Organize for strength in choosing reverse chronological, functional/skills, or accomplishment/highlights approach.
- Preferably write the résumé without personal pronouns, make the parts parallel grammatically, and use words that help sell your abilities.
- Present the information with good visual appeal, selecting fonts that show the importance of the headings and the information.

In preparing the scannable résumé, follow these procedures:

- Include industry-specific keywords.
- Choose precise nouns over action verbs.
- Present the information in a form that can be read accurately by scanners.

In preparing the electronic résumé, follow these procedures:

- Use the electronic format the receiver specifies or prefers.
- Remove all contact information except your email address.
- Consider adding a last updated notation.
- Extend the HTML format to include colors, graphics, video, and sound as appropriate.

5 Write targeted cover messages that skillfully sell your abilities.

5. As the cover message is a form of sales message, plan it as you would a sales message.
   - Study your product (you) and your prospect (the employer) and think out a strategy for persuasion.
   - Begin with words that gain attention, begin applying for the job, and set up the presentation of your sales points (briefly describe your qualifications).
   - Adapt the tone and content to the job you seek.
   - Present your qualifications, fitting them to the job you seek.
   - Choose words that enhance the information presented.
   - Drive for an appropriate action—an interview, further communication, reference checks.

6 Explain how you can participate effectively in an interview.

6. Your major contact with a prospective employer is the interview. For best results, you should do the following:
   - Research the employer in advance so you can impress the interviewer.
   - Present a good appearance through appropriate dress and grooming.
   - Try to anticipate the interviewer's questions and to plan your answers.
   - Make a good impression by being at ease.
   - Help the interviewer establish a dialogue with questions and comments that enable you to present the best information about you.

7 Write application follow-up messages that are appropriate, friendly, and positive.

7. You may need to write other messages in your search for a job.
   - Following the interview, a thank-you message is appropriate.
   - Also appropriate is an inquiry about the status of an application.
   - You also may need to write messages accepting, rejecting, or resigning a job.
   - Write these messages much as you would the messages reviewed in preceding chapters: direct order for good news, indirect order for bad.

8 Maintain your job-search skills.

8. To learn information about the changes occurring in their field and to be aware of better job opportunities, you should
   - Maintain your résumé.
   - Read both job ads and professional journals.

CRITICAL THINKING QUESTIONS

1 "Building a network of contacts to help one find jobs appears to be selfish. It involves acquiring friendships just to use them for one's personal benefit." Discuss this view. **(LO1)**

2 Maryann Brennan followed a broad program of study in college and received a degree in general studies. She did her best work in English, especially in the writing courses. She also did well in history, sociology, and psychology. As much as she could, she avoided math and computer courses.

   Her overall grade point average of 3.7 (4.0 basis) placed her in the top 10 percent of her class. What advice would you give her as she begins her search for a career job? **(LO1, 2, 3)**

3 Discuss the value of each of the sources for finding jobs to a finance major (*a*) before an internship (*b*) right after graduation and (*c*) after 20 years of work in his or her specialty. **(LO1, 2, 3)**

4 Assume that in an interview for the job you want, you are asked the questions listed in the text under the heading "Anticipating Questions and Preparing Answers." Answer these questions. **(LO6)**

5 The most popular arrangement of résumé information is the three-part grouping: education, experience, and personal details. Describe two other arrangements. When would each be used? **(LO4)**

6 Distinguish between the print résumé and the electronic résumé. When would each be most appropriate? **(LO4)**

7 What is meant by *parallelism of headings?* **(LO4)**

8 Describe the cover message and résumé you would write (*a*) immediately after graduation, (*b*) 10 years later, and (*c*) 25 years later. Point out similarities and differences, and defend your decisions. **(LO2, 4, 5)**

9 What differences would you suggest in writing cover messages for jobs in (*a*) accounting, (*b*) banking, (*c*) advertising copy writing, (*d*) management, (*e*) sales, (*f*) consulting, and (*g*) information systems? **(LO5)**

10 Discuss the logic of beginning a cover message with these words: "This is to apply for . . ." and "I would like to . . . ."

11 "In writing cover messages, just present the facts clearly and without analysis and interpretation. The facts alone will tell the employer whether he or she wants you." Discuss this viewpoint. **(LO5)**

12 When should the drive for action in a cover message (*a*) request the job, (*b*) request an interview, and (*c*) request a reference check? **(LO5)**

13 Discuss some of the advantages that writing a thank-you note to the interviewer gives the writer. **(LO8)**

14 Identify some of benefits one gains from continuing to read professional journals for job information after one is employed. **(LO8)**

CRITICAL THINKING EXERCISES

1 Criticize the following résumé parts. (They are not from the same résumé.) **(LO4)**

a. **Work Experience**

2009–2012	Employed as sales rep for Lloyd-Shanks Tool Company
2006–2009	Office manager, Drago Plumbing Supply, Toronto
2003–2006	Matson's Super Stores. I worked part time as sales clerk while attending college.

b. **References**

Mr. Carl T. Whitesides
Sunrise Insurance, Inc.
317 Forrest Lane
Dover, DE 19901-6452

Patricia Cullen
Cullen and Cullen Realtors
2001 Bowman
Dr. Wilmington, DE 19804

Rev. Troy A. Graham
Asbury Methodist Church
Hyattsville, MD 20783

D. W. Boozer
Boozer Industries
Baltimore, MD 21202

c. **Education**

2012	Graduated from Tippen H.S. (I was in top 10 percent of class.)
2012	B.S. from Bradley University with major in marketing
2012 to present	Enrolled part time in M.B.A. program at the University of Phoenix

d. **Qualifications**

Know how to motivate a sales force. I have done it.

Experienced in screening applicants and selecting salespeople.

Know the pharmaceutical business from 11 years of experience.

Knowledgeable about realistic quota setting and incentives.

Proven leadership ability.

2 Criticize these sentences from cover messages: **(LO5)**

Beginning Sentences

a. Please consider this my application for any position for which my training and experience qualify me.

b. Mr. Jerry Bono of your staff has told me about a vacancy in your loan department for which I would like to apply.

c. I am that accountant you described in your advertisement in today's *Times-Record.*

d. I want to work for you!

Sentences Presenting Selling Points

e. From 2008 to 2012 I attended Bradley University where I took courses leading to a B.S. degree with a major in finance.

f. I am highly skilled in trading corporate bonds as a result of three years spent in the New York office of Collins, Bragg, and Weaver.

g. For three years (2009–2012) I was in the loan department at Bank One.

h. My two strongest qualifications for this job are my personality and gift of conversation.

Sentences from Action Endings

i. I will call you on the 12th to arrange an interview.

j. If my qualifications meet your requirements, it would be greatly appreciated if you would schedule an interview for me.

k. Please call to set up an interview. Do it now—while it is on your mind.

PROBLEM-SOLVING CASES

1 You have successfully prepared yourself for the career of your choice, but the recruiters visiting your school have not yet offered you a job. Now you must look on your own. So by searching newspapers, online job databases, and company website announcements, find the best job for which you believe you are qualified. Write two cover messages that you might use to present your qualifications for this job: one for print presentation and one for email. Attach a copy of the job description to the messages. Write the résumé and reference sheet to accompany the message.

2 Project yourself three years past your graduation date. During those years, you have had good experience working for the company of your choice in the field of your choice. (Use your imagination to supply this information.)

Unfortunately, your progress hasn't been what you had expected. You think that you must look around for a better opportunity. Your search through the classified advertisements in your area newspapers, online, and in *The Wall Street Journal,* and you turn up one promising possibility (you find it). Write a cover message that skillfully presents your qualifications for this job. (You may make logical assumptions about your experience over the three-year period.) For class purposes, attach the advertisement to your message. Write the résumé and reference sheet to accompany the message.

3 Assume you are in your last term of school and graduation is just around the corner. Your greatest interest is in finding work that you like and that would enable you to support yourself now and to support a family as you win promotions.

No job of your choice is revealed in the want ads of newspapers and trade magazines. No career center has provided anything to your liking. So you decide to do what any good salesperson does: survey the product (yourself) and the market (companies that could use a person who can do what you are prepared to do) and then advertise (send each of these companies a résumé with a cover message). This procedure sometimes creates a job where none existed before, and sometimes it establishes a basis for negotiations for the "big job" two, three, or five years after graduation. And very frequently, it puts you on the list for the good job that is not filled through advertising or from the company staff. Write the cover message. Write the résumé and reference sheet to accompany the message.

4 Move the calendar to your graduation date so that you are now ready to sell your working ability in the job market for as much as you can get and still hold your own. Besides canvassing likely firms with the help of prospecting messages and diligently following up family contacts, you have decided to look into anything that appears especially good in the ads of newspapers, online sources, and magazines. The latest available issues of large city publications and online services yield the jobs listed below.

Concentrate on the ad describing the job you would like most or could do best—and then write a cover message that will get you that job. Your message will first have to survive the filtering that eliminates dozens (sometimes hundreds) of applicants who lack the expected qualifications. Toward the end you will be getting into strong competition in which small details may give you the little extra margin of superiority that will get you an interview and a chance to campaign further.

Study your chosen ad for what it says and even more for what it implies. Weigh your own preparation even more thoroughly than you weigh the ad. You may imagine far enough ahead to assume completion of all the courses that are planned for your degree. You may build up your case a bit beyond what you actually have. Sort out the things that line you up for the one job, organize them strategically, and then present them in a cover letter. Write a résumé and reference sheet to accompany your message.

a. *Office manager.* Currently seeking an office manager with initiative and flexibility for work in a fast-paced environment. Must have an outgoing personality and excellent communication skills and be a team player. Must be a "power user" of Word and Excel and have excellent Internet search skills. Knowledge of PowerPoint a plus. Some overtime expected during crunch periods. Send application materials to Chris Eveland at ceveland@qconline.com.

b. *Assistant webmaster.* Outstanding information technology, organizational, and interpersonal skills are needed for work on a company portal. Mastery of HTML and PHP, experience with website design including graphic design, and knowledge of client/server technology are vital. Candidates also must possess excellent writing skills and the ability to effectively manage multiple projects while interfacing with company employees. A bachelor's degree with a background in information systems, marketing, or communications is required. Please send résumé to Megan Adami in Human Resources, 7165 North Main Street, (your city), or fax it to 1-888-444-5047, or email it to megan_adami@cnet.com.

c. *Management trainee.* Named by *Fortune* magazine as one of the best places to work, this constantly expanding international company uses shared decision making and clear career paths so that employees can be productive and well rewarded. The challenging management training program requires candidates with good communications skills and high energy

levels to be successful. Applicants must be computer literate and possess good interpersonal skills. Fax résumé to Don Zatyko at 1-888-399-2569.

d. *Staff accountant—payroll specialist.* We are looking for an accountant who desires to grow and move up the ladder. One should be motivated and willing to work in a fast-paced, multitasking environment. An associate's degree in accounting or finance is required. Additionally, the ideal candidate will be detail-oriented and able to meet deadlines. The job involves coordinating transfers of time worked data from time collection systems to payroll systems. Must have extended knowledge of Excel to compute withholdings and deductions, and must stay up to date on multiple state laws regarding payroll. Excellent compensation package and benefits. Apply to Carolynn Workman, accounting director, at carolynn_workman@adelphia.net.

e. *Staff accountant.* Successful candidate should have a B.S. in accounting and be proficient in QuickBooks and/or Excel. Would be responsible for performing account analysis for corporate accounts, assisting in consolidation of subsidiaries, and assisting in the preparation of annual and quarterly financial statements and financial reports for certain subsidiaries. Experience in the local environment of small business is desirable. If you are concerned with order, quality, and accuracy, please contact us by mail at Administrative Partner, Winship and Acord, P.C., 3013 Stonybrook Drive, (your city), or by email at CWA@msn.com, or by fax at 1-217-399-2569.

f. *Network specialist.* We seek someone who can help deliver reliable, secure, and integrated networks. Must be able to bring together data and voice, WAN and LAN, fiber optics and wireless. Opportunity to learn newest technologies. Must have network certification such as MCP, MCSE, CNA, or CNE as well as a college degree or the equivalent experience. Requires excellent interpersonal and problem-solving skills. Experience with multiplatform computing is preferred. Will be expected to develop technical documentation and help establish network policies, procedures, and standards to ensure conformance with information systems and client objectives and strategy. Qualified applicants should send application documents to Robert Edwards at redwards@tyt.com.

g. *Technology analyst/consultant.* A fast-growing, highly regarded information technology assessment/consulting firm has a position for someone with expertise in client/server technology and Access. Must have excellent written communication and interpersonal skills. Vendor or user organization experience is highly desirable. Position is in the Bay Area. Send or fax your résumé to director of human resources at 500 Airport Road, Suite 100, (your city), or 415-579-1022.

h. *Financial analyst.* An eastern-based investment firm is seeking an analyst to help with the evaluation of potential private equity investments and marketing of an existing and a new leveraged buyout fund. Should have a bachelor's degree from a good school and some experience in banking. Ideal candidates will have strong analytical capabilities and excellent computer skills, particularly spreadsheet, statistics, and database. Please fax résumé and cover letter to 203-869-1022 or send an email file to andrew-winston@fidelity.com.

i. *Trade show exhibits coordinator.* Position reports to the national sales manager and requires an individual who can work independently as well as part of a team. Professional telephone and computer skills are essential. Coordinator will maintain exhibitor contact databases, serve as an internal liaison to accounting and as an external liaison to vendors, and assist the on-site floor managers with various exhibitor-related responsibilities. Also must create exhibitor and attendee pre- and post-show surveys, collect data, and compile results. Trade show, association, or convention services experience is a plus. Some limited travel is expected. Send your résumé to lmiller@aol.com.

j. *Sales representative.* Major pharmaceutical company is expanding and looking for a sales representative in your area. Ideal candidate will have a successful record of sales experience, preferably in a business-to-business environment. Candidate must be well versed in science and willing to continually learn about new products. Good knowledge of your area is highly desirable. Send your résumé to Jane_Adami@pfizer.com.

k. *Internet programmer.* Seeking a professional individual with experience in complex HTML/DHTML, strong web development, and a thorough understanding of ajax and PHP. Will design, write, modify, test, and maintain programs and scripts for a suite of server applications. Must be comfortable in a UNIX environment and possess some competency in SQL. Any experience with data warehousing would be a plus. Additionally, a qualified candidate should be a team player and self-motivated and possess excellent speaking and writing skills. Send all application documents to James.Andrews@menshealth.com.

l. *Marketing professional.* An international, rapidly growing consumer and trade publisher is seeking a self-motivated individual to help us reach our goal of doubling revenues by the year 2015. Ideal candidate will be an innovative, results-oriented professional willing to take the challenge of developing new markets. Should be good at packaging and repackaging information products for a large and expanding customer base. We are looking for those with some experience, creative writing talent, leadership skills, good communication skills, and strong interpersonal

skills. Sell yourself through your cover message and résumé. Send a rich media text to Thomas McLaughlin, corporate vice president, Blackhawk Publishing at tjmclaughlin@blackhawk.com.

m. *Executive administrative assistant.* Vice president of a Fortune 500 manufacturing company seeks a highly competent, personable, organized, and dependable executive assistant. College degree desired. Must have excellent communication skills and thorough command of Internet navigation as well as word processing and presentation programs. In addition to basic business knowledge in accounting, economics, computer systems, finance, marketing, and management, an understanding of manufacturing in a global market would be desirable. Apply to director of human resources, P.O. Box 3733, (your city).

n. *Graphic artist.* An employee-owned systems integration firm has an immediate need for a graphic artist. A bachelor's degree or an associate's degree with some experience desired. Must be proficient in PhotoShop and Illustrator, preferably in a Windows environment. Will prepare presentation and curriculum support graphics for government customer. Knowledge of project management software is a plus. Must have a work portfolio. Send résumé to the attention of KML, P.O. Box 900, (your city).

o. *MIS specialist.* A local medical clinic is seeking an individual to manage a multisite, multiplatform computer system. Will be responsible for troubleshooting and coordinating problems in a Windows Vista environment and writing reports for management. A background in the health care/medical field combined with a good knowledge of computing is highly desirable. Send résumé to (your city's name) Community Clinic, 1113 Henderson, (your city) or fax to 888-316-1026.

p. *Financial manager.* Multispecialty medical group (60 doctors) needs dedicated professional to work in providing financial planning and control in a growing organization. Join a team of financial specialists who bear responsibility for budgeting, general accounting, reimbursement, billing processes, and external reporting. Also responsible for development of long- and short-range financial goals and evaluation of their impact on strategic objectives and service mission. Degree in accounting/finance. Technical and team skills needed. Competitive salary and benefits package. Send letter and résumé to Mount Renault Medical Group, Box 14871, New York, NY 00146.

q. *Accountant.* A major real estate developer and property management company seeks an accountant. Must have a bachelor's degree in accounting. Will assist in financial reporting, tax preparation, cash flow projections, and year-end audit workpaper preparation. Mastery of Excel is required as are good communication skills. Some work experience in accounting is desirable; internship experience in an accounting or real estate environment is also desirable. Send your résumé and cover letter to TPL, P.O. Box 613, (your city) or email it to tpl@hotmail.com.

r. *Accounting majors.* Multinational consumer electronics firm seeks entry-level accountant for work in its controller's division. This person must be knowledgeable in financial and managerial accounting, internal auditing, budgeting, and capital investments. A multinational orientation, degree in accounting, and progress toward completion of CPA or CMA are a plus. Good communication skills (written and oral) and computer applications are required. Interested applicants should send letter and résumé to hrdirector@circuitcity.com.

s. *Bank examiner.* Federal Reserve Bank (nearest to your location) seeks career-oriented individuals. Persons hired will conduct on-site examinations of foreign banks operating in the U.S. in their lending activities, derivative products, bank operations, and financial information. Applicants must possess a bachelor's degree in accounting, finance, or economics. Evidence of cross-cultural sensitivity and foreign language proficiency is preferred. Travel 30–50 percent of the time. Excellent oral/written skills and U.S. citizenship required. Apply with letter, résumé, and reference sheets to Federal Reserve Board, Human Resources Department, (your region).

t. *Proposal writer.* Global leader in high-technology asset management needs individual to prepare proposals for clients. Person selected must be a team player, thrive on high-tech challenges in fast-paced environment, and possess a state-of-the-art solution orientation. Excellent writing skills essential, along with BBA degree and experience with various hardware/software technologies. Job includes coordinating appropriate persons to define solutions and preparing program plans with cost estimation for clients. Send letter, résumé, and writing sample to Department SAS, (your city).

u. *Assistant to operations manager.* Proven leader in the insurance industry seeks a highly motivated assistant to the operations manager of regional service center. Technical skills include proficiency in Internet use and Microsoft Word, Excel, PowerPoint, Access, and other database applications. College training preferred with good people skills. Person selected must be able to develop and maintain effective working relationships with internal and external customers. Apply to H R Department, Box 7438, (your city) or email to hrdirector@statefarm.com.

v. *Environmental safety and health assistant.* World leader in battery manufacturing is looking for an individual to work in safety and health area of production plant and distribution center. The successful candidate will need to have a business or environmental engineering degree and possess excellent organizational and people skills. Job duties involve administering health/safety programs, conducting training, and working with governmental agencies and regulatory personnel. Excellent opportunity for results-oriented individual seeking to work for a safe, attractive, and sanitary environment. Send cover message and résumé to Box SH, (your city).

w. *Account executive for display advertising.* State business journal invites applications for career-oriented individuals. Qualified candidates must be college graduates (business preferred) and have work background to demonstrate reliability and commitment. Job scope involves selling display advertising in creative ways for specialized business print and online publications. Applicants should be of high energy, aggressive, and creative. Send applications to Drawer HBD, (your city) or salesmgr@busjrnl.com.

x. *Financial consultant.* Large communications services company needs qualified person to provide communication-based utility automation consulting to electric utilities. Must have comprehensive financial management knowledge. Perform economic analyses on current and proposed projects; assist in development of budgets; evaluate budget to actual performance; prepare monthly reports. Demonstrated knowledge of strategic planning, valuation techniques, accounting principles, and economic forecasts. Must communicate well orally and in writing. Email letter, résumé, and references to applications@alc.com.

y. *SEO Blogger.* New website is seeking a writer/intern for its search engine optimization (SEO) blog. This new site, which has free SEO tools, is attracting a growing worldwide interest. We are seeking two writers for three to five posts per week. Must have a background in SEO and be abreast of the field in order to write on current topics. Telecommuting is OK. Please send samples of your work or links to it along with your SEO credentials to jobs@nonbot.com.

z. *Corporate trainer.* Exciting opportunity is available for a professional with strong presentation skills, good organizational skills, and excellent written and oral communication skills. Successful trainer will be able to effectively communicate technical information to both technical and nontechnical users. Should be able to design classroom training modules and measure their effectiveness. Good time management and use of Outlook are required. Some travel to clients' sites may be required. Application documents including a sample PowerPoint presentation should be sent to Sharon Garbett, President, Sedona Training, P.O. Box 1308, Moline, Illinois 61266.

5 You are looking ahead to your graduation soon. You've decided to begin to look for jobs online. Tap into a system that you know posts jobs in your major or a corporate website that posts job openings. (See textbook website for links to some of these sites.) Browse through the jobs until you see one that appeals to you and for which you will be qualified when you graduate. Print (or save) a copy of the ad so you will have it handy when you write your résumé and cover messages. Address the points covered in the ad and explain that you learned about the position from a particular online system. Plan to send your résumé digitally, creating both an ASCII text and an HTM file.

6 Using visual CV or a similar tool of your choice, create a webpage profile complete with links that provide supporting details. Take care that your online portfolio is easy to navigate as well as pleasing to view.

7 You are seeking an internship in your field. Using your school's career services office, online internship sites, personal contacts, or other sources, find an internship in your field that you are currently qualified to hold. Write a résumé, references list, and cover letter for the position. Print a copy of the position description for your instructor. If you find the information through a personal contact or have no official job posting to print, write a brief paragraph describing the position. Be sure the description includes your personal contact's name, job title, company name, and contact information as well as a list of job duties and qualifications.

8 You are seeking an internship but have not yet found a job posting that fits your interests and abilities. However, you have always wanted to work for _____ (pick a real company), and even though the company has no positions advertised, you decide to send an unsolicited cover letter, résumé, and references to this company. Before you write the letter and résumé, though, you will want to analyze your purpose and goals; your audience; and the skills, experience, and qualifications you could bring to an internship with this company. Submit this analysis in a short memo to your instructor. When you turn in your job application materials.

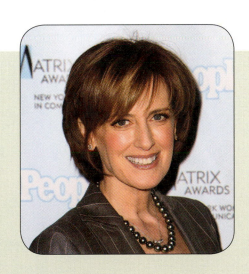

Anne Sweeney, President of Disney Channel Worldwide and President of ABC Cable Networks Group, began her television career at age 19 as a network page and as a researcher studying children who liked *Sesame Street* magazine. The research led her to enroll in Harvard's School of Education, where she learned the benefits of investigation for shaping both television programming and business strategy. Named by *Fortune* magazine as one of the most powerful women in business in 2005, Sweeney considers curiosity to be the most important factor in her success.

Research of "tween" viewers helped Disney add one million new subscribers per month for five years.

"We had been hearing from kids from the research we were conducting that there was an age group of kids that felt too old for Nickelodeon and too young for MTV. I'm always really interested in what's missing, so we probed deeper. We looked at a lot of lifestyle information, we looked at how kids spent their days, and at what time they came home from school. We took a very hard look at who they are and what was going on in their lives. [That research] really launched our live-action programming strategy."

Anne Sweeney, President of Disney Channel Worldwide and President of ABC Cable Networks Group

chapter ten

Basics of Report Writing

Upon completing this chapter, you will be able to prepare well-organized, objective reports. To reach this goal, you should be able to

1 State a problem clearly in writing.

2 List the factors involved in a problem.

3 Explain the common errors in interpreting data and develop attitudes and practices conducive to good interpreting.

4 Organize information in outline form, using time, place, quantity, factor, or a combination of these as bases for division.

5 Turn an outline into a table of contents whose format and wording are logical and meaningful.

6 Write reports that are focused, objective, consistent in time viewpoint, smoothly connected, and interesting.

7 Prepare reports collaboratively.

Report Writing

Introduce yourself to the subject of report writing by assuming the role of administrative assistant to the president of Technisoft, Inc. Much of your work at this large software company involves getting information for your boss. Yesterday, for example, you looked into the question of excessive time spent by office workers on Web surfing. A few days earlier, you worked on an assignment to determine the causes of unrest in one of the local branches. Before that assignment you investigated a supervisor's recommendation to change an evaluation process. You could continue the list indefinitely, for investigating problems is a part of your work.

You must write a report on each of your investigations. You write such reports for good reasons. Written reports make permanent records. Thus, those who need the information contained in these reports can review and study them at their convenience. Written reports also can be routed to a number of readers with a minimum of effort. Unquestionably, such reports are a convenient and efficient means of transmitting information.

Your report-writing work is not unique to your job. In fact, report writing is common throughout the company. For example, the engineers often report on the technical problems they encounter. The accountants regularly report to management on the company's financial operations. From time to time, production people report on various aspects of operations. The salespeople regularly report on marketing matters. And so it is throughout the company. Such reporting is vital to your company's operations—as it is to the operations of all companies.

Writing to external audiences can also be critical to an organization's success. If the organization is a consulting firm, reports to the client may be its primary deliverable. If the company is publicly traded, it is required by law to publish financial reports to the government and to shareholders. Depending on the nature of its business, a company may have to write reports to various agencies about its impact on the environment, its hiring practices, or its compliance with quality standards.

Sometimes reports are written by individuals. Increasingly, however, they are prepared in collaboration with others. Even if one person has primary responsibility for a report, he or she will often need contributions from many people. Indeed, report writing draws on a wide variety of communication skills, from getting information to presenting it clearly.

This and the following chapter describe the structure and writing of this vital form of business communication.

REPORTS AND YOUR FUTURE

How often you write reports in the years ahead will depend on the size and nature of the organization you work for. If you work for a very small organization (say, one with fewer than 10 employees), you will probably write only a few. But if you work for a midsize or larger organization, you are likely to write many. The larger the organization, the greater its complexity; and the greater the complexity, the greater the need for information to manage the organization.

- Reports are vital to larger organizations.

The nature of the business can also influence the number and type of reports you will write. The Securities and Exchange Commission requires all publicly traded businesses to write certain financial reports at regular intervals. A consulting firm's whole business effort may be directed toward informational and advisory reports to its clients. A business performing work under government contracts will also have special reporting needs. The frequency with which you will write reports, and the kinds you will write, will depend on your employer. But you can be fairly certain that report writing will figure significantly in your business career.

- The nature of the business also determines how many and what kinds of reports are needed.

- Report writing is likely to be important in your career.

DEFINING REPORTS

You probably have a good idea of what reports are. Even so, you might have a hard time defining them. Some people define reports to include almost any presentation of information; others limit reports to only the most formal presentations. We use this middle-ground definition: *A business report is an orderly and objective communication of factual information that serves a business purpose.*

- A business report is an orderly and objective communication of factual information that serves a business purpose.

As an *orderly* communication, a report is prepared carefully. Thus, care in preparation distinguishes reports from casual exchanges of information. The *objective* quality of a report is its unbiased approach. Reports seek to present facts. They avoid human biases as much as possible. The word *communication* in our definition is broad in meaning. It covers all ways of transmitting meaning: speaking, writing, using graphics. The basic ingredient of reports is *factual information*. Factual information is based on events, statistics, and other data. Not all reports are business reports. Research scientists, medical doctors, ministers, students, and many others write them. To be classified as a business report, a report must *serve a business purpose*.

This definition is specific enough to be meaningful, yet broad enough to account for the variations in reports. For example, some reports (information reports) do nothing more than present facts. Others (analytical reports) go a step further by including interpretations, sometimes accompanied by conclusions. Recommendation reports go further yet, presenting advice for future action. There are reports that are highly formal both in writing style and in physical appearance. And there are reports that show a high degree of informality. Our definition permits all of these variations.

DETERMINING THE REPORT PURPOSE

- Work on a report begins with a business need (problem).

Your work on a report logically begins with a need, which we refer to generally as the *problem* in the following discussion. Someone or some group (usually your superiors) needs information for a business purpose. Perhaps the need is for information only; perhaps it is for information and analysis; or perhaps it is for information, analysis, and recommendations. Whatever the case, someone with a need (problem) will authorize you to do the work. The work may be authorized orally or in writing.

- Your first task is to get the problem clearly in mind.

After you have been assigned a report problem, your first task should be to get your problem clearly in mind. Elementary and basic as this task may appear, all too often it is done haphazardly. And all too often a report fails to reach its goal because of such haphazardness.

The Preliminary Investigation

- To do this, you should begin by gathering all the information you need to understand the problem.

Getting your problem clearly in mind is largely a matter of gathering all the information needed to understand it and then applying your best logic to it. Gathering the right information can involve many tasks, depending on the problem. It may mean gathering material from company files, talking over the problem with experts, searching through print and electronic sources, and discussing the problem with those who authorized the report. In general, you should continue this preliminary investigation until you have the information you need to understand your problem.

Need for a Clear Statement of the Problem

- Then you should express the problem clearly, preferably in writing.

After you understand your problem, your next step is to state it clearly. Writing the problem statement is good practice for several reasons. A written statement serves as a helpful touchstone, keeping you on track as you continue through the project. In addition, a written statement can be reviewed, approved, and evaluated by people whose assistance may be valuable. Most important of all, putting the problem in writing forces you to think it through.

- The problem statement may be (1) an infinitive phrase, (2) a question, or (3) a declarative statement.

The problem statement normally takes one of three forms: infinitive phrase, question, or declarative statement. To illustrate each, we will use the problem of determining why sales at a certain store have declined:

Infinitive phrase: To determine the causes of decreasing sales at Store X.

Question: What are the causes of decreasing sales at Store X?

Declarative statement: Store X sales are decreasing, and management wants to know why.

COMMUNICATION MATTERS

Report-Writing Practices and the Sarbanes-Oxley Act

Changes in the regulatory environment can have a significant impact on the kinds of reporting that companies must do. One of the most major changes in recent history was the adoption of the Sarbanes-Oxley Act in 2002.* The law, which applies to all publicly traded companies, is intended to prevent financial scandals like those involving Enron, Arthur Andersen, Tyco, and WorldCom and to restore investor confidence. It requires companies to submit periodic reports on their financial practices to outside audit committees and assessments of those practices to the Securities and Exchange Commission (SEC), beyond the financial reports they were already submitting (such as their annual 10-K reports).

But chief financial officers are not the only ones writing more reports. Managers, office personnel, and information technology professionals also must do much more reporting on procedures and controls involving financial transactions and recordkeeping. And the process of bringing these companies into compliance has generated thousands of internal directives and reports.

You will not be able to predict all the kinds of reports you may be asked to write. At any moment, your company, its needs, or its environment may change. You must be ready to adapt with your problem-analysis, data-gathering, interpreting, and writing skills.

*For further information, see the Securities and Exchange Commission website at <http://www.sec.gov/> and the Beginner's Guide website at <http://beginnersguide.com/accounting/sarbanesoxley/>.

You may use any of the three forms for stating the report problem. One way to make sure you have the problem clearly in mind is to state it in one form (say the infinitive phrase) and then state it again in another form (say the question form). No differences in meanings should exist between the two problem statements. If there are differences, you should rethink the report problem for clarity before you proceed further in the report process.

- State the problem in several forms. The meaning should be the same.

Understand, though, that no matter how earnestly you've tried to frame the problem correctly, your conception of it may change as you continue with your research. As Chapters 1 and 5 point out, effective writing often involves a certain amount of revisiting earlier steps (*recursivity*). You may need to revise your conception of the problem as you gather more information. But a clear statement of your problem-solving purpose at any given point is essential, both to guide your research and to let others know where you are headed. It will also be an essential component of the introduction for your finished report and of other front matter intended to orient your readers (for example, the letter of transmittal and executive summary).

- You may need to revise your problem statement as you continue your research.

DETERMINING THE FACTORS

After stating the problem, you determine what needs to be done to solve it. Specifically, you look for the factors of the problem. That is, you determine what subject areas you must look into to solve the problem.

- Next, you should determine the factors of the problem.

What factors a problem involves can vary widely, but we can identify three common types. First, they may be subtopics of the overall topic about which the report is concerned. Second, they may be hypotheses that must be tested. Third, in problems that involve comparisons, they may be the bases on which the comparisons are made.

- The factors may be subtopics of the overall topic, hypotheses, or bases for comparison.

Use of Subtopics in Information Reports

If the problem concerns a need for information, you will need to figure out the areas about which information is needed. Illustrating this type of situation is the problem of preparing a report that reviews Company X's activities during the past quarter. Clearly, this is an informational report problem—that is, it requires no analysis, no

- Subtopics of the overall topic are the factors in information reports.

conclusion, no recommendation. It requires only that information be presented. The main effort in this case is to determine which subdivisions of the overall topic should be covered. After thoroughly evaluating the possibilities, you might come up with a plan like this:

Problem statement: To review operations of Company X from January 1 through March 31.

Subtopics:
1. Production
2. Sales and promotion
3. Financial status
4. Computer systems
5. Product development
6. Human resources

Hypotheses for Problems Requiring Solution

- Hypotheses (possible explanations of the problem) may be the factors in problems requiring solution.

Some problems concern why something bad is happening and perhaps how to correct it. In analyzing problems of this kind, you should seek explanations or solutions. Such explanations or solutions are termed *hypotheses.* Once formulated, hypotheses are tested, and their applicability to the problem is either proved or disproved.

To illustrate, assume that you have the problem of determining why sales at a certain store have declined. In preparing to investigate this problem, you would think of the possible explanations (hypotheses) for the decline. Your task would be one of studying, weighing, and selecting, and you would brainstorm such explanations as these:

- For example, these hypotheses could be suggested to explain a store's loss in sales.

Problem statement: Sales at the Springfield store have declined, and management wants to know why.

Hypotheses:
1. Activities of the competition have caused the decline.
2. Changes in the economy of the area have caused the decline.
3. Merchandising deficiencies have caused the decline.
4. Changes in the environment (population shifts, political actions, etc.) have caused the decline.

In the investigation that follows, you would test these hypotheses. You might find that one, two, or all apply. Or you might find that none is valid. If so, you would have to generate additional hypotheses for further evaluation.

Bases of Comparison in Evaluation Studies

- For evaluation problems, the bases for evaluating are the factors.

When the problem concerns evaluating something, either singularly or in comparison with other things, you should look for the bases for the evaluation. That is, you should determine what characteristics you will evaluate. In some cases, the procedure may concern more than naming the characteristics. It also may include the criteria to be used in evaluating them.

- This illustration shows the bases for comparing possible sites for expansion.

Illustrating this technique is the problem of a company that seeks to determine which of three cities would be best for expansion. Such a problem obviously involves a comparison of the cities. The bases for comparison are the factors that determine success for the type of work involved. After careful mental search for these factors, you might come up with a plan such as this:

Problem statement: To determine whether Y Company's new location should be built in City A, City B, or City C.

Comparison bases:
1. Availability of skilled workers
2. Tax structure

Report writing requires hard work and clear thinking in every stage of the process. To determine the problem and to gather facts, you will need to consult many sources of information.

3. Community attitude

4. Transportation facilities

5. Nearness to markets

Each of the factors selected for investigation may have factors of its own. In the last illustration, for example, the comparison of transportation in the three cities may well be covered by such subdivisions as water, rail, truck, and air. Workers may be compared by using such categories as skilled workers and unskilled workers. Breakdowns of this kind may go still further. Skilled workers may be broken down by specific skills: engineers, programmers, technical writers, graphic designers. The subdivisions could go on and on. Make them as long as they are helpful.

- The factors sometimes have factors of their own. That is, they also may be broken down.

GATHERING THE INFORMATION NEEDED

For most business problems, you will need to investigate personally. A production problem, for example, might require gathering and reviewing the company's production records. A sales problem might require collecting information through discussions with customers and sales personnel. A computer problem might require talking to both end users and programmers. A purchasing problem might require getting product information, finding prices, compiling performance statistics, and so on. Such a personal investigation usually requires knowledge of your field of work, which is probably why you were assigned the problem.

- The next step is to conduct the research needed. A personal investigation is usually appropriate.

Some business problems require a more formal type of research, such as an experiment or a survey. The experiment is the basic technique of the sciences. Business uses experiments primarily in the laboratory, although experiments have some nonlaboratory applications in marketing. Surveys are more likely to be used in business, especially in solving marketing problems. If you are called on to use experiments or surveys, it will probably be because your training has prepared you to use them. If you should need these techniques in this course, you will find them summarized in Chapter 18.

- Experiments or surveys are sometimes needed.

One of the newest features in Word 2007—the Reference tab—helps writers manage their sources. Although not as full-featured as dedicated citation managers such as ProCite, EndNote, or even the Web-based RefWorks, it can take some of the grunt work out of managing and citing sources.

When you select the type of source to cite, it will open a form prompting you for the information needed. Once you've entered the data and selected the style you prefer (APA, Chicago, MLA, etc.), Word will create your citations as well as create a Bibliography or Works Cited page for you.

Careful, though: these tools are not perfect. Always check their citations against an authoritative style manual. See Chapter 18 and Appendix E for further advice.

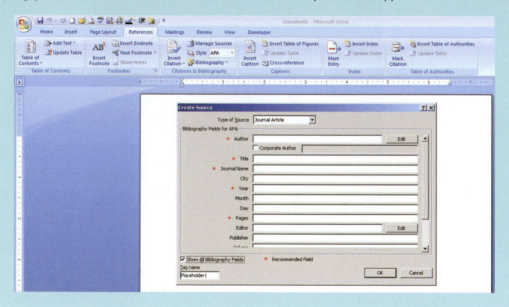

- Sometimes library research is used.

In some cases, you may use library and online research to find the information you need. Perhaps you have a good working knowledge of the techniques of research. If you do not, you will find these techniques also summarized in Chapter 18. To present facts from published sources in reports, you will need to use still other techniques: constructing a bibliography, citing references, quoting, paraphrasing, and so on. These techniques are covered in Appendix E.

- The Internet gives you access to many information sources. Quality may vary.

With the computer, you can search for electronically stored information. By using the Internet, a worldwide collection of networks, you can connect to information sources throughout the world. For example, you can work with others at different locations, you can access databases, you can use larger computers to help in your research, or you can browse any number of library catalogs. As noted in Chapter 18, the Internet is a vital source for information gathering in business reports. Information quality varies widely on the Internet, however. You should make sure the sources you consult are reliable. You will find more information on evaluating sources in Chapter 18.

- Apply the research techniques needed for the problem.

In any event, your task is to apply whatever research techniques are required to get the information you need for your problem.

INTERPRETING THE FINDINGS

- Next, interpret the information in light of your problem and your readers' needs.

The next major stage of the report-writing process is to interpret the information you've gathered. Actually, you will have done a good bit of interpreting already by the time you reach this stage. You had to interpret the elements of the situation to come up with

your conception of the problem. You also had to interpret your data as you were gathering them to make sure that you were getting appropriate and sufficient information. But when your research is finished, you will need to come up with the interpretations that will guide the shape and contents of your report. To do this, keep both your problem and your readers in mind. Your findings will need to apply clearly to the given problem in order to be viewed as logical solutions. But they will also need to meet the readers' needs in order to be viewed as relevant and helpful. If you have kept your reader-based problem statement in mind while doing your research, making logical, reader-based analyses of your data should follow naturally.

Interpretation is obviously a mental process, and how you interpret your data will vary from case to case. Still, the following general advice can help you with this process.

Advice for Avoiding Human Error

The first advice is to avoid certain human tendencies that lead to error in interpretation, described in the following list:

1. *Report the facts as they are.* Do nothing to make them more or less exciting. Adding color to interpretations to make the report more interesting compromises objectivity.

2. *Do not think that conclusions are always necessary.* When the facts do not support a conclusion, you should just summarize your findings and conclude that there is no conclusion. All too often report writers think that if they do not conclude, they have failed in their investigation.

3. *Do not interpret a lack of evidence as proof to the contrary.* The fact that you cannot prove something is true does not mean that it is false.

4. *Do not compare noncomparable data.* When you look for relationships between sets of data, make sure they have similarities—that you do not have apples and oranges.

- How you will interpret your data will vary specifically from case to case, but you can benefit from the following advice.

- Avoid human error by remembering these fundamentals:

- 1. Report the facts as they are.

- 2. Do not think that conclusions are always necessary.

- 3. Do not interpret a lack of evidence as proof to the contrary.

- 4. Do not compare noncomparable data.

You're right. This report does make you look like a fool.

Source: © 1985 Dean Vietor. Used with permission.

5. Do not draw illogical cause–effect conclusions.

5. *Do not draw illogical cause–effect conclusions.* The fact that two sets of data appear to affect each other does not mean they actually do. Use your good logic to determine whether a cause–effect relationship is likely.

6. Beware of unreliable and unrepresentative data.

6. *Beware of unreliable and unrepresentative data.* Much of the information to be found in secondary sources is incorrect to some extent. The causes are many: collection error, biased research, recording mistakes. Beware especially of data collected by groups that advocate a position (political organizations, groups supporting social issues, and other special interest groups). Make sure the sources you uncover are reliable. And remember that the interpretations you make are no better than the data you interpret.

7. Do not oversimplify.

7. *Do not oversimplify.* Most business problems are complex, and all too often we neglect some important parts of them.

8. Make only those claims that your evidence can support.

8. *Tailor your claims to your data.* There's a tendency among inexperienced report writers to use too few facts to generalize far too much. If you have learned about a certain phenomenon, do not assume that your interpretations can automatically be applied to similar phenomena. Or if your research has revealed the source of a problem, do not assume that you can also propose solutions. Finding solutions can be a separate research project altogether. Make only those claims that are well supported by your evidence, and when you are not sure how strong to make them, use such qualified language as "may be," "could be," and "suggest."

Appropriate Attitudes and Practices

Adopt the following attitudes and practices:

In addition to being alert to the most likely causes of error, you can improve your interpretation of findings by adopting the following attitudes and practices:

1. Maintain a judicial attitude.

1. *Maintain a judicial attitude.* Play the role of a judge as you interpret. Look at all sides of every issue without emotion or prejudice. Your primary objective is to form the most reliable interpretations of the situation.

2. Consult with others.

2. *Consult with others.* It is rare indeed when one mind is better than two or more. Thus, you can profit by talking over your interpretations with others.

3. Test your interpretations.

3. *Test your interpretations.* While the ultimate test of your interpretations' validity will be how well they hold up in their actual application to a company problem, you can perform two tests to help you make reasonable inferences from your data.

Use the test of experience—reason.

First is the test of experience. In applying this test, you use the underlying theme in all scientific methods—reason. You ponder each interpretation you make, asking yourself, "Does this appear reasonable in light of all I know or have experienced?"

Second is the negative test, which is an application of the critical viewpoint. You begin by making the interpretation that is directly opposite your initial one. Next, you examine the opposite interpretation carefully in light of all available evidence, perhaps even building a case for it. Then you compare the two interpretations and retain the one that is more strongly supported.

● Use the negative test—question your interpretations.

Statistical Tools for Data Analysis

In many cases, the information you gather is quantitative—that is, expressed in numbers. Such data in their raw form usually are voluminous, consisting of tens, hundreds, even thousands of figures. To use these figures intelligently, you first must find ways of simplifying them so that your reader can grasp their general meaning. Statistical techniques provide many methods for analyzing data. By knowing them, you can improve your ability to interpret. Although a thorough review of statistical techniques is beyond the scope of this book, you should know the more commonly used methods described in the following paragraphs.

● Statistics permit you to examine a set of facts.

Possibly of greatest use to you in writing reports are *descriptive statistics*—measures of central tendency, dispersion, ratios, and probability. Measures of central tendency—the mean, median, and mode—will help you find a value that roughly represents the whole. The measures of dispersion—ranges, variances, and standard deviations—should help you describe how spread out the data are. Ratios (which expresses proportionate relationship) and probabilities (which determine how many times something will likely occur out of the total number of possibilities) can also help you give meaning to data. Inferential and other statistical approaches are also useful but go beyond these basic elements. You will find descriptions of these and other useful techniques in the help documentation of your spreadsheet and statistics software as well as in any standard statistics textbook.

● Descriptive statistics should help the most.

A word of caution, however: Your job as a writer is to help your reader interpret the information. Sometimes unexplained statistical calculations—even if elementary to you—may confuse the reader. Thus, you must explain your statistical techniques explicitly with words and visuals when needed. You must remember that statistics are a help to interpretation, not a replacement for it. Whatever you do to reduce the volume of data deserves careful explanation so that the reader will receive the intended meaning.

● Do not allow statistical calculations to confuse; they should help the reader interpret.

ORGANIZING THE REPORT INFORMATION

When you have interpreted your information, you know the message of your report. Now you are ready to organize this message for presentation. Your goal here is to arrange the information in a logical order that meets your reader's needs.

● After you know what your findings mean, you are ready to construct an outline.

The Nature and Benefits of Outlining

An invaluable aid at this stage of the process is an outline. A good one will show what things go together (grouping), what order they should be in (ordering), and how the ideas relate in terms of levels of generality (hierarchy). Although you can outline mentally, a written plan is advisable for all but the shortest reports. Time spent on outlining at this stage is time well spent because it will make your drafting process more efficient and orderly. For longer reports, your outline will also form the basis for the table of contents.

● An outline helps you group and order the information and distinguish main from supporting points.

If you have proceeded methodically thus far, you probably already have a rough outline. It is the list of topics that you drew up when planning how to research your problem. You may also have added to this list the findings that you developed when interpreting your data. But when it's time to turn your research plan into a report plan, you need to outline more deliberately. Your goal is to create the most logical, helpful pattern of organization for your readers.

● When you reach the main organizing stage, you will probably have already done some of the work.

Software Tools Assist the Writer in Both Identifying Factors and Outlining

Inspiration is a conceptmapping tool aimed at helping business executives create and outline business documents. The example shown here demonstrates how individuals or groups can brainstorm the factors of a report that investigates which color laser printer a product design department should purchase. Using either the diagram or outline view (or both), a report writer would list as many ideas as possible. Later the items and relationships can be rearranged by dragging and moving pointers.

The software will update the outline symbols as changes are made. Users can toggle between the different views to work with the mode that works best for them. When ready to write, users can export the outline or diagram to Word or RTF format.

You can download a free 30-day trial version from <http://www.inspiration.com/freetrial>. You can also experiment with the new online version, Webspiration, at <http://mywebspiration.com> (currently in "Public Beta," or trial, form).

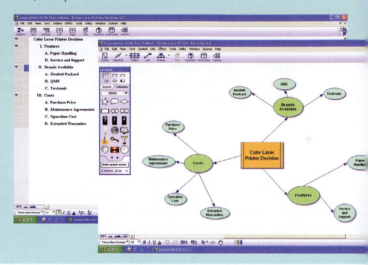

• Your outline should usually be written. It can later provide your headings and table of contents.

In constructing your outline, you can use any system of numbering or formatting that will help you see the logical structure of your planned contents. If it will help, you can use the conventional or the decimal symbol system to mark the levels. The conventional system uses Roman numerals to show the major headings and letters of the alphabet and Arabic numbers to show the lesser headings, as illustrated here:

Conventional System

• This conventional symbol system is used in marking the levels of an outline.

   I. First-level heading
      A. Second level, first part
      B. Second level, second part
         1. Third level, first part
         2. Third level, second part
            a. Fourth level, first part
               (1) Fifth level, first part
                   (a) Sixth level, first part
  II. First-level heading
      A. Second level, first part
      B. Second level, second part
        Etc.

The decimal system uses whole numbers to show the major sections. Whole numbers followed by decimals and additional digits show subsections. That is, the digits to the right of the decimal show each successive level in the outline, as shown here:

Decimal System

• This decimal system is also used.

  1.0 First-level heading
      1.1 Second level, first part
      1.2 Second level, second part
           1.2.1 Third level, first part

```
      1.2.2  Third level, second part
           1.2.2.1  Fourth level, first part
                 1.2.2.1.1  Fifth level, first part
                       1.2.2.1.1.1  Sixth level, first part
  2.0  First-level heading
     2.1  Second level, first part
     2.2  Second level, second part
     Etc.
```

Bear in mind that the outline is a tool for you, even though it is based on your readers' needs. Unless others will want to see an updated outline as you work, spend minimal time on its appearance. Allow yourself to change it, scribble on it, depart from it—whatever seems appropriate as your report develops. For example, you might want to note on your outline which sections will contain visuals, or to jot down a particularly good transition between sections that came to mind. The time to sweat over the outline's format and exact wording will be when you use it to create the headings and the table of contents for your finished report.

● The outline is a tool for you. Use it in any way that will help you write a good report.

Organization by Division

One methodical way to create an outline is to use the process of dividing the contents into smaller and smaller sections. With this method, you begin by looking over all your information. You then identify its major parts. This first level of division gives you the major outline parts indicated in Figure 10–1 by the Roman numerals (I, II, III, and so on).

● You may view organizing as a process of division. First, you divide the whole into parts.

Next, you find ways to subdivide the contents in each major section, yielding the second-level information (indicated by A, B, C). If practical, you keep dividing the contents, generating more levels. This method helps you divide your report into digestible chunks while also creating a logical and clear structural hierarchy.

● Then you divide the parts into subparts. You may subdivide further.

Division by Conventional Relationships

In dividing your information into subparts, you have to find a way of dividing that will produce approximately equal parts. Time, place, quantity, and factor are the general bases for these divisions.

● Time, place, quantity, and factor are the bases for the process of division.

Whenever the information you have to present has some time aspect, consider organizing it by *time*. In such an organization, the divisions are periods of time. These time periods usually follow a sequence. Although a past-to-present or present-to-past sequence is the rule, variations are possible. The periods you select need not be equal in duration, but they should be about equal in importance.

● When the information has a time basis, division by time is possible.

A report on the progress of a research committee illustrates this possibility. The period covered by this report might be broken down into the following comparable subperiods:

    The period of orientation, May–July
    Planning the project, August
    Implementation of the research plan, September–November

The happenings within each period might next be arranged in order of occurrence. Close inspection might reveal additional division possibilities.

If the information you have collected has some relation to geographic location, you may use a *place* division. Ideally, this division would be such that the areas are nearly equal in importance.

● When the information is related to geographic location, a place division is possible.

A report on the U.S. sales program of a national manufacturer illustrates a division by place. The information in this problem might be broken down by these major geographic areas:

    New England
    Atlantic Seaboard

Figure 10–1

Procedure for Constructing an Outline by Process of Division

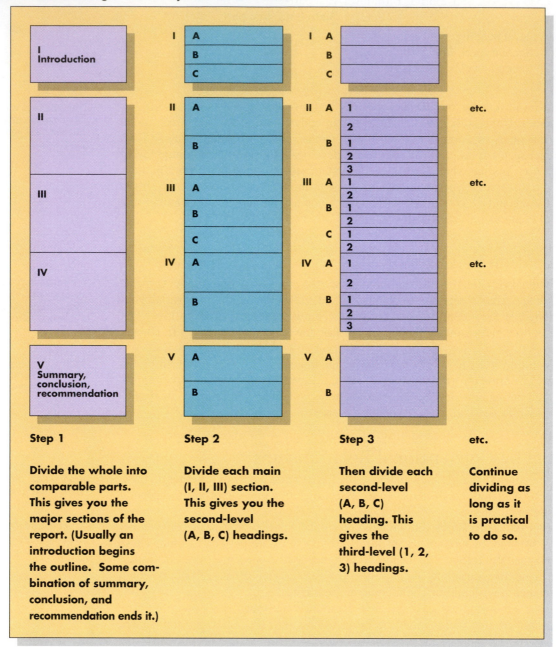

Step 1

Divide the whole into comparable parts. This gives you the major sections of the report. (Usually an introduction begins the outline. Some combination of summary, conclusion, and recommendation ends it.)

Step 2

Divide each main (I, II, III) section. This gives you the second-level (A, B, C) headings.

Step 3

Then divide each second-level (A, B, C) heading. This gives the third-level (1, 2, 3) headings.

etc.

Continue dividing as long as it is practical to do so.

South
Southwest
Midwest
Rocky Mountains
Pacific Coast

Another illustration of organization by place is a report on the productivity of a company with a number of customer service branches. A major division of the report might be devoted to each of the branches. The information for each branch might be broken down further, this time by sections, departments, divisions, or the like.

Quantity divisions are possible for information that has quantitative values. To illustrate, an analysis of the buying habits of potential customers could be divided by such income groups as the following:

• Division based on quantity is possible when the information has a number base.

Under $30,000
$30,000 to under $45,000
$45,000 to under $60,000
$60,000 to under $85,000
$85,000 to under $100,000
$100,000 and over

Another example of division on a quantitative basis is a report of a survey of men's preferences for shoes, in which an organization by age groups might be used to show variations in preference by ages. Perhaps the following divisions would be appropriate:

Youths, under 18
Young adults, 18–30
Adults, 31–50
Senior adults, 51–70
Elder adults, over 70

Problems often have few or no time, place, or quantity aspects. Instead, they require that certain factors, or information areas, be investigated. Such areas may consist of questions that must be answered in solving a problem, or of subjects that must be investigated and applied to the problem.

- Factors (areas to be investigated) are a fourth basis for dividing information.

An example of a division by factors is a report that seeks to determine which of three locations is the best for a new office for property management. In arriving at this decision, one would need to compare the three locations based on the factors affecting the office location. Thus, the following organization of this problem would be a possibility:

Location accessibility
Rent
Parking
Convenience to current and new customers
Facilities

Another illustration of organization by factors is a report advising a manufacturer whether to begin production of a new product. The solution of this problem will be reached through careful consideration of the factors involved. Among the more likely factors are these:

Production feasibility
Financial considerations
Strength of competition
Consumer demand
Marketing considerations

Combination and Multiple Division Possibilities

Not all division possibilities are clearly time, place, quantity, or factor. In some instances, combinations of these bases of division are possible. In a report on the progress of a sales organization, for example, the information collected could be arranged by a combination of quantity and place:

- Combinations of time, place, quantity, and factor are sometimes logical.

Areas of high sales activity
Areas of moderate sales activity
Areas of low sales activity

Some reports on sales of cyclical products might use the following combination of time and quantity:

Periods of low sales
Periods of moderate sales
Periods of high sales

Some problems can be organized in more than one way. For example, take the problem of determining the best of three locations for an annual sales meeting. It could be organized by site or by the bases of comparison. Organized by sites, the bases of comparison would probably be the second-level headings:

Site A
    Airport accessibility
    Hotel accommodations
    Meeting facilities
    Favorable weather
    Costs
    Restaurant/entertainment options
Site B
    Airport accessibility
    [And so on]
Site C
    Airport accessibility
    [And so on]

Organized by bases of comparison, cities would probably be the second-level headings:

● Here, it is organized by
  factors (the bases of
  comparison).

Airport accessibility
    Site A
    Site B
    Site C
Hotel accommodations
    Site A
    Site B
    Site C
Meeting facilities
    Site A
    Site B
    Site C

● The second plan is
  better because it makes
  comparison easy.

At first glance, both plans appear logical. Close inspection, however, shows that organization by cities separates information that has to be compared. For example, you must examine three different parts of the report to find out which city has the best hotel accommodations. In the second outline, the information that has to be compared is close together. You can determine which city has the best hotel accommodations after reading only one section of the report.

Nevertheless, these two plans show that some problems can be organized in more than one way. In such cases, you must compare the possibilities carefully to find the one that best presents the report information.

From Outline to Table of Contents

● A table of contents
  requires rigorous
  attention to detail.

When you are ready to prepare the table of contents for your report, you will be, in essence, turning the outline that helped you write into an aid for the reader. Because it will be your public outline, the table of contents needs to be carefully formatted and worded.

True, you will probably design the table of contents late in the report-writing process. We discuss it here as a logical conclusion to our discussion of outlining. But in the event that others involved in the project want to see a well-prepared outline before your report is done, you can use the following advice to prepare that outline. Note also that what we say about preparing the headings for the table of contents also applies to writing the headings for the report sections. The two sets of headings, those in the table of contents and those in the report itself, should match exactly. Using the Outline view in Word with the Table of Contents generator will assure that these are exact matches.

Formatting Decisions. Whatever format you used for your outline, you now need to choose a format that your reader will find instructive, readable, and appropriate. You create an *instructive* format by clearly indicating the hierarchy of the information. Rely mostly on form (font selection, size, style, and color as well as on effects) and placement to distinguish among the levels of your contents, as the sample in Chapter 11 shows. You make the format *readable* by using ample vertical white space between topics and enabling readers to see at a glance how the report is organized. Using leaders (dots with intervening spaces) between your topics and your page numbers can also enhance readability.

An *appropriate* format is one that your reader expects. Some business readers view the conventional outlining system (Roman numerals, letters, and Arabic numbers) and the decimal system (as in 1.2.1) as adding unnecessary clutter to the table of contents. Instead, they prefer the use of form and placement to show them how the parts relate to each other. However, in the military and some technical environments, the decimal system is expected, and in other contexts, your readers may want the full numerals and letters of the conventional system. In our examples, we use format rather than numbering to indicate levels of information, but be sure to get a sense of what your particular readers will prefer.

- Make your format instructive, readable, and appropriate.

Topic or Talking Headings. In selecting the wording for your table of contents headings, you have a choice of two general forms: topic headings and talking headings. *Topic headings* are short constructions, frequently consisting of one or two words. They merely identify the topic of discussion. Here is a segment of a topic-heading table of contents:

- You may use topic or talking headings. Topic headings give only the subject of discussion.

Present armor unit
    Description and output
    Cost
    Deficiencies
Replacement effects
    Space
    Boiler setting
    Additional accessories
    Fuel

Like topic headings, *talking headings* (or *popular headings* as they are sometimes called) identify the subject matter covered. But they go a step further. They also indicate what is said about the subject. In other words, talking headings summarize the material they cover, as in this illustration:

- Talking headings identify the subject and tell what is said about it.

Operation analyses of armor unit
    Recent lag in overall output
    Increase in cost of operation
    Inability to deliver necessary steam
Consideration of replacement effects
    Greater space requirements
    Need for higher boiler setting
    Efficiency possibilities of accessories
    Practicability of firing two fuels

The following table of contents excerpt is made up of headings that talk:

Introduction to the problem
    Authorization by board action
    Problem of locating a woolen mill
    Use of miscellaneous government data
    Factors as bases of problem solution
Community attitudes toward the woolen industry
    Favorable reaction of all towns to new mill
    Mixed attitudes of all towns toward labor policy

Labor supply and prevailing wage rates
    Prevalence of unskilled labor in San Marcos
    Concentration of skilled workers in San Marcos
    Generally confused pattern of wage rates
Nearness to the raw wool supply
    Location of Ballinger, Coleman, and San Marcos in the wool area
    Relatively low production near Big Spring and Littlefield
Availability of utilities
    Inadequate water supply for all towns but San Marcos
    Unlimited supply of natural gas for all towns
    Electric rate advantage of San Marcos and Coleman
    General adequacy of all towns for waste disposal
Adequacy of existing transportation systems
    Surface transportation advantages of San Marcos and Ballinger
    General equality of airway connections
A final weighting of the factors
    Selection of San Marcos as first choice
    Recommendation of Ballinger as second choice
    Lack of advantages in Big Spring, Coleman, and Littlefield

This contrasting version uses topic headings:

Introduction
    Authorization
    Purpose
    Sources
    Preview
Community attitudes
    Plant location
    Labor policy
Factors of labor
    Unskilled workers
    Skilled workers
    Wage rates
Raw wool supply
    Adequate areas
    Inadequate areas
Utilities
    Water
    Natural gas
    Electricity
    Waste disposal
Transportation
    Surface
    Air
Conclusions
    First choice
    Alternative choice
    Other possibilities

● Headings making up a level of division should be parallel grammatically.

Parallelism of Construction. As a general rule, you should write headings at each level of the table of contents in the same grammatical form. In other words, equal-level headings should be parallel in structure. This rule is not just an exercise in grammar; its purpose is to show similarity. As you will recall from the discussion of conventional relationships of data, equal-level headings are divided consistently using time, place, quantity, factor, or combinations. You want to show consistently such equal-level divisions through parallel headings. For example, if the first major heading is a noun phrase, all other major headings should be noun phrases. If the first second-level heading under a major head is an *-ing* phrase, all second-level headings in this section should be *-ing* phrases. However, authorities also permit varying the form from one section and level to another; that is, the second-level heads in one section need to match, but they do not need to match the second-level heads in the other sections, and the third-level heads do not need to match the second-level heads.

The following headings illustrate violations of parallelism:

Programmer output is lagging (sentence).

Increase in cost of labor (noun phrase)

Unable to deliver necessary results (decapitated sentence—no subject)

You may correct this violation in any of three ways: by making the headings all sentences, all noun phrases, or all decapitated sentences. If you desire all noun phrases, you could construct such headings as these:

Lag in programmer output

Increase in cost of labor

Inability to deliver necessary results

Or you could make all the headings sentences, like this:

Programmer output is lagging.

Cost of labor is increasing.

Information systems cannot deliver necessary results.

Conciseness in Wording. Your talking headings should be the shortest possible word arrangement that also can meet the talking requirement. Although the following headings talk well, their excessive length obviously hinders their communication effectiveness:

- Make the talking headings concise.

Personal appearance enhancement is the most desirable feature of contact lenses that wearers report.

The drawback of contacts mentioned by most people who can't wear them is that they are difficult to put in.

More comfort is the most desired improvement suggested by wearers and nonwearers of contact lenses.

Obviously, the headings contain too much information. Just what should be left out depends on your judgment. Here is one possible revision:

Most desirable feature: Personal appearance

Prime criticism: Difficulty of insertion

Most desired improvement: Comfort

Variety of Expression. In wording of headings, as in all other forms of writing, you should use some variety of expression. Repeating words too frequently makes for monotonous writing. The following outline excerpt illustrates this point:

- Repeating words in headings can be monotonous.

Oil production in Texas

Oil production in California

Oil production in Louisiana

As a rule, if you make the headings talk well, there is little chance of monotonous repetition. Since your successive sections would probably not be presenting similar

- Talking headings are not likely to be monotonous.

or identical information, headings really descriptive of the material they cover would not be likely to use the same words. The headings in the preceding example can be improved simply by making them talk:

> Texas leads in oil production.
> California holds runner-up position.
> Rapidly gaining Louisiana ranks third.

As we say, the same guidelines that make for an informative, logical, and interesting table of contents also apply to the headings for your report.

WRITING THE REPORT

- You will already have done a lot of writing when you "start to write" your report.

When you write your report, you will have already done a good deal of writing. You will have written—and probably rewritten—a problem statement to guide you through your research. You will have collected written data or recorded your findings in notes, and you will have organized your interpretations of the data into a logical, reader-centered structure. Now it is time to flesh out your outline with clearly expressed facts and observations.

- In writing the report, communicate clearly and quickly.

- When drafting, get the right things in the right order. Do not strive for a perfect first draft.

When you draft your report, your first priority is to get the right things said in the right order. As Chapter 5 advises, you do not need to strive for a perfect draft the first time around. Understand that some pieces will seem to write themselves, while others will be much more difficult. Allow yourself to move along, stitching together the pieces. Once you have a draft to work with, you can perfect it.

- Your finished report should communicate clearly and quickly.

When revising, let the advice in the previous chapters be your guide. As with all the business messages previously discussed, reports should communicate as clearly and quickly as possible. Your readers' time is valuable, and you risk having your report misread or even ignored if you do not keep a healthy respect for this fact in mind. Use both words and formatting to get your contents across efficiently.

- Also give it these characteristics: objectivity, time consistency, transition, and interest.

You can help your reader receive the report's message clearly by giving your report some specific qualities of well-written reports. Two critical ingredients are a reader-centered beginning and ending. Such characteristics as objectivity, consistency in time viewpoint, coherence, and interest can also enhance the reception of your report. We review these topics next.

Beginning and Ending

- The beginning and ending of your report will probably be the most important and most frequently read parts.

Arguably the most critical parts of your report will be the beginning and ending. In fact, researchers agree that these are the most frequently read parts of a report. Chapter 11 goes into detail about beginnings and endings, but some general advice is in order here.

- Early on, your report should convey what you studied, how you studied it, and what you found out.

Whatever other goals it may achieve, the opening of your report should convey what problem you studied, how you studied it, and (at least generally) what you found out. Why? Because these are the facts that the reader most wants to know when he or she first looks at your report.

Here is a simple introduction that follows this pattern:

> In order to find out why sales were down at the Salisbury store, I interviewed the manager, observed the operations, and assessed the environment. A high rate of employee turnover appears to have resulted in a loss of customers, though the deteriorating neighborhood also seems to be a contributing factor.

In a formal report, some brief sections may precede this statement of purpose (for example, facts about the authorization of the study), and there might be extensive front matter (for example, a title page, letter of transmittal, table of contents, and executive summary). What follows the core problem statement can also vary depending on the size and complexity of the report (for example, it may or may not be appropriate to go into more detail about the research methods and limitations, or to announce specifically how the following sections will be organized). But whatever kind of report you are writing, make sure that the beginning gets across the subject of the report, what kind of data it is based upon, and its likely significance to the reader.

Your ending will provide a concise statement of the report's main payoff—whether facts, interpretations, or recommendations. In a short report, you may simply summarize your findings with a brief paragraph, since the specific findings will be easy to see in the body of the report. In a longer report, you should make this section a more thorough restatement of your main findings, formatted in an easy-to-digest way. The gist ("so what did you find out?") and significance ("and why should I care?") of your report should come through loud and clear.

- Make sure the ending of your report provides efficient answers to the reader questions "what did you find out?" and "why should I care?"

Being Objective

Good report writing presents facts and interprets them logically. It avoids presenting the writer's opinions, biases, and attitudes. In other words, it is objective. You can make your report objective by putting aside your prejudices and biases, by approaching the problem with an open mind and looking at all sides of every issue, and by fairly reviewing and interpreting the information you have uncovered. Your role should be much like that of a fair-minded judge presiding over a court of law. You will leave no stone unturned in your search for the best information and the most reasonable interpretations.

- Good report writing is objective.

Objectivity as a Basis for Believability. An objective report has an ingredient that is essential to good report writing—believability. Biased writing in artfully deceptive language may at first glance be believable. But if bias is evident at any place in a report, the reader will be suspicious of the entire report. Maintaining objectivity is, therefore, the only sure way to make report writing believable.

- Objective writing is believable.

The Question of Impersonal versus Personal Writing. Recognizing the need for objectivity, the early report writers worked to develop an objective style of writing. Since the source of bias in reports was people, they reasoned that objectivity was best attained by emphasizing facts rather than the people involved in writing and reading reports. So they tried to take the human beings out of their reports. The result was impersonal writing, that is, writing in the third person—without *I*s, *we*s, or *you*s.

- Historically, objective writing has meant writing impersonally (no *I*'s, *we*'s, *you*'s).

In recent years, some writers have opposed this approach. They argue that personal writing is more forceful and direct than impersonal writing. They point out that writing is more conversational and therefore more interesting if it brings both the reader and the writer into the picture. They contend that objectivity is an attitude—not a matter of person—and that a report written in personal style can be just as objective as a report written in impersonal style. These writers argue that impersonal writing frequently leads to an overuse of the passive voice and a dull writing style. (While this last claim may be true, impersonal writing need not be boring. One has only to look at the lively style of writers for newspapers, newsmagazines, and journals to see that impersonal writing can be interesting.)

- Recently, some writers have argued that personal writing is more interesting than impersonal writing and just as objective.

As with most controversies, the arguments on both sides have merit. In some situations, personal writing is better. In other situations, impersonal writing is better. And in still other situations, either type of writing is good.

- There is merit to both sides. You would be wise to do what your reader expects of you.

Your decision should be based on the facts of each report situation. First, you should consider the expectations of those for whom you are preparing the report. If your readers prefer an impersonal style, use it—and vice versa. Then you should consider the formality of the situation. You should use personal writing for informal situations and impersonal writing for formal situations.

- Good advice is to use personal style for routine reports and impersonal style for more formal reports.

Here are contrasting examples of the personal and impersonal style:

Personal

Having studied the advantages and disadvantages of using coupons, I recommend that your company not adopt this practice. If you used coupons, you would have to pay for them. You also would have to hire additional employees to take care of the increase in sales volume.

Impersonal

A study of the advantages and disadvantages of using coupons supports the conclusion that the Mills Company should not adopt this practice. The coupons themselves would cost extra money. Also, use of coupons would require additional personnel to take care of the increase in sales volume.

Notice that both are active, clear, and interesting. Strive for these effects no matter which you choose.

Being Consistent with Time

- Keep a consistent time viewpoint throughout the report.

Presenting information in the right time order is essential to your report's clarity. Not doing so confuses the reader. Thus, it is important that you maintain a consistent time viewpoint.

- There are two time viewpoints: past and present. Select one, and do not change.

You have two main choices of time viewpoint: past and present. Although some authorities favor one or the other, either viewpoint can produce a good report. The important thing is to be consistent—to select one time viewpoint and stay with it. In other words, you should view all similar information in the report from the same position in time.

- The past-time viewpoint views the research and the findings as past, and prevailing concepts and proven conclusions as present.

If you adopt the past-time viewpoint, you treat the research, the findings, and the writing of the report as past. Thus, you would report the results of a recent survey in past tense: "Twenty-two percent of the managers *favored* a change." You would write a reference to another part of the report this way: "In Part III, this conclusion *was reached.*" Your use of the past-time viewpoint would have no effect on references to future happenings. It would be proper to write a sentence like this: "If the current trend continues, 30 percent *will favor* a change by 2012." Prevailing concepts and proven conclusions are also exceptions. You would present them in present tense. For example, you would write "Solar energy *is* a major potential source of energy" and "The findings *show* conclusively that managers are not adequately trained."

- The present-time viewpoint presents as current all information that can be assumed to be current at the time of writing.

Writing in the present-time viewpoint presents as current all information that can logically be assumed to be current at the time of writing. All other information is presented in its proper place in the past or future. Thus, you would report the results of a recent survey in these words: "Twenty-two percent of the managers *favor* a change." You would refer to another part of the text like this: "In Part III, this conclusion *is reached.*" In referring to an old survey, you would write: "In 2006 only 12 percent *held* this opinion." And in making a future reference, you would write: "If this trend continues, 30 percent *will hold* this opinion by 2012."

Including Transitions

A well-written report reads as one continuous story. The parts connect smoothly. Much of this flow is the result of good, logical organization. But more than logical order is needed in long reports. As you will see in Chapter 11, a special coherence plan may be needed in such reports. In all reports, however, lesser transitional techniques are useful to connect information.

By *transition* we mean a "bridging across." Transitions are words or sentences that show the relationships of succeeding parts. They may appear at the beginning of a part as a way of relating this part to the preceding part. They may appear at the end of a part as a forward look. Or they may appear within a part as words or phrases that help move the flow of information.

Before we comment more specifically on transitions, we should make one point clear: Use them mechanically. You should use them only when they are needed—when leaving them out would produce abruptness. For example, avoid such boring, unnecessary transitions as "The last section discussed Topic X. In the next section, Y will be analyzed."

Sentence Transitions. Throughout the report you can improve the connecting network of thought by the wise use of sentence transitions. You can use them especially to connect parts of the report. The following example shows how a sentence can explain the relationship between Sections A and B of a report. Note that the first words draw a conclusion for Section B. Then, with smooth tie-in, the next words introduce Section C and relate this part to the report plan. The words in brackets explain the pattern of the thought connections.

> [Section B, concluded] . . . Thus, the data show only negligible differences in the cost for oil consumption [subject of Section B] for the three models of cars.

> [Section C] Even though the costs of gasoline [subject of Section A] and oil [subject of Section B] are the more consistent factors of operation expense, the picture is not complete until the costs of repairs and maintenance [subject of Section C] are considered.

In the following examples, succeeding parts are connected by sentences that make a forward-looking reference and thus set up the next subject. As a result, the shift of subject matter is smooth and logical.

> These data show clearly that alternative fuel cars are the most economical. Unquestionably, their operation by gas and hydrogen and their record for low-cost maintenance give them a decided edge over gas-fueled cars. *Before a definite conclusion about their merit is reached, however, one more vital comparison should be made.*

(The final sentence clearly introduces the subsequent discussion of an additional comparison.)

> . . . *At first glance the data appear convincing, but a closer observation reveals a number of discrepancies.*

(Discussion of the discrepancies is logically set up by this sentence.)

Placing topic sentences at key points of emphasis is another way of using sentences to link the various parts of the report. Usually the topic sentence is best placed at the paragraph beginning. Note in the following example how topic sentences maintain the flow of thought by emphasizing key information.

> *The Acura accelerates faster than the other two brands, both on a level road and on a 9 percent grade.* According to a test conducted by *Consumer Reports,*

- You should use transitions to connect the parts of the report.

- *Transition* means a "bridging across."

- They should not be used mechanically.

- For connecting large parts, transition sentences may be used.

- Use of topic sentences also helps improve thought flow.

Acura reaches a speed of 60 miles per hour in 13.2 seconds. To reach the same speed, Toyota requires 13.6 seconds, and Volkswagen requires 14.4 seconds. On a 9 percent grade, Acura reaches the 60-miles-per-hour speed in 29.4 seconds, and Toyota reaches it in 43.3 seconds. Volkswagen is unable to reach this speed.

Because it carries more weight on its rear wheels than the others, Acura has the best traction of the three. Traction, which means a minimum of sliding on wet or icy roads, is important to safe driving, particularly during the cold, wet winter months. Since traction is directly related to the weight carried by the rear wheels, a comparison of these weights should give some measure of the safety of the three cars. According to data released by the Automobile Bureau of Standards, Acura carries 47 percent of its weight on its rear wheels. Nissan and Toyota carry 44 and 42 percent, respectively.

> • Transitional words show relationships between lesser parts.

Transitional Words. Although the most important transition problems concern connection between the major parts of the report, transitions are needed between the lesser parts. If the writing is to flow smoothly, you will need to connect clause to clause, sentence to sentence, and paragraph to paragraph. As Chapter 3 points out, transitional words and phrases generally serve to make such connections.

Numerous transitional words are available. The following list shows such words and how you can use them. With a little imagination to supply the context, you can easily see how these words relate ideas. For better understanding, the words are grouped by the relationships they show between what comes before and what follows.

> • This partial list shows how words explain relationships.

Relationship	Word Examples
Listing or enumeration of subjects	In addition
	First, second, and so on
	Besides
	Moreover

Relationship	Word Examples
Contrast	On the contrary
	In spite of
	On the other hand
	In contrast
	However
Likeness	Also
	Likewise
	Similarly
Cause–result	Thus
	Because of
	Therefore
	Consequently
	For this reason
Explanation or elaboration	For example
	To illustrate
	For instance
	Also
	Too

Maintaining Interest

Like any other form of writing, report writing should be interesting. Actually, interest is as important as the facts of the report, because communication is not likely to occur without it. Readers cannot help missing parts of the message if their attention is allowed to stray. (If you have ever tried to read dull writing when studying for an exam, you know the truth of this statement.)

Perhaps writing interestingly is an art. But if so, it is an art you can develop by working at it. To develop this ability, you need to avoid the rubber-stamp jargon so often used in business and instead work to make your words build concrete pictures. You need to cultivate a feeling for the rhythmic flow of words and sentences. You need to remember that in back of every fact and figure there is life—people doing things, machines operating, a commodity being marketed. A technique of good report writing is to bring that life to the surface by using concrete words and active-voice verbs as much as possible. You also should work to achieve interest without using more words than are necessary.

But you can overdo efforts to make report writing interesting. Such is the case whenever your reader's attention is attracted to how something has been said rather than to what has been said. Effective report writing simply presents information in a clear, concise, and interesting manner. Perhaps the purpose and definition of report-writing style are best summarized in this way: Report-writing style is at its best when the readers are prompted to say "Here are some interesting facts" rather than "Here is some beautiful writing."

- Report writing should be interesting. Interesting writing is necessary for good communication.

- Interesting writing is the result of careful word choice, rhythm, concreteness—in fact, all the good writing techniques.

- But efforts to make writing interesting can be overdone. The writing style should never draw attention away from the information.

COLLABORATIVE REPORT WRITING

In your business career, you are likely to participate in numerous collaborative writing projects, and many of them are likely to be reports. Group involvement in report preparation is becoming increasingly significant for a number of reasons. For one, the specialized knowledge of different people can improve the quality of the work. For another, the combined talents of the members are likely to produce a document better than any one of the members could produce alone. A third reason is that dividing the work can reduce the time needed for the project. And fourth, new software tools allow groups to collaborate easily and well from different places.

- Collaborative report preparation is common for good reasons.

COMMUNICATION MATTERS

Does Your Group Have Emotional Intelligence?

Ever since the publication of Daniel Goleman's *Emotional Intelligence: Why It Can Matter More Than IQ* in 1995, companies have been looking for ways to cultivate the emotional intelligence (EI) of its members.

But groups can enhance their collective EI, too. According to Vanessa Urch Druskat and Steven B. Wolff of the *Harvard Business Review*, "Group EI norms build the foundation for true collaboration and cooperation—helping otherwise skilled teams fulfill their highest potential."

What kinds of things should a group do to channel its members' insights and emotions into positive results? Here's a partial list from Druskat and Wolff:

- Encourage all members to share their perspectives before making key decisions.
- Handle confrontation constructively. If team members fall short, call them on it by letting them know the group needs them.
- Regularly assess the group's strengths, weaknesses, and modes of interaction.
- Create structures that let the group express its emotions.
- Cultivate an affirmative environment.
- Encourage proactive problemsolving.

And try to keep things fun. In one company, the industrial-design firm IDEO, participants throw stuffed toys at anyone who prematurely judges ideas during brainstorming sessions.

Source: "Building the Emotional Intelligence of Groups," *Harvard Business Review* 1 Mar. 2001, *HarvardBusiness.org,* Harvard Business Publishing, Web, 15 June 2009.

Determining the Group Makeup

- Groups should have five or fewer members and include all pertinent specialization areas.

As a beginning step, the membership of the group should be determined. The availability and competencies of the people in the work situation involved are likely to be the major considerations. At a minimum, the group will consist of two. The maximum will depend on the number actually needed to do the project. As a practical matter, however, a maximum of five is a good rule, for larger groups tend to lose efficiency. More important than size, however, is the need to include all major areas of specialization involved in the work to be done.

- Preferably, the group will have a leader.

In most business situations the highest ranking administrator in the group serves as leader. In groups made up of equals, a leader usually is appointed or elected. When no leader is so designated, the group works together informally. In such cases, however, an informal leader usually emerges. Especially with group writing projects, it is a good idea to have one person in charge overseeing the entire process.

Creating the Ground Rules

- Ground rules help the group function positively and productively.

In organizations where teamwork is common, the ground rules for participation in a group may be understood. But students and working professionals alike may find it helpful to establish explicit guidelines for the participants.

Some rules may govern the members' interactions. For example, a rule might be "Listen respectfully and actively to what others are saying, without interrupting." Or it might instruct members to use "I" language ("I think . . .") rather than "you" language ("The problem with your idea is . . .") when disagreeing. Others might cover more logistical issues, such as conscientiously doing one's share of the work, keeping the group informed if problems arise, and being on time with one's contributions.

Ideally, the group will generate its own ground rules to which all members will agree. Some instructors find that actually drawing up a contract and having each member sign it is a good way to get group work off to a good start and prevent problems down the line.

Choosing the Means of Collaboration

Not that many years ago, groups needed numerous face-to-face meetings in order to get their work done. Today there are many other venues for group interactions. Your group should put careful thought into the choice of media that will enable effective collaboration while taking into account members' time constraints, distance from each other, and technological preferences.

If possible, you should have at least two face-to-face meetings—one at the start of the project and another near the end (for example, when doing the final revisions). But the bulk of the collaborating may take place by email, by discussion board, or through such online collaborative authoring tools as Google Docs or wikis (see Chapter 17). You might even use a live-meeting application or Skype to converse with each other. Whatever tools you use, it is vitally important that you choose them consciously and create any ground rules that will apply to their use.

- Many means of collaboration exist. Choose yours with care.

Making a Project Plan

Especially when the desired outcome is a coherent, effective report, the group should structure their tasks to meet the project's goals. Using the steps discussed in the next section and any additional considerations, the group should prepare a timeline that clearly states or shows the deadline for each task. A Gantt chart can be very useful along these lines (see Chapter 17), but even a simple list or table can suffice. In addition, your plan should make clear who is responsible for what. If your group has taken an inventory of its strengths before its planning, you can match members up with what they do best (for example, doing research or revising a document).

Your plan can also describe in some detail the desired form and style of the final document (such as which template it will use or whether or not it will use "you"). The

- A project plan helps members and the group as a whole stay on track.

Many reports written in business are produced in collaboration with others. Although you will do some work individually, you can expect to plan, organize, and revise the report as a group.

The commenting and reviewing tools in most word processors help people work together on documents asynchronously. When others review content and edit your document digitally, the commenting tool allows them to express opinions and concerns while the tracking tool makes their editing changes clearly visible. In fact, the tools allow you to accept or reject their suggestions individually or en masse.

In the example shown here, the reviewer clicked the Review tab to reveal commenting and reviewing tools.

Using this tool on a Tablet PC enables the reviewer to input comments using the keyboard or digital ink. The tracking system allows reviewers to use a variety of colors so that others can easily determine whom the changes belong to. The commenting tool inserts identifying information, too. Reviewers can also insert voice comments; the user can simply click a speaker icon to listen to the comment.

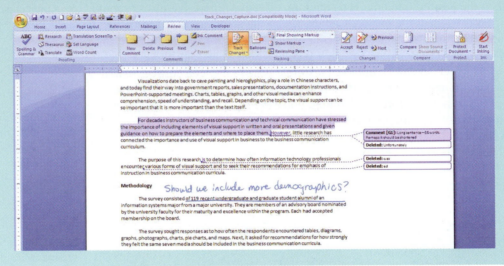

more the group determines such matters up front, the less scrambling it will need to do at the end to generate a coherent, consistent-looking report.

Writing the Report

- The following activities normally occur, usually in this sequence.

Whatever number of meetings is scheduled, the following activities typically occur, usually in the sequence shown. Of course, they will vary depending on the project and the situation.

- First, determine the report purpose.

Determine the Purpose. As with all report projects, the participants must determine just what the report must do. Thus, the group should follow the preliminary steps of problem definition discussed previously. They also need to develop a coherent, shared sense of the report's intended readers and their needs.

- Next, derive the factors involved.

Identify the Factors. The group next determines what is needed to achieve the purpose. This step involves determining the factors of the problem, as described earlier in the chapter. An advantage of collaboration is that several minds are available for the critical thinking that is so necessary for identifying the factors of the problem.

- If necessary, make a plan for gathering the information needed.

Gather the Information Needed. Before the group can begin work on the report, it must get the information needed. This activity could involve conducting any of the research designs mentioned earlier in this chapter and in Chapter 18. In some cases, group work begins after the information has been assembled, thus eliminating this step.

Interpret the Information. Determining the meaning of the information gathered is the next logical step for the group. In this step, the participants apply the findings to the problem, thereby selecting the information to be used in the report. In applying the findings to the problem, they also give meaning to the facts collected. The facts do not speak for themselves. Rather, group participants must think through the facts, apply them to the problem, derive logical meaning from the facts, and see them from the readers' points of view. Interpretations are no better than the thinking of the people in the group.

- The members interpret the information, applying it to the problem.

Organize the Material. Just as in any other report-writing project, the group next organizes the material selected for presentation. They will base the report's structure on the time, place, quantity, factor, or other relationships in the data.

- They organize the information for presentation in the report.

Plan the Writing. A next logical step is that of planning the makeup of the report. In this step the formality of the situation and the audience involved determine the decision. In addition, matters of writing such as tone, style, and formality are addressed. The need for coherence, time consistency, and interesting writing should be kept in mind.

- They plan the writing of the report.

Assign Parts to Be Written. After the planning has been done, the group next turns its attention to the writing. The usual practice is to assign each person a part of the report.

- They assign themselves report parts to write.

Write Parts Assigned. Next comes a period of individual work. Each participant writes his or her part. Each will apply the ideas in Chapters 2 and 3 about word selection, sentence design, and paragraph construction to writing the assigned parts.

- The members then write their parts.

Revise Collaboratively. The group meets either face to face or virtually and reviews each person's contribution and the full report. This should be a give-and-take session with each person actively participating. It requires that every person give keen attention to the work of each participant, making constructive suggestions wherever appropriate. It requires courteous but meaningful criticisms. It also requires that the participants be open-minded, remembering that the goal is to construct the best possible document. In no case should the group merely give automatic approval to the work submitted. In cases of controversy, the majority views of the group should prevail.

- The group members collaboratively review the writing.

Edit the Final Draft. After the group has done its work, one member usually is assigned the task of editing the final draft. This gives the document consistency. In addition, the editor serves as a final proofreader. The editor should probably be the most competent writer in the group.

- A selected member usually edits the final draft.

If all the work has been done with care and diligence, this final draft should be a report better than anyone in the group could have prepared alone. Those who study groups use the word *synergistic* to refer to groups that function this way. The final report is better than the sum of the individual parts.

SUMMARY BY LEARNING OBJECTIVES

1. Your work on a report begins with a problem (purpose, goal, objective).
   - Get the problem in mind by gathering all the information you need about it.
   - Then develop a problem statement from the information.
   - Phrase this statement as an infinitive phrase, a question, or a declarative statement.
   - Understand that you may need to revise your problem definition as you proceed with your research.

1 State a problem clearly in writing.

2. From the problem statement, determine the factors involved.
   - These may be subtopics in information reports.
   - They may be hypotheses (possible explanations) in problems requiring a solution.
   - They may be bases of comparison in problems requiring evaluations.

3. After you have gathered the information needed, interpret it as it applies to the problem.
   - Interpret the information in light of your problem and your readers' needs.
   - Heed this advice for avoiding human error:
     — Report the facts as they are.
     — Do not think that conclusions are always necessary.
     — Do not interpret a lack of evidence as proof to the contrary.
     — Do not compare noncomparable data.
     — Do not draw illogical cause–effect conclusions.
     — Beware of unreliable and unrepresentative data.
     — Do not oversimplify.
     — Tailor your claims to your data.
   - Adopt these attitudes and practices:
     — Maintain a judicial attitude.
     — Consult with others.
     — Test your interpretations by applying the test of experience (reason) and the negative test (question them).
     — Use statistical analysis to help you interpret numerical data.

4. Next, organize the information (construct an outline).
   - An outline helps you group and order the information and create an information hierarchy.
     — Your research plan and interpretation notes can help you make your report outline.
     — You may choose to use conventional outline symbols (I, A, 1, a) or numeric symbols (1, 1.1, 1.1.1), but any outline format is fine if it helps you write a well-organized draft.
     — The outline is a tool to help you—feel free to mark it up and revise it.
   - Organize the report body (the part between the introduction and the ending section) by a process of division.
     — Look over the findings for ways of dividing on the basis of time, place, quantity, factor, or combinations.
     — Then divide, forming the major parts of the report.
     — Next, look at these divisions for ways of dividing them.
     — Continue to subdivide as far as necessary.
     — The end result is your outline.

5. Turn your outline into a table of contents.
   - Use a format that your reader will find instructive, readable, and appropriate.
   - Use the topic form (identifies topic).
   - Or use the talking form (identifies topic and says something about it).
   - Make the wording of comparable parts parallel grammatically.
   - Prune each heading for conciseness.
   - Avoid excessive repetition of words.

6. From the outline, write the report.
   - Draft to get the right information in the right order; then revise for perfection.
   - Make your beginning and ending reader centered.
     — Write a beginning that tells what problem you studied, how you studied it, and what you found out.
     — Write an ending that summarizes the main findings and their significance to the readers.
   - Maintain objectivity (no bias).
     — An impersonal writing style (third person) has long been associated with objectivity.
     — But some authorities question this style, saying that a personal style is more interesting.
     — The argument continues, although most formal reports are written in the impersonal style.
   - Be consistent in time viewpoint—either past or present.
     — Past-time viewpoint views the research and findings as past and prevailing concepts and conclusions as present.
     — Present-time viewpoint presents as current all that is current at the time of writing.
   - Use transitions to make the report parts flow smoothly.
     — Between large parts, you may need to use full sentences to make connections.
     — Topic sentences also can help the flow of thought.
     — Use transitional words and phrases to connect the lesser parts.
   - Work to make the writing interesting.
     — Select words carefully for best effect.
     — Follow techniques of good writing (e.g., correctness, rhythmic flow of words, vigorous words).
     — Do not overdo these efforts by drawing attention to how you write rather than what you say.

7. Expect that you will sometimes prepare reports collaboratively in groups.
   - Groups (two to five members) may produce better reports than individuals if all things go well.
   - Members of groups (leaders and participants) should have clear roles.
   - Groups should establish their ground rules, choose their means of collaboration, and make a project plan.
   - Groups should follow this procedure in writing reports collaboratively:
     — Determine report purpose.
     — Identify factors.
     — Collect facts for the report.
     — Interpret the facts.
     — Organize the facts.
     — Plan for writing.
     — Assign parts to members.
     — Write assigned parts.
     — Revise members' contributions collaboratively.
     — Edit the final draft.

6 Write reports that are focused, objective, consistent in time viewpoint, smoothly connected, and interesting.

7 Prepare reports collaboratively.

1 What kinds of reports do you expect to write in your chosen profession? Why?

2 Explain the concept of outlining as a division process. **(LO4)**

3 In what ways can the format of the table of contents aid in reader comprehension? Find some examples of helpfully formatted tables of contents. **(LO5)**

4 You are writing a report on the progress of your local cable company's efforts to increase sales of five of its products through extensive advertising in print and online newspapers and magazines and on television and radio. Discuss the possibilities for major headings. Evaluate each possibility. **(LO2, LO4)**

5 Not all business reports are written objectively. In fact, many are deliberately biased. Why, then, should we stress objectivity in a college course that includes report writing? **(LO3, LO6)**

6 Explain the difference between personal and impersonal writing. Which is "better"? Argue both sides. **(LO6)**

7 Explain the differences between the present-time viewpoint and the past-time viewpoint. **(LO6)**

8 Is it incorrect to have present, past, and future tense in the same report? In the same paragraph? In the same sentence? Discuss. **(LO6)**

9 "Transitional sentences are unnecessary. They merely add length to a report and thus run contrary to the goal of conciseness." Discuss. **(LO6)**

10 "Reports are written for business executives who want them. Thus, you don't have to be concerned about holding your reader's interest." Discuss. **(LO6)**

11 "Collaborative reports are better than reports written by an individual because they use many minds rather than one." Discuss. **(LO7)**

12 "Disagreements in groups are counterproductive." Discuss. **(LO7)**

1 For each of the following problem situations, write a clear statement of the problem and list the factors involved. When necessary, you may use your imagination logically to supply any additional information needed. **(LO1, LO2)**

  a. A manufacturer of breakfast cereals wants to determine the characteristics of its consumers.

  b. The manufacturer of a toothpaste wants to learn what the buying public thinks of its product in relation to competing products.

  c. Wal-Mart wants to give its stockholders a summary of its operations for the past calendar year.

  d. A building contractor engaged to build a new office for Company X submits a report summarizing its monthly progress.

  e. The Able Wholesale Company must prepare a report on its credit relations with the Crystal City Hardware Company.

  f. The supervisor of Department X must prepare a report evaluating the performance of a secretary.

  g. Baker, Inc., wants a study made to determine why its employee turnover is high.

  h. An executive must rank three subordinates on the basis of their suitability for promotion to a particular job.

  i. The supervisor of production must compare three competing machines that are being considered for use in a particular production job.

  j. An investment consultant must advise a client on whether to invest in the development of a lake resort.

  k. A consultant seeks to learn how a restaurant can improve its profits.

2 Select a hypothetical problem with a time division possibility. What other division possibilities does it have? Compare the two possibilities as the main bases for organizing the report. **(LO2)**

3 Assume that you are writing the results of a survey conducted to determine what styles of shoes are worn throughout the country on various occasions by women of all ages. What division possibilities exist here? Which would you recommend? **(LO4)**

4 For the problem described in the preceding exercise, use your imagination to construct topic headings for the outline. **(LO4)**

5 Point out any violations of grammatical parallelism in these headings: **(LO4)**

   a. Region I sales lagging.

   b. Moderate increase seen for Region II.

   c. Sales in Region III.

6 Point out any error in grammatical parallelism in these headings: **(LO4)**

   a. High cost of operation.

   b. Slight improvement in production efficiency.

   c. Maintenance cost is low.

7 Which of the following headings is logically inconsistent with the others? **(LO4)**

   a. Agricultural production continues to increase.

   b. Slight increase is made by manufacturing.

   c. Salaries remain high.

   d. Service industries show no change.

8 Select an editorial, feature article, book chapter, or other document that has no headings. Write talking headings for it. **(LO4)**

9 Assume that you are writing a report that summarizes a survey you have conducted. Write a paragraph of the report using the present-time viewpoint; then write the paragraph using the past-time viewpoint. The paragraph will be based on the following information: **(LO6)**

Answers to the question about how students view the proposed Aid to Education Bill in this survey and in a survey taken a year earlier (in parentheses):

For, 39 percent (21); Against, 17 percent (43).

No answer, undecided, etc., 44 percent (36).

10 What are the advantages and disadvantages of the different means of writing collaboratively? Choose three and discuss.

   a. Face-to-face meetings

   b. Email

   c. Discussion boards

   d. Online editing tool (ea. Google Docs).

   e. Website (e.g., blog or wiki).

   f. live online interaction (e.g., Skype or IM-ing) **(LO7)**

chapter eleven

Types of Business Reports

Upon completing this chapter, you will be able to write well-structured business reports. To reach this goal, you should be able to

1   Explain the makeup of reports relative to length and formality.

2   Discuss the four major differences involved in writing short and long reports.

3   Choose an appropriate form for short reports.

4   Adapt the procedures for writing short reports to routine operational, progress, problem-solving, and audit reports as well as minutes of meetings.

5   Write longer reports that include the appropriate components, meet the readers' needs, and are easy to follow.

Types of Business Reports

Assume again the position of assistant to the president of Technisoft and the report-writing work necessary in this position. Most of the time, your assignments concern routine, everyday problems: human resource policies, administrative procedures, work flow, and the like. Following what appears to be established company practice, you write the reports on these problems in simple email form.

Occasionally, however, you have a more involved assignment. Last week, for example, you investigated a union charge that the company showed favoritism to the nonunion workers on certain production jobs. Because your report on this formal investigation was written for the benefit of ranking company administrators as well as union leaders, you used a more formal style and format.

Then there was the report you helped prepare for the board of directors last fall. That report summarized pressing needs for capital improvements. A number of executives contributed to this project, but you were the coordinator. Because the report was important and was written for the board, you made it as formal as possible.

Clearly, reports vary widely. This chapter will help you determine your reports' makeup, style, form, and contents. It will then focus on the types of reports that are likely to figure in your business-writing future.

AN OVERVIEW OF REPORT COMPONENTS

As you prepare to write any report, you will need to decide on its makeup. Will it be a simple email? Will it be a long, complex, and formal report? Or will it fall between these extremes?

- Length and formality determine the form and components of the report.

Your decisions will be based on the needs of your situation. Those needs are related to report length and the formality of the situation. The longer the problem and the more formal the situation, the more elaborate the report is likely to be. The shorter the problem and the more informal the situation, the less elaborate the report is likely to be. Such adjustments of report makeup to length and formality help meet the reader's needs in each situation.

To help you understand your choices, we first explain how to decide which components to use for a given report. We then briefly review the purpose and contents of each of these components.

The Report Classification Plan

The diagram in Figure 11–1 can help you construct reports that fit your specific need. At the top of the "stairway" are the most formal, full-dress reports. Such reports have a number of pages that come before the text material, just as this book has pages that come before the first chapter. These pages serve useful purposes, but they also dress up the report. Typically, these *prefatory pages,* as they are called, are included when the problem situation is formal and the report is long. The exact makeup of the prefatory pages may vary, but the most common arrangement includes these parts: title fly, title page, letter of transmittal, table of contents, and executive summary. Flyleaves (blank pages at the beginning and end that protect the report) also may be included.

- Figure 11–1 helps you see the range of report forms.

- Long, formal reports are at the top. Prefatory pages dress up these reports.

As the need for formality decreases and the problem becomes smaller, the makeup of the report changes. Although the changes that occur are far from standardized, they follow a general order. First, the title fly drops out. This page contains only the report title, which also appears on the next page. Obviously, the title fly is used primarily for reasons of formality.

- As reports become shorter and less formal, changes occur in this general order.

- The title fly drops out.

Next in the progression, the executive summary and the letter of transmittal are combined. When this stage is reached, the report problem is short enough to be summarized

- The executive summary and the letter of transmittal are combined.

Figure 11–1

**Changes in Report
Makeup as Formality
Requirements and Length
Decrease**

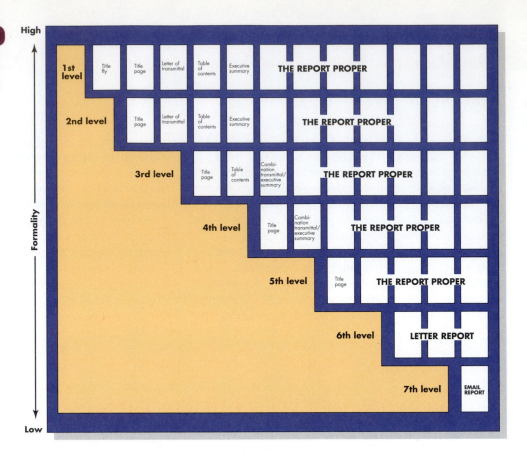

in a short space. As shown in Figure 11–1, the report at this stage has three prefatory parts: title page, table of contents, and combination transmittal letter and executive summary.

At the fourth step, the table of contents drops out. Another step down, as formality and length requirements continue to decrease, the combined letter of transmittal and executive summary drops out. Thus, the report commonly called the *short report* now has only a title page and the report text. The title page remains to the last because it serves as a very useful cover page. In addition, it contains the most important identifying information. The short report is a popular form in business.

Below the short-report form is a form that reinstates the letter of transmittal and summary and presents the entire report as a letter—thus, the *letter report*. And finally, for short problems of more informality, the *email* or memo form is used.

This is a general analysis of report change; it does not cover every report situation. Most reports, however, will fit within the framework of the diagram. Knowledge of the basic relationship of formality and length to report makeup should help you understand and plan reports.

The Report Components

To be able to decide which parts of a long, formal report to include in your reports, you need a basic understanding of each part. This section describes the different report components represented in Figure 11–1.

The first two pages of a long, formal report—the *title fly* and *title page*—contain identification information. As we have said, the title fly contains only the report title; it is included simply to give a report the most formal appearance. The title page, as illustrated on pages 350 and 378, is more informative. It typically contains the title, identification of the writer and reader, and the date.

- Next, the table of contents is omitted.

- The combined letter of transmittal and executive summary drops out, and what is left is the basic short report.

- The next step is the letter report, and the step after that is the email report.

- The title fly contains only the title.

Creating a Report Title with the 5 Ws and 1 H

As this chapter says, the five Ws (*who, what, where, when, why*) and one H (*how*) can help you craft a report title that is precise and informative.

For example, to generate a title for a recommendation report about sales training at Nokia, you might ask yourself . . .

Who?   Nokia

What?   Sales training recommendations

Where?   Implied (Nokia regional offices)

When?   2012

Why: Implied (to improve sales training)

How?   Studied the company's sales activities

From this analysis would come the title "Sales Training Recommendations for Nokia," with the subtitle "Based on a 2012 Study of Company Sales Activities."

Although constructing title pages is easy, composing the title is not. In fact, on a per-word basis, the title requires more time than any other part of the report. A good title efficiently and precisely covering the contents. For completeness of coverage, consider building your title around the five Ws: *who, what, where, when,* and *why*. Sometimes *how* may be important as well. You may not need to use all the Ws, but they can help you check the completeness of your title. Remember that a good title is concise as well as complete, so be careful not to make your title so long that it is hard to understand. A subtitle can help you be both concise and complete, as in this example: "Employee Morale at Florida Human Resource Offices: Results from a 2011 Survey."

- Construct the title to make it describe the report precisely.
- As a checklist, use *who, what, where, when, why,* and sometimes *how*.

In addition to displaying the report title, the *title page* identifies the recipient and the writer (and usually their titles and company names). The title page also contains the date unless it is already in the title of the report. Your word-processing program probably includes some attractive templates for title pages, like those used in the sample reports in this chapter.

- The title page includes the title, identification of the reader and writer, and the date.

As the label implies, the *letter of transmittal* is a letter that transmits the report. In less formal situations, the report can be transmitted orally or by email. Whatever the case, you should think of the transmittal as a personal message from the writer to the reader, with much the same contents you would use if you were handing the report over in a face-to-face meeting with the recipient. Except in cases of extreme formality, you should use personal pronouns (*you, I, we*) and conversational language.

- The transmittal message is a personal message from the writer to the reader.

The transmittal letters on pages 351 and 379 illustrate the usual structure for this component. Begin with a brief paragraph that says, essentially, "Here is the report." Briefly identify the report's contents and purpose and, if appropriate, its authorization (who assigned the report, when, and why). Focus the body of the message on the key points of the report or on facts about the report that could be useful for your readers to know. If you are combining the transmittal message with the executive summary, as represented by the third and fourth levels of Figure 11–1, here is where you will include that summary. At the end of the message, you should provide a pleasant and/or forward-looking comment. You might express gratitude for the assignment, for example, or offer to do additional research.

If your short report goes much over five pages (or 1,500 words), you might consider including a brief *table of contents*. This, of course, is a listing of the report's contents. As Chapter 10 points out, it is the report outline in finished form, with page numbers to indicate where the parts begin. The formatting should reflect the report's structure, with main headings clearly differentiated from subheadings. The section titles should state each part's contents clearly and match the report's headings exactly. The table of contents may also include a list of illustrations (or, if long, this list can stand alone). If

- A table of contents is helpful for longer reports.

Figure 11–2

Diagram of the Executive Summary in Indirect and Direct Order

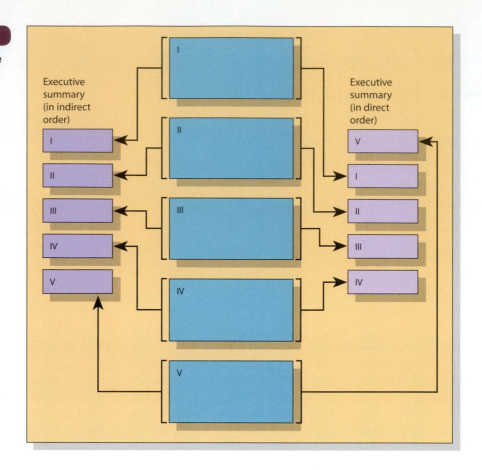

a separate table of contents would be too formal, you can just list the topics that your report will cover in its introductory section.

The *executive summary* (also called *synopsis, abstract, précis,* or *digest*) is the report in miniature. For some readers it serves as a preview to the report, but for others—such as busy executives who may not have time to read the whole report—it's the only part of the report they will read. Because of this latter group of readers, the summary should be self-explanatory; that is, readers shouldn't have to read other parts of the report in order to make sense of the summary. As pointed out previously, whether the executive summary is one of the prefatory parts (as illustrated on page 381), is included in the transmittal message (see page 351), or is part of the report proper will depend on how long and how formal the report is.

You construct the executive summary by reducing the parts of the report in order and in proportion. You should clearly identify the topic, purpose, and origin of the report; state at least briefly what kind of research was conducted; present the key facts, findings, and analysis; and include the main conclusions and recommendations. While some writers follow this order, which usually matches the order of the report contents, others put the conclusions and recommendations first and then continue with the other information. Figure 11–2 shows the difference between these two structures, and Figures 11–3 and 11–4 give examples. Whichever order you choose, the executive summary will need to be a masterpiece of economical writing.

It may be desirable to include other report components not discussed here—for example, a copy of the message that authorized the report, various appendices containing supplementary material, a glossary, or a bibliography. These have not been considered in Figure 11–1 or this discussion because their inclusion depends on the information needs of the reader, not on the report's length and formality. As with any writing task, you will need to decide what parts to provide given the facts of the situation and your readers' preferences.

- The executive summary summarizes the report.

- It includes the report purpose research highlights, and key findings.

- It may be either direct or indirect.

- Additional parts may also be necessary.

Figure 11–3

An Executive Summary in Direct Order

EXECUTIVE SUMMARY

To enhance the performance of Nokia's salespeople, this report recommends adding the following topics to Nokia's sales training program:

- Negative effects of idle time
- Projection of integrity
- Use of moderate persuasion
- Value of product knowledge

Supporting these recommendations are the findings and conclusions drawn from a five-day observational study of 20 productive and 20 under-performing salespeople. The study also included an exit interview and a test of the salesperson's product knowledge.

The data show that the productive salespeople used their time more effectively than did the under-performing salespeople. Compared with the latter, the productive salespeople spent less time being idle (28% vs. 53%). They also spent more time in contact with prospects (31.3% vs. 19.8%) and more time developing prospects (10.4% vs. 4.4%).

Observations of sales presentations revealed that productive salespeople displayed higher integrity, used pressure more reasonably, and knew the product better than under-performing salespeople. Of the 20 productive salespeople, 16 displayed images of moderately high integrity (Group II). Under-performing group members ranged widely, with 7 in Group III (questionable) and 5 each in Group II (moderately high integrity) and Group IV (deceitful). Most (15) of the productive salespeople used moderate pressure, whereas the under-performing salespeople tended toward extremes (10 high pressure, 7 low pressure). On the product knowledge test, 17 of the productive salespeople scored excellent and 3 fair. In the other group, 5 scored excellent, 6 fair, and 9 inadequate.

Figure 11–4

An Executive Summary in Indirect Order

EXECUTIVE SUMMARY

Midwestern Research associates was contracted to study the performance of Nokia's salespeople. A team of two researchers observed 20 productive and 20 under-performing salespeople over five working days. The study also included an exit interview and a test of the salesperson's product knowledge.

The data show that the productive salespeople used their time more effectively than did the under-performing salespeople. Compared with the latter, the productive salespeople spent less time in idleness (28% vs. 53%). They also spent more time in contact with prospects (31.3% vs. 19.8%) and more time developing prospects (10.4% vs. 4.4%).

Observations of sales presentations revealed that productive salespeople displayed higher integrity, used pressure more reasonably, and knew the product better than under-performing salespeople. Of the 20 productive salespeople, 16 displayed images of moderately high integrity (Group II). Members of the under-performing group ranged widely, with 7 in Group III (questionable) and 5 each in Group II (moderately high integrity) and Group IV (deceitful). Most (15) of the productive salespeople used moderate pressure, whereas the under-performing salespeople tended toward extremes (10 high pressure, 7 low pressure). On the product knowledge test, 17 of the productive salespeople scored excellent and 3 fair. In the other group, 5 scored excellent, 6 fair, and 9 inadequate.

On the basis of these findings, this report recommends adding the following topics to Nokia's sales training program:

- Negative effects of idle time
- Projection of integrity
- Use of moderate persuasion
- Value of product knowledge

CHARACTERISTICS OF SHORTER REPORTS

The shorter report forms (those at the bottom of the stairway) are by far the most common in business. These are the everyday working reports—those used for the routine information reporting that is vital to an organization's communication. Because these reports are so common, our study of report types begins with them.

● The shorter report forms are the most common in business.

Little Need for Introductory Information

Most of the shorter, more informal reports require little or no introductory material. These reports typically concern day-to-day problems. Their lives are short; that is, they are not likely to be kept on file very long. They are intended for only a few readers, and these readers know the problem. They are likely to need little introduction.

● Shorter reports have little need for introductory material.

This is not to say that all shorter reports have no need for introductory material. Some do need it. In general, however, the need is likely to be small.

Determining what introductory material is needed is simply a matter of answering one question: What does my reader need to know before reading the information in this report? In very short reports, an incidental reference to the problem, authorization of the investigation, or the like provides sufficient introduction. In extreme cases, however, you may need a detailed introduction comparable to that of the more formal reports.

Reports need no introductory material if their very nature explains their purpose. This holds true for personnel actions. It also holds true for weekly sales reports, inventory reports, and some progress reports.

Predominance of the Direct Order

Because the shorter reports usually solve routine problems, they are likely to be written in the direct order. By *direct order* we mean that the report begins with its most important information—usually the conclusion and perhaps a recommendation.

● The shorter reports usually begin directly— with conclusions and recommendations up front.

Many routine reports are submitted from the field on hand-held devices like the one shown here.

FRANK & ERNEST©

Source: Reprinted by permission of *United Features Syndicate, Inc.*

Business writers use this order because they know that their readers' main concern is to get the information needed to make a decision, so they present this information right away.

The form that the direct order takes in longer reports is somewhat different. The main findings will be somewhere up front—either in the letter of transmittal, executive summary, or both—but the report itself may be organized indirectly. The introduction will present the topic and purpose of the report, but the actual findings may not come out until the body sections, and their fullest statement will usually appear in the conclusions or recommendations section. As one moves down the structural ladder toward the more informal and shorter reports, however, the need for the direct order in the report itself increases. At the bottom of the ladder, the direct order is more the rule than the exception.

Because order is so vital a part of constructing the shorter reports, we'll compare the direct arrangement and the indirect arrangement in more detail.

The direct arrangement presents the most important part of the report right away. This is the answer—the achievement of the report's goal. Depending on the problem, the direct beginning could consist of a summary of facts, a conclusion, a recommendation, or some combination of summary, conclusion, and recommendation.

Whatever background information is needed usually follows the direct opening. As noted previously, sometimes little or none is needed in everyday, routine reports. Next come the supporting facts and analyses, organized logically (as described in Chapter 10).

Illustrating this arrangement is the following beginning of a report on a short and simple personnel problem:

> Clifford A. Knudson, administrative assistant in the accounting department, should be fired. This conclusion has been reached after a thorough investigation brought about by numerous incidents during the past two months. . . .
>
> The recommended action is supported by this information from his work record for the past two months:
>
> • He has been late to work seven times.
> • He has been absent without acceptable excuse for seven days.
> • Twice he reported to work in a drunken and disorderly condition.
> • [And so on].

In contrast, the indirect arrangement begins with whatever introductory material is needed to prepare the reader for the report. Then comes the presentation of facts, with analyses when needed. Next comes the part that accomplishes the goal of the report. If the goal is to present information, this part summarizes the information. If the goal is to reach a conclusion, this part reviews the analyses and draws a conclusion from them. And if the goal is to recommend an action, this part reviews the analyses, draws a conclusion, and, on the basis of the conclusion, makes a recommendation.

Using the simple personnel problem from the last example, the indirect arrangement would appear like this:

• Longer reports are often indirect, but that is because the letter of transmittal and/or executive summary can foreground the findings.

• The direct order gives the main message first.

• Then it gives background (if any), facts, analyses, conclusions, and recommendations (if any).

• The indirect order has this sequence: introduction/background, facts and analyses, conclusions, and recommendations (if any).

Numerous incidents during the past two months appeared to justify an investigation of the work record of Clifford A. Knudson, administrative assistant in the accounting department.

The investigation of his work record for the past two months revealed these points:

- He has been late to work seven times.
- He has been absent without acceptable excuse for seven days.
- Twice he reported to work in a drunken and disorderly condition.
- [And so on, to the conclusion that Knudson should be fired].

Deciding whether to use the direct order is best based on a consideration of your readers' likely use of the report. If your readers need the report conclusion or recommendation as a basis for an action that they must take, directness will speed their effort by enabling them to quickly receive the most important information. If they have confidence in your work, they may choose not to read beyond this point and to proceed with the action that the report supports. Should they desire to question any part of the report, however, the material is there for their inspection.

On the other hand, if there is reason to believe that it would be better for your readers to arrive at the conclusion or recommendation only after a logical review of the analysis, you should organize your report in the indirect order. This arrangement is especially preferable when you will be recommending something that you know your readers will not favor or want to hear. Presenting the supporting data before the recommendation will get them ready to accept your solution to the report problem.

- Use the direct order when the conclusions or recommendations will serve as a basis for action.

- Use the indirect order when you believe you should take readers through the analysis before presenting your conclusions or recommendations.

TECHNOLOGY IN BRIEF

Templates Help Writers Format Reports

Templates for word processors help report writers format reports attractively and consistently. Once a template is selected, report writers can concentrate on the report message and let the software create a professional-looking document.

These templates contain margin settings, font type and size for headings and text, and even graphic layouts. Most are designed to help the writer present a report that communicates its message with a professional look. Although standard templates can be used, some companies design their own templates to give their reports consistent and distinct images.

Templates readily set up both short and long reports. In addition to the installed templates, you can find more on the Web. Here you see some templates installed in Microsoft's Word 2007 and one of the templates open in Word.

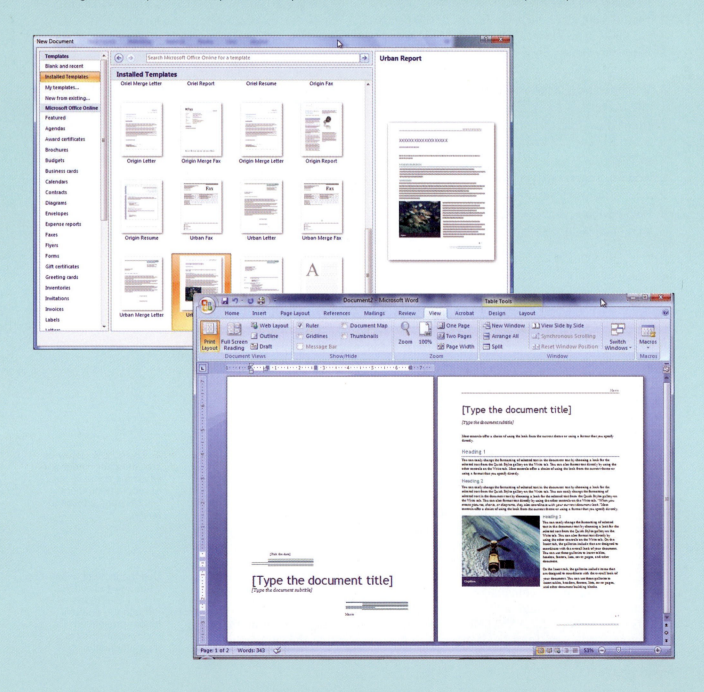

More Personal Writing Style

Although the writing for all reports is much the same, the writing in shorter reports tends to be more personal. That is, the shorter reports are likely to use the personal pronouns *I, we,* and *you* rather than only the third person.

There are several reasons for this tendency toward personal writing in shorter reports. In the first place, short-report situations usually involve personal relationships. Such reports tend to be from and to people who know each other and who normally address each other informally when they meet. In addition, shorter reports are apt to involve personal investigations and to represent the observations, evaluations, and analyses of their writers. Finally, shorter reports tend to deal with day-to-day, routine problems. These problems are by their very nature informal. It is logical to report them informally, and personal writing tends to produce this informal effect.

As explained in Chapter 10, your decision about whether to write a report in personal or impersonal style should be based on the situation. You should consider the expectations of those who will receive the report. If they expect formality, you should write impersonally. If they expect informality, you should write personally. If you do not know their preferences, you should consider the formality of the situation. Convention favors impersonal writing for the most formal situations. Like the direct and indirect order, the question of personal versus impersonal style involves the matter of relating to the reader in ways that he or she prefers.

Most short-report situations, however, are likely to justify personal writing because of their relatively routine nature.

- Personal writing is common in the shorter report forms.

- The reasons are that the shorter reports usually (1) involve personal relationships, (2) include personal interpretations, and (3) are routine.

- Write impersonally when (1) your reader prefers it and (2) the situation is formal.

Less Need for a Structured Coherence Plan

A long, formal report usually needs what we call a "structured coherence plan"—a network of introductions, conclusions, and transitions that guide the reader through the report. Creating such a plan means giving the overall report an overview and a conclusion, providing the same for the individual sections, and devising transitions that bridge each section to the next. Such devices enable the reader to know, at every point, where he or she is in the report and how the current section is related to the overall goal of the report.

Short reports, because they are short, generally do not need an elaborate coherence plan. Readers will not need many reminders of what they just read or previews of what they're about to read. The report introduction (which should contain an overview), clear headings, and brief transitional devices (such as "Second," "next," and quick references to previous points) will usually be sufficient to keep readers on track.

- Shorter reports need fewer overviews, conclusions, and transitional devices.

FORMS OF SHORTER REPORTS

As noted earlier, the shorter report forms are by far the most numerous and important in business. In fact, the three forms represented by the bottom three steps of the stairway in Figure 11–1—short reports, letter reports, and email (or memo) reports—make up the bulk of the reports written.

- Following is a review of the more popular shorter reports.

The Short Report

One of the more popular of the less formal report forms is the short report. Representing the fifth step in the diagram of report progression, this report consists of only a title page and text. Its popularity may be explained by the middle-ground impression of formality that it conveys. Including the most important prefatory part gives the report at least some appearance of formality. And it does this without the tedious work of preparing the other prefatory pages. The short report is ideally suited for the short but somewhat formal problem.

- The short report consists of a title page and the report text.

A Mid-length Recommendation Report. This report, with its title page and combined letter of transmittal and executive summary, would fall on the fourth level of Figure 11–1. It is organized indirectly in order to prepare the reader for the students' recommendations.

Increasing Student Patronage at Kirby's Grocery

Title makes the topic and purpose of the report clear.

April 28, 2010

Prepared for:

Mr. Claude Douglas, Owner
Kirby's Grocery
38 Lance Avenue
Crestview, IN 45771

Page uses an attractive but simple template.

Prepared by:

Kirsten Brantley, Business Communication Student
College of Business
P. O. Box 236
Metropolitan University
Crestview, IN 45770-0236

(continued)

METROPOLITAN UNIVERSITY

College of Business, P. O. Box 236, Crestview, IN 45770-0236
Phone: (421)555-5555, Fax: (421)555-5566

May 28, 2010

Mr. Claude Douglas
Kirby's Grocery
319 Lance Avenue
Crestview, IN 45771

Dear Mr. Douglas:

As you requested, our Business Communication class conducted a study to determine ways to increase Metropolitan University students' awareness of Kirby's Grocery and attract more students to your store. This report presents the results.

Identifies the project and "hands over" the report.

To gather our information, we first interviewed assistant manager Bradley Vostick, who leads the store's marketing efforts. To get a veteran customer's perspective, we also interviewed our professor, Beth Rawson, a long-time Kirby's customer. Next we researched MU campus events, publications, transportation issues, demographics, and the Lance Avenue area surrounding Kirby's. Finally, the class did walkthroughs of Kirby's to gain firsthand reactions to the store as well as quantified data in the form of an exit survey on overall reactions to Kirby's.

We found that Kirby's is part of a niche market that offers a wide variety in a small space, much like the surrounding Lance Avenue area. Given these findings, we recommend the following:

- Targeting health-conscious, older MU students who enjoy shopping.
- Using Internet-based media to reach these potential customers.
- Focusing on your strengths to make these shoppers aware of the experience that is Kirby's Grocery.

Combines letter of transmittal and executive summary.

Thank you for allowing us the opportunity to do this real-world project. We enjoyed learning about your store and hope that our research will bring many more MU students to Kirby's Grocery.

Ends with goodwill comments.

Sincerely,

Kirsten Brantley

Kirsten Brantley
For Professor Beth Rawson's Business Communication Class

Increasing Student Patronage at Kirby's Grocery

Introduction

Objective of the study

Kirby's Grocery is a full-service neighborhood grocery store in the vicinity of Metropolitan University. With its appealing range of products and proximity to the university, its potential to attract student customers is great. Yet according to a survey conducted by Professor Beth Rawson's Fall 2009 Business Communication class, only one in three MU students has ever shopped at Kirby's. As a follow-up to this study, our Business Communication class conducted research to determine how Kirby's might attract more MU student shoppers. This report presents our results and recommendations.

Opening gives the context and purpose in a nutshell.

Research methods

The research for this study was conducted in three phases:

■ Phase One: As preparation for the observational part of the study, the class gathered supplemental information about a variety of topics related to Kirby's. It was carried out by groups of three to four students, with each group focusing on one of seven particular "beats." These beats included MU campus events and publications, MU's demographic information, and interviews with Kirby's customers and Bradley Vostick of Kirby's.

■ Phase Two: This was the main phase of our research. For this phase, 13 pairs of students visited Kirby's during the week of March 7–14, 2010, to gather observational data. Each pair consisted of an observer, who made oral comments about any and all aspects of the store, and a recorder, who recorded these observations. On average, each pair spent approximately 40 minutes in the store, and each pair was required to make a small purchase. At the end of their visits, the observers all completed exit surveys to quantify their overall reactions to Kirby's and to provide some demographic information about themselves.

■ Phase Three: Given our findings, we gathered information to develop our recommendations for marketing Kirby's to MU students.

Detailed description of research builds confidence in the validity of the findings.

The following sections describe the study participants, present the observational data, and offer our recommendations.

Preview adds to report's coherence.

Demographics of the Participants

Previews table.

While our observer number of 13 was very small in comparison to the entire MU population of 33,000, it was actually a fairly representative sample in terms of student diversity, gender, and age. The following table shows how these observers compared to the general MU population.

Lone table in nonacademic report does not need to be numbered.

Demographics of Store Observers		
	Study Participants	**MU Population**
Diversity	77% (11) European-American, 23% (2) African American	71.5% European-American, 12% African American
	77% (11) US citizens	83% US citizens
Gender	47% (6) female, 54% (7) male	54.2% female, 45.8% male
Average Age	24	23

Report includes a special section to further support the validity of the findings.

Paragraphs interpret and elaborate on the table.

Compared to the MU population, our sample of 13 was relatively diverse. In addition to including 2 African-American participants, it included 2 non-US participants, one from Russia and one from Sweden.

The gender ratios were also relatively close. The MU population is 54.2% female to 45.8% male. Again, our observers came very close to this ratio, with 47% female and 54% male.

The average age for full-time students at Midwestern University is 23. The average age of our observers was 24. This included a student who is 41 years old, but even without this outlier, our group closely represented the average MU student in terms of age.

In addition, all students in our class (26) were juniors and seniors at MU, and most were business students with some background in marketing. Through class discussion, we were able to bring our collective perspective as MU students to bear on our observations.

Qualitative Findings

Section preview adds coherence.

This section presents the qualitative results from our observational research, broken down into two categories: perceived strengths and perceived weaknesses.

2

(continued)

Perceived Areas of Strength

Three main positive reactions came out of this research:

- Students were impressed with the wide product variety.
- Students were happy to see organic and health food products.
- Kirby's employees provided excellent service to their customers.

Section starts with a helpful summary.

Product variety was seen as the strongest asset of Kirby's. Of the 13 observation surveys, 11 mentioned the large variety of products offered by Kirby's as a positive aspect of the store. Overall, the consensus was that the selection offered by Kirby's in such a small space was impressive. This was especially apparent in the beer aisle, which received the most praise of any section in Kirby's for a selection that rivals that of specialty stores.

Organic and health food products also received a large positive reaction, being mentioned by almost two-thirds of the observers. While health may not be the main concern of the stereotypical college student, it is certainly appealing to older students. Since the average age of an MU student is 23, it is likely that Kirby's organic and health food selection can also be a strong selling point for getting more students into the store.

Paragraphs present and interpret data.

Customer service was the third most mentioned positive aspect of Kirby's. During observations, employees at Kirby's were consistently happy and helpful. The long-time customer we interviewed, Professor Rawson, cited Kirby's excellent customer service as one of the reasons she continues to shop there. She commented that the employees of Kirby's care more about their customers' shopping experiences than employees of other stores, and the data compiled by the class supported this claim.

Not only were students asked if they needed help, but they also observed that employees knew their customers, which makes the customer feel more like family than just another person wanting groceries. When observers made their small purchases, they noted that they were treated in the same friendly manner as customers who were checking out with filled carts.

Perceived Areas of Weakness

Two main negative reactions came out of this research:

- Students observed a number of dirty shelves and floors.
- The placement of some products was confusing.

Another helpful summary.

About half of the observers made note of areas of Kirby's that seemed to need a good cleaning, with specific remarks about stained floor tiles, produce on the floor

3

(continued)

that hadn't been swept up, and dusty shelves. This was a significant negative for several student shoppers, as dirty floors and shelves don't shed the kindest light on the products for sale, especially when compared to the seeming sterility of larger grocery stores like Kroger's and Biggs.

More helpful data and interpretation.

But the largest negative reaction to Kirby's concerned the random-seeming placement of a variety of products. Examples included cakes next to whole turkeys, freezers next to greeting cards, and hot peppers next to candies. This confused student shoppers because the placement of some of these products did not fall in line with the aisle signs. While Kirby's is a smaller grocery store and is certainly impacted by the limits of space, the class as a whole felt that more could be done to eliminate this random product layout.

Quantitative Findings

Introduces figure.

The following figure contains the composite results of the 13 exit surveys. Students were asked to rate their Kirby's experience on a variety of topics on a scale of one to five, with one being the worst and five being the best. The observers took the survey immediately after completing their walkthroughs of the store.

Lone figure in a nonacademic report does not need to be numbered.

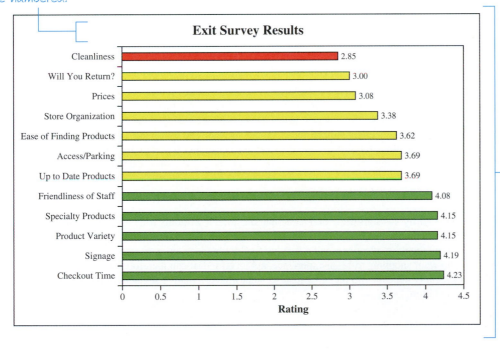

Exit Survey Results

Category	Rating
Cleanliness	2.85
Will You Return?	3.00
Prices	3.08
Store Organization	3.38
Ease of Finding Products	3.62
Access/Parking	3.69
Up to Date Products	3.69
Friendliness of Staff	4.08
Specialty Products	4.15
Product Variety	4.15
Signage	4.19
Checkout Time	4.23

Rating

Visual, textual, and numerical elements work together to present specific findings clearly.

4

Paragraphs help reader interpret the findings.

These results simply quantify what was discovered in the qualitative phase of the observation. Checkout time, friendliness, variety, and specialty products were the highest scorers, while cleanliness received the lowest rating. Still, Kirby's scored above average in all categories, which is an important positive result.

Along these lines, the "Will You Return?" score is encouraging. Though it may seem negative when compared to the other reactions, a score of 3.00 is actually above average. This means that with only one trip through Kirby's, there is a better than average chance that students will return to purchase groceries.

Prices ranked just above "Will You Return?" at 3.08. Again, its comparative rating is low, but it is still above average. Price is an important consideration for student shoppers, and Kirby's has a tough time competing with prices offered by the nearby Kroger store, its main competitor. Even given these two facts, though, observers felt that Kirby's had slightly better than average prices, which is another important positive result.

Interesting to note are the scores for Signage, Ease of Finding Products, and Store Organization. Signage was rated high at 4.19, while Ease of Finding Products was rated lower (3.62), and Store Organization even lower (3.38). These numbers correlate with the student shopper reactions. While Kirby's has excellent signs, some of the aisles are difficult to find because of displays blocking them, and the placement of certain products adjacent to other unrelated products only increases this confusion.

Recommendations

Summarizes main impression and leads into recommendations.

From our compiled data on Kirby's Grocery, we learned that Kirby's is not a large, faceless grocery chain that slashes prices in order to make up for poor customer service and variety. Rather, Kirby's is a niche-market store that offers wide variety and excellent service for a decent price. Yet only about a third of the MU population is aware of its excellent variety and customer service. The following recommendations for Kirby's aim to increase its customer base through targeted awareness-raising advertising that focuses on promoting the store's uniqueness.

Whom to Target

Since Kirby's is something of a niche-market store, it will only truly appeal to a niche market of MU students. Kirby's should focus on attracting those shoppers who want variety, healthy selections, and a familiar feel. Kirby's is a grocery store for people who want shopping to be an experience, not an errand. It can therefore be especially appealing to the more mature, somewhat alternative segment of the MU population.

5

(continued)

How to Reach Them

While Kirby's has been using the MU Coupon Book for campus ads and participating in campus events such as Welcome Week, the store's marketing efforts do not take advantage of a key fact about modern students: they are heavy users of Internet-based social-networking sites. To cite one study, over 85% of college students use Facebook, where they spend over six hours per week and which they visit over six times per day (Ana M. Martinez Aleman and Katherine Link Wartman, *Online Social Networking on Campus,* 2008). Such sites thus represent a huge opportunity for Kirby's to reach its student market.

You can take advantage of these sites in two main ways: creating a profile page and advertising.

Creating a Free Online Profile

Kirby's currently has an attractive website, but it is unlikely to receive many student visitors. Free social-networking websites such as Facebook (*www.facebook.com*) and MySpace (*www.myspace.com*) can help you build a student fan base and generate a buzz about your store. These sites require only that one register in order to create and post a "profile" page. A company can feature its major selling points, photos, directions, customer testimonials, special promotions, a link to its website, and other material on its profile page, which these sites' templates makes relatively easy to do.

Once the page is posted, users can learn about your site using the search engine. If they like what they see and want to be kept updated about special offerings, they can click a link to include Kirby's in their network. This will place your logo and name on their own profile pages, where all their friends will see it and perhaps consider becoming "fans" of Kirby's themselves. In this way, your store can take advantage of "viral marketing."

Using Paid Advertising

It is also possible to advertise on social-networking websites. For example, with Facebook, the most popular site among college students, you can use an easy-to-complete template to design a brief advertisement. You can then target the ad to the Facebook users you want to reach—for example, those between the ages of 18 and 25 in the MU area. When those users visit their Facebook pages, they will see your ad displayed in the right-hand Ad Space.

The cost for these ads varies depending on whether you choose to pay per view (how many times users see your ad) or per click (how many times users click on your ad to go visit your website or profile), as well as on what other advertisers targeting the same market are offering to pay. The current minimum cost per click is $.01; the current minimum cost per 1,000 views is $.02, though these low "bids" will not be accepted if other businesses are competing for the same space with the same users. Facebook's "Ads: Campaign Cost and Budgeting" page can help you plan your campaign given whom you want to reach and what you are willing to spend each day.

6

Recent research supports claim.

Shows knowledge of the store's current efforts.

Briefly citing sources in the text is acceptable in an informal report.

Links make it easy to go learn more.

Paragraphs adapt research to reader's needs.

(continued)

What to Say

Kirby's advertisements need to focus on promoting the store's variety and uniqueness to the MU student body. It has to separate itself from the idea that it is simply another grocery store and emphasize that it encompasses a wide variety in a small space, just like the eclectic Lance Avenue area in which it is located.

Promotions for students should focus on its wide beer selection (perhaps mentioning the exact number of domestic and imported brands offered), on its organic and health food selection, and on its unique products such as sushi and fresh peanut butter. These advertisements will not appeal to the entire MU student body, but it will make the students who are likely to value Kirby's strengths aware of these and give them a desirable, convenient alternative to shopping at a giant superstore.

Conclusion

We found that Kirby's Grocery offers a shopping experience that simply cannot be found at larger grocery stores. The variety and customer service are top notch, and this makes a trip to Kirby's an experience rather than an errand (perhaps this could be a slogan?). By taking advantage of the large-scale marketing opportunities offered by the Internet, Kirby's can raise awareness of its many positive qualities among the MU student body well beyond what it currently achieves with its current outreach efforts. This strategy is also appealing because it can greatly increase Kirby's visibility at no to very little cost.

Paragraphs use main findings to suggest a marketing strategy.

Ending wraps up report in a positive way.

7

Like most of the less formal report forms, the short report may be organized in either the direct or indirect order. But the direct order is more common. This plan usually begins with a quick summary of the report, including and emphasizing conclusions and recommendations. Such a beginning serves much the same function as the executive summary of a long, formal report.

It is usually in the direct order, beginning with the conclusions.

Following the summary comes whatever introductory remarks are needed. Sometimes this part is not needed. Usually, however, a single paragraph covers the facts of authorization and a brief statement of the problem and its scope. After the introductory words come the findings, analyzed and applied to the problem. From all this comes a conclusion and, if needed, a recommendation. These last two elements—conclusions and recommendations—should be restated or summarized at the end even though they also appear in the beginning summary. Omitting them would end the report too abruptly.

The introduction comes next, then the findings and analyses, and finally the conclusion.

The mechanics of constructing the short report are much the same as the mechanics of constructing the more formal, longer types. The short report uses the same form of title page and page layout. Like the longer reports, it uses headings. But because of the short report's brevity, the headings rarely go beyond the two-division level. In fact, one level of division is most common. Like any other report, the short report uses graphics, an appendix, and a bibliography when these are needed.

Letter Reports

The second of the more common shorter report forms is the letter report—that is, a report in letter form. Letter reports are used primarily to present information to persons outside the organization, especially when the information is to be sent by mail or fax. For example, a company's written evaluation of its experience with a particular product may be presented in letter form and sent to the person who requests it. An outside consultant may write a report of analyses and recommendations in letter form. Or the officer of an organization may report certain information to the membership in a letter.

Letter reports are reports in letter form.

Typically, the length of letter reports is three or four pages or less. But no hard-and-fast rule exists on this point.

They usually cover short problems.

As a general rule, letter reports are written personally, using *I*, *you*, and *we* references (see page 349). Exceptions exist, of course, such as letter reports for very important readers—for example, a company's board of directors. Otherwise, the writing style recommended for letter reports is much the same as that recommended for any other reports. Certainly, clear and meaningful expression is a requirement for all reports.

They are usually written in personal style.

Letter reports may be in either the direct order or the indirect order. If such a report is to be mailed, there is some justification for using the indirect order. Because such reports arrive unannounced, it is logical to begin with a reminder of what they are, how they originated, and the like. A letter report written to the membership of an organization, for example, might appropriately begin as follows:

Most of them begin indirectly.

As authorized by your board of directors last January 6, this report reviews member company expenditures for travel.

If a letter report is begun in the direct order, a subject line is appropriate. The subject line consists of identifying words appearing at the top of the letter, usually right after the salutation. Although subject lines may be formed in many ways, one acceptable version begins with the word *subject* and follows it with words that identify the situation. As the following example illustrates, this identifying device helps overcome any confusion that the direct beginning might otherwise create.

Subject lines are appropriate to begin them.

Subject: Travel Expenditures of Association Members, Authorized by Board of Directors, January 2012

Association members are spending 11 percent more on travel this year than they did the year before. Current plans call for a 10 percent increase for next year.

Regardless of which type of beginning is used, the organizational plans for letter reports correspond to those of longer, more formal types. Thus, the indirect-order letter

The organizational plans of letter reports are much like those of longer reports.

A Letter Report. This direct-order letter report compares two hotels for a meeting site. Organized by the bases used in determining the choice, it evaluates the pertinent information and reaches a decision. The personal style is appropriate.

INTERNATIONAL COMMUNICATION ASSOCIATION

314 N. Capitol St. NW • Washington, DC 20001 • 202.624.2411

October 26, 2010

Professor Helen Toohey
Board of Directors
International Communication Association
Thunderbird American Graduate School of International Management
15249 N. 59th Ave.
Glendale, AZ 85306-6000

Dear Professor Toohey:

Subject: Recommendation of Convention Hotel for the 2011 Meeting

The Hyatt Hotel is my recommendation for the International Communication Association meeting next October. The Hyatt has significant advantages over the Marriott, the other potential site for the meeting.

Direct order emphasizes decision.

First, the Hyatt has a definite downtown location advantage, and this is important to convention goers and their spouses. Second, accommodations, including meeting rooms, are adequate in both places, although the Marriott's rooms are more modern. Third, Hyatt room costs are approximately 15 percent lower than those at the Marriott. The Hyatt, however, would charge $500 for a room for the opening session. Although both hotels are adequate, because of location and cost advantages the Hyatt appears to be the better choice from the members' viewpoint.

Preview describes the structure of the upcoming information.

Origin and Plan of the Investigation

In investigating these two hotels, as was my charge from you at our October 7 board meeting, I collected information on what I believed to be the three major factors of consideration in the problem. First is location. Second is adequacy of accommodations. And third is cost. The following findings and evaluations form the basis of my recommendation.

Bases of comparison (factors) permit hotels (units) to be compared logically.

The Hyatt's Favorable Downtown Location

The older of the two hotels, the Hyatt is located in the heart of the downtown business district. Thus it is convenient to the area's major mall as well as the other downtown shops. The Marriott, on the other hand, is approximately nine blocks from the major shopping area. Located in the periphery of the business and residential area, it provides little location advantage for those wanting to shop. It does, however, have shops within its walls that provide for virtually all of the guests' normal needs. Because many members will bring spouses, however, the downtown location does give the Hyatt an advantage.

Short sentences and transitional words increase readability and move ideas forward.

(continued)

Alternate placement of topic sentences offers pattern variety.

Board of Directors   -2-   October 26, 2010

Adequate Accommodations at Both Hotels

Talking headings (all noun phrases) help interpretation.

Both hotels can guarantee the 600 rooms we will require. Because the Marriott is newer (built in 2006), its rooms are more modern and, therefore, more appealing. The 9-year-old Hyatt, however, is well preserved and comfortable. Its rooms are all in good condition, and the equipment is up to date.

The Marriott has 11 small meeting rooms and the Hyatt has 13. All are adequate for our purposes. Both hotels can provide the 10 we need. For our opening session, the Hyatt would make available its Capri Ballroom, which can easily seat our membership. It would also serve as the site of our presidential luncheon. The assembly facilities at the Marriott appear to be somewhat crowded, although the management assures me that their largest meeting room can hold 600. Pillars in the room, however, would make some seats undesirable. In spite of the limitations mentioned, both hotels appear to have adequate facilities for our meeting.

Paragraph length shows good organization.

Lower Costs at the Hyatt

Text analysis relates facts to problem.

Both the Hyatt and the Marriott would provide nine rooms for meetings on a complimentary basis. Both would provide complimentary suites for our president and our executive director. The Hyatt, however, would charge $500 for use of the room for the opening session. The Marriott would provide this room without charge.

Convention rates at the Hyatt are $169 for singles, $179 for double-bedded rooms, and $229 for suites. Comparable rates at the Marriott are $189, $199, and $350. Thus, the savings at the Hyatt would be approximately 15 percent per member.

Cost of the dinner selected would be $35 per person, including gratuities, at the Hyatt. The Marriott would meet this price if we would guarantee 600 plates. Otherwise, they would charge $38. Considering all of these figures, the total cost picture at the Hyatt is the more favorable one.

In conclusion, while both hotels would meet our needs, the significant location and cost advantages of the Hyatt make it the more desirable site for next year's conference.

Repetition of the key point provides a sense of closure.

Sincerely,

Willard K. Mitchell

Willard K. Mitchell
Executive Secretary

report follows its introduction with a logical presentation and analysis of the information gathered. From this presentation, it develops a conclusion or recommendation, or both, in the end. The direct-order letter report follows the initial summary-conclusion-recommendation section with whatever introduction is appropriate. For example, the direct beginning illustrated previously could be followed with these introductory sentences:

> These are the primary findings of a study authorized by your board of directors last January. Because they concern information vital to all of us in the Association, they are presented here for your confidential use.

- Supporting facts and analyses follow an appropriate introduction.

Following such an introduction, the report would present the supporting facts and their analyses. The writer would systematically build the case supporting the opening comment. With either the direct or indirect order, a letter report may close with whatever friendly, goodwill comment fits the occasion.

Email Reports

- Email (internal written messages) is widely used.

As we noted in Chapter 5, email is a heavily used form of written communication in business. Although often directed toward outside parties, email dominates internal written communication. That is, email is written by and to people in an organization.

- Most email messages are written informally.

Because email is primarily communication between people who know each other, it is usually informal. In fact, many are hurried, casual messages. Some email, however, is formal, especially reports directed to readers high in the administration of the organization.

- Some resemble letters and follow letter form.

As indicated in Chapter 5, some email messages resemble letters. Others, however, are more appropriately classified as reports. Most email reports tend to be more formal and factual. In fact, some email reports rival the longer forms in formality. Like the longer forms, they may use headings to display content and graphics to support the text. For the longer email reports, writers will often choose to make the report itself an attached document and use the email message as a transmittal message.

- Some are reports. Such email reports tend to be formal, factual, and problem related.

Because they are largely internal, email reports tend to be problem-solving reports. They are intended to help improve operations, lay the groundwork for an innovation, solve a problem, or otherwise assist decision makers in the organization.

A Progress Report in Email Form. This email report summarizes a sales manager's progress in opening a new district. It begins with the highlights—all a busy reader may need to know. Organized by three categories of activity, the factual information follows. The writer–reader relationship justifies a personal style.

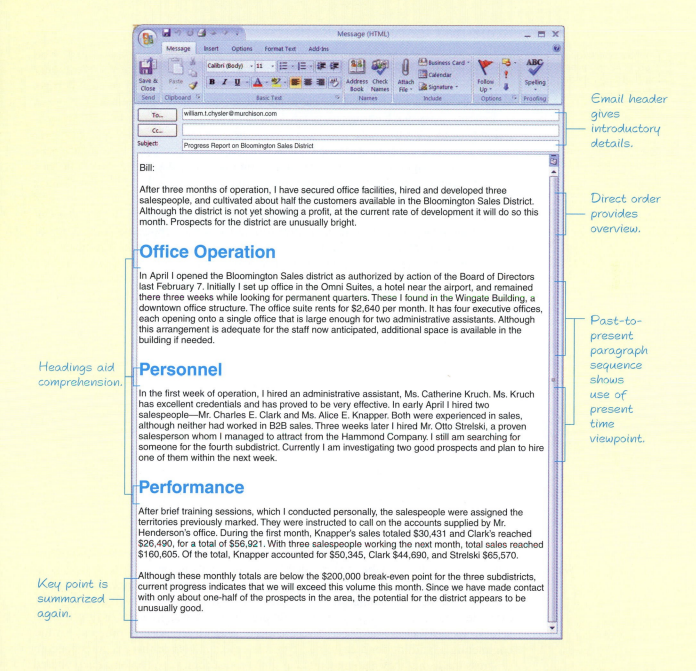

Email header gives introductory details.

To... william.t.chysler@murchison.com

Cc...

Subject: Progress Report on Bloomington Sales District

Bill:

Direct order provides overview.

After three months of operation, I have secured office facilities, hired and developed three salespeople, and cultivated about half the customers available in the Bloomington Sales District. Although the district is not yet showing a profit, at the current rate of development it will do so this month. Prospects for the district are unusually bright.

Office Operation

Headings aid comprehension.

In April I opened the Bloomington Sales district as authorized by action of the Board of Directors last February 7. Initially I set up office in the Omni Suites, a hotel near the airport, and remained there three weeks while looking for permanent quarters. These I found in the Wingate Building, a downtown office structure. The office suite rents for $2,640 per month. It has four executive offices, each opening onto a single office that is large enough for two administrative assistants. Although this arrangement is adequate for the staff now anticipated, additional space is available in the building if needed.

Past-to-present paragraph sequence shows use of present time viewpoint.

Personnel

In the first week of operation, I hired an administrative assistant, Ms. Catherine Kruch. Ms. Kruch has excellent credentials and has proved to be very effective. In early April I hired two salespeople—Mr. Charles E. Clark and Ms. Alice E. Knapper. Both were experienced in sales, although neither had worked in B2B sales. Three weeks later I hired Mr. Otto Strelski, a proven salesperson whom I managed to attract from the Hammond Company. I still am searching for someone for the fourth subdistrict. Currently I am investigating two good prospects and plan to hire one of them within the next week.

Performance

After brief training sessions, which I conducted personally, the salespeople were assigned the territories previously marked. They were instructed to call on the accounts supplied by Mr. Henderson's office. During the first month, Knapper's sales totaled $30,431 and Clark's reached $26,490, for a total of $56,921. With three salespeople working the next month, total sales reached $160,605. Of the total, Knapper accounted for $50,345, Clark $44,690, and Strelski $65,570.

Key point is summarized again.

Although these monthly totals are below the $200,000 break-even point for the three subdistricts, current progress indicates that we will exceed this volume this month. Since we have made contact with only about one-half of the prospects in the area, the potential for the district appears to be unusually good.

TYPES OF SHORT REPORTS

- There are many types of short reports. Here we cover five common types.

Because organizations depend heavily on short reports, there are many varieties, written for many different purposes. We cover some of the most common types here, but the form they take will vary from company to company. Also, most companies will have developed certain unique report forms for their special purposes. Always study your company's ways of reporting before contributing a report yourself.

Routine Operational Reports

- Routine operational reports keep others informed about company operations.

The majority of the reports written within companies are routine reports that keep supervisors, managers, and team members informed about the company's operations. These can be daily, weekly, monthly, or quarterly reports on the work of each department or even each employee. They can relate production data, information on visits to customers, issues that have arisen, or any kind of information that others in the organization need on a routine basis.

- The form and contents will vary, depending on the company.

The form and contents of these reports will vary from company to company and manager to manager. Many will be submitted on predesigned forms. Others may not use forms but will follow a prescribed format. Still others will be shaped by the writer's own judgment about what to include and how to present it.

The nature and culture of the organization can heavily influence the forms taken by these reports. For example, one innovative format for weekly reporting is the 5-15 report.[1] The name comes from the fact that it is intended to be read in 5 minutes and written in 15 minutes. Its typical three-part contents are a description of what the employee did that week, a statement about the employee's morale and that of others he or she worked with, and one idea for how to improve operations. Clearly, this format would work best in an organization where employees have nonroutinized jobs and the management values the employees' opinions.

- These reports should deliver the required information efficiently, clearly, and on time.

Whatever the form, the routine operational report should convey clearly and quickly what readers most need and want to know about the time period in question. It is also an opportunity for you, the writer, to showcase your ability to gather needed information on deadline.

- Your word-processing program's template macro or merge feature can save you time on routine reports.

When using standardized forms for periodic reports, you should consider developing a template macro or merge document with your word processing software. A macro would fill in all the standard parts for you, pausing to let you fill in the variable information. A template merge document would prompt you for the variables first, merging them with the primary document later. However standardized the process, you will still need to be careful to gather accurate information and state it clearly.

Progress Reports

- Progress reports review progress on an activity.

You can think of an internal progress report as a routine operational report except that it tends to be submitted on an as-needed basis, and, as its name implies, it focuses on progress toward a specific goal. If you are working on a project for an external client, you may also need to submit progress reports to show that your work is on track. For example, a fund-raising organization might prepare weekly summaries of its efforts to achieve its goal. Or a building contractor might prepare a report on progress toward completing a building for a customer. Typically, the contents of these reports concern progress made, but they also may include such related topics as problems encountered or anticipated and projections of future progress.

- Most are informal and narrative; some are formal.

Progress reports follow no set form. They can be quite formal, as when a contractor building a large manufacturing plant reports to the company for whom the plant is being built. Or they can be very informal, as in the case of a worker reporting by email to his or her supervisor on the progress of a task being performed. Some progress

---

[1] For a fuller description and history, see Joyce Wycoff, "5-15 Reports: Communication for Dispersed Organizations," *Innovation Network,* InnovationNetwork, 2001, Web, 15 June 2009.

reports are quite routine and structured, sometimes involving filling in blanks on forms devised for the purpose. Most, however, are informal, narrative reports, as illustrated by the example on page 363.

As with most reports, you have some choice about the tone to use when presenting your information. With progress reports, you want to emphasis the positive if possible. The overall message should be "I (or we) have made progress." The best way to convey this message confidently, of course, is to be sure that you or your team has in fact made some progress on the issue at hand.

Problem-Solving Reports

Many short reports are *problem-solving reports*. These reports help decision makers figure out what to do any time a problem arises within an organization—which is often. For example, a piece of equipment may have broken down, causing mayhem on the production line. Or employees may have gotten hurt on the job. Or, less dramatically, a company procedure may have become outdated, or a client company may want to know why it's losing money. If we define *problem* as an issue facing the company, we could include many other scenarios as well—for example, whether or not a company should adopt flextime scheduling or what location it should choose for a new store. Whatever the context, the writer of a problem-solving report needs to gather facts about the problem or issue, define it clearly, research solutions, and recommend a course of action.

Like progress reports, problem-solving reports can be internal or external. Internal problem-solving reports are usually assigned, but sometimes employees may need to write unsolicited problem-solving reports—for example, if they must recommend that a subordinate be fired or if they feel that a change in procedures is necessary. External problem-solving reports are most often written by consulting companies for their clients. In these cases, the report is the main product that the client is paying for.

A type of problem-solving report that deserves special attention is a *feasibility study*. For these reports, writers study several courses of action and then propose the most feasible, desirable one. For instance, you might be asked to compare Internet service providers and recommend the one that suits the company's needs and budget best. Or you might investigate what type of onsite childcare center, if any, is feasible for your organization. Sometimes feasibility studies are not full-blown problem-solving reports. They may offer detailed analysis but stop short of making a recommendation. The analysis they provide nevertheless helps decision makers decide what to do.

In fact, many short reports that help solve company problems may not be complete problem-solving reports. Decision makers who assign research reports may not want recommendations. They may want only good data and careful analysis so that they can formulate a course of action themselves. Whether you are preparing an internal or external report, it is important to understand how far your readers want you to go toward proposing solutions.

You have some latitude when deciding how direct to make your opening in a problem-solving report. If you believe that your readers will be open to any reasonable findings or recommendations, you should state those up front. If you think your conclusions will be unexpected or your readers will be skeptical, you should still state your report's purpose and topic clearly at the beginning but save the conclusions and recommendations until the end, after leading your readers through the details. Figure 11–5, a pattern for a problem-solving report used by the U.S. military, follows this more indirect route. As always, try to find out which method of organization your readers prefer.

While they usually propose action, problem-solving reports are not true persuasive messages. Because they have either been assigned or fall within an employee's assigned duties, the writer already has a willing reader. Furthermore, the writer has no obvious personal stake in the outcome the way he or she does with a persuasive message. However, when writing a problem-solving report, especially one that makes recommendations, you do need to show that your study was thorough and your reasoning sound. The decision makers may not choose to follow your advice, but your work, if it is carefully performed, still helps them decide what to do and reflects positively on you.

- With progress reports, you want to emphasize the positive.

- Problem-solving reports help decision makers choose a course of action.

- These reports can be internal or external.

- A special type of problem-solving report is a feasibility study.

- Whether or not you should make a recommendation will depend on the situation.

- You will need to decide whether to use a direct or indirect approach.

- Even though they are not overtly persuasive, problem-solving reports still need to be convincing.

Figure 11–5

Military Form For Problem-Solving Report

DEPARTMENT OF THE AIR FORCE
HEADQUARTERS UNITED STATES AIR FORCE
WASHINGTON, DC 20330

REPLY TO
ATTN OF   AFODC/Colonel Jones

SUBJECT   Staff Study Report

TO:

PROBLEM

1. --
--.

FACTORS BEARING ON THE PROBLEM

2. Facts.

a.--
--.

b--.

3. Assumptions.

4. Criteria.

5. Definitions.

DISCUSSION

6. ---.

7. ---.

8. ---.

CONCLUSION

9. ---.

ACTION RECOMMENDED

10. --.

11. ---.

JOHN J. JONES, Colonel, USAF   2 Atch
Deputy Chief of Staff, Operations   1. -----------------------
                                         2. -----------------------

Audit Reports

- Audit reports hold organizations accountable to certain standards.

- The most common type is the financial audit written by accounting firms.

- Short financial audits follow a standardized format.

- Longer audit reports vary in form and contents.

- The Sarbanes-Oxley Act has increased the need for audit reports.

A specialized type of report is the audit report. This type is written to hold an organization accountable to certain standards that they are required to meet. While audit reports can be assessments of an organization's finances, operations, or compliance with the terms of a contract, and while they can be written by internal or external auditors, the most common type of audit report is that written by an accounting firm to verify the truthfulness of a company's financial reports. These reports are short and standardized. You can find such reports in almost any corporate annual report. But accounting firms are also contracted to write longer, less standardized reports that help the company assess its financial health and adopt better accounting practices. Long-form audit reports vary greatly in their makeup, but, like other reports, they tend to include an executive summary followed by an introduction, methodology and standards used, findings, discussion, and conclusions or recommendations.

As Chapter 10 notes, the Sarbanes-Oxley Act of 2002 has had an enormous impact on financial recordkeeping and reporting. This new set of federal regulations was prompted by the financial scandals of Enron, WorldCom, and other publicly traded companies. To restore and maintain investor confidence in companies' financial reports, Sarbanes-Oxley requires companies to have not only their financial records but also their financial reporting practices audited by external parties. As an employee, you may find yourself having to write reports related to this kind of audit. If you are an accountant working for an independent accounting firm, you may well find yourself involved in writing such audit reports.

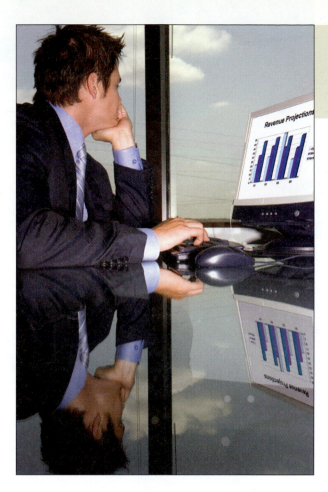

Meeting Minutes

Many short reports in business, especially internal ones, do not recommend or even analyze. Instead, they describe. Trip reports, incident reports, and the like are meant to provide a written record of something that happened. Whatever their type and specific purpose, they all share the need to be well organized, easy to read, and factual. Perhaps the most common of these reports is minutes for meetings. We thus single them out for special emphasis.

Minutes provide a written record of a group's activities and decisions, a history that includes announcements, reports, significant discussions, and decisions. Minutes might report who will do what and when, but they are primarily a summary that reports the gist of what happened, not a verbatim transcript. Minutes include only objective data; their writer carefully avoids using descriptive adjectives such as *brilliant, intelligent, reasonable,* and so on. However, if the group passes a resolution that specific wording be officially recorded, a writer would then include it. Accurate minutes are important because they can have some legal significance as to whether decisions are binding.

The physical form is typically a memo or email, but the layout varies among organizations. Basically, it should enable the reader to easily focus on the content as well as easily retrieve it. Some writers find that numbering items in the minutes to agree with the numbering of a meeting's agenda helps in retrieving and reviewing specific discussions. Subheads are often useful, especially if they are bold, italicized, or underlined to make them stand out. Most important, minutes should provide an adequate record. Additional advice on writing minutes can be found on page 451.

- Meeting minutes are a common type of descriptive report.

- Minutes provide a written record of a group's activities

- Most are distributed by memo or email, but their layout varies among organizations.

Illustration of Meeting Minutes

Minutes of the Policy Committee
Semiannual Meeting
November 21, 2010, 9:30–11:30 A.M., Conference Room A

Present: Megan Adami (chair), D'Marie Simon, DeAnne Overholt, Michelle Lum, Joel Zwanziger, Rebecca Shuster, Jeff Merrill, Donna Wingler, Chris Woods, Tim Lebold (corporate attorney, guest).

Absent: Joan Marian, Jeff Horen (excused), Leonna Plummer (excused)

Complete preliminary information provides a good record.

Minutes

Minutes from the May 5, 2010, meeting were read and approved.

Subheads help readers retrieve information.

Announcements

Chris Woods invited the committee to a reception for Milton Chen, director in our Asia region. It'll be held in the executive dining room at 3:00 P.M. tomorrow. Chris reminded us that Asia is ahead of the United States in its use of wireless technology. He suggested that perhaps we can get an idea of good policies to implement now.

Old Business—Email Policy

Joel Zwanziger reported the results of his survey on the proposed new email policy. While 16 percent of the employees approved implementing the policy, 84 percent were not opposed. The committee approved a January 1, 2011, implementation subject to its distribution to all employees before the Christmas break.

Discussions are summarized and actions taken are included.

Web Surfing Policy

D'Marie Simon reported on the preliminary findings of other companies in the industry. Most have informal guides but no official policies. The guidelines generally are that all surfing must be related to the job and that personal surfing should be done on breaks. The committee discussed the issue at length. It approved a policy that reflects the current general guidelines.

Temp Policy

Tim Lebold presented the legal steps we need to take to get our old and new temporary employees to sign a nondisclosure agreement prior to working here as we've been discussing in relation to a new temp policy. The committee directed Tim to begin the process so that the policy could be put in force as soon as possible.

New Business—Resolution

Michelle Lum proposed that a resolution of thanks be added to the record recognizing Megan for her terrific attention to detail as well her clear focus on keeping the committee abreast of policy issues. It was unanimously approved.

Resolutions often include descriptive language.

Next Meeting

The next meeting of the committee will be May 3, 2011, from 9:30–11:30 A.M. in Conference Room A.

Closing gives reader complete needed facts.

Adjournment

The meeting was adjourned at 11:25 A.M.

Respectfully submitted,

Megan Adami
Megan Adami

Signing signifies the minutes are an official record.

The sample on page 368 illustrates typical minutes. The following preliminary, body, and closing items may be included.

- Typical minutes include common preliminary, body, and closing items.

Preliminary Items

- Name of the group.
- Name of the document.
- Type of meeting (monthly, emergency, special).
- Place, date, and time called to order.
- Names of those attending including guests (used to determine if a quorum is present).
- Names of those absent and the reasons for absence.

Body Items

- Approval of the minutes of previous meeting.
- Meeting announcements.
- Old business—Reports on matters previously presented.
- New business—Reports on matters presented to the group.

Closing Items

- Place and time of the next meeting.
- Notation of the meeting's ending time.
- Name and signature of the person responsible for preparing the minutes.

When you are responsible for preparing the minutes of a meeting, you can take several steps to make the task easier. First, get an agenda in advance. Use it to complete as much of the preliminary information as possible, including the names of those expected to attend. If someone is not present, you can easily move that person's name to the absentee list. You might even set up a table in advance with the following column headings to encourage you to take complete notes.

- Preparing ahead of time makes the job easier and encourages more complete notes.

Topic	Summary of Discussion	Action/Resolution

Bear in mind that meeting minutes, while they look innocent enough, almost always have political implications. Because minutes are the only tangible record of what happened, meeting participants will want their contributions included and cast in a positive light. Since you cannot record every comment made, you will need to decide which ones to include, whether or not to credit a particular speaker, how to capture the group's reaction, and so forth. Use your good judgment when translating a rich oral event into a written summary.

- Be aware of the political dimension of minutes.

COMPONENTS OF LONG, FORMAL REPORTS

Although not as numerous as short reports, long, formal reports are highly important in business. They usually concern major investigations, which explains their length. They are usually prepared for high-level executives, which explains their formality.

- Long, formal reports are important in business.

The advice in Chapter 10 about creating reports—determining the purpose, gathering information, and choosing a logical structure adapted to the readers—applies to long, formal reports as well. Here we will focus on the special components of formal reports, emphasizing their purpose and design. For any given case, you will need to decide which of these components to use and whether or not your report or proposal needs different special elements. As always, the facts of the situation and your readers' preferences should be your guide.

- See Chapter 10 for advice about developing the contents and structure of reports.

The first parts in your case are the prefatory pages described on pages 339–342. As noted in Figure 11–1, the longest, most formal reports contain all of these. As the length of the report and the formality of the situation decrease, certain changes occur. As the report architect, you must decide which arrangement of prefatory parts meets the length and formality requirements of your situation.

- The need for the prefatory parts decreases as reports become shorter and less formal.

Since these elements have already been discussed, the rest of this section will focus on other components.

The Report Introduction

- The introduction should prepare the readers.

The introduction is the first section of the report itself. Its purpose is to prepare the readers to receive the report. Whatever will help achieve this goal is appropriate content. Giving your readers what they need makes a good first impression and displays good you-viewpoint.

- In deciding what to include, consider all likely readers.

In determining what content is appropriate, consider all the likely readers of your report. As we noted earlier, the readers of many shorter reports are likely to know the problem well and have little or no need for an introduction. But such is not often the case for longer reports. Many of these reports are prepared for a large number of readers, some of whom know little about the problem. These reports often have long lives and are kept on file to be read in future years. Your introductory material will need to prepare both immediate and later readers.

Playing possum doesn't work anymore, Stephmeyer! I want that report by 5 P.M. or else!

Source: © Tribune Media Services. All rights reserved. Reprinted with permission.

Determining what should be included is a matter of judgment. You should ask yourself what you would need or want to know about the problem if you were in your readers' shoes. As the report's author, you know more about the report than anyone else. So you will work hard not to assume that readers have the same knowledge of the problem that you do. In selecting the appropriate information, you would do well to use the following checklist of likely introduction contents. Remember, though, that it is only a checklist. Only on rare occasions, such as in the longest, most complex reports, would you include all the items.

● Then determine what those readers need to know. Use the following checklist.

Origin of the Report. The first part of your introduction might well include a review of the facts of authorization. Some writers, however, leave this part out. If you decide to include it, you should present such facts as when, how, and by whom the report was authorized; who wrote the report; and when the report was submitted. Information of this kind is particularly useful in reports that have no transmittal message.

● 1. Origin—the facts of authorization.

Problem and Purpose. A vital part of almost every report is a statement of its problem. The *problem* is the need that prompted the investigation.

● 2. Problem—what prompted the report.

You may state the problem of your report in three ways, as shown in Chapter 10. One common way is to word it in the infinitive form: "To determine standards for corporate annual reports." Another common way is to word it as a question: "What retail advertising practices do Springfield consumers disapprove of?" Still another way is to word it as a declarative statement: "Company X wants to know the characteristics of the buyers of Y perfume as a guide to its advertising planning." Any of the three should give your reader a clear picture of the problem your report addresses.

● The problem is commonly stated in infinitive, question, or declarative form.

But the problem statement is not the only sentence you include. You will need to put the problem into context and bring out its significance to your readers. Closely related to *what* you are discussing is *why* you are discussing it. The *purpose* (often called by other names such as *objective, aim, goal*) tells the reason for the report. For example, you might be determining standards for the corporate annual report *in order to streamline the production process*. You will need to weave the what and why of the report together for a smooth flow of thoughts. See the first four paragraphs of the sample formal report for an example (page 382).

● The purpose is the end reason for the report.

Scope. If the scope of your report is not clearly covered in any of the other introductory parts, you may need to include it in a separate part. By *scope* we mean the boundaries of your investigation. In this part of the introduction—in plain, clear language—you should describe what parts of the problem you studied and what parts you didn't.

● 3. Scope—the boundaries of the problem.

Limitations. In some reports, you will need to explain limitations. By *limitations* we mean things that keep your report from being an ideal treatment of the problem. Of course, in reality there is no such thing as an ideal treatment. No real-world problem can be completely explored, and because different writers will approach the same problem differently, what seems complete to one person may not seem complete to another. Everyone understands that no report can provide coverage of a given topic in an absolute sense. But in certain cases, you will want to state explicitly what forms of research were not employed so that your readers will know how to evaluate your information.

● 4. Limitations—anything that limits the report's treatment of the problem.

For example, if time constraints permitted only a quick email survey rather than in-depth interviews of your sources, you would say so. Or if a major source of information was unavailable (perhaps a key informant had left the company or relevant industry reports were too expensive), you would note this limitation in your report.

Be frank in this section but not too negative. State clearly what was not done and why, but do so without apology or such negative wording as "impair" or "compromised the validity of our findings." If you have done a good job with the resources at your disposal, this section of the report can use a directness that shows confidence in the report's usefulness despite its limitations.

The table of contents generator tool in today's word-processing software frees writers from both the physical formatting and the accuracy tasks. Just a few clicks produces and formats the table of contents, along with leaders and page numbers. Additionally, today's generators add links so that those reading the report on the screen rather than on paper can easily navigate to a particular section or page by simply clicking it in the table of contents.

The table of contents generator works with built-in styles, which you use as tags to mark the different levels of headings that will be included in the table of contents. If you are using a standard report template, styles are already incorporated in it. If you are creating your own report from a blank document, you could use predefined styles or define your own styles to create titles, headings, and subheads. Styles provide consistency so that headings at certain levels always appear the same, helping the reader see the relationship of the parts of your report.

Furthermore, if you decide to change the material in your report after you have generated the table of contents, you simply regenerate it to update page numbers with only a few clicks.

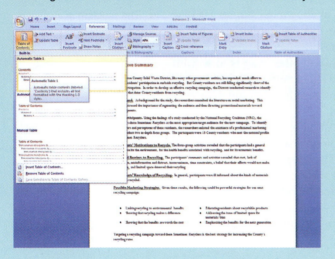

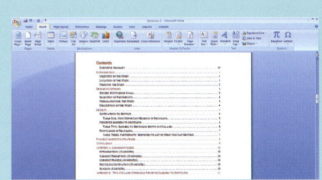

5. History—how the problem developed and what is known about it.

Historical Background. Knowledge of the history of the problem is sometimes essential to understanding the report. Thus, you may need to cover that history in your introduction. You will need to do more than merely list and present facts. You will need to organize and interpret them for the readers. Your general aim in this part is to acquaint the readers with how the problem developed and what has been done about it. Your discussion here should bring out the main issues. It should review what past investigations have determined about the problem, and it should lead to what still needs to be done.

6. Sources and methods—how you got the information.

Sources and Methods of Collecting Information. You usually need to tell the readers how you collected the information in the report. That is, you explain your research methodology and you justify it. You specify whether you used published research, surveys, experiments, or a combination of methods, and you describe the steps you followed. In general, you describe your work in enough detail to allow your readers to judge it. You tell them enough to convince them that your work was done competently.

Sometimes it is necessary to cite sources.

In a simple case in which you gathered published research, you need to say little. If most of your findings came from a few sources, you could name the sources. If you used a large number of sources, you would be wise to note that you used secondary research and refer to the report's bibliography.

More complex research usually requires a more detailed description. If you conducted a survey, for example, you probably would need to explain all parts of the investigation. You would cover how you chose your sample, how you developed the survey, and how you administered it. In fact, you would include whatever detail would be needed to gain the readers' confidence in your work.

Definitions, Initialisms, and Acronyms. If you use words, initialisms, or acronyms that are likely to be unfamiliar to readers of the report, you should define these words and initials. You can do this in either of two ways: you can define each term in the text or as a footnote when it is first used in the report, or you can define all unfamiliar terms in a separate part of the introduction. This part begins with an introductory statement and then lists the terms with their definitions. If the list is long, you may choose to arrange the terms alphabetically.

Report Preview. In very long reports, a final part of the introduction should preview the report structure. In this part you tell the readers how the report will be presented—what topics will be taken up first, second, third, and so on. You also give your reasons for following this plan—that is, you explain the *strategy* of your report. In short, you give your readers a clear picture of the road ahead. As you will see later in the chapter, this part of the introduction is a basic ingredient of the coherence plan of the long report. An illustration of a report preview appears in the discussion of this plan (pages 374–375).

The Report Body

In the report body, the information collected is presented and related to the problem. Normally, this part of the report comprises most of its content. In a sense, the report body is the report. With the exception of the conclusion or recommendation part, the other parts of the report are attached parts.

Advice presented throughout this book will help you prepare this part of the report. Its organization was discussed extensively in Chapter 10. It is written in accord with the instructions on style presented in Chapter 10 and with the general principles for clear writing presented in the early chapters. It may use the components of the shorter reports already discussed. Any sources used must be appropriately noted and documented as illustrated in Appendix E. It uses good presentation form as discussed in Appendix B and elsewhere, and it follows the guidelines for use of figures and tables discussed in Chapter 12. In short, writing this major section of the long, formal report will require virtually all your organizing, writing, and formatting skills.

The Ending of the Report

You can end your report in any of a number of ways: with a summary, a conclusion, a recommendation, or a combination of the three. Your choice depends on the purpose of your report. You should choose the way that enables you to satisfy that purpose.

Ending Summary. When the purpose of the report is to present information, the ending is logically a summary of the major findings. There is usually no attempt to interpret at this point. Informational reports often have minor summaries at the end of the major sections. When this arrangement is followed, the ending summary basically justs restates these summaries.

You should not confuse the ending summary with the executive summary. The executive summary is a prefatory part of the report; the ending summary is a part of the

- More complex research requires a thorough description.

- 7. Definitions of unfamiliar words, acronyms, or initialisms used.

- 8. Preview—a description of the route ahead.

- The report body presents and analyzes the information gathered.

- Preparing this part will employ much of the advice in this book.

- Reports can end in various ways.

- Informational reports usually end with a summary of the major findings.

- The ending summary is not as complete as the executive summary.

report text. Also, the executive summary is more complete than the ending summary. The executive summary reviews the entire report, usually from the beginning to the end. The ending summary reviews only the highlights of the report.

Conclusions.

- Reports that seek an answer end with a conclusion.

- The structure of the conclusion varies by problem.

Conclusions. Some reports must do more than just present information. They must analyze the information in light of the problem; and from this analysis, they must reach a conclusion. Such reports typically end with this conclusion.

The makeup of the conclusion section varies from case to case. In problems for which a single answer is sought, the conclusion section normally reviews the preceding information and analyses and, from this review, arrives at the answer. In problems with more than one goal, the report plan may treat each goal in a separate section and draw conclusions in each section. The conclusion section of such a report might well summarize the conclusions previously drawn. There are other arrangements. In fact, almost any plan that brings the analyses together to reach the goals of the report is appropriate.

- Include recommendations when the readers want or expect them.

Recommendations. When the goal of the report is not only to draw conclusions but also to present a course of action, a recommendation is in order. You may organize it as a separate section following the conclusion section, or you may include it in the conclusion section. Regardless, if you have several recommendations, you may want to bullet them for easy reading. In some reports, the conclusion is the recommendation— or at least a logical interpretation of it. Whether you include a recommendation should be determined by whether the readers want or expect one.

Appended Parts

- Add an appendix or a bibliography when needed.

Sometimes you will need to include an appendix, a bibliography, or both at the end of the report. Whether you include these parts should be determined by need.

- The appendix usually contains auxiliary information.

Appendix. The appendix, as its name implies, is a tacked-on part. You use it for supplementary information that supports the body of the report. Possible appendix contents are questionnaires, working papers, summary tables, additional references, and other reports.

- Visuals that directly support the report belong in the text of the report.

As a rule, the appendix should not include the charts, graphs, and tables that directly support the report. These should be placed in the body of the report where they can support the findings. Because it is not convenient for readers to look to the appendix for the facts they need, put in the appendix only those graphics that are too large or complex to insert into the body of the report.

- Include a bibliography if you make heavy use of published sources.

Bibliography. When your investigation makes heavy use of published sources, you normally include either footnotes, a bibliography, or both. The construction of these is described in Appendix E of this book.

THE STRUCTURAL COHERENCE PLAN

- Longer reports need extra structural coherence devices.

As we have noted, the writing in the longer reports is much like the writing in the shorter ones. In general, the instructions given in earlier chapters apply to the longer reports. But the longer reports have one writing need that is not present in the shorter ones—the need for a structural coherence plan.

- These are a network of explanations, introductions, summaries, and conclusions.

By *structural coherence plan* we mean a network of explanations, introductions, summaries, and conclusions that guide the reader through the report. Of course, you will also employ the devices for coherent writing discussed in Chapters 3 and 4. But because of the formal report's length, your reader will probably need additional help relating the parts of the report to each other or keeping track of where he or she is in the report. A structural coherence plan provides this extra help. Although you should

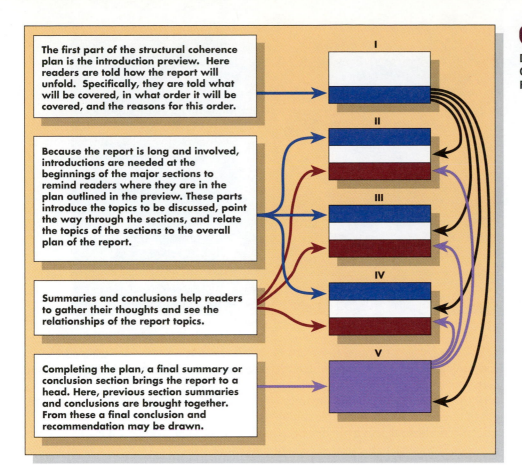

The first part of the structural coherence plan is the introduction preview. Here readers are told how the report will unfold. Specifically, they are told what will be covered, in what order it will be covered, and the reasons for this order.

Because the report is long and involved, introductions are needed at the beginnings of the major sections to remind readers where they are in the plan outlined in the preview. These parts introduce the topics to be discussed, point the way through the sections, and relate the topics of the sections to the overall plan of the report.

Summaries and conclusions help readers to gather their thoughts and see the relationships of the report topics.

Completing the plan, a final summary or conclusion section brings the report to a head. Here, previous section summaries and conclusions are brought together. From these a final conclusion and recommendation may be drawn.

not use its components mechanically, it is likely to follow the general plan illustrated in Figure 11–6.

The coherence plan begins with the report preview in the introduction. The preview covers three things: the topics to be discussed, their order, and the logic of that order. With this information in mind, the readers know how the parts of the report will relate to one another. The following paragraphs do a good job of previewing a report comparing four automobiles to determine which is the best for a company's sales fleet.

- The coherence plan begins with the preview, which describes the route ahead.

> To identify which light car Allied Distributors should buy, this report compares the cars under consideration on the basis of three factors: cost, safety, and performance. Each of these factors is broken down into its component parts, which are applied to the specific models being considered.
>
> Because cost is the most tangible factor, it is examined in the first major section. In this section, the four automobiles are compared for initial and trade-in values. Then they are compared for operating costs, as determined by mileage, oil use, and repair expense. In the second major section, the safety of the four makes is compared. Driver visibility, special safety features, brakes, steering quality, acceleration rate, and traction are the main considerations here. In the third major section, the dependability of the four makes is compared on the basis of repair records and salespersons' time lost because of automobile failure. In the final major section, weights are assigned to the foregoing comparisons, and the automobile that is best suited to the company's needs is recommended.

In addition to the preview in the introduction, the plan uses introductory and summary sections at convenient places throughout the report. Typically, these sections are at the beginning and end of major divisions, but you should use them wherever they are needed. Such sections remind the readers where they are in the report. They tell the

- Introductions to and summaries of the report sections keep readers informed of where they are in the report.

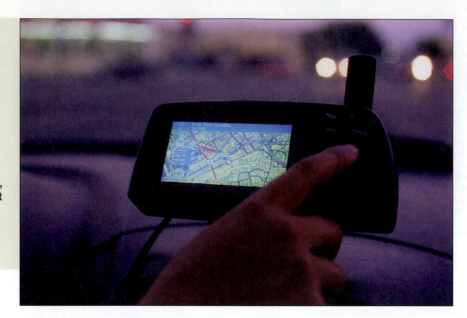

readers where they have been, where they are going, and perhaps why they are going there.

Illustrating this technique is the following paragraph, which introduces a major section of a report. Note how the paragraph ties in with the preceding discussion, which concerned industrial activity in three geographic areas. Note also how it justifies covering secondary areas in the next section of the report.

> Although the great bulk of industry is concentrated in three areas (Grand City, Milltown, and Port Starr), a thorough industrial survey needs to consider the secondary, but nevertheless important, areas of the state. In the rank of their current industrial potential, these areas are the Southeast, with Hartsburg as its center; the Central West, dominated by Parrington; and the North Central, where Pineview is the center of activities.

● The final major section of the report brings together the preceding information and applies it to the goal.

Completing the coherence plan is the final major section of the report. In this section, you achieve the goal of the report. Here you recall from the preceding section summaries all the major findings and analyses. Then you apply them to the problem and present the conclusion. Sometimes you will make recommendations. Thus, you complete the strategy explained in the introduction preview and recalled at convenient places throughout the report.

● Use coherence helpers naturally—when they are needed.

Wisely used coherence helpers can form a network of connections throughout the report. You should keep in mind, however, that these helpers should be used only when they are needed. That is, you should use them when your readers need help in seeing relationships and in knowing where they are and where they are going. If you use them well, they will appear as natural parts of the report story. When paragraphs are combined with sentence and word transitions, as discussed in Chapters 3, 4, and 10, the total plan should guide your readers smoothly and naturally through the report.

THE LONG ANALYTICAL REPORT ILLUSTRATED

Illustrating the long analytical report is the following report written by a communications professional in a waste-management agency. The report's structure includes many of the formal elements described in the preceding pages.

A Long, Formal Report. This report, with its many prefatory parts, exemplifies the top level of Figure 11–1. It is intended not only for the writer's boss but also for those in other recycling agencies and organizations. (Some names, dates, and sources have been fictionalized.)

Behaviors and Perceptions of Sometimes Recyclers in Hamilton County, Ohio

Title fly-for the most formal reports.

Behaviors and Perceptions of Sometimes Recyclers in Hamilton County, Ohio

Title page repeats title...

Prepared for:

Jeanine Smart
Solid Waste Manager
Hamilton County Solid Waste Management District

and adds additional information.

Prepared by:

Michelle Tonney
Community Outreach Coordinator
Hamilton County Solid Waste Management District

March 7, 2010

(continued)

HAMILTON COUNTY ENVIRONMENTAL SERVICES

250 William Howard Taft Road, First Floor, Cincinnati, OH 45219
Ph: 513-946-7777 | Fax: 513-946-7778
Ph: Toll Free in Ohio 1-800-889-0474

March 7, 2010

Jeanine Smart
Solid Waste Manager
Hamilton County Solid Waste District

Dear Jeanine:

Here is an in-depth qualitative study of Hamilton County residents' attitudes toward recycling, which you authorized on 3 December 2009.

We contracted the services of Advanced Marketing, a Cincinnati marketing firm, to conduct the study in collaboration with four representatives from the District. The study revealed positive and negative attitudes that Sometimes Recyclers in Hamilton County have toward recycling. This report describes their attitudes in detail.

In light of these findings, the report identifies several strategies that can be implemented to make our next recycling campaign a success.

Thank you for authorizing this research. I look forward to working with you to create our most effective campaign ever.

Sincerely yours,

Michelle Tonney

Michelle Tonney
Community Outreach Coordinator

Letter of transmittal "hands over" the report.

Contents

Entries match the report headings.

Table of contents previews report structure.

iv

(continued)

Executive Summary

The Hamilton County Solid Waste District of southeastern Ohio has expended much effort to promote residents' participation in curbside recycling. But county residents are still falling significantly short of the desired participation. In order to develop an effective recycling campaign, the District conducted research to identify the factors that deter county residents from recycling.

Identifies context and research goal.

Background. As background for the study, the researchers consulted the literature on social marketing. This literature stressed the importance of segmenting the audience and then directing promotional materials toward specific segments.

Research Methods. Using the findings of a study conducted by the National Recycling Coalition (NRC), the researchers chose Sometimes Recyclers as the most appropriate target audience for the new campaign. To identify the behaviors and perceptions of these residents, the researchers enlisted the assistance of a professional marketing firm to conduct two in-depth focus groups. The participants were 18 county residents who met the national profile for Sometimes Recyclers.

Participants' Motivations to Recycle. The focus-group activities revealed that the participants had a general appreciation for the environment, for the health benefits associated with recycling, and for its economic benefits.

Identifies key sections/ findings.

Presents the report in brief, using the indirect pattern.

Perceived Barriers to Recycling. The participants' comments and activities revealed that cost, lack of information, misinformation and distrust, inconvenience, time constraints, a belief that their efforts would not make a difference, and limited space deterred their recycling.

Participants' Knowledge of Recycling. In general, participants were ill informed about the kinds of materials that can be recycled.

Possible Marketing Strategies. Given these results, the following could be powerful strategies for the District's next recycling campaign:

- Linking recycling to environmental benefits
- Showing that recycling makes a difference
- Showing that the benefits are worth the cost
- Educating residents about recyclable products
- Addressing the issue of limited space for materials/bins
- Emphasizing the benefits for the next generation

Recommendations and conclusion come at the end in the indirect pattern.

Targeting a recycling campaign toward these Sometimes Recyclers is the best strategy for increasing the county's recycling rates.

v

CASE ILLUSTRATION

Behaviors and Perceptions of Sometimes Recyclers in Hamilton County, Ohio

Introduction

Local governments have numerous motivations to increase recycling rates. Some want to reach state-mandated recycling goals while others wish to improve the bottom line and reduce landfill-tipping fees. Still other communities want to add a few more years to the life of their landfill. Almost all local governments recognize the societal benefits of recycling: reduced pollution, saved energy, and a stronger economy. However, local governments have struggled to increase recycling rates in communities since curbside-recycling collection began in the early 1990s.

Identifies context and report problem.

To identify deterrents to recycling, the Hamilton County Solid Waste Division studied county residents participating in two focus groups. The results, presented here, can be used to develop a more effective recycling campaign.

Objective of the Study

Explains and justifies the study's specific purpose.

Promotional materials designed to increase recycling rates can be described as a type of social marketing, the use of marketing techniques to persuade an audience to change their behavior in a way that benefits society as a whole. In their study of social marketing methods, Kotler, Roberto, and Lee stress the importance of segmenting the intended audience and understanding the different segments' behaviors. "This important and often-skipped step explores current knowledge, beliefs, and behaviors of target audiences."[1] Traditional local government advertising, however, directs promotional materials to all residents, failing to segment the audience. By leaving the target audience broad and undefined, local government advertising loses its potential to influence specific segments of the population.

The need to segment the population is especially true in recycling outreach. Portions of the population have different attitudes toward recycling and clearly have different recycling behaviors. This research project thus aimed to build on previous knowledge about one specific segment—Sometimes Recyclers. Understanding the recycling knowledge, beliefs, and behaviors of this significant portion of the population will enable the district to do more effective social marketing.

Location of the Study

The research took place in Hamilton County, Ohio, located in the southeastern corner of the state. According to the U.S. Census, Hamilton County has an estimated 346,790 households in 49 different political jurisdictions, including the City of Cincinnati. The Hamilton County Solid Waste Management District is a county organization, established by state law, responsible for ensuring that the county achieves state mandated goals for recycling and waste reduction. The Solid Waste District includes 48 of the 49 political jurisdictions.

Provides helpful background for secondary readers.

Each of the 48 political jurisdictions decides what type of recycling program to offer their residents. Approximately half of the municipalities contract for recycling services with a private waste hauler, making recycling no additional cost to the residents. Residents in communities with a recycling contract can receive weekly curbside recycling collection without having to pay a monthly fee. However, the other half of the municipalities, mostly townships, has a subscription-based recycling program. Residents in subscription communities have to subscribe for curbside recycling and trash services by calling their waste hauler and paying an additional fee of approximately $3.00 a month.

Citations footnotes are convenient for readers.

---

[1]Philip Kotler, Ned Roberto, and Nancy Lee, *Social Marketing: Improving the Quality of Life* (Thousand Oaks, CA: Sage, 2002) 38, print.

(continued)

Need for the Study

Several studies have been conducted that shed light on local recycling habits:

- 61% of Hamilton County residents say they participate in some sort of recycling.[2]
- In 2008, Hamilton County communities recycled 35,116 tons of material.[3]
- Approximately 60% of the material entering the landfill is recyclable.[4]

Although 61% of residents claim to recycle, the volume of recyclables collected shows that residents fall short of recycling everything possible. Communities with strong, established recycling programs in Hamilton County regularly average 500 to 600 pounds of material set out for recycling per household per year. If 61% of the households recycled at this high volume, the county would recycle 52,885 tons of material a year—or 17,769 tons more than it currently does. The shortfall becomes even more significant considering that 60% of what enters the landfill could be easily recycled through a curbside recycling program.

So why are household recycling rates so low? The National Recycling Coalition (NRC) may have identified the cause. NRC separates people who claim to participate in recycling into two categories: Always Recyclers and Sometimes Recyclers. Always Recyclers consistently recycle everything possible and have difficulty throwing an item away if they know it is recyclable. A Sometimes Recycler, however, only recycles certain materials and has little difficulty throwing an item away if it is inconvenient to recycle. These residents do not see themselves as typical recyclers and recycle only when it is convenient.

Uses research and good logic to justify the study.

Sometimes Recyclers care about health and environmental issues and support charitable causes. According to the NRC research, these residents want to feel connected to others and need to believe that their efforts make a difference. But they are stuck between trial recycling and consistent recycling. They often do not connect the dots between recycling and benefits and therefore do not see the relevance of recycling to them.[5]

Sometimes Recyclers outnumber Always Recyclers by two and half times. Using a national survey estimate, Hamilton County has roughly 257,000 Sometimes Recyclers compared to roughly 107,000 Always Recyclers,[6] making them an ideal audience for an outreach campaign.

Past outreach campaigns of the District did not define a clear target audience but tried to reach all residents of Hamilton County. By choosing a target audience, the District will be able to profile the behaviors of the audience and shape the message to match their behaviors.

---

[2]Tom Hall, *Greater Cincinnati Survey 55, Fall 2006* (Cincinnati, OH: University of Cincinnati Institute for Policy Research, 2007), print.

[3]Data collected through the Residential Recycling Incentive program for the Hamilton County Solid Waste Management District.

[4]Ohio Department of Natural Resources, *State of Ohio Waste Characterization Study* (Columbus, OH: Engineering Solutions and Designs, Inc., 21 April 2007), print.

[5]Joan Cook, "Uncovering the Drivers of Consumer Recycling Behavior," National Recycling Coalition Annual Congress and Expo, Washington, DC, June 2009, presentation.

[6]Cook.

(continued)

Research Methods

The NRC data on Sometimes Recyclers did not provide specific information that could be applied to a local context. To better understand the target audience, the researchers conducted two focus groups with local Sometimes Recyclers. Conducting focus groups allowed the researchers to gather in-depth data about Sometimes Recyclers' recycling behaviors and motivations.

Specific Knowledge Goals

The specific objectives of the study were to

- Identify motivations to recycling
- Understand perceived barriers to recycling
- Understand what would encourage participants to recycle
- Learn where and when the participants find current information about recycling and where they would like to find it in the future

Selection of Participants

Using NRC identifiers for Sometimes Recyclers,[7] the researchers recruited participant groups within the following parameters:

- Homeowners
- Ages 30-55
- Half male, half female
- Support charitable causes through donation or volunteering
- Participate in some type of recycling but not avid recyclers
- Hamilton County, Ohio, residents
- Married
- Voters
- Some college education

Although these identifiers are by no means descriptive of all residents falling into the Sometimes Recyclers group, they enabled researchers to choose residents who met the national profile. Approximately three-fourths (14) of the participants came from townships where residents are charged for recycling services.

Preparation for the Study

Since the District has a limited staff and limited resources, they contracted the service of finding participants to a professional marketing firm in Cincinnati, Advanced Marketing. By reading past surveys conducted locally as well as national research on recycling behavior, the researchers prepared a list of questions for the focus groups and organized the questions in a logical manner. A volunteer moderator not related to the project moderated the focus group so the researchers would

Well-organized research specifics build confidence in the study and help with interpretation of results.

---

[7]Cook.

(continued)

not influence the answers of the participants.[8,9] The researchers met with the moderator beforehand to further refine the questions and tailor them to the objectives of the study. The appendix to this report shows the final draft of the discussion guide for the focus groups.

Description of the Study

On January 30, 2010, the researchers conducted two focus groups, with 10 participants in the first group and 8 participants in the second. The contracted company provided a space with one-sided glass for observation, as well as a recorded DVD of the session for later review.[10]

Each focus group was questioned for approximately one hour and participated in exercises that followed the predetermined outline. The moderator had experience with the level of questioning to ask and with drawing out participants who were not contributing.[11]

After asking general questions, the moderator asked participants to take part in these exercises:

- clipping pictures from magazines that express the primary barriers they perceive to recycling,
- drawing their process involved in recycling,
- writing down all the materials they know are recyclable, and
- reviewing a preprinted list of recyclables to mark items they did not know were recyclable.

Participants were also asked to evaluate a series of slogans related to recycling.

Four staff members from Hamilton County Environmental Services attended the focus group: two from the Solid Waste District and two from the Public Affairs Department. In addition, two staff members of Keep Cincinnati Beautiful also attended because the two organizations coordinate their recycling outreach efforts. All staff members took notes and recorded their observations from behind one-way glass.

Afterward, all the observers met to discuss their impressions, share notes, and reach consensus on the key findings. The next section presents the results.

Results

This section groups the main findings into three categories: participants' motivations to recycle, their perceived barriers to recycling, and their knowledge of recyclable materials.

Section preview adds coherence.

Motivations to Recycle

When asked why they recycle, participants responded, "Recycling is good for the environment" and "I want to take responsibility." Some said they want to save resources. Two participants said that recycling spared their families trash bags and time taking out the trash. Several parents expressed concern about "leaving a better place for their kids" or said "I do it for my children's future."

---

[8]Richard A. Krueger and Mary Anne Casey, *Focus Groups: A Practical Guide for Applied Research*, 4th ed. (Thousand Oaks, CA: Sage, 2009) 87, print.

[9]Frank I. Luntz, "Voices of Victory, Part II: The Makings of a Good Focus Group," *The Polling Report*, 30 May 1994, Web, 18 Feb. 2009.

[10]Krueger and Casey 144, 96.

[11]Luntz.

(continued)

Most participants saw the environmental and health benefits as the biggest motivators to recycle. Several participants commented that they were not "tree-huggers" but they did have a general concern for the environment. One mentioned that he wanted an "opportunity to give back to the environment." Several said recycling is "good for everyone" or "I want to make a difference." Some responded that they didn't want to add to the landfill.

Specific quotes add authenticity.

Several participants mentioned that they collect recyclables for local charities. Their charitable recycling included removing the tabs from aluminum cans and then donating the cans to Children's Hospital and collecting paper for local school and church paper drives.

Many of the participants collect their metal cans to bring to a metal scrap dealer. Almost all participants that described doing this explained that they rinsed and crushed the cans before driving them to the drop-off and receiving compensation for the cans.

Participants were asked to identify the primary benefit of recycling. Table 1 provides a numerical summary of the benefits identified by the two groups.

Previews table.

Table 1: Most Important Benefit of Recycling			
Benefit	Group One	Group Two	Total
Environmental	4	3	7
Economic	1	1	2
Health	3	3	6

At the table shows, many participants listed environmental and health benefits as the most important. (Two participants in group one and one participant in group two did not respond.) In both groups, participants said that environmental and health benefits were connected.

Interprets and adds to table data.

Perceived Barriers to Recycling

Much of the discussion in the focus groups related to barriers to recycling. Participants identified several of these, both in the magazine activity and in response to the question "Is recycling an easy or difficult thing to do? Tell me why."

- **Cost.** One of the most often talked about barriers was the cost of recycling. Participants said, "Why do they charge when they make money?"; "I don't recycle because of the charge"; and "Why does the hauler make you pay?" The perception of recycling is that it is expensive. Several participants used drop-off recycling centers or used their neighbor's recycling bin to avoid paying for curbside recycling. Additionally, the participants felt that waste management companies were profiting from residents' recycling efforts.

- **Lack of Information.** Participants mentioned that they were confused about what is recyclable. One woman said the recycling symbol was hard to locate on the product. Even when she found it, the symbol confused her; she asked "What does PET mean?" Several people also mentioned

(continued)

confusion over the number system, saying "I don't know all the stuff that can be recycled" and "I don't know how much you have to pay for recycling."

- **Myths and Distrust.** One participant commented that "Products made out of recycled materials are not as good," to which several others nodded in response. Another participant expressed disbelief that the material was going to be recycled, saying, "It all ends up in the landfill."

- **Perception That It Is Not Convenient.** This perception was revealed through such comments as "I don't like separating my waste," "I don't like rinsing my cans," "The recycling container is too far away," and "I don't have enough space in my kitchen." Several participants admitted that they were just too lazy. Many also mentioned that it was inconvenient and even "gross" to have to rinse the containers. Another woman mentioned it was too cold to recycle; she didn't want to go to her garage.

- **Time Constraints.** Many participants talked about being too busy to recycle. This was especially true when the participant had children with many activities to attend. They did not think recycling fit easily within their daily routine. Some participants responded by saying "I have too many things on my plate."

- **Perception That It Is Not Important.** Participants made such statements as "I have other things to do," "Sometimes I just don't care," or "I guess I should care more about it." They did not think their effort really made a difference. Participants also wanted a reward for recycling; one said "Make it worth my while," and another said "What's in it for us?"

- **Space Constraints.** Another barrier mentioned was limited space. Comments along these lines were "Why don't they give you an extra bin?" and "The bin is too small."

Helpful, well-organized qualitative data.

Participants made collages from magazines to express what they felt were the biggest barriers to recycling for them. By far the most popular images were of a watch or busy people. Table 2 summarizes the results of this activity.

Tables are numbered consecutively throughout report.

Table 2: Barriers to Recycling Shown in Collages			
	Group One	Group Two	Total
Not enough time	4	7	11
Not enough information	2		2
Materials aren't recyclable	2	1	3
Critters	1		1
Cost	1	1	2
Laziness		1	1

Knowledge of Recycling

The moderator asked participants to list what materials they knew were recyclable on a sheet of paper. After they completed their lists, the moderator then gave them a list of the materials that can currently be recycled in a curbside bin. The moderator asked the participants to circle the materials

Adds helpful procedural details.

387

CASE ILLUSTRATION

(continued)

they did not know were recyclable and place a star by the materials they will start recycling after becoming aware that the item is recyclable. Table 3 shows the results of this exercise broken down according to group. The list of items in the leftmost column is the list that the moderator gave the participants.

Lead-in prepares readers to interpret the table.

Table 3: Participants' Responses to List of Items You Can Recycle				
	Focus Group One		Focus Group Two	
Item	Surprised	Will start recycling	Surprised	Will start recycling
Plastic bottles and jugs				
Glass bottles and jars				
Empty aerosol cans	4	5	8	2
Aluminum cans				
Steel cans			1	1
Tin cans				
Paperboard	1	1	1	1
Junk mail	6	2		1
Envelopes	1			
Magazines	2	2		1
Newspaper				
Cardboard				
Office paper				
Brown grocery bags				
Writing paper				
File folders	2	1		
Post-it notes	3	1		2
Index cards	1	1		2
Phone books		1		3

In both groups, most participants were surprised to learn that aerosol cans are recyclable, and in the first group, 6 of 10 participants were surprised that junk mail is recyclable. Some of the other

Helps readers identify the noteworthy data.

(continued)

CASE ILLUSTRATION

paper items also elicited surprise for being recyclable. This is likely because several years ago these items were not recyclable and the participants remembered those rules.

In general, the "will start recycling" responses were positive; most people who were surprised that something could be recycled said they would start recycling it. But in the second group, only 2 of the 8 people who were surprised that aerosol cans are recyclable said that they would start recycling the cans.

Possible Marketing Strategies

With the information from the focus group, the researchers were able to generate ideas for an outreach campaign targeted toward Sometimes Recyclers. First, the barriers should be addressed and if possible, broken down. Then the campaign needs to appeal to Sometimes Recyclers' motivations for recycling and extend that motivation into further involvement.

- **Linking Recycling to Important Environmental Benefits**

  One of the most significant barriers that the focus group participants discussed was the lack of time for and the inconvenience of recycling. They feel their lives are hectic and that recycling is just one more thing to add to their list of things to do. But do Always Recyclers have less hectic lives than Sometimes Recyclers? What helps Always Recyclers transcend this barrier is the relative importance they place on recycling. A related barrier the participants discussed was not feeling recycling was important or not feeling they were making a difference. Sometimes Recyclers do not make the connection between recycling and the environmental benefits.

  The barrier of not completely believing the importance of recycling ties into one of the chief motivations for recycling that the Sometimes Recyclers expressed: the opportunity to give back to the environment and make a difference. Sometimes Recyclers seem to have a surface belief that recycling betters the environment, but they cannot explain exactly how or why. The outreach campaign needs to overcome these barriers to recycling by connecting recycling to the environmental benefits in ways that Sometimes Recyclers can understand.

- **Showing that Individual Recycling Makes a Difference**

  The moderator asked participants what message would most motivate them to start recycling. Participants wanted to see results. They responded that they wanted to see numbers that expressed the tangible benefits of recycling. They wanted to know that little things do make a difference. They wanted to know what immediate impact their actions made, not just how it would benefit the future of the planet. Including actual numbers on the immediate environmental benefits of recycling could address this need. Making the numbers personally relevant by using a per-household or per-item scale could also help residents understand that their actions can make a difference.

- **Showing that the Benefits Are Worth the Cost**

  Although cost was a major barrier discussed by participants, addressing this issue is difficult on the level of recycling outreach. Individual communities can make the decision to contract the recycling service and lower the cost to help overcome this barrier. Similarly, myths about and distrust of the hauler are difficult barriers to address with an outreach campaign. These barriers would make for interesting future research. How can a community build trust for recycling and

Recommendations are closely tied to research findings.

(continued)

the processes involved? What type of message is needed to convey the idea that while recycling is not free, the benefits outweigh the cost? The answers could help recyclers transcend this barrier.

■ **Educating Residents about Recyclable Products**
Lack of information pertaining to what is recyclable arose as a barrier in several of the collages. The lack of knowledge about what can be recycled was also apparent in the activities involving the list of recyclables. Communities wishing to address this barrier should examine the method by which the message is delivered. For example, would a magnet with a list of recyclables be more effective than a radio advertisement?

■ **Addressing the Space Issue**
Another barrier the participants addressed was lack of space. The 14- or 18-gallon recycling bin provided in local curbside recycling programs seems to be inadequate to contain all of the materials participants could recycle. This concept could explain why many Sometimes Recyclers do not create the volume of recycling that one would expect with an Always Recycler. Once the bin is full, the Sometimes Recycler simply throws the item in the trash while the Always Recycler finds creative solutions for recycling more, such as purchasing an additional container to store recyclables. Communities can address this issue by providing an additional recycling bin at no charge or by providing larger recycling containers, such as 64-gallon wheeled carts.

■ **Emphasizing the Benefits for the Next Generation**
Many participants also mentioned that their children were their primary mode of receiving information about recycling. This is good news for all the environmental educators working so hard to teach children about the importance of recycling. Motivating children to recycle and educating them on what materials can be recycled seems to have permeated their home life. Targeting the participants' motivation to leave a better place for their children combined with continuing environmental education in the schools could be a powerful strategy.

Conclusion

While this study involved a small number of people representing a small portion of the Sometimes Recyclers in Hamilton County, the 18 participants all met the NRC's profile of Sometimes Recyclers, and the research methods used enabled them to express their opinions in depth. The perceptual data collected can be immensely helpful in shaping and directing an outreach campaign.

Research limitations are acknowledged but de-emphasized.

The ultimate goal of the outreach campaign is to motivate Sometimes Recyclers to adopt consistent recycling behaviors and beliefs that elevate them to the Always Recyclers status. They should want to recycle every piece of waste they generate that is recyclable, whether through a curbside program or a community drop-off.

In order to reach the Sometimes Recyclers, a campaign needs to make the connection between their daily recycling actions and benefits to the environment, both immediate and in the future. By identifying the target audience of Sometimes Recyclers and directing outreach efforts specifically toward them, local governments can come one step closer to converting Sometimes Recyclers to Always Recyclers and increasing residential recycling rates.

Ending reiterates main point of the report and uses motivational language to spark action.

Works Cited

Cook, Joan. "Uncovering the Drivers of Consumer Recycling Behavior." National Recycling Coalition Annual Congress and Expo. Washington, DC. June 2009. Presentation.

Hall, Tom. *Greater Cincinnati Survey 55 Fall 2006*. Cincinnati, OH: University of Cincinnati Institute for Policy Research, 2007. Print.

Kotler, Philip, Ned Robert, and Nancy Lee. *Social Marketing: Improving the Quality of Life*. Thousand Oaks, CA: Sage, 2002. Print.

Krueger, Richard A., and Mary Anne Casey. Focus Groups: *A Practical Guide for Applied Research*. 4th ed. Thousand Oaks, CA: Sage, 2009. Print.

Luntz, Frank I. "Voices of Victory, Part II: The Makings of a Good Focus Group." *The Polling Report* 30 May 1994: n. pag. Web. 18 Feb. 2009.

Ohio Department of Natural Resources. *State of Ohio Waste Characterization Study*. Columbus, OH: Engineering Solutions and Designs, Inc., 21 Apr. 2007. Print.

Though not absolutely necessary with citation footnotes, a bibliography is included as a convenience to readers.

(continued)

Appendix: Focus Group Discussion Guide

Introduction (10 minutes)

Have participant make introductions (name, # in household, where you live).
Ask participants to name an idea they have seen that helps the environment.
Transition to recycling; ask them what they know about recycling and its benefits.
First activity: Have participants draw their recycling process using any item as an example. Use very basic pictures to draw cycle from when they are finished with the item to when the recyclables leave their hands.

Current Perception (20 minutes)

"Why is recycling important to you?"
"How long have you been recycling and what influenced you to start?"
"Is recycling an easy or difficult thing to do? Tell me why."
Second activity: "Cut out pictures from a magazine that describe your biggest barrier to recycling. Discuss the pictures."

Current Process (20 minutes)

Third Activity: "On a piece a paper write everything that you know you can recycle."
Pass out list of recyclable material (in normal curbside program) and have participants flag what they are surprised about and what they will start doing now that they know.
"What determines if something goes into your recycling bin?"
"How do you feel when you throw something in the trash that you know is recyclable? Does it invoke any emotions?"
"Where do you keep your recycling bin?"
"How do you go about getting a bin?"
"Do you know where a drop-off is that is close to you?"
"What type of schedule do you have for recycling (weekly, monthly, etc.)?"
"Does anyone recycle at work?"
"What do you know about materials that use recycled content? What do you feel about the quality of those products?"
"What is your impression of how much profit companies make on recycling?"

Recycling Motivation (20 minutes)

Fourth Activity: "Write down the benefit you feel is the most important benefit of recycling—economic, environmental, health."
"Raise your hand if you knew recycling had economic benefits. Can you explain them?"
"Raise your hand if you knew recycling had environmental benefits. Can you explain them?"
"Raise your hand if you knew recycling had health benefits. Can you explain them?"
"What could someone tell you to influence you to start recycling? What would make the message more persuasive?"
"How can recycling be made more relevant to you?"
"Where do you look for recycling information?"

Slogans (5 minutes)

Read slogans and ask them their reaction. Ask what they like and don't like.
Have them write their top two favorite slogans on their paper.

Appendix includes helpful supplementary material.

1. Length and formality determine the following general progression of report structure:

   1 Explain the makeup of reports relative to length and formality.

   - The very long ones have prefatory pages.
     - Title fly—a page displaying only the title.
     - Title page—a page displaying the title, writer and reader's names and their titles/organizations, and date.
     - Authorization message—included only when a written message authorized the report.
     - Transmittal message—a personal message "handing the report over" to the reader.
     - Table of contents, list of illustrations—a listing of the report parts and illustrations with page numbers.
     - Executive summary—the report in miniature; written in direct or indirect order.
   - As reports become shorter and less formal, the composition of the prefatory parts section changes, generally in this order:
     - First, the title fly drops out.
     - Then, in succession, the executive summary and letter of transmittal are combined.
     - The table of contents is omitted.
     - The combined letter of transmittal and executive summary is dropped.
   - Even less elaborate are the letter report and the short email report.

2. The shorter and by far the most common reports are much like the longer ones except for these four differences:

   2 Discuss the four major differences involved in writing short and long reports.

   - They have less need for introductory material.
   - They are more likely to begin directly (conclusion and recommendation first).
   - They are more likely to use a personal style.
   - They have less need for a formal coherence plan.

3. The shorter reports come in three main forms.

   3 Choose an appropriate form for short reports.

   - The short report form can be for any situation of mid-level formality and complexity.
     - It consists of a title page and report text.
     - Usually it begins with a summary or conclusion.
     - Then it presents findings and analyses.
   - Letter reports tend to be written to those outside the company.
     - They tend to use a personal style.
     - Usually they are written in the indirect order.
   - Email reports are usually written to those within the organization.
     - They are usually informal but can also be formal.
     - They tend to be problem-solving reports.

4. Among the varieties of short reports, five types stand out.

   4 Adapt the procedures for writing short reports to routine operational, progress, problem-solving, and audit reports as well as minutes of meetings.

   - Routine operational reports keep others informed about company operations.
     - Their form and content will vary, depending on the organization.
     - They should deliver the required information efficiently, clearly, and on time.
     - Special word-processing features can assist you with standardized reports.

- Progress reports review progress on an activity.
  - Most are informal and in narrative form, but some are formal.
  - They should emphasize the positive.
- Problem-solving reports help decision makers choose a course of action.
  - They can be internal or external.
  - You will need to decide whether or not to make recommendations.
  - You will need to decide whether to take a direct or indirect approach.
  - Though not persuasive per se, these reports do need to convince with their good data and analysis.
- Audit reports hold organizations accountable to certain standards.
  - The most common type is the financial audit prepared by an accounting firm.
  - Short financial audits follow a standardized format.
  - Longer audit reports vary in form and content.
  - The Sarbanes-Oxley Act has increased the need for audit reports.
- Meeting minutes, a type of descriptive report, provide a written record of a group's activities and decisions.
  - Most are distributed by memo or email, but their layout varies.
  - Typical minutes include common preliminary, body, and closing items.
  - Minutes have political implications. Use good judgment when preparing them.

5 Write longer reports that include the appropriate components, meet the readers' needs, and are easy to follow.

5. Longer reports need to include the appropriate elements, meet the readers' needs, and facilitate easy reading.
   - They include the prefatory parts that are appropriate for the report's length, formality, and reader.
   - The report introduction prepares the readers to follow and interpret the report.
     - Include whatever helps with this goal.
     - Use these items as a checklist for content: purpose, scope, limitations, problem history, methodology, definitions, preview.
     - A preview telling the order and reasoning for the order is useful in longer, more involved reports.
   - Preparing the body of a long, formal report will require virtually all your organizing, writing, and formatting skills.
   - The ending of the report achieves the report purpose.
     - Use a summary if the purpose is to review information.
     - Use a conclusion if the purpose is to reach an answer.
     - Use a recommendation if the purpose is to determine a desirable action.
   - An appendix and/or bibliography can follow the report text.
     - The appendix contains items that support the text but have no specific place in the text (such as questionnaires, working papers, summary tables).
     - The bibliography is a descriptive list of the secondary sources that were used in the investigation.
   - The longer reports need various structural devices to give them coherence.
     - These devices consist of a network of explanations, introductions, summaries, and conclusions that guide the reader through the report.
     - Begin the coherence plan with the introduction preview, which tells the structure of the report.
     - Then use the introductions and summaries in following parts to tell readers where they are in this structure.

1 Discuss the effects of formality and problem length on report makeup as described in the chapter. **(LO1)**

2 Which of the prefatory pages of reports appear to be related primarily to the length of the report? Which to the need for formality? **(LO1)**

3 Describe the role and content of a transmittal message. **(LO1)**

4 Why is personal style typically used in the transmittal message? **(LO1)**

5 Explain how to write the executive summary of a report. **(LO1)**

6 Why does the executive summary include key facts and figures in addition to the analyses and conclusions drawn from them? **(LO1)**

7 Explain why some routine report problems require little or no introduction. **(LO2)**

8 Why is the direct order generally used in the shorter reports? When is the indirect order desirable for such reports? **(LO2)**

9 Describe the organization of the conventional short report. **(LO3)**

10 What types of problems are written up as letter reports? As email reports? Explain the differences. **(LO3)**

11 What kinds of information might go into routine operational reports for different kinds of organizations? Why would these organizations need this information regularly? **(LO4)**

12 Given what you've learned about progress reports, suggest an appropriate structure for these reports. What might go into the beginning? What might the middle parts be? What would the conclusion do? **(LO4)**

13 How might an internal problem-solving report that has been assigned differ from one on the same subject that an employee generated on his or her own? **(LO4)**

14 Study the audit reports in several companies' annual reports. What seem to be the common features of such audit reports? **(LO4)**

15 Discuss the pros and cons of including a list of absentees in meeting minutes. **(LO4)**

16 Give examples of long-report problems whose introduction could require coverage of methods of collecting data, historical background, and limitations. **(LO5)**

17 Explain how the advice in Chapter 10 can help you prepare the body of a long report. **(LO5)**

18 Give examples of report problems that would require, respectively, (*a*) an ending summary, (*b*) an ending conclusion, and (*c*) an ending recommendation. **(LO5)**

19 Using as a guide the diagram in Figure 11–6, summarize the coherence plan of the long, formal report. **(LO5)**

1 Review the following report situations and determine for each the makeup of the report you would recommend for it. **(LO1)**

a. A professional research organization has completed a survey of consumer attitudes toward BankOne. The survey results will be presented to the bank president in a 28-page report, including seven charts and three tables.

b. Joan Marion was asked by her department head to inspect the work area and report on safety conditions. Her report is two pages long and written in personal style.

c. Bill Wingler has an idea for improving a work procedure in his department at McLaughlin Body Company. His department head suggested that Bill present his idea in a report to the production superintendent. The report is almost five pages long, including a full-page diagram. It is written in the personal style.

d. Karen Canady, a worker in the corporate library of Accenture, was asked by Doug Edmunds, its president, for current inventory information on a number of subscriptions. Her report is less than a full page and consists mostly of a list of items and numbers.

e. Bryan Toups, a sales manager for Johnson and Johnson, was asked by the vice president of marketing to prepare an analysis of the results of a promotional campaign conducted in Toups's district. The report is six pages long (including one chart) and is written in the personal style.

2 Following is a report that was written for the manager of a large furniture retail store by the manager's assistant. The manager was concerned about customer complaints of late deliveries of furniture purchased and wanted to know the cause of the delays. Critique this report. **(LO2, LO4)**

11-17-04

TO: Martina Kalavoda

FROM: Anthony Dudrow

SUBJECT: Investigation requested 11-17-04

This morning at staff meeting it was requested that an investigation be made of the status of home deliveries and of the causes of the delays that have occurred. The investigation has been made with findings as follows.

Now that a new driver's helper, Morris Tunney, has been hired, there should be no more delays. This was the cause of the problem.

Over the past two weeks (10 working days), a total of 143 deliveries were made; and of these, 107 were made on or before the date promised. But some of the deliveries were late because of the departure two weeks ago of the driver's helper, Sean Toulouse, who had to be fired because of dishonesty and could not be replaced quickly with a permanent, qualified helper. Now that a permanent, qualified helper has been hired, there should be no more delays in delivery as this was the cause of the problem.

The driver was able to find a temporary helper, a man by the name of Rusty Sellers, for some help in the unloading work, but he got behind and couldn't seem to catch up. He could have caught up by working overtime, in the opinion of the writer, but he refused to do so. Of the 36 deliveries that were late, all were completed within two days. The problem is over now that the driver has a helper, so there should be no additional delays.

3 Making any assumptions needed, construct complete yet concise titles for the reports described below. **(LO5)**

a. A report writer reviewed records of exit interviews of employees at Marvel-Floyd Manufacturing Company who quit their jobs voluntarily. The objective of the investigation was to determine the reasons for their leaving.

b. A researcher studied data from employee personnel records at Magna-Tech, Inc., to determine whether permanent (long-term) employees differ from short-term employees. Some of the differences found would be used in hiring employees in the future. The data studied included age, education, experience, and scores on pre-employment tests.

c. A report writer compared historical financial records (1965 to the present) of Super Saver Foods to determine whether this grocery chain should own or rent store buildings. In the past it did both.

4 Criticize the following beginning sentences of transmittal messages. **(LO5)**

a. "In your hands is the report you requested January 7 concerning . . ."

b. "As you will recall, last January 7 you requested a report on . . ."

c. "That we should open a new outlet in Bragg City is the conclusion of this report, which you authorized January 7."

5 In a report comparing four automobiles (Alpha, Beta, Gamma, and Delta) to determine which one is the best buy for a company, Section II of the report body covered these cost data: (*a*) initial costs, (*b*) trade-in values, and (*c*) operating expenses. Section III presented a comparison of these safety features of the automobiles: (*a*) standard safety features, (*b*) acceleration data, (*c*) weight distribution, and (*d*) braking quality. **(LO5)**

a. Criticique this introductory paragraph at the beginning of Section III:

In the preceding section was presented a thorough analysis of the cost data. Now safety of the cars will be compared. Although costs are important, Warren-Burke also is concerned about the safety of its salespeople, who spend almost half their work time driving.

Now write a more appropriate introductory paragraph.

b. The next section of the report (Section IV) covered these topics: (*a*) handling, (*b*) quality of ride, and (*c*) durability.

Criticique this introductory paragraph for the section:

This section of the report presents a comparison of the overall construction of the four automobiles. These considerations also are important because they affect how a car rides, and this is important. Thus, we will take up in this order: handling, general riding quality, and construction qualities.

Now write a more appropriate introductory paragraph.

c. Criticique this final paragraph (a preview) of the introduction of the report described above:

This report compares the automobiles on three factors. These are costs, safety, and comfort and construction, in that order. Costs include initial expenditure, trade-in value, and operating expense. Safety covers safety devices, acceleration, weight distribution, and braking. Comfort and construction includes handling, ride quality, and durability. A ranking is derived from this comparison.

Shorter Reports

1 You started working for AmCrane, an industrial crane rental and sales company, as an office clerk when you were in high school. You're in college now, but you still work there part time, and you've noticed that the management of the company seems to respect your opinion and judgment a little more each day.

Today you and some others were hanging around the coffeemaker with one of the owners, who mentioned that he'd seen a big U.S. flag hanging from the crane of a competitor in a nearby city. "I wonder what the rules are for displaying a U.S. flag?" he asks. "I'm kind of surprised you can hang one from a crane." After a moment of thought, he turns to you. "Will you find out how we can do that?" he asks. "And see if there's anything else we should know? Also, where would we get a big U.S. flag? I wonder if they're expensive."

You tell him you'll look into the matter and send him an email about it. Do the appropriate research, and tell your boss everything he needs to know to decide whether and how to move forward with this idea.

2 Take advantage of the many resources about careers to research what the career outlook is in your field. Research the employment prospects, typical jobs, advancement opportunities, salary range, career advantages/disadvantages, typical responsibilities—whatever you can find. You might start with the U.S. Government's *Occupational Outlook Handbook* (<www.bls.gov/OCO/>). Professional societies also sometimes have excellent statistics on salaries and working conditions in their fields. And don't neglect such job-search sites as *monster.com*. If your instructor directs, interview someone in your field who can give you an insider's view. Write up your findings as a well-organized short report, and be sure to interpret your findings in terms of their likely significance to you.

3 The graphic design shop where you work as the account manager is doing well. Just last year, the owner hired three new designers and a receptionist, bringing the total number of employees to 14. But with growth come certain headaches—and one of them is figuring out how to regulate employees' Internet use.

The owner's IT person has alerted him to several problems. One is that the designers are downloading any and all software that they think sounds "cool"—even software in beta versions that still have a lot of kinks. As a result, their computers lock up or malfunction, and the IT person has to spend hours troubleshooting the problem. Your IT person is also worried about security breaches resulting from these downloads and from other Internet activities. And of course there's always the worry that employees will be looking at Internet sites inappropriate for the workplace.

It's time for an Internet-use policy, and your boss thinks you're just the person to help write it. Your assignment is to study the current wisdom on workplace Internet policies and send your findings to your boss and the IT person in an email report. You three will then use the report as the basis for a meeting on the subject next week.

4 It's almost time for the annual award brunch for the _____ (you pick the city) Literacy Network. Each year, your boss, the director of the local chapter, presents the volunteer of the year with a gift book.

This year's winner is a woman who helped three high-school-aged participants earn the General Educational Development (GED) certificate, the equivalent of a high school diploma. She is a favorite among the teenagers, with whom she clearly loves to work.

Your boss has asked you to recommend four books that could work as this year's gift book. Write him a brief email report describing four appropriate books and helping him see their relative strengths.

5 To give back to the community, and to enhance your résumé, you have decided to volunteer your time this summer to a worthy charity. Habitat for Humanity is one you have great respect for, so you contacted the volunteer coordinator. The meeting was a disaster. Habitat for Humanity staff interrupted the interview no fewer than six times in ten minutes. The coordinator apologized profusely, explaining that the project manager for the upcoming annual fundraiser/auction had resigned last week. Now the interviewer is responsible for finding an appropriate location for the event, and she is overwhelmed.

You are sure that you can help. Just last fall you organized a very successful fundraiser for your college soccer club, raising more than $1,000. The coordinator is thrilled with your offer. She hands to you a file filled with the former project manager's research.

As you study the file, you begin to consider your strategy. The theme of the event is "Lawyers, Nails, and Money," with the goal of encouraging leaders in the legal community to step up and help those in need. This group consists of members across the economic spectrum, but you will probably want to appeal to those at the more affluent end. At the same time, there has been some downsizing in the legal community, so you wouldn't want to go overboard. Last year the event drew 300 attendees at the price of $100 per ticket, but both numbers can go up or down depending on the appeal of the venue. A sit-down dinner is planned. A silent auction is also part of the festivities, from which the organization hopes to bring in as much as $50,000, based on the success of past events.

Your predecessor narrowed the choice of venue down to two locations. The first is the ballroom at the Hyatt. The Hyatt has a nice ambience, and the location is close to the suburbs, where many law partners reside. It's pretty much ready as is, but for $4,000 for the night, you expect that. The room's seating capacity of 450 guests is certainly a plus if your tickets sales are strong, but miss your mark and there will be a big empty feeling. You are sure your guests will appreciate the valet parking, but the $30 fee could somewhat erode that giving feeling you seek. A nice four-course meal can be provided for $60 per plate.

The second option is the VFW hall. It is located in the warehouse district with upscale lofts nearby, but crime is a concern. Two armed security officers are part of the package, but you do see that only street parking is available. You would have to do some decorating to make the VFW hall work, since it has a bit of a gymnasium feel. Maybe you can work that into the theme of the event. You certainly do like the $2,000 price tag. The hall has no kitchen, but you can cater in from a nearby restaurant at $40 per plate for a nice three-course meal.

The coordinator asks you to write a memo report comparing the two locations and recommending the better one for the event. You accept. Use your imagination to fill in any gaps. For more information on the organization see <www.habitat.org>.

---

6 As a Senior Buyer at Darcy's, a national department store company, Sasha Warner manages the buyers in the eastern U.S. region. You're currently working under her as a sales co-op student. She drops by your office to chat one day and brings up a subject she's been wondering about. "Do you know anything about Skype?" she asks. You nod, having used this online international phone service yourself. "I hear it's totally free and really easy to use," she continues, "so I'm thinking about recommending that all my buyers subscribe to it. Then maybe they could talk to each other and to international designers and merchandisers more easily. Is there any downside? Maybe security issues?" You're not sure—but you offer to look into the matter for her.

Do the necessary research—and, if you haven't yet done so, try this service yourself—and then write Sasha a report giving her the information she needs to decide whether or not to pursue this idea further. She may want to share your report with other managers in the company, so be sure you give it your best effort.

---

7 You work for the owner of three local coffee and tea shops, one of which opened a few months ago. The newest one has already developed quite a nice regular clientele—mostly those in or near the neighborhood who want an alternative to the big-coffee-chain experience—but your boss thinks its sales need a bump. So she's considering holding an in-store promotion there—her first ever. Since she knows you're an Internet whiz, she turns to you for help. "How do you run one of these events?" she wants to know. "How much do they cost? Are they worth the effort and expense? What are my options? Do such promotions have lasting effects? How can I maximize the results?"

You turn to the Internet and find a lot of great stuff about in-store promotions—so much, in fact, that you decide to present your findings to your boss in writing. Tell her what she needs and wants to know in a clear, well-organized report. Having the information in writing will also be helpful if she wants to share it with other employees. Be sure she can go to your sources and read more if she wants to.

---

8 You work in the marketing department of a mid-sized accounting firm in San Diego. The marketing manager stops by your office early one morning with news that three high-level CPAs from a competing firm just jumped ship to your team. This is big. These first-rate resources will allow your firm to go head-to-head with the national accounting firms. When word gets out about this new talent, your boss expects a huge jump in business. It's crucial that you reach out to large businesses to let them know that there is a new accounting firm in the game.

Most of the ads placed by your company until now have been with local media. Your boss wants to reach a wider audience. He believes it is time to advertise in *The Wall Street Journal*. He does, though, have some questions. Should your firm advertise in only the western region of the *WSJ*? Or how about the U.S. edition? Should you include the online edition? In any case, what's the deadline for next Monday's edition? What sizes of ads are available for purchase, and at what cost?

Write a memo to your boss giving the necessary details about placing an ad in *The Wall Street Journal*. Provide as much information as you believe is necessary to make a sound decision, covering circulation, rates, specifications, and demographics. Information is available at <www.wsj.com>.

---

9 In an effort to cut down on waste and expenses, the campus food service company at your university implemented a new policy a month ago, in the middle of the fall term: no more trays. Instead of going from station to station loading their trays up with food, students must now get their food carrying only a plate and/or bowl (but they can use as many plates and bowls and visit the stations as often as they like).

After a month has passed, the director of the campus food service wants to know two things: Is there significantly less food waste, and how do the students feel about the new policy? He asks you, his trusty assistant, to find out and write up your findings in a report that he can share with university administrators.

You gather the information in two ways. First, you ask the managers of the three campus eateries how many 13-gallon bags of food waste (not including paper) they threw out during the last week before the policy was implemented and during the fourth week afterwards. Since the managers have been asked to keep track of this information, they are ready for your question. The manager at the smallest dining hall reports 6.5 bags for the "before" week and 5 bags for the "after" week. At the mid-sized hall, the "before" figure is 10 bags and the "after" figure is 8. At the largest facility, the "before" figure is 14 bags and the "after" figure is 11.5. The total number of students served for the "before" week was 3,042; for the "after" week it was 2,890.

Next, you send a brief online survey to the 3,050 students who are on a campus meal plan. In fact, you send it out twice to encourage as much participation as possible. Altogether, 840 students participate (though a few do not answer all the questions). In response to the question "I waste less food now that the trays are gone," 35 students pick strongly disagree, 78 disagree, 390 agree, and 360 strongly agree. In response to the question "I eat less now that the trays are gone," 18 pick strongly disagree, 37 disagree, 460 agree, and 320 strongly agree. In response to the question "I favor the new trayless policy," 24 students pick strongly disagree, 55 disagree, 381 agree, and 372 strongly agree. In response to the question "My attitude toward being on a meal plan is more positive now," 24 pick strongly disagree, 57 disagree, 590 agree, and 139 strongly agree. In response to the open-ended question inviting feedback on the new policy, you get many positive comments about the university's effort to reduce waste, to help the environment, and to keep up with the times. A few even praise the university's effort to help students not overeat. The negative comments are about the loss of convenience, the difficulty of getting enough food on one plate, and the awkwardness of carrying a stack of dishes to the dishwashing area. A few students comment that for the high price they're paying, the food service should at least include trays.

Now that you have your data, organize and interpret it for your boss, being careful to use qualified language (e.g., "perhaps," "may be") where appropriate.

---

10 You're assistant HR director at a large, successful construction company in _____ (you pick the city). For some time now, you and your boss, Mike Stanton, have been discussing starting a formal employee-volunteer program in the company. Your main competitors in the area feature their extensive community service efforts on their websites and in their print literature, but thus far your company's contributions have been random and relatively sparse. Your boss thinks it's time to propose to the owners that the company create a focused, well-organized, appealing employee-volunteer program that will generate positive publicity—and business—for the company.

For this proposal, your boss is going to need expert information and persuasive arguments. And that's where you come in. Mike has asked you to review the literature on such programs and harvest information that will be useful for his proposal. He particularly wants to know the features

of successful programs and the business benefits of such programs.

You decide you'll start your research with three good resources Mike told you about: the book *Leveraging Goodwill* by Alice Korngold, the website for the Boston College Center for Corporate Citizenship (<www.bcccc.net/>), and <www.serviceleader.org>. Then you'll look at other sources, including the Corporate Volunteer Council websites for various cities—and of course your competitors' websites. (If your instructor directs, you may also interview the director of a company's employee-volunteer program.) Once you believe you've found everything useful, you'll digest it, interpret it, and present the results in a well-organized, well-written report to Mike. Keep your report to about four pages, but be sure to include your sources so Mike can cite them in his proposal or consult them himself if he wants.

---

11 Many managers today are realizing that there really is something distinctive about "Gen Y" or "Millenial" employees (the children of the "baby boomers"—who were themselves children of the World War II generation). Find a real client or invent a realistic company to use as your client.

Then review the literature on Gen Y employees and write your client a report in which you describe the distinctive traits of this segment of the workforce and recommend ways to recruit, manage, and retain them.

---

12 Write a report to your instructor in which you argue for or against one of the following:

a. All business students should be required to purchase laptops for classroom/educational use.

b. Students graduating with business degrees should be required to pass a proficiency exam in the use of Microsoft Word, Excel, PowerPoint, and Access.

c. Business writing/presentations/communications courses should have a minimum grade requirement of a B-.

d. All business students should be required to complete a professional internship to graduate.

e. To be prepared for today's global business environment, all business students should be required to speak a foreign language proficiently (the equivalent of five semesters of study) or complete a study abroad experience.

---

13 Your company does not offer flexible spending accounts (FSAs) for its employees. Your boss wonders if your company (you pick the name) should. Are FSAs a good idea for businesses and employees? Prepare a report to your boss in which you analyze the advantages and disadvantages of FSAs so that she can decide whether to offer FSAs to your employees.

---

14 You work in human resources for Clear Water Design, a company of 75 employees that offers both single-person and family health insurance plans. Twenty-three percent of the employees do not take the health insurance benefit. If an employee declines health insurance upon employment, he or she forfeits the benefit—no other benefits are offered in its place. Last week you hired Maria Reese. You sent her the standard paperwork that all new hires complete. When Maria stopped by today to submit her paperwork, she said that she had turned down the health insurance, as she has health insurance coverage through her spouse. In telling you this, she mentions that her spouse's company offers an annuity the equivalent of a single-person premium as an alternative benefit for employees who decline the health insurance and wants to know if Clear Water Design will do the same for her. The cost of a single-person premium per month is $410.

You present the idea to your boss, who initially says "absolutely not" but then decides that you should research the issue first. What are the advantages and disadvantages for the employee and for the company? How much will this potentially cost if other employees choose an annuity over health insurance? What if the cost of a single-person premium increases? Can you go back? That is, can you decide to discontinue this benefit at any time? Present your research in a report so your boss can make an informed decision.

---

15 As a student trustee on the governing board of your college, you make sure that students' concerns are heard on all academic matters. A proposal was just introduced by the Academic Senate to change the grading system from straight letter grades (A, B, C . . .) to plus/minus grading (A, A-, B+, B . . .). This proposal appears to be sailing through the committee that was assigned to this task. As the representative of the students, you believe you'd better weigh in on this issue.

Write a short report for or against the plus/minus grading system. Explain why you feel one is better than the other for the students.

---

16 Recently a repair person from a heating and air conditioning company visited your workplace to find out why the furnace wasn't working. The verdict was that your company needs to replace the antiquated furnace. Now your boss has come to you, her assistant, for help. "The repair person tried to sell me a new furnace on the spot," she says, "but I decided we'd better do some research first. I don't have any idea how big a furnace we need or what the good brands are. Plus, I didn't understand some of the lingo—'heat exchanger,' '2-stage gas valve,' 'variable speed fan motor,' and the like. Would you look into some good options for us and help me make an informed decision?"

The company building is a smallish three-story house—you figure about 2,000 square feet—with a basement. After figuring out on what bases to compare furnaces, decide on two reasonable choices for the company and help your boss decide which one to purchase. Email her your report. (If your instructor permits, you may choose a different kind of appliance/equipment.)

---

17 You are quite comfortable in your position as supervisor at a small accounting office in your hometown, but you find some tasks a bit more challenging than others. Mary, your lead auditing clerk, is one of those challenges.

Mary is a terrific auditor—in fact, she is the best you have. Losing her would have a detrimental impact on office productivity. Unfortunately, she is frequently late to her shift, causing others to work overtime, an added expense and a nuisance. To make things worse, you've noticed recently that others in the office are arriving late to work too because, you believe, they see that Mary has not suffered any consequences for her actions.

You ask your boss for some guidance with this matter, and she points out that no company policy exists that deals directly with tardiness. She asks you to do some research and to present some options.

Write a report to your supervisor investigating the many options available to managers when it is necessary to discipline tardy employees. The options can range from termination to demotion to doing nothing. Address in a general sense any legal challenges you may encounter.

Longer Reports

18 The University Career Center is a great place to begin your career in Human Resources Management, so you were thrilled to land a part-time position as an assistant to the lead counselor. Your boss selected you because she is concerned that the office is a bit "old fashioned" and she expects you to help bring in their operations into the digital age.

On your first day of work, you were surprised to learn that no electronic/online résumé resources were available to students. You know that many of these sites exist—such as <www.gigtide.com>—and some can be quite helpful. You are certain this type of resource will help students with their job searches, so you decide to present a report to your supervisor explaining the many electronic/online résumé options available. Some are better than others, so you choose three and compare them based on several factors including cost, ease of use, effectiveness, compatibility, and any other factors you believe important.

Write a long report comparing the three resources. This report will be passed up to the head of the department, so write a formal report with all of the necessary components.

19 For your team project in your Entrepreneurship class you and two classmates wrote a business plan for a service that delivers gardening materials—including plants, fertilizer, and gardening tools—to home-gardening enthusiasts. Your research shows that your college community has many active gardeners, but the nearest garden store, Armstrong's, is 30 miles from town.

You professor loves the idea and suggests that you make it work. All you need is some seed money. Fortunately, the mother of one of your teammates has a business acquaintance, Jim Daugherty, who is willing to help you look for some sound investments. One problem, though: The section of your business plan that discusses the purchase of a delivery vehicle is not well developed, and it's a considerable piece of the start-up costs. Mr. Daugherty won't shop your plan to potential investors until that topic is thoroughly addressed.

Write an analytical report for Mr. Daugherty and your teammates comparing three vehicles that might meet your needs. Good gas mileage is important. Safety, too, ranks right up there. And you certainly can't afford for this vehicle to break down, so reliability is key. Choose three vehicles that might meet your needs and compare them, adding any other factors you believe are important. You'll write the report in a relatively formal style since parts of it are likely to be added to your business plan.

20 Every employee at Fairway Software Solutions needs to be current in his or her field. As a developer of medical practice management software for hospitals, clinics, and private practices, Fairway requires everyone from the programmers to the sales staff to the communications specialists be up to date on current practices, trends, and client needs so that the company can survive in an extremely competitive industry.

To ensure that its employees have the most current knowledge, Fairway invests a lot of money in employees' continuing education, which includes workshops, seminars, and continuing education courses at two-year colleges and four-year colleges and universities; the company has even paid for some employees' courses toward an MBA. Wherever the education is, Fairway sends its employees.

This practice for continuing education has become too costly. Your boss, the director of education and training, has done some research and has found that high-quality online workshops, webinars, and courses are much more cost effective. As a result, the company has decided that nearly all employees can remain current in their fields by taking advantage of more cost-effective online opportunities.

The issue, though, is selling the concept to the employees. In talking with a few department heads and employees informally, your boss senses some resistance to online learning. Your boss wants to learn whether there really is widespread resistance to online learning and where the points of resistance are. Your boss also wants to know some best practices for promoting online training opportunities as valid options for continuing education. You have been assigned the task of gathering the information your boss requires and presenting both the information and recommendations for ensuring that employees see online education opportunities as useful.

You surveyed your 2,500 employees and received 524 responses. The survey results (primary data) are provided below. The numbers represent frequency data (the number of respondents, not percentages). You will also need to gather secondary research (as many sources as your instructor requires) regarding best practices for promoting online education. Cite your sources in the style required by your instructor.

Q1: In what department do you work?

- 109 Research and Development
- 204 Sales
- 15 Communications
- 39 Accounting
- 14 Training and Education
- 21 Marketing
- 14 Human Resources
- 46 Customer Relations
- 51 Information Technology
- 11 Legal

Q2: What is the nature of your position?

- 87 Manager
- 92 Supervisor
- 276 Subject matter expert (accountants, technical writers, programmers, salespeople)
- 69 Clerical/Support

Q3: Have you ever participated in any of the following online education opportunities? Check all that apply.

- 0 Online workshop
- 91 Webinar (online seminar)
- 51 Online course
- 15 Other (please specify): 9 bachelor's degree from an online university or a face-to-face university with an online program; 6 technical/vocational degree through an online program

Q4: Do you participate in any of the following? Check all that apply.

- 102 Professionally related blog
- 321 Professionally related online social networking site (e.g., Twitter, LinkedIn, Facebook)

Q5: What is your *perception* of the workload in online seminars/workshops/courses?

- 198 More work than face-to-face opportunities
- 102 About the same work as face-to-face opportunities
- 224 Less work than face-to-face opportunities

Q6: What is your *perception* of the quality of online seminars/workshops/courses?

- 147 Better quality than face-to-face opportunities
- 175 About the same quality as face-to-face opportunities
- 202 Less quality than face-to-face opportunities

Q7: Indicate your level of agreement with this statement: People can learn as much in an online environment as they can in a face-to-face environment.

- 75 Strongly agree
- 124 Agree
- 42 Neither agree nor disagree
- 257 Disagree
- 26 Strongly disagree

Q8: Indicate your level of agreement with this statement: If the following online continuing education opportunity presented itself, I would willingly take it:

An online seminar (1–2 hours)

- 62 Strongly agree
- 312 Agree
- 13 Neither agree nor disagree
- 73 Disagree
- 64 Strongly disagree

An online workshop (1–2 days)

- 37 Strongly agree
- 112 Agree
- 207 Neither agree nor disagree
- 149 Disagree
- 19 Strongly disagree

An online course (1–3 weeks)

- 187 Strongly agree
- 172 Agree
- 44 Neither agree nor disagree
- 63 Disagree
- 58 Strongly disagree

An online course (4–8 weeks)

- 159 Strongly agree
- 208 Agree
- 75 Neither agree nor disagree
- 67 Disagree
- 15 Strongly disagree

An online course (9–16 weeks)

- 92 Strongly agree
- 133 Agree

151 Neither agree nor disagree

110 Disagree

  38 Strongly disagree

Q9: My general attitude toward online learning in any form is

  67 Strongly Positive

107 Positive

129 Neutral

128 Negative

  93 Strongly negative

Cross tabulations for "Q9: My general attitude toward online learning in any form is":

  67 Strongly Positive (24 managers, 20 supervisors, 17 subject matter experts, 6 clerical/support staff)

107 Positive (37 managers, 33 supervisors, 30 subject matter experts, 7 clerical/support staff)

129 Neutral (20 managers, 14 supervisors, 75 subject matter experts, 20 clerical/support staff)

128 Negative (6 managers, 20 supervisors, 100 subject matter experts, 2 clerical support staff)

  93 Strongly negative (0 managers, 5 supervisors, 54 subject matter experts, 34 clerical support staff)

Employee comments on the survey:

- I enjoy the opportunity to meet others in my field and network. I can't do that online.
- Getting away from the company for a few days of training is a nice break from the routine.
- I can't imagine being able to learn when I can't see the instructor or other students.
- This is just one more way for the company to cut costs and quality. I can't see online learning as having the same quality as the face-to-face seminars and courses I attend.
- How can online learning use the hands-on activities we do in face-to-face workshops?
- I have taken an online course and several webinars. I like that I don't have to leave my family or my office for workshops and seminars.
- Online seminars are great! Today's technology is so good that it's just like being in the same room with other participants.
- I just finished a webinar and loved it! I've had face-to-face experiences that weren't as good. I think it depends on the quality of the course and the instructor, not whether the location is face-to-face or online.

---

21 Your marketing internship with Ride Snowboards will be over in three weeks, but you hope your accomplishments during your time there will result in a full-time marketing position with the company. Your supervisor, Laurie Alexy, is well aware of your desire, so she assigns you a final project that she says just might get the attention of upper management.

Laurie explains that Ride Snowboards will be sponsoring the 2011 Snowboarding International Championship. The contest will result in tremendous exposure for Ride, so its success is crucial.

"We expect 100 contestants from around the world, all world-class boarders, so the location must offer challenging slopes for our contestants," Laurie says. "As many as 10,000 spectators, including 300 VIPs from media agencies around the country, are expected, so the surrounding town must have adequate accommodations. It's crucial that the mountain have enough snow and the overall weather conditions be appropriate for spectators to be reasonably comfortable."

"The top eight members of our executive team will be working around the clock, so their comfort is important," continues Laurie. "Be sure to arrange accommodations for this group at a five-star resort—cost is no object for these rooms. A conference room that holds at least 50 is necessary for the product strategy meeting we have scheduled for the final evening. Some of our team will be joined by their spouses and children, so appropriate activities for them should be explored."

Three snowboarding resorts should be compared and contrasted to give upper management an idea of the options available. Accommodations, transportation, and mountain conditions are a few of the factors that should be considered. One of the three resorts should be located outside of the United States. Gather the necessary information and write a report that compares and contrasts three resorts. This report will make it to the CEO, so be sure to prepare it accordingly.

---

22 Choose a company and assume the role of a specialist in the Human Resources Department. Universal Casualty Insurance, which insures your company, has requested a copy of your emergency preparedness plan for protecting your facilities, employees, and data in the event of a disaster or accident. Your boss knows your company has an evacuation plan for tornados or fires and that the IT department backs up the system every day, but the plan needs to be updated and made more thorough. Your boss has asked you to research an emergency preparedness plan for your company. After you have done the research on what an emergency preparedness plan should contain for a company of your size and nature, write a report to your boss in which you report your findings. Based on your research, also present a policy and include it as an appendix.

23 You work for a nonprofit organization (you may pick the organization). You and your boss know that many nonprofit organizations in your area make a lot of money selling food and beverages at the local summer festivals. You and your boss decide to host a booth at one festival this summer to see if this is a fund-raising opportunity you might want to pursue regularly. Research three possible sites in your area where your organization could host a food booth. Ideally, you would like to sell burgers, hot dogs, chips, beverages, and candy bars. Your boss will need information regarding the cost for space, any restrictions on what you can do in setting up your site or what you can serve, insurance requirements, permit and license requirements, and so on. Your boss will use the information to decide which site to choose.

24 Research three trends in your field using primary or secondary research as your instructor directs. Analyze what these trends mean for graduates in your field. What should students in your field do to prepare for these trends?

25 In the last year your company has launched a corporate fitness program. The results have been tremendous. Your employees have lost a collective 5,367 pounds, and the employees have had fewer sick days and paid less for medical care. The problem? Many of the sales and management staff members entertain clients at business breakfasts, lunches, and dinners. These employees have expressed concern that their hard work in the fitness program is sabotaged when they entertain clients and dine on food loaded with fat, calories, cholesterol, carbohydrates, and sodium. They also worry that hidden "hazards" in certain foods (e.g., dressings, sauces) may cause them to make poor food choices even when they are attempting to make good ones. Your boss has assigned you the task of researching the nutritional content of menus for at least six restaurants where employees may entertain clients and submit a report that presents healthy choices for breakfast, lunch, and dinner at these restaurants.

26 The nonprofit organization you manage, Washington Community Center, provides meals, a literacy program, youth and teen activities, parenting classes, a computer lab, sports and art activities, and several other opportunities for people in your community. You recently received a $15,000 bequest from the estate of Ted Germain who said in his will that the center helped him 20 years ago when he was unemployed by giving him meals and helping him get the literacy skills he needed to earn his high school diploma. He continued his education and eventually became a computer programmer. The only stipulation on the donation is that it go for programs (e.g., a literacy initiative) and not for capital improvements (e.g., a new roof). The Washington Community Center's board of directors has asked you for a report on how the money should be spent. Write a report to the board recommending a plan for spending the money.

27 Pick a website for any company. Review Part 2: Fundamentals of Business Writing (Chapters 2–4) and conduct some research on what makes a website good in terms of content, design, navigation, and usability. Then evaluate this company's website according to your research and your knowledge of business communication fundamentals. Assess its strengths and weaknesses and recommend improvements.

28 You're the bookkeeper for a small but successful legal firm. The three owners manage their 11 employees' 401(k) (retirement) accounts with the help of an investment advisor, but sometimes they decide on their own to add or remove companies from their investment portfolio. Recently they received an intriguing piece of sales literature from The Vanguard Group, a premier mutual fund. They want you to look into the company and see what you think about the wisdom of their purchasing some of the company's shares.

You go to *Hoover*'s *Online,* a great research tool you learned about in college, and you see that Vanguard has two main competitors in the mutual-funds business: FMR (Fidelity) and T. Rowe Price. You decide to compare the three companies on such criteria as longevity, recent performance, mix of funds, clarity of their information—or any factor that you think would be of interest to your employers.

Using your resourcefulness and great research skills, scout out the three companies and write a clear, well-organized, helpful report for your bosses.

29 The management of Hathaway Hotels, a national chain of mid-priced hotels, wants to know why some of its hotels are doing much better than others. They have contracted the services of your company, Quality Research Associates (QRA), to find out.

As a senior researcher for QRA, you and a team of four associates have been researching the problem for four weeks. As authorized by Julio Alvarez, VP of Sales for Hathaway, your team visited 20 hotels in the eastern United States, the region that Hathaway selected as the site of the study. The hotels, which Hathaway also chose, were roughly equal in size, traffic flow past the hotel, and facilities. But they differed in one crucial way: 10 of the hotels were underperforming on sales, while the other 10 were thriving.

To find the reasons for high or low sales volumes, you worked out a detailed plan for collecting data. First you had your investigators—all of whom were trained hospitality evaluators—visit each hotel posing as customers and spend one night in the hotel. While they were there, they observed and recorded data on such features as hotel appearance, cleanliness, and service. The evaluations were based on a detailed assessment guide. Later, the researchers returned to interview the manager to gather pertinent information on the hotel's personnel.

The research is done and you have the summary tabulations before you. Your next step is to put these data into a meaningful order. Then you will analyze them in light of the problem. From these analyses you hope to identify possible reasons for the different sales volumes of the two groups of hotels. Finally, you will prepare a report presenting the information to Mr. Alvarez. (You'll be careful to refrain from making any specific recommendations for corrective action, since you have neither the information nor the expertise to make such recommendations.)

The summary findings are presented below (S = satisfactory hotels, U = unsatisfactory hotels). Use your logic and imagination to develop any additional details you may need

Check-in experience	S	U
Courtesy/helpfulness of staff:		
Unusually courteous	3	1
Above average	7	6
Below average	1	3
Check-in wait time:		
No waiting	3	4
1–5 minutes	4	6
Over 5 minutes	3	—
Curb appeal		
Visibility/condition of sign:		
Excellent	6	4
Average	4	5
Poor	—	1
Outdoor lighting:		
Excellent	8	6
Average	2	3
Poor	—	1
Cleanliness:		
Excellent	8	6
Average	2	2
Poor	—	2
Grounds:		
Excellent	8	5
Average	2	3
Poor	—	2
Breakfast area		
Cleanliness:		
Excellent	8	5
Average	2	3
Poor	—	2
Food display:		
Appealing	6	2
Average	3	6
Unappealing	1	2
Food quality:		
Excellent	7	5
Average	2	2
Poor	1	3
Restocking of items:		
Excellent	6	4
Average	4	3
Poor	—	3

Preparation of room:	S	U
Excellent	4	2
Above average	6	5
Below average	—	3
Qualifications of managers		
Education:		
Some high school	—	—
High school graduate	2	3
Some college	2	4
College graduate	6	3
Experience:		
Less than 1 year	1	2
1–5 years	4	4
Over 5 years	5	4
Age:		
21–25	—	1
26–30	1	1
31–40	5	1
41–50	3	5
Over 50	1	2
Grades on Manager's Aptitude Test:		
Did not take test	—	3
Below 40 (poor)	—	—
40–59 (acceptable)	2	4
60–79 (good)	4	2
80–100 (outstanding)	4	2
Maintenance personnel		
Appearance:		
Excellent	6	2
Average	4	4
Poor	—	3
Friendliness:		
Excellent	7	2
Average	2	4
Poor	1	4
Desk clerk experience		
Less than 6 months	2	2
6 months–1 year	5	3
Over a year	3	5
Check-out experience		
Excellent	7	3
Average	3	6
Poor	—	1

to write a successful report. For example, in describing your research procedure you may add specifics that your reader would find helpful, and you may generate some plausible specifics when discussing your findings. You can assume that the tabulations and notes for each of the 20 hotels are attached as an appendix.

---

30 Your boss, Mike Stanton, succeeded in gaining approval for launching an employee-volunteer program in the construction company where you serve as Assistant HR Director (see problem 10 above). You have been working on phase one of the plan: surveying the 400 employees to find out what kind of program they would be most likely to support. You designed an online survey to gather this information, and you got 300 replies. Here are the aggregate results:

Q1: Do you currently volunteer in the community?

Yes: 180   No: 120

If yes,

> **About how many hours per week do you volunteer?** 1.2

> **Where do you volunteer? Choose all that apply.**

School: 38	National nonprofit organization: 9
Church: 110	Local nonprofit organization: 26
Neighborhood/community: 80	Other: 7

> **What type(s) of activity do you do? Choose all that apply.**

Tutoring/teaching: 30	Mentoring: 12
Construction/maintenance: 49	Organizing/promoting a cause: 20
Help at food pantry/homeless shelter: 34	Coaching: 31
Beautification work: 34	Other: 4

> **Why do you volunteer? Rate each reason on a scale from 1 (not important) to 7 (very important).**

> It's important to give: 5.5

> I'm needed: 6.5

> It broadens my world: 4

> It makes me feel good to share what I'm good at: 5

> I learn new things: 3

> It feels good to work with others for a good cause: 6.5

> I meet others and make friends: 3.5

> Other: [Use your imagination to invent plausible write-ins.]

If no,

> **Why not? Rate each reason on a scale from 1 (not important) to 7 (very important).**

> I'm too busy: 6.5

> I feel I give enough to others already: 4

> It's too hard to find the right volunteer opportunity for me: 4.5

> It just sounds like more work: 5

> Other: [Use your imagination to invent plausible write-ins.]

Q2: How appealing would you find the following incentives for volunteering? Rate each on a scale from 1 (not important) to 7 (very important).

Time off for volunteering (unpaid): 5

Paid time off for volunteering: 6

Volunteers are celebrated in the company: 3.5

Volunteers can win awards: 4

Volunteers can earn company grants for the organizations where they volunteer: 4.5

Volunteers have advancement opportunities: 3.5

Others in the company, including management, are volunteering: 4.5

Volunteering counts in my performance review or toward my job security: 3.5*

*On this question, the responses were dramatically spread out; 118 employees chose 1 or 2, 100 chose 6 or 7, and 82 chose something in between.

Q3: If the company were to create a volunteer program, how would you feel about each of the following types? Rate each on a scale from 1 (not very positive) to 7 (very positive). (There were only 274 responses to this question.)

Individuals volunteer on their own time: 3

Individuals volunteer for an hour or two of paid time off per month: 4.5

The company holds a special volunteer event (e.g., community fix-up day): 6

Individuals take a paid "service sabbatical" for an extended period (one to 12 months) for special projects: 2

Q4: If the company were to create a volunteer program, what types of employee volunteer opportunities should be supported? Choose one. (There were only 274 responses to this question.)

Any and all service in the community should be supported: 115

Only certain company-approved types of service should be supported: 49

The company should sponsor one or two major community service events: 110

Q5: My general attitude toward a company volunteer program in any form is

Strongly positive: 59

Positive: 79

Neutral: 76

Negative: 60

Strongly negative: 26

Write Mike a report that helps him interpret these data and decide what kinds of parameters the new program should have.

---

31 Write a recommendation report to help solve a problem on your campus or at your workplace. Choose a problem that you can reasonably investigate in the time you have, and find out who the most appropriate recipient for your report will be. Then carefully study both the problem and possible solutions, using any and all appropriate forms of research (including consulting with your intended recipient). Finally, prepare your findings and recommendations in a formal report. (Your instructor may request a progress report midway through your project.)

---

32 Your hard work as assembly worker at a local electronics firm had finally paid off. You were recently promoted to the assistant manager position, and you had heard that another promotion was not too far off.

That was two weeks ago. This morning the company president announced that sales last quarter were the lowest in five years. Lower-priced competitors have saturated the local market, and the sales outlook for the coming year is bleak. Without any new orders by the end of the year, he'll have to reduce the workforce by 25 percent. Your promotion, too, will be gone.

You read in *The Wall Street Journal* that more U.S. manufacturing companies are pursuing markets in Europe. In fact, Germany (or any other county you choose to investigate) appears to be a promising market for your products. Prepare a long, formal report investigating the positives and negatives of trading with Germany. Consider competition, currency exchange, trade restrictions, and treaties. This report should land on the CEO's desk, so include all necessary components of a formal report.

---

33 Your father just called to tell you that his hours at work have been reduced, so you're going to have to find a summer job to help pay for next year's tuition. One of your Facebook friends from your Business Marketing group who knows of your passion for reading tells you about a part-time position available at a local used-book store. You jump at the chance to combine two things you love: business and books.

The job interview with the store manager was not quite what you had expected. Instead of shelving books and ringing up sales, she has a special project for you. Your online résumé, she said, was quite impressive. She especially appreciated the links to your most recent marketing research project dealing with online marketing. She says that sales at the store have been in a free fall for the past several years. As she sees it, they must move their sales to the Internet or they will be out of business by the end of the year. She asks you to compare two established retail Internet sites (e.g., *Craigslist.com* and *Amazon.com*), and recommend the one that best meets the needs of a small business wanting to expand online. Some of her concerns include set-up costs, customer support, reliability, and consumer privacy. She also wants to know which one is the least complicated to use since she is not especially computer literate.

The best part is that she'll pay you $2,500! Write a memo report comparing these sites and recommending the one best for her.

ADDITIONAL TOPICS FOR REPORTS

Following are suggestions for additional report problems ranging from the simple to the highly complex. You can convert them into realistic business problems by supplying details and/or adapting them to real-life business situations. For most of these problems, you can obtain the needed information through secondary research. The topics are arranged by business field, although many of them cross fields.

Accounting

1 Report on current depreciation accounting practices, and recommend depreciation accounting procedures for Company X.

2 Recommend measures that Company X, which recently went public, should take to comply with the Sarbanes-Oxley Act.

3 Report to Company X executives on how tax court decisions handed down over the past six months will affect their firm.

4 What security measures should Company X take regarding access to its accounting data online?

5 Advise the managers of X Company on the accounting issues that they can anticipate when the company begins overseas operations.

6 Analyze break-even analysis as a decision-making tool for X Company.

7 Explain to potential investors which sections in Company X's most recent annual report they should review most carefully.

8 Analyze the relative effects on income of the first-in, first-out (FIFO) and last-in, first-out (LIFO) methods of inventory valuation during a prolonged period of inflation.

9 Write a report for the American Accounting Association on the demand for accountants with computer systems training.

10 Develop information for accounting students at your college that will help them choose between careers in public accounting and careers in private accounting.

11 Advise the management of X Company on the validity of return on investment as a measure of performance.

12 Report on operations research as a decision-making tool for accountants and managers.

13 Report to the management of X Company on trends in the content and design of corporate annual reports.

14 Report to an association of accountants the status of professional ethics in accounting.

15 Report to management of X Company on the communication skills important to accounting.

16 Investigate the matching principle and its effects on financial statements for Company X.

17 Report to the board of directors at Company X on whether the balance sheet fails to recognize important intangible assets.

18 Explain the extent to which the accounting practices in Company X reflect the intent of the company's business decisions.

19 Review for Company X whether disclosure could be an effective substitute for recognition in financial statements.

20 Report to the management of Company X on whether intangible assets have finite or infinite lives.

21 Advise the founders of new Company X on income tax considerations in the selection of a form of business organization.

22 Review for Company X the pros and cons of current methods of securities evaluation.

General Business

23 Evaluate the adequacy of current college programs for developing business leadership.

24 Which business skills should schools and colleges teach, and which should companies teach?

25 What should be the role of business leaders in developing courses and curricula for business schools?

26 Report on ways to build and use good teams in the workplace.

27 Identify the criteria Company X should use in selecting a public relations firm.

28 Investigate the impact of electronic signatures on the business community.

29 How does today's business community regard the master of business administration (MBA) degree?

30 Evaluate the contribution that campus business and professional clubs make to business education.

31 How effective is online training in education for business?

32 Should education for business be specialized, or should it provide a generalized, well-rounded education?

33 What can X Company do to improve the quality of its product or service?

34 Advise Company X on the problems and procedures involved in exporting its products to _____ (your choice of country).

35 Determine how to get and use permission for music, text, and visuals (online, audio, and print) added to business presentations.

36 Determine which of three franchises (your instructor will select) offer the best opportunity for investment.

37 Recommend guidelines to supervisors, managers, and employees of Company X for avoiding sexual harassment cases.

38 Determine cultural issues likely to be encountered by employees going to work in _____ (a foreign country).

39 Should Company X use the U.S. Postal Service or a private courier (Federal Express, United Parcel Service)?

40 For an instructor, answer the question of whether IM-ing should be used as a class teaching tool.

41 Advise a client on whether to invest in a company producing renewable energy (wind, solar, etc.).

42 Recommend for X Company a city and hotel for its annual sales meeting.

Labor

43 For the executives of the National Association of Manufacturers (or a similar group), report on the outlook for labor–management relations in the next 12 months.

44 For the officers of a major labor union, research and report progress toward decreasing job discrimination against minorities.

45 For X Union, project the effects that a particular technology (you choose) will have on traditionally unionized industries by the year 2015.

46 Advise the management of X Company on how to deal with Y Union, which is attempting to organize the employees of X Company.

47 Interpret the change in the number of union members over the past _____ years.

48 Report on the successes and failures of employee-run businesses.

49 Report on the status and effects of "right to work" laws.

50 Evaluate the effects of a particular strike (your choice) on the union, Company X, the stockholders, and the public. Write the report for your boss in Company Y.

51 For Union X, prepare an objective report on union leadership in the nation during the past decade.

52 Layoffs based on seniority are causing a disproportionate reduction in the number of women, minority, and older workers at Company X. Investigate alternatives that the company can present to the union.

53 Investigate recent trends relative to the older worker and the stands that unions have taken in this area.

54 Review the appropriateness of unionizing government workers, and recommend to a body of government leaders the stand they should take on this issue.

55 Report on the role of unions (or management) in politics, and recommend a course for them to follow.

56 Reevaluate _____ (unions or employment relations—your instructor will specify) for the management of X Company.

57 Analyze the changing nature of work for the leaders of _____ union (your instructor will designate).

58 Report on the blending of work and family issues for X Union.

Finance

59 As a financial consultant, evaluate a specific form of tax shelter for a client.

60 Review the customer-relations practices of banks and recommend customer-relations procedures for Bank X.

61 Review current employee loan practices and recommend whether Company X should make employee loans.

62 Report on what Company X needs to know about financial matters in doing business with _____ (foreign country).

63 Give estate planning advice to a client with a unique personal situation.

64 Advise X Company on whether it should lease capital equipment or buy it.

65 Advise Company X on whether it should engage in a joint venture with a company overseas.

66 Should Company X accept major credit cards or set up its own credit card system?

67 Advise Company X on how to avoid a hostile take-over.

68 Which will be the better investment in the next three years: stocks or bonds?

69 Advise Company X on whether it should list its stock on a major stock exchange.

70 Advise Company X, which is having problems with liquidity, on the pros and cons of factoring accounts receivable.

71 Recommend the most feasible way to finance a start-up restaurant.

Management

72 Investigate the likely advantages and disadvantages of requiring workers to wear uniforms at Company X.

73 Develop for Company X a guide to ethical behavior in its highly competitive business situation.

74 After reviewing pertinent literature and experiences of other companies, develop a plan for selecting and training administrators for an overseas operation for Company X.

75 Survey the current literature and advise Company X on whether its management should become politically active.

76 After reviewing the pros and cons, advise X Company on whether it should begin a program of hiring individuals with disabilities or the disadvantaged.

77 Report on the behavioral and psychological effects of introducing wellness programs to Company X.

78 The executives of X Company (a manufacturer of automobile and truck tires) want a report on recent court decisions relating to warranties. Include any recommendations that your report justifies.

79 Report on the issues involved in moving Company X headquarters from _____ (city) to _____ (city).

80 After reviewing current practices regarding worker participation in management, advise Company X on whether it should permit such participation.

81 Should Company X outsource for _____ (service) or establish its own department?

82 Review the advantages and disadvantages of rotating executive jobs at Company X, and then make a recommendation.

83 What should be Company X's policy on office romances?

84 Develop an energy conservation or recycling plan for X Company.

85 Evaluate the effectiveness of a portal for handling internal communications for Company X.

86 Recommend security measures for preventing computer espionage at Company X, a leader in the highly competitive _____ industry.

87 Evaluate the various methods for determining corporate performance and select the one most appropriate for Company X.

88 Advise X Company on the procedures for incorporating in _____ (state or province).

89 Report to Company X on the civil and criminal liabilities of its corporate executives.

90 Report on the quality awards being given to businesses.

91 Determine how diversity enrichment is addressed at Company X.

92 Determine for a legislative committee the extent of minority recruiting, hiring, and training in the industry.

93 As a consultant for an association of farmers, evaluate the recent past and project the future of growing, raising, or bioengineering _____ (your choice—cattle, poultry, wheat, soybeans, or the like).

94 Develop a plan for reducing employee turnover for Company X.

95 Investigate the feasibility of hiring older workers for part-time work for Company X.

Personnel/Human Resource Administration

96 Report on and interpret for Company X the effects of recent court decisions on the testing and hiring of employees.

97 Survey company retirement practices and recommend retirement policies for Company X.

98 Report on practices in compensating key personnel in overseas assignments and recommend policies for the compensation of such personnel for Company X.

99 Report on what human resource executives look for in application documents.

100 Report on the advantages and disadvantages of Company X's providing on-site day care for children of employees.

101 After reviewing the legal and ethical questions involved, recommend whether Company X should use integrity tests in employee hiring.

102 Review what other companies are doing about employees suffering from drug or alcohol abuse, and recommend a policy on the matter for Company X.

103 Report on effective interviewing techniques used to identify the best people to hire.

104 Investigate the impact of the Family Leave Act on Company X.

105 Compare the pros and cons of alternative methods of dispute resolution.

106 What can Company X do to improve employee retention?

107 Review the literature on employee and executive burnout and recommend remedies for it.

108 Investigate the pros and cons of hiring physically and or mentally challenged workers for Company X.

109 Report on ways Company X can link performance improvement plans to discipline and pay.

110 Investigate the impact of the legal aspects of human resource management (EEO, ADA, wrongful termination, harassment, family care and medical leave, workplace violence—your instructor will select one or several) on Company X.

111 Analyze the impact of changing work priorities in a culturally diverse workplace for Company X.

112 Report on recent issues in employee communication for Company X.

113 Investigate the problem of employee absenteeism at Company X and recommend ways to decrease it.

Marketing

114 Review the available literature and advise Company X on whether it should franchise its _____ business.

115 Select a recent national marketing program and analyze why it succeeded or failed.

116 Advise the advertising vice president of Company X on whether the company should respond to or ignore a competitor's direct attack on the quality of its product.

117 Review the ethical considerations involved in advertising to children and advise Company X on the matter.

118 Determine for Company X the social and ethical aspects of pricing for the market.

119 Explore the possibilities of trade with _____ (a foreign country) for Company X.

120 Determine for a national department store chain changing trends in the services that customers expect when shopping online.

121 Prepare a report to help a contingent of your legislature decide whether current regulation of advertising should be changed.

122 Determine the problems X Company will encounter in introducing a new product to its line.

123 Report on the success of rebates as a sales stimulator and advise Company X on whether it should use rebates.

124 Should Company X buy or lease minivans for distributing its products?

125 Determine the trends in packaging in the _____ industry.

126 Should X Company establish its own sales force, use manufacturer's agents, or use selling agents?

127 How should Company X evaluate the performance of its salespeople?

128 Determine for X Company how it can evaluate the effectiveness of its (online, print, or radio) advertising.

129 Select the best channel of distribution for new product Y and justify your choice.

130 Should X Company establish its own advertising department or use an advertising agency?

131 Conduct a market study of _____ (city) to determine whether it is a suitable location for _____ (a type of business).

132 Report to X Company on drip marketing and recommend whether it should use drip marketing to increase sales.

133 Investigate the factors to consider when marketing online through the Internet to children.

134 Compare the effectiveness of three different types of online advertising and recommend one for Company X.

135 Determine whether any of the products of Company X are good candidates for infomercials.

Computer Applications

136 Recommend a handheld computer for use by the salespeople of Company X.

137 Determine whether Company X should purchase or lease its computer equipment.

138 Report to the president of Company X the copyright and contract laws that apply to the use of computer programs.

139 Investigate the possibility of using the majority of office applications from the Internet rather than continually purchasing and upgrading programs.

140 Determine which positions Company X should designate as possible telecommuting candidates.

141 Report on the future developments of robotics in the _____ industry.

142 Review and rank for possible adoption three software programs that Company X might use for its _____ work (name the field of operations).

143 Determine for Company X the factors it should consider in selecting computer insurance.

144 Compare three online programs/courses for training your employees on _____ (name the topic) and recommend one.

145 Your Company is considering the purchase of smart phones for its sales representatives. Evaluate three brands and recommend one for purchase.

146 Do a cost/benefit analysis of purchasing Tablet PCs for use by sales representatives at Company X.

147 Explore the procedures and methods for measuring information system effectiveness and productivity for Company X.

148 Investigate how to improve information security and control for Company X.

149 Identify and recommend Web-based survey tools that would be appropriate for Company X.

Business Education

150 Evaluate the effect of remodeling your new office site using both ergonomic and feng shui principles.

151 Report on ways companies now use and plan to use desktop meeting applications.

152 Analyze the possibility of instituting companywide training on etiquette, covering everything from handling telephone calls, to sexual harassment, to dining out.

153 Advise management on the importance of the air quality in its offices.

154 Investigate ways to complete and submit company forms on the Web or the company portal.

155 Evaluate the reprographic services and practices at your school from an environmental perspective.

156 Report on ways to hire and keep the best employees in the computer support center.

157 Report on ways to improve literacy in the workplace.

158 Report on the availability and quality of online training programs.

159 Report on ways to improve the communication of cross-cultural work groups.

160 Analyze the possibility of using voice-recognition software with the products available today.

161 Determine for Company X whether it should replace the laptop computers of its sales reps with tablet PCs.

162 Evaluate at least three data visualization programs and recommend one for use at Company X.

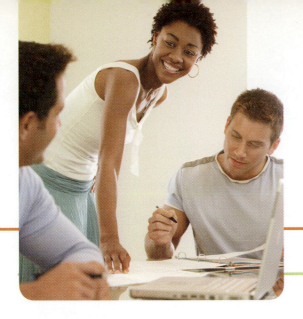

chapter twelve

Graphics in Reports and Other Documents

Upon completing this chapter, you will be able to use graphics effectively in business reports. To reach this goal, you should be able to

1. Plan which parts of your report or other document should be communicated by graphics.

2. Explain the general mechanics of constructing graphics—size, layout, type, rules and borders, color and cross-hatching, clip art, background, numbering, titles, title placement, and footnotes and acknowledgments.

3. Construct textual graphics such as tables, pull quotes, flowcharts, and process charts.

4. Construct and use visual graphics such as bar charts, pie charts, line charts, scatter diagrams, and maps.

5. Avoid common errors and ethical problems when constructing and using graphics.

6. Place and interpret graphics effectively.

Graphics in Reports and Other Documents

In your management job at Pinnacle, you proofread reports prepared by your co-workers. Because Pinnacle uses chemicals in its products, many of the reports are highly technical and complex. Many others, especially those coming from finance and sales, are filled with facts and figures. In your judgment, most of the reports you have proofread are hard to understand.

The one you are looking at now is packed with page after page of sales statistics. Your mind quickly gets lost in the mass of details. Why didn't the writer take the time to summarize the more important figures in a chart? And why didn't the writer put some of the details in tables? Many of the other reports you have been reading, especially the technical ones, are in equal need of graphics. Bar charts, pie charts, and maps would certainly help explain some of the concepts discussed. If only report writers would understand that words alone sometimes cannot communicate clearly—that words sometimes need to be supplemented with visual communication techniques. If the writers of your reports studied the following review of graphics, your job would be easier and more enjoyable. So would the jobs of the readers of those reports.

- A graphic is any form of illustration.

In many of your reports and other business documents, you will need to use graphics to help convey information quickly and accurately. Graphics also grab attention and help the reader retain information. By *graphics* we mean any form of illustration (e.g., charts, pictures, diagrams, maps, tables, or bulleted lists). Although some situations call for decorative graphics, graphics in business tend to be functional. Our focus is therefore on graphics that communicate.

PLANNING THE GRAPHICS

- You should plan the use of graphics as you plan your document.

You should plan the graphics for a document soon after you organize your findings. Your planning of graphics should be guided largely by your communication purpose. Graphics can clarify complex or difficult information, emphasize facts, add coherence, summarize data, and provide interest. Additionally, today's data mining and visualization tools help writers filter the vast amount of data that is gathered and stored regularly. Of course, well-constructed graphics also enhance the document's appearance.

- In planning their use, look for information that they can help communicate.

In selecting graphics, you should review the information that your document will contain, looking for any possibility of improving communication of the material through the use of graphics. Specifically, you should look for complex information that visual presentation can make clear, for information too detailed to be covered in words, and for information that deserves special emphasis.

- Plan graphics with your reader in mind.

Of course, you will want to plan with your reader in mind and choose graphics appropriate to both the content and context where they are presented. You should construct graphics to help the intended reader understand the information more quickly, easily, and completely. Keep in mind that the time and money you spend gathering information or creating a graphic should be balanced in terms of the importance of the message you want to convey.

- But remember that graphics supplement and do not replace the writing

As you plan the graphics, remember that some graphics can stand alone, but others will supplement the writing or speaking—not take its place. Graphics in documents or oral reports should help the wording by covering the more difficult parts, emphasizing the important points, and presenting details. But the words should carry the main message—all of it.

DETERMINING THE GENERAL MECHANICS OF CONSTRUCTION

In constructing graphics, you will be concerned with various mechanical matters. The most common are summarized in the following paragraphs.

Size

One of the first steps you must make in constructing a graphic is determining its size. This decision should not be arbitrary, and it should not be based on convenience. You should give the graphic the size that its contents and importance justify. If a graphic is simple (with only two or three quantities), a quarter page might be more than enough. But if a graphic must display complex or detailed information, a full page might be justified.

With extremely complex, involved information, you may need to use more than a full page. When you do, make certain that this large page is inserted and folded so that the readers can open it easily. The fold you select will be determined by the size of the page. You simply have to experiment until you find a convenient fold.

- Make each graphic the size that its contents justify.

- Graphics larger than a page are justified if they contain enough information.

Layout

You should determine the layout (shape) of the graphic by considering its size and contents. Sometimes a tall orientation (portrait) is the answer; sometimes the answer is a wide orientation (landscape). Simply consider the logical possibilities and select the one that appears best.

- Size and contents determine the shape of graphics.

Type

The type used in graphics throughout a report should generally be consistent in terms of style and font. Style refers to the look of the type such as bold or italics; font refers to the look of the letters such as with or without feet (*serif* or *sans serif*). Occasionally you may want to vary the type, but do so by design for some special reason. Be aware that even the design of the font you choose will convey a message, a message that should work with the text content and design. If your reader will be viewing the document on screen in Word 2007 or on a Vista computer with ClearType, be sure to use one of the fonts optimized for use with ClearType such as Cambria or Calibri. They were designed to render well on the screen, and Microsoft's research has confirmed that they enable

- Choose a type to help convey the message clearly.

"This is where we added high-caffeine cappuccino in our office coffee machines."

people to read faster and more accurately, leading to a 7 percent average increase in productivity.[1]

Size is another variable to watch. The size you choose should look appropriate in the context in which it is used. Your top priority when choosing type style, font, and size should always be readability.

- Choose a type size that is readable.

Rules and Borders

- Use rules and borders when they improve the graphic's appearance.

You should use rules and borders when they help the appearance of the graphic. Rules help distinguish one section or graphic from another, while borders help separate graphics from the text. In general, you should place borders around graphics that occupy less than a full page. You also can place borders around full-page graphics, but such borders serve little practical value. Except in cases in which graphics simply will not fit into the normal page layout, you should not extend the borders of graphics beyond the normal page margins.

Color and Cross-Hatching

- Color and cross-hatching can improve graphics.

Color and cross-hatching, appropriately used, help readers see comparisons and distinctions (see Figure 12–1). In fact, research has found that color in graphics improves the comprehension, retention, and ease of extracting information. Also, color and cross-hatching add to the attractiveness of the report. Because color is especially effective for this purpose, you should use it whenever practical and appropriate.

Clip Art

- Use clip art to help your reader understand your message.

Today you can get good-looking clip art easily—so easily in fact that some writers often overuse it. Although clip art can add interest and bring the reader into a graphic effectively, it also can overpower and distract the reader. The general rule is to keep in mind the purpose your clip art is serving: to help the reader understand the content. It should be appropriate in both its nature and size. It also should be appropriate in its representation of gender, race, and age. Also, if it is copyrighted, you need permission to use it.

Background

- Background color, photos, and art should enhance the message of the graphic.

Background colors, photos, and art for your graphics should be chosen carefully. The color should provide high contrast with the data and not distract from the main message. Photos, especially washout photos that are well chosen, can add interest and draw the reader in. As with any photos or art, backgrounds should create a positive, professional impression. Additionally, when graphics are used cross-culturally, you will want to be sure the message your background sends is the one you intended by testing or reviewing it with the intended receivers.

Figure 12–1

Color versus Cross-Hatched Pie

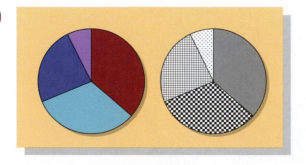

---

[1] Bill Hill, video interview, *Microsoft.com,* Microsoft, 2005, Web, 29 May 2006.

COMMUNICATION MATTERS

Adding Some "Spark (lines)" to Your Text

As with any visual, sparklines are intended to get the reader's attention and communicate information more concisely and clearly than spoken or written text. Unlike other graphics that stand separately from the text in a document, sparklines generally run with text or within a table and are not labeled as tables or figures. Invented by Edward Tufte, they are tiny graphics that, as he describes them, "can be embedded in-line in a sentence, summarizing millions of points of data in the space of a word." Many times they represent financial data, such as the day's market performance below:

The color and bar graphs provide the reader with an immediate understanding of the market performance throughout the day. Imagine the amount of work the reader would have to do to understand the performance of the market by viewing an hour-by-hour representation of discrete data in a standard table or bar graph! If a reader needs this information, then of course an expanded table or figure is necessary, but if the reader needs only a quick understanding of the information, a sparkline could likely do a better job of meeting the reader's needs.

Bissantz SparkPro 4 lets writers create sparklines in Excel, Word, PowerPoint, and HTML documents. Some examples of sparklines provided at its website include the following:

As you consider the possibilities for graphics in your documents, be sure you add sparklines to your list.

Sources: Adam Aston, "Tuft's Invisible yet Ubiquitous Influence," *BusinessWeek*, McGraw-Hill Companies, 10 June 2009, Web, 16 June 2009.

"SparkMaker 4: SparkMaker 4Sparklines for Excel, Word, PowerPoint, and HTML Documents," *Bissantz.de,* Bissantz, 2009, Web, 16 June 2009.

Numbering

Pull quotes, clip art, and other decorative visuals do not need to be numbered. Neither does a lone table or figure in a document. Otherwise, you should number all the graphics. Many schemes of numbering are available to you, depending on the types of graphics you have.

- Number graphics consecutively by type.

If you have many graphics that fall into two or three categories, you may number each of the categories consecutively. For example, if your report is illustrated by six tables, five charts, and six maps, you may number these graphics Table I, Table II, . . . Table VI; Chart 1, Chart 2, . . . Chart 5; and Map 1, Map 2, . . . Map 6.

However, if your graphics comprise a wide mixture of types, you may number them in two groups: tables and figures. Figures, a miscellaneous grouping, may include all types other than tables. To illustrate, consider a report containing three tables, two maps, three charts, one diagram, and one photograph. You could number

- Figures are a miscellaneous grouping of types. Number tables separately.

these graphics Table I, Table II, and Table III and Figure 1, Figure 2, . . . Figure 7. By convention, tables are not grouped with other types of graphics. But it would not be wrong to group and number as figures all graphics other than tables even if the group contained sufficient subgroups (charts, maps, and the like) to permit separate numbering of each of them.

Construction of Titles and Captions

- The titles should describe content clearly (consider the five Ws: *who, what, where, when, why*).

Every graphic should have a title or caption that adequately describes its contents. A title is used with graphics displayed in oral presentations; a caption is used with graphics included in print documents. Like the headings used in other parts of the report, the title or caption of the graphic has the objective of concisely covering the contents. As a check of content coverage, you might well use the journalist's five Ws: *who, what, where, when,* and *why,* and sometimes you also might use *how.* But because conciseness also is desired, it is not always necessary to include all the Ws in the title. The title or caption of a chart comparing the annual sales volume of the Texas and California territories of the Dell Company for the years 2009–10 might be constructed as follows:

Who: Dell Company
What: Annual sales
Where: Texas and California branches
When: 2009–10
Why: For comparison

The title or caption might read, "Comparative Annual Sales of Texas and California Territories of the Dell Company, 2009–10." For even more conciseness, you could use a major title and subtitle. The major title might read, "A Texas and California Sales Comparison"; the subtitle might read, "Dell Company 2009–10." Similarly, the caption might read "A Texas and California Sales Comparison: Dell Company 2009–10."

An alternative to this kind of topic heading is a talking heading. As you learned in Chapter 10, the talking heading tells the reader the nature of what is to follow. The same holds true for a graphic. In this case a talking heading might read, "Texas Leads California in Total Annual Sales for 2009." In a sense, it gives the reader the main message of the graphic.

Placement of Titles and Captions

- The conventional placement of titles is at the top for tables and at the bottom for charts, but many place all titles at the top.

In documents, titles of tables conventionally appear above the tabular display; captions of all other types of graphics may appear above or below them. Most software programs automatically place titles and captions at the top. When typing these, use title case (the kind of capitalization used for book titles).

Footnotes and Acknowledgments

- Use footnotes to explain or elaborate.

Parts of a graphic sometimes require special explanation or elaboration. When this happens, as when similar situations arise in connection with the text of the document, you should use footnotes. Such footnotes are concise explanations placed below the illustration and keyed to the part explained by means of a superscript (raised) number or symbol (asterisk, dagger, double dagger, and so on). Footnotes for tables are best placed immediately below the graphic presentation. Footnotes for other graphic forms follow the illustration when the title or caption is placed at the bottom of the graphic (see Figure 12–2).

- Acknowledge the source of the data in a footnote.

Usually, a source acknowledgment is the bottom-most component of a graphic. By *source acknowledgment* we mean a reference to the body or authority that deserves the credit for gathering the data used in the illustration. The entry consists of the word *Source* followed by a colon and the source information (in some cases,

Figure 12–2

Good Arrangement of the Parts of a Typical Table

Table number and title → **Table 1. Top 10 US Brands Advertised on Radio by Number of Ad Plays**
Week of July 27, 2009

Column heads →

Rank Last Period	Rank This Period	Brand Advertised	Category	Plays This Period	Plays Last Period	Share of Market	Change in Plays	% Change
1	1	GEICO INSURANCE	INSURANCE: AUTO	50,364	62,171	2.7%	-11,807	-19%
2	2	HOME DEPOT / EXPO DESIGN CENTER	RETAIL & E-TAIL STORES: HARDWARE / HOME IMPROVEMENT	47,568	44,643	2.6%	2,925	7%
3	3	MCDONALD'S RESTAURANT	RESTAURANTS / FOOD SERVICE: QUICK SERVICE RESTAURANT - NATIONAL	36,592	37,312	2.0%	-720	-2%
4	9	AUTOZONE AUTO PARTS STORE	AUTOMOTIVE PRODUCTS & SERVICES: PARTS & ACCESSORIES STORES	24,113	14,172	1.3%	9,941	70%
5	5	HD RADIO	MASS MEDIA: BROADCAST RADIO	22,903	21,333	1.2%	1,570	7%
6	66	WALMART DEPARTMENT STORES	RETAIL & E-TAIL STORES: DEPARTMENT STORES	20,773	4,399	1.1%	16,374	372%
7	16	KOHL'S DEPARTMENT STORES	RETAIL & E-TAIL STORES: DEPARTMENT STORES	19,090	11,080	1.0%	8,010	72%
8	17	VERIZON	TELECOMMUNICATIONS: TELEPHONE - WIRELESS PROVIDERS, SERVICE & PRODUCTS	18,783	10,752	1.0%	8,031	75%
9	8	WELLS FARGO / WACHOVIA BANKS	FINANCIAL SERVICES: BANKS & CREDIT UNIONS	17,316	15,647	.9%	1,669	11%
10	6	AT&T	TELECOMMUNICATIONS: TELEPHONE - WIRELESS PROVIDERS, SERVICE & PRODUCTS	16,962	17,086	.9%	-124	-1%

Source acknowledgment → Source: Mediaguide Inc., "Top 10 US Brands Advertised on Radio by Number of Ad Plays," *Marketing Charts*, Watershed Publishing, 7 Aug. 2009, Web, 20 Aug. 2009.

simply the source name will suffice). See Figure 12–2 for an illustration of source acknowledgment.

If you or your staff collected the data, you may either omit the source note or give the source as "Primary," in which case the note would read like this:

Source: Primary.

- "Source: Primary" is the proper note for data you gathered.

CONSTRUCTING TEXTUAL GRAPHICS

Graphics for communicating report information fall into two general categories: those that communicate primarily through textual content (words and numerals) and those that communicate primarily through some form of visual. Included in the textual group are pull quotes and a variety of process charts (e.g., Gantt, flow, organization).

- Graphics fall into two general categories: (1) textual (words and numerals) and (2) visual (pictures).

Tables

A *table* is an orderly arrangement of information in rows and columns. As we have noted, tables are textual graphics (not really pictures), but they communicate like graphics, and they have many of the characteristics of graphics.

- A table is an orderly arrangement of information.

Two basic types of tables are available to you: the general-purpose table and the special-purpose table. General-purpose tables cover a broad area of information. For example, a table reviewing the answers to all the questions in a survey is a general-purpose table. Such tables usually belong in the appendix.

- You may use general-purpose tables (those containing broad information),

Special-purpose tables are prepared for one special purpose: to illustrate a particular part of the report. They contain information that could be included with related information in a general-purpose table. For example, a table presenting the answer to one of the questions in a survey is a special-purpose table. Such tables belong in the report text near the discussion of their contents.

- or you may use special-purpose tables (those covering a specific area of information).

Aside from the title, footnotes, and source designation previously discussed, a table contains heads, columns, and rows of data, as shown in Figure 12–2. Row heads are the titles of the rows of data, and column heads are the titles of the columns.

- See Figure 12–2 for labeled table components.

The construction of text tables is largely influenced by their purpose. Nevertheless, a few rules generally apply:

- If rows are long, the row heads may be repeated at the right.

- The em dash (—) or the abbreviation *n.a.* (or *N.A.* or *NA*), but not the zero, is used to indicate data not available.

- Since footnote numbers in a table full of numbers might be confusing, footnote references to numbers in the table should be keyed with asterisks (*), daggers (†), double daggers (‡), section marks (§), and so on. Small letters of the alphabet can be used when many references are made.

- Totals and subtotals should appear whenever they help readers interpret the table. The totals may be for each column and sometimes for each row. Row totals are usually placed at the right; but when they need emphasis, they may be placed at the left. Likewise, column totals are generally placed at the bottom of the column, but they may be placed at the top when the writer wants to emphasize them. A ruled line (usually a double one) separates the totals from their components.

- The units in which the data are recorded must be clear. Unit descriptions (e.g., bushels, acres, pounds) appropriately appear above the columns, as part of the headings or subheadings. If the data are in dollars, however, placing the dollar mark ($) before the first entry in each column is sufficient.

● Tabular information also can be presented as (1) leaderwork (as illustrated here), or

Tabular information need not always be presented in formal tables. In fact, short arrangements of data may be presented more effectively as parts of the text. Such arrangements are generally made as either leaderwork or text tabulations.

Leaderwork is the presentation of tabular material in the text without titles or rules. (*Leaders* are the repeated dots with intervening spaces.) Typically, a colon precedes the tabulation, as in this illustration:

The August sales of the representatives in the Western Region were as follows:

> Charles B. Brown $33,517
> Thelma Capp 39,703
> Bill E. Knauth 38,198

Text tabulations are simple tables, usually with column heads and sometimes with rules and borders. But they are not numbered, and they have no titles. They are made to read with the text, as in this example:

● (2) text tabulations (as illustrated here).

In August the sales of the representatives in the Western Region increased sharply from those for the preceding month, as these figures show:

Representative	July Sales	August Sales	Increase
Charles B. Brown	$32,819	$33,517	$ 698
Thelma Capp	37,225	39,703	2,478
Bill E. Knauth	36,838	38,198	1,360

Pull Quotes

● Pull quotes emphasize key concepts.

The pull quote is a textual visual that is often overlooked yet extremely useful in emphasizing key points. It is also useful when the text or content of the report does not lend itself naturally or easily to other graphics. By selecting a key sentence, copying it to a text box, enlarging it, and perhaps even enhancing it with a new font, style, or color, a writer can break up the visual boredom of a full page or screen of text. Software lets users easily wrap text around shapes as well as along curves and irregular lines. Figure 12–3 shows an example that is simple yet effective in both drawing the reader's attention to a key point and adding visual interest to a page.

Bullet Lists

● Bullet lists show points set off by a bullet symbol.

Bullet lists are listings of points arranged with bullets (•) to set them off. These lists can have a title that covers all the points, or they can appear without titles, as they appear at various places in this book. When you use this arrangement, make the points grammatically parallel. If the points have subparts, use sub-bullets for them. Make the

Figure 12–3

Illustration of a Pull Quote

beating down the doors to join his group. In terms of execution, his track record was flawless: He and his team had met or surpassed their numbers in each of the past five years. Additionally, they had successfully implemented every major corporate program during that time, and his division had recently been selected to serve as the pilot site for an SAP installation. When he'd learned of these last two GM assignments, he'd also been told that he had a great future with the company and that with a little "seasoning," he'd be ready for advancement. He'd tried several times to get the real scoop on why he hadn't been promoted, only to hear vague comments about improving his "communication skills" and demonstrating more "executive presence" and "leadership." It seemed to him that the company valued people who could look and sound good in the boardroom more than it cared about the year-over-year results of proven performers like himself.

As for Kelly? She'd hired some top people in the past couple of years, but Ralph knew that she had a reputation for being tough on her reports and having "sharp elbows." To Ralph, the promotion wasn't much of an expression of the company's leadership competency model, posted on his office wall: "Display ethics and integrity, envision the future, deliver results, focus on customers, engage in teamwork and collaboration, and develop talent." Ralph bore Kelly no ill will, but it looked as though it was time to update his résumé and rekindle some relationships in his network. Distasteful as it was, testing the job market seemed to be the only way to advance.

The Unwritten Rules

Ralph's situation is surprisingly common, especially among people who aren't politically inclined. Few organizations spell out the criteria for advancement.

Though Ralph had been considered for the GM role both times, in each instance there were bona fide concerns about his readiness. The vague feedback

IDEA IN BRIEF

- Decisions about who gets promoted can seem mysterious and arbitrary. Stellar performance reviews and a strong track record – and you still get passed over. What's going on?

- In most companies feedback is vague and confusing – sometimes intentionally, so as not to demoralize. It's up to you to ferret out the real reasons you're not getting the job.

- For example, think twice when you're told you need to work on "leadership" or gain more "seasoning." These can be code words masking more specific concerns, like a failure to demonstrate strategic thinking or an inability to delegate.

about his communication skills actually alluded to tensions with peers in other units: He could be overly competitive and slow to resolve conflict, whereas Kelly's powers of persuasion allowed her to manage discord and achieve superior results. She was also known for developing talent. Working for her was not for the faint of heart, but she challenged her staff members, and they grew in the process. Ralph didn't recognize that his

Under the heading of "leadership" lurked questions regarding Ralph's strategic thinking. He was a go-to guy for implementing corporate initiatives, a master of continuous improvement. But senior management had seen no evidence of his ability to conceive a large-scale change that would produce a quantum leap in performance. Can strategic thinking be developed? That's open to debate, but the fact was that Ralph had always worked for visionaries who never gave him the chance to flex his own strategic muscles, a problem everyone had overlooked.

The information void wasn't a matter of malice; rather, it was due to assumptions that nobody thought to make explicit and an all-too-human reluctance to deliver bad news. Managers and HR professionals often provide intentionally vague feedback for fear of losing a good employee. Further, although most leadership competency models refer in some way to important management skills and attributes, they typically fail to distinguish nice-to-have from non-negotiable skills.

What's more, such models usually don't spell out how leadership skills should be demonstrated at different levels or how the relative importance of those qualities will change as you rise

> ## Managers may provide vague feedback to avoid losing a good employee.

popularity reflected, in part, his reputation for being a little easy on people – he didn't stretch them to grow and develop. Managers flocking to his unit were often B players who knew he'd cut them some slack. He was luring talent that was good but not great; Kelly was attracting A players who wanted a push. The company's competency model included "develop talent" but didn't specify that having a track record for doing so was nonnegotiable for anyone who wanted to rise beyond Ralph's level.

in the hierarchy. For example, in middle management, teamwork – defined as the ability to maintain cohesion and morale within one's group – is a vital competency. At higher levels, where Ralph hopes to play, it matters less. In fact, at most companies, cohesion tends to fall short at senior levels thanks to rivalry and ego, but teams function pretty well nonetheless. Acquiring and developing talent is the executive's imperative, and teamwork becomes a nice-to-have. Ralph's ability to orchestrate

Source: *Harvard Business Review,* "Why Didn't You Get that Promotion, John Beeson, June 1, 2009: 102.

sub-bullets different by color, size, shape, or weight. Darts, check marks, squares, or triangles can be used for the secondary bullets.

Flowcharts and Process Charts

If you have studied business management, you know that administrators use a variety of specialized charts in their work. Often these charts are a part of the information presented in reports. Perhaps the most common of these is the *organization chart* (see Figure 12–4). These charts show the hierarchy of levels and positions in an organization. As the word implies, a *flowchart* (see Figure 12–5) shows the sequence of activities in a process. Traditionally, flowcharts use specific designs and symbols to show process variations. A variation of the organization and flowchart

- Various specialized management charts are useful in reports—for example, organization charts, flowcharts, and Gantt charts.

Figure 12–4

Illustration of an Organization Chart

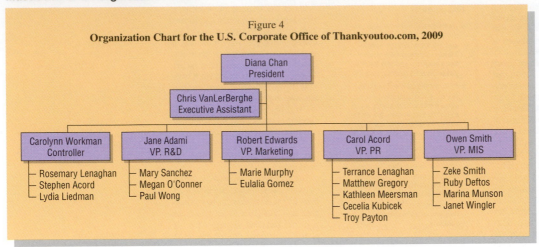

Figure 4
Organization Chart for the U.S. Corporate Office of Thankyoutoo.com, 2009

Figure 12–5

Illustration of a Flowchart

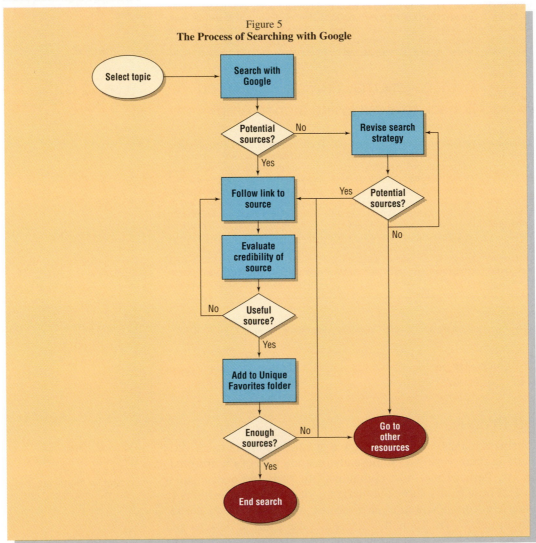

Figure 5
The Process of Searching with Google

Figure 12–6

Illustration of a Gantt Chart

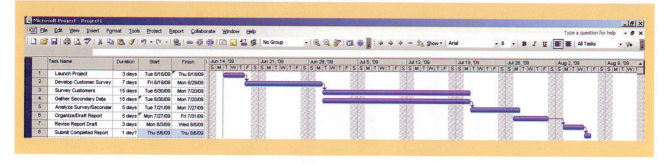

is the *decision tree*. This chart helps one follow a path to an appropriate decision. *Gantt charts* are graphic presentations that show planning and scheduling activities (see Figure 12–6). You can easily construct these charts in a variety of applications.

CONSTRUCTING VISUAL GRAPHICS

The truly visual types of graphics include a variety of charts and illustrations. Charts are graphics built with raw data and include bar, pie, and line charts and all their variations and combinations. Illustrations include maps, diagrams, drawings, photos, and cartoons.

- Visual graphics include data-generated charts, photographs, and artwork.

Bar and Column Charts

Simple bar and *column charts* compare differences in quantities using differences in the lengths of the bars to represent those quantities. You should use them primarily to show comparisons of quantity changes at a moment in time.

As shown in Figure 12–7, the main parts of the bar chart are the bars and the grid (the field on which the bars are placed). The bars, which may be arranged horizontally or vertically (also called a column chart), should be of equal width. You should identify each bar or column, usually with a caption at the left or bottom. The grid (field) on which the bars are placed is usually needed to show the magnitudes of the bars, and the units (e.g., dollars, pounds, miles) are identified by the scale caption below.

When you need to compare quantities of two or three different values in one chart, you can use a *clustered* (or *multiple*) *bar chart*. Cross-hatching, colors, or the like on the bars distinguish the different kinds of information (see Figure 12–8). Somewhere

- Simple bar and column charts compare differences in quantities by using varying bar lengths.

- Clustered bar charts are useful in comparing two or three kinds of quantities.

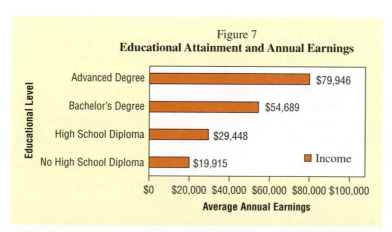

Figure 7
Educational Attainment and Annual Earnings

Source: "Earnings Gap Highlighted by Census Bureau Data on Educational Attainment," *U.S. Census Bureau*, U.S. Census Bureau News, 15 Mar. 2007, Web, 20 Aug. 2009.

Figure 12–7

Illustration of a Bar Chart

Figure 12–8

Illustration of a Clustered Bar Chart

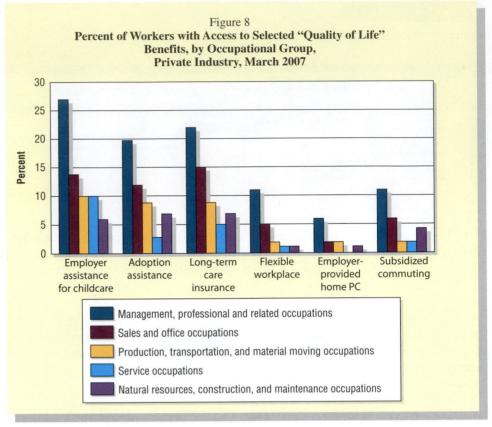

Figure 8
**Percent of Workers with Access to Selected "Quality of Life"
Benefits, by Occupational Group,
Private Industry, March 2007**

Legend:
- Management, professional and related occupations
- Sales and office occupations
- Production, transportation, and material moving occupations
- Service occupations
- Natural resources, construction, and maintenance occupations

Source: George I. Long, "Employer-provided 'Quality-of-life' Benefits for Workers in Private Industry," *Compensation and Working Conditions,* Bureau of Labor Statistics, 24 Oct. 2007, Web, 19 Aug. 2009.

within the chart, a legend (explanation) gives a key to the different bars. Because clustered bar charts can become cluttered, usually you should limit comparisons to three to five kinds of information in one of them.

- When you need to show plus and minus differences, bilateral column charts are useful.

When you need to show plus and minus differences, you can use *bilateral column charts*. The columns of these charts begin at a central point of reference and may go either up or down, as illustrated in Figure 12–9. Bar titles appear either within, above, or below the bars, depending on which placement fits best. Bilateral column charts are especially good for showing percentage changes, but you may use them for any series in which plus and minus quantities are present.

- To compare subdivisions of columns, use a stacked bar chart.

If you need to compare subdivisions of columns, you can use a *stacked (subdivided) column chart*. As shown in Figure 12–10, such a chart divides each column into its parts. It distinguishes these parts by color, cross-hatching, or the like; and it explains these differences in a legend. Subdivided columns may be difficult for your reader to interpret since both the beginning and ending points need to be found. Then the reader has to subtract to find the size of the column component. Clustered column charts or pie charts do not introduce this possibility for error.

- Two-dimensional columns on two-dimensional axes are easiest for readers to use.

Another feature that can lead to reader error in interpreting bar and column chart data is the use of three dimensions when only two variables are being compared. In one study, university students were asked questions regarding two-dimensional and three-dimensional graphics in a PowerPoint presentation. Students more accurately interpreted the two-dimensional graphs—especially when the information was complex.[2] Therefore, unless more than two variables are used, choosing the two-dimensional presentation over the three-dimensional form is usually better.

---

[2] Michelle Stewart Brandie, Lisa Ann Best, and Jessica Marie Cipolla, "Extraneous Information and Graph Comprehension: Implications for Effective Design Choices," *Campus-Wide Information Systems* 26.3 (2009): 191–200, print.

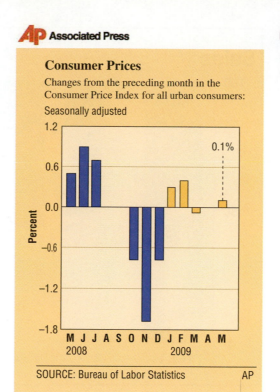

AP Associated Press

Consumer Prices

Changes from the preceding month in the Consumer Price Index for all urban consumers: Seasonally adjusted

0.1%

SOURCE: Bureau of Labor Statistics   AP

Figure 12–9

Illustration of a Bilateral Column Chart

Chart shows percent change in the Consumer Price Index from prior month, seasonally adjusted.

Source: "Consumer Prices," *Hosted News,* Google, 2009, Web, 16 June 2009.

Figure 10
Spending by Student Type, 2008

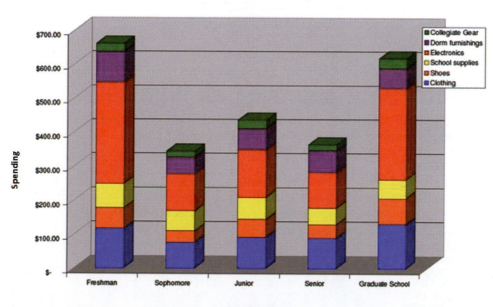

Figure 12–10

Illustration of a Stacked Column Chart

Source: "Back to School College Spending to Surpass $47 Billion," *Marketing Charts*, Watershed Publishing, 2009, Web, 16 June 2009.

A special form of stacked (subdivided) column chart is used to compare the subdivisions of percentages. In this form, all the bars are equal in length, for each represents 100 percent. Only the subdivisions within the bars vary. The objective of this form is to compare differences in how wholes are divided. The component parts may be labeled, as in Figure 12–11, or explained in a legend.

• You also can use such a chart for comparing subdivisions of percentages.

Figure 12–11

Illustration of a
100 Percent Stacked
Column Chart

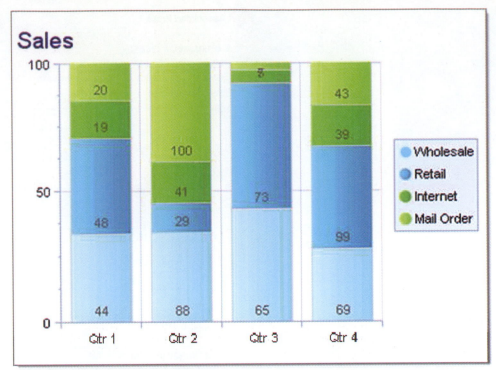

Source: "Stacked Bar 100% Charts," *RadChart for WinForms,* Telerik, 2009, Web, 19 Aug. 2009.
<http://www.telerik.com/help/winforms/understandingtypesstackedbar100.html>.

Pictographs

● Pictographs are bar or column charts made with pictures.

A *pictograph* is a bar or column chart that uses bars made of pictures. The pictures are typically drawings of the items being compared. For example, the number of senators in Figure 12–12 is shown by the image of a single person for each senator instead of by ordinary bars.

Figure 12–12

Illustration of a Pictograph

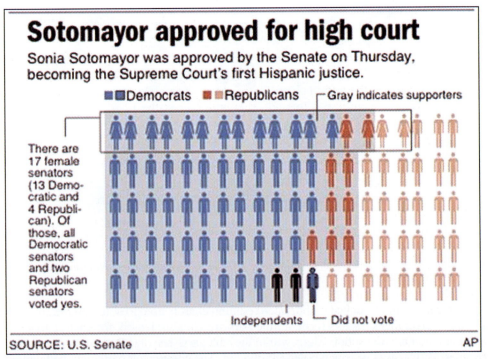

Source: D. Morris, "Sotomayor Approved for High Court," *The Washington Post,* The Washington Post Company, 7 Aug. 2009, Web, 20 Aug. 2009.

PART 4   Fundamentals of Report Writing

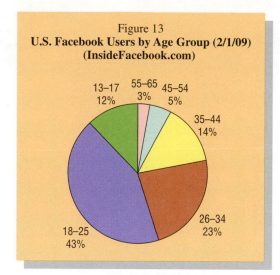

Figure 12–13

Illustration of a Pie Chart

Figure 13
U.S. Facebook Users by Age Group (2/1/09)
(InsideFacebook.com)

13–17
12%

55–65
3%

45–54
5%

35–44
14%

26–34
23%

18–25
43%

Source: "Women Over 55 Take Facebook by Storm," *Marketing Charts*, Watershed Publishing, Feb. 2009, Web, 16 June 2009.

In constructing a pictograph, you should follow the procedures you used in constructing bar and column charts and two special rules. First, you must make all the picture units equal in size. The human eye is grossly inaccurate when comparing geometric designs that vary in more than one dimension, so show differences by varying the number, not the size, of the picture units. Second, you should select pictures or symbols that fit the information to be illustrated. In comparing the cruise lines of the world, for example, you might use ships. In comparing computers used in the world's major countries, you might use computers. The meaning of the drawings you use must be immediately clear to the readers.

- In constructing pictographs, follow the procedure for making bar and column charts, plus two special rules.

Pie Charts

The most frequently used chart in comparing the subdivisions of wholes is the *pie chart* (see Figure 12–13). As the name implies, pie charts show the whole of the information being studied as a pie (circle) and the parts of this whole as slices of the pie. The slices may be distinguished by labeling and color or cross-hatching. A single slice can be emphasized by exploding—pulling out—a piece. Because it is hard to judge the values of the slices with the naked eye, it is good to include the percentage values within or near each slice. Also, placing a label near each slice makes it quicker for the reader to understand the items being compared than using a legend to identify components. A good rule to follow is to begin slicing the pie at the 12 o'clock position and then to move around clockwise.

- Pie charts show subdivisions of a whole.

Line Charts

Line charts are useful in showing changes of information over time. For example, changes in prices, sales totals, employment, or production over a period of years can be shown well in a line chart.

In constructing a line chart, draw the information to be illustrated as a continuous line on a grid. The grid is the area in which the line is displayed. It is scaled to show time changes from left to right across the chart (X-axis) and quantity changes from bottom to top (Y-axis). You should clearly mark the scale values and the time periods. They should be in equal increments.

You also may compare two or more series on the same line chart (see Figure 12–14). In such a comparison, you should clearly distinguish the lines by color or form (e.g., dots, dashes, dots and dashes). You should clearly label them on the chart or by a legend somewhere in the chart. But the number of series that you may compare on one line chart is limited. As a practical guide, the maximum number is around five.

- Line charts show changes over time.

- The line appears on a grid (a scaled area) and is continuous.

- Two or more lines may appear on one chart.

Figure 12–14

Illustration of a Line Chart

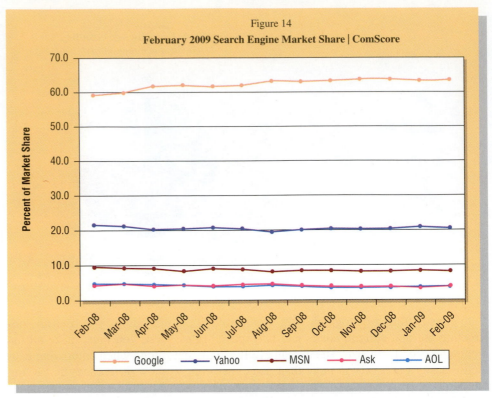

Source: "February 2009 Search Engine Market Share/ComScore", *E-Marketing Performance*, PolePosition Marketing, Feb. 2009, Web, 16 June 2009. © Pole Position Marketing. Used by permission.

• Area charts show the makeup of a series.

It is also possible to show parts of a series by use of an *area* chart. Such a chart, though, can show only one series. You should construct this type of chart, as shown in Figure 12–15, with a top line representing the total of the series. Then, starting from the base, you should cumulate the parts, beginning with the largest and ending with the smallest or beginning with the smallest and ending with the largest. You may use cross-hatching or coloring to distinguish the parts.

Figure 12–15

Illustration of an Area Chart

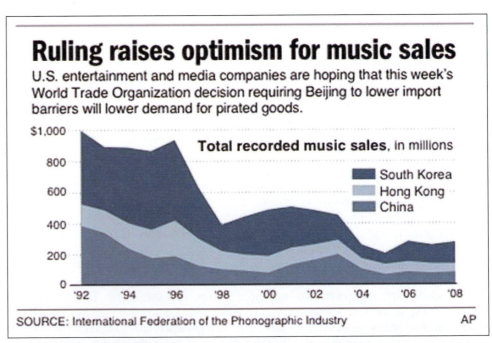

Source: R. Segal, "Ruling Raises Optimism for Music Sales," *The Washington Post,* The Washington Post Company, 15 Aug. 2009, Web, 20 Aug. 2009.

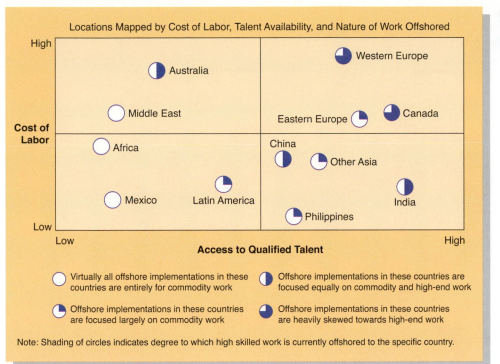

Figure 12–16

Illustration of a Scatter Diagram

Locations Mapped by Cost of Labor, Talent Availability, and Nature of Work Offshored

Cost of Labor — High / Low

Access to Qualified Talent — Low / High

Western Europe
Australia
Middle East
Eastern Europe — Canada
Africa
China
Other Asia
Mexico — Latin America
India
Philippines

Virtually all offshore implementations in these countries are entirely for commodity work

Offshore implementations in these countries are focused equally on commodity and high-end work

Offshore implementations in these countries are focused largely on commodity work

Offshore implementations in these countries are heavily skewed towards high-end work

Note: Shading of circles indicates degree to which high skilled work is currently offshored to the specific country.

Source: "The Globalization of White-Collar Work: The Facts and Fallout of Next-Generation Offshoring," Booz & Company/Duke University Offshoring Network 2006 Survey, Web, 20 Aug. 2009, <http://www.booz.com>.

Line charts that show a range of data for particular times are called *variance* or *hi-lo* charts. Some variance charts show high and low points as well as the mean, median, or mode. When used to chart daily stock prices, they typically include closing price in addition to the high and low. When you use points other than high and low, be sure to make it clear what these points are.

- Variance charts show high and low points— sometimes more.

Scatter Diagrams

Scatter diagrams are often considered another variation of the line chart. Although they do use X and Y axes to plot paired values, the points stand alone without a line drawn through them. For example, a writer might use a scatter diagram in a report on digital cameras to plot values for price and resolution of several cameras. While clustering the points allows users to validate hunches about cause and effect, they can only be interpreted for correlation—the direction and strength relationships. The points can reveal positive, negative, or no relationships. Additionally, by examining the tightness of the points, the user can see the strength of the relationship. The closer the points are to a straight line, the stronger the relationship. In Figure 12–16, the paired values are *Cost of Labor* and *Access to Qualified Talent*.

- Scatter diagrams show direction and strength of paired values.

Maps

You also may use *maps* to communicate quantitative as well as physical (or geographic) information. Statistical maps are useful primarily when quantitative information is to be compared by geographic areas. On such maps, the geographic areas are clearly outlined, and some graphic technique is used to show the differences between areas (see Figure 12–17). Quantitative maps are particularly useful in illustrating and analyzing complex data. Traffic patterns on a website could be mapped as well as patterns in a retail store. Physical or geographic maps (see Figure 12–18) can

- Maps show quantitative and geographic information.

Illustration of a Map (Quantitative)

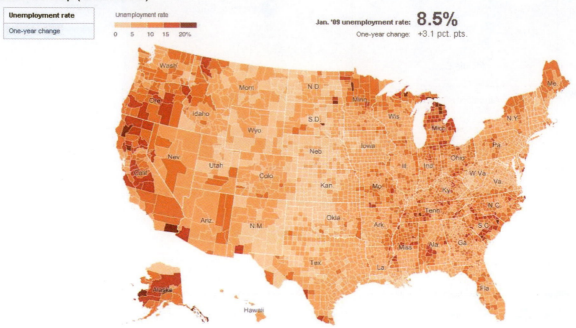

Source: "Geography of a Recession," *The New York Times,* The New York Times, 3 Mar. 2009, Web, 16 June 2009.

Illustration of a Map (Physical)

Source: "Google Maps," *Google.com,* Google, 16 June 2009, Web, 16 June 2009.

show distributions as well as specific locations. Of the numerous techniques available to you, these are the most common:

● Here are some specific instructions for statistical maps.

• Showing differences of areas by color, shading, or cross-hatching is perhaps the most popular technique (see Figure 12–17). Of course, maps using this technique must have a legend to explain the quantitative meanings of the various colors, cross-hatchings, and so forth.

Figure 12–19

Illustration of a Combination Chart, Comparing the Dow Jones Average to the Volume and Weekly Change Range of Deere Common Stock

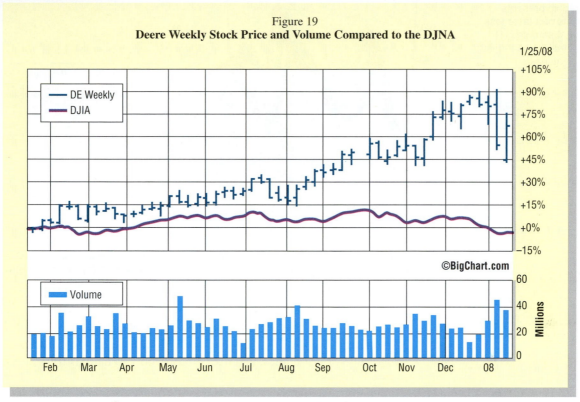

Figure 19
Deere Weekly Stock Price and Volume Compared to the DJNA

Source: "Deere Weekly Stock Price and Volume Compared to the DJNA," *Big Charts,* MarketWatch, 25 Jan. 2008, Web, 27 Jan. 2008.

- Graphics, symbols, or clip art may be placed within each geographic area to depict the quantity for that area or geographic location.

- Placing the quantities in numerical form within each geographic area is another widely used technique.

Combination Charts

Combination charts often serve readers extremely well by allowing them to see relationships of different kinds of data. The example in Figure 12–19 shows the reader the price of stock over time (the trend) as well as the volume of sales over time (comparisons). It allows the reader to detect whether the change in volume affects the price of the stock. This kind of information would be difficult to get from raw data.

> Sometimes a combination of chart types is effective.

Three-Dimensional Graphics

Until now you have learned that three-dimensional graphs are generally undesirable. However, we have mostly been referring to the three-dimensional effect applied to graphics with two variables. But when you actually have three or more variables, presenting them in three dimensions is an option if doing so will help your readers see the data from multiple perspectives and gain additional information. In fact, Francis Crick, a Nobel prize-winner for discovering the structure of

> With multiple variables, 3D graphics can help readers understand the data better.

Figure 12–20

Illustration of a Three-Dimensional Graphic
This graphic presents the results of a taste test involving 4 samples, 11 types of taste, and varying levels of intensity.

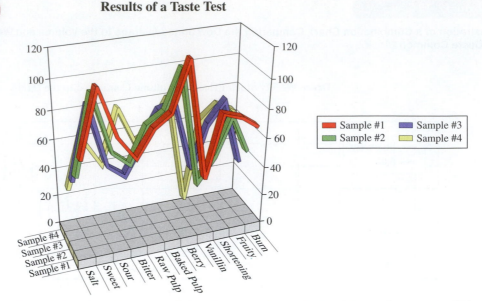

Results of a Taste Test

Source: "3 Dimensional Line Graph," *Sensory Computer Systems,* Sensory Computer Systems, 2009, Web, 2 Nov. 2009. Graph courtesy of Sensory Computer Systems, <www.SIMS2000.com>; <www.sensoryTest.com>.

DNA, once revealed it was not until he and his collaborators took a sheet of paper, cut it, and twisted it that they understood the configuration of DNA. Today we have sophisticated statistics, graphics, and data mining tools to help us filter and see our data from multiple perspectives.

- 3D graphics facilitate analyzing large data sets.

These three-dimensional tools are beginning to make their way from science labs into business settings. Several factors seem to be driving the trend. Businesses large and small are collecting and attempting to analyze extremely large amounts of detailed data. They are analyzing not only their own data but also data on their competitors. And advances in hardware, software, and Web-based applications are making it easier to graphically represent both quantitative and qualitative data.

- 3D graphics facilitate seeing data from a new perspective.

Although 3D graphics help writers display the results of their data analysis, they change how readers look at information and may take some time getting used to. These tools enable users both to see data from new perspectives and to interact with it. They allow users to free themselves from two dimensions and give them ways to stretch their insights and see new possibilities. These graphics can help businesses make timely decisions through leveraging their corporate information assets.

- Tools allow users to interact with their data.

Figure 12–20 shows a three-dimensional line graph. The three dimensions are the kinds of taste (*x* axis), the samples (*y* axis), and the intensity of each kind of taste for each sample (*z* axis). Notice how easy it is to see at a glance how the four samples compared. If these data had been displayed on a two-dimensional graph, the lines would have overlapped too much to be distinguishable. To make sure the data are absolutely clear, you would need to accompany this visual with a table, enable the reader to rotate the graphic, or both.

In deciding whether to use a three-dimensional representation or a two-dimensional one, you need to consider your audience, the context, and goal of your communication. Overall, multidimensional presentation on paper is difficult; multiple representations can be made from separate two-dimensional views, but not always effectively. Moreover, if the 3D graphic is being presented online or digitally where the reader can rotate it to see perspectives, it is likely to be much more effective with a larger number of readers.

Photographs

Cameras are everywhere today. If we do not have them in our phones, we might have them in a credit-card size or even smaller. And free and for-fee photos are readily available on

Figure 12–21

Illustration of a Photo

the Internet, too. In documents, photos can serve useful communication purposes. They can be used to document events as well as show products, processes, or services. The photo in Figure 12–21 illustrates how a simple visual creates a message. What does the context created by the trees and sidewalk void of people suggest to you?

Today photos, like data-generated graphics, can easily be manipulated. A writer's job is to use them ethically, including getting permission when needed and presenting them objectively.

Other Graphics

The types of graphics discussed thus far are the ones most commonly used. Other types also may be helpful. *Diagrams* (see Figure 12–22) and drawings may help simplify a complicated explanation or description. *Icons* are another useful type of graphic. You can create new icons, or you can select one from an existing body of icons with easily recognized meanings, such as ⊘. Even carefully selected *cartoons* can be used effectively. *Video clips* and *animation* are now used in electronic documents. For all practical purposes, any graphic is acceptable as long as it helps communicate the intended story.

- Other graphics available to you are diagrams, drawings, and even cartoons.

Visual Integrity

In writing an objective report, you are ethically bound to present data and visuals in ways that enable readers to interpret them easily and accurately. By being aware of some of the common errors made in presenting graphics, you learn how to avoid them

- Business writers are ethically bound to present data that readers can extract easily and accurately.

Figure 12–22

Illustration of a Diagram

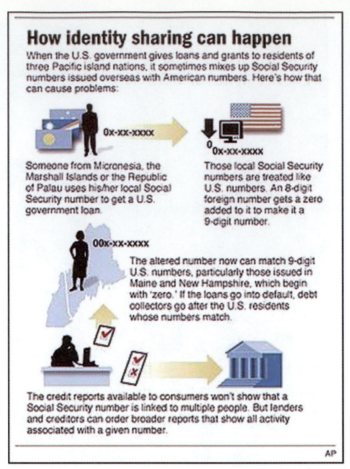

How identity sharing can happen

When the U.S. government gives loans and grants to residents of three Pacific island nations, it sometimes mixes up Social Security numbers issued overseas with American numbers. Here's how that can cause problems:

0x-xx-xxxx

Someone from Micronesia, the Marshall Islands or the Republic of Palau uses his/her local Social Security number to get a U.S. government loan.

0
0x-xx-xxxx

Those local Social Security numbers are treated like U.S. numbers. An 8-digit foreign number gets a zero added to it to make it a 9-digit number.

00x-xx-xxxx

The altered number now can match 9-digit U.S. numbers, particularly those issued in Maine and New Hampshire, which begin with 'zero.' If the loans go into default, debt collectors go after the U.S. residents whose numbers match.

The credit reports available to consumers won't show that a Social Security number is linked to multiple people. But lenders and creditors can order broader reports that show all activity associated with a given number.

AP

Source: J. Bell, "How Identity Sharing Can Happen," *The Washington Post*, The Washington Post Company, 17 Aug. 2009. Web, 20 Aug. 2009.

as well as how to spot them in other documents. Even when errors are not deliberately created to deceive a reader, they make you lose credibility—casting doubt on the document as well as on other work you have completed. Writers need to be diligent in applying high quality standards when creating visuals.

- Common errors are errors of scale, format, and context presentation.

Avoiding Errors in Graphing Data. Two categories of common errors in using graphs are errors of scale and errors of format. Another category of error is inaccurate or misleading presentation of context.

Errors of scale include problems with uniform scale size, scale distortion, and zero points. You need to be sure that all the dimensions from left to right (X axis) are equal and that the dimensions from the bottom to the top (Y axis) are equal. Otherwise, as you see here, an incorrect picture would be shown.

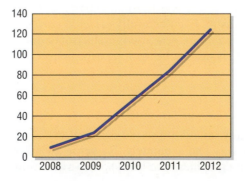

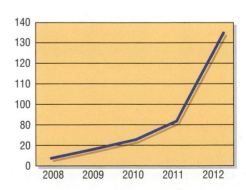

Subjective Interpretations of Color by Different Audiences

Color is a great way to make your visuals clearer and more interesting to your audience. One of the most important considerations in your color selection will be the effect the color will have on your audience. Many business communicators may already know that colors may have different connotations across cultures. But have you considered the importance of color within certain professions or social settings? In *How to Lie with Charts,* Gerald E. Jones offers the following:

Color	Movie Audience	Financial Managers	Health Care Professionals	Control Engineers
		Interpretation		
Blue	Tender	Corporate, reliable	Dead	Cold, water
Cyan	Leisurely	Cool, subdued	Cyanotic, deprived of oxygen	Steam
Green	Playful	Profitable	Infected, bilious	Nominal, safe
Yellow	Happy	Highlighted item, important	Jaundiced	Caution
Red	Exciting	Unprofitable	Healthy	Danger
Magenta	Sad	Wealthy	Cause for concern	Hot, radioactive

Jones notes that "Liars are skilled at sensing the mood of an audience and then manipulating it to their own ends" and reminds us that ethical communicators use color appropriate for the audience and the context.

Source: Gerald E. Jones, *How to Lie with Charts,* 2nd ed. (booksurge.com: Book Surge Publishing, 2006) 205–206, print.

Scale distortion occurs when a graphic is stretched excessively horizontally or vertically to change the meaning it conveys to the reader. Expanding a scale can change the appearance of the line. For example, if the values on a chart are plotted one-half unit apart, changes appear much more suddenly. Determining the distances that present the most accurate picture is a matter of judgment. Notice the different looks of the graphic show here when stretched vertically and horizontally.

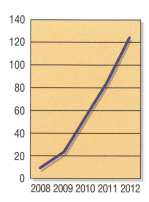
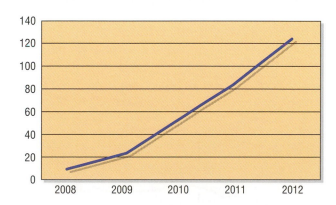

Finally, another type of scale error is violating the zero beginning of the series. For accuracy you should begin the scale at zero. But when all the information shown in the chart has high values, it is awkward to show the entire scale from zero to the highest value. For example, if the quantities compared range from 1320 to 1350 and the chart shows the entire area from zero to 1350, the line showing these quantities would be almost straight and very high on the chart. Your solution in this case is not to begin the scale at a high number (say 1300), which would distort the information, but to begin at zero and show a scale break. Realize, however, that while this makes the differences easier to see, it does exaggerate the differences. You can see this here.

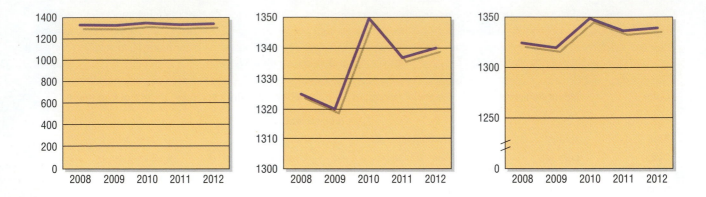

Occasionally, though, a writer needs to use his or her judgment when the guides for using graphics do not appear to fit the situation. For example, a writer may want to begin a scale at a number other than 0 when looking at the increase in life expectancy for the past several decades (see Figure 12–23). The line chart shows an upward trend in the average age. However, to present the trend by beginning the scale at 0 and at five-year increments thereafter appears to serve no purpose given that the average age at the beginning of the time period examined begins near 60. In this context, presenting the data with a scale that begins at 60 efficiently presents the data while maintaining its integrity.

Figure 12–23

Illustration of a Line Graph That Considers Context

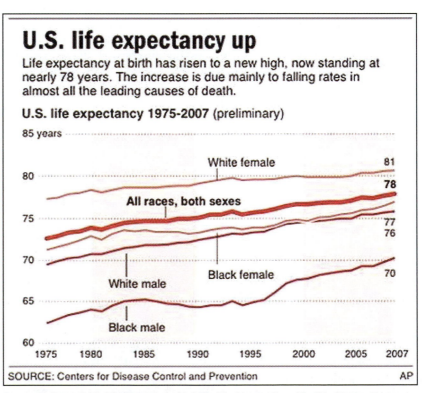

Source: N. Rapp, "U.S. Life Expectancy Up," *The Washington Post*, The Washington Post Company, 19 Aug. 2009, Web, 20 Aug. 2009.

COMMUNICATION MATTERS

The Periodic Table of Visualization Methods

This chapter presents many of the most common options for using graphics to present your text and data. The Periodic Table of Visualization Methods provides an array of many other possibilities to help you choose the best graphic as well. To see your options, just visit the website <http://www.visual-literacy.org/periodic_table/periodic_table.html>, move your mouse over any of the graphic types, and view the example that appears. As you view the many creative options, you may be tempted to choose a graphic format based on its novelty rather than its functionality. Remember, though, that the main purpose of any graphic is to communicate. Choose wisely. You want your graphics to look good, but more importantly you want them to be appropriate for your message.

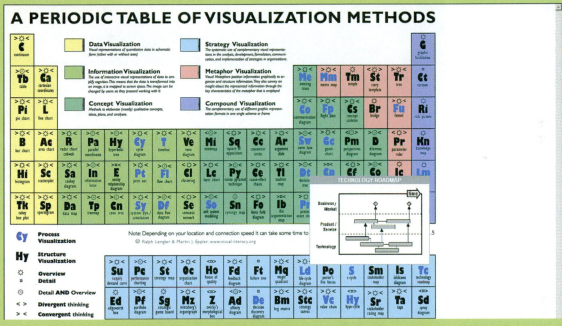

Source: Ralph Lengler and Martin J. Eppler, <www.visual-literacy.org>. Used with permission.

Errors of format come in a wide variety. Some of the more common ones are choice of wrong chart type, distracting use of grids and shading, misuse of typeface, and problems with labels. If a company used pie charts to compare expenses from one year to the next, readers might be tempted to draw conclusions that would be inappropriate because, although the pies both represent 100 percent of the expenses, the size of the business and the expenses may have grown or shrunk drastically in a year's time. If one piece of the pie is colored or shaded in such a way as to make it stand out from the others, it could mislead readers. And, of course, small type or unlabeled, inconsistently labeled, or inappropriately labeled graphics clearly confuse readers. You need to be careful to present graphics that are both complete and accurate.

Another ethical challenge is accurately representing the context. Politicians are often deliberately guilty of framing the issue to suit their cause. Business writers can avoid this deception both by attempting to frame the data objectively and by presenting the data with the reader in mind.

Avoiding Other Ethical Problems. There are other ethical issues to consider. Writers need to be careful when choosing the information to represent and the visual elements to represent it. One area writers need to watch is appropriate selection of the contents. Are people or things over- or underrepresented? Are the numbers of men and women appropriate for the context? Are their ages appropriate? Is ethnicity represented appropriately? Have colors been used appropriately and not to evoke or manipulate emotions? What about volume and size? Are the number of visuals and size appropriate for the emphasis the topic deserves? Are visuals presented accurately, free of distortion or alteration? Have photos been cropped to be consistent with the context? Today's computerized tools for creating visuals, such as the one shown in Figure 12–24, provide many options for generating interesting graphics but also make

Figure 12–24

Computerized Tools for Creating Visuals.
Today's data mining tools, such as IBM's ManyEyes Web-based application shown here, give writers many options for presenting data but also require good judgment.

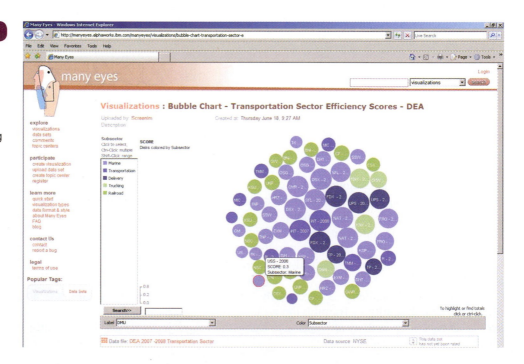

PART 4   Fundamentals of Report Writing

misrepresentation easy. Writers need to carefully select and design visuals to maintain high integrity.

PLACING AND INTERPRETING THE GRAPHICS

For the best communication effect, you should place each graphic near the place where it is covered in writing. Exactly where on the page you should place it, however, should be determined by its size. If the graphic is small, you should place it within the text that discusses it. If it is a full page, you should place it on the page following the first reference to the information it covers.

- Place the graphics near the first place in the text where you refer to them.

Some writers like to place all graphics at the end of a the report, usually in the appendix. This arrangement may save time in preparing the report, but it does not help the readers. They have to flip through pages every time they want to see a graphic. Common sense requires that you place graphics in such a way as to help readers understand the report.

- Placing graphics at the end of the report does not help the readers.

Sometimes you may need to include graphics that do not fit a specific part of the report. For example, you may have a graphic that is necessary for completeness but is not discussed in the report. Or you may have summary charts or tables that apply to the entire report but to no specific place in it. When such graphics are appropriate, you should place them in the appendix. And you should refer to the appendix somewhere in the report.

- Graphics not discussed in the report belong in the appendix.

Graphics communicate most effectively when the readers view them at the right point in their reading. Thus, you should tell the readers when to look at a graphic and what to see. Of the many wordings used for this purpose, these are the most common:

- At the right place, incidentally invite the readers to look at the graphics.

> . . . , as shown in Figure 4, ...
> . . . , indicated in Figure 4, ...
> . . . , as a glance at Figure 4 reveals, ...
> . . . (see Figure 4) . . . .

If your graphic is carrying the primary message, as in a detailed table, you can just make an incidental reference to the information in the graphic, as in "Our increased sales over the last three years. . . ."

However, if the words are carrying the primary message such as in the area chart in Figure 12–15, you might start with a reference to the chart followed closely by a thorough interpretation. One good presentation strategy to use is GEE, standing for generalization, example, and exception.[3] You'll start with a summary statement that reveals the big picture. In the case of Figure 12–15, you might say, "As Figure 12–15 shows, the amount of recorded music sales decreased from 1992 to 2008." After presenting the figure, you'll give one or more supporting examples that call your readers' attention to key findings. Then you will give the exception to the general trend, if there is one.

- Interpret using a generalization, example, exception (GEE) strategy.

Your readers will appreciate well-chosen, well-designed, and well-explained graphics, and you will achieve powerful communication results.

---

[3] Jane E. Miller, "Implementing 'Generalization, Example, Exceptions (GEE),'" *The Chicago Guide to Writing about Numbers: The Effective Presentation of Quantitative Information* (Chicago: The University of Chicago Press, 2004) 265, print.

1 Plan which parts of your report or other document should be communicated by graphics.

2 Explain the general mechanics of constructing graphics—size, layout, type, rules and borders, color and cross-hatching, clip art, background, numbering, titles, title placement, and footnotes and acknowledgments.

3 Construct textual graphics such as tables, pull quotes, flowcharts, and process charts.

4 Construct and use visual graphics such as bar charts, pie charts, scatter diagrams, and maps.

1. Because graphics are a key part of communicating information, you should plan them when you plan your document.
   - But remember that they supplement the writing; they do not replace it.
   - Use them wherever they help communicate the report information.
2. Construct each graphic carefully, following these general instructions:
   - Give each the size and arrangement that its contents and importance justify.
   - Choose a readable type. New Clear Type fonts such as Calibri or Cambria improve on-screen readability.
   - Use rules, borders, and color when they help.
   - Use clip art and background appropriately.
   - Number the graphics consecutively by type.
   - Construct topic titles for them using the five Ws (*who, what, where, when, why*) and one H (*how*) as a checklist. Alternatively, use the main message as a talking heading.
   - Use footnotes and acknowledgments when needed, placing them below the graphic.
3. Choose textual graphics to display data that are largely text based.
   - Use general-purpose tables for information that is broad in scope.
   - Use special-purpose tables for information that is specific in scope.
   - Use leaderwork or tabulations for short arrangement of data.
   - Use pull quotes to emphasize a key idea.
   - Use bullet lists to set off points.
   - Use flowcharts and process charts to show activity sequences.
4. In selecting a graphic, consider these primary uses of each:
   - *Simple bar* or *column chart*—shows quantity comparisons over time or over geographic distances.
   - *Clustered bar* or *column chart*—shows two or three quantities on one chart.
   - *Bilateral column chart*—shows plus and minus differences and is especially good for showing percentage changes.
   - *Stacked* or *subdivided bar chart*—used to compare differences in the division of wholes.
   - *Pictograph*—shows quantitative differences in picture form.
   - *Pie chart*—used to show how wholes are divided.
   - *Line chart*—useful in showing changes over time.
   - *Scatter diagram*—compares pairs of values.
   - *Map*—shows quantitative and physical differences by area.
   - *Combination chart*—used to show relationships between separate data sets.
   - *Three-dimensional graphic*—used to analyze and interpret large data sets with three or more variables.
   - *Photograph*—used to document events or show products, processes, and services.

   Employ other graphics to serve special needs:
   - Diagrams and drawings.
   - Icons.
   - Cartoons.
   - Video clips and animation.

5. Make sure that your graphics have visual integrity.
- To present data objectively, avoid these common errors:
  — *Errors of scale*—no uniform scale size, scale distortion, missing zero point.
  — *Errors of format*—wrong chart type, distracting use of grids and shading, misuse of typeface, and problems with labels.
  — *Errors in representing context.*
- Also consider the ethical use of the following:
  — *Selection.*
  — *Color.*
  — *Volume and size.*
  — *Distortion, dropping, and alterations.*
6. Place and interpret graphics effectively.
- Place graphics near to the text part they illustrate.
- Place in the appendix those that you do not discuss in the text.
- Invite the readers to look at them at the appropriate place.
- Interpret using a generalization, example, exception strategy.

5 Avoid common errors and ethical problems when constructing and using graphics.

6 Place and interpret graphics effectively.

CRITICAL THINKING QUESTIONS

1 For the past 20 years, Professor Clark Kupenheimer has required that his students include five graphics in the long, formal report he assigns them to prepare. Evaluate this requirement. **(LO1)**

2 Because it was easier to do, a report writer prepared each of the graphics on a full page. Some of these graphics were extremely complex; some were very simple. Comment on this practice. **(LO1, 6)**

3 A report has five maps, four tables, one chart, one diagram, and one photograph. How would you number these graphics? **(LO2)**

4 How would you number these graphics in a report: seven tables, six charts, nine maps? **(LO2)**

5 Discuss the techniques that may be used to show quantitative differences between areas on a statistical map. **(LO4)**

6 Give examples of data that are ideally suited for presentation in three dimensions. Explain why use of a data visualization is good for this case. **(LO4)**

7 Discuss the advantages and disadvantages of using pictographs. **(LO4)**

8 Find a graph that uses scale breaks. Discuss the possible effects of its use on the reader. **(LO5)**

9 Find a graphic with errors in format. Tell how you would correct the errors to present the chart's data more clearly to the reader. **(LO5)**

10 "I have placed every graphic near the place I write about it. The reader can see the graphic without any *additional* help from me. It just doesn't make sense to direct the reader's attention to the graphics with words." Evaluate this comment. **(LO6)**

CRITICAL THINKING EXERCISES

1 Construct a complete, concise title for a bar chart showing annual attendance at home football (or basketball, or soccer) games at your school from 2003 to the present. **(LO2)**

2 The chart prepared in Exercise 1 requires an explanation for the years 2006 to the present: In each of those years, one extra home game was played. Provide the necessary explanation. **(LO6)**

3 For each of the types of information described below, which form of graphic would you use? Explain your decision. **(LO1, 3, 4)**

a. Record of annual sales for the Kenyon Company for the past 20 years.

b. Comparison of Kenyon Company sales, by product, for this year and last year.

c. Monthly production of the automobile industry in units.

d. Breakdown of how the average middle-income family in your state (or province) disposes of its income dollar.

e. How middle-income families spend their income dollar as compared with how low-income families spend their income dollar.

f. Comparison of sales for the past two years for each of the B&B Company's 14 sales districts. The districts cover all 50 states, Canada, and Puerto Rico.

g. National production of trucks from 1950 to present, broken down by manufacturer.

h. Relationship between list price and gas mileage of alternative and gasoline-fueled cars.

4 For each of the following sets of facts, (a) determine the graphic (or graphics) that would be best, (b) defend your choice, and (c) construct the graphic. **(LO1, 2, 3, 4, 5)**

a. Average (mean) amount of life insurance owned by Mutual Life Insurance Company policyholders. Classification is by annual income.

Income	Average Life Insurance
Under $30,000	$ 40,000
$30,000–34,999	97,500
$35,000–39,999	112,500
$40,000–44,999	129,000
$45,000–49,999	142,500
$50,000 and over	225,000

b. Profits and losses for Whole Foods Stores, by store, 2008–2012, in dollars.

	Store			
Year	Able City	Baker	Charleston	Total
2008	234,210	132,410	97,660	464,280
2009	229,110	−11,730	218,470	435,850
2010	238,430	−22,410	216,060	432,080
2011	226,730	68,650	235,510	530,890
2012	230,080	91,450	254,820	576,350

c. Share of real estate tax payments by ward for Bigg City, 2008 and 2012, in thousands of dollars.

	2008	2012
Ward 1	17.1	21.3
Ward 2	10.2	31.8
Ward 3	19.5	21.1
Ward 4	7.8	18.2
City total	54.6	92.4

d. Percentage change in sales by employee, 2011–2012, District IV, Abbott, Inc.

Employee	Percentage Change
Joan Abraham	+7.3
Helen Calmes	+2.1
Edward Sanchez	−7.5
Clifton Nevers	+41.6
Wilson Platt	+7.4
Clara Ruiz	+11.5
David Schlimmer	−4.8
Phil Wirks	−3.6

5 The basic blood types are O, A, B, and AB. These can be either positive or negative. With some basic research, determine what percentage of each type people in the United States have. Choose an appropriate graph type and create it to convey the data. **(LO1, 2, 3, 4, 5)**

6 Through your research, find the approximate milligrams of caffeine in the following items and create an appropriate graphic for Affiliated Food Products, Inc., to illustrate your findings. **(LO2, 3, 4, 5)**

5-oz. cup of coffee (drip brewed)

7-oz. glass of iced tea

6-oz. glass of soda with caffeine

1-oz. dark chocolate, semisweet

7 Choose five or six outdoor summer sport activities. In a graphic identify the activity and whether it affects cardiovascular, arms, legs, back, or abdominals. You can assume these activities can affect more than one fitness zone. You work for the Parks and Recreation Department of a city of your choosing. Provide an interpretation of your graphic. **(LO1, 2, 3, 4, 5, 6)**

part five

Oral Forms of Business Communication

13 Oral and Interpersonal Communication

14 Oral Reporting and Public Speaking

Considered one of Fortune 500's "Most Powerful Black Executives" at age 39, Pamela Thomas-Graham was the first black woman to become a partner at management consulting firm McKinsey & Company. Between this position and her current ones, she served as an executive vice president of NBC, president and CEO of CNBC, and Group President for Liz Claiborne, Inc. Thomas-Graham recognizes the importance of communicating informally to gather information and harvest good ideas.

"It's very important to have a lot of interaction with people at every level of the company. You should spend time walking around talking with people, and have meetings that bring together different groups of people, either from different areas of the company or from different levels within the company. And my basic philosophy is, 'The best idea wins.' It doesn't matter where it comes from."

Pamela Thomas-Graham,
Director, The Clorox Company
Director, Idenix Pharmaceuticals, Inc.
Managing Director, Private Equity Group,
Angelo, Gordon, & Co.

chapter thirteen

Oral and Interpersonal Communication

LEARNING OBJECTIVES

Upon completing this chapter, you will be able to understand and use good talking techniques, lead and participate in meetings, communicate effectively by telephone, dictate messages effectively, listen well, and understand nonverbal communication. To reach these goals, you should be able to

1 Discuss talking and its key elements.

2 Explain the techniques for conducting and participating in meetings.

3 Describe good phone and voice mail techniques.

4 Describe the techniques of good voice input.

5 Explain the listening problem and how to solve it.

6 Describe the nature and types of nonverbal communication.

Oral Communication on the Job

Your job as assistant director in the Public Relations Department at Mastadon Chemicals, Inc., seems somewhat different from what you anticipated. It makes full use of your specialized college training, as you expected, but it also involves duties for which you did not train because you did not expect them. Most of these duties seem to involve some form of oral communication. In fact, you probably spend more of your work time talking and listening than performing any other activity.

To illustrate, take today's activities. Early this morning, you discussed a morale problem with some of your supervisors. You don't think they understood what you said. After that, you conducted a meeting of the special committee to plan the department's annual picnic. As chairperson, you ran the meeting. You felt if was a disaster—everybody

talking at once, interrupting, arguing. It was a wonder that the committee made any progress. It seemed that everybody wanted to talk but nobody wanted to listen.

In the afternoon, you had other job duties involving oral communication. After you returned from lunch, you must have had a phone conversation every 20 minutes or so. You felt comfortable with most of these calls, but you thought some of the callers needed a lesson or two in phone etiquette. Also, using speech recognition in Word, you dictated a few messages and emails between phone calls.

You certainly do a lot of talking (and listening) on your job, as do most of the people at Mastadon and just about everywhere else. Oral communication is a vital part of your work. Perhaps you can become better at it by studying the following review of oral communication techniques.

THE PREVALENCE OF ORAL COMMUNICATION

As you know, your work will involve oral as well as written communication. Although you may find written communication more challenging and may spend a lot of time planning, drafting, and revising, you are likely to spend more time in oral communication than in any other work activity.

- You will spend more time talking than writing in business.

Much of the oral communication that goes on in business is the informal, person-to-person communication that occurs whenever people get together. Obviously, we all have experience with this form of communication, and most of us do it reasonably well. But all of us can improve our informal speaking and listening with practice.

- Most of your oral communication will be informal.

In addition to informal talking and listening, various kinds of other interpersonal oral communication take place in business. Sometimes businesspeople conduct and participate in committee meetings, conferences, and group discussions. Often they call one another on the phone. Even their messages and reports may begin orally as spoken dictation, and frequently, they are called upon to make more formal presentations such as speeches, lectures, and oral reports. All these kinds of oral communication are a part of the work that businesspeople do.

- But some of it will be formal, as in meetings, phone calls, dictation, speeches, and oral reports.

This and the following chapter cover these kinds of oral communication. This chapter reviews the more interpersonal kinds: informal talking, listening, participating in meetings, talking by phone, and dictating. The following chapter presents the two most formal kinds: oral reporting and public speaking. Together, the two chapters should give you an understanding of the types of oral communication situations you will encounter in business. Remember, though, that whether you are in a less formal or more formal situation, your oral communication must meet your audience's needs and project a professional image.

- This and the following chapter cover these types of oral communication.

INFORMAL TALKING

As noted previously, most of us do a reasonably good job of informal talking. In fact, we do such a good job that we often take talking for granted and overlook the need for improving our talking ability. To improve our talking, we need to be aware of its nature and qualities. Then we need to work to overcome our shortcomings.

- Most of us talk reasonably well, but probably we can do better.

Voice Input Saves Writers Time Creating Documents

Voice recognition programs are a great way to compose messages quickly. The cost and features of these programs vary, but e-speaking (shown here) is free and works with several programs including Word, PowerPoint, Excel, and Outlook.

Source: "Screenshot by kind permission of Jeff Kandra, www.e-speaking.com.

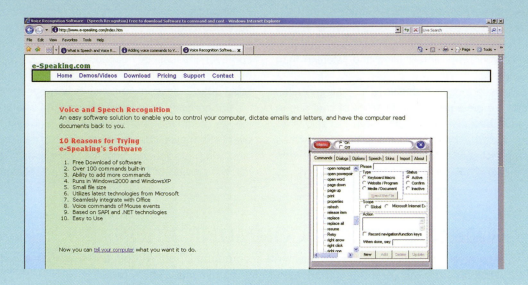

As a first step in improving your talking ability, think for a moment about the qualities you like in a good talker—one with whom you would enjoy talking in ordinary conversation. Then think about the opposite—the worst conversationalist you can imagine. With these two images in mind, you can form a good picture of the characteristics of good talking. The following section covers the most important of these.

- Think about the best and worst speakers you can imagine. This contrast should give you the qualities of good talking: voice quality, speaking style, word choice, adaptation.

Elements of Good Talking

The techniques of good talking use four basic elements: (1) voice quality, (2) style, (3) word choice, and (4) adaptation to your audience.

- Good voice quality helps one communicate. It involves pitch, delivery speed, and volume.

Voice Quality. Primarily, voice quality refers to the pitch and resonance of the sounds a speaker makes and the sounds an audience hears, but it also includes speed and volume. Because we cover these topics in Chapter 14, we need only to say here that voices vary widely—from the unpleasant to the melodious. Each of us must work with the voice given us, but we can work for improvement.

- Study the quality of your voice and compare it with what experience tells you is good. Then correct the shortcomings.

Perhaps the best way of improving voice quality is first to refer to your life experiences. From these you have learned to know good and bad voice quality when you hear them. You know the effect of talking that is too fast or too slow. You know the effect of talking in a monotone. You know the effect of a high-pitched voice, a guttural voice, a melodious voice. With this knowledge in mind, you should analyze your own voice, perhaps with the assistance of a recorder. Listen carefully to yourself. Then make a conscious effort to improve what you hear.

How Executives Feel about Graduates' Communication Skills

The Conference Board, along with Corporate Voices for Working Families, the Partnership for 21st Century Skills, and the Society for Human Resource Management, asked several executives to indicate the skills they felt were very important for new graduates to have in the workplace. The top five skills were oral communications (95.4%); teamwork/collaboration (94.4%); professionalism/work ethic (93.8%); written communications (93.1%); and critical thinking/problem solving (92.1%).

The executives were also asked to rate graduates' skills in the above areas as "excellent" or "deficient." Interestingly, when rating four-year graduates, 46.3 percent of the respondents gave an "excellent" rating to graduates' skills in information technology application (which was 11th on the executives' list of important skills, with 81.0%), but only 24.8 percent gave an "excellent" rating to graduates' oral communication skills (first on the list). Written communication, writing in English, and leadership skills appeared on the "deficient" list.

The results of this study encourage us to keep working to improve our communication skills. This chapter and several others in this book provide many useful strategies and tips for doing so.

Source: The Conference Board, *Are They Really Ready To Work? Employers' Perspectives on the Basic Knowledge and Applied Skills of New Entrants to the 21st Century U.S. Workforce,* The Conference Board, 2006, Web, 30 June 2009.

Style. Style refers to a set of voice behaviors that give each person a unique voice. It is the way that pitch, speed, and volume combine to give personality to one's oral expression.

From the self-analysis described in our review of voice quality, you also should have a good idea of your talking style. What is the image your talking projects? Does it project sincerity? Is it polished? Smooth? Rough? Dull? After your honest assessment, you should be able to determine your style deficiencies so that you can improve.

- Style is the blending of pitch, speed, and volume to form a unique talking personality.

- A self-analysis of your talking should show you your talking style and the image it projects.

Word Choice. A third quality of talking is word choice. Of course, word choice is related to one's vocabulary. The larger the vocabulary, the more choices one has. Even so, you should keep in mind the need for the recipient to understand the words you choose. You should choose words you know he or she will understand. In addition, the words you choose should be appropriate. They should convey courtesy and respect for the listener's knowledge of the subject matter—that is, they should not talk down to or above the listener. Consider, too, that the vocabulary you use with your friends outside the workplace may not be professionally appropriate for use in the workplace—no matter how friendly you are with your co-workers, superiors, or subordinates.

- Choose words in your listener's vocabulary. Select those that appropriately convey courtesy and respect for the listener's knowledge.

Adaptation. Adaptation is the fourth quality of good talking. As you learned in earlier chapters, adaptation means fitting the message to the intended listener. Primarily this means fitting the words to the listener's interpretive world, but it also can include voice and style. To illustrate, the voice, style, and words in an oral message aimed at children would be different for the same message aimed at adults. Similarly, these qualities might vary in messages delivered in different cultures as well as different social situations, work situations, and classrooms.

- Adaptation is fitting the message to the listener. It includes word selection, but here we refer to the combined effect of words, voice, and style.

Courtesy in Talking

Our review of talking would not be complete without a comment about the need for courtesy. Good relations between human beings require courtesy. We have all been frustrated by talkers who drown out others with their loud voices, who interrupt while

- Good talkers are courteous. They don't attempt to dominate.

others are talking, who attempt to dominate others in conversation. Good talkers encourage others to make their voices heard.

This emphasis on courtesy does not suggest that you should be submissive in your conversations—that you should not be aggressive in pressing your points. It means that you should accord others the courtesy that you expect of them.

- They are assertive, but they treat others as they want to be treated.

CONDUCTING AND PARTICIPATING IN MEETINGS

- Meetings involve oral communication.

From time to time, you will participate in business meetings. These will range from extreme formality to extreme informality. On the formal end will be conferences and committee meetings, while discussions with groups of fellow workers will be at the informal end. Whether formal or informal, the meetings will obviously involve communication, and the quality of the communication will determine their success. As noted in Chapter 10, collaborative report-writing groups should use the suggestions for conducting effective meetings.

- In a meeting you will be either a leader or a participant.

Your role in a meeting will be that of either leader or participant. Of course, the leader's role is the primary one, but good participation is also vital. The following paragraphs review the techniques of performing well in either role.

Techniques of Conducting Meetings

- To lead some formal meetings, you should know parliamentary procedure. So study the subject.

How you conduct a meeting depends on the formality of the occasion. Meetings of such groups as formal committees, boards of directors, and professional organizations usually follow generally accepted rules of conduct called *parliamentary procedure*. These very specific rules are too detailed for review here. When you are involved in a formal meeting, you would do well to study one of the many books covering parliamentary procedure before the meeting so that you know, for example, what it means to make a motion or call for a vote. In addition, you should know and practice the following techniques. For less formal meetings, you

Collaborative Tools Support Virtual Meetings

Virtual meetings are becoming common in small and large business alike. No longer do businesses need sophisticated teleconferencing equipment to work together from different locations. A typical desktop or laptop with an Internet connection will work nicely. With the proper system configuration, meeting participants can both see and hear others as well as see and work with various software applications.

Businesses are using this technology with their employees, their suppliers, and their customers. Some of the uses include training, sales presentations, review meetings, product demonstrations, and much more—sometimes even just-in-time meetings. All uses help businesspeople do their jobs while saving both time and travel costs.

One such meeting tool is Cisco's WebEx, which can accommodate up to 25 participants in a meeting.

Source: "Annual Report," *Cisco WebEx Meeting Center,* Cisco, 2009, Web, 30 June 2009.

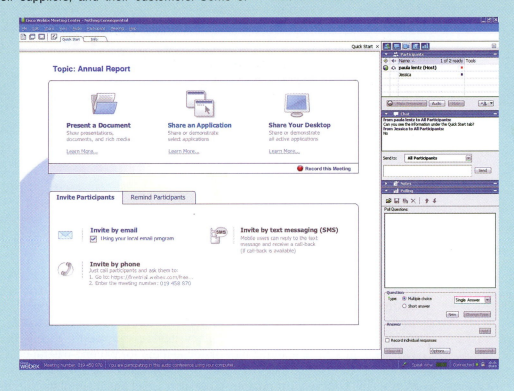

can depart somewhat from parliamentary procedure and those techniques. But you should keep in mind that every meeting has goals and that such departures should never hinder you from reaching them.

Plan the Meeting. A key to conducting a successful meeting is to plan it thoroughly. That is, you develop an agenda (a list of topics to be covered) by selecting the items that need to be covered to achieve the goals of the meeting. Then arrange these items in the most logical order. Items that explain or lead to other items should come before the items that they explain or lead to. After preparing the agenda, make it available to those who will attend. For informal meetings, you may find having a mental agenda satisfactory. Figure 13–1 shows an agenda created for a student organization meeting. An agenda does not need all of these items. You can tailor an agenda to whatever will best help you accomplish your goals. Word processing programs also have templates that may be helpful.

- In addition, you should do the following: (1) plan the items to be covered (the agenda),

Figure 13–1

Example of a Meeting
Agenda

Agenda

International Association of Business Communicators (IABC)
Executive Board Meeting
February 23, 2009
Clearwater Room, 7 p.m.

I. **Officer Reports**
    A.   President
    B.   Vice president
    C.   Secretary
    D.   Treasurer

II. **Committee Reports**
    A.   Public Relations Committee
    B.   Web Development Committee
    C.   Social Committee

III. **Old Business**
    A.   Bake sale fundraisers
    B.   Community service project

IV. **New Business**
    A.   Election of new officers
    B.   Attendance at exec board meetings
    C.   Hot chocolate promo

V. **Adjournment**

- (2) follow the plan item by item,

Follow the Plan. You should follow the plan for the meeting item by item. In most meetings the discussion tends to stray and new items tend to come up. As leader, you should keep the discussion on track. If new items come up during the meeting, you can take them up at the end or perhaps postpone them for a future meeting.

- (3) move the discussion along,

Move the Discussion Along. As leader, you should control the agenda. After one item has been covered, bring up the next item. When the discussion moves off subject, move it back on subject. In general, do what is needed to proceed through the items efficiently, but do not cut off discussion before all the important points have been made. You will have to use your good judgment. Your goal is to permit complete discussion on the one hand and to avoid repetition, excessive details, and off-topic comments on the other.

- (4) allow no one to talk too much,

Control Those Who Talk Too Much. Keeping certain people from talking too much is likely to be one of your harder tasks. A few people usually tend to dominate the discussion. Your task as leader is to control them. Of course, you want the meeting to be democratic, so you will need to let these people talk as long as they are contributing to the goals of the meeting. However, when they begin to stray, duplicate, or bring in irrelevant matter, you should step in. You can do this tactfully by asking for other viewpoints or by summarizing the discussion and moving on to the next topic.

- (5) encourage everybody to take part,

Encourage Participation from Those Who Talk Too Little. Just as some people talk too much, some talk too little. In business groups, those who say little are often in positions lower than those of other group members. Your job as leader is to encourage these people to participate by asking them for their viewpoints and by showing respect for the comments they make.

Control Time. When your meeting time is limited, you need to determine in advance how much time will be needed to cover each item. Then, at the appropriate times, you should end discussion of the items. You may find it helpful to announce the time goals at the beginning of the meeting and to remind the group members of the time status during the meeting.

- (6) control time when time is limited, and

Summarize at Appropriate Places. After a key item has been discussed, you should summarize what the group has covered and concluded. If a group decision is needed, the group's vote will be the conclusion. In any event, you should formally conclude each point and then move on to the next one. At the end of the meeting, you can summarize the progress made. You also should summarize whenever a review will help the group members understand their accomplishments.

- (7) at appropriate places, summarize what the group has covered and concluded.

Take Minutes. What is said and what is heard in a meeting may not be remembered consistently by participants. People at meetings may hear or interpret what is said differently. In addition, you may need to refer to the discussions or to the decisions made at a meeting long after the meeting when people's memories are even less reliable. To ensure you have an accurate, objective account of the topics covered and decisions made at a meeting, assign the task of recording the meeting events (taking minutes) to someone. In particularly contentious or detailed discussions, it is important that everyone have a shared understanding of what has transpired, especially if you need to vote on the group's decisions.

- Minutes can provide a shared understanding of what happened at a meeting.

The format of meeting minutes will depend on the nature of the meeting, group preferences, and company requirements. Some minutes are highly formal, with headings and complete sentences, while others might simply resemble casually written notes to oneself. As pointed out in Chapter 11 (pages 367–369), the minutes of a meeting usually list the date, time, and location along with those persons who attended and those who were supposed to attend but were absent; some minutes may also note excused or unexcused absences. If there is an agenda, the minutes will usually summarize the discussion of each agenda topic. Figure 13–2 provides an example of minutes based on the meeting agenda presented in Figure 13–1. (See page 368 for another example.) Generally, the person who takes minutes sends them to those who attended the meeting and requests corrections, or he or she presents the minutes at the next meeting and asks for changes or corrections at that time. Group members may also vote on whether to accept the minutes as they were recorded.

- Minutes can be written many ways. Regardless of their format, the minutes must be accurate and reliable.

Techniques for Participating in a Meeting

From the preceding discussion of the techniques that a leader should use, you can infer some of the things that a participant should do. The following review emphasizes them.

- As a participant in a meeting you should

Follow the Agenda. When an agenda exists, you should follow it. Specifically, you should not bring up items not on the agenda or comment on such items if others bring them up. When there is no agenda, you should stay within the general limits of the goal for the meeting.

- (1) follow the agenda,

Participate. The purpose of meetings is to get the input of everybody concerned. Thus, you should participate. Your participation, however, should be meaningful. You should talk only when you have something to contribute, but you should talk whenever you have something to contribute. Practice professional etiquette as you work courteously and cooperatively with others in the group.

- (2) participate in the meeting,

Figure 13–2

Example of Meeting Minutes

Minutes

International Association of Business Communicators (IABC)
Executive Board Meeting
February 23, 2009
Clearwater Room, 7 p.m.

Attended: Jim Solberg, Aaron Ross, Linda Yang, Tyler Baines, Sara Ryan
Absent: Jenna Kircher (excused) Rebecca Anderson (unexcused)

I. Officer Reports

A. *President*: Jim Solberg. Jim received a message from the director of university programs reminding him to view IABC's officer roster. He reviewed it on February 16 and signed the required forms.

B. *Vice president*: Linda Yang. Linda compiled job descriptions for all officer positions. Jenna put them on the IABC Web site. The link to the description of the secretary's position was not working. She is contacting Jenna to fix the link.

C. *Secretary*: Aaron Ross. Minutes of the last meeting were read and approved. He sent a thank-you note to Village Pizza for letting us have our last social there. Our average general meeting attendance is 15 even though we have 27 people who have paid dues. At the next executive board meeting, we should discuss ways to improve attendance.

D. *Treasurer*: Rebecca Anderson. No report.

II. Committee Reports

A. *Public Relations Committee:* Tyler Baines. The committee wants to have a public relations campaign in place for next fall. He will be asking for volunteers at the next general meeting.

B. *Web Development Committee:* Jenna Kircher. No report

C. *Social Committee:* Sara Ryan. The next social will be at the campus bowling alley on March 12 at 7 p.m.

III. Old Business

A. *Bake sale fundraisers:* The $76 we earned this time is less than the $102 we earned at the last one. We will discuss creative fundraising ideas at the next general meeting.

B. *Community service project:* Linda has the forms for participating in IABC's Relay for Life team on April 26–27. She will present them at the next general meeting and ask for volunteers.

IV. New Business

A. *Election of new officers:* Linda. Officers will be elected at the April meeting. We need to encourage people to run.

B. *Attendance at exec board meetings:* Jim. Rebecca has missed every executive board meeting this semester without an excuse. The bylaws state that anyone with more than three unexcused absences in an academic year can be removed from the exec board and office. Jim sent Rebecca an email reminding her of the bylaws, but she did not respond. The Executive Board voted unanimously to remove Rebecca from the board and office. Jim will send her a letter thanking her for her service and telling her she is off the board and no longer treasurer.

C. *Hot chocolate promo*: Sara. Sara requested $20 to buy supplies to serve hot chocolate on the quad from 7:30–9:30 a.m. on Monday, March 9, to promote IABC. Linda moved to spend the $20. Jim seconded the motion. Motion carried unanimously.

V. Adjourn

The meeting adjourned at 8:30 p.m. The next general meeting will be Monday, March 2, at 7 p.m. in the Alumni Room. The next exec board meeting will be Monday, March 9, at 7 p.m. in the Clearwater Room.

Respectfully submitted,

Aaron Ross

Do Not Talk Too Much. As you participate in the meeting, be aware that other people are attending. You should speak up whenever you have something to say, but do not get carried away. As in all matters of etiquette, always respect the rights of others. As you speak, ask yourself whether what you are saying really contributes to the discussion. Not only is the meeting costing you time, but it is costing other people's time and salaries, as well as the opportunity costs of other work they might be doing.

● (3) avoid talking too much,

Cooperate. A meeting by its very nature requires cooperation from all the participants. Respect the leader and her or his efforts to make progress. Respect the other participants, and work with them in every practical way.

● (4) cooperate with all concerned, and

Be Courteous. Perhaps being courteous is a part of being cooperative. In any event, you should be courteous to the other group members. Specifically, you should respect their rights and opinions, and you should permit them to speak.

● (5) practice courtesy.

USING THE PHONE

At first thought, a discussion of business phone techniques may appear to be unnecessary. After all, most of us have had long experience in using the phone and may feel that we have little to learn about it. No doubt, some of us have excellent phone skills. But you have only to call a few randomly selected businesses to learn that not everyone who talks on the phone does so proficiently. You will get some gruff, cold greetings, and you will be subjected to a variety of discourtesies. And you will find instances of inefficient use of time (which, of course, is costly). This is not to say that the problem is major, for most progressive businesses are aware of the need for good phone habits. But poor phone techniques are found often enough to justify a review of the subject here.

● Some businesspeople are discourteous and inefficient in phone communication.

Professional Voice Quality

In reviewing good phone techniques, keep in mind that a phone conversation is a unique form of oral communication. Only voices are heard; the speakers are not seen. Impressions are received only from the words and the quality of the voices. Thus, when speaking by phone, you must work to make your voice sound pleasant and friendly.

● Because only sound is involved, friendly voices are important.

One often-suggested way of improving your phone voice is to talk as if you were face-to-face with the other person—even smiling and gesturing as you talk if this helps you be more natural. In addition, you would do well to put into practice the suggestions given earlier in this chapter concerning the use of the voice in speaking (voice quality, variation in pitch, and speed). Perhaps the best advice is to record one of your phone conversations. Then judge for yourself how you come across and what you need to do to improve.

● So talk as if you were in a face-to-face conversation.

Courtesy

If you have worked in business for any length of time, you have probably experienced most of the common phone discourtesies. You probably know that most of them are not intended as discourtesies but result from ignorance or lack of concern. The following review should help you avoid them and incorporate business etiquette into your phone conversations.

● Be courteous.

The recommended procedure when you are calling is to introduce yourself immediately and then to ask for the person with whom you want to talk:

● When calling, immediately introduce yourself and ask for the person you want (or explain your purpose).

"This is Wanda Tidwell of Tioga Milling Company. May I speak with Mr. José Martinez?"

If you are not certain with whom you should talk, explain the purpose of your call:

"This is Wanda Tidwell of Tioga Milling Company. We have a question about your service warranty. May I speak with someone who can help me?"

- When receiving a call, identify your company or office; then offer assistance.

When an administrative assistant or someone else who is screening calls answers the phone, the recommended procedure is to first identify the company or office and then to offer assistance:

"Rowan Insurance Company. How may I help you?"

"Ms. Santo's office. May I help you?"

When a call goes directly into the office of the executive, the procedure is much the same, except that the executive identifies herself or himself:

"Bartosh Realty. Toby Bartosh speaking. May I help you?"

- Assistants should avoid offending callers by asking misleading questions, by making misleading comments, or

When an assistant answers for an executive (the usual case), special care should be taken not to offend the caller. Following a question like "Who is calling?" by "I am sorry, but Mr. Gordon is not in" leaves the impression that Gordon may be in but does not want to talk with this particular caller. A better procedure would be to state directly "Mr. Gordon is not in right now. May I ask him to return your call?" Or perhaps "May I tell him who called?" or "Can someone else help you?" could be substituted for the latter sentence.

- by being inconsiderate in placing callers on hold. Let the callers choose, and check on the hold status continually.

Especially irritating to callers is being put on hold for unreasonable periods of time. If the person being called is on another line or involved in some other activity, it may be desirable to place the caller on hold or ask if the caller would like to leave a message. But good business etiquette dictates that the choice should be the caller's. If the hold continues for a period longer than anticipated, the assistant should check back with the caller periodically to show concern and offer assistance. Equally irritating is the practice of having an assistant place a call for an executive and then put the person called on hold until the executive is free to talk. Although it may be efficient to use assistants for such work, as a matter of courtesy and etiquette the executive should be ready to talk the moment the call goes through.

Assistants to busy executives often screen incoming calls. In doing so, they should courteously ask the purpose of the calls. The response might prompt the assistant to refer the caller to a more appropriate person in the company. It also might reveal that the executive has no interest in the subject of the call, in which case the assistant should courteously yet clearly explain this to the caller. If the executive is busy at the moment, the assistant should explain this and either suggest a more appropriate time for a call or promise a callback by the executive. But in no case should the assistant promise a callback that will not be made. Such a breach of etiquette would likely destroy any goodwill between the caller and the company.

- Assistants often screen calls. They should do this courteously and honestly.

Effective Phone Procedures

At the beginning of a phone conversation that you have initiated, state the purpose of the call. Then cover systematically all the points involved. For really important calls, you should plan your call, even to the point of making notes of the points to cover. Then follow your notes to make certain you cover them all.

Courteous procedure is much the same in a telephone conversation as in a face-to-face conversation. You listen when the other person is talking, refrain from interrupting, and avoid dominating the conversation. And perhaps most important of all, you cover your message quickly, saving time (and money) for all concerned.

- When calling, state your purpose early. Then cover your points systematically. Plan important calls.

- Be considerate, listen, and do not dominate. Use time efficiently.

Effective Voice Mail Techniques

Sometimes when the person you are calling is not available, you will be able to leave a voice message in an electronic voice mailbox. Not only does this save you the time involved in calling back the person you are trying to reach, but it also allows you to leave a more detailed message than you might leave with an assistant. However, you need to be prepared for this to be sure your message is both complete and concise.

You begin the message nearly the same way you would a telephone call. Be as courteous as you would on the telephone and speak as clearly and distinctly as you can. Tell the listener in a natural way your name and affiliation. Begin with an overview of the message and continue with details. If you want the listener to take action, call for it at the end. If you want the listener to return your call, state that precisely, including when you can be reached. Slowly give the number where your call can be returned. Close with a brief goodwill message. For example, as a program coordinator for a professional training organization, you might leave this message in the voice mailbox of one of your participants:

- Voice mail is becoming common in business.

- Use it much as you would any other telephone call.

This is Ron Ivy from Metroplex Development Institute. I'm calling to remind Ms. Melanie Wilson about the Chief Executive Round Table (CERT) meeting next week (Wednesday, July 20) at the Crescent Hotel in Dallas. Dr. Ken Cooper of the Dallas Aerobics Center will present the program on Executive Health in the 21st Century. We will begin with breakfast at 7:30 AM and conclude with lunch at noon. Some of the CERT members will play golf in the afternoon at Dallas Country Club. If Ms. Wilson would like to join them, I will be glad to make a tee time for her. She can contact me at 940-240-1003 before 5:00 PM this Friday. We look forward to seeing her at our Chief Executive Round Table meeting next Wednesday. Thank you.

Cell Phones and Their Courteous Use

In recent years the use of cell phones has become ubiquitous. In fact, according to a 2009 poll conducted by the Marist Institute of Public Opinion, 87% of all Americans own a cell phone. To say the least, the benefits of this technology have greatly expanded our ability to communicate. Even so, their use has become an annoyance to

- Cell phones are widely used. Their use can be annoying.

82 percent of Americans and 87 percent of cell phone users.[1] Each of us should be aware of these annoyances and do what we can to reduce them.

- You can avoid annoying others by following these suggestions.

1. Turn off the ringer in meetings and other places where it would be disruptive.
2. Do not use the cell phone at social gatherings.
3. Do not place the phone on the table while eating.
4. Avoid talking whenever it will annoy others. Usually this means when within earshot of others.
5. Avoid discussing personal or confidential matters when others can hear you.
6. Do not talk in an excessively loud voice.
7. Preferably call from a quiet place, away from other people.
8. If you must talk while around people, be conscious of them. Don't hold up lines or get in the way of others.
9. Avoid using the phone while driving (the law in some states).

USING SPEECH RECOGNITION FOR MESSAGES AND REPORTS

- Dictation is an underutilized input method.

Dictating messages and reports is probably one of the most underutilized input methods for writers today. Speech recognition software has been improved to allow continuous speech and short setup periods with little training. Additionally, it works with most standard software applications, and it is inexpensive compared to the value it offers writers. Not only does such technology spell correctly, it can quickly learn specialized vocabularies. It is generally faster for most people than writing by hand or keying information because most people can speak 140 to 160 words per minute. Although proofreading dictated documents is a bit different because it involves looking for homophones (words that sound alike) rather than misspelled or misused words, most programs offer users the ability to play back the dictation, which will help them catch other errors.

- Today's software make the process easy . . .

- and inexpensive.

If you haven't started dictating documents yet, one of the best ways to learn is to use voice recognition software to handle your email. If you are using Office XP or higher, you already have the software; you simply need a microphone and a few minutes for training. However, the Word Help feature in Word 2007 says that speech recognition is not available in Office 2007 and directs users to Windows Speech Recognition in Windows Vista. Other excellent programs are e-Speaking, Dragon NaturallySpeaking, and Simply Speaking. Once you have the tools, you can use the following steps to dictate effectively.

Source: ©ZITS PARTNERSHIP. KING FEATURES SYNDICATE.

---

[1] Lee Rainie and Scott Keeter, "Cell Phone Use," *Pew Internet Project,* Pew Internet, April 2006, Web, 21 June 2006.

Techniques of Dictating

Gather the Facts. Your first logical step in dictating is to get all the information you need for the message so you can work efficiently and quickly. This step involves such activities as getting past correspondence from files, consulting with other employees, and ascertaining company policy.

You should (1) get all the information you need to avoid interruption later;

Plan the Message. Having gathered the information, you next plan the message. You may prefer to do this step in your mind or to jot down a few notes or an outline. Whatever your preference, your goal in this step is to decide what your message will be and how you will present it. In this step, you apply the procedures covered in our earlier reviews of message and report writing.

(2) plan the message following the processes described in preceding chapters;

Make the Words Flow. Your next step is to talk through the message. Simple as this step appears, you are likely to have problems with it. Thinking out loud even to the computer frightens most of us at first. The result is likely to be slow and awkward dictation.

(3) talk through the message,

Overcoming this problem requires self-discipline and practice. You should force yourself to concentrate and to make the words flow. Your goal should be to get the words out—to talk through the message. You need not be too concerned about producing a polished work on the first effort. You will probably need to revise, perhaps several times. After you have forced your way through several messages, your need to revise will decrease, and the speed and quality of your dictation will improve.

forcing the words to flow if necessary (you can revise later);

Speak Clearly. Because your dictation must be heard clearly by your system, you should speak distinctly. Even small improvements in accuracy—say, from 95 percent to 99 percent—will yield significant time savings.

(4) speak distinctly for improved accuracy;

Give Paragraphing, Punctuation, and Other Instructions as Needed. How much of the paragraphing, spelling, punctuation, and other mechanics you dictate depends on how well trained your system is. The more often you use the software, the more it knows your dictation style and the fewer instructions it will need. If you take care to spell out words unknown to your system in addition to training your system, it will serve you better.

(5) give the paragraphing, punctuation, and other instructions as the system needs;

Play Back as Needed. Although you should try to talk through the message without interruption, you will sometimes need to stop and get a playback of what you have dictated. But do this only when necessary. More than likely, the need for a playback results from confused thinking. When you are learning to dictate, however, some confused thinking is normal. Until you gain experience, you may profit from playbacks.

(6) play back when necessary; and

Proofread for Accuracy. You will find a playback especially helpful at the end of the message to give you a check on the overall effect of your words. Additionally, conducting playbacks while visually reading your final document will help you proofread your document for homophone errors (for example, using "there" for "their").

(7) play back to proofread for accuracy, especially checking for homophone errors.

Illustration

Many of the preceding techniques are illustrated in the following transcript of a dictated routine email message. This example shows all the dictator's words, including punctuation, paragraphing, and corrections, that were spoken after the microphone was activated. Note that the dictator spells out words that might not be in the program's vocabulary. However, if the word were the name of a client one expected to have for

Here is the exact transcript of a short confirmation message.

a long time, the name could be added to the program for future use. Also, note that the program attempts to learn your usage patterns, even the usage of homophones. For example, if most of the time you used the word *sweet* rather than *suite,* the program would first supply *sweet.* As the software improves and as your dictation speed improves, the program may be able to select the correct word forms based on context. At first, though, careful proofreading is essential.

> Dear Payton *spell that* p-a-y-t-o-n *cap that comma new paragraph* Three crates of orchard *hyphen* fresh Florida oranges should be in your store sometime Wednesday morning as they were shipped today by Greene *spell that* g-r-e-e-n-e *cap that* motor *cap that* freight *cap that period new paragraph* As you requested in your August 29 order *comma* the three hundred sixty-one dollars and sixty cents *left paren* invoice *cap that* 14721 *right paren* was credited to your account *period new paragraph* Your customers will go for these large *comma* tasty oranges *comma* I am sure *period* They are the best we have handled in months *period new paragraph* Thanks *comma* Payton *comma* for another opportunity to serve you *period new paragraph* Sincerely *comma new line* Alex

LISTENING

- Poor listening is a major cause of miscommunication.

Up to this point, our review of oral communication has been about sending information (talking). Certainly, this is an area in which businesspeople need help. But evidence shows that the receiving side (listening) causes more problems.

The Nature of Listening

- Listening involves sensing, filtering, and remembering.

When listening is mentioned, we think primarily of the act of sensing sounds. In human communication, of course, the sounds are mainly spoken words. Viewed from a communication standpoint, however, the listening process involves the addition of filtering and remembering.

- How well we sense spoken words is determined by (1) our ability to sense sounds and

Sensing. How well we sense the words around us is determined by two factors. One factor is our ability to sense sounds—how well our ears can pick them up. As you know, we do not all hear equally well, although mechanical devices (hearing aids) can reduce our differences in this respect.

- (2) our attentiveness.

The other factor is our attentiveness to listening. More specifically, this is our mental concentration—our will to listen. Our mental concentration on the communication symbols that our senses can detect varies from moment to moment. It can range from almost totally blocking out those symbols to concentrating on them very intensely. From your own experience, you can recall moments when you were oblivious to the words spoken around you and moments when you listened with all the intensity you could muster. Most of the time, your listening fell somewhere between these extremes.

- Filtering is the process of giving symbols meanings through the unique contents of each person's mind.

Filtering. From your study of the communication process in Chapter 1, you know that interpretation enables you to give meanings to the symbols you sense. In this process, the contents of your mind serve as a sort of filter through which you give meaning to incoming messages. This filter is formed by the unique contents of your mind: your knowledge, emotions, beliefs, biases, experiences, and expectations. Thus, you sometimes give messages meanings that are different from the meanings that others give them.

- Remembering what we hear is a part of listening.

Remembering. Remembering what we hear is the third activity involved in listening. Unfortunately, we retain little of what we hear. We remember many of the comments we hear in casual conversation for only a short time—perhaps for only a few minutes or hours. Some we forget almost as we hear them. According to authorities,

What's in a Handshake?

Have you practiced your handshake recently? If not, you may want to perfect this very important nonverbal communication skill. CareerBuilder.com cites research indicating that prospective employers are more likely to overlook body piercings and tattoos than they are a poor handshake and that employers are two times more likely to remember you if you shake hands than if you don't. You want to avoid handshakes that are too strong, too weak, or too long, as well as those that involve only the fingers rather than the whole hand. In addition, make sure your hands are not cold, clammy, or sweaty; and be sure to keep your right hand free so that you don't have to shake with your left hand. Lastly, watch the number of rings you wear, as they can lead to a very painful handshake for both you and the recipient.

What should you do instead? CareerBuilder.com advises the following for U.S. communicators:

- As you're approaching someone, extend your right arm when you're about three feet away. Slightly angle your arm across your chest, with your thumb pointing up.
- Lock hands, thumb joint to thumb joint. Then, firmly clasp the other person's hand.
- Pump the other person's hand two to three times and let go.

When communicating cross-culturally, another greeting entirely may be expected. Be sure to do your homework for such situations (see Chapter 15).

Source: Rachel Zupek, "What Does Your Handshake Say About You? 10 Worst Grips," *CareerBuilder.com*, CareerBuilder, 24 Apr. 2007, Web, 30 June 2009.

we even quickly forget most of the message in formal oral communications (such as speeches), remembering only a fourth after two days.

Improving Your Listening Ability

Improving your listening is largely a matter of mental conditioning—of concentrating on the activity of sensing. If you are like most of us, you are often tempted not to listen or you just find it easier not to listen. Listening may seem like a passive activity, but it can be hard work.

- To improve your listening, you must be willing to work on it.

After you have decided that you want to listen better, you must make an effort to pay attention. Force yourself to be alert, to pay attention to all the words spoken. Active listening is one technique individuals can use successfully. It involves focusing on what is being said and reserving judgment. Other components include sitting forward and acknowledging with "um-hm" and nodding. Back-channeling (repeating what you think you heard) is a variation of this technique that groups can use. Communicators can use technologies such as chat and blogs to comment on and enhance presentations in real time, which helps keep people focused on what is being said. Whatever technique you choose, improvement requires effort.

- Be alert. Force yourself to pay attention.

In addition to working on the improvement of your sensing, you should work on the accuracy of your interpreting. To do this, you will need to think in terms of what words mean to the speakers who use them rather than what the dictionary says they mean or what they mean to you. You must try to think as the speaker thinks—judging the speaker's words by considering the speaker's knowledge, experiences, culture, and viewpoints. Like improving your sensing, improving your ability to hear what is intended requires conscious effort.

- Concentrate on improving your interpreting.

- Think from the speaker's viewpoint.

Remembering what you hear also requires conscious effort. Certainly, there are limits to what the mind can retain, but authorities agree that few of us come close to them. By taking care to hear what is said and by working to make your interpreting process give more accurate meanings to the words you hear, you hear more accurately.

- Consciously try to remember.

Improve your listening skills by focusing your attention on the speaker and listening actively.

● In addition, follow these practical guidelines (summarized in italics).

In addition to the foregoing advice, various practical steps may prove helpful. Assembled in a classic document titled "The Ten Commandments of Listening,"[2] the following list summarizes the most useful of them:

1. *Stop talking.* Even when we are not talking, we are inclined to concentrate on what to say next rather than on listening to others. So you must stop talking (and thinking about talking) before you can listen.

2. *Put the talker at ease.* If you make the talker feel at ease, he or she will do a better job of talking. Then you will have better input to work with.

3. *Show the talker you want to listen.* If you can convince the talker that you are listening to understand rather than oppose, you will help create a climate for information exchange. You should look and act interested. Doing such things as reading, looking at your watch, and looking away distracts the talker.

4. *Remove distractions.* Other things you do also can distract the talker. So don't doodle, tap with your pencil, or shuffle papers.

5. *Empathize with the talker.* If you place yourself in the talker's position and look at things from the talker's point of view, you will help create a climate of understanding that can result in a true exchange of information.

6. *Be patient.* You will need to allow the talker plenty of time. Remember that not everyone can get to the point as quickly and clearly as you. And do not interrupt. Interruptions are barriers to the exchange of information.

7. *Hold your temper.* Anger impedes communication. Angry people build walls between each other; they harden their positions and block their minds to the words of others.

8. *Go easy on argument and criticism.* Argument and criticism tend to put the talker on the defensive. He or she then tends to "clam up" or get angry. Thus, even if you win the argument, you lose. Rarely does either party benefit from argument and criticism.

---

[2] To some anonymous author goes a debt of gratitude for these classic and often-quoted comments about listening.

Voice input systems allow writers to concentrate on word choice and message composition, freeing them from typing and spelling concerns. But careful proofreading is still essential, especially for easily confused words and sound-alikes.

9. *Ask questions.* By frequently asking questions, you display an open mind and show that you are listening. And you assist the talker in developing his or her message and in improving the correctness of your interpretation.

10. *Stop talking!* The last commandment is to stop talking. It was also the first. All the other commandments depend on it.

From the preceding review it should be clear that to improve your listening ability, you must set your mind to the task. Poor listening habits are ingrained in our makeup. We can alter these habits only through conscious effort.

THE REINFORCING ROLE OF NONVERBAL COMMUNICATION

In your role of either speaker or listener in oral communication, you will need to be aware of the nonverbal—nonword—part of your communication. In face-to-face communication, nonverbal communication accounts for a larger part of the total message than do the words you send or receive. Usually, we use nonverbal communication to supplement and reinforce our words. Sometimes, nonverbal communication communicates by itself. Because it is so important to our communication, we will look at the nature of nonverbal communication and some types of it.

• In face-to-face communication, nonverbal communication accounts for more of the total message than words do.

The Nature of Nonverbal Communication

Nonverbal or nonword communication means all communication that occurs without words. The "vocabulary" for these types of "language" is broad and imprecise. For

• Nonverbal (nonword) communication means all communication without words. It is broad and imprecise.

instance, a frown on someone's forehead is sometimes interpreted to mean worry. But could it be that the person has a headache? Or is the person in deep thought? No doubt, there could be numerous meanings given to the facial expression.

The number of possible meanings is multiplied even more when we consider the cross-cultural side of communication. As noted in Chapter 15, culture teaches us about body positions, movements, and various factors that affect human relationships (e.g., intimacy, space, time). Thus, the meanings we give to nonverbal symbols will vary depending on how our culture has conditioned us.

Because of these numerous meanings, you need to be sensitive to what others intend with nonverbal communication, and you need to make some allowance for error in the meanings you receive from nonverbal symbols. As a listener, you need to go beyond the obvious to determine what nonword symbols mean. Just as we have said about word symbols, you need to see what people intend with their nonverbal symbols. Perhaps one good way to grasp the intent of this suggestion is to look at the intended meanings you have for the nonverbal symbols you use.

Think for a few moments about a sample gesture you might make. What do you mean by it? What could it mean to others? Is it exactly as you intend? Could it be interpreted differently? Could someone from a different culture give a different meaning to it? Only if you look at nonverbal symbols through the prism of self-analysis and realize their multiple meanings can you get some idea of how they might be interpreted differently. And when you become aware of the many differences, you then can become sensitive to the meaning intended by the nonverbal communication.

To help you become sensitive to the myriad of nonverbal symbols, we will look at four types of nonverbal communication.

Types of Nonverbal Communication

Although there are many ways to classify nonverbal communication, we will examine four of the more common types: body language, space, time, and paralanguage. These four types are especially relevant to our discussion of speaking and listening.

Body Language. Much of what we say to others without using words is sent through the physical movements of our bodies. When we wave our arms and fingers, wrinkle our foreheads, stand erect, smile, gaze at another, or wear a coat and tie, we convey certain meanings; and others convey meanings to us in return. In particular, the face and eyes, gestures, posture, and physical appearance reflect the inner workings of emotions in our bodies.

The face and eyes are by far the most important features of body language. We look to the face and eyes to determine much of the meaning behind body language and nonverbal communication. For example, happiness, surprise, fear, anger, and sadness usually are accompanied by definite facial expressions and eye patterns. You should be aware of these two aspects of body language as you speak and listen to others.

Gestures are another way we send nonword messages through our body parts. *Gestures* are physical movements of our arms, legs, hands, torsos, and heads. Through the movement of each of these body parts, we can accent and reinforce our verbal messages. And we can observe how others punctuate their verbal efforts with gestures. For example, observe the hand movements of another person while he or she is talking. As you observe these gestures, you will get a good picture of the emotional state of the person. Moreover, speaking and gestures appear to be linked. In general, the louder someone speaks, the more emphatic the gestures used, and vice versa.

Another area of body language is physical appearance—our clothing, hair, and accessories. The appearance of our bodies can affect how our body movements are seen. Consider, for example, how you might perceive a speaker at a formal banquet dressed in faded blue jeans. Everything the speaker says or does would be perceived in relation to this attire. Accordingly, you want to make sure that your appearance fits the situation. And you want to remember that appearance is an important part of the body messages that are sent and received in oral communication.

- Cross-cultural aspects give many meanings to nonverbal communication.

- Be sensitive to intended nonverbal meanings. Go beyond the obvious.

- Realize that nonverbal symbols can have many meanings.

- Four common types of nonverbal communication are (1) body language, (2) space, (3) time, and (4) paralanguage.

- Our bodies send nonword messages—through arms, fingers, expressions, posture, and so on.

- The face and eyes are the most important.

- Gestures (physical movements of the arms, legs, torso, and head) send nonword messages.

- Physical appearance—clothing, hair, jewelry, cosmetics, and so on—also communicates.

Space. Another type of nonverbal communication involves space. How we use space and what we do in certain spaces we create tell much about us. Thus, each of us has a space language just as we do a body language. This space language is heavily influenced by our culture.

Authorities tell us that we create four different types of space: intimate (physical contact to 18 inches); personal (18 inches to 4 feet); social (4 to 12 feet); and public (12 feet to the outer range of seeing and hearing). In each of these spaces, our communication behaviors differ and convey different meanings. For example, consider the volume of your voice when someone is 18 inches from you. Do you shout? Whisper? Now contrast the tone of your voice when someone is 12 feet away. Unquestionably, there is a difference, just because of the distance involved.

You will need to be sensitive to the spaces of others—especially those from different cultures. As noted in Chapter 15, when people's attitudes toward space are different, their actions are likely to be misinterpreted.

Time. A third type of nonverbal communication involves time. Just as there are body language and space language, there is also a time language. That is, how we give meaning to time communicates to others. To illustrate, think about how you manage your daily schedule. Do you arrive early for most appointments? Do you prioritize phone calls? Do you prepare agendas for meetings? Your response to time in these ways communicates to others, and, of course, others' use of time communicates to you. In terms of nonverbal communication, you should recognize that time orientations are not always the same—especially in cross-cultural situations—but they do communicate. For Americans, Canadians, and many others from English-speaking countries, time values are monochronic. Monochronic people tend to view time as linear and always moving ahead. They expect events to happen at scheduled times. Polychronic people—such as those from Asian, Arabic, and Spanish-speaking countries—have a more indefinite view of time. Unlike the monochronic person who expects a meeting to start precisely at 9:00 AM, the polychronic person sees a 9:00 AM meeting as an objective to be accomplished if possible. Such time orientations are parts of the messages we send to and receive from one another.

Paralanguage. *Paralanguage,* meaning "along with language," is a fourth type of nonverbal communication. Of all the types, it is the closest to communication with word symbols. It has to do with the sound of a speaker's voice—those hints and signals in the way words are delivered, such as emphasis, pitch, and volume, that also give meaning to a speaker's message.

To illustrate, read the following series of statements, emphasizing the underscored word in each.

I am a good communicator.
I am a good communicator.
I am a good communicator.
I am a good communicator.
I am a good communicator.

By emphasizing the underscored word in each statement, you change the meaning of that statement from the others even though you used the same words. You do so by the way in which the word sequence sounds. As another example, try counting from 1 to 10 a number of times, each time expressing a different emotional state—say anxiety, anger, or happiness. The way you state each sequence of numbers will show what you intend quite accurately.

Paralanguage is the communication effect of the speed, pitch, volume, and connectivity of spoken words. Are they fast or slow? Are they high pitched or deep? Are they loud and forceful or barely audible? Are they smooth or disjointed? These questions are examples of the types you would ask to analyze the nonverbal symbols of paralanguage. The symbols become a part of the meaning that is conveyed by a spoken message.

- Space is another type of nonverbal language.

- Four types of space exist: (1) intimate, (2) personal, (3) social, and (4) public. Communication behavior differs in each.

- Communication behaviors are learned from cultures.

- Time is a third type of nonverbal communication.

- Paralanguage involves *how* we say something.

- You can change the meaning of spoken sentences by accenting different words in each.

- Paralanguage creates meanings because of speed, pitch, volume, and connection of words.

- Degrees of consistency between what and how someone says something convey meaning.

Paralanguage meanings also are conveyed by consistencies and inconsistencies in what is said and how it is said. Depending on the circumstance, a person's voice may or may not be consistent with the intended word meanings. Consistency between the words you choose and how you deliver them to create clear meaning should be your goal.

- Expectancies about background, appearance, and personality are part of paralanguage.

All communicators have certain assumptions about how a message should sound. Whether real or imagined, people infer background factors (race, education, etc.); physical appearance (age, height, gender); and personality (introversion, social orientation, etc.) when they hear and interpret voice patterns. When you speak, you should do whatever you can to influence these assumptions positively. Many of the suggestions in this chapter and the following one should help you deliver a consistent and effective message. Active listeners will also want to listen between the lines of a spoken message to determine the true meaning a speaker is sending.

- Two other nonverbal types exist, but they are minor. One is color.

Other Types of Nonverbal Communication. The preceding four types are the primary forms of nonverbal communication, but others exist. For example, artists, interior decorators, and "image consultants" believe that different colors project different meanings. What meanings do you get from red, yellow, black, blue? That you can answer at all should prove that colors influence meaning. The colors in visual aids, wardrobe, and office decor all send nonverbal messages. Thus, you should give more than casual attention to color as a type of nonverbal communication.

- Another is physical context—furniture carpeting, decorations, and other features.

Still another type of nonverbal communication involves the structure of our physical context—its layout and design. In an office, the physical arrangements—furniture, carpeting, size, location, and decorations—all communicate meaning to us and to others. These elements provide the context for many of our speaking and listening activities. We should therefore consider them as part of the messages we send and receive as well.

SUMMARY BY LEARNING OBJECTIVES

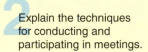

Discuss talking and its key elements.

1. Good talking depends on four critical factors:
   - Voice quality—talking with variations in pitch, delivery, and volume.
   - Speaking style—blending voice quality and personality.
   - Word choice—finding the right vocabulary for the situation.
   - Adaptation—fitting a message to the listener.

Explain the techniques for conducting and participating in meetings.

2. In business, you are likely to participate in meetings, some formal and some informal.
   - If you are in charge of a meeting, follow these guidelines.
     — Know parliamentary procedure for formal meetings.
     — Plan the meeting; develop an agenda and circulate it in advance.
     — Follow the plan.
     — Keep the discussion moving.
     — Control those who talk too much.
     — Encourage participation from those who talk too little.
     — Control time, making sure the agenda is covered.

— Summarize at appropriate times.

— Take minutes.

- If you are a participant at a meeting, follow these guidelines:

    — Stay with the agenda; do not stray.

    — Participate fully.

    — But do not talk too much.

    — Cooperate.

    — Be courteous.

3. To improve your phone and voice mail techniques, consider the following:

3 Describe good phone and voice mail techniques.

- Cultivate a pleasant voice.

- Talk as if in a face-to-face conversation.

- Follow courteous procedures.

    — When calling, introduce yourself and ask for the person you want.

    — State your purpose early.

    — Cover points systematically.

    — When receiving a call, identify your company or office and offer assistance.

    — When answering for the boss, do not offend by asking questions or making comments that might give a wrong impression; and do not neglect callers placed on hold.

    — When screening calls for the boss, be courteous and honest.

    — Listen when the other person is talking.

    — Do not interrupt or dominate.

    — Plan long conversations, and follow the plan.

- For good voice mail messages, follow these suggestions:

    — Identify yourself by name and affiliation.

    — Deliver a complete and accurate message.

    — Speak naturally and clearly.

    — Give important information slowly.

    — Close with a brief goodwill message.

- Demonstrate courtesy when using cell phones by following these general guidelines:

    — Turn off the ringer where it could disrupt others.

    — Avoid use at social gatherings.

    — Keep the phone off the table during meals.

    — Talk only in places where others won't be in earshot.

    — Avoid talking about confidential or private business.

    — Keep voice volume down.

    — Initiate calls in quiet places away from others.

    — Be conscious of others when you talk.

    — Avoid talking while driving, especially if it is against the law.

4. In dictating messages and reports, follow these suggestions.

4 Describe the techniques of good voice input.

- First, gather all the information you will need so you will not have to interrupt your dictating to get it.

- Next, plan (think through) the message.

- Until you are experienced, force the words to flow—then revise.

- Remember, also, to speak in a strong, clear voice.

- Give punctuation and paragraphing in the dictation.
- Play back only when necessary.
- Proofread for accuracy.

5 Explain the listening problem and how to solve it.

5. Listening is just as important as talking in oral communication, but it causes more problems.
    - Listening involves how we sense, filter, and retain incoming messages.
    - Most of us do not listen well because we tend to avoid the hard work that good listening requires.
    - You can improve your listening with effort.
    - Put your mind to it and discipline yourself to be attentive.
    - Make a conscious effort to improve your interpretation of incoming messages; strive to retain what you hear.
    - Follow the practical suggestions offered in "The Ten Commandments of Listening."

6 Describe the nature and types of nonverbal communication.

6. Nonverbal (nonword) communication is the communication that occurs without words.
    - One major type is body language—the movements of our arms, fingers, facial muscles, and other physical components.
        - Our face and eyes are the most expressive parts of body language.
        - Gestures also send messages.
        - Our physical appearance (clothing, cosmetics, jewelry, hairstyle) communicates about us.
    - Space is a second major type of nonverbal communication.
        - We create four unique types of spaces: (1) intimate, (2) physical, (3) social, and (4) public.
        - We communicate differently in each space, as influenced by our culture.
    - How we give meaning to time is a third type of nonverbal communication.
    - The meanings that the sounds of our voices convey (paralanguage) are a fourth type.
    - Color and physical context are also nonverbal forms of communication.
    - In our speaking, we should use nonverbal communication to accent our words.
    - In listening, we need to "hear" the nonverbal communication of others.

CRITICAL THINKING QUESTIONS

1 Talking is a natural occurrence, so we should give it little attention. Discuss. **(LO1)**

2 How can being conscious of the elements of talking help us communicate better? **(LO1)**

3 Being able to start a conversation is especially important when meeting clients in social settings. Discuss the types of topics that would and would not be appropriate. **(LO1, 2)**

4 The people attending a meeting—not the leader—should determine the agenda. Discuss. **(LO2)**

5 As meetings should be democratic, everyone present should be permitted to talk as much as he or she wants without interference from the leader. Discuss. **(LO2)**

6 Describe an annoying phone practice that you have experienced or know about (other than the ones discussed in the chapter). Explain and/or demonstrate how it should be corrected. **(LO3)**

7 Describe the strengths and weaknesses of voice mail systems with which you are familiar. **(LO3)**

8 Discuss why we have difficulty listening well. **(LO5)**

9 What can you do to improve your listening? **(LO5)**

10 Explain how each type of nonverbal communication relates to speaking and to listening. **(LO6)**

Talking

1 Record yourself in conversation with three different audiences (e.g., a friend, your parents, a customer or client at work, an instructor). Conduct a SWOT analysis of your talking using the four elements of good talking discussed in this chapter. What are your *strengths*? What are your *weaknesses*? Identify *opportunities* for improving your talking. Discuss *threats* to improving your talking (e.g., nervousness, lack of interest). What will you do to address the threats? Present your analysis in a memo report to your instructor. Be sure to explain to your audiences why you're recording your conversation and seek permission as appropriate.

2 Record an example of talking done by someone you think has good voice quality and someone you think has poor voice quality. You may find talk shows or news programs helpful sources. You may also be able to think of a movie in which someone speaks poorly or speaks well. Analyze the speaker's voice quality in terms of the features discussed in this chapter. As your instructor requests, present your analysis to your class or a small group or to your instructor in the form of a memo. Your instructor may also require that you assess each person's nonverbal communication skills.

Meetings

3 For one of the topics below, develop a specific problem that would warrant a group meeting. (Example: For student government, the problem might be "To determine the weaknesses of student government on this campus and what should be done to correct them.") Then lead the class (or participate) in a meeting on the topic. Class discussion following the meeting should reinforce the text material and bring out the effective and ineffective parts of the meeting.

a. Student drinking

b. Scholastic dishonesty

c. Housing regulations

d. Student–faculty relations

e. Student government

f. Library

g. Grading standards

h. Attendance policies

i. Varsity athletics

j. Intramural athletics

k. Degree requirements

l. Parking

m. Examination scheduling

n. Administrative policies

o. University calendar

p. Homework requirements

q. Tuition and fees

r. Student evaluation of faculty

s. Community–college relations

t. Maintaining files of old examinations for students

u. Wireless Internet availability

4 Using one of the topics in the above exercise (or another topic as your instructor directs), work in groups of four to present a solution to the problem you decide to address. You should meet at least four times. One person should be designated to establish an agenda for and lead each meeting and another to take minutes at each meeting. Each person in the group should take a turn leading a meeting and taking minutes. After each meeting, group members should evaluate the group leader's abilities. Let your reader know of at least one strength and one area needing improvement. Submit your agendas, minutes, and leader evaluations to your instructor as directed. Present your group's solution to your class as a short presentation or to your instructor in a memo.

5 Working in groups of four or five, debate the following statement. *As long as the information they provide is truthful, employers should be able to give a negative reference without fear of lawsuits or other negative effects for a former employee seeking employment with another company.* Examine arguments that might lead you to agree with the statement or disagree with it, and come to a consensus. Tape (video or DVR so that you have both sound and picture) the meeting and analyze the group members' performances. You may analyze the recording as a group or individually as your instructor directs. Who emerged as the leader of the discussion? How could you tell this person was the leader? Did anyone dominate the discussion? Did anyone not participate or participate very little? Why do you think this person did not participate as much as he or she could have? What could people in the group do to improve their skills? What did they do well?

Phoning

6 Make a list of bad phone practices that you have experienced or heard about. With a classmate, first demonstrate the bad practice and then demonstrate how you would handle it. Some possibilities: putting a caller on hold tactlessly, harsh greeting, unfriendly voice quality, insulting comments (unintended), attitude of unconcern, cold and formal treatment.

7 Think about your outgoing message on your cell phone or answering machine. For whom is your message appropriate? Are the voice quality, style, and word choice appropriate? Is it courteous? Is there anyone you would not want to hear this message (e.g., a potential employer)? Does the message contain sufficient detail? Is it too detailed or too long? In a memo to your instructor, include the text of your current outgoing message. If your message needs revision, include the text of your revised message. Explain why you are revising the message and describe the audience you are making the message more appropriate for. If you do not believe your message needs revision, explain how your message meets the needs of your current audiences. If you do not have a cell phone or answering machine, borrow a friend's.

Dictating

8 Working with the voice recognition feature in Office XP or higher (or any other your instructor specifies), select a writing case from the problems following the chapters on messages (Chapters 6, 7, and 8). Then dictate a message. You may need to train the software before using it. After you have finished your dictation, proofread it carefully. Then play back the message for review one final time.

9 Use the Internet to gather information and present a report on recent developments in voice-recognition technology.

Listening

10 After the class has been divided into two (or more) teams, the instructor reads some factual information (newspaper article, short story, or the like) to only one member of each team. Each of these team members tells what he or she has heard to a second team member, who in turn tells it to a third team member—and so on until the last member of each team has heard the information. The last person receiving the information reports what she or he has heard to the instructor, who checks it against the original message. The team able to report the information with the greatest accuracy wins.

11 This exercise is similar to exercise 2 under Talking, but in this exercise, you will analyze your listening skills. Reflect on a recent conversation with a friend, oral instructions you received from your boss, or a class lecture where you demonstrated what you believe is representative of your listening skills in general. Use a SWOT analysis to evaluate your listening skills. What are your *strengths* as a listener? What are your *weaknesses*? Identify some *opportunities* for improving your skills. Identify possible *threats* (e.g., physical limitations, lack of interest) that may hinder your ability to improve your skills. What can you do to address these threats? Present your analysis in a memo report to your instructor.

Nonverbal

12 Using a digital camera or pictures from magazines, get three to five pictures of men and women with different facial expressions (happiness, sadness, anger, etc.) or gestures. Ask those native to your area to identify the emotions or the meanings of the gestures the pictures convey. Then ask at least three others from different countries (preferably different continents) to identify the emotions. Report your results to the class.

13 Go to a public place (e.g., your school's cafeteria, the library, a park, or a mall). Observe the interaction between two people whom you can see but whom you cannot hear. In a short memo to your instructor, describe the setting, the participants, the interaction, and the nonverbal behaviors. Analyze their nonverbal communication and present two possible interpretations of these behaviors. Be sure to justify your interpretations with evidence from your observation.

14 Record yourself in some type of oral communication setting (e.g., the meetings described in previous exercises, a mock job interview with your school's career services office, your next presentation for this or another course). Watch the recording without the sound, and pay attention to your nonverbal behaviors. In a short memo to your instructor, describe what you saw and evaluate what you do well and what you will work to improve.

chapter fourteen

Oral Reporting and Public Speaking

LEARNING OBJECTIVES

Upon completing this chapter, you will be able to use good speaking and oral-reporting techniques. To reach this goal, you should be able to

1   Define oral reports and differentiate between them and written reports.

2   Select and organize a subject for effective formal presentation to a specific audience.

3   Describe how audience analysis and personal aspects contribute to formal presentations.

4   Explain the use of voice quality and physical aspects such as posture, walking, facial expression, and gestures in effective oral communication.

5   Plan for visuals (graphics and slides) to support speeches and oral reports.

6   Work effectively with a group in preparing and making a team presentation.

7   Plan and deliver effective virtual presentations.

Formal Speaking

In addition to your interpersonal speaking and listening activities at Mastadon Chemicals, you have more formal ones involving oral communication.

For example, last week, at the monthly meeting, Mastadon's executive committee asked you for a special oral report from your department. The report concerns the results of a survey that your department conducted to determine opinions about a dispute between Mastadon and its union. This report is not just for the executives at your Mastadon branch; it is also for the managers at all 10 Mastadon locations across the U.S. You must find a way to give your report to all these audiences simultaneously.

Then today, Marla Cody (your boss) asked you to do something very special for the company. It seems that each year Mastadon Chemicals awards a $5,000 scholarship to a deserving business student at State University. The award is presented at the business school's annual Honors Day Convocation, usually by Ms. Cody. To show the business school's appreciation for the award, its administration requested that Ms. Cody be the speaker at this year's convocation. But Ms. Cody has a conflicting engagement, so you got the assignment. You are excited but nervous about this challenge.

Such assignments are becoming more and more a part of your work as you move up the administrative ladder at Mastadon. The following review of formal oral presentations (reports and speeches) should help you do them well.

MASTERING FORMAL SPEAKING

Researchers consistently note the growing importance of oral communication skills even as technologies such as email, blogs, and other social networking opportunities demand more of our writing skills. According to a recent textbook, "some experts have estimated that speakers address audiences an astonishing 33 million times each day . . . and businesspeople give an average of 26 presentations a year."[1]

While Chapter 13 addressed the informal, interpersonal types of oral communication you might encounter in business, this chapter addresses the more formal types of oral communication—oral reports and speeches—that you will be likely to prepare in any professional setting. As with the written forms of communication discussed in this book, oral reports and formal speeches require careful planning and polishing.

REPORTING ORALLY

- The oral report is a form of speech.

The ability to give effective oral reports is a critical skill in business. In the words of one expert, "Presentations have become the de facto business communication tool. Companies are started, products are launched, climate systems are saved—possibly based on the quality of presentations. Likewise, ideas, endeavors, and even careers can be cut short due to ineffective communication."[2]

The following sections will help you master the art of the oral report in business.

Defining Oral Reports

- An oral report is an oral presentation of factual information.

In its broadest sense, an oral report is any presentation of facts and their interpretation using the spoken word. Oral business reports cover much of the information and analysis exchanged daily in the conduct of business. They vary widely in formality. At one extreme, they cover the most routine and informal reporting situations. At the other, they include highly formal presentations. Because the more informal oral

---

[1] Ronald B. Adler and Jeanne Marquardt Elmhorst, *Communicating at Work: Principles and Practices for Business and the Professions* (New York: McGraw-Hill, 2010) 303, print.

[2] Nancy Duarte, *slide:ology: The Art and Science of Creating Great Presentations* (Beijing: O'Reilly, 2008) xviii.

exchanges are similar to routine conversations, the emphasis in the following pages is on the more formal ones.

Understanding the Differences between Oral and Written Reports

If you have the choice between giving an oral or written report, consider the following differences.

Visual and Verbal Cues. As you have learned, readers rely on visual cues to interpret written reports. To help them, you can use paragraphing to show the structure of the message and to make the thought units stand out. In addition, you can use punctuation to help show relationships, subordination, and qualification.

When you make an oral presentation, you cannot use many of these techniques. However, you can use inflection, pauses, volume emphasis, and changes in the rate of delivery. In addition, many speakers incorporate visual cues in their presentations by using slides, photos, and other supporting material.

Degree of Reader Control. A significant difference between oral and written reports is that the readers of a written report, unlike the listeners of an oral report, control the pace of the communication. They can pause, reread, change their rate of reading, or stop as they choose. Since the readers set the pace, writing can be complex and still communicate. However, since the listeners for an oral report cannot control the pace of the presentation, they must grasp the intended meaning as the speaker presents the words. For this reason, good presenters keep their reports concise and use handouts or other written material for detailed information that might need careful review.

Formality in Oral and Written Reports. As with written reports, your use of correct grammar in oral reports is a reflection of your competence. However, it is often acceptable to use a less formal style in oral reports. Colloquialisms, contractions, and even slang can be effective with certain audiences. Do not make the mistake of lapsing into incorrectness in your effort to be engaging.

Considering the differences between writing and speaking in terms of—verbal and visual cues, degree of reader control, and level of formality—can help you identify which type of report—written or oral—to prepare.

Planning the Oral Report

As with written reports, planning is the logical first step in your work on oral reports. For short, informal oral reports, planning may be minimal. But for the more formal oral reports, particularly those involving audiences of more than one, proper planning is likely to be as involved as that for a comparable written report.

Determining the Report Objective. Logically, your first task in planning an oral report is to determine your objective. As prescribed for the written report in Chapter 10, you should state the report objective for yourself in clear, concise language. Then you should determine the factors involved in achieving this objective. This procedure gives you a guide to the information you must gather and to the framework around which you will build your presentation.

In determining your report objective, you must be aware of your general objective. That is, you must decide on your general purpose in making the presentation. Is it to persuade? To inform? To recommend? This decision will have a major influence on your development of material for presentation and perhaps even on the presentation itself.

Organizing the Content. The procedure for organizing oral reports is similar to that for organizing written reports. You have the choice of using either the direct or indirect order. Even so, the same information is not necessarily presented in the same

----

- Oral reports differ from written reports in three ways:

- (1) writing and speaking have unique advantages and disadvantages;

- (2) the speaker controls the pace of an oral report, and the reader controls the pace of a written report; and

- (3) written reports place more stress on correctness.

- Planning is the first step in preparing oral reports.

- First determine the objective and what must be done to reach it.

- Next organize content. Either the indirect or direct order is all right,

way orally and in writing. Time pressure, for example, might justify direct presentation for an oral report on a problem that, presented in writing, might be better arranged in the indirect order. Readers in a hurry can always skip to the conclusion or ending of the report. Listeners do not have this choice.

- but the indirect order is more common.

In general, though, oral reports are more likely to be delivered indirectly than are written reports. In an oral presentation, you will usually state the purpose, give any helpful background information, present the facts and analysis, and then give the conclusions or recommendations. Even when an oral report is in the direct order, you will probably need to preface your presentation with introductory remarks that provide the context for what you're about to say.

- The organization of oral and written reports is much the same, except that oral reports usually have a closing summary.

In the body of the oral report, as with written reports, you should use a logical structure. Dividing the subject matter logically, preparing a helpful introduction, and constructing an appropriate conclusion are equally important to both forms.

A major difference in the organization of the written and the oral report is in the ending. Both forms may end with a conclusion, a recommendation, a summary, or a combination of the three. But the oral report is likely to have a final summary, whether or not it has a conclusion or a recommendation. In a sense, this final summary serves the purpose of an executive summary by bringing together all the really important information, analyses, conclusions, and recommendations in the report. It also assists the memory by emphasizing the points that should stand out. Oral and nonverbal emphasis techniques should help your audience remember your key points.

MAKING FORMAL SPEECHES

- Speeches are difficult for most of us. The following techniques should help you.

The most difficult kind of oral communication for many people is a formal speech. Most of us do not feel comfortable speaking before others, and some do a poor job of it. We can improve our formal speaking abilities by learning what good speaking techniques are and then putting those techniques into practice.

Selecting the Topic

- Your topic may be assigned.

Your first step in formal speaking is to determine the topic of your presentation. In some cases, you will be assigned a topic, usually one within your area of specialization. In fact, when you are asked to make a speech on a specified topic, it is likely because of your knowledge of the topic. In some cases, your choice of topic will be determined by the purpose of your assignment, as when you are asked to welcome a group or introduce a speaker.

- If you must select a topic, consider (1) your knowledge, (2) your audience, and (3) the occasion.

If you are not assigned a topic, then you must find one on your own. In your search for a suitable topic, you should be guided by three basic factors. The first is your background and knowledge. Any topic you select should be one with which you are comfortable—one within your areas of proficiency. The second basic factor is the interests of your audience. Selecting a topic that your audience can appreciate and understand is vital to the success of your speech. The third basic factor is the occasion of the speech. Is the occasion a meeting commemorating a historic event? A monthly meeting of an executives' club? An annual meeting of a hairstylists' association? Whatever topic you select should fit the occasion. A speech about Japanese management practices might be quite appropriate for the members of the executives' club but not for the hairstylists. Your selection should be justified by all three factors.

Preparing the Presentation

- Conduct research to get the information you need.

After you have decided what to talk about, you should gather the information you need for your speech. This step may involve searching your mind for experiences or ideas, conducting research in a library or in company files, gathering information online, or consulting people in your own company or other companies. In short, you do whatever is necessary to get the information you need.

**"My presentation lacks power and it has no point.
I assumed the software would take care of that!"**

When you have that information, you are ready to begin organizing your speech. Although variations are sometimes appropriate, you should usually follow the time-honored order of a speech: *introduction, body, conclusion*. This is the order described in the following paragraphs.

• Then organize the information.

Although not really a part of the speech, the first words usually spoken are the greeting. Your greeting, of course, should fit the audience. A simple "good morning" or "good evening" may suffice. Some speakers eliminate the greeting and begin with the speech, especially in more informal and technical presentations. If you have not been introduced to your audience, be sure to introduce yourself.

• The greeting usually comes first.

Introduction. The introduction of a speech has much the same goal as the introduction of a written report: to prepare the listeners (or readers) to receive the message. But it usually has the additional goal of arousing interest. Unless you arouse interest at the beginning, your presentation is likely to fail. The situation is somewhat like that of the sales message. At least some of the people with whom you want to communicate are not likely to be interested in receiving your message. As you recall from Chapter 13, speakers can easily lose the audience's attention. To prove the point, ask yourself how many times your mind has drifted away from the speaker's words when you have been part of an audience. There is no question about it: You, the speaker, will have to work to gain and hold the attention of your audience.

• Gain attention in the opening.

The techniques of arousing interest are limited only by the imagination. One possibility is a human-interest story. For example, a speaker presenting a message about the opportunities available to people with original ideas might open this way: "Nearly 150 years ago, an immigrant boy of 17 walked the streets of our town. He had no food, no money, no belongings except the shabby clothes he wore. He had only a strong will to work—and an idea."

• There are many opening possibilities: human interest,

Humor, another possibility, is probably the most widely used technique. To illustrate, an investment broker might begin a speech on investment strategy as follows: "What you want me to give you today is some 'tried and trusted' advice on how to make money in the stock market. This reminds me of the proverbial 'tried

• humor,

Virtual Presentations

As we mentioned in Chapter 13, many technologies enable business communicators to meet virtually rather than face-to-face. Many companies now find that virtual environments also provide a cost-effective means of hosting seminars, which, in the virtual environment, are called "Webinars." Microsoft's Live Meeting, shown below, is one such technology that enables companies to reach as many as a thousand people at once. Many of the features simulate what participants might encounter in a face-to-face environment: a white board, chat, the opportunity to vote on a topic, slide shows, and a seating chart. In fact, the seating chart feature contains a "mood indicator" where participants can change their seat colors to indicate whether they understand the presenter—a useful nonverbal cue in an environment where a presenter may not see the participants.

- quotations, and questions.

and trusted' bank teller. He was trusted; and when they caught him, he was tried." Humor works best and is safest when it is closely related to the subject of your presentation.

Other effective ways for gaining attention at the opening are by using quotations and questions. By quoting someone the audience would know and view as credible, you build interest in your topic. You also can ask questions. One kind of question is the rhetorical question—the one everyone answers the same, such as "Who wants to be freed of burdensome financial responsibilities?" Another kind of question gives you background information on how much to talk about different aspects of your subject. With this kind of question, you must follow through by basing your presentation on the response. If you asked "How many of you have IRAs?" and nearly everyone raised a hand, you wouldn't want to talk about the importance of IRAs. You could skip that part of your presentation, spending more time on another aspect, such as managing an IRA effectively.

Yet another possibility is the startling statement. Illustrating this possibility is the beginning of a speech to an audience of merchants on a plan to reduce shoplifting:

"Last year, right here in our city, in your stores, shoplifters stole over $3.5 million of your merchandise! And most of you did nothing about it."

In addition to arousing interest, your opening should lead into the theme of your speech. In other words, it should set up your message as the examples above do.

The opening should set up your subject.

Following the attention-gaining opening, it is appropriate to tell your audience the subject (theme) for your speech. In fact, in cases where your audience already has an interest in what you have to say, you can begin here and skip the attention-gaining opening. Presentations of technical topics to technical audiences typically begin this way. Whether you lead into a statement of your topic or begin with it, that statement should be clear and complete.

Tell the subject of your speech . . .

Because of the nature of your subject, you may find it undesirable to reveal a position early. In such cases, you may prefer to move into your subject indirectly—to build up your case before revealing your position. This inductive pattern may be especially desirable when your goal is to persuade—when you need to move the views of your audience from one position to another. But in most business-related speeches you should state your theme early in the speech.

unless you have reason not to, as when you must persuade or deliver negative news.

Body. Organizing the body of your speech is much like organizing the body of a report (see Chapter 10). You take the whole and divide it into comparable parts. Then you take those parts and divide them. You continue to divide as far as it is practical to do so. In speeches, however, you are more likely to use factors rather than time, place, or quantity as the basis of division because in most speeches your presentation is likely to be built around issues and questions that are subtopics of the subject. Even so, time, place, and quantity subdivisions are possibilities.

Organize most speeches by factors, as you would a report.

You need to emphasize the transitions between the divisions because, unlike the reader who can see them, the listener may miss them if they are not stressed adequately. Without clear transitions, you may be talking about one point, and your listener may think you are still on the previous point.

Emphasize transitions between parts.

Good presenters project their personal qualities—confidence, sincerity, friendliness, enthusiasm, and interest.

Conclusion. Like most reports, the speech usually ends by drawing a conclusion. Here you bring all that you have presented to a head and achieve whatever goal the speech has. You should consider including these three elements in your close: (1) a restatement of the subject, (2) a summary of the key points developed in the presentation, and (3) a statement of the conclusion (or main message). Bringing the speech to a climactic close—that is, making the conclusion the high point of the speech—is usually effective. Present the concluding message in strong language—in words that gain attention and will be remembered. In addition to concluding with a summary, you can give an appropriate quote, use humor, or call for action. The following close of a speech comparing two companies' management techniques illustrates this point: "These facts make my conclusion clear. We are not the Miller Company. We do not have the Miller corporate culture. Most Miller management methods have not worked—cannot work—will not work—in our company."

Choosing the Presentation Method

With the speech organized, you are ready to prepare its delivery. At this time, you need to decide on your method of presentation—that is, whether to present the speech extemporaneously, to memorize it, or to read it.

Presenting Extemporaneously. Extemporaneous presentation is by far the most popular and effective method. With this method, you first thoroughly prepare your speech, as outlined above. Then you prepare notes and present the speech from them. You usually rehearse, making sure you have all the parts clearly in mind, but you make no attempt to memorize. Extemporaneous presentations generally sound natural to the listeners, yet they are (or should be) the product of careful planning and practice.

Memorizing. The most difficult method is memorizing. If you are like most people, you find it hard to memorize a long succession of words. And when you do memorize, you are likely to memorize words rather than meanings. Thus, when you make the speech, if you miss a word or two, you become confused—and so does your speech. You even may become panic-stricken.

Few speakers who use this method likely memorize the entire speech. Instead, they memorize key passages and use notes to help them through the speech. A delivery of this kind is a cross between an extemporaneous presentation and a memorized presentation.

Reading. The third presentation method is reading. Unfortunately, most of us tend to read aloud in a dull monotone. We also miss punctuation marks, fumble over words, lose our place, and so on. Of course, many speakers overcome these problems, and with effort you can, too. One effective way is to practice with a recorder and listen to yourself. Then you can be your own judge of what you must do to improve your delivery. You would be wise not to read speeches until you have mastered this presentation method. In most settings, it is a breach of etiquette to read. Your audience is likely to be insulted, and reading is unlikely to be as well received as an extemporaneous delivery. However, when you are in a position where you will be quoted widely, such as president of the United States or the CEO of a major company, reading from a carefully prepared speech is recommended. Many top executives today use teleprompters when delivering read speeches, and many of these appear well done, especially with practice.

PREPARING TO SPEAK

Whether you give your presentation or speech extemporaneously, memorize it, or read it, be sure you are prepared to deliver it. Of course, the content of a message must be solid, but if your delivery is poor, people may ignore or simply miss your most important points. The following sections provide strategies for ensuring that your audience receives and understands your message.

Presentation Delivery Tools Help You Convey Your Message Effectively

Delivery tools can help you do a better job preparing and delivering oral presentations. One tool within PowerPoint, Presenters View, should help you plan, practice, and deliver good presentations. You can see its major tools in the screenshot here. As your audience sees only the slide, you are seeing the presenter's view. You see the current slide being projected and its slide notes. Additionally, you see the title to the upcoming slide as well as the elapsed time since the beginning of the presentation. Furthermore, along the right column are several buttons that allow you to start or end the show on one click, black out that screen to bring the attention back to you, and perform other actions. As the presenter, you have the flexibility to skip slides or change the ordering on the fly. The slider bar at the bottom enables you easily to pull up slides during question and answer sessions as well.

In PowerPoint 2007 you can access the presenter's view by going to the Slide Show tab > Monitors box > Use presenter view. *Note:* You may need to configure PowerPoint to use this view. Simply searching "presenter's view" in the Help feature will provide you with step-by-step instructions for doing so.

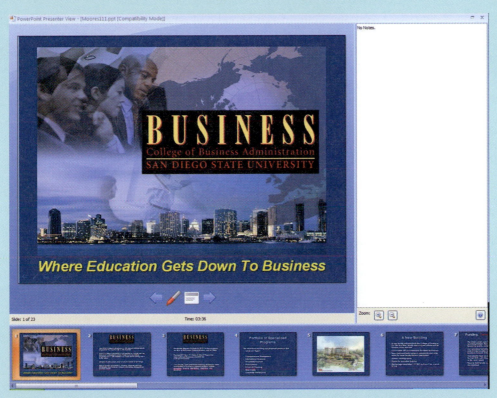

Audience Analysis

As with written messages and reports, a critical component of good presentations is knowing your audience. You should study your audience both before and during the presentation.

Preliminary Analysis. Analyzing your audience before the presentation requires that you size it up—that you search for audience characteristics that could affect how you should present your speech.

For example, the size of your audience is likely to influence how formal or informal your speech should be. As a rule, large audiences require more formality. Personal characteristics of your audience, such as age, gender, nationality, education, experience,

- You should know your audience.

- Size up the audience in advance. Look for audience characteristics that will affect your speech—things like the size, gender, nationality, age, education, and knowledge of the subject.

and knowledge of subject matter, also should influence how you make your speech—affecting the words, illustrations, and level of detail you use. Like writing, speeches should be adapted to the audience. And the more you know about the audience, the better you will adapt your presentation to them.

● Analyze the audience's reactions during the speech (called *feedback*). Facial expressions, movements, and noises give you feedback information that helps you adapt to the audience.

Analysis during the Presentation. Your audience analysis should continue as you make the speech. *Feedback* is information about how your listeners are receiving your words. Armed with this information, you can adjust your presentation to improve the communication result.

Your eyes and ears will give you feedback information. For example, facial expressions will tell you how your listeners are reacting to your message. Smiles, blank stares, and movements will give you an indication of whether they understand, agree with, or accept it. You can detect from sounds coming (or not coming) from them whether they are listening. If questions are in order, you can learn directly how your message is coming across. In general, you can learn much from your audience by being alert, and what you learn can help you make a better speech.

Consideration of Personal Aspects

● A logical preliminary to speechmaking is to analyze yourself as a speaker. You are a part of the message.

An important preliminary to good oral reports or speeches is to analyze yourself as a speaker. In oral presentations you, the speaker, are a very real part of the message. The members of your audience take in not only the words you communicate but also what they see in you. And what they see in you can significantly affect the meanings that develop in their minds. Thus, you should carefully evaluate your personal effect on your message. You should do whatever you can to detect and overcome your shortcomings and to sharpen your strengths.

The following qualities of effective speakers should help you pinpoint and deal with your problem areas.

● Remember the following as you deliver your presentations:

● (1) Confidence in yourself is important. So is having the confidence of your audience.

Confidence. A primary characteristic of effective oral reporting is confidence—your confidence in yourself and the confidence of your audience in you. The two are complementary: Your confidence in yourself tends to produce an image that gives your audience confidence in you and your audience's confidence in you can give you a sense of security that increases your confidence in yourself.

● You must earn the confidence of your audience, project the right image, and talk in a strong, clear voice.

Typically, you earn your audience's confidence through repeated contact with them. But there are things you can do in a speech to project an image that builds confidence. For example, preparing your presentation diligently and practicing it thoroughly gives you confidence in yourself. That confidence leads to more effective communication, which increases your listeners' confidence in you. Another confidence-building technique is an appropriate physical appearance. Unfair and illogical as it may seem, certain types of dress and hairstyles create strong images in people's minds, ranging from highly favorable to highly unfavorable. Thus, if you want to communicate effectively, you should analyze the audience you seek to reach. And you should work to develop the physical appearance that projects an image in which that audience can have confidence. Yet another confidence-building technique is simply to talk in strong, clear tones. Although most people can do little to change their natural voice, they can use sufficient volume to project a confident tone.

● (2) Sincerity is vital. You convey an image of sincerity by being sincere.

Sincerity. Your listeners are quick to detect insincerity. And if they detect it in you, they are likely to give little weight to what you say. On the other hand, sincerity is valuable to conviction, especially if the audience has confidence in your ability. The way to project an image of sincerity is clear and simple: You must *be* sincere. Pretense of sincerity is rarely successful.

● (3) Thoroughness— giving your listeners all they need—helps your image.

Thoroughness. Generally, a thorough presentation is better received than a scanty or hurried presentation. Thorough coverage gives the impression that time and care have been taken, and this tends to make the presentation believable. But thoroughness can be overdone. Too much detail can drown your listeners in a sea of information.

Successful oral presentations to large audiences are the result of thorough preparation.

The secret is to leave out unimportant information. This, of course, requires good judgment. You must ask yourself just what your listeners need to know and what they do not need to know. Striking such a balance is the secret to achieving integrity in your presentation.

Friendliness. A speaker who projects an image of friendliness has a significant advantage in communicating. People simply like friendly people, and they are generally receptive to what such people say. Like sincerity, friendliness is hard to feign and must be honest to be effective. Most people are genuinely friendly, but some have trouble projecting a friendly image. By watching yourself as you practice speaking, you can find ways to improve your projection of friendliness.

● (4) Projecting an image of friendliness helps your communication effort.

These are but a few of the characteristics that should assist you as a speaker. There are others: *interest, enthusiasm, originality, flexibility,* and so on. But the ones discussed are the most significant and the ones that most speakers need to work on. Through self-analysis and dedicated effort, you can improve your speaking ability.

Appearance and Physical Actions

As your listeners hear your words, they are looking at you. What they see is a part of the message and can affect the success of your speech. What they see, of course, is you and what surrounds you. In your efforts to improve the effects of your oral presentations, you should understand the communication effects of what your listeners see. Some of the effects that were mentioned in Chapter 13 are expanded on here because they are particularly important to speeches and oral reports.

● Your audience forms impressions from these six factors:

The Communication Environment. Much of what your audience sees is the physical things that surround you as you speak: the stage, lighting, background, and so on. These things tend to create a general impression. Although not visual, outside noises have a related influence. For the best communication results, the factors in your communication environment should contribute to your message, not detract from it. Your own experience as a listener will tell you what factors are important.

● (1) all that surrounds you (stage, lighting, and the like),

• (2) your personal appearance,

Personal Appearance.

Your personal appearance is a part of the message your audience receives. Of course, you have to accept the physical traits you have, but most of us do not need to be at a disadvantage in appearance. All that is necessary is to use what you have appropriately. Specifically, you should dress in a manner appropriate for the audience and the occasion. You should also be sure that nothing about your appearance (e.g., hairstyle or jewelry) is distracting.

• (3) your posture,

Posture.

Posture is likely to be the most obvious of the things that your audience sees in you. Even listeners not close enough to detect such things as facial expressions and eye movements can see the general form of the body.

You probably think that no one needs to tell you about good posture. You know it when you see it. The trouble is that you are not likely to see it in yourself. One solution is to have others tell you whether your posture needs improvement. Another is to practice speaking before a mirror or watch yourself on video.

In your efforts to improve your posture, keep in mind what must go on within your body to form a good posture. Your body weight must be distributed in a way consistent with the impression you want to make. You should keep your body erect without appearing stiff and comfortable without appearing limp. You should appear naturally poised and alert.

• (4) your manner of walking,

Walking.

Your audience also forms an impression from the way you walk. A strong, sure walk to the speaker's position conveys an impression of confidence. Hesitant, awkward steps convey the opposite impression. Walking during the presentation can be good or bad, depending on how you do it. Some speakers use steps forward and to the side to emphasize points. Too much walking, however, attracts attention and detracts from the message. You would be wise to walk only when you are reasonably sure that this will have the effect you want. You would not want to walk away from a microphone.

• (5) facial expressions (smiles, frowns, eye contact), and

Facial Expression.

As noted in Chapter 13, probably the most apparent and communicative physical movements are facial expressions. The problem, however, is that you may unconsciously use facial expressions that convey unintended meanings. For example, if a speaker appears frightened, the image detracts from the entire communication effort. A smile, a grimace, and a puzzled frown all convey clear messages. Of course, you should choose those expressions that best convey your intended meaning.

Eye contact is important. The eyes, which have long been considered "mirrors of the soul," provide most listeners with information about the speaker's sincerity, goodwill, and flexibility. Some listeners tend to shun speakers who do not look at them. On the other hand, discriminate eye contact tends to show that you have a genuine interest in your audience.

Gestures. Like posture, gestures contribute to the message you communicate. Just what they contribute, however, is hard to say, for they have no definite or clear-cut meanings. A clenched fist, for example, certainly adds emphasis to a strong point. But it also can be used to show defiance, make a threat, or signify respect for a cause. And so it is with other gestures. They register different meanings, as discussed in Chapters 13 and 15.

- (6) gestures.

Even so, gestures are strong, natural aids to speaking. It appears natural, for example, to emphasize a plea with palms up and to show disagreement with palms down. Raising first one hand and then the other reinforces a division of points. Slicing the air with the hand shows several divisions. Although such gestures are generally clear, we do not all use them in exactly the same way.

- Gestures have various meanings, but they communicate.

In summary, physical movements can help your speaking. Just which physical movements you should use, however, is hard to say. The appropriateness of physical movements is related to personality, physical makeup, and the size and nature of the audience. A speaker appearing before a formal group should generally use relatively few physical movements. A speaker appearing before an informal group should use more. Which physical movements you should use on a given occasion is a matter for your best judgment.

- In summary, your physical movements help your speaking.

Voice

Good voice is an obvious requirement of good speaking. Like physical movements, the voice should not hinder the listener's concentration on the message. More specifically, it should not detract attention from the message. Voices that cause such difficulties generally fall into these areas of fault: (1) lack of pitch variation, (2) lack of variation in speed, (3) lack of vocal emphasis, and (4) unpleasant voice quality. Although these areas are mentioned in Chapter 13, we will examine them here because of their significance to formal oral communication.

- Good voice is a requirement of good speaking. Four faults affect voice:

Lack of Pitch Variation. Speakers who talk in monotone are not likely to hold the interest of their listeners for long. Since most voices are capable of wide variations in pitch, the problem usually can be corrected. The failure to vary pitch generally is a matter of habit—of voice patterns developed over years of talking without being aware of their effect.

- (1) lack of variation in pitch (usually a matter of habit),

Lack of Variation in Speaking Speed. Determining how fast to talk is a major problem. As a general rule, you should present the easy parts of your message at a fairly fast rate and the hard parts and the parts you want to emphasize at a slower rate. The reason for varying the speed of presentation should be apparent: it is more interesting. A slow presentation of easy information is irritating; hard information presented fast may be difficult to understand.

- (2) lack of variation in speed (cover the simple quickly, the hard slowly),

A problem related to the pace of speaking is the incorrect use of pauses. Properly used, pauses emphasize upcoming subject matter and are effective means of gaining attention. But frequent pauses for no reason are irritating and break the listeners' concentration. Pauses become even more irritating when the speaker uses fillers such as *uh, like, you know,* and *OK.*

Lack of Vocal Emphasis. A secret of good speaking is to give words their proper emphasis by varying the manner of speaking. You can do this by (1) varying the pitch of your voice, (2) varying the pace of your presentation, and (3) varying the volume of your voice.

- (3) lack of vocal emphasis (gain emphasis by varying pitch, pace, and volume), and

COMMUNICATION MATTERS

PowerPoint Keyboard Shortcuts

Sometimes PowerPoint presentations, just like oral communication, are more circular than linear—the speaker needs to go backward or forward to answer a question or make a point or perhaps just wants to change the order of the presentation. As Dusti Howell notes, making these changes can be awkward and frustrating. Howell provides four tips to make these movements smoothly: (1) use key commands to navigate the presentation rather than leaving the slide show to view individual slides, (2) switch to a blank white or black screen if you want to talk without the slides or if you need to pause the presentation, (3) use the pen feature to draw circles and arrows that capture the listeners' attention and make your presentation more exciting, and (4) make sure the beginning and ending of your presentation are strong by opening your presentation in slide show mode and ending with something useful to the audience such as an email address or invitation for questions. Keyboard shortcuts enable presenters to control the openings and endings of presentations more quickly. Howell offers a list of PowerPoint Keyboard Shortcuts that will likely be helpful as you perfect your presentation style.

Source: Dusti Howell, "Four Key Keys to Powerful Presentations in PowerPoint: Take Your Presentations to the Next Level," *TechTrends* Nov./Dec. 2008: 44–46, print.

PowerPoint Keyboard Shortcuts	
Can you go back, please?	Previous — Press Left Arrow (or Up Arrow).
Let's move on.	Next — Press Right Arrow (or Down Arrow).
Go to a specific slide by typing in the slide number, then press Enter.	Example: To go to slide 28, type 2, then 8, then Enter.
Go back to the first slide in the presentation.	Press <1 + Enter>.
(Vista only) Go back to the first slide in a presentation.	Press Right and Left mouse buttons for two seconds (2 Buttons + 2 Seconds).
(Vista only) Open an All Slides dialog box to see the titles of all the slides. Scroll through the list and choose the slide you want to go to.	Press <Ctrl + S>.
For a Black blank slide	Press B (or b); press B or Esc to return.
For a White blank slide	Press W (or w); press W or Esc to return.
To turn on the pen feature	Press <Ctrl + P> (Mac: <Cmd + P>).
To erase the drawings, turn off the pen feature, and retrieve the arrow	Press E .
To change the pen to an eraser	Press <Ctrl + E> (In Vista, press E).
To retain the drawings, turn off the pen feature, and retrieve the arrow	Press <Ctrl +A> (Mac: Cmd + A).
To retain the drawings, leave the pen feature on, and advance or back up in the presentation	Press an advance arrow (right or up) or a return arrow (left or down).
Begin the slideshow on the first slide.	Press F5 (2008: Crtl + Shift + S).
Begin the slideshow on the current slide.	Press <Shift + F5> (2008: Crtl + Shift + B).
Go to the final slide in the slideshow.	Press 9, 9, 9. Press Enter.
End a slide show.	Press ESC.
Bring up the shortcut menu.	Press F1, or right-click (Mac: <Ctrl + click>).

You must talk loudly enough for your entire audience to hear you, but not too loudly. Thus, the loudness—voice volume—for a large audience should be greater than that for a small audience. Regardless of audience size, however, variety in volume is good for interest and emphasis. It produces contrast, which is one way of emphasizing the more important subject matter. Some speakers incorrectly believe that the only way to show emphasis is to get louder and louder. But you can also show emphasis by going from loud to soft. The contrast with what has gone on earlier provides the emphasis. Again, variety is the key to making the voice more effective.

Unpleasant Voice Quality. It is a hard fact of communication that some voices are more pleasant than others. Fortunately, most voices are reasonably pleasant. But some are raspy, nasal, or unpleasant in another way. Although therapy often can improve such voices, some speakers must live with them. But concentrating on variations in pitch, speed of delivery, and volume can make even the most unpleasant voice acceptable.

- (4) unpleasant voice (improvement is often possible).

Improvement through Self-Analysis and Imitation. You can overcome any of the foregoing voice faults through self-analysis. In this day of audio and video recorders, it is easy to hear and see yourself talk. Since you know good speaking when you hear it, you should be able to improve your vocal presentation. One of the best ways to improve your presentation skills is through watching others. Watch your instructors, your peers, television personnel, professional speakers, and anyone else who gives you an opportunity. Today you can even watch top corporate executives on webcasts and video presentations. Analyze these speakers to determine what works for them and what does not. Imitate those good techniques that you think would help you and avoid the bad ones. Take advantage of any opportunity you have to practice speaking.

- You can correct the foregoing faults through self-analysis and work.

Visuals

The spoken word is severely limited in communicating. Sound is here briefly and then gone. A listener who misses the vocal message may not have a chance to hear it again. Because of this limitation, speeches often need strong visual support: slides with talking points, charts, tables, film, and the like. Visuals may be as vital to the success of a speech as the words themselves.

- Visuals can sometimes help overcome the limitations of spoken words.

Proper Use of Visuals. Effective visuals are drawn from the message. They fit the one speech and the one audience.

In selecting visuals, you should search through your presentation for topics that appear vague or confusing. Whenever a visual of some kind will help eliminate vagueness or confusion, you should use it. You should use visuals to simplify complex information and improve cohesiveness, as well as to emphasize or add interest. Visuals are truly a part of your message, and you should look at them as such.

- Use visuals for the hard parts of the message.

Types to Consider. After deciding that a topic deserves visual help, you determine what form that help should take. That is, should the visual be an outline, a chart, a diagram, a picture, or what? You should select your visuals primarily on the basis of their ability to communicate content. Simple and obvious as this suggestion may appear, people violate it all too often. They select visuals more for appearance and dramatic effect than for communication effect.

Because no one type of visual is best for all occasions, you should have a flexible attitude toward visuals. You should know the strengths and weaknesses of each type, and you should know how to use each type effectively.

In selecting visuals, you should keep in mind the available types. You will mainly consider the various types of graphics—the charts, line graphs, tables, diagrams, and pictures—discussed in Chapter 12. Each of these types has its strengths and weaknesses and can be displayed in various ways. Nonprojected techniques include such media as posters, flip charts, models, and handouts; projected techniques include slides, transparencies, and computer projections.

- Use the type of visual (outline, chart, diagram, picture) that communicates the information best.

- Select from the various available types of visuals.

Audience Size, Cost, and Ease of Preparation Considerations. Your choice of visuals also should be influenced by the audience size and formality, the cost of preparing and using the media (visuals), and the ease and time of preparation. The table below illustrates how the different media fare on these dimensions, helping guide you to the best choice for your particular needs.

	Media	Image Quality	Audience Size	Cost	Ease of Preparation
Nonprojected	Poster	Very good	Small	$$	Medium
	Flip chart	Good	Small	$	Short
	Presentation board	Good	Small	$	Short
	Real object or model	Very good	Small	$–$$$$	Short to long
	Chalkboard or whiteboard	Fair	Medium	$	None
	Photos	Very good	Medium	$$	Short to medium
	Handouts	Excellent	Large	$–$$	Short to long
Projected	35 mm slides	Very good	Large	$	Medium
	Overhead transparencies	Very good	Medium	$	Short
	Visual presenters (e.g., PowerPoint)	Very good	Medium to large	None*	None
	TVs/VCRs	Excellent	Medium to large	$–$$$$	Short to long
	Computer projection	Very good	Medium to large	None*	Short to long
	Document camera	Fair to excellent	Medium to large	None*	Short to long

*This assumes that the technology is already in place.

Techniques in Using Visuals. Visuals usually carry key parts of the message. Thus, they are points of emphasis in your presentation. You blend them in with your words to communicate the message. How you do this is to some extent an individual matter, but you should keep in mind the following dos and don'ts:

● Make the visuals points of interest in your presentation.

- Make certain that everyone in the audience can see the visuals. Too many or too-light lines on a chart, for example, can be hard to see. An illustration that is too small can be meaningless to people far from the speaker. Even fonts must be selected and sized for visibility.

● Here are specific suggestions for using visuals.

- Explain the visual. Remember that the visual helps you communicate content.

- Organize the visuals as a part of the presentation. Fit them into the presentation plan.

- Emphasize the visuals. Point to them with physical action and words. Use laser presenter tools and slide animations to emphasize. Most presentation software and tablet PCs let you annotate slides easily.

- Talk to the audience—not to the visuals. Look at the visuals only when the audience should look at them. When you want the audience to look at you, you can regain attention by covering the visual or making the screen in PowerPoint white or black (toggle the W or B keys).

- Avoid blocking the listeners' views of the visuals. Make certain that the listeners' views are not blocked by lecterns, pillars, or furniture. Take care not to stand in anyone's line of vision.

Use of PowerPoint. PowerPoint is likely the most common presentation software for business communicators. Though it has helped many communicate their message more clearly and thoroughly, it has also hindered many presenters who have relied on the software to do their job of relating to their audience. Can software that reduces content to a few words in a bulleted list really capture the nuances of your message? Can a graphic or animation on a slide really be more interesting than you, the presenter? Can software develop a relationship with the audience that is stronger than one you can develop? Of course it can't, and your audience is smart enough to recognize a poorly conceived idea no matter how attractive the slides. Remember that the audience wants to hear *you,* the speaker.

● PowerPoint should supplement the content of a presentation. It is not a substitute for content.

In other words, your content should drive what is presented in PowerPoint; PowerPoint should not drive what happens to the content. Only after you have carefully planned your message can you think about how PowerPoint will help you. Figure 14–1 provides a helpful checklist for ensuring that PowerPoint is a useful tool. Remember that a good slide show helps the listener follow your presentation. To do so, the listener needs clear, readable text. Generally, dark text on a white background works well, though light text on a dark background can work in certain conditions. A readable slide will also have minimal text. Though guidelines vary, we recommend not more than six bulleted lines with no more than four words per bullet on any slide. In addition, fonts should be no smaller than 24 points, and the text in a graphic must be readable from the back of the room. Figure 14–2 is an example of an attractive, readable PowerPoint slide.

● Keep PowerPoint slides simple and uncluttered.

If graphics contain too much data to fit clearly on a slide, consider using a handout for them. Furthermore, although sound and animations can add humor and get an audience's attention, they are annoying if they have no relevance to the content. Lastly, though it's fun to use decorative graphics, save those graphics for a title slide. Use graphics in your PowerPoint presentation that are functional—that represent the content or direct the audience's attention. Otherwise, your graphics can make a slide seem cluttered.

Simply put, think about your role in the presentation and PowerPoint's role, and organize and practice according to the tips in this chapter. Your audience will be impressed by a presenter who is considerate of their needs.

Figure 14–1

Tips for Effective PowerPoint Presentations

Guidelines for Preparing/Editing PowerPoint Slides

Questions about the presentation as a whole:

- Is there an attractive, clearly worded, readable title slide?
- Does the writer make good use of an outline slide? Is it titled effectively, and are the items in the list of topics grammatically parallel?
- Do the slides seem to cover all the important information?
- Do the slides seem to be in the most logical order?
- Is there a final slide that sums things up and/or leaves people with a significant thought/finding?
- Does the whole presentation have a consistent look?

Questions about every slide:

- Is there a strong contrast between the background and the text color?
- Is there any type that is too small to be read? (Remember, no typeface should be smaller than 24 points.) Conversely, is any type too big (yelling)? Is any typeface hard to read (as with italics or too fancy a font)?
- Is there too much or too little information on any slide? Should any slides be combined or divided up? If a topic is covered in more than one slide, the title on the subsequent slides should include "(cont'd)."
- Is every slide accurately/informatively titled?
- Has the writer managed the hierarchy of the information well (not using more than two levels of information and making clear which is on the top level and which is on the secondary level)?
- Are all headings on the same level grammatically parallel? Are items in all lists grammatically parallel?
- Is the wording on each slide clear and grammatically correct?
- If there are borrowed facts or quotes, are the sources named clearly on the slides?
- Is each slide visually clean and attractive? Should/could the writer add visuals anywhere? Are all visuals appropriately used and clearly labeled?
- Are the dynamic elements (e.g., slide transitions) appropriate for the topic/audience? Would you recommend any more or less at any point?

Figure 14–2

An Attractive, Readable Slide Using PowerPoint 2007

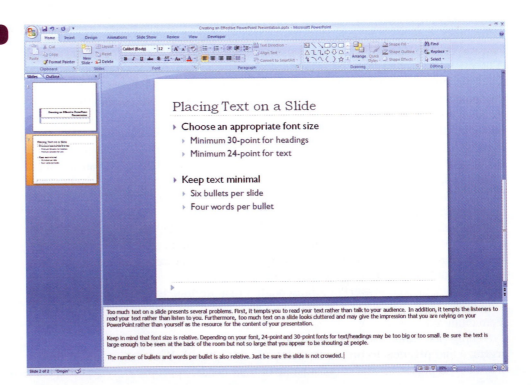

PART 5   Oral Forms of Business Communication

A Summary List of Speaking Practices

The preceding review of business speaking has been selective because the subject is broad. In fact, entire books have been devoted to it. This review has covered the high points, especially those that you can easily transfer into practice. Perhaps even more practical is the following list of what to do and not to do in speaking.

- This review has covered the high points of speaking.

- This summary checklist of good and bad speaking practices should prove helpful.

- Organize the presentation or report so that it leads the listeners' thoughts logically to the conclusion.

- Use language specifically adapted to the audience.

- Articulate clearly, pleasantly, and with proper emphasis. Avoid mumbling and the use of fillers such as *ah, er, uh, like* and *OK*.

- Speak correctly, using accepted grammar and pronunciation.

- Maintain an attitude of alertness, displaying appropriate enthusiasm and confidence.

- Employ body language to best advantage. Use it to emphasize points and to assist in communicating concepts and ideas.

- Be relaxed and natural. Avoid appearing stiff or rigid.

- Look the listeners in the eye and talk directly to them.

- Keep still. Avoid excessive movements, fidgeting, and other signs of nervousness.

- Punctuate the presentation with reference to visuals. Make them a part of the speech text.

- Even when faced with hostile questions or remarks, keep your temper. To lose your temper is to lose control of the presentation.

- Move surely and quickly to the conclusion. Do not leave a conclusion dangling, repeat unnecessarily, or appear unable to close.

- Choose visuals that are appropriate to your topic and enhance the audience's understanding of the material.

- Remember that PowerPoint helps the speaker convey the important ideas; it is not a substitute for a carefully prepared speech.

GIVING TEAM (COLLABORATIVE) PRESENTATIONS

Another type of presentation you may be asked to give is a group or team presentation. To give this type of presentation, you will need to use all you have learned about giving individual speeches. Also, you will need to use many of the topics discussed in Chapter 10 on collaborative writing groups. But you will need to adapt the ideas to an oral presentation setting. Some of the adaptations should be obvious. We will mention others to which you should give special thought in your team presentation.

First, you will need to take special care to plan the presentation—to determine the sequence of the presentation as well as the content of each team member's part. You also will need to select supporting examples carefully to build continuity from one part of the presentation to the next.

Groups should plan for the physical aspects of the presentation, too. You should coordinate the type of delivery, use of notes, graphics, and attire to present a good image of competence and professionalism. You should also plan transitions so that the team will appear coordinated.

Another presentation aspect—physical staging—is important as well. Team members should know where to sit or stand, how visuals will be handled, how to change or adjust microphones, and how to enter and leave the speaking area.

Attention to the close of the presentation is especially strategic. Teams need to decide who will present the close and what will be said. If a summary is used, the member who presents it should attribute key points to appropriate team members.

- Group presentations require individual speaking skills plus planning for collaboration. Adapt the ideas on collaborative writing in Chapter 10 to team presentations.

- Plan for the order of the presentation and each member's part.

- Plan for the physical factors.

- Plan for the physical staging.

- Plan for the close.

If there is to be a question-and-answer session, the team should plan how to conduct it. For example, will one member take the questions and direct them to a specific team member? Or will the audience be permitted to ask questions to specific members? Some type of final note of appreciation or thanks needs to be planned with all the team nodding in agreement or acknowledging the final comment in some way.

- Plan to rehearse the presentation.

In all of their extra planning activities, teams should not overlook the need to plan for rehearsal time. Teams should consider practicing the presentation in its entirety several times as a group before the actual presentation. During these rehearsals, individual members should critique thoroughly each other's contributions, offering specific ways to improve. After first rehearsal sessions, outsiders (nonteam members) might be asked to view the team's presentation and critique the group. Moreover, the team might consider videotaping the presentation so that all members can evaluate it. In addition to a more effective presentation, the team can enjoy better team spirit by rehearsing the presentation. Successful teams know the value of rehearsing and will build such activity into their presentation planning schedules.

These points may appear trivial, but careful attention to them will result in a polished, coordinated team presentation.

PRESENTING VIRTUALLY

- Both organizational and technogical factors are driving the growth of virtual presentations.

A relatively new venue for oral presentations is the virtual or online venue. While videoconferencing has been around for years, several factors seem to be driving the use of this technology now. Some of these factors are organizational—high costs of travel in both dollars and time and widely dispersed business operations. But there are technological reasons as well. With better hardware and faster, more widely accessible connections to the Internet, several companies have developed easy-to-use, Web-based applications. WebEx, once the de facto standard in this area, now has competitors with such products as Citrix's GoToMeeting, Microsoft's Live Meeting, Adobe's Acrobat ConnectPro, Wimba, and more. The affordable costs make this technology attractive to both large and small businesses for presentations to both large and small audiences.

Understanding the nature of this technology, the differences between virtual and face-to-face presentations, and some techniques to use with it will become more important as its use in business grows.

Defining Virtual Presentations

A virtual presentation is one usually delivered from a desktop over the Internet to an audience located anywhere in the world. While it could be delivered with both audio and video components so the audience could see and hear the presenter, users may also view PowerPoint slides on the Internet and listen over a phone line. Usually no other special hardware or costly software is needed. These presentations can also be recorded, allowing audiences to view them at different times as well at different places.

Virtual presentations are being used in businesses in many of the same ways face-to-face presentations are used—to inform and to persuade. They can improve productivity by giving even remote employees up-to-date information and training, avoiding down time for travel, and reducing travel costs. They can allow sales people to reach broader audiences as well as highly targeted specialized audiences worldwide.

Delivering Virtual Presentations

The major difference between face-to-face and virtual presentations is that the dynamics have changed—the speaker may not be able to see the audience, and sometimes the audience cannot see the speaker. Some argue that being able to see the presenter is not critical and that the technology has given us some tools to help the speaker get feedback from the audience. In the screenshot on page 474, you can see some of the tools available to the viewer using Microsoft's LiveMeeting. Each viewer can configure the screen to his or her preference.

To deliver a virtual presentation effectively, a presenter needs to do some preliminary, delivery, and closing activities. First is to choose a user-friendly, simple technology. Then send out announcements of the presentation along with a note encouraging the audience to pretest their systems before the designated start time for the presentation. If needed, you might want to have a technical person on hand to troubleshoot, anticipating that some will have trouble connecting, others will fall behind, and occasionally your time will expire. Also, you'll need to arrange ahead of time for an assistant if you need one. You may want to create something for early arrivers at your presentation to view in the first 5 to 10 minutes before you start. This could be an announcement, news of an upcoming presentation, or information about your products and services. You will also want to tell participants where additional information is available, including your slides, video recording of the presentation, and other business links.

The delivery of your presentation will be much like that for other presentations, except you will be doing it from your desktop using a headphone. You may want to use the highlighter or an animation effects tool in PowerPoint to help you emphasize key points that you would otherwise physically point to in a face-to-face presentation. You will want to plan breaks where you will poll or quiz the audience or handle questions that have come in through the chat tool. If you use the presenter's view in PowerPoint, you can set the timer to help you do this at regular intervals as well as gauge the timing through the questions and speed feedback.

In the closing, you will want to allow time to evaluate the success of your presentation as well as to handle questions and answers. Watching your time is critical because some systems will drop you if you exceed your requested time.

Overall, presenting virtually requires the same keys to success as other presentations—careful planning, attentive delivery, and practice.

- A virtual presentation can be delivered and viewed anywhere there is access to the Internet.

- Virtual presentations can inform and persuade both on-site and remote users.

- Virtual presenters may not see their audience; some audiences today may not see the presenter.

- Effective virtual presenters employ some unique preliminary, delivery, and closing techniques.

- Effective virtual presenters often use a variety of technological tools to keep their audiences attention.

- Effective virtual presenters manage the timing carefully.

1 Define oral reports and differentiate between them and written reports.

1. Business oral reports are spoken communications of factual business information and its interpretation.

   - Written and oral reports have the following differences:
     — Written reports permit the use of such visual cues as paragraphing and punctuation; oral reports allow voice inflection, pauses, and the like.
     — Oral reports permit the speaker to exercise greater control over the pace of the presentation; readers of a written report control the pace.
     — Both oral and written reports should be correct, but oral reports may be less formal.
   - Plan oral reports just as you do written ones.
     — First, determine your objective and state its factors.
     — Next, organize the report, using either indirect or direct order.
     — Divide the body based on your purpose, keeping the divisions comparable and using introductory/concluding paragraphs, logical order, and the like.
     — End the report with a final summary—a sort of ending executive summary.

2 Select and organize a subject for effective formal presentation to a specific audience.

2. Consider the following suggestions in selecting and organizing a speech.

   - Begin by selecting an appropriate topic—one in your area of specialization and of interest to your audience.
   - Organize the message (probably by introduction, body, conclusion).
   - Consider an appropriate greeting ("Good morning").
   - Design the introduction to meet these goals:
     — Arouse interest, perhaps with a story, humor, quotation, or question.
     — Introduce the subject (theme).
     — Prepare the reader to receive the message.
   - Use indirect order presentation to persuade and direct order for other cases.
   - Organize like a report: divide and subdivide, usually by factors.
   - Select the most appropriate ending, usually restating the subject and summarizing.
   - Consider using a climactic close.
   - Choose the best manner of presentation.
     — Extemporaneous is usually best.
     — Memorizing is risky.
     — Reading is difficult unless you are skilled.

3 Describe how audience analysis and personal aspects contribute to formal presentations.

3. To improve your speaking, take these steps:

   - Know your audience.
     — When preparing the presentation, analyze your audience, looking for characteristics that affect your presentation (gender, age, education).
     — During the presentation, continue to analyze them and adapt.
   - Work on these characteristics of a good speaker:
     — Confidence.
     — Sincerity.
     — Thoroughness.
     — Friendliness.

4. What the listeners see and hear affects the communication.
   - They see the physical environment (stage, lighting, background), personal appearance, posture, walking, facial expressions, gestures, and such.
   - They hear your voice.
     — For best effect, vary the pitch and speed.
     — Give appropriate vocal emphasis.
     — Cultivate a pleasant voice quality.
5. Use visuals whenever they help communicate.
   - Select the types that do the best job.
   - Blend the visuals into your speech, making certain that the audience sees and understands them.
   - Organize your visuals as a part of your message.
   - Emphasize the visuals by pointing to them.
   - Talk to the audience, not the visuals.
   - Do not block your audience's view of the visuals.
   - Use PowerPoint to enhance content.
6. Group presentations present special challenges.
   - They require all the skills of individual presentation.
   - In addition, they require extra planning to
     — Reduce overlap and provide continuity.
     — Provide smooth transitions between presentations.
     — Coordinate questions and answers.
7. Advances in hardware and software along with high-speed Internet access have spawned the growth of virtual presentations in business.
   - In virtual presentations the speaker cannot see the audience and often the audience cannot see the speaker. But today's software helps bridge this gap.
   - Before delivering a virtual presentation, the speaker should plan for the technology being used, announcements mailed to the audience ahead of the meeting, system testing, assistance for presentation support from technical and nontechnical sides, and material for early arrivers to view.
   - During the delivery, the speaker should plan interaction with polling or quizzing, take regular breaks for feedback and questions, and be attentive to the feedback from the audience on speed of delivery.
   - In closing, the speaker should allow ample time for both questions and evaluation.
   - Overall, the virtual presentation like the face-to-face presentation requires planning, attentive delivery, and practice.

4 Explain the use of voice quality and physical aspects such as posture, walking, facial expression, and gestures in effective oral communication.

5 Plan for visuals (graphics and slides) to support speeches and oral reports.

6 Work effectively with a group in preparing and making a team presentation.

7 Plan and deliver effective virtual presentations.

CRITICAL THINKING QUESTIONS

1 Explain the principal differences between written and oral reports. **(LO1)**

2 Compare the typical organization plans of oral and written reports. Note the major differences between the two kinds of plans. **(LO1)**

3 Assume that you must prepare a speech on the importance of making good grades for an audience of college students. Develop some attention-gaining ideas for the introduction of this speech. Do the same for a climactic close for the speech. **(LO2, 3)**

4 When is an extemporaneous presentation desirable? When should a speech be read? Discuss. **(LO2)**

5 Explain how a speaker's personal characteristics influence the meanings of his or her spoken words. **(LO3)**

6 An employee presented an oral report to an audience of 27 middle- and upper-level administrators. Then she presented the same information to three top executives. Note some of the probable differences between the two presentations. **(LO1, 3)**

7 Explain how feedback can be used in making a speech. **(LO3)**

8 "One's manner of dress, choice of hairstyle, physical characteristics, and the like are personal. They should have no influence on any form of oral communication." Discuss. **(LO4)**

9 By description (or perhaps by example), identify good and bad postures and walking practices for speaking. **(LO4)**

10 Explain how facial expressions can miscommunicate. **(LO4)**

11 Give some illustrations of gestures that can be used to communicate more than one meaning. Demonstrate them. **(LO4)**

12 "We are born with voices—some good, some bad, and some in between. We have no choice but to accept what we have been given." Comment. **(LO4)**

13 What should be the determining factors in the use of visuals (graphics)? **(LO5)**

14 Discuss (or demonstrate) some good and bad techniques of using visuals. **(LO5)**

15 In presenting an oral report to a group composed of fellow workers as well as some bosses, a worker is harassed by the questions of a fellow worker who is trying to embarrass him. What advice would you give the worker? Would your advice be different if the critic were one of the bosses? What if the speaker were a boss and the critic a worker? Discuss. **(LO3, 4)**

16 Give examples of ways a team could provide continuity between members through the use of supporting examples. Be specific. **(LO6)**

17 Explain the principal differences between face-to-face and virtual presentations. **(LO7)**

CRITICAL THINKING EXERCISES

Oral Reports (Face-to-face or Virtual)

Most of the written report problems presented in the problem section following Chapter 11 also can serve as oral report problems. The following problems, however, are especially suitable for oral presentation.

1 Survey the major business publications for information about the outlook for the national (or world) economy for the coming year. Then present a summary report to the directors of Allied Department Stores, Inc.

2 Select a current technological innovation for business use and report it to a company's top administrators (you select the company). You will describe the innovation and point out how it will benefit the company. If appropriate, you may recommend its purchase.

3 Report to a meeting of a wildlife-protection organization on the status of an endangered species. You will need to gather the facts through research, probably in wildlife publications.

4 A national chain of _____ (your choice) is opening an outlet in your city. You have been assigned the task of reviewing site possibilities. Gather the pertinent information and make an oral recommendation to the board of directors.

5 The Future Business Leaders Club at your old high school has asked you to report to it on the nature and quality of business study at your college. You will cover all the factors that you think high school students need to know. Include visuals in your presentation.

6 As representative of a travel agency, present a travel package on _____ (place or places of your choice) to the members of the Adventurer Travel Club. You will describe places to be visited, and you will cover all the essential details: dates, hotels, guide service, meals, costs, manner of travel, and so on.

7 As a member of an investment club, report to the membership on whether the club should purchase shares of Time Warner (TWX), Clear Channel Communications (CCU), and Yahoo (YHOO). Your report will cover past performance, current status, and future prospects for the short and long run.

8 Look through current newspapers, magazines, the Web, and so on, and get the best available information on the job outlook for this year's college graduates. You will want to look at each major field separately. You also may want to show variations by geographic area, degree, and schools. Present your findings in a well-organized and illustrated oral report.

9 Present a plan for improving some phase of operations on your campus (registration, academic honesty, housing, grade appeals, library, cafeteria, traffic, curricula, athletics, computer labs, or the like).

10 Present an objective report on some legislation of importance to business (right-to-work laws, ethics, environmental controls, taxes, or the like). Take care to present evidence and reasoning from all the major viewpoints. Support your presentation with facts, figures, and so on whenever they will help. Prepare visual supports.

11 Assume that you are being considered by a company of your choice for a job of your choice. Your prospective employer has asked you to make a _____ -minute report (your instructor will specify) on your qualifications. You may project your education to the date you will be on the job market, making assumptions that are consistent with your record to date.

12 Prepare and present a report on how individuals may reduce their federal or state income tax payments. You probably will want to emphasize the most likely sources of tax savings, such as tax sheltering and avoiding common errors.

13 Make a presentation to a hypothetical group of investors that will get you the investment money you need for a purpose of your choice. Your purpose could be to begin a new business, to construct a building, to develop land—whatever interests you. Make your presentation as real (or realistic) as you can. And support your appeal with visuals.

14 As chairperson of the site-selection committee of the National Federation of Business Executives, present a report on your committee's recommendation. The committee has selected a city and a convention hotel (you may choose each). Your report will give your recommendation and the reasons that support it. For class purposes, you may make up whatever facts you may need about the organization and its convention requirements and about the hotel. But use real facts about the city.

15 As a buyer of men's (or women's) clothing, report to the sales personnel of your store on the fashions for the coming season. You may get the necessary information from publications in the field.

16 The top administrators of your company have asked you to look into the matter of whether the company should own automobiles, lease automobiles, or pay mileage costs on employee-owned automobiles. (Automobiles are used by sales personnel.) Gather the best available information on the matter and report it to the top administrators. You may make up any company facts you need, but make them realistic.

17 The career services center at your school is conducting a series of brief presentations on companies both local and national/international that students might want to learn about as potential employees. Your business communication teacher has gotten wind of this initiative and has offered to have her class prepare and deliver some of these as their report assignments. The director of the center has enthusiastically agreed! In this pretend scenario, you'll be preparing an oral report about a company of your choice for students at your school who are entering the job market. Your instructor and the director of your career services center are your secondary audiences.

Carefully plan your report to be between 8 to 10 minutes long. Support your talk with PowerPoint slides that have the following:

- An introductory slide to identify your company.
- An overview slide, listing the topics your talk is going to cover.
- A slide for each main section of your talk.
- A closing slide with the main point you want to leave with people.

The following kinds of information might be appropriate to include in your talk:

- Company's outputs (products/services); the industry to which it belongs.
- Company's size (dollars in sales/revenue; number of employees), ownership, financial health.
- Company's plants/facilities/location.
- Company's history (how founded? When? By whom? Main achievements and/or crises in the company's history?).
- Company's structure (if possible, include an organizational chart at the end of the report and refer to it in your report).
- Company's employees (labor force, unionized or not, kinds of expertise, values).
- Company's position in its industry or main competitors; company's market/customers.
- Company's culture/missions/policies/management style/work environment.

- Current problems/challenges facing this company.
- Any unique traits of this company or industry that are important to mention to the prospective employee.

Include at least two Web and two non-Web references in your report (that is, material in a publication or database).

Formal Speeches

Since a speech can be made on almost any topic, you or your instructor can generate any number of interesting and timely topics in a short time. Whatever topic you select, you will need to determine the goals clearly, to work out the facts of the situation, and to set a time limit.

Named one of the "25 Most Influential Global Executives" (*Time* magazine/CNN) and one of *Fortune* magazine's "50 most powerful women in business," Andrea Jung is widely recognized for connecting Avon's international operations into a global "Company for Women." By setting up and listening to an advisory council from every level of the company, Jung has revitalized the 140-country sales force and increased sales around the globe. Being able to adapt to cultural and market differences is essential to communicating with customers.

"Avon does business in more than 100 countries, and engaging in an active dialogue with women is critical in helping us meet the beauty and lifestyle aspirations of our 5 million Avon Sales Representatives and 300 million customers from diverse cultures. We are a major global corporation but our roots are in local communities, and the person-to-person relationships we build through our direct sales model are a source of competitive advantage."

Andrea Jung, Chairman and CEO,
Avon Products, Inc.

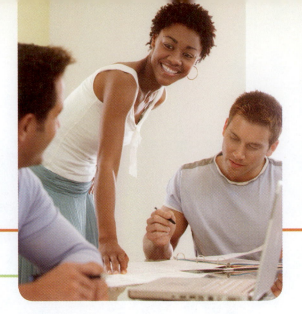

chapter fifteen

Cross-Cultural Communication

Upon completing this chapter, you will be able to describe the major issues in cross-cultural communication and prepare yourself to communicate with international partners. To reach these goals, you should be able to

1 Explain why communicating clearly across cultures is important to business.

2 Define culture and explain its effects on cross-cultural communication.

3 Describe cultural differences in body positions and movements and use this knowledge effectively in communicating.

4 Describe cultural differences in views and practices concerning human relations and use this knowledge effectively in communicating.

5 Explain the language equivalency problem and techniques for minimizing its effects.

6 Describe what one can do to enhance one's cross-cultural communication skills.

Cross-Cultural Communication

To introduce yourself to this chapter, assume that you're a recently hired trainer for a U.S. company that has a new branch office in Sweden. You've been sent to the office to facilitate the training of new employees.

After what seemed a fruitful brainstorming session with the leadership team, you ask the Swedish head manager, Andreas, to appoint a contact person in the group to help you launch the training project. Andreas turns to the HR manager, Prasan, who is from India, and says that he will be your key contact from here on out. You describe the process you want to follow and the documents you'll need in order to go forward. Then you ask Prasan if you can expect the documents by the next day.

Hesitating, Prasan replies, "Yes, I can send everything to you by the end of the day tomorrow." His boss suddenly intervenes: "No, that's not going to happen. You know you have a lot of work right now and won't be able to meet that deadline." Turning to you, the Swedish manager continues, "You can expect the material you need in two weeks." Prasan looks somewhat embarrassed but nods in agreement.

Back in the Andreas's office, you ask, "What just happened? Why did Prasan agree to such an unrealistic deadline?" Andreas explains that the Indian wanted to save face by giving a pleasing answer. Such an answer would keep you from appearing to be demanding and would keep him from appearing to be slow. "He values face-saving more than accuracy," the Swede says—implying that he himself does not. You wonder if such clashes of cultural preference could be handled more gracefully than the one you just witnessed. This chapter will introduce you to cross-cultural communication issues that may arise in business situations and help prepare you to meet them successfully.

THE GROWING IMPORTANCE OF CROSS-CULTURAL COMMUNICATION

As Chapter 1 points out and you surely already know, globalization is one of the major trends in business today. The spread of the Internet and other communication systems has only fueled this trend. And it isn't just for big businesses. According to Laurel Delaney, founder of GlobeTrade.com, "It's the small business owners of the world who are busting borders, discovering unlimited potential for growth and profit, and changing the shape of the world economy."[1]

- Business has become more global.

Both large and small businesses want you to be able to communicate clearly with those from other cultures, for several reasons. A primary reason is that businesses sell their products and services both domestically and internationally. Being able to communicate with others will help you be more successful in understanding customers' needs, communicating how your company can meet these needs, and winning their business. Another reason is that in addition to being a more effective employee, you will be more efficient both within and outside your company. You will be able to work harmoniously with those from other cultures, creating a more comfortable and productive workplace. Furthermore, if cultural barriers are minimized, you will be able to hire a wider variety of good people. Also, you will avoid problems stemming solely from misinterpretations. A final reason is that your attention to communicating clearly with those from other cultures will enrich your business and personal life.

- Communicating across cultures effectively improves your productivity and efficiency and promotes harmonious work environments.

In preparing to communicate with people from other cultures, you might well begin by reviewing the instructions given in this book. Adapting your words, sentences, and overall message to your audience is always important, and never more so than in cross-cultural situations. Clarity, courtesy, and correctness are appreciated everywhere. But how to achieve these goals can vary by culture; in one culture, for example, it might be appropriate to imply the main point, while in another you should state the point directly and explicitly. Thus, learning about the ways cultures differ is an important foundation

- Cross-cultural communication involves understanding cultural differences and overcoming language problems.

---

[1] Laurel Delaney, *The World Is Your Market: Small Businesses Gear up for Globalization, Scribd,* Scribd, 2004, Web, 3 July 2009.

for communicating globally. In addition, you must look at the special problems that our language presents to those who use it as a second language. It is around these two topic areas that this review of cross-cultural communication is organized.

DIMENSIONS OF CULTURAL DIFFERENCE

Dutch sociologist Geert Hofstede, probably the most respected expert on cross-cultural differences, defines culture as "the collective programming of the mind which distinguishes the members of one category of people from another," and national culture as "that component of our mental programming which we share with more of our compatriots as opposed to most other world citizens."[2] In other words, cultures are "shared ways in which groups of people understand and interpret the world."[3] Our dominant culture affects almost everything about us—from the way we think and communicate to the way we hold our bodies or establish our personal space. Certainly the spread of capitalism, advances in technology and science, and the explosive growth of electronic media have eroded national differences. The title of a popular book on international business claims that "the world is flat,"[4] and many would agree that we seem to have more and more in common globally. But cultural differences are still strong in many places and situations.

Of course, even within one culture there can be many subcultures. With only a moment's reflection on regional, ethnic, and even gender differences within any culture, you will realize that this is true. Plus, the person with whom you are communicating may be completely unrepresentative of his or her culture of origin. National borders are more permeable, and workplaces more diverse, than they have ever been. Still, an understanding of your communication partner's cultural roots will greatly enhance your interpretive and interaction skills.

Following the advice of Canning, a UK-based communication consulting firm, we recommend starting your cross-cultural education with the big picture.[5] Instead of trying to memorize such isolated facts as a culture's typical greeting or attitude toward punctuality, try to create a holistic picture. What is the *topography* of the country you are studying? In our Internet-influenced age, it may be difficult to believe, but topography still has a profound influence on what types of people live in a certain place. For instance, many natural borders around a country make for a more insular culture than changing, indistinct borders, and life under a broiling sun creates different habits and values than life in a darker, colder environment. What is the country's *history*? Have there been certain events or systems of government that have affected the national memory? And what about *religion or religions*? Think for a moment about how religious values have shaped the Middle East, different Asian countries, or even the United States. Knowing something about these three topics—topography, history, and religion—can tell you a great deal about the outlook of a country's or region's natives.

These broad cultural factors can have a major effect on businesspeople's communication practices and preferences. If you know your audience is Islamic, for example, you will be prepared to interpret their behavior when they do not take notes at an important business meeting (they tend to favor oral communication and the use of memory rather than writing), or when they exhibit a certain fatalistic attitude (since, in Islam, the success of human projects always depends on God's will).

Keep in mind, though, that businesspeople the world over share many goals and problems. All are interested in keeping their businesses financially viable, hiring and retaining good employees, developing marketable products, finding reliable suppliers, and so forth. Your efforts to understand your cross-cultural audience—like those

Margin notes

- Culture is the shared ways that groups of people view the world.

- A culture may contain subcultures as well.

- When learning about a culture, start with the big picture.

- Remember that you share many goals with your cross-cultural communication partners.

---

[2] Geert Hofstede, "National Cultures and Corporate Cultures," *Communication Between Cultures*, ed. Larry A. Samovar and Richard E. Porter (Belmont, CA: Wadsworth, 1984) 51, print.

[3] Fons Trompenaars and Peter Woolliams, *Business Across Cultures* (London: Capstone, 2003) 53, print.

[4] Thomas L. Friedman, *The World Is Flat: A Brief History of the Twenty-First Century* (New York: Farrar, Straus, and Giroux, 2005), print.

[5] John Mattuck, ed., *Cross-Cultural Communication: The Essential Guide to International Business*, rev. 2nd ed. (London: Kogan Page, 2003) 15–23, print.

TECHNOLOGY IN BRIEF

Web Tools for Cross-Cultural Communication

The Internet is a rich source of cross-cultural information for business communicators. Not only can you find information about places where you might be doing business, but you can use some Web-based tools to help you with your communication.

One of these, shown top right, is a currency converter, allowing you to convert from one currency to another. In this example, U.S. dollars are converted to Indian rupees. These converters are set up to use regularly updated exchange rates, so you can quote prices in both U.S. dollars and other currency.

The screenshot at the bottom shows an electronic translator, Babylon 8, in action. After downloading the software for free, you can easily translate words or whole websites without leaving your current window by using control>right click. Shown here is Babylon's pop-up window translating the Dutch word for *press release*. Or, you can use the online translator available through Word 07. Just right click, choose Look Up . . ., and pick your translation options.

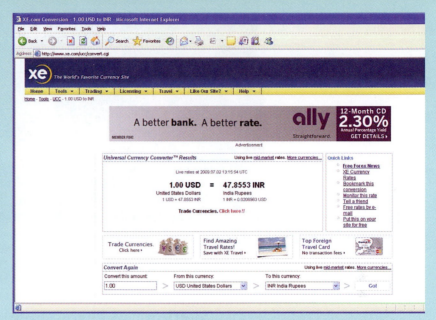

Source: <http://www.xe.com/ucc>. The XE.com. Universal Currency Converter, copyright © 2009 XE Corporation. XE and Universal Currency Converter are registered trademarks of XE Corporation.

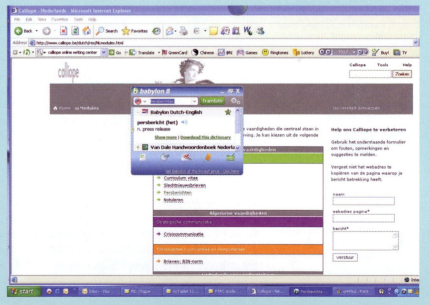

Source: By kind permission of Mr. Luuk Van Waes, University of Antwerp, <http://www.calliope.be/dutch/res/NLmodules.html>

to understand communication partners from your own culture—can lead to many profitable and mutually beneficial relationships.

To assist you in these efforts, we will briefly discuss various dimensions of cultural difference, starting with physical differences and then moving to mental and social ones. Sensitivity to these dimensions will help you avoid *ethnocentrism*—the tendency

- Learning about other cultures' habits and values will help you avoid *ethnocentrism* and enhance your cross-cultural communication.

Remember that, despite cultural differences, businesspeople around the world share many of the same goals.

to see only your own cultural programming as "normal"—and make you a better cross-cultural communicator.

Body Positions and Movements

• Body positions and movements differ among cultures. For example, in some cultures, people sit; in other cultures, they squat.

One might think that the positions and movements of the body would be much the same for all people. But such is not the case. These positions and movements differ by culture, and the differences can affect communication. For example, in the United States most people sit when they wish to remain in one place for some time, but many of the world's people squat when doing business. Because we do not squat, we tend to view squatting as primitive. This view obviously would affect our communication with people who squat. But how correct is this view? Actually, squatting is a very normal body position. Who is to say that sitting is more advanced or better?

• Manners of walking differ among cultures.

To take another example, people from the United States who visit certain Asian countries are likely to view the fast, short steps taken by the inhabitants as peculiar and to view their own longer strides as normal. And when people from those countries encounter U.S. natives who do not bow on meeting and leaving each other, they are likely to interpret the omission as rude. Similarly, people from the United States see standing up as the appropriate thing to do on certain occasions (as when someone enters the room), whereas people from some other cultures do not.

• Communication with body parts (hands, arms, head, etc.) varies by culture.

As you know, movements of certain body parts (especially the hands) are a vital form of human communication. Some of these movements have no definite meaning even within a culture. But some have clear meanings, and these meanings may differ by culture. In the United States an up-and-down movement of the head means yes and a side-to-side movement of the head means no. These movements may mean nothing at all or something quite different to people from cultures in which thrusting the head forward, raising the eyebrows, jerking the head to one side, or lifting the chin are used to convey similar meanings.

• Hand gestures differ by culture.

Hand gestures can have many different meanings. The two-fingered sign that means "victory" or "peace" in the United States is considered vulgar in Australia, and the "OK" sign is insulting in such diverse countries as Russia, Germany, and Brazil.[6] Even

---

[6] Roger E. Axtell, *Gestures: The Do's and Taboos of Body Language around the World* (New York: John Wiley & Sons, 1998) 43, print.

COMMUNICATION MATTERS

Carefully Present and Receive a Business Card in Japan

In Japan, it is considered bad manners to go to a business meeting without a business card, or *meishi*. There are a number of ways to present the card, but receiving it is an art, too. If you want to make a good impression on the presenter, receive it in both hands, especially when the other party is senior in age or status or a potential customer.

Be careful not to fiddle with the card or put it in your rear pocket—that is considered crude. Put it in some distinctive case. Those who do business in both countries often have their business cards translated on the back, as the examples here show.

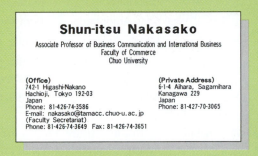

the use of fingers to indicate numbers can vary by culture. In the United States, most people indicate "1" by holding up the forefinger, whereas in parts of Europe, "1" is the thumb, "2" is the forefinger, and so forth. To point to themselves, the Japanese point to their faces, while the Chinese point to their noses and Americans point to their chests.[7] And holding up both hands with the palms facing outwards can mean either "ten," "I surrender," "I'm telling the truth," or "up yours—twice!" depending on where you are.[8]

Even meanings of eye movements vary by culture. In North America, we are taught not to look over the heads of our audience but to maintain eye contact when giving formal speeches. In informal talking, we are encouraged to look at others but not to stare. In Indonesia, looking directly at people, especially those in higher positions and older, is considered disrespectful. On the other hand, our practices of eye contact are less rigorous than those of the British and Germans. Unless one understands these cultural differences, how one uses eye movement can be interpreted as being impolite on the one hand or being shy on the other.

- So do eye movements,

Touching and particularly handshaking differences are important to understand in cross-cultural communication. Some cultures, like the Chinese, do not like much touching. They will give a handshake that Westerners might perceive as weak. Other

- touching, and handshaking.

---

[7] Wang De-hua and Li Hui, "Nonverbal Language in Crosscultural Communication," *Sino-US English Teaching* 4.10 (2007): 67, *www.linguist.org.cn*, Web, 3 July 2009.
[8] Allan Pease and Barabara Pease, *The Definitive Book of Body Language* (New York: Bantam, 2006) 111, print.

cultures that like touching will give greetings ranging from full embraces and kisses to nose rubbing. If you can avoid judging others from different cultures on their greeting based on your standards for others like you, you can seize the opportunity to access the cultural style of another. Here are some types of handshakes by culture:

Culture	Handshakes
Americans	Firm, five to seven pumps
Germans	Brusque, firm, single pump, repeated upon arrival and departure
French	Light, quick, not offered to superiors, repeated upon arrival and departure, may include a double kiss
British	Soft, three to five pumps
Hispanics	Moderate grasp, repeated frequently
Latin Americans	Firm, long-lasting
Middle Easterners	Gentle, repeated frequently
Asians	Gentle; for some, shaking hands is unfamiliar and uncomfortable (an exception to this is the Korean, who generally has a firm handshake)
Arabs	Gentle, longlasting, sometimes with kisses on both cheeks

- A smile can be a sign of weakness, and the left hand may be taboo.

In our culture, smiles are viewed positively in most situations. But in some other cultures (notably African cultures), a smile is regarded as a sign of weakness in certain situations (such as bargaining). Receiving a gift or touching with the left hand is a serious breach of etiquette among Muslims, who view the left hand as unclean, but many cultures attach no such meaning to the left hand. And so it is with other body movements—arching the eyebrows, positioning the fingers, raising the arms, and many more. All cultures use body movements in communicating, but in different ways.

Views and Practices Concerning Factors of Human Relationships

- Differing attitudes toward various factors of human relationships cause communication problems.

Probably causing even more miscommunication than differences in body positions and movements are the different attitudes of different cultures toward various factors of human relationships. For illustrative purposes, we will review seven major factors: time, space, odors, frankness, intimacy of relationships, values, and expression of emotions.

- Views about time differ widely. Some cultures stress punctuality; some do not.

Time. In the United States, people tend to be monochronic. They regard time as something that must be planned for the most efficient use. They strive to meet deadlines, to be punctual, to conduct business quickly, and to work on a schedule.

In some other cultures (especially those of the Middle East and some parts of Asia), people are polychronic, viewing time in a more relaxed way. They see planning as unwise and unnecessary. Being late to a meeting or a social function is of little consequence to them. In fact, some of them hold the view that important people should be late to show that they are busy. In business negotiations, the people in these cultures move at a deliberately slow pace, engaging in casual talk before getting to the main issue. It is easy to see how such different views of time can cause people from different cultures to have serious communication problems.

- Space is viewed differently by different cultures. In some cultures, people want to be far apart; in other cultures, they want to be close.

Space. People from different cultures often vary in their attitudes toward space. Even people from the same culture may have different space preferences, as noted in Chapter 13. North Americans tend to prefer about two feet or so of distance between themselves and those with whom they speak. But in some cultures (some Arabian and South American cultures), people stand closer to each other; not following this practice is considered impolite and bad etiquette. To take another example, North Americans view personal space as a right and tend to respect this right of others; thus, they stand in line and wait their turn. People from some other cultures view space as belonging

High-Context versus Low-Context Cultures: Edward T. Hall

An extremely influential model of cross-cultural differences comes from U.S. anthropologist Edward T. Hall. With *Beyond Culture* (1976), as well as two earlier books (*The Silent Language* [1959], about perceptions of space and time, and *The Hidden Dimension* [1966], focusing on the use of space), Hall essentially launched the field of cross-cultural communication. His most lasting contribution to this field has been his dividing of the cultures of the world into low- and high-context communicators.

Low-context communicators, in Hall's model, tend to express themselves in concrete, direct, and explicit ways. The gist of the message and everything one needs in order to interpret it are all there in the message. American, German, Scandinavian, Swiss, and Finnish people tend to fall into this category. They use and value a straightforward communication style.

High-context communicators use a more multimodal style. Rather than putting everything they mean into words, they use eye movements, body language, tone of voice, and other nonverbal elements to give interpretational cues. Though they communicate implicitly, they expect you to be able to interpret their points by drawing on your knowledge of their cultural context. French, Japanese, Indian, Irish, British, and Arabic people tend to be high-context communicators—though of course their contexts can differ dramatically.

Lately Hall's model has come under fire for being unsupported by formal research. In an extensive review of the topic, Peter Cardon has shown that Hall's generalizations arose from unsystematic observation and have often been contradicted. On the other hand, Cardon's study also shows that Hall's theory of contexting is the most cited theory in cross-cultural communication. The fact that so many researchers, teachers, and consultants have found it useful suggests that, despite its flaws, the model has a certain tried-and-true appeal. So put it into your cross-cultural communication tool box—and apply with caution.

Sources: Penny Carte and Chris Fox, *Bridging the Culture Gap: A Practical Guide to International Business Communication*, 2nd ed. (London: Canning, 2008) 18, print; Peter W. Cardon, "A Critique of Hall's Contexting Model: A Meta-Analysis of Literature on Intercultural Business and Technical Communication," *Journal of Business and Technical Communication* 22.4 (2008): 399–428, print.

to all. Thus, they jostle for space when boarding trains, standing at ticket counters, or shopping. In encounters between people whose cultures have such different attitudes toward space, actions are likely to be misinterpreted.

Odors. People from different cultures may have different attitudes toward body odors. To illustrate, Americans work hard to neutralize body odors or cover them up and view those with body odors as dirty and unsanitary. On the other hand, in some Asian cultures people view body odors not as something to be hidden but as something that friends should experience. Some of the people from these cultures believe that it is an act of friendship to "breathe the breath" of the person with whom they converse and to feel their presence by smelling. Clearly, encounters between people with such widely differing attitudes could lead to serious miscommunication.

- Some cultures view body odors as bad; others view them as normal.

Frankness. North Americans tend to be relatively frank or explicit in their relationships with others, quickly getting to the point and perhaps being blunt and sharp in doing so. Germans and Israelis are even more frank than Americans. Asians tend to be far more reticent or implicit and sometimes go to great lengths to save face or not to offend. Americans belong to a low-context culture, a culture that explicitly shares all relevant background information when communicating. Asians, on the other hand, belong to a high-context culture, which leads them to limit background information and communicate more implicitly.[9] Thus, Asians may appear evasive, roundabout, and indecisive to North Americans; and North Americans may appear harsh, impolite, and aggressive to Asians. Phone customs may be an exception, especially among

- Low-context cultures are more frank and explicit than high-context cultures.

[9] Linda Beamer and Iris Varner, *Intercultural Communication in the Global Workplace*, 4th ed. (New York: McGraw-Hill/Irwin, 2008) 34–35, print.

Greetings vary among cultures, as do many other behaviors. Consult print resources and those with international experience to learn the preferred ways of interacting in different cultures—and take a cue from your communication partner as well.

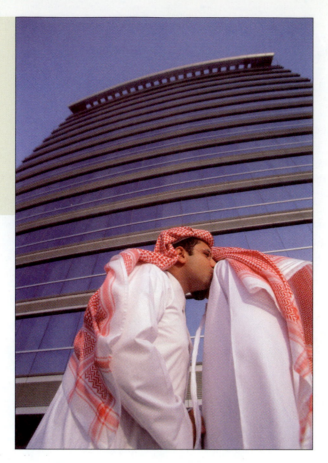

the Chinese, who tend to end telephone calls abruptly after their purpose has been accomplished. North Americans, on the other hand, tend to move on to friendly talk and clearly prepare the listener for the end of the call.

- Intimacy among people varies across cultures.

Intimacy of Relationships. In many cultures, strict social classes exist, and class status determines how intimately people are addressed and treated in communication. For this reason, a person from such a culture might quiz a person from another culture to determine that person's class status. Questions concerning occupation, income, title, and origin might be asked. People from cultures that stress human equality are apt to take offense at such questioning about class status. This difference in attitude toward class status is also illustrated by differences in the familiarity of address. Some Americans are quick to use first names. This practice is offensive to people from some other cultures, notably the English and the Germans, who expect such intimate address only from long-standing acquaintances.

- How people view superior–subordinate relations also differs.

Similarly, how people view superior–subordinate relations can vary by culture. The dominant arrangement in Latin America, for example, is a strong boss with weak subordinates doing as the boss directs. In sharp contrast is the somewhat democratic work arrangement of the Japanese in which much of the decision making is by consensus. Most in our culture view as appropriate something between these extremes. These widely differing practices have led to major communication problems in joint business ventures involving people from these cultures.

- So does the role of women.

The role of women varies widely by culture. In North America, we continue to move toward a generally recognized goal of equality. In some Islamic cultures or subcultures, the role of women is quite different. To many in our culture, the practices of the people of these other cultures suggest severe restriction of human rights. In the view of the people of these cultures, their practices are in accord with their heritage and religious convictions. The increasing spread of Western values has made such cultures more hospitable to businesswomen, but they may still encounter serious barriers.

Five Dimensions of Culture: Geert Hofstede

Between 1967 and 1973, Dutch sociologist Geert Hofstede collected 116,000 questionnaires about business practices and attitudes from IBM employees in over 50 countries. The result was the hugely influential *Culture's Consequences* (1980), one of the most cited works in cross-cultural communication literature.

The book identified four dimensions of culture, to which a fifth was later added. These have become mainstays in the field of international business. Here they are briefly explained:

- *Power distance.* To what extent do the less powerful members of a culture or organization expect that power will be distributed unevenly? If this is a normal expectation, it means that the company or culture exhibits "high power distance" and values hierarchy and obedience. If not, the company or culture has "low power distance."

- *Individualism vs. collectivism.* An individualistic culture is one in which people are expected to look after themselves and their families, while a collectivist culture promotes strong identification with social groups.

- *Masculinity vs. femininity.* At the feminine end of the spectrum is a "modest, caring" attitude, while at the masculine end is assertiveness and competitiveness.

- *Uncertainty avoidance.* This label refers to the extent to which "a culture programs its members to feel either uncomfortable or comfortable in unstructured situations." Uncertainty-avoiding cultures try to prevent such situations with strict rules and core values. Uncertainty-accepting cultures tend to be more relaxed, more tolerant of differences, and less rule-bound.

- *Long-term vs. short-term orientation.* This dimension was found in a study conducted by Chinese researchers. People with a long-term orientation are more oriented toward the future. They value persistence and thrift. Those with a short-term orientation value the past and present—respecting traditions, fulfilling social obligations, and saving face in social situations.

It is tempting to see whole cultures as falling at one end or the other on these dimensions. But as with other models, one must use this one only as a rough, preliminary guide. As one business executive puts it, "In my own practice, I look upon Hofstede's data as would an airplane passenger looking down upon mountain ranges. . . . These represent country cultures. Smaller ranges represent subcultures within countries. But to understand individuals, you have to land at the nearest airport and meet them at the ground level, taking into account their unique qualities."

Sources: Geert Hofstede and Jean-Claude Usunier, "Hofstede's Dimensions of Culture and Their Influence on International Business Negotiations," 1989, *International Business Negotiations*, ed. Pervez N. Ghauri and Jean-Claude Usunier, 2nd ed. (Amsterdam: Pergamon, 2003) 137–153, print; John W. Bing, "Hofstede's Consequences: The Impact of His Work on Consulting and Business Practices," *Academy of Management Executive* 2004 (18.1): 80–87, print.

Values. Also differing by culture are our values—how we evaluate the critical matters in life. Americans, for example, have been steeped in the Protestant work ethic. It is the belief that if one puts hard work ahead of pleasure, success will follow. The product of this thinking is an emphasis on planning, working efficiently, and maximizing production. Of course, not all of us subscribe to this ethic, but it is a strong force in the thinking of many in our culture. The prevailing view in some other cultures is quite different. In India, for example, the major concern is for spiritual and human well-being. The view of work is more relaxed, and productivity is a secondary concern.

Views about the relationships of employers and employees also may differ by culture. North American workers expect to change companies in their career a number of times; and they expect companies to fire them from time to time. Employees expect to move freely from job to job, and they expect employers to hire and fire as their needs change. Expectations are quite different in some other cultures. In Japan, for example, employment tends to be for a lifetime. The company is viewed much like a family, with loyalty expected from employees and employer. Such differences have caused misunderstandings in American–Japanese joint ventures.

How employees view authority is yet another question that cultures view differently. We North Americans generally accept authority, yet we fiercely maintain the

- Each culture has different values concerning such matters as attitude toward work,

- employee–employer relations,

- and authority.

COMMUNICATION MATTERS

Linear-actives, Multi-actives, and Reactives: Richard D. Lewis

British linguist Richard D. Lewis, founder of a highly successful cross-cultural communication consulting firm, has developed a three-part model for categorizing the world's many cultures. He believes they can be generally described as linear-active, multi-active, or reactive.

Linear-actives are those who tend to follow a linear path toward a desired goal. They "plan, schedule, organize, pursue action chains, do one thing at a time." Lewis cites the Germans and Swiss as exemplars of this group.

Multi-actives are those who have several things going at the same time—and not all of them overtly business related. According to Lewis, they are "lively, loquacious people who do many things at once, planning their priorities not according to a time schedule, but according to the relative thrill or importance that each appointment brings

with it." He puts Italians, Latin Americans, and Arabs in this group.

Then there are the *reactives*—those who listen and ponder carefully and move with caution. In Lewis's words, they "prioritize courtesy and respect, listening quietly and calmly to their interlocutors and reacting carefully to the other side's proposals." The Chinese, Japanese, and Finns would be in this group.

Knowing which style your communication partner prefers can help you adjust your expectations and communication style accordingly. But as with all categorizing schemes, use this one only as a general guide, paying careful attention to the actual situation you're in.

Source: Richard D. Lewis, *When Cultures Collide: Leading Across Cultures*, 3rd ed. (Boston: Nicholas Brealey International, 2006), print.

rights of the individual. In many developing countries, workers accept a subservient role passively. Autocratic rule is expected—even wanted.

- Social behavior varies by culture, such as practices concerning affection, laughter, and emotion.

Expression of Emotions. From culture to culture, differences in social behavior have developed. To illustrate, some Asian cultures strongly frown upon public displays of affection—in fact, they consider them crude and offensive. Westerners, on the other hand, accept at least a moderate display of affection. To Westerners, laughter is a spontaneous display of pleasure, but in some cultures (Japanese, for one), laughter also can be a controlled behavior—to be used in certain social situations. Even such emotional displays as sorrow are influenced by culture. In some Middle Eastern cultures, sorrow is expressed with loud, seemingly uncontrolled wailing. In similar situations, Westerners typically respond with subdued and controlled emotions, which could be seen as cold and uncaring by Middle Easterners.

We all have observed the emotion and animation that people of the Mediterranean cultures display as they communicate. And we have seen the more subdued communication of others—notably northern Europeans. The first group tends to see the second as uninterested and lacking in friendliness. The second sees the first as excitable, emotional, perhaps even unstable.

- Many more social differences exist.

Many more such differences exist. Some cultures combine business and social pleasure; others do not. Some expect to engage in aggressive bargaining in business transactions; others prefer straightforward dealings. Some talk loudly and with emotion; others communicate orally in a subdued manner. Some communicate with emphasis on economy of expression; others communicate with an abundance of verbiage.

- We must recognize them, look for them, and understand them.

There are countless differences between cultures. But it is not necessary that you know them all. What is important is that you recognize their existence, respect them, and study them when necessary. Only then can you adapt your communication style accordingly.

Effects on Business Communication

- Cultural differences affect communication.

Because cultural differences will affect communication between people of different cultures, the communication advice presented in this book should be modified to fit the cultures involved.

Keep in mind that this book was written largely for U.S. readers. Much of what we say does not apply to other cultures, especially our coverage of the basic message situations—those concerning directness and indirectness. People in Asian cultures, for example, generally favor a somewhat indirect approach for messages we would treat directly. They begin with an identification of context—that is, a description of the situation the message concerns.[10] They use what appears to us as exaggerated politeness and slowness in moving to the point. In fact, some of our direct messages would be regarded as rude by people in these cultures.[11]

• Our communication techniques are not universally acceptable.

Our persuasive appeals may be rejected in India, where they view themselves as having a more highly developed morality than we do.[12] Even the British, whose culture we think of as resembling our own, have message practices that differ from ours. They especially differ in the treatment of negative situations. They prefer an approach that we would regard as blunt and calloused. They would regard our goodwill strategies as insincere and evasive.

• The Indians and even the British have practices different from ours.

And so it is with the many other cultures of the world. Our practices just do not fit into them. What to do about this problem? You have no choice but to become a student of culture. You must learn the cultures of those with whom you communicate. Don't expect them to understand your culture, although many of them do. With your recipient's culture in mind, you then modify your communication accordingly.

• You must modify your communications to fit the culture of your recipient.

PROBLEMS OF LANGUAGE

The people on earth use more than 3,000 languages. Because few of us can learn more than one or two other languages well, problems of miscommunication are bound to occur in international communication.

• Communication problems are caused by the existence of many languages.

Lack of Language Equivalency

Unfortunately, wide differences among languages make precisely equivalent translations difficult. One reason for such differences is that languages are based on the concepts, experiences, and views of the cultures that developed them. And different cultures have different concepts, experiences, and views. For example, we think of a florist as someone who sells flowers and related items in a store. In some cultures, however, flowers are sold by street vendors, mainly women and children. Obviously, our *florist* does not have a precise equivalent in the language of such cultures.

• Language differences make equivalent translations difficult.

Similarly, our *supermarket* has no equivalent in some languages. The French have no word to distinguish between *house* and *home, mind* and *brain,* and *man* and *gentleman.* The Spanish have no word to distinguish between a *chairman* and a *president,* while Italians have no word for *wishful thinking.* And Russians have no words for *efficiency, challenge,* and *having fun.* However, Italians have nearly 500 words for types of pasta. And so it is with words for many other objects, actions, and concepts (for example, *roundup, interview, strike, tough, monopoly, domestic, feminine, responsible, aloof*).

Another explanation for the lack of language equivalency is the grammatical and syntactic differences among languages. Some languages (Urdu, for example) have no gerunds, and some have no adverbs and/or adjectives. Not all languages deal with verb mood, voice, and tense in the same way. The obvious result is that even the best translators often cannot find literal equivalents between languages.

• Grammar and syntax differences add to the difficulty.

Adding to these equivalency problems is the problem of multiple word meanings. Like English, other languages have more than one meaning for many words. Think, for example, of our numerous meanings for the simple word *run* (to move fast, to compete for office, a score in baseball, a break in a stocking, a fading of colors, and many more). The Oxford English Dictionary uses over 15,000 words to define *what.* Unless one knows a language well, it is difficult to know which of the meanings is intended.

• So do the multiple meanings of words.

---

[10] Beamer and Varner 168.
[11] Richard M. Hodgetts, Fred Luthans, and Jonathan Doh, *International Management: Culture, Strategy, and Behavior* (New York: McGraw-Hill/Irwin, 2006) 190, print.
[12] Beamer and Varner 173.

COMMUNICATION MATTERS

Blundering with Words

Companies can make blunders in international business through their products, practices, and words. Here are some of those where words were the culprit.

- When Coca-Cola first attempted to market its drink in China, the characters representing it sounded like Coca-Cola but translated to "a wax-flattened mare." Now the characters that represent it translate to "happiness in the mouth."

- Olympia tried to introduce a copier in Chile under the name "Roto," which is the Spanish word for *broken.*

- American Motor Company's Matador translated into "killer" in Puerto Rico, clearly not a good name in a place with high traffic fatality rates.

- Toyota's MR2 did well in most countries, but in France it is often pronounced merde, meaning *human waste.*

- Ford encountered problems when it introduced a low-cost truck it named "Fiera." The name translates to "ugly old woman."

- Bacardi developed and launched a fruity drink, calling it Pavian. In German it means *baboon.*

- When Nike attempted to place a graphic of flames on its shoes, it discovered that the illustration resembled the Arabic script meaning *Allah,* the word for God. The Council on American-Islamic Relations demanded an apology and withdrawal of the shoes from the market.

Selected from David A. Ricks, *Blunders in International Business,* 4th ed. (Malden, MA: Blackwell Publishing, 2006), print.

- Certain of our expressions don't mean what their dictionary and grammatical structures say they mean.

Within a culture, certain manners of expression may be used in a way that their dictionary translations and grammatical structures do not explain. Those within the culture understand these expressions; those outside may not. For example, we might say, "Business couldn't be better," meaning business is very good. One from another culture might understand the sentence to mean "Business is bad" (impossible to improve). Or we might say, "We could never be too nice to our customers," meaning try as we may, we couldn't be overly nice. To one from another culture, the sentence might mean "We cannot be nice to our customers."[13]

- Even words with the same meaning can differ in usage by culture.

Similarly, like-meaning words can be used in different ways in different cultures. One example is the simple word *yes,* a word that has an equivalent in all languages. "The Chinese *yes,* like the Japanese *yes,* can often be understood by Americans and British as their English *yes.* But the Chinese *yes* often means 'I am listening.' Or it may be understood in English as the opposite. For example, when an American says to a Chinese counterpart, 'I see you don't agree with this clause,' the Chinese will usually reply, 'Yes' meaning a polite agreement with the negative question: 'Yes, you are right. I do not agree with the clause.' "[14]

- Overcome such language problems by knowing languages well and by questioning.

Overcoming such language problems is difficult. The best way, of course, is to know your partner's language well, but the competence required is beyond the reach of many of us. Thus, your best course is first to be aware that translation problems exist and then to ask questions—to probe—to determine what the other person understands. For very important messages, you might consider using a procedure called *back translating.* This procedure involves using two translators, one with first-language skills in one of the languages involved and one with first-language skills in the other language. The first translator translates the message into his or her language, and the second translator then translates the message back into the original. If the translations are good, the second translation matches the original.

- Use back translating for important communications.

---

[13] Jensen J. Zhao, "The Chinese Approach to International Business Negotiation," *Journal of Business Communication* 37 (2000): 225, print.

[14] Zhao 225.

Difficulties with English

English is the primary language of international business. This is not to say that other languages are not used in international business, for they are. When business executives from different countries have a common language, whatever it may be, they are likely to use it. For example, an executive from Iraq and an executive from Saudi Arabia would communicate with each other in Arabic, for Arabic is their common first language. For the same reason, an executive from Venezuela would use Spanish in dealing with an executive from Mexico. However, when executives have no common language, they are likely to use English. The members of the European Free Trade Association conduct all their business in English. In the words of one international authority, "English has emerged as the *lingua franca* of world commerce in much the same way that Greek did in the ancient world of the West and Chinese did in the East."[15]

We must keep in mind, though, that English is not the primary language of many of those who use it. Since many of these users have had to learn English as a second language, they are likely to use it less fluently than native speakers and to experience problems in understanding it. Some of their more troublesome problems are reviewed in the following pages.

Two-Word Verbs. One of the most difficult problems for nonnative speakers of English is the use of two-word verbs. By *two-word verbs* we mean a wording consisting of (1) a verb and (2) a second element that, combined with the verb, produces a meaning that the verb alone does not have. For example, take the verb *break* and the word *up*. When combined, they have a meaning quite different from the meanings the words have alone. And look how the meaning changes when the same verb is combined with other words: *break away, break out, break in, break down.* Figure 15–1 lists some of the more common words that combine with verbs.

Of course, nonnatives studying English learn some of these word combinations, for they are part of the English language. But many of them are not covered in language textbooks or listed in dictionaries. It is apparent that we should use these word combinations sparingly when communicating with nonnative speakers of English. Whenever possible, we should substitute for them words that appear in standard dictionaries. Following are some two-word verbs and suggested substitutes:

Two-Word Verbs	Suggested Substitutes
give up	surrender
speed up, hurry up	accelerate
go on, keep on	continue
put off	defer, delay
take off	depart, remove
come down	descend
go in, come in, get in	enter
go out, come out, get out	exit, leave
blow up	explode
think up	imagine
figure out	solve
take out, take away	remove
go back, get back, be back	return

- English is the primary language of international business.

- But many nonnatives have problems using English.

- Two-word verbs are hard for nonnatives to understand.

- Use two-word verbs sparingly. Find substitutes, as shown here.

[15] Naoki Kameda, *Business Communication toward Transnationalism: The Significance of Cross-Cultural Business English and Its Role* (Tokyo: Kindaibungeisha Co., 1996) 34, print.

Figure 15–1

Some Two-Word Verbs That Confuse Nonnative Speakers

Verb Plus *Away*	Verb Plus *In*	Verb Plus *Out*	Verb Plus *Up*
give away	cash in	blow out	blow up
keep away	cave in	clean out	build up
lay away	close in	crowd out	call up
pass away	dig in	cut out	catch up
throw away	give in	die out	cover up
Verb Plus *Back*	run in	dry out	dig up
	take in	even out	end up
cut back	throw in	figure out	fill up
feed back		fill out	get up
keep back	**Verb Plus *Off***	find out	hang up
play back		give out	hold up
read back	break off	hold out	keep up
take back	brush off	lose out	look up
turn back	buy off	pull out	mix up
win back	check off	rule out	pick up
Verb Plus *Down*	clear off	tire out	save up
	cool off	wear out	shake up
calm down	cut off	work out	shut up
die down	finish off		slow up
hand down	let off	**Verb Plus *Over***	wrap up
keep down	mark off		**Verb Plus**
let down	pay off	check over	**Miscellaneous**
lie down	run off	do over	**Words**
mark down	send off	hold over	
pin down	slow off	pass over	bring about
play down	shut off	put over	catch on
put down	sound off	roll over	get across
run down	start off	run over	pass on
shut down	take off	stop over	put across
sit down	write off	take over	put forth
wear down		talk over	set forth
		think over	
		win over	

Additional problems result from the fact that some two-word verbs have noun and adjective forms. These also tend to confuse nonnatives using English. Examples of such nouns are *breakthrough, cover-up, drive-in,* and *show-off.* Examples of such adjectives are *going-away* (a going-away gift), *cover-up* (cover-up tactics), *cleanup* (cleanup work), and *turning-off* (turning-off place). Fortunately, some nouns and adjectives of this kind are commonly used and appear in standard dictionaries (words such as *hookup, feedback, breakthrough, lookout,* and *takeover*). In writing to nonnative readers, you will need to use sparingly those that do not appear in standard dictionaries.

● Some two-word verbs have noun and adjective forms. Use these sparingly.

● Slang and colloquialisms cause problems.

Slang and Colloquialisms. As Chapter 2 points out, slang and colloquialisms can cause problems when your reader or listener is unfamiliar with them. The odds of this being the case are dramatically increased in cross-cultural communication.

For example, will non-U.S. communicators understand the expressions *nerd, couch potato, control freak, 24/7, pumped,* or *basket case*? How about words derived from U.S. sports, such as *kickoff, over the top, out in left field, strike out, touch base,* and *get the ball rolling*? Such expressions are sometimes defined on English as a Second Language (ESL) websites, but rarely in dictionaries. They would be risky to use except with those very familiar with U.S. English.

head for home	shoot from the hip	in a rut
seal the deal	over the top	priming the pump
grasp at straws	on the same page	make heads or tails of it
flat-footed	back to the drawing board	tearjerker
on target	start at square one	countdown
out to pasture	a flop (or bust)	shortcut
sitting duck	up the creek without a paddle	educated guess
in the groove	a fish out of water	all ears
nuts (crazy)	a chicken with its head cut off	slower than molasses
circle the wagons	in the ball park	break the ice

In the United States, we tend to use colloquial expressions often in our everyday communicating, which is all right. They are colorful, and they can communicate clearly to those who understand them. But when you are communicating with non-native English speakers, try to replace them with words that are clearly defined in the dictionaries that these people are likely to use in translating your message. Following are some examples:

- We use such words in everyday communication. But avoid them in cross-cultural correspondence.

Not This	**But This**
That's just off the top of my head.	Here's a quick idea.
He frequently shoots from the hip.	He frequently acts before he thinks.
We would be up the creek without a paddle.	We would be in a helpless situation.
They couldn't make heads or tails of the report.	They couldn't understand the report.
The sales campaign was a flop.	The sales campaign was a failure.
I'll touch base with you on this problem in August.	I'll talk with you about this problem in August.
Take an educated guess on this question.	Answer this question to the best of your knowledge.
We will wind down manufacturing operations in November.	We will end manufacturing operations in November.
Your prediction was right on target.	Your prediction was correct.
Don't let him get your goat.	Don't let him upset you.

ADVICE FOR COMMUNICATING ACROSS CULTURES

As the preceding sections make clear, cross-cultural communication is fraught with potential barriers and misunderstandings. And even with the best effort on your part, not every act of cross-cultural communication will succeed. Like other kinds of communication, cross-cultural communication involves people—and people are unpredictable. In every culture, some persons are uncooperative, deceitful, prejudiced, or insensitive, while others are respectful, welcoming, sincere, and harmony-seeking. You can only make sure that you are as prepared as possible.

Keeping in mind the following words of advice will help.

- Cross-cultural communication is challenging. To increase your chances of success,

Do Your Research

This chapter cites many helpful resources on different cultures and their communication practices, and Figure 15–3 lists additional websites and books. Before any international business encounter, be sure you have done your homework. Learn something

- do your research,

Figure 15–3

Additional Resources for Cross-Cultural Communication

Websites:

<http://www.state.gov>. The U.S. government's main diplomatic website, with a wealth of information about countries and travel. The "Countries" link on the main menu bar gives you access to the site's Backgound Notes. These provide extensive, frequently updated information on the land, people, government, history, and so forth of all countries with whom the United States has relations.

<https://www.cia.gov/library/publications/the-world-factbook/>. Resources from the U.S. Central Intelligence Agency. The site "provides information on the history, people, government, economy, geography, communications, transportation, military, and transnational issues for 266 world entities."

<http://trade.gov/index.asp>. Website of the International Trade Administration, U.S. Department of Commerce, whose purpose is to promote international trade. Through the "Press and Publications" link on the main menu bar, you can access the agency's latest publications, including its monthly newsletter, as well as previous articles and reports.

<http://www.export.gov/>. Website of the U.S. Commercial Service (under the International Trade Administration), offering assistance of all types on international trade. Of particular value are its Country Commercial Guides, regularly updated for each country (access these through "Find Opportunities > Market Research" on the left menu bar and then click the "Market Research Library" link).

<http://www.sba.gov/aboutsba/sbaprograms/internationaltrade/exportlibrary/index.html>. Resources from the U.S. government for small businesses interested in doing international trade.

<http://www.oecd.org/home/0,3305,en_2649_201185_1_1_1_1_1,00.html>. Website for the Organisation for Economic Co-operation and Development (OECD)—originally the Organisation for European Economic Co-operation (OEEC)—an organization of 30 member countries who share their knowledge and resources on "more than 70 developing and emerging market economies." Can search for information by topic or country.

<http://www.uscib.org>. Website of the United States Council for International Business, a nongovernmental organization. Can access recent issues of the USCIB's journal *International Business* and news articles for free (must belong to a member company, law firm, or organization to access additional material).

<http://www.fita.org/index.html>. Site of the Federation of International Trade Organizations, another nongovernmental organization promoting international trade. Has links to over 8,000 international trade-related websites on such topics as maps and geography, weights and measures, international business terms, trade law, currencies, and many more. (A good place to start is "Really Useful Links" in the "Tools of Trade" section of the left-hand main menu bar.) Some links lead to free resources; some are for paying members only.

<http://globaledge.msu.edu/>. Sponsored by Michigan State University in the United States. Can find extensive resources by country and state, including not only geography, history, and vital statistics but also news, trade, and industry information.

<http://www.ciber.uiuc.edu/>. Center for International Businesss Education and Research (CIBER), hosted by the University of Illinois, Urbana-Champaign, and sponsored by the U.S. Department of Education. Particularly helpful is "Country Resources," found under the "Resources" link on the left-hand menu bar.

<http://timeticker.com>. Can find out what time it is in any country or which countries are in any time zone. (Be ready to click the "mute ticking" link at the left if you don't like the site's audio.)

<http://www.NationMaster.com>. A popular educational website started by an Australian statistics enthusiast. Offers maps, flags, and country profiles, but its greatest strength is statistics on many countries, which the site will graph for you.

<http://www.calliope.be/>. An online learning center for international communication at the University of Antwerp. Offers theory, exercises, and cases on intercultural communication in three languages: Dutch, English, and French. Using an electronic translator (or your own foreign-language skill), you can see what readers in these different cultures prefer to see in such documents as résumés, press releases, and persuasive messages.

Books:

William B. Gudykunst and Young Yun Kim, *Communicating with Strangers: An Approach to Intercultural Communication,* 4th ed. (New York: McGraw-Hill, 2002). Focuses more on cognitive and psychological issues than other approaches to this topic. See additional books by Gudykunst (e.g., *Theorizing about Intercultural Communciation* [Thousand Oaks, CA: Sage, 2004]) for more advanced reading.

Brooks Peterson, *Cultural Intelligence: A Guide to Working with People from Other Cultures* (Yarmouth, ME: Intercultural Press, 2004). Adapts and synthesizes concepts developed by cross-cultural researchers to offer five scales for analyzing others' and one's own culture-based tendencies.

Mustafa F. Ozbilgin and Ahu Tatli, *Global Diversity Management: An Evidence-Based Approach* (London: Palgrave Macmillan, 2008). Full of case studies and advice concerning many countries and issues.

Mary Murray Bosrock, *Asian Business Customs & Manners: A Country-by-Country Guide* (Minnetonka, MN: Meadowbrook, 2007). The latest in a series by this popular author; other books focus on Europe, United States, Mexico/Canada, Russia, and the Middle East.

Lillian H. Chaney and Jeanette S. Martin, *Global Business Etiquette: A Guide to International Communicaton and Customs* (Westport, CT: Praeger, 2008). Comprehensive guide to world business communication and behavior.

Terri Morrison and Wayne A. Conaway, *Kiss, Bow, or Shake Hands: How to Do Business in Sixty Countries*, 2nd ed. (Avon, MA: Adams Media, 2006). An alphabetically arranged country-by-country guide describing the overall culture, behavioral styles, negotiating techniques, protocol, and business practices of each country.

Roger E. Axtell, Tami Briggs, Margaret Corcoran, and Mary Beth Lamb, *Do's and Taboos Around the World for Women in Business* (New York: John Wiley & Sons, 1997). Like Axtell's *Gestures: Do's and Taboos Around the World*, is somewhat dated but still gives useful advice on communication and behavior in international business.

Jag Bhalla, *I'm Not Hanging Noodles on Your Ears and Other Intriguing Idioms from Around the* World (Washington, DC: National Geographic, 2009). A compilation of colorful expressions in different languages.

about the topography, climate, and location of your potential partners' countries of origin. Learn something about their language—and learn to speak it if you can. Study descriptions of their history, their ways of life, their values, their manners, even their food and recreation.

Besides doing library and online research, talk with people who have had experience with those in other cultures, and if they have writing samples, ask to see them. Take an intercultural business course or even a course designed for those preparing to do business in a specific country. Pursue opportunities to socialize or do teamwork with nonnatives in your own country. There is simply no excuse for undertaking an important cross-cultural event without having done all the research you can reasonably do.

Know Yourself and Your Company

As several books by international communication experts point out, a frequent mistake made by those preparing to do business abroad is that they focus all their research on people in the culture they're about to engage with and forget to research themselves. Yet knowing yourself is a good way to anticipate and prevent likely frustrations. For example, if you know you tend to be a "low-context," "low power distance," "individualistic," "masculine," "long-term goals" kind of person, you will be less caught off guard by people at the opposite ends of these dimensions. You can remind yourself to watch and listen carefully for visual and vocal cues, to be patient, to show respect and act with due dignity yourself, and so forth.

● know yourself and your company,

It is also very important to understand the business you represent. Is yours a rule-bound, procedure-governed operation or one that is more loose and trusting? Do you solve problems by leaving them to management, by hiring an expert, or by pooling everyone's ideas? Does your company avoid mixing business with pleasure, do employees socialize only with their peers, or does everyone in the company feel free to relax together? Does your company tend to take a straight, efficient route to its goals or learn and adjust as it goes? Just as you will view your international business partner as representative of his or her company, so he or she will view you. Be sure you send accurate signals.

Be Aware—and Wary—of Stereotypes

One of the most sensitive issues in cross-cultural communication is the extent to which generalizing about a culture perpetuates stereotypes. We have come to regard stereotyping as negative, with good reason: Stereotyping can prejudice us and blind us to someone's true nature. But the reason stereotypes are powerful is that they are based to some degree on observable likenesses within groups of people. They appeal because they are tempting mental shortcuts. But as the Canning consultants point out, that is also their downside. They "are fixed and conventionalized," and for that reason "suggest a failure to learn from experience." Canning recommends using well-researched cultural stereotypes as models that you can then adjust as you accumulate additional information. The generalizations can be a beginning point of reference, but you should quickly let them go when someone clearly doesn't represent the general type.[16]

● be aware—and wary—of stereotypes

Another reason it is important to be aware of stereotypes is that your prospective international business partners are likely to see *you* through the lens of a cultural stereotype. The more familiar you are with the way people from your culture or country are seen by those in another, the better prepared you will be to show them the ways in which you differ from that "norm."

---

[16] Mattock 14–15.

● adapt your English to your audience, and

Adapt Your English to Your Audience

The nonnative English speakers you meet will vary widely in their skill. Some may speak better English than you do, while others may have only the barest grasp of the language. As we have suggested, erring on the side of simplicity is your best bet for clear communication. Write or talk simply and clearly. Talk slowly and enunciate each word. Remember that because most nonnative speakers learned English in school, they are acquainted mainly with primary dictionary meanings and are not likely to understand slang words or shades of difference in the meanings we give words. They will understand you better if you avoid these pitfalls.

You also will communicate better if you carefully word your questions. Be sure your questions are not double questions (for example, avoid a question like "Do you want to go to dinner now or wait until after the rush hour is over?"). Also, avoid the yes/no question that some cultures may have difficulty answering directly. Use more open-ended questions such as "When would you like to go to dinner?" And avoid negative questions such as "Aren't you going to dinner?" In some cultures a yes response confirms whether the questioner is correct; in other cultures the response is directed toward the question being asked.

Finally, try to check and clarify your communication through continuous confirmation. Even in Britain, whose culture similar to ours in the United States, similar words can have vastly different meanings. For example, we use a billion to mean 1,000,000,000 whereas the British use it to mean 1,000,000,000,000. If a British English speaker asks to *table* an item, an American English speaker will probably interpret that as a request to put it off, when the real request is to bring it to attention.[17] Continually checking for meaning and using written summaries can help ensure the accuracy of the communication process.

Be Open to Change

● be open to change.

International communication can be a broadening experience if you approach it with openness and tolerance. In addition to learning about new and better ways to do business, you can also grow personally and enlarge your world.

Is adapting to the practices of one's international partners always feasible? No. You may find that the culture of the company you represent will simply not mesh with those of some potential business partners. Is adapting to others' practices always ethical? Here, too, the answer is no. For example, Frenchman Jean-Claude Usunier lists several practices to avoid in international negotiations, including bribery, buying information, buying influence, giving misleading information, exploiting the other party's ignorance, undermining the competition by buying out their people, and negotiating without intending to keep any promises.[18] Unfortunately, these practices are all fairly widespread, even though some have been made expressly illegal by such acts as the U.S. Foreign Corrupt Practices Act. And other ethical problems—racism, sexism, homophobia, disregard for the environment, exploitation of labor, and so forth—may arise. If put in a situation where you must choose between making a deal or behaving ethically and legally, seek advice from others in your company. You are likely to be advised to do the ethical thing—not only because most businesspeople are honorable but also because, in the Internet age, news about scandalous company dealings travels fast, often with disastrous results.

If approached patiently, humbly, and sincerely, forming international business relations can be incredibly exciting. Be ready to make and acknowledge mistakes, and to forgive them in others. Mutual respect is key—perhaps *the* key—to successful cross-cultural communication.

---

[17] Danielle Medina Walker, Thomas Walker, and Joerg Schmitz, *Doing Business Internationally: The Guide to Cross-Cultural Success,* 2nd ed. (New York: McGraw-Hill/Irwin, 2003) 211, print.

[18] Jean-Claude Usunier, "Ethical Aspects of International Business Negotiations," *International Business Negotiations,* ed. Pervez N. Ghauri and Jean-Claude Usunier, 2nd ed. (Amsterdam: Pergamon, 2003) 437–38, print.

1. Businesses are becoming increasingly global in their operations.
   - Being able to communicate across cultures is necessary in these operations.
   - Specifically, it helps in gaining additional business, in hiring good people, and generally in understanding and satisfying the needs of customers.

1 Explain why communicating clearly across cultures is important to business.

2. *Culture* may be defined as "the shared ways in which groups of people understand and interpret the world."
   - Cultures may have different subcultures.
   - When learning about a culture, start with the big picture.
   - Remember that business people the world over share many of the same goals.
   - Learn about others' cultures to avoid *ethnocentrism* and to enhance your cross-cultural communication.

2 Define culture and explain its effects on cross-cultural communication.

3. How people use body positions and body movements varies across cultures.
   - How people walk, gesture, smile, and touch differs from culture to culture.
   - Understanding others' body movements is important in cross-cultural communication.

3 Describe cultural differences in body positions and movements and use this knowledge effectively in communicating.

4. People in different cultures differ in their ways of relating to people.
   - Specifically, they differ in their practices and thinking concerning time, space, odors, frankness, relationships, values, and social behavior.
   - We should not use our own culture's practices as standards for determining meaning.
   - Instead, we should try to understand the other culture.

4 Describe cultural differences in views and practices concerning human relations and use this knowledge effectively in communicating.

5. Language equivalency problems are another major cause of miscommunication in cross-cultural communication, but you can minimize them.
   - About 3,000 languages exist.
   - They differ greatly in grammar and syntax.
   - As in English, most words in other languages have multiple meanings.
   - As a result, equivalency in translation is difficult.
   - The best advice is to master the language of the nonnative English speakers with whom you communicate.
   - Ask questions carefully to make sure you are understood.
   - Try to avoid two-word verbs and colloquial expressions.
   - Continually check the accuracy of the communication.

5 Explain the language equivalency problem and techniques for minimizing its effects.

6. Keep in mind the following advice about cross-cultural communication:
   - Do your research.
   - Know yourself and your company.
   - Adapt your English to your audience.
   - Be open to change.

6 Describe what one can do to enhance one's cross-cultural communication skills.

CRITICAL THINKING QUESTIONS

1 Put yourself in the shoes of the trainer described in this chapter's Introductory Situation. What might have been a better way to handle the situation? Explain why. **(LO4)**

2 What are the prevailing attitudes in our culture toward the following, and how can those attitudes affect our communication with nonnatives? Discuss. **(LO4)**

a. Negotiation methods

b. Truth in advertising

c. Company–worker loyalty

d. Women's appropriate roles in society

e. The Protestant work ethic

3 Some of our message-writing techniques are said to be unacceptable to people from such cultures as those of Japan and England. Which techniques in particular do you think would be most inappropriate in these cultures? Why? **(LO2, LO4)**

4 Think of English words (other than text examples) that probably do not have precise equivalents in some other culture. Tell how you would attempt to explain each of these words to a person from that culture. **(LO5)**

5 Select a word with at least five meanings. List those meanings and tell how you would communicate each of them to a nonnative. **(LO5)**

6 From newspapers or magazines, find and bring to class 10 sentences containing words and expressions that a nonnative English speaker would not be likely to understand. Rewrite the sentences for this reader. **(LO5)**

7 Is conversational style appropriate in writing to nonnative readers? Discuss. **(LO4, LO5)**

8 Interview a nonnative speaker of English about communication differences between cultures he or she has experienced. Report your findings to the class in a 10-minute presentation. **(LO2, LO3, LO4)**

9 Research a non-English-speaking country on the Internet or in your library. Look for ways in which business communication can vary by culture. Report your work to the class in a short presentation. **(LO2, LO6)**

10 Research differences in business etiquette between your country and another one. Report your findings to the class. **(LO2, LO4, LO6)**

11 On a recent trip to India, Mr. Yang, a prominent Chinese executive, dined with his client Himanshu Jain. Mr. Yang commented that the food was spicy, which Mr. Jain interpreted as an opportunity to discuss Indian cuisine. After lengthy explanations, Mr. Yang commented again that the food was spicy.

What happened here? What barrier is likely getting in the way of clear communication? (Adapted from Danielle Medina Walker, Thomas Walker, and Joerg Schmitz, *Doing Business Internationally: The Guide to Cross-Cultural Success* [New York: McGraw-Hill, 2003] 237, print.) **(LO2, LO4)**

CRITICAL THINKING EXERCISES

Instructions: Rewrite the following sentences for a nonnative English speaker. **(LO5)**

1 Last year our laboratory made a breakthrough in design that really made our sales skyrocket.

2 You will need to pin down Mr. Wang to get him to tighten up expenses.

3 Recent losses have us on the ropes now, but we expect to get out of the hole by the end of the year.

4 We will kick off the advertising campaign in February, and in April we will bring out the new products.

5 Maryellen gave us a ballpark figure on the project, but I think she is ready to back down from her estimate.

6 We will back up any of our products that are not up to par.

7 Mr. Maghrabi managed to straighten out and become our star salesperson.

8 Now that we have cut back on our telemarketing, we will have to build up our radio advertising.

9 If you want to improve sales, you should stay with your prospects until you win them over.

10 We should be able to haul in a savings of 8 or 10 grand.

chapter sixteen

Correctness of Communication

LEARNING OBJECTIVES

Upon completing this chapter, you will be able to use the accepted standards of English grammar and punctuation in written business communications. To reach this goal, you should be able to

1. Punctuate messages correctly.

2. Write complete, grammatically correct sentences, avoiding such problems as awkward construction, dangling modifiers, and misuse of words.

3. Determine when to spell out numbers and when to express them in numeral form according to standards of correctness.

4. Spell words correctly by applying spelling rules and using a dictionary or spell checker.

5. Use capital letters for all proper names, first words of sentences, and first words of complimentary closes.

The Effects of Correctness on Communication

Play the role of Mike Rook, a purchasing agent for Hewlett-Packard, and read through today's mail. The first letter comes from Joe Spivey, sales manager, B and B Manufacturing Company. You have not met the writer, though you talked to him on the phone a few days ago. At that time, you were favorably impressed with Spivey's enthusiasm and ability and with B and B. In fact, you assumed that after he gave you the information you needed about B and B's products and services, you would begin buying from it.

As you read Spivey's letter, however, you are startled. "Could this be the same person I talked with?" you ask yourself. There in the first paragraph is an *it don't,* a clear error of subject–verb agreement. Farther down, an *it's* is used to show possession rather than *its*. Spivey apparently uses the sprinkle system for placing commas—that is, he sprinkles them wherever his whims direct. His commas often fall in strange places. For example, he writes, "Our salespeople, say the Rabb Company engineers, will verify the durability of Ironskin protective coating," but you think he means "Our salespeople say the Rabb Company engineers will verify the durability of Ironskin protective coating." The two sentences, which differ only in their punctuation, have distinctly different meanings. Spivey's message is filled with such errors.

In general, you now have a lower opinion of Spivey and his company. Perhaps you'll have to take a long look at B and B's products and services. After all, the products and services that a company provides are closely related to the quality of its people.

The problem just described is a very real one in business. Image does influence the success of both companies and people. And correctness in writing influences image. Thus, you will want to make certain that your writing is correct so that it helps form a favorable image both of you and of your company. The material presented in the pages that follow should help you in that effort.

THE IMPORTANCE OF CORRECTNESS

- People judge you and your company by the correctness of your communication.

The correctness of your communication will be important to you and your company. It will be important to you because people will judge you by it, and how they judge you will help determine your success in life. It will be important to your company because it will help convey the image of competence that companies like. People judge a company by how its employees act, think, talk, and write. Company executives want such judgments to be favorable.

THE NATURE OF CORRECTNESS

- Businesspeople expect you to follow the generally accepted standards of English.

Not all people agree that there are standards for correct communication. In fact, some people think there should be no general standards of this kind—that whatever communicates in a given case is all right. Businesspeople, however, generally accept the standards for correct usage that educated people have developed over the years. These are the standards that you have studied in your English composition classes and that appear in textbooks. Businesspeople expect you to follow them.

- These standards of correctness assist in communicating.

These standards of correctness have one basic purpose: to assist in communicating. They are designed to reduce misunderstanding—to make communication more precise. When you communicate precisely, you practice good ethics by meeting your reader's needs for understandable messages.

The practical value of these standards is easily illustrated. Take, for example, the following two sentences. Their words are the same; only their punctuation differs. But what a difference the punctuation makes!

"The teacher," said the student, "is careless."
The teacher said, "The student is careless."

Can You Detect the Difference that Punctuation Makes?

Call me Karla.
Call me, Karla.

The groom was asked to call the guests names as they arrived.
The groom was asked to call the guests' names as they arrived.

A clever dog knows it's master.
A clever dog knows its master.

Everyone, I know, has a problem.
Everyone I know has a problem.

Do not break your bread or roll in your soup.
Do not break your bread, or roll in your soup.

She ate a half-fried chicken.
She ate a half fried chicken.

I left him convinced he was a fool.
I left him, convinced he was a fool.

The play ended, happily.
The play ended happily.

Thirteen people knew the secret, all told.
Thirteen people knew the secret; all told.

Or what about the following pair of sentences? Who is speaking, the Democrats or the Republicans? The commas make a difference.

The Democrats, say the Republicans, will win.
The Democrats say the Republicans will win.

Because the standards of correctness are important to your communication in business, this chapter reviews them. Much more space would be needed for complete coverage, but the major standards—those that most often present problems in your writing—are covered. The standards are coded with symbols (letters and numbers) so that your instructor can use them as grading marks to identify errors.

- The following review covers the major standards.

You probably already know many of the standards of correctness. To help you determine how much you know and do not know, you should take the self-analysis test at the end of the chapter (page 544) or on the textbook website. This will enable you to study the standards selectively. Because the self-analysis test covers only the more frequently used standards, however, you would be wise to review the entire chapter.

- Take the self-analysis test to determine your present knowledge of the standards.

STANDARDS FOR PUNCTUATION

The following explanations cover the most important standards for correctness in punctuation. For reasons of accuracy, the explanations use some grammatical terms. Even so, the illustrations should make the standards clear.

Apostrophe: Apos 1

Use the apostrophe to show the possessive case of nouns and indefinite pronouns. Whether the apostrophe goes before or after the *s* depends on whether the possessive noun is singular or plural.

If the possessive noun is singular, just add an *'s*.

- Use the apostrophe to show possession.

one company's sales
one employee's desk
someone's pen
one boss's policy
Texas's state laws
Sue Jones's car
Joe's report

If the possessive noun is plural and already ends in an *s*, just add the apostrophe after the *s*.

Singular	Plural	Plural Possessive
company	companies	six companies' sales
employee	employees	three employees' desks
boss	bosses	two bosses' policies
Jones	Joneses	the Joneses' cars

If the possessive noun does not end in an *s*, add an *'s*.

Singular	Plural	Plural Possessive
child	children	children's
person	people	people's

Note: A popular practice is to place only an apostrophe at the end of singular possessive nouns that end in *s* (e.g., one boss' policy). However, until you're comfortable distinguishing between singular and plural possessives, you may prefer to use the more standard punctuation. If a noun is singular, you don't have to think about putting the apostrophe inside or outside the *s*; just add the *'s* and move on because you'll know that your punctuation is correct.

Apos 2

● Indicate omissions in contractions with the apostrophe.

Use an apostrophe to mark the place in a contraction where letters are omitted. Do not use it to make personal pronouns possessive (its, hers).

> it is = it's
> has not = hasn't
> cannot = can't

Apos 3

● Use the apostrophe to indicate time, value, or measurement of a noun.

Use the apostrophe to indicate time, value, or measurement of a noun. The placement of the apostrophe before or after the *s* depends on whether the possessive is singular or plural (see Apos 1).

> today's newspaper
> three weeks' vacation
> last year's sales
> 20 pounds' worth

Brackets: Bkts

● Use brackets to set off words that you insert in a quotation.

Set off in brackets words that you wish to insert in a quotation.

> "The use of this type of mentor [the personal coach] may still be increasing."
> "Direct supervision has diminished in importance during the past decade [the report was written in 2005], when 63 percent of the reporting business firms that started programs used teams."

Colon: Cln 1

● Use the colon to introduce formal statements.

Use the colon to introduce an enumeration, a formal quotation, or a statement of explanation.

> *Enumeration:* Working in this department are three classes of support: clerical support, computer support, and customer support.
> *Formal quotation:* President Hartung had this to say about the proposal: "Any such movement that fails to get the support of the workers from all divisions fails to get my support."

Explanation: At this time the company was pioneering a new marketing idea: It was attempting to sell customized products directly to consumers through its website.

Cln 2

An independent clause (complete sentence) should precede a colon. Do not use the colon when the thought of the sentence should continue without interruption. If introducing a list by a colon, the colon should be preceded by a word that explains or identifies the list.

- Do not use the colon when it breaks the thought flow.

> *Not this:* Cities in which new sales offices are in operation are: Fort Smith, Texarkana, Lake Charles, Jackson, and Biloxi.
>
> *But this:* Cities in which new sales offices are in operation are Fort Smith, Texarkana, Lake Charles, Jackson, and Biloxi.
>
> *Or this:* Cities with new sales offices are as follows: Fort Smith, Texarkana, Lake Charles, Jackson, and Biloxi.

Comma: Cma 1

Use the comma to separate independent (main) clauses connected by a coordinating conjunction. Some coordinating conjunctions are *and, but, or,* and *nor.* (An independent clause has a subject and a verb and stands by itself as a sentence. A coordinating conjunction connects clauses, words, or phrases of equal rank.)

- Use the comma to separate independent clauses connected by *and, but, or,* and *nor.*

> Only two components of the index declined, and these two account for only 12 percent of the total weight of the index.
>
> New hybrid automobiles are moving at record volumes, but used-car sales are lagging behind the record pace set two years ago.

Make exceptions to this rule, however, in the case of compound sentences consisting of short and closely connected clauses.

> We sold and the price dropped.
>
> Sometimes we win and sometimes we lose.

Cma 2–1

Separate the items listed in a series by commas. In order to avoid misinterpretation of the rare instances in which some of the items listed have compound constructions, it is always good to include the comma between the last two items (before the final conjunction).

- Use the comma to separate (1) items in a series and

> Good copy must cover facts with accuracy, sincerity, honesty, and conviction.
>
> Direct advertising can be used to introduce salespeople, fill in between salespeople's calls, cover territory where salespeople cannot be maintained, and keep pertinent reference material in the hands of prospects.

CHAPTER 16 Correctness of Communication

The DuPont Color Popularity Report conducted in 2005 indicated that silver, white, blue, and black were the top four car colors favored by the public.

Cma 2–2

● (2) adjectives in a series.

Separate coordinate adjectives in a series by commas if they modify the same noun and if no *and* connects them. A good test to determine whether adjectives are coordinate is to insert an *and* between them. If the *and* does not change the meaning, the adjectives are coordinate.

> Miss Pratt has been a reliable, faithful, efficient employee for 20 years.
>
> We guarantee that this is a good, clean car.
>
> Blue office furniture is Mr. Orr's recommendation for the new conference room. (*Blue* and *office furniture* does not make sense.)
>
> A big crescent wrench proved to be best for the task. (The *and* won't fit between *big* and *crescent*.)

Cma 3

● Use commas to set off nonrestrictive clauses (those that could be left out without changing the meaning of the sentence).

Set off nonrestrictive clauses with commas. By a *nonrestrictive clauses* we mean a clause (a group of words with a subject and a verb) that could be omitted from the sentence without changing its meaning. Restrictive clauses (those that restrict the words they modify to one particular object) are not set off by commas. A restrictive clause cannot be left out of the sentence without changing its meaning.

> *Restrictive:* The salesperson *who sells the most* will get a bonus. (Not every salesperson will get a bonus. Only the person who sells the most will get a bonus. Therefore, the clause restricts the meaning of the sentence.)
>
> *Nonrestrictive:* Diana Chan, *who was the company's top salesperson for the year*, was awarded a bonus. (If the clause *who was the company's top salesperson for the year* is omitted, the meaning of the sentence is not changed.)
>
> J. Ward & Company is the firm *that employs most of the seasonal workers in this area*.
>
> J. Ward & Company, *which employs most of the seasonal workers in this area*, has gained the admiration of the community.

Notice that some clauses can be either restrictive or nonrestrictive, depending on the writer's intended meaning.

> *Restrictive:* All the cars that were damaged in the flood were sold at a discount. (Not all cars were sold at a discount, only the cars damaged in the flood.)
>
> *Nonrestrictive:* All the cars, which were damaged by the flood, were sold at a discount. (Implies that the entire fleet of cars was damaged.)

Note: That usually indicates a restrictive clause that is not set off with commas. *Which* usually indicates a nonrestrictive clause that is set off with commas. *Who,* which should be used to refer to people, may indicate either a restrictive or nonrestrictive clause.

Cma 4–1

● Use commas to set off (1) parenthetical expressions (comments "stuck in"),

Use commas to set off parenthetical expressions. A parenthetical expression consists of words that interrupt the normal flow of the sentence. In a sense, they appear to be "stuck in." In many instances, they are simply words out of normal order. For example, the sentence "A full-page, black-and-white advertisement was run in the *Daily Bulletin*" contains a parenthetical expression when the word order is altered: "An advertisement, full-page and in black and white, was run in the *Daily Bulletin*."

> This practice, it is believed, will lead to financial ruin.
>
> Merck, as *The Wall Street Journal* reports, has sharply increased its alliance activity.

PART 6 Cross-Cultural Communication, Correctness, Technology, Research

Although in such cases you may use dashes or parentheses in place of commas, the three marks differ in the degree to which they separate the enclosed words from the rest of the sentence. The comma is the weakest of the three, and it is best used when the material set off is closely related to the surrounding words. Parentheses and dashes are used to more obviously separate material from the rest of the sentence than would be indicated by commas. Parentheses are used when a writer wants to de-emphasize the material, while dashes are used to emphasize material.

Cma 4–2

Use commas to set off an appositive (a noun or a noun and its modifiers inserted to rename another noun) from the rest of the sentence. In a sense, appositives are parenthetical expressions because they interrupt the normal flow of the sentence.

● (2) appositives (words renaming another word),

> UPS, our primary shipper, is leasing a new distribution center in China.
> St. Louis, home office of our Midwest district, will be the permanent site of our annual sales meeting.
> President Cartwright, a self-educated woman, is the leading advocate of online training for employees.

But appositives that are required for the sentence meaning are not set off by commas.

> The word *liabilities* is not understood by most people.
> Our next shipment will come on the ship *Alberta*.

Cma 4–3

Set off parenthetical words including such transitional expressions as *however, in fact, of course, for example,* and *consequently* with commas.

● (3) certain parenthetical words (*in fact, however*), and

> It is apparent, therefore, that the buyers' resistance was caused by an overvigorous sales campaign.
> After the first experiment, for example, the traffic flow increased 10 percent.
> The company, however, will be forced to adopt a more competitive pricing strategy.

Included in this group of parenthetical words may be introductory interjections (*oh, alas*) and responsive expressions (*yes, no, surely, indeed, well,* and *and so on*). But if the words are strongly exclamatory or are not closely connected with the rest of the sentence, they may be punctuated as a sentence. (*No. Yes. Indeed.*)

> Yes, the decision to increase product placement advertising has been made.
> Oh, contribute whatever you think is appropriate.

Cma 4–4

When more than one unit appears in a date or an address, set off the units by commas.

● (4) units in a date or address.

> *One unit:* December 30 is the date of our annual inventory.
> *One unit:* The company has one outlet in Ohio.
> *More than one unit:* December 30, 1906, is the date the Johnston Company first opened its doors.
> *More than one unit:* Tuesday, June 30, is the project deadline.
> *More than one unit:* Richmond, Virginia, is the headquarters of the new sales district.

Cma 5–1

Use the comma after a subordinate clause that precedes the main clause. A subordinate clause is a dependent clause (subordinating conjunction + subject + verb). Examples of subordinating conjunctions are *although, since, because,* and *while.*

● Use the comma after (1) introductory subordinate clauses and

Although it is durable, this package does not have eye appeal.

Since there was little store traffic on aisle 13, the area was converted into storage space.

Cma 5–2

- (2) introductory phrases.

Place a comma after an introductory phrase. An introductory phrase may be a participle, an infinitive, or a prepositional phrase of five words or more.

Participle phrase: Realizing his mistake, Ron instructed his direct reports to keep a record of all salvaged equipment.

Infinitive phrase: To increase the turnover of automobile accessories, we must first improve their display area.

Prepositional phrase: Before the annual ABC board meeting, we met to discuss the agenda.

Cma 6–1

- Do not use the comma without good reason, such as between the subject and the verb.

Use the comma only for good reason. As a rule, the use of commas should be justified by one of the standard practices previously noted.

In particular do not be tricked into putting a comma between the subject and the verb.

The thought that he could not afford to fail spurred him on. (No comma after *fail.*)

Cma 6–2

- Use the comma wherever it helps clarity.

Take exception to the preceding standards wherever the insertion of a comma will help clarity of expression.

Not this: From the beginning inventory methods of Hill Company have been haphazard.
But this: From the beginning, inventory methods of Hill Company have been haphazard.

Not this: Ever since she has been a model worker.
But this: Ever since, she has been a model worker.

Dash: Dsh 1

- Use the em dash to show interruption or emphasis.

Use the em dash to set off an element for emphasis or to show interrupted thought. In particular, use it with long parenthetical expressions or parenthetical expressions containing internal punctuation (see Cma 4–1).

Budgets for some past years—2006, for example—were prepared without consulting the department heads.

The test proved that the new process is simple, effective, accurate—and more expensive.

Only one person—the supervisor in charge—has authority to approve a policy exception.

If you want a voice in the government—vote.

Dsh 2

- Use the en dash to indicate ranges of dates, times, and page numbers.

The en dash is longer than a hyphen but shorter than an em dash and is used to indicate ranges such as those that involve dates, times, or page numbers. Generally, if you can use the words *to* or *through* between dates, times, or page numbers, you can use the en dash.

The conference will be held Monday–Thursday.

Please read pages 1–50 before tomorrow's meeting.

See *Technology in Brief,* page 529, for tips on how to use Word to help you insert em dashes and en dashes correctly.

Exclamation Mark: Ex

Use the exclamation mark at the end of a sentence or an exclamatory fragment to show strong emotion. But use it sparingly; never use it with trivial ideas.

> We've done it again!
>
> Congratulations! Your outstanding performance review qualifies you for merit pay.

- Use exclamation marks to show strong feeling.

Hyphen: Hpn 1

Use the hyphen to indicate the division of a word at the end of the line. You must divide between syllables. It is generally impractical to leave a one-letter syllable at the end of a line (*a-bove*) or to carry over a two-letter syllable to the next line (*expens-es*).

If you turn on the hyphenation feature of your word processing software, you can let it automatically take care of hyphenating words. This feature permits you to set a hyphenation range. The wider the range, the fewer words that will be hyphenated and the more ragged your margin; the narrower the range, the more words that will be hyphenated and the smoother your right margin. You also have the option of controlling the hyphenation you desire. You can accept what the program recommends, suggest a different place to hyphenate, or tell it not to hyphenate.

- Mark word divisions with hyphens.

Hpn 2–1

Place hyphens between the parts of some compound words. Generally, the hyphen is used whenever its absence would confuse the meaning of the words.

> *Compound nouns:* brother-in-law, cure-all, city-state, foreign-born
>
> *Compound numbers twenty-one through ninety-nine:* fifty-five, eighty-one
>
> *Compound adjectives* (two or more words used before a noun as a single adjective): *long-term* contract, *50-gallon* drum, *five-day* grace period, *end-of-month* clearance
>
> *Prefixes* (most have been absorbed into the word): co-organizer, ex-chairperson, anti-inflation, self-sufficient

- Place hyphens between the parts of compound words.

Hpn 2–2

A proper name used as a compound adjective needs no hyphen or hyphens to hold it together as a visual unit for the reader. The capitals perform that function.

> *Correct:* a Lamar High School student
>
> *Correct:* a United Airlines pilot

- Do not place hyphens (1) between proper names and

Hpn 2–3

Two or more modifiers in normal grammatical form and order need no hyphens. Particularly, a phrase consisting of an unmistakable adverb (one ending in *ly*) modifying an adjective or participle that in turn modifies a noun shows normal grammatical order and is readily grasped by the reader without the benefit of the hyphen. But an adverb not ending in *ly* is joined to its adjective or participle by the hyphen.

> *No hyphen needed:* a poorly drawn chart
>
> *Use the hyphen:* a well-prepared chart

- (2) after words that end in *ly*.

Italics: Ital 1

For the use of italics for book titles, see QM 4. Note that italics also are used for titles of periodicals, works of art, long musical compositions, and names of naval vessels and aircraft.

- Use italics for (1) publication titles,

Becoming an expert in grammar is much like becoming an expert in sports or music—it takes a lot of practice. Indeed, even experts seek opportunities to practice and keep their skills sharp. Technology certainly makes practice more convenient. Whenever you're online and have a few minutes, consider taking a quick quiz or listening to a short podcast. If you have more time, you may want to visit a business writing blog to learn from the answers to others' questions or even to share your expertise by responding to someone's post or discussing a topic. You could also get the RSS feeds available at many sites so that the topics come right to you. The websites here are only a few of the many available. Whether you use these or others, you'll likely find that your practice results in sharp, polished business documents that elicit a positive response from your audiences.

Online Quizzes

- Capital Community College: <http://grammar.ccc.commnet.edu/GRAMMAR/quiz_list.htm>
- The Purdue Online Writing Lab: <http://owl.english.purdue.edu/owl/>
- GrammarBook.com <http://www.grammarbook.com/interactive_quizzes_exercises.asp>

- Facebook Business Writing Daily Quiz: <http://www.facebook.com/home.php?#/pages/Writing-for-Business-Daily-Grammar-Quiz/33633651366?ref=ts>

Grammar Podcasts

- Grammar Girl: <http://grammar.quickanddirtytips.com/>. (See the screenshot below.)
- Grammar Grater (Minnesota Public Radio): <http://minnesota.publicradio.org/radio/podcasts/grammar_grater/>

Business Writing Blogs

- Writing for Business: <http://itknowledgeexchange.techtarget.com/writing-for-business/>
- Business Writing: <http://www.businesswritingblog.com/>
- Society for the Protection of Good Grammar: <http://spogg.org/> (The blog is not specific to business writing, but many of the examples on the blog are from professional contexts.)

General Business Writing Tips:

- Business Writer's Free Library: <http://managementhelp.org/commskls/cmm_writ.htm>

Source: Screenshot of "Grammar Girl" from GRAMMAR GIRL'S QUICK AND DIRTY TIPS FOR BETTER WRITING by Mignon Fogarty. Copyright © 2007 by Macmillan Publishing Group, LLC. Reprinted by permission of Henry Holt and Company, LLC.

Ital 2

Italicize rarely used foreign words—if you must use them (*wunderbar, keiretsu, oobeya*). After a foreign word is widely accepted, however, it does not need to be italicized (carpe diem, faux pas, verboten). A current dictionary is a good source for information on which foreign words are italicized.

- (2) foreign words and abbreviations, and

Ital 3

Italicize a word, letter, or figure used as its own name. Without this device, we could not write this set of rules. Note the use of italics throughout to label name words.

- (3) a word used as its own name.

> The little word *sell* is still in the dictionary.
>
> The pronoun *which* should always have a noun as a clear antecedent. (Without the italics, this one becomes a fragment.)

Parentheses: Parens

Use parentheses to set off words that are inserted to explain or supplement the principal message (see Cma 4–1).

- Set off supplemental words with parentheses.

> David Rick's phenomenal illustrations (*Blunders in International Business,* 2006) show readers that even large corporations make disastrous mistakes.
>
> As soon as Owen Smith was elected chairperson (the vote was almost 2 to 1), he introduced his plan for reorganization.

Period: Pd 1

Use the period to indicate the end of a declarative sentence or an imperative statement.

- End a declarative sentence or an imperative statement with a period.

> *Declarative sentence:* The survey will be completed and returned by October 26.
> *Imperative statement:* Complete and return the survey by October 26.

Pd 2

Use periods after abbreviations or initials.

- Use periods in abbreviations.

> Ph.D., Co., Inc., a.m., etc.

But omit the periods and use all capitals in the initials or acronyms of agencies, networks, associations, and such: IRS, NBC, OPEC, EEC.

Pd 3

Use ellipses (a series of periods) to indicate the omission of words from a quoted passage. If the omitted part consists of something less than a sentence, three periods are customarily placed at the point of omission (a fourth period is added if the omission is a sentence or more). If the omitted part is a paragraph or more, however, a full line of periods is used. In all cases, the periods are separated by spaces.

- Use a series of periods to show omissions.

> Logical explanations, however, have been given by authorities in the field. Some attribute the decline . . . to recent changes in the state's economy. . . .
>
> . . . .
>
> Added to the labor factor is the high cost of raw material, which has tended to eliminate many marginal producers. Moreover, the rising cost of electric power in recent years may have shifted the attention of many industry leaders to other forms of production.

Question Mark: Q

- End direct questions with the question mark.

Place a question mark at the end of sentences that are direct questions.

> What are the latest quotations on Disney common stock?
> Will this campaign help sell Microsoft products?

But do not use the question mark with indirect questions.

> The president was asked whether this campaign would help sell Microsoft products.
> He asked me what the latest quotations on Disney common stock were.

Quotation Marks: QM 1

- Use quotation marks to enclose a speaker's or writer's exact words.

Use quotation marks to enclose the exact words of a speaker or, if the quotation is short, the exact words of a writer.

Short written quotations are quotations of four lines or less, although authorities do not agree on this point. Some suggest three lines; others, up to eight. Longer written quotations are best displayed without quotation marks and with an indented right and left margin.

> *Short written quotation:* Ben Bernanke sums up his presentation with this statement: "The central bank will remain vigilant to ensure that recent increases in inflation do not become chronic."
> *Oral quotation:* "This really should bring on a production slowdown," said Ms. Kuntz.

If a quotation is broken by explanation or reference words, each part of the quotation is enclosed in quotation marks.

> "Will you be specific," he asked, "in recommending a course of action?"

QM 2

- Use single quotation marks for a quotation within a quotation.

Enclose a quotation within a quotation with single quotation marks.

> Professor Dalbey said, "It has been a long time since I have heard a student say, 'Prof, we need more writing assignments.' "

QM 3

- Periods and commas go inside quotation marks; semicolons and colons go outside; question marks and exclamation points go inside when they apply to the quoted part and outside when they apply to the entire sentence.

Always place periods and commas inside quotation marks. Place semicolons and colons outside the quotation marks. Place question marks and exclamation points inside if they apply to the quoted passage only and outside if they apply to the whole sentence.

> "If we are patient," he said, "we will reach this year's goals." (The comma and the period are within the quotation marks.)
> "Is there a quorum?" he asked. (The question mark belongs to the quoted passage.)
> Which of you said, "I know where the error lies"? (The question mark applies to the entire sentence.)
> I conclude only this from the union's promise to "force the hand of management": A strike will be its trump card.

QM 4

- Use quotation marks to enclose titles of parts of a publication.

Enclose in quotation marks the titles of parts of publications (articles in a magazine, chapters in a book). But italicize the titles of whole publications or underline if you are handwriting.

> The third chapter of the book *Elementary Statistical Procedure* is titled "Concepts of Sampling."
> Anne Fisher's timely article, "Fatal Mistakes When Starting a New Job," appears in the current issue of *Fortune.*

TECHNOLOGY IN BRIEF

Hyphen, Small Dash, or Big Dash?

The hyphen, en dash, and em dash are regularly confused. Visually, the hyphen is the shortest. The em dash (the width of the letter *m* in the font you're using) is the longest, and the length of the en dash (the width of the letter *n* in the font you're using) is in between. This chapter discusses the use of the hyphen, em dash, and en dash, so if you know when to use them, the trick becomes how to insert them into your documents. Microsoft Word will occasionally help. In fact, you may have noticed that when you type two hyphens, Word sometimes automatically inserts the em dash. However, sometimes the software does not convert hyphens to a dash or may convert the hyphens to an en dash when you really need an em dash or vice versa. To ensure that you control the dash and use it correctly, use the *Symbols* list in Microsoft Word. Whether you are in Word 2007 or an earlier version, just go to Insert>Symbol>More Symbols>Special Characters. You can then select the mark you need based on whether you're dividing a word or connecting adjectives (hyphen), emphasizing information (em dash), or indicating a range (en dash). Generally, when you insert the hyphen or dash, you do not need a space before or after the mark.

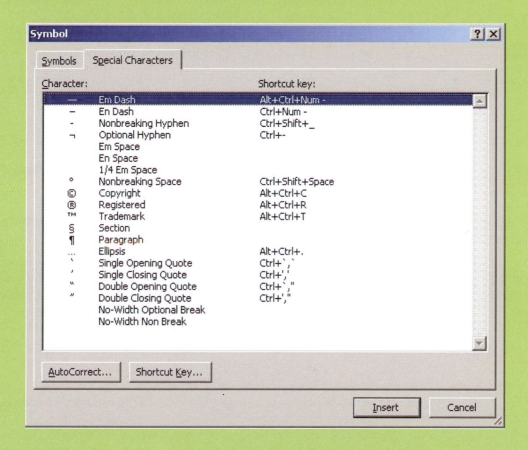

Semicolon: SC 1

Use the semicolon to separate closely related independent clauses that are not connected by a conjunction. Although writers generally use periods to separate independent clauses, a semicolon can be used to indicate a smaller break in thought than a period would.

- Use the semicolon to separate independent clauses not connected by a conjunction.

> The new contract provides wage increases; the original contract emphasized shorter hours.

Covered by this standard are independent clauses connected by conjunctive adverbs (transitional expressions) such as *however, nevertheless, therefore, then, moreover,* and *besides.*

> The survey findings indicated a need to revise the policy; nevertheless, the president did not approve the proposed revision.
>
> Small-town buyers favor the old model; therefore, the board concluded that both models should be marketed.

SC 2

- You may sometimes use a semicolon to separate independent clauses joined by a conjunction.

You may use the semicolon to separate independent clauses joined by *and, but, or,* or *nor* (coordinating conjunctions) if the clauses are long or if they have other punctuation in them. In such situations, you may need the semicolon to make your message clear. If you visualize the example below with a comma instead of a semicolon, you can see that your message would be visually confusing.

> The OCAW and the NUPNG, rivals from the beginning of the new industry, have shared almost equally in the growth of membership; but the OCAW predominates among workers in the petroleum-products crafts, including pipeline construction and operation, and the NUPNG leads in memberships of chemical workers.

SC 3

- Use the semicolon to separate items in a list when the items contain commas.

Separate by semicolons the items in a list when the items have commas in them.

> The following gains were made in the February year-to-year comparison: Fort Worth, 7,300; Dallas, 4,705; Lubbock, 2,610; San Antonio, 2,350; Waco, 2,240; Port Arthur, 2,170; and Corpus Christi, 1,420.
>
> Elected for the new term were Anna T. Zelnak, attorney from Cincinnati; Wilbur T. Hoffmeister, stockbroker and president of Hoffmeister Associates of Baltimore; and William P. Peabody, a member of the faculty of the University of Georgia.

SC 4

- Use the semicolon only between equal units.

Use the semicolon between equal (coordinate) units only. Do not use it to attach a dependent clause or phrase to an independent clause.

> *Not this:* The flood damaged much of the equipment in Building 113; making it necessary for management to close the area and suspend some employees.
>
> *But this:* The flood damaged much of the equipment in Building 113, making it necessary for management to close the area and suspend some employees.
>
> *Or this:* The flood damaged much of the equipment in Building 113; thus, it was necessary for management to close the area and suspend some employees.

STANDARDS FOR GRAMMAR

Like the review of punctuation standards, the following summary of grammatical standards is not intended as a complete handbook on the subject. Rather, it is a summary of the major trouble spots that business writers encounter. If you learn these grammatical principles, you should be able to write with the correctness expected in business.

Adjective–Adverb Confusion: AA

- Do not use adjectives for adverbs.

Do not use adjectives for adverbs or adverbs for adjectives. Adjectives modify only nouns and pronouns; and adverbs modify verbs, adjectives, or other adverbs.

Possibly the chief source of this confusion occurs in statements in which the modifier follows the verb. If the modifier refers to the subject, an adjective should be used. If it refers to the verb, an adverb is needed.

> *Not this:* She filed the records *quick.*
>
> *But this:* She filed the records *quickly.* (Refers to the verb.)

Not this: John doesn't feel *badly*.

But this: John doesn't feel *bad*. (Refers to the noun.)

Not this: The new cars look *beautifully*.

But this: The new cars look *beautiful*. (Refers to the noun.)

It should be noted that many words are both adjective and adverb (*little, well, fast, much*).

Adverb: The time went fast.

Adjective: She drives a fast car.

Subject–Verb Agreement: Agmt SV

Nouns and their verbs must agree in number. A plural noun must have a plural verb form; a singular noun must have a singular verb form.

- Verbs must agree in number with their subjects.

Nouns in prepositional phrases (i.e., phrases that begin with words such as *for, of, on, with, in, about,* and *between*) and nouns in phrases that are separated from the sentence with commas will not be the subjects of your sentences.

Not this: Expenditures for miscellaneous equipment *was* expected to decline. (*Expenditures* is plural, so its verb must be plural.)

But this: Expenditures for miscellaneous equipment *were* expected to decline.

Not this: The *president,* as well as the staff, *were* not able to attend. (*President* is the subject, and the number is not changed by the modifying phrase.)

But this: The *president,* as well as the staff, *was* not able to attend.

In a "there is" or "there are" sentence, the subject follows the verb.

Not this: There's several reasons why we should act.

But this: There are several reasons why we should act.

Compound subjects joined by *and* require plural verbs.

- Compound subjects require plural verbs.

Not this: The *salespeople* and their *manager is* in favor of the proposal. (*Salespeople* and *manager* make a compound subject, but *is* is singular.)

But this: The *salespeople* and their *manager are* in favor of the proposal.

Not this: Received in the morning delivery *was* an *ink cartridge* and two *reams* of copy paper. (*Ink cartridge* and *reams* are the subjects; the verb must be plural.)

But this: Received in the morning delivery *were* an *ink cartridge* and two *reams* of copy paper.

When a sentence has a compound subject joined with *or,* the singular or plural nature of the verb is determined by the subject closest to the verb.

- When a sentence has a compound subject joined with *or,* make the verb match the subject closest to the verb.

Not this: Either the shift supervisors or the department's manager *are* allowed to alter a time card. (Even though there are two subjects, the verb *or* means that you need to look only at the subject closest to the verb.)

But this: Either the shift supervisors or the department's manager *is* allowed to alter a time card. (*Manager* is closer to the verb and is singular, so the singular verb *is* is correct.)

Or this: Either the department's manager or the shift supervisors *are* allowed to alter a time card. (*Supervisors* is closer to the verb and is plural, so the plural verb *are* is correct.)

Collective nouns may be either singular or plural, depending on the meaning intended.

- Collective nouns may be singular or plural.

The *committee have* carefully *studied* the proposal. (*Committee* is thought of as separate individuals.)

The *committee has* carefully *studied* the proposal. (The *committee* is thought of as a unit.)

- The indefinite pronouns listed here are singular.

An indefinite pronoun does not refer specifically to another person or object or to groups of people and objects but to people, objects, or groups more generally. Some indefinite pronouns are always singular (e.g., *each, every, either, neither*, and any pronoun ending in *body, one,* or *thing,* such as (*anyone, anybody, anything, everyone, everybody, everything, someone, somebody, something, no one, nobody,* and *nothing*).

> *Either* of the campaigns *is* costly. (*Note:* If you have trouble finding the subject, remember that anything in a prepositional phrase can't be the subject of your sentence. *Campaigns* is in a prepositional phrase, so it cannot be the subject of your sentence.)
> *Nobody* who watches the clock *is* successful.

- The indefinite pronouns listed here are plural.

Other indefinite pronouns such as *both, few, many,* and *several* are always plural.

> *Many were* qualified for the job, but only three did well in the interview.

- Some indefinite pronouns are either singular or plural.

Some indefinite pronouns are either singular or plural (e.g., *all, any, most, none, some*), depending on what they refer to.

> *None* of the workers *were* ready for their assignments.
> *None* of the work *was* completed.

Adverbial Noun Clause: AN

- Do not use an adverbial clause as a noun clause.

Do not use an adverbial clause as a noun clause. Clauses beginning with *because, when, where, if,* and similar adverbial connections are not properly used as subjects, objects, or complements of verbs.

> *Not this:* The reason was *because* he did not submit a report.
> *But this:* The reason was *that* he did not submit a report.

> *Not this:* A time-series graph is *where* (or *when*) changes in an index such as wholesale prices are indicated.
> *But this:* A time-series graph is the picturing of . . .

Awkward: Awk

- Avoid awkward writing.

Avoid awkward writing. By *awkward writing* we mean word arrangements that are unconventional, uneconomical, or simply not the best for quick understanding.

Dangling Modifiers: Dng

- Avoid dangling modifiers (those that do not clearly modify a specific word).

Avoid the use of modifiers that do not clearly modify the right word in the sentence. Such modifiers are said to dangle. You can usually correct sentences containing dangling constructions by inserting the noun or pronoun that the modifier describes or by changing the dangling part to a complete clause.

> *Not this:* Believing that credit customers should have advance notice of the sale, special letters were mailed to them.
> *But this:* Believing that credit customers should have advance notice of the sale, we mailed special letters to them. (Inserting the pronoun *we* makes clear who did the believing.)
> *Or this:* Because we believed that credit customers should have advance notice of the sale, special letters were mailed to them. (Changing the dangling element to a complete clause makes clear who did the believing.)

Dangling modifiers are of four principal types: participial phrases, elliptical clauses, gerund phrases, and infinitive phrases.

> *Not this:* Believing that District 7 was not being thoroughly covered, an additional salesperson was assigned to the area. (Dangling participial phrase.)
> *But this:* Believing that District 7 was not being thoroughly covered, the sales manager assigned an additional salesperson to the area.

Not this: By working hard, your goal can be reached. (Dangling gerund phrase.)
But this: By working hard, you can reach your goal.

Not this: To succeed at this job, long hours and hard work must not be shunned. (Dangling infinitive phrase.)
But this: To succeed at this job, one must not shun long hours and hard work.

Not this: While waiting on a customer, the watch was stolen. (Dangling elliptical clause—a clause without a noun or verb.)
But this: While the salesperson was waiting on a customer, the watch was stolen.

However, several generally accepted introductory phrases are permitted to dangle. Included in this group are *generally speaking, confidentially speaking, taking all things into consideration,* and such expressions as *in boxing, in welding,* and *in farming.*

- Some introductory phrases are permitted to dangle.

Generally speaking, business activity is at an all-time high.
In farming, the land must be prepared long before planting time.
Taking all things into consideration, this applicant is the best for the job.

Misplaced Modifiers: Mispl

Unlike dangling modifiers, which do not clearly modify anything, misplaced modifiers do have a clear referent but are placed in the sentence in such a way that the sentence reads awkwardly or is unclear. Frequently, misplaced modifiers are prepositional phrases (e.g., phrases that begin with prepositions such as *in, on, with, for, over, under, near,* or *by*) or are adverbs such as *only, just, almost,* or *often.*

- Avoid misplaced modifiers (modifiers that are confusingly placed).

Unclear: New employees who demonstrate initiative *often* are promoted more quickly than those who don't.
Better: New employees who *often* demonstrate initiative are promoted more quickly than those who don't.
Better: New employees who demonstrate initiative are *often* promoted more quickly than those who don't.

Mixed Construction: MixCon

A mixed construction occurs when a writer inappropriately changes point of view, voice, tense, or sentence structure.

- Avoid mixed constructions—constructions that inappropriately change point of view, voice, tense, or sentence structure.

Mixed: If one is often late for work, it will detract from your performance review. (The sentence mixes third person, *one,* and second person, *you.*)
Consistent: If you are often late for work, it will detract from your performance review.

See Chapter 3, page 58, for additional examples.

Incomplete Constructions: IncCon

An incomplete construction occurs when a writer sets up a sentence that promises a certain kind of content but then does not deliver that content.

- Avoid incomplete constructions—those that do not complete an expected sentence pattern.

Incomplete: More companies in the food and beverage industry are using viral marketing. (*More* than what?)
Better: More companies in the food and beverage industry are using viral marketing than ever before.
Or: More companies in the food and beverage industry are using viral marketing than those in the construction business.

See Chapter 3, page 59, for additional examples.

Sentence Fragment: Frag

Avoid the sentence fragment. Although the sentence fragment may sometimes be used to good effect, as in sales writing, it is best avoided by all but the most skilled writers.

- Avoid sentence fragments (words used as a sentence that are not a sentence).

The sentence fragment consists of any group of words that are used as if they were a sentence but are not a sentence. Probably the most frequent cause of sentence fragments is the use of a subordinate clause as a sentence.

Not this: Believing that you will want an analysis of sales for November. We have sent you the figures.

But this: Believing that you will want an analysis of sales for November, we have sent you the figures.

Not this: He declared that such a procedure would not be practical. And that it would be too expensive in the long run.

But this: He declared that such a procedure would not be practical and that it would be too expensive in the long run.

Pronouns: Pn 1

- A pronoun should refer clearly to a preceding word.

Make certain that the word each pronoun refers to (its antecedent) is clear. Failure to conform to this standard causes confusion, particularly in sentences in which two or more nouns are possible antecedents or the antecedent is far away from the pronoun.

Not this: When the president objected to Mr. Carter, he told him to mind his own business. (Who told whom?)

But this: When the president objected to Mr. Carter, Mr. Carter told him to mind his own business.

Not this: The mixture should not be allowed to boil; so when you do it, watch the temperature gauge. (*It* doesn't have an antecedent.)

But this: The mixture should not be allowed to boil; so when conducting the experiment, watch the temperature gauge.

Not this: The Model *Q* is being introduced this year. Ads in *USA Today, The Wall Street Journal,* and big-city newspapers over the country are designed to get sales off to a good start. It is especially designed for the businessperson who is not willing to pay a big price.

But this: The Model *Q* is being introduced this year. Ads in *USA Today, The Wall Street Journal,* and big-city newspapers over the country are designed to get sales off to a good start. The new model is especially designed for the business-person who is not willing to pay a big price.

Confusion may sometimes result from using a pronoun with an implied antecedent.

Not this: Because of the disastrous freeze in the citrus belt, it is necessary that most of them be replanted.

But this: Because of the disastrous freeze in the citrus belt, most of the citrus orchards must be replanted.

- Usually avoid using *which, that,* and *this* to refer to broad ideas.

Except when the reference of *which, that,* and *this* is perfectly clear, avoid using these pronouns to refer to the whole idea of a preceding clause. Many times you can make the sentence clear by using a clarifying noun following the pronoun.

Not this (following a detailed presentation of the writer's suggestion for improving the company suggestion plan): This should be put into effect without delay.

But this: This suggested plan should be put into effect right away.

When a noun can be either singular or plural because it refers to a group of people, use a singular pronoun if group members are acting as one and a plural pronoun if they are acting as individual group members.

Not this: The committee gave their decision on the new proposal they reviewed.

But this: The committee gave its decision on the new proposal it reviewed.

For reference to the group as individual units:

Not this: The presenter polled the audience for its interpretation of the data.

But this: The presenter polled the audience for their interpretation of the data.

Pn 2

The number of the pronoun should agree with the number of its antecedent (the word it stands for). If the antecedent is singular, its pronoun must be singular. If the antecedent is plural, its pronoun must be plural.

● The number of a pronoun should be the same as that of the word to which the pronoun refers.

> *Not this:* Taxes and insurance are expenses in any business, and it must be considered carefully in anticipating profits.
>
> *But this:* Taxes and insurance are expenses in any business, and they must be considered carefully in anticipating profits.
>
> *Not this:* Everybody should plan for their retirement. (Such words as *everyone, everybody,* and *anybody* are singular.)
>
> *But this:* Everybody should plan for his or her retirement.

Pn 3

Take care to use the correct case of the pronoun. If the pronoun serves as the subject of the verb, or if it follows a form of the linking verb *be,* (e.g., *is, are, was, were, being, have been*), use a pronoun in the nominative case. (The nominative personal pronouns are *I, you, he, she, it, we, who, whoever,* and *they*).

● Use the correct case of pronoun.

> He will record the minutes of the meeting.
> I think it will be he.

If the pronoun is the object of a preposition or a verb, use the objective case. (The objective personal pronouns are *me, you, him, her, it, us, whom, whomever,* and *them.*)

> *Not this:* This transaction is between you and he. (*He* is nominative and cannot be the object of the preposition *between.*)
>
> *But this:* This transaction is between you and him.
>
> *Not this:* Because the investigator praised Ms. Smith and I, we were promoted.
>
> *But this:* Because the investigator praised Ms. Smith and me, we were promoted.

Many writers are intimidated by the use of *who* and *whom.* However, their use is really no different from that of any other pronoun. As with all other pronouns, their use depends on whether they function as subjects or objects. *Who* and *Whoever* are nominative pronouns and are used as subjects or following a form of the linking verb *be* (e.g., *is, are, were, was being*). *Whom* and *Whomever* are objective pronouns and are used as objects of verbs or prepositions. One trick for using who/whom is to substitute a common personal pronoun for the word and then choose who/whom based on which form of the substituted pronoun worked.

> Example: George Cutler is the salesperson *who* won the award. (*He*, nominative, could be substituted for *who* because the pronoun is the subject of the verb *won*. You could say "*he* won the award"; therefore, *who* is the right choice.)
>
> Example: *Whom* should we notify? (Turn the question into a statement: We should notify *whom*. *Him*, objective, could be substituted for *whom* because the pronoun is the object of the verb *should notify*. You could say "we should notify *him*"; therefore, *whom* is the right choice).

Sometimes, though, the choice is not as clear. What would you choose in the following case?

> George is the person who/whom you recommended.

If you substitute *he/him* here, you might not know whether to choose *who* or *whom* because the substitution of *he* or *him* sounds equally awkward. The solution is to notice that who/whom is part of its own clause (*who/whom you recommended*). To identify how who/whom is being used in the clause, see if it already has a subject. If it does, then you probably need *whom* because the clause won't need two subjects in a row. In the example above, *you* is the subject of the dependent clause, so the correct solution is *whom*:

> George is the person whom you recommended.

Here is a contrasting example:

> George is the person who recruited the most volunteers. (Here, the verb of the dependent clause, *recruited,* has no other possible subject, so *who* is the subject of the clause.)

And here is the exception:

> I can't remember who the president was. (Using the advice above, you might think the correct form would be *whom* since, otherwise, the clause would seem to have two subjects, *who* and *president*. But notice that the verb is a form of *be*. In such cases, you need the nominative [subject] form.)

The possessive case is used for pronouns that immediately precede a gerund (a verbal noun ending in *ing*).

> *Our* selling of the stock frightened some of the conservative members of the board.
> *Her* accepting the money ended her legal claim to the property.
> I appreciate *your* offering to take my place on the committee.

Parallelism: Prl

- Express equal thoughts in parallel (equal) grammatical form.

Parts of a sentence that express equal thoughts should be parallel (the same) in grammatical form. Parallel constructions are logically connected by the coordinating conjunctions *and, but,* and *or.* Care should be taken to see that the sentence elements connected by these conjunctions are of the same grammatical type. That is, if one of the parts is a noun, the other parts also should be nouns. If one of the parts is an infinitive phrase, the other parts also should be infinitive phrases.

> *Not this:* The company objectives for the coming year are to match last year's sales volume, higher earnings, and improving customer relations.
> *But this:* The company objectives for the coming year are to match last year's sales volume, to increase earnings, and to improve customer relations.

> *Not this:* Writing copy may be more valuable experience than to make layouts.
> *But this:* Writing copy may be more valuable experience than making layouts.

> *Not this:* The questionnaire asks for this information: number of employees, what is our union status, and how much do we pay.
> *But this:* The questionnaire asks for this information: number of employees, union affiliation, and pay rate.

Tense: Tns

- The tense of each verb should show the logical time of happening.

The tense of each verb, infinitive, and participle should reflect the logical time of happening of the statement. Every statement has its place in time. To communicate that place exactly, you must select your tenses carefully.

Tns 1

- Use present tense for current happenings.

Use present tense for statements of fact that are true at the time of writing.

> *Not this:* Boston was not selected as a site for the headquarters because it *was* too near the coast. (Boston is still near the coast, isn't it?)
> *But this:* Boston was not selected as a site for the headquarters because it *is* too near the coast.

Tns 2

- Use past tense for past happenings.

Use past tense in statements covering a definite past event or action.

> *Not this:* Mr. Burns *says* to me, "Bill, you'll never become an auditor."
> *But this:* Mr. Burns *said* to me, "Bill, you'll never become an auditor."

Tns 3

The time period reflected by the past participle (*having been* . . .) is earlier than that of its governing verb. The present participle (*being* . . .) reflects the same time period as that of its governing verb.

> *Not this:* These debentures are among the oldest on record, *being* issued in early 1937.
>
> *But this:* These debentures are among the oldest on record, *having been* issued in early 1937.
>
> *Not this:* Ms. Sloan, *having been* the top salesperson on the force, was made sales manager. (Possible but illogical.)
>
> *But this:* Ms. Sloan, *being* the top salesperson on the force, was made sales manager.

- The past participle (*having been* . . .) indicates a time earlier than that of the governing verb, and the present participle (*being* . . .) indicates the same period as that of the governing verb.

Tns 4

Verbs in combined clauses should be in the same tense. For instance, when the first verb is in the past tense, you should usually also place the second verb in a past tense (past, past perfect, or present perfect).

> I *noticed* [past tense] the discrepancy, and then I *remembered* [same time as main verb] the incidents that had caused it.

If the time of a subordinate clause is earlier than that of the main verb in past tense, use past perfect tense for the subordinate verb.

> *Not this:* In early July we *noticed* [past] that he *exceeded* [logically should be previous to main verb] his quota three times.
>
> *But this:* In early July we *noticed* that he *had exceeded* his quota three times.

The present perfect tense is used for the subordinate clause when the time of this clause is subsequent to the time of the main verb.

> *Not this:* Before the war we *contributed* [past] generously, but lately we *forget* [should be a time subsequent to the time of the main verb] our duties.
>
> *But this:* Before the war we *contributed* generously, but lately we *have forgotten* our duties.

- Verbs in the principal clause govern those in subordinate clauses.

- Present perfect tense (*have* . . .) refers to the indefinite past.

Tns 5

The present perfect tense does not logically refer to a definite time in the past. Instead, it indicates time somewhere in the indefinite past.

> *Not this:* We *have audited* your records on July 31 of 2005 and 2006.
>
> *But this:* We *audited* your records on July 31 of 2005 and 2006.
>
> *Or this:* We *have audited* your records twice in the past.

- Use of present perfect tense indicates time somewhere in the indefinite past.

Word Use: WU

Misused words call attention to themselves and detract from the writing. The possibilities of error in word use are infinite; the following list contains only a few of the common errors of this kind.

- Use words correctly.

Don't Use	Use
a long ways	a long way
and etc.	etc.
anywheres	anywhere
continue on	continue
different than	different from
have got to	must

Don't Use	Use
in back of	behind
in hopes of	in hope of
in regards to	in regard to or regarding
inside of	within
kind of satisfied	somewhat satisfied
nowhere near	not nearly
nowheres	nowhere
over with	over
seldom ever	seldom
try and come	try to come

Wrong Word: WW

- Check the spelling and meanings of words carefully.

Be careful not to use one word but mean another. Sometimes these words are confused by their spelling and sometimes by their meanings. Since the spell checker won't find these errors, you need to proofread carefully to eliminate them. Here are a few examples:

affect	effect
among	between
bow	bough
capital	capitol
cite	sight, site
collision	collusion
complement	compliment
cooperation	corporation
deferential	differential
desert	dessert
except	accept
implicit	explicit
imply	infer
plane	plain
principal	principle
stationary	stationery

STANDARDS FOR THE USE OF NUMBERS: NO

Quantities may be spelled out or expressed as numerals. Whether to use one form or the other is often a perplexing question. It is especially perplexing to business writers, whose work often deals with quantitative subjects.

No 1

- Spell out numbers nine and under, and use figures for higher numbers, except as follows:

Although authorities do not agree on number usage, business writers would do well to follow the rule of nine. By this rule, you spell out numbers nine and below. You use figures for numbers ten and above.

> The auditor found 13 discrepancies in the stock records.
> The auditor found nine discrepancies in the stock records.

Apply the rule to both ordinal and cardinal numbers:

> She was the seventh applicant.
> She was the 31st applicant.

No 2

Make an exception to the rule of nine when a number begins a sentence. Spell out all numbers in this position.

> Seventy-three bonds and six debentures were destroyed.
> Eighty-nine strikers picketed the north entrance.

• Spell out numbers that begin a sentence.

No 3

If you have numbers in a sentence or paragraph that refer to related items, be consistent. If one of the numbers is ten or greater, use numbers for all of the related items even if the other items are nine or fewer.

> We managed to salvage 3 printers, 1 scanner, and 13 monitors.

• Keep in the same form for all numbers in comparisons.

No 4

Use numerals for all percentages.

> Sales increases over last year were 9 percent on automotive parts, 14 percent on hardware, and 23 percent on appliances.

On whether to use the percent sign (%) or the word, authorities differ. One good rule to follow is to use the percentage sign in papers that are scientific or technical and the word in all others. Also, the convention is to use the sign following numbers in graphics and presentations. Consistent use of either is correct.

• Use numerals for percentages.

No 5

Present days of the month in figure form when the month precedes the day.

> June 29, 2008.

When days of the month appear alone or precede the month, they may be either spelled out or expressed in numeral form according to the rule of nine. The *th, rd,* and *st* follow the day only when the day is used by itself or precedes the month. These suffixes are never used when the month precedes the day.

> I will be there on the 13th.
> The union scheduled the strike vote for the eighth.
> Ms. Millican signed the contract on July 7.
> Sales have declined since the 14th of August.

• Use figures for days of the month when the month precedes the day.

No 6

Use either of two accepted orders for date information. One, preferred by *The Chicago Manual of Style,* is day, month, and year:

> On 29 June 2008 we introduced a new product line.

The other is the sequence of month, day, and year. This order requires that the year be set off by commas:

> On June 29, 2008, we introduced a new product line.

• For dates, use either the day, month, year or month, day, year sequence, the latter with year set off by commas.

No 7

Present money amounts as you would other numbers. If you spell out the number, also spell out the unit of currency.

> Twenty-seven dollars

If you present the number as a figure, use the $ with U.S. currency and the appropriate abbreviation or symbol with other currencies.

• Present amounts like other numbers, spelling units when numbers are spelled and using appropriate symbols or abbreviations when in figures.

U.S., Canada, and Mexico	US $27.33, Can $27.33, Mex $27.33
Euro countries	€ 202.61
Japan	¥2,178.61
Thailand	฿7,489.91

No 8

- Usually spell out indefinite numbers and amounts.

Usually spell out indefinite numbers and amounts.

> Over a million people live there.
> The current population is about four hundred thousand.
> Bill Gates's net worth is in the billions.

No 9

- Spell out fractions that stand alone or begin a sentence. Use numerics with whole numbers and in technical contexts.

Spell out a fraction such as *one-half* that stands alone (without a whole number) or begins a sentence. Represent mixed numbers as figures.

> Two-thirds of all jobs in the United States are jobs in the information industry.
> The median price of a home rose by 6½ percent this year.

No 10

- Use both words and figures only for legal reasons.

Except in legal documents, do not express amounts in both figures and words.

> *For legal purposes:* 25 (twenty-five)
> *For business use: either the figure or the word, depending on circumstance*

No 11

- Follow accepted ways of representing time.

Represent times as follows:

> 2:00, 2:30   two o'clock
> 2 p.m., 2:30 p.m.   *not:* 2:00 o'clock
> 2 o'clock

SPELLING: SP

- Spell words correctly. Use the dictionary.

Misspelling is probably the most frequent error in writing. And it is the least excusable. It is inexcusable because all one needs to do to virtually eliminate the error is to use a dictionary or a spell checker. Unfortunately, spell checkers cannot detect a correctly spelled but misused word.

- See Figure 16–1 for the 80 most commonly misspelled words.

You can improve your spelling significantly with relatively little effort. Studies show that fewer than 100 words account for most spelling errors. So if you will learn to spell these most troublesome words, you will go a long way toward solving your spelling problems. Eighty of these words appear in Figure 16–1. Although English spelling follows little rhyme or reason, a few helpful rules exist. You would do well to learn and use them.

Rules for Word Plurals

1. To form the plurals of most words, add *s*.

> price, prices
> quote, quotes

- These three rules cover plurals for most words.

2. To form the plurals of words ending in *s, sh, ch,* and *x,* usually add *es* to the singular.

> boss, bosses
> relinquish, relinquishes
> glitch, glitches
> tax, taxes

Figure 16–1

Eighty of the Most
Frequently Misspelled
Words

absence	desirable	irritable	pursue
accessible	despair	leisure	questionnaire
accommodate	development	license	receive
achieve	disappear	misspelling	recommend
analyze	disappoint	necessary	repetition
argument	discriminate	ninety	ridiculous
assistant	drunkenness	noticeable	seize
balloon	embarrassment	occasionally	separate
benefited	equivalent	occurrence	sergeant
category	exceed	panicky	sheriff
cede	existence	parallel	succeed
changeable	forty	paralyze	suddenness
committee	grammar	pastime	superintendent
comparative	grievous	persistent	supersede
conscience	holiday	possesses	surprise
conscious	incidentally	predictable	truly
deductible	indispensable	privilege	until
definitely	insistent	proceed	vacuum
dependent	irrelevant	professor	vicious
description	irresistible	pronunciation	weird

3. To form the plural of words ending in *y*, if a consonant precedes the *y*, drop the *y* and add *ies*. But if the *y* is preceded by a vowel, add *s*.

    company, companies

    medley, medleys

    key, keys

Other Spelling Rules

1. Words ending in *ce* or *ge* do not drop the *e* when *ous* or *able* is added.

    charge, chargeable

    change, changeable

    notice, noticeable

    service, serviceable

2. Words ending in *l* do not drop the *l* when *ly* is added.

    final, finally

    principal, principally

3. Words ending in silent *e* usually drop the *e* when a suffix beginning with a vowel is added.

    have, having

    believe, believable

    dine, dining

    time, timing

4. Place *i* before *e* except after *c*.

    relieve   conceive

    believe   receive

    Exception: when the word is sounded as long *a*.

    neighbor   weigh

- These rules cover four other trouble areas of spelling.

CHAPTER 16   Correctness of Communication

541

Exceptions:

either	Fahrenheit	height
seize	surfeit	efficient
sufficient	neither	foreign
leisure	ancient	seizure
weird	financier	codeine
forfeit	seismograph	sovereign
deficient	science	counterfeit

CAPITALIZATION: CAP

● Capitalize all proper names and the beginning words of sentences.

In text and instant messaging environments, writers may forego standard capitalization in informal circumstances. In other all communication situations, standard capitalization is expected. Always capitalize the first word of a sentence, a person's name, and the pronoun *I*. Generally, the more specific the noun, the more likely it is to require capitalization. The following table presents a guide for basic principles of capitalization; however, capitalization practices vary widely, so be sure to know your company's preferences.

Capitalize	Don't Capitalize
Proper names: • Richard Thompson	Common names: • the dean
Geographic places: • St. Paul, Minnesota, United States • Streets: 317 East Boyd Avenue • Chippewa River • Midwest, East Coast	General directions: • north side of town • travel east on Highway 29
Companies: • Qualcomm, Microsoft	Company names that intentionally begin with a lowercase letter: • eBay, iOmega
Titles *preceding* names when the title and name are not separated by commas: • President Watkins	Titles separated from the name by a comma: • Karen Watkins, president of the company, • company president, Karen Watkins
Important words in book, article, and poem titles: • *Getting Things Done*: *The Art of Stress-Free Productivity*	Conjunctions (*a, an, the*) and short prepositions (*in, on, to, for*) in book, article, and poem titles unless they are the first or last word of the title or the first word after a colon
Words *preceding* most numbers: • Room 418 • No. 10 envelopes • Figure 2	Words preceding page, verse, and paragraph numbers: • page 32 • paragraph three
Official department names: • the Department of Human Resources	General references to a department: • the human resources department
Official degree names and course titles: • Bachelor of Business Administration • Principles of Accounting	Majors, minors, and general references to degrees or courses: • bachelor's degree • accounting class • marketing major
Races, nationalities, and ethnicities: • Caucasian, African American • German, Japanese	*White* and *black* when referring to people
Names of months • November	Names of seasons • winter, spring, fall, summer
First words of complimentary closes: • Sincerely yours,	Subsequent words of complimentary closes: • Yours truly

As noted earlier, other standards are useful in clear communication. But those covered in the preceding pages will help you through most of your writing problems. By using them, you can give your writing the precision that good communication requires. For further references on this topic, you will find several links to more detailed sources on the textbook website. You also will find some interactive self-tests there to help you review this material.

CRITICAL THINKING QUESTIONS

Correct any punctuation or grammar errors you can find in the following sentences. Explain your corrections, **LO1–LO5**

1 Charles E. Baskin the new member of the advisory committee has been an employee for seven years.

2 The auditor asked us, "If all members of the work group had access to the petty cash fund?"

3 Our January order consisted of the following items; two dozen Post-it pads, cube size, one dozen desk blotters, 20 by 32 inches, and one dozen gel roller pens, permanent black.

4 The truth of the matter is, that the union representative had not informed the workers of the decision.

5 Sales for the first quarter were the highest in history, profits declined for the period.

6 We suggest that you use a mild soap for best results but detergents will not harm the product.

7 Employment for October totaled 12,741 an increase of 3.1 percent over September.

8 It would not be fair however to consider only this point.

9 It is the only shrink resistant antiwrinkle and inexpensive material available.

10 Todd Thatcher a supervisor in our company is accused of the crime.

11 Mr. Goodman made this statement, "Contrary to our expectations, Smith and Company will lose money this year."

12 I bought and he sold.

13 Soon we saw George Sweeney who is the auditor for the company.

14 Sold in light medium and heavy weight this paper has been widely accepted.

15 Because of a common belief that profits are too high we will have to cut our prices on most items.

16 Such has been the growth of the cities most prestigious firm, H.E. Klauss and Company.

17 In 2006 we were advised in fact we were instructed to accept this five year contract.

18 Henrys goofing off has gotten him into trouble.

19 Cyrus B. Henshaw who was our leading salesperson last month is the leading candidate for the position.

20 The sales representative who secures the most new accounts will receive a bonus.

21 The word phone which is short for telephone should be avoided in formal writing.

22 In last months issue of Fortune appeared Johnson's latest article Tiger! The Sky's the Limit for Golf.

23 Yes he replied this is exactly what we mean.

24 Why did he say John it's too late?

25 Place your order today, it is not too late.

26 We make our plans on a day to day basis.

27 There is little accuracy in the 60 day forecast.

28 The pre Christmas sale will extend over twenty six days.

29 We cannot tolerate any worker's failure to do their duty.

30 An assortment of guns, bombs, burglar tools, and ammunition were found in the seller.

31 If we can be certain that we have the facts we can make our decision soon.

32 This one is easy to make. If one reads the instructions carefully.

33 This is the gift he received from you and I.

34 A collection of short articles on the subject were printed.

35 If we can detect only a tenth of the errors it will make us realize the truth.

36 She takes criticism good.

37 There was plenty of surprises at the meeting.

38 It don't appear that we have made much progress.

39 The surface of these products are smooth.

40 Everybody is expected to do their best.

41 The brochures were delivered to John and I early Sunday morning.

42 Who did he recommend for the job.

43 We were given considerable money for the study.

44 He seen what could happen when administration breaks down.

45 One of his conclusions is that the climate of the region was not desirable for our purposes.

46 Smith and Rogers plans to buy the Moline plant.

47 The committee feels that no action should be taken.

48 Neither of the workers found their money.

49 While observing the employees, the work flow was operating at peak perfection.

50 The new building is three stories high, fifteen years old, solid brick construction, and occupies a corner lot.

51 They had promised to have completed the job by noon.

52 Jones has been employed by Kimberly Clark for twenty years.

53 Wilson and myself will handle the job.

54 Each man and woman are expected to abide by this rule.

55 The boiler has been inspected on April 1 and May 3.

56 To find problems and correcting them takes up most of my work time.

57 The case of canned goods were distributed to the homeless.

58 The motor ran uneven.

59 All are expected except John and she.

60 Everyone here has more ability than him.

A SELF-ADMINISTERED DIAGNOSTIC TEST OF CORRECTNESS

The following test is designed to give you a quick measure of your ability to handle some of the most troublesome punctuation and grammar situations. First, correct all the errors in each sentence. Then turn to Appendix A for the recommended corrections and the symbols for the punctuation and grammar standards involved. Next, review the relevant standards.

1 An important fact about this keyboard is, that it has the patented "ergonomic design".

2 Goods received on Invoice 2741 are as follows; 3 dozen blue denim shirts, size 15–33, 4 mens gortex gloves, brown, size large, and 5 dozen assorted socks.

3 James Silver president of the new union had the priviledge of introducing the speaker.

4 We do not expect to act on this matter however until we hear from you.

5 Shipments through September 20, 2007 totaled 69,485 pounds an increase of 17 percent over the year ago total.

6 Brick is recommended as the building material but the board is giving serious consideration to a substitute.

7 Markdowns for the sale total $34,000, never before has the company done anything like this.

8 After long experimentation a wear resistant high grade and beautiful stocking has been perfected.

9 Available in white green and blue this paint is sold by dealers all over the country.

10 Julie Jahn who won the trip is our most energetic salesperson.

11 Good he replied, sales are sure to increase.

12 Hogan's article Retirement? Never!, printed in the current issue of Management Review, is really a part of his book A Report on Worker Security.

13 Formal announcement of our Labor Day sale will be made in thirty two days.

14 Each day we encounter new problems. Although they are solved easily.

15 A list of models, sizes, and prices of both competing lines are being sent to you.

16 The manager could not tolerate any employee's failing to do their best.

17 A series of tests were completed only yesterday.

18 There should be no misunderstanding between you and I.

19 He run the accounting department for five years.

20 This report is considerable long.

21 Who did you interview for the position?

22 The report concluded that the natural resources of the Southwest was ideal for the chemical industry.

23 This applicant is six feet in height, 28 years old, weighs 165 pounds, and has had eight years' experience.

24 While reading the report, a gust of wind came through the window, blowing papers all over the room.

25 The sprinkler system has been checked on July 1 and September 3.

chapter seventeen

Technology-Enabled Communication

LEARNING OBJECTIVES

Upon completing this chapter, you will be able to describe the role of technology in business communication. To reach this goal, you should be able to

1   Explain how technology helps in constructing messages.

2   Identify appropriate tools for different stages in the writing process.

3   Discuss considerations for writing electronic and print documents.

4   Discuss how technology facilitates the development of online content.

5   Describe how technology assists in collaboration.

6   Discuss what impact future developments in technology might have on business communication.

Using Technology in Communication Tasks

The company that hired you after your recent graduation is looking into ways the information technology (IT) department can empower its employees with technological support. Your new boss has asked you to be on the team that is to propose new ideas. One of the main focuses will be on identifying ways to help employees improve their day-to-day communication.

This chapter discusses ways to use technology to make your writing process easier and more effective. It also helps you consider the differences between print and online writing.

TECHNOLOGICAL SUPPORT FOR WRITING TASKS

- Technology assists with both the tedious and creative writing tasks.

Technological tools can enhance your communication. But as with any set of tools, how one uses them determines their degree of effectiveness.

When you think of enhancing the communication process with technology, you probably first think of using word processing software on a personal computer. Although this is your most important tool, numerous other tools can help improve your communication. These tools help with the various stages of the writing process as well as with collaboration. Because we incorporated our discussion of oral communication technologies into Chapters 13 and 14, we focus our discussion here on technologies that facilitate written communication.

TOOLS FOR CONSTRUCTING MESSAGES

- Computer tools can be used throughout the writing process.

Computer tools for constructing written messages can be associated with the different stages of the writing process: planning, gathering and collecting information, analyzing and organizing information, and writing and rewriting. In the past, many of these tools were discrete tools. But today, they often work seamlessly together. Of course, these tools work on a variety of devices attached to networks. The more skilled you become with each of these tools, the better they serve you.

Computer Tools for Planning

- Outlining or brainstorming programs help in planning the content of a message.

Whether you are writing a short message or a long report, you can use a computer to help you plan both the document and the writing project. In planning the content of the document, *outlining* or *concept-mapping* tools are useful. You can brainstorm, listing your ideas as they occur to you. Later you tag related ideas, asking the software to group them. Outlining tools are included in most word processors.

One way to use an outliner is with a split screen, as shown in Figure 17–1. In one part of the screen you'll see one part of your outline and in the other part, a different piece of your outline. Today's large-screen monitors make this an effective use. Another way you can use an outliner is as a separate document. In this case your outline is held in memory; you can toggle back and forth to view it or work with the outline and document side by side using a widescreen display.

A specialty tool for planning is a concept-mapping/idea-generation program. As you see in Figure 17–2 on the next page, the program Inspiration (also shown in Chapter 10) provides both a visual and an outlining mode, which allows users to toggle back and forth or work primarily in the mode that suits their particular tasks. You can also use these tools on your handheld personal digital assistant (PDA) or smartphone.

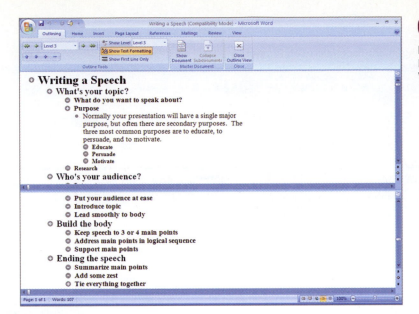

Figure 17–2

Illustration of a Concept-Mapping Tool for Planning

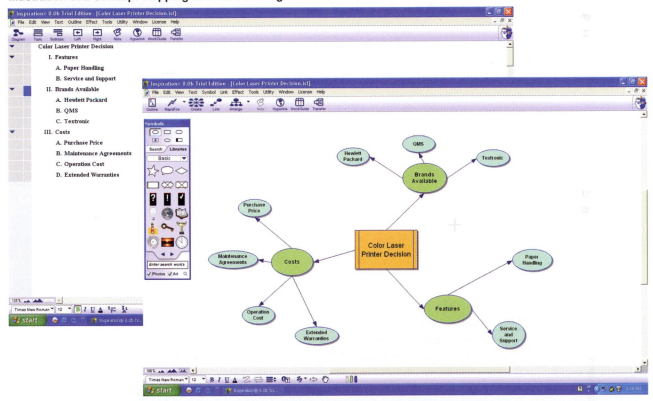

When you are working on a long writing project, several projects, or one carried over a long time, *project management programs* are excellent for planning the project. They allow you to identify all the tasks needed to complete the project, to determine how much time each task might take, and to generate a time-and-task chart (commonly called a Gantt chart). Also, they help you keep track of your progress and determine how to reallocate your resources to complete the project on time or within budget. You can see an example of a Gantt chart and network diagram created using Microsoft Project in Figure 17–3.

- Project management
  programs assist in
  identifying tasks and
  allocating resources.

Figure 17–3

Illustration of a Project Management Tool (Microsoft Project)

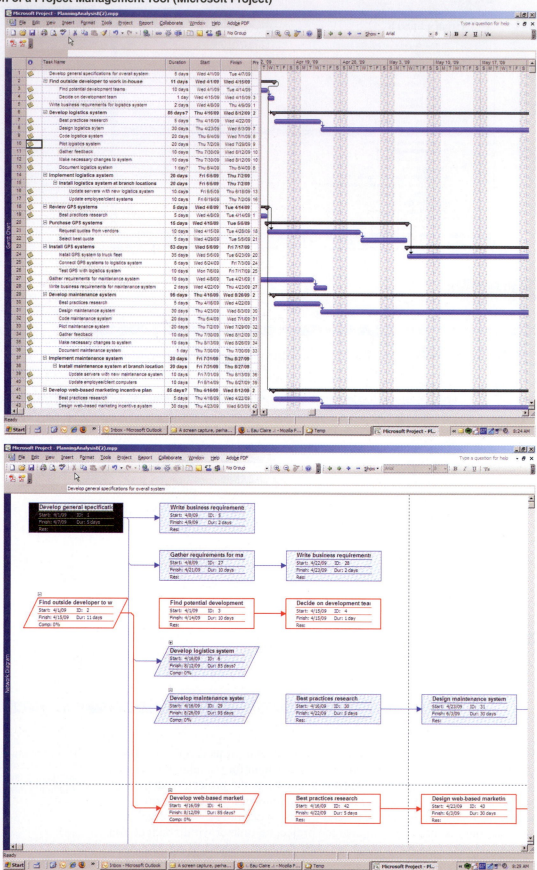

Figure 17–4

Illustration of a Personal Information Manager for Planning

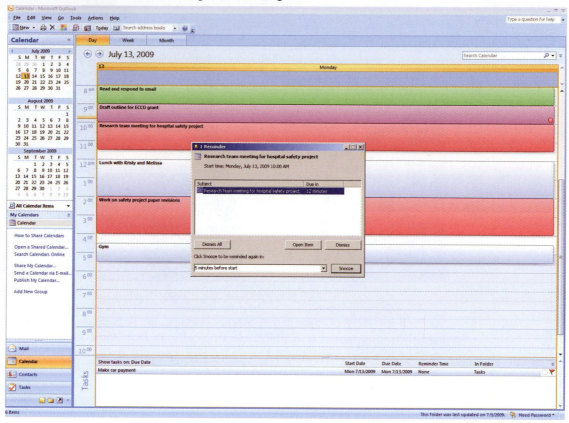

Finding time for writing, of course, is one of the major challenges for business-people. By using *personal information management (PIM)* tools, you can plan time for completing writing projects. These time-management tools are essentially annotated electronic calendars. However, they are excellent planning tools for scheduling your writing tasks. They will remind you of tasks to complete and days remaining before a document needs to be finished.

These tools are readily available. One such desktop tool is Microsoft Outlook. It can be synchronized with many handheld PDAs and smartphones as well as Web-based PIM sites. But you can choose from a slew of other time-management tools as well. These offer a variety of ways to help you plan time for writing tasks, from day-to-day scheduling to longer-term planning. Figure 17–4 shows Microsoft Outlook's calendar. The bell icon in the title bar of the dialog box shows that this writer set an alarm to have the computer remind her when it was time to work. The alarm sounds and the window opens at the designated time with a precise message of what needs to be done.

Some research identifies planning as the primary step that separates good writers from others. Using the powerful features that both project management and PIM tools provide will give you the potential to produce high-quality work in a timely fashion.

- Personal information management programs assist with time management.

Computer Tools for Gathering and Collecting Information

Before you can write, you have to have something to say. Sometimes you may be writing about your own ideas, but often you will supplement them with facts. Gathering facts or data is one of the most important jobs of the writer. Today you will want to combine your manual search for facts with electronic searches. The computer can help

- When you need information for a writing task, consider conducting an electronic search.

you find a variety of information quickly and accurately because today much of our published information is available electronically. In fact, some kinds of information are only available electronically. In Chapter 18, you will learn ways to find and evaluate the information you find online and in commercial databases.

- Data can be gathered from internal or external computers.

Using Internal and External Databases. The facts you need may be found in either internal or external databases. Your report due today at 1 PM might be on the current inventory of your off-site manufacturing product line. You could simply connect to your company's computer at noon and download the most recent data before completing your report. However, if you need to project the number of completed units by the end of the month, you may also need to connect to your supplier's computer to check the inventory of the parts you will need to complete your units. In this case, you will be using your computer to find facts both internally (from within your company) and externally (from your suppliers).

Most libraries now allow both internal and external access to their online catalogs and databases. This means you can use the online catalog from within the library or from anywhere outside the library. Most college networks also allow you to connect to the library resources from campus computer labs, dormitories, and remote offices. And many colleges are installing wireless networks, allowing users within range and with wireless capabilities on laptops, PDAs, and smartphones to access their library resources.

You can also gather facts on the Internet. This expands your resources immensely beyond your local library. Not only can you reach the Library of Congress, but you can also search libraries in other countries. You can gather information from blogs and other sources not available in any library anywhere. While you do need to be especially critical of the sources of your facts, knowing how to use the Internet effectively to gather information can give you a tremendous advantage. Chapter 18 gives you more details on using the Internet to gather business information.

Currently you can use technology such as Google News Alert or RSS feeds to push the information you want to you. By completing a profile at a content provider's website, you will create a filter so that the kind of information pushed to you is the kind you want. You also can use software agents to monitor sources and notify you when information you specify is available. And, of course, you can rerun the results page that you have saved from a search using a well-designed search strategy. The new results page will be updated to reflect the information available at the moment.

Another tool that can help writers manage and retrieve information is OneNote. This tool enables users to collect all types of digital files from handwritten, typed, and scanned text to photos as well as audio and video records. Its powerful search function retrieves words from text, pictures, and even recordings. Furthermore, the digital notebooks can be shared and used simultaneously from any place. You can see a video demo of this tool online as well as take a self-paced, e-learning course.

Organizing Your Data. Once you have gathered the facts, you will want to store them in some organized fashion so you can retrieve them readily when needed. *Database tools* will help you immensely here. If your company is interested in developing a new product for a newly defined market niche, you may want to collect information about the targeted market, potential suppliers of components of your new product, sites for producing the product, projected labor costs, and so on. You could do this simply by entering the facts of publication and abstracted information in your individually designed form created with database tools. The source information you have collected will be available whenever you need it. You can search and sort it on any of the categories (called fields) you set up on your data entry screen.

- Database tools provide a convenient way to collect information.

Variations of the generic database are specialty tools such as EndNote, ProCite, and RefWorks. These specialty programs allow you to transfer bibliographic information automatically from a wide variety of online databases. Microsoft Word 2007 also provides a database for managing sources, as shown in Figure 17–5. To use the database, click References>Citations & Bibliography tab>Insert Citation. After you have inserted your citations, you can organize them by clicking the Manage Sources icon. (An advisory, though: The bibliography of your sources is saved in a master list in an .xml file on the computer where you created the list. The list does not travel with your document if you save the document somewhere else, such as on a flash drive. You will need to copy and paste the bibliography.xml file from its location on the computer where you created it to the new location where you will be working on your document.)

- Specialty tools help you collect facts, too.

In Chapter 18, which discusses business research methods, you will learn about other tools for gathering and managing business information. The major point to remember is that in business it is not necessarily what you know that really counts but what you can find out and later retrieve. No one can know all there is to know about a subject, but those who are skilled at using a computer to find and store information will find it a real asset.

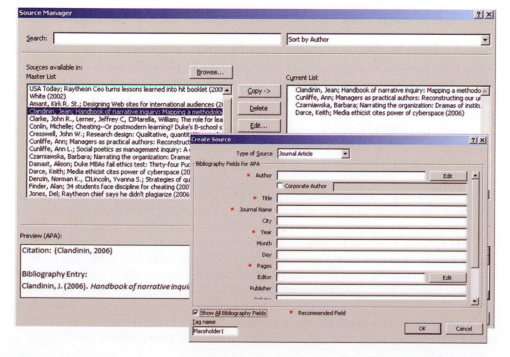

Figure 17–5

Illustration of the References Tool in Word 2007

Computer Tools for Analyzing and Organizing

Three tools that writers find useful in analyzing data are statistics, graphics, and spreadsheet tools. Since sometimes you cannot say very much about raw numbers, combining them or viewing them in different ways gives you a clearer picture of their meaning. Today, some very sophisticated *statistical programs,* such as SPSS and SAS, have been made user-friendly, allowing those with little computer expertise to use them easily. Some programs will even query you about the nature of your data and recommend which statistical tests to use. Also, most *spreadsheet programs,* such as Excel, will compute a broad range of statistics to help writers give meaningful interpretations to data.

Graphics programs help writers in several ways. First, graphics reveal trends and relationships in data that are often hard to cull from raw data. This helps writers understand clearly the meaning of their data. New data visualization tools, which allow users to graph and parse huge amounts of data, go further. These tools give users the power to explore what their data mean from multiple perspectives and reveal where no meaningful data exist. These tools help users gain insights that other tools cannot provide. Second, graphics programs help writers explain more clearly to readers what the data mean. For example, you can direct the reader to look at the red and blue lines for the last five years on a line chart, noting the trend of increasing rate of return. Also, most of these tools have features that allow you to annotate the graphic, directing the reader's attention to some particular aspect of the graph. You no longer have to be a graphic artist to create clear, good-looking graphics.

Outlining or *concept-mapping programs* that you use for planning a document are organizing tools for the writer as well. Once you have captured your ideas and grouped related ideas, you can rearrange items into a meaningful order, organizing with the reader in mind. You also can collapse or expand the outline to view as few or as many levels as you want. This lets you see a macro, or top-level, view of your document as well as a micro, or detailed, view so that you can check for consistency at all levels.

Computer Tools for Drafting

You are likely familiar with Microsoft Word or another word processing software program as a technology for creating your documents. In addition to the basics of using the software to open files, draft, edit, cut and paste, change a font size and style, and print a document, this software offers many more options for helping you with the drafting process. Because of its popularity, we reference Microsoft Word, but many of the tools we discuss are readily available in other word processing software programs as well.

Use the *Help* Menu. When using your software, be sure that you control the software rather than letting it control you. That is, if you need your software to do something, there is usually a way to accomplish the task. "The computer wouldn't let me" is really not an issue anymore. For example, in Microsoft Word 2007, the default line spacing is 1.15 spaces, and the default paragraph spacing is 10 points. If you are not a proficient user of Word, you may think that you are stuck with this spacing. However, if you search the *Help* menu or think logically that the controls for line and paragraph spacing would be under *Paragraph,* you can quickly make changes.

Take Advantage of Built-in Styles and Themes. Word processing software programs also offer a variety of styles, document themes, and templates that you may use to ensure consistency in your documents. The built-in styles in Word 2007 are particularly useful not only in ensuring consistency but also in creating a table of contents. If you use the styles (or create your own using the *Styles* tool), Word will use them to automatically generate a table of contents. If you use the themes and templates, though, be aware that many of these themes and templates have specially set formatting for line and paragraph spacing, bullets, and alignment. You can manipulate these settings to meet your preferences, but if you are not comfortable doing so, you may find it easier to create your own formatting. Again, the *Help* menu can help you make these changes.

Explore Other Interesting Features. Microsoft Word 2007 offers the following features (if you use other word processing software, you may have access to similar features as well):

- Equation builder: lets you write equations.
- Quick Parts (also called QuickWords and AutoText in other software): lets you create a collection of information that you frequently use in documents so that you do not have to retype the information every time you create a document.
- Word count: allows you to keep track of your document's length.
- Collaboration: enables you to merge, view, or compare multiple documents.
- Digital signature: validates the authenticity of the writer much like the signature on a printed document.
- Smart Art, Clip Art, Charts: let you create visually appealing, informative graphics.
- Multiple *Save* options: allow you to save your document as a Word file, .pdf, or .html file. Word 2007 also enables users to create blog posts.

Figure 17–6 shows the various ribbons and their tools in Word 2007. Some people may find it useful to take courses to learn how to use word processing software, but many learn successfully by navigating the software and the *Help* menu to accomplish their tasks.

Save Your Document Correctly. If your readers are getting printed copies of your document, you can save your file in whatever software format you are using. However, if your readers will view your document electronically, you need to save it in a format that your reader's software will recognize. For instance, Word 2007 files save as .docx files. If your reader has an earlier version of Word that recognizes only .doc files, he or she will not be able to open your file without first downloading a special utililty program. You will need to do a *Save As* and save your document as a .doc file. In addition, if you save your .docx file as a .doc, you may lose some of the formatting from the themes or Smart Art that are not recognized by earlier versions of Word. Likewise, if your reader's software is not compatible with Word at all, you may want to save your document as a .pdf (portable document format). As with the actual composing process itself, saving your documents is an audience-centered effort. You don't want your reader to be angry and frustrated at not being able to open your documents, nor do you want to spend time (and the reader's time) backtracking to save the document in another format and then resending it.

> • Software programs contain many advanced features to help the writing process.

> • Save your document in a format that your audience can access.

Figure 17–6

Illustration of the Many Tools in MS Word 2007

Computer Tools for Revising and Editing

Word processing software also offers several tools for proofing and editing your documents. If your editing consists of reading from the computer monitor or printing a document and simply reading it, you may be missing issues or errors that could be quickly fixed. Furthermore, although your software may help you identify some of the things you need to revise, the software can be unreliable in catching or correctly identifying errors. Again, we use Word 2007 as our reference, but the tools we address are readily available in other software as well.

- Rather than rely on the software to catch your errors, use the software to help you catch and fix errors on your own.

The *Find* Feature. The *Find* feature (Ctrl+F or Home>Editing>Find) can search for and highlight parts of the text you want to check. Let's say that you are writing a letter, and you know you have a problem with comma splices. You could have the software find and highlight every comma in the letter and then check to see whether you have two independent clauses on either side of the comma. If you do, then you could replace the comma with a period or semicolon.

- The *Find* and *Find and Replace* features help you edit a lot of text simultaneously.

The *Find and Replace* Feature. This feature (Ctrl+H or Home>Editing> Replace) allows you to make multiple changes simultaneously (see Figure 17–7). You can find and replace words or text formatting. If, for example, you spelled *internet* with a lowercase "*i*" and want to capitalize it instead, you would tell Word to search for all instances of *internet* and replace them with *Internet*. You can also find and replace line spacing, paragraph formatting, tabs, styles, and special characters much more efficiently than selecting all individual instances of a word, sentence, or paragraph and making changes one at a time.

- Use *Comments* and *Track Changes* to keep a record of your edits.

The *Comments* and *Track Changes* Features. Though these features can be used separately, they are often used together when writers want to collaborate on documents (see Chapter 10); however, you may also want to use them to leave comments for yourself (e.g., "check the date of this source") or keep a record of your changes. Because you can accept or reject the changes, you are not committed to them, and because you still have a record of your earlier work, you can simply reject a change and revert to your original version.

Figure 17–7

Illustration of the *Find and Replace* Feature

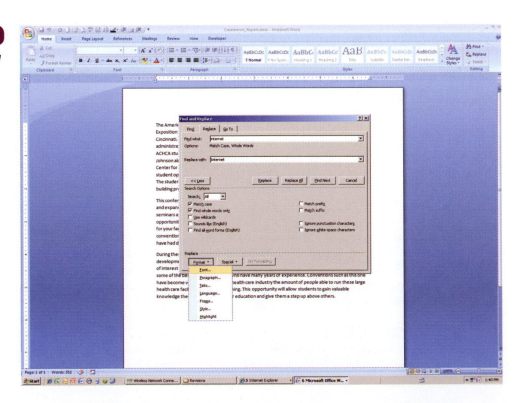

TECHNOLOGY IN BRIEF

Backing Up Frequently Is the Writer's Responsibility

Most writers know how difficult it is to create a document, much less recreate it, so they are willing to spend a little time to protect their investment. In the Save Options dialog box of Word (Microsoft Office Button>Word Options>Save in Office 2007), a writer can set up the program to fit his or her needs. Here a writer elected to have Word always create a backup file, to run these backups every 10 minutes, and to do it in the background. This writer could have also asked Word to allow fast saves, which saves only the changes but take more disk space. This type of saving helps protect you from systems that go down unexpectedly whether from crashes, power outages, accidents, or viruses.

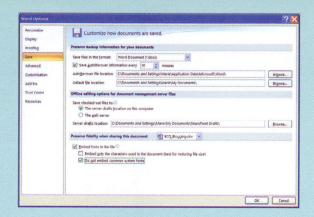

To protect your documents further, you might want to vary the backup media you use. If your computer is damaged or becomes infected with a computer virus, you still have copies of your files. This media could range from simple backups on disks or USB drives to backups at offsite locations. Individuals can do this with subscriptions on Internet hosts, such as idrive, or on school networks or space provided by an Internet service provider.

Backing up is an easy, inexpensive form of insurance for a writer.

***Auto Correct* Features.** As we discussed in Chapter 6, the *Auto Correct* feature lets you enable the software to recognize common errors you may make. For example, if you type quotation marks inside a period (e.g., *".*) , you can set the auto correct features to always correct your text to read *."* instead.

> • Set your *Auto Correct* features to catch mistakes you're likely to make.

Spelling Checkers. Along with Quick Parts, AutoText, and QuickWords, spelling checkers are tools business writers rely on daily. However, they are effective only if the writer uses them. And they are only effective at identifying words that are not in their dictionary. Therefore, spellers could miss some of your mistakes. Mistakes you will want to watch out for include wrong-word errors such as *compliment* for *complement* or *imply* for *infer*. A spell checker also will miss errors such as *desert* for *dessert* or misused words such as *good* for *well*. In addition, if any misspelled words have inadvertently been added to its dictionary, the speller will skip those words too. Therefore, careful proofreading is still in order after a document has been checked with a spelling program. Proofreading carefully is a simple courtesy your reader will appreciate.

> • Spelling checkers supplement proofreading but do not replace it.

Thesaurus Software. While a few serious writers may have a bound thesaurus on hand, most now use a digital thesaurus. The ease of popping up a window with suggested synonyms is hard to beat. Most word processors include a thesaurus; however, several good Web-based programs are available. For example, the Merriam-Webster website (www.m-w.com) includes a free online thesaurus, as well as a dictionary and other tools. The thesaurus is a powerful writing aid, and the computer has made it faster to use and easier to access.

> • The electronic thesaurus gives easy access to synonyms.

Grammar and Style Checkers. The value of grammar and style checkers is often debated. Unlike spelling programs, which are easily able to identify "wrong" words (words that are not in their dictionaries), grammar and style checkers identify "possible problems" and give "suggestions" for revision. It is then your responsibility to decide whether

> • Grammar and style checkers are only suggestion systems.

Figure 17–8

Illustration of a Spelling and Grammar Checker for Writing

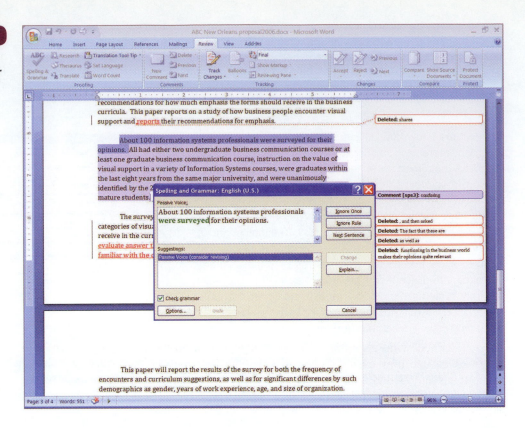

the "possible problem" is a problem and whether the "suggestion" is the best solution. Making this decision requires that you have a good understanding of basic grammar.

- They also evaluate a variety of other elements of writing quality.

In addition to checking grammar, style, word usage, and punctuation, these programs now report readability, strength, descriptive, and jargon indexes. They also perform sentence structure analysis, suggesting that you use simpler sentences, vary the sentence beginnings, use more or fewer prepositional phrases, and make various other changes. Grammar and style checkers also identify "possible problems" with specific words that might be slang, jargon, misspelled, misused, negative, or difficult for readers to understand. A complementary feature, Word Count, reports statistics for number of pages, words, characters, paragraphs, and lines. An example of the interactive use of one grammar checker is shown in Figure 17–8.

- Although often criticized, this tool is improving.

While the debate goes on, the tool is getting better. Recent versions address some of the issues concerning writers. For example, recent versions of grammar and style checkers are much more flexible than older versions. If you are writing in an environment where your boss finds beginning sentences with "And" and "But" acceptable, you can turn off the rule that would identify those beginnings as problems. Also, you can choose the level of writing your intended audience wants. These are just a few examples of the flexibility in the newest versions of grammar and style checkers.

Grammar and style checkers are definitely important for the business writer. But, as with all tools, the more appropriately you use them, the better the job they do for you.

- A wide variety of reference material is available for easy access.

Reference Programs. Reference programs are just what their name suggests—programs that access or act like reference books such as dictionaries, style manuals, and ZIP code directories. While once these reference programs were on CDs, many dictionaries, thesauruses, encyclopedias, books of quotations, ZIP code directories, world almanacs, and other references are now on the Web. They include such elements as pronunciation of words in audio form and pictures, including video and animation. Chapter 18 and the textbook website identify many of these tools.

- Speech input is new technology that will free the writer from keying messages.

Speech Recognition Tools. Recently several companies have introduced some good tools for continuous voice input. Although they are priced favorably, they have

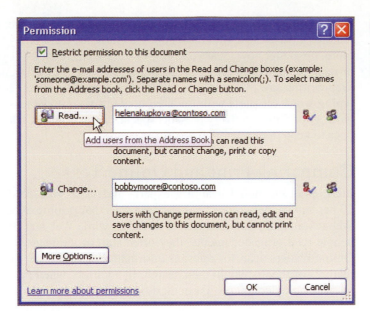

Figure 17–9

Illustration of Information Rights Management for Writing

not yet gained wide acceptance in most businesses. However, as businesspeople begin to realize how easily they can compose their messages by talking to their computer systems and even editing through voice commands, their acceptance is likely to grow. Chapter 13 discussed how business communicators can use speech recognition tools.

Information Rights Management (IRM). Following the lead of Microsoft's Office Professional 2003, many writing programs now give writers the ability to specify how their documents are shared, controlled, and used. Until this time writers had little control over a document once it was transmitted; one could password protect a document or perhaps encrypt it, but both were awkward and a bit complicated to do. The new set of IRM tools is easy to use and much more powerful than these old methods. As you can see in Figure 17–9, the permission dialog box allows users to easily set a variety of features.

Writers can determine how their documents are shared by specifying who can read, change, or have full control over them. Additionally, the writer can set an expiration date on these permissions. Not only do these features help businesses prevent sensitive information from getting into the wrong hands either accidentally or intentionally, but they also give writers control over documents once they leave their computers. If only certain people have permissions, forwarded and copied files will be protected from unauthorized use just as print copies can be.

IRM tools have prompted many businesses to establish practices or policies on the kinds of permissions required for various types of information to protect their intellectual property. These tools also help decrease in-box clutter because they force writers to think about who really needs the document and for how long.

Technology is certainly an important tool for constructing messages. While word processing is the writer's primary tool, a wide variety of other tools can help in the planning, gathering and collecting, analyzing and organizing, and writing stages.

PRINT VERSUS ONLINE DOCUMENTS

Much of what we have discussed in this text references printed documents (e.g., letters, memos, reports). However, as you well know, you will also find yourself doing business electronically, whether you write emails; engage in social networking such as a blog, Twitter, or Facebook; or develop websites. The basic principles of business writing apply to both print and electronic text; that is, your text must be reader-centered, accessible, complete, concise, and accurate. Though electronic documents often have

● As with print documents, electronic documents must be reader centered.

the opportunity for more creative and interactive features than print documents, these features are useless if your reader does not have the technology to access them. Furthermore, no matter how great your blog or your website looks, if your message is unclear or incomplete, your blog or site serves no purpose. In fact, Janice Redish, an expert in Web writing says, "Writing successful Web [or other online] content doesn't start with typing words. It starts with finding out about your audiences and their needs."[1] Still, writing for online delivery presents special considerations. The following are the main ones to keep in mind.

Comparing Print and Online Text

- Readers are more likely to scan text in an electronic document than read it.

Jakob Nielsen, noted usability expert, finds that Web readers read an average of 20 percent of the words on a page.[2] He says that print text can be distinguished from Web text in that print text tends to be linear, while Web text is nonlinear. That is, when people read print documents, they often start at the beginning and finish at the end. Online readers scan for relevant information and may be diverted by links or other features of the display in their search. In addition, when people look for information in electronic documents, particularly on the Web, they do so not necessarily to read what an author has to say about an issue but to accomplish a specific task (e.g., locate a statistic, fill out a form). Online text, then, needs to facilitate the reader's ability to find and use information.

- Online readers tend to be task oriented.
- Online documents can present a lot of information in a small space.
- Print text requires complete sentences; electronic text may allow fragments and abbreviations.

Furthermore, online text can produce comprehensive data more concisely than a print document. Because technology allows writers to embed links to relevant or related information rather than include that information in a paragraph or on a page, electronic documents can incorporate a lot of information in a relatively small space. Print documents, though, could become quite long and unwieldy if an author were to try to include every fact, statistic, or resource related to the topic at hand.

Lastly, print documents generally require that thoughts be expressed in complete sentences, with occasional bulleted lists added for clarity and visual appeal. In electronic documents, writers tend to rely much more on bulleted lists and other terse forms of text. Depending on the medium, they may use fragments and frequent abbreviations.

Organizing Content

- Favor the inverted pyramid structure for online content.

Redish notes that most people visit Web pages because they need to *do* something. Consequently, they do not read as much as they scan for information, and they want what they need quickly, which means that writers are "writing information, not documents."[3] As with print documents, online information must be organized well. Redish advocates organizing Web pages in the inverted pyramid style, where the main point is presented first, followed by supporting information and then by any historical or background information (see Figure 17–10). Other kinds of electronic documents can benefit from this advice as well. If readers are merely scanning for information, they may not scroll for information, which means that the main point must stand out. Similar to information in printed business documents, information in electronic documents should be chunked in short paragraphs and contain headings and lists that emphasize a logical structure and presentation of the information.

Presenting the Content

- Font and line length should accommodate the average monitor resolution for most readers.

Design conventions (font, color, and graphics) depend on your audience. Redish notes that one of the important differences between print and electronic documents is that the resolution, or sharpness of the letters and images, is drastically lower on a screen than in print. Computer printers will print about 600 dpi (dots per inch), while

---

[1] Janice Redish, *Letting Go of the Words: Writing Web Content That Works* (San Francisco: Elsevier, (2007) 12, print.
[2] Jakob Nielsen, "Writing Style for Print vs. Web," *Alert Box*, Jakob Nielsen, 7 June 2008, Web, 12 July 2009.
[3] Redish, 69.

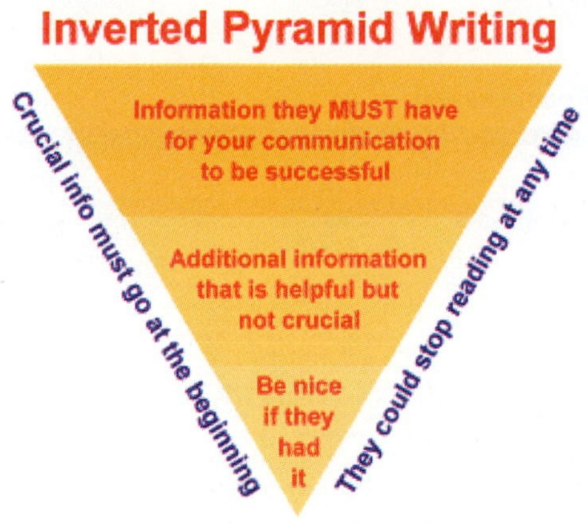

Inverted Pyramid Writing

Information they MUST have for your communication to be successful

Crucial info must go at the beginning

They could stop reading at any time

Additional information that is helpful but not crucial

Be nice if they had it

Figure 17–10

Illustration of the "Inverted Pyramid" Structure
Source: "Inverted Pyramid Writing," *Google Images,* Google, 2009, Web, 13 July 2009.

computer monitors have an approximate resolution of 100 dpi. Thus, while you can use a variety of serif and sans serif fonts in a variety of sizes in print documents, you will want to choose sans serif fonts (those without tails at the ends of the letters) in at least a 12-point size for most online documents so that the serifs do not obscure the text. In addition, readers usually see printed documents on 8½ × 11 paper, but online readers may see electronic documents in windows of varying sizes. For this reason, Redish recommends a line length of 50 to 70 characters or 8 to 10 words. Short lines are also more quickly and easily read, though you do not want lines so short that your text does not capture the main point.

Likewise, text formatting conventions differ in print and electronic environments. In print environments, writers can use underlining, italics, or bold text for emphasis. However, because underlining also represents links in electronic environments, writers should prefer italics or bold text in that context.

- Colors, graphics, and text formatting should be appropriate for print and electronic text.

In addition, as with printed text, writers should also use colors that are appropriate for an audience's culture and are easy on the eyes. For most readers, this will be a dark text on a light background.

Making Your Products Accessible

Many businesses have seen the wisdom of ensuring that their websites are accessible by people with disabilities; in fact, in some cases, accessibility is required by law. Many features of the Web that we take for granted may present difficulties for those with disabilities. For instance, how do people with hearing impairments access audio content on a website? How do people with visual disabilities access text? How does a person with a motor impairment use a mouse? Incorporating text along with audio files gives people who have hearing impairments access to a site, while incorporating text with visuals enables the screen readers of those with visual impairments to "read" the visual for the user. People with motor disabilities can be helped with voice-activated features or key commands rather than mouse-controlled navigation.

- Websites should accommodate those with hearing, visual, or mobility impairments.

COMPUTER TOOLS FOR CREATING ELECTRONIC DOCUMENTS

Just as computer tools such as Microsoft Word can help you with the planning, drafting, and editing of your printed documents, so, too, can they help you with the development of your electronic documents. The mapping and outlining tools discussed earlier in this chapter can help you organize the structure of a blog, an individual Web page, or an entire website. Word will let you publish your document as a blog post, and both Word and Microsoft Publisher (a document design program) will let you save your work as an .html (Web) document. Even if you publish your Word documents as .doc or .docx files rather than in .html format, you can include hyperlinks to websites that your online reader can access if he or she has Internet access.

- Computer tools can help you write effective electronic text.

Figure 17–11

Illustration of a Web Editor (Dreamweaver)

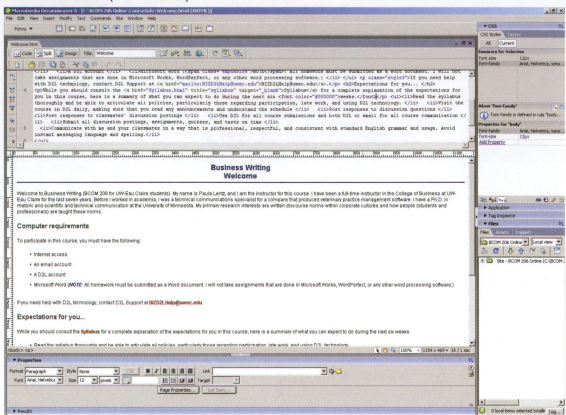

Figure 17–12

Illustration of Zemanta, a Blog- and Email-enhancing Tool

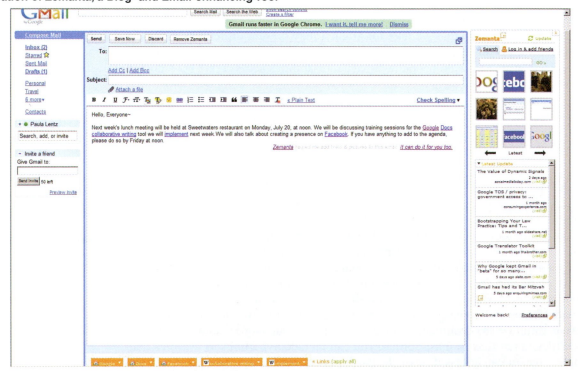

© ZITS Partnership. King Features Syndicate.

However, software programs specifically designed for creating Web documents are also available. Software such as Dreamweaver (see Figure 17–11) and FrontPage are just a few packages available, but there are programs at varying costs that accommodate all levels of expertise. Some, such as those at thefreecountry.com (<http://www.thefreecountry.com/webmaster/htmleditors.shtml>), are free and also accommodate those with little or no experience in Web development.

- Web editing programs accommodate a variety of users' abilities.

Technology can also work within websites or blogs to facilitate communication. Zemanta (see Figure 17–12), for instance, works with blogs, Gmail, and Yahoo! mail to incorporate links and pictures your reader may find useful. Some blogs and websites also use RSS (Really Simple Syndication) feeds to automatically inform users of new posts, information, or news articles. This saves the reader the time of having to go to each of his or her favorite sites to see if anything new has been posted. An example you may be familiar with is Facebook, which sends RSS feeds to your email inbox informing you of new messages on your or your friends' walls. The RSS feeds save you the time of going to Facebook and checking your home page or friends' walls individually; you just open the email messages of the posts you wish to read.

- Tools within websites can also improve the efficiency and effectiveness of your messages.

Sometimes you need to attach or embed documents within an email, Web page, or blog. As we have discussed, documents in .pdf format are easily accessed, as the Adobe Reader a user needs to view the file is free and already installed on most computers. If you are using Office 2007, you can save your Word, PowerPoint, or Publisher files as .pdf files. If your software does not let you save your files in .pdf format, you can download and use CutePDF Writer (cutepdf.com) for free to save your files in this form.

The types and varieties of software are many. As we have mentioned, your audience's needs should drive the technology you use to communicate; the technology should not drive or limit what or how you communicate.

COMPUTER TOOLS FOR COLLABORATION

As discussed in Chapter 10, collaborative writing or group writing tasks occur regularly in business, and they vary widely in terms of the form and nature of the work. However, a wide range of computer tools is available to support various aspects of the process. These tools for computer-supported collaborative writing may allow members to work in asynchronous or synchronous environments. Asynchronous tools are used for different-time/different-place collaboration; synchronous tools, on the other hand, are used for same-time/anyplace collaboration.

- Computer tools assist groups with a wide variety of tasks.

Many tools for collaborative writing have already been discussed in this text: blogs, other social networks, Word's *Comments* and *Track Changes* features, and virtual meeting programs such as Microsoft's Live Meeting. The following tools may also be helpful.

Figure 17–13

Illustration of Office Live Workspace, an Online Collaboration Tool

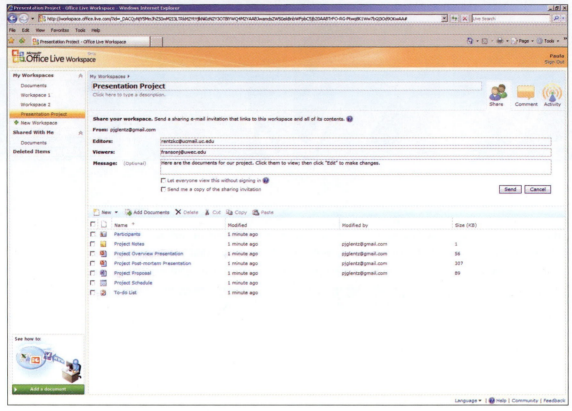

Collaborative Writing Programs

- Several computer tools support collaborative writing.

Google Docs, Zoho Writer, Please Write, Writeboard, Gobby, Socialtext, and Microsoft Groove are just a few of the collaborative writing tools available. Some of these are free and let you edit documents, spreadsheets, .html documents, and images. Other features may include simultaneous editing, chat options, RSS feeds, privacy and security settings, and email updates. Programs such as Google Docs allow users to upload documents and edit them simultaneously only with other team members whom you have invited to edit the document.

Some programs such as Microsoft Office Live Workspace (see Figure 17–13) let you upload all documents associated with a project such as a schedule and to-do list. By locating all of your documents centrally, you and your team members do not have to deal with multiple versions of a document or multiple email attachments. Plus, everyone can have access to a common schedule, and contact among group members is convenient. These collaborative programs can streamline your writing process, save time, and make the writing process more efficient.

Discussion Boards

- Discussion boards are useful for storing documents and for communicating online.

Discussion boards such as those in blogs or an online learning platform such as Blackboard, WebCT, or Desire2Learn are also useful when groups have a difficult time meeting due to distance and time. To begin, the lead writer enters some text. Others access the system, review the text, and enter their own comments that other group members can view. In some systems, group members are anonymous, but others maintain audit trails so comments can be attributed to a specific group member.

Unlike blogs, which list posts chronologically, discussion boards generally list postings by threaded topics. If you are in a discussion board, it is helpful to coordinate with

Smaller, smarter technology may enable future businesspeople to wear their computers.

other group members to devise a strategy for threading and naming posts. For instance, if you and your group members are collaborating on a draft and every member names his or her part of the report "My Section," group members may become confused regarding which draft to view. Deciding on naming conventions in advance can prevent a lot of confusion.

A LOOK TO THE FUTURE

Given the recent explosion of communication-related technologies, you will probably not be surprised to learn that you can anticipate further rapid advancements. While some of this innovation is happening in academic institutions such as MIT's Media Lab, much of it is happening at large companies such as IBM, Intel, Microsoft, Yahoo!, and Google. These companies have some of their brightest, most creative people working on technologies for both the near term and the longer term. According to one blog, the information technology company Gartner, Inc., reports that "by 2012, 50 percent of traveling workers will leave their notebooks at home in favor of other devices."[4] Internet TV and video will soon become a more widely used technology. And email will get better, too. Not only will offensive, malicious, and deceptive email become a thing of the past, but through the use of data mining tools, businesses will be able to better understand their people and their strengths. They will be able to identify experts on a variety of subjects as well as discover new ideas.

- Computer tools will continue to enhance the communication process.

Many of us are used to downloading software to our computers and creating and saving documents to our own machines. *Cloud computing,* though, is changing the way business communicators access and store their software and their work. In cloud computing, the *cloud* is essentially a metaphor for the Internet. Software and information are stored on websites—*in the cloud*—rather than on your computer. Google's gmail, Yahoo! mail, Microsoft's Webmail, SurveyMonkey, and various customer-relationship management (CRM) tools are examples of such Web-based applications. You do not have to download software to your computer to use these programs; all you need is the Internet connection that lets you access the service.

- *Cloud computing,* or the use of Internet-based applications, is becoming more and more popular.

[4] Beatenetworks, "Gartner: Technology Opportunities . . .," weblog comment, *The Network: The Latest on the Immersive Web,* 5 Feb 2008, Web, 17 July 2009.

Some Microsoft applications can now be accessed as Web applications. Because cloud applications have no system requirements and require no software on the user's computer, they can be a cost-effective, efficient means of accessing programs; however, because the information is on the Internet, security can be an issue, as can the problem of server crashes. Thus, if you use cloud applications, be sure that you have a plan for backing up your data just as you would if you were working locally from your own computer.

- Humans will still need to control the communication.

Whatever technologies develop, human minds will still need to control the communication using good judgment and skill. In fact, there is no evidence whatsoever that the need for well-crafted communication will decrease. Business communication is here to stay. In fact, the increasing advancement of the technology of the future is likely to require more—not less—of it.

SUMMARY BY LEARNING OBJECTIVES

1 Explain how technology helps in constructing messages.

1. Technology helps a writer construct messages through every step of the writing process including
   - Planning,
   - Gathering and collecting information,
   - Analyzing and organizing information, and
   - Writing and rewriting.

2 Identify appropriate tools for different stages in the writing process.

2. Each stage of the writing process has a set of tools most appropriate for the tasks in that stage. These include the following:
   - Outlining or concept-mapping, project management, and personal information management programs for planning;
   - Database programs and reference managers for gathering and collecting information; and
   - Statistical, spreadsheet, graphics, and outlining or concept-mapping tools for analyzing and organizing information; and word processing, spelling, thesaurus, grammar and style checking, reference, graphics, drawing, and voice recognition, and information rights management programs for writing.

3 Discuss considerations for writing electronic and print documents.

3. Although writing electronic documents and print documents is similar in many ways, electronic documents present additional considerations.
   - Online readers are task oriented and tend to scan rather than read material.
   - Online content should be written in the inverted pyramid order.
   - Fonts, colors, and graphics should be chosen to promote readability.
   - Print documents have a much higher resolution than electronic documents and are more easily read.
   - Good Web writers will make text accessible to people with hearing, vision, or motor disabilities.

4 Discuss how technology facilitates the development of online content.

4. Technology facilitates the development of online content.
   - Office programs such as Word and Publisher can help you plan and create electronic documents.
   - Programs such as Dreamweaver and FrontPage are used for creating websites. Many free programs are available as well to enhance a document's content and presentation.

- RSS feeds can be used to coordinate and organize news, emails, or blog updates.
- Using .pdf files can ensure that your reader has access to your electronic documents.

5. A range of software tools assists groups of writers in asynchronous and synchronous writing environments.
   - Software such as Google Docs, Writeboard, and Groove let writers collaborate asynchronously or simultaneously to compose, edit, and publish documents.
   - Discussion boards can also support collaborative writing efforts.

6. Business leaders believe technology will continue to advance. Future developments are expected to enhance present technologies, making them better and easier to use. Researchers at large companies are working on a variety of projects, including many search and social networking areas. Future developments will likely mean more need for good basic communication skills.

5 Describe how technology assists in collaboration.

6 Discuss what impact future developments in technology might have on business communication.

CRITICAL THINKING QUESTIONS

1 Explain how technology can help the writer with both creative and tedious writing tasks. **(LO1)**

2 Identify specific software tools that assist with constructing written messages. Explain what each does. **(LO2)**

3 Word processing programs are the writer's primary tool. Identify five basic features and two advanced features useful to business writers. **(LO2)**

4 Discuss the advantages and disadvantages of spelling checkers and grammar and style checkers. **(LO2)**

5 Brainstorm some practices or policies that businesses might develop for using the Information Rights Management (IRM) tool effectively. **(LO2)**

6 Explain the similarities and differences between preparing print and electronic business documents. **(LO3)**

7 Discuss the various technologies that can be used to develop electronic messages. **(LO4)**

8 How can technology assist in collaboration? **(LO5)**

9 How might cloud computing and other technologies affect the future of business communication? **(LO6)**

CRITICAL THINKING EXERCISES

1 Investigate your school and/or local libraries to determine what current (or future) computer sources will help one find information for business. Report your findings to the class.

2 Compile an annotated list of at least 10 websites with good links to business sources. Three of these links should be for local business information.

3 Locate six examples of video and audio clips you might use in a business document. Describe the examples along with a brief explanation of a good use in a business document.

4 Identify where computers, printers, scanners, wireless hot spots, and other tools are available at or around your college. Prepare a table with this information, listing times available as well as any costs. Also, be sure to include computer configurations and programs available.

5 Choose a feature from your word processor (such as index, table of contents, templates, or citation builder) that you have not used much. Learn how to use it and create an example of its use in a business document. Write a brief description of its application.

6 Select a dozen idioms from a reference book (found online or in print) that seem common to you. Type these into your word processor and run the file through a grammar and style checker. Print a copy of the results and bring it to class for discussion.

7 From a current computer magazine, find an article that relates to communication in business. Write a one-paragraph reaction to it and post it to a blog specified by your instructor.

chapter eighteen

Business Research Methods

LEARNING OBJECTIVES

Upon completing this chapter, you will be able to design and implement a plan for conducting the research needed for a business report. To reach this goal, you should be able to

1 Explain the difference between primary and secondary research.

2 Gather secondary sources using direct and indirect research methods.

3 Evaluate websites for reliability.

4 Describe the procedures for searching through company records.

5 Conduct an experiment for a business problem.

6 Design an observational study for a business problem.

7 Use sampling to conduct a survey.

8 Construct a questionnaire, develop a working plan, and conduct a pilot test for a survey.

9 Explain the purpose of focus groups and personal interviews.

10 Analyze and interpret information clearly and completely for your reader.

11 Explain the ethical considerations for work with human subjects.

Business Research Methods

Introduce yourself to this chapter by assuming the position of administrative assistant to Carmen Bergeron, the vice president for human resources for Pinnacle Industries. Today at a meeting of administrators, someone commented about the low morale among sales representatives since last year's merger with Price Corporation. The marketing vice president immediately came to the defense of her area, claiming that there was no proof of the statement—that in fact the opposite was true. Others joined in with their views, and in time a heated discussion developed. In an effort to ease tensions, Ms. Bergeron suggested that her office conduct a survey of employees "to learn the truth of the matter." The administrators liked the idea.

After the meeting, Ms. Bergeron called you in to tell you that you would be the one to do the research. And she wants the findings in report form in time for next month's meeting. She didn't say much more. No doubt she thinks your college training equipped you to handle the assignment.

Now you must do the research. This means you will have to choose appropriate methods and develop a plan for implementing them. Specifically, you will have to select a sample, construct a questionnaire, devise an interview procedure, conduct interviews, record findings—and more. All these activities require much more than a casual understanding of research. How to do this research effectively is the subject of this chapter.

CONDUCTING BUSINESS RESEARCH

As Chapter 10 pointed out, you are likely to write many business reports in your career. To prepare these reports, as well as other business documents, you must often search for the most reliable, timely, and useful information. Sometimes your research can be informal, as when you quickly review the earlier correspondence on a problem. But sometimes your search will need to be more systematic. This chapter focuses on the latter type.

- In business, you will often need to search for reliable, timely, and useful information.

The first step in understanding formal research is to distinguish between the two main types: secondary research and primary research. Secondary research is research utilizing material that someone else has published—for example, periodicals, brochures, books, and electronic publications. This research may be the first form of research that you use for some problems (see Chapter 10). Primary research is research that uncovers information firsthand. It is research that produces new findings.

- The two basic forms of research are secondary research (getting information from published sources) and primary research (getting information firsthand).

To be effective as a report writer, you should be familiar with the techniques of both secondary and primary research. A discussion of each follows.

SECONDARY RESEARCH

Secondary research materials are potentially the least costly, the most accessible, and the most complete sources of information. However, to take full advantage of the available materials, you must know what you are looking for and where and how to find it.

- Secondary research can be a rich source of information if you know what to look for and where to look.

The task can be complex and challenging. You can meet the challenge if you become familiar with the general arrangement of a library or other sources of secondary materials and if you learn the techniques of finding those materials. Also, research must be orderly if it is to be reliable and complete.

In the past, researchers used a card system to help them keep track of the sources they identified. This card system could be combined with and adapted to a computer system quite easily. The manual system of organization required that the researcher complete two sets of cards. One set was simply a bibliography card set, containing complete information about sources. A researcher numbered these cards consecutively as the sources were identified. A second set of cards contained the notes from each source. Each of these cards was linked to its source through the number of the source in the bibliography card set.

- Keep track of the sources you gather in an orderly way.

Since the computer systems in today's libraries often allow users to print, download, email, or transfer directly the citations they find from the indexes and databases, it makes sense to identify each with a unique number rather than recopy the source to a card. Not only is the resulting list more legible than one's handwriting, but it is also complete. Some researchers cut their printouts apart and tape them to a master sheet. Others enter these items in databases they build. And still others export items directly into specialty databases, letting the software organize and number them. With the widespread use of notebook and laptop computers, most researchers now take notes on computers rather than cards. These notes can be linked to the original source by number as in the manual system.

Whether you use a manual, combined, or computer system, using an orderly system is essential.

Finding Publication Collections

- A library is the natural place to begin secondary research.

The first step in an orderly search for printed information is to determine where to begin. The natural place, of course, is a library. However, since different types of libraries offer different kinds of collections, it is helpful to know what types of libraries are available and to be familiar with their contents.

- General libraries offer the public a wide variety of information sources.

General Libraries. *General libraries* are the best known and the most accessible. General libraries, which include college, university, and most public libraries, are called *general* to the extent that they contain all kinds of materials. Many general libraries, however, have substantial collections in certain specialized areas.

- Special libraries have limited collections and circulation and can be owned by
- private business,

Special Libraries. Libraries that limit their collections to one type or just a few types of material are considered *special libraries*. Many such libraries are private and do not invite routine public use of their materials. Still, they will frequently cooperate on research projects that they consider relevant and worthwhile.

Among the special libraries are those libraries of private businesses. As a rule, such libraries are designed to serve the sponsoring company and provide excellent information in the specialized areas of its operations. Company libraries are less accessible than other specialized libraries, but a written inquiry explaining the nature and purpose of a project or an introduction from someone known to the company can help you gain access to them.

- associations, and

Special libraries are also maintained by various types of associations—for example, trade organizations, professional and technical groups, chambers of commerce, and labor unions. Like company libraries, association libraries may provide excellent coverage of highly specialized areas. Although such libraries develop collections principally for members or a research staff, they frequently make resources available to others engaged in reputable research.

- research organizations.

A number of public and private research organizations also maintain specialized libraries. The research divisions of big-city chambers of commerce and the bureaus of research of major universities, for example, keep extensive collections of material containing statistical and general information on a local area. State agencies collect similar data. Again, though these materials are developed for a limited audience, they are often made available upon request.

- Consult a directory to determine what special libraries offer.

Directories. Several guides are available in the reference department of most general libraries to help you determine what these research centers and special libraries offer and whom to contact for permission to use their collections. The *American Library Directory* is a geographic listing of libraries in the United States and Canada. It gives detailed information on libraries, including special interests and collections. It covers all public libraries as well as many corporate and association libraries. Also, the Special Libraries Association has chapters in many large cities that publish directories for their chapter areas. Particularly helpful in identifying the information available in research centers is *The Research Centers Directory*. Published by The Gale Group, it lists the research activities, publications, and services of thousands of university-related and other nonprofit organizations. It is supplemented between editions by a related publication, *New Research Centers*.

Taking the Direct Approach

When you have found the appropriate library for your research, you are ready for the next challenge. With the volume of material available, how will you find what you need? Many cost-conscious businesses are hiring professionals to find information for them. These professionals' charges range from $60 to $120 per hour in addition to any online charges incurred. Other companies like to keep their information gathering more confidential; some employ company librarians, and others expect their employees to gather the information. If you know little about how material is arranged in a library or online, you will waste valuable time on a probably fruitless search. However, if you are familiar with certain basic reference materials, you may be able to proceed directly to the information you seek. And if the direct approach does not work, there are several effective indirect methods of finding the material you need.

● You can begin your research using the direct approach, but you must be familiar with basic references.

Taking the direct approach is advisable when you seek quantitative or factual information. The reference section of your library is where you should start. There, either on your own or with the assistance of a research librarian, you can discover any number of timely and comprehensive sources of facts and figures. Although you cannot know all these sources, as a business researcher you should be familiar with certain basic ones. These sources are available in either print or electronic forms. You should be able to use both.

● The direct approach is especially effective with quantitative or factual information.

Encyclopedias. Encyclopedias are the best-known sources of direct information and are particularly valuable when you are just beginning a search. They offer background material and other general information that give you a helpful introduction to the area under study. Individual articles or sections of articles are written by experts in the field and frequently include a short bibliography.

● Encyclopedias offer both general and detailed information.

Of the general encyclopedias, two worthy of special mention are *Encyclopedia Americana* and *Encyclopaedia Britannica. Britannica* online now requires a subscription at britannica.com. Others that are widely used are *World Book* and *Microsoft Encarta* (though note that Microsoft will not be updating *Encarta* after 2009). Also helpful are such specialized encyclopedias as the *Encyclopedia of Banking and Finance,* the *Encyclopedia of Business and Finance,* the *Encyclopedia of Small Business,* the *Encyclopedia of Advertising,* and the *Encyclopedia of Emerging Industries.*

Biographical Directories. A direct source of biographical information about leading figures of today or of the past is a biographical directory. The best-known biographical directories are *Who's Who in America* and *Who's Who in the World,* annual publications that summarize the lives of living people who have achieved prominence. Similar publications provide coverage by geographic area: *Who's Who in the East* and *Who's Who in the South and Southwest,* for example. For biographical information about prominent Americans of the past, the *Dictionary of American Biography* is useful. You also can find biographical information under the reference section of *Lexis-Nexis Academic Universe.* In addition to links to biographical directories, links to news stories about the person also are provided.

● Biographical directories offer information about influential people.

Specialized publications will help you find information on people in particular professions. Among the most important of these are *Who's Who in Finance and Industry*; *Standard & Poor's Register of Corporations, Directors, and Executives*; *Who's Who in Insurance*; and *Who's Who in Technology.* Nearly all business and professional areas are covered by some form of directory.

Almanacs. Almanacs are handy guides to factual and statistical information. Simple, concise, and selective in their presentation of data, they should not be underestimated as references. *The World Almanac and Book of Facts,* published by Funk & Wagnalls, is an excellent general source of facts and statistics. The *Time Almanac* is another excellent source for a broad range of statistical data. One of its strongest areas is information on the world. The *New York Times Almanac* presents much of its data in tables. It has excellent coverage of business and the economy.

● Almanacs provide factual and statistical information.

Almanacs are available online as well. Infoplease.com offers broad coverage of topics, including a business section at <http://www.infoplease.com/almanacs.html>.

- Trade directories publish information about individual businesses and products.

Trade Directories. For information about individual businesses or the products they make, buy, or sell, directories are the references to consult. Directories compile details in specific areas of interest and are variously referred to as *catalogs, listings, registers,* or *source books.* Some of the more comprehensive directories indispensable in general business research are the following: *The Million Dollar Directory* (a listing of U.S. companies compiled by Dun & Bradstreet), *Thomas Register of American Manufacturers* (free on the web at <http://www.thomasregister.com>), and *The Datapro Directory.* Some directories that will help you determine linkages between parent entities and their subsidiaries include *America's Corporate Families* and *Who Owns Whom* (both compiled by Dun & Bradstreet) as well as the *Directory of Corporate Affiliations.* Thousands of directories exist—so many, in fact, that there is a directory called *Directories in Print.*

- Governments (national, state, provincial, etc.) publish extensive research materials.

Government Publications. Governments (national, state, local, etc.) publish hundreds of thousands of titles each year. In fact, the U.S. government is the world's largest publisher. Surveys, catalogs, pamphlets, periodicals—there seems to be no limit to the information that various bureaus, departments, and agencies collect and make available to the public. The challenge of working with government publications, therefore, is finding your way through this wealth of material to the specifics you need. That task sometimes can be so complex as to require indirect research methods. However, if you are familiar with a few key sources, the direct approach will often produce good results. And at this time, many government publications are moving rapidly to the Web. You can see links to many of these in Figures 18–1 and 18–2.

- The U.S. government publishes guides to its publications.

In the United States, it may be helpful to consult the *Monthly Catalog of U.S. Government Publications.* Issued by the Superintendent of Documents, it includes a comprehensive listing of annual and monthly publications and an alphabetical index of the issuing agencies. It can be searched online at <http://www.gpoaccess.gov/databases/>. The Superintendent of Documents also issues *Selected United States Government Publications,* a monthly list of general-interest publications that are sold to the public.

- These government publications are invaluable in business research.

Routinely available are a number of specialized publications that are invaluable in business research. These include *Census of Population, Census of Housing, Annual Housing Survey, Consumer Income, Population Characteristics, Census of Governments, Census of Retail Trade, Census of Manufacturers, Census of Agriculture,*

Figure 18–1

Website of the U.S. Census Bureau. This is a rich source of business information that is easily accessible.
Source: *U.S. Census Bureau,* home page, U.S. Department of Commerce, 2009, Web, 16 July 2009.

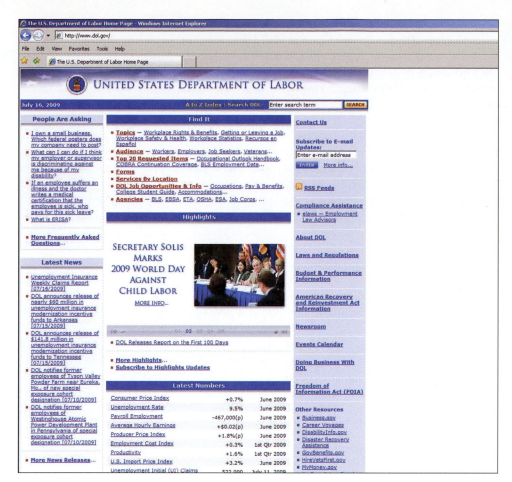

Figure 18–2

The U.S. Department of Labor's Website. You can find useful publications here, as well as news, statistics, and more.
Source: *United States Department of Labor,* home page, U.S. Department of Labor, 2009, Web, 16 July 2009.

Census of Construction Industries, Census of Transportation, Census of Service Industries, Census of Wholesale Trade, and *Census of Mineral Industries.* The *Statistical Abstract of the United States* is another invaluable publication, as are the *Survey of Current Business,* the *Monthly Labor Review,* the *Occupational Outlook Quarterly,* and the *Federal Reserve Bulletin.* To say the least, government sources are extensive.

Dictionaries. Dictionaries are helpful for looking up meanings, spellings, and pronunciations of words or phrases. Electronic dictionaries add other options; they include pronunciation in audio files and let you find words when you know the meaning only. Dictionaries are available in both general and specialized versions. While it might be nice to own an unabridged dictionary, an abridged collegiate or desk dictionary will answer most of your questions.

● Dictionaries provide meanings, spellings, and pronunciations for both general and specialized words and phrases.

You should be aware that the name *Webster* can be legally used by any dictionary publisher. Also, dictionaries often include added features such as style manuals, signs, symbols, and weights and measures. Because dictionaries reflect usage, you want to be sure the one you use is current. Not only are new words being added, but spellings and meanings change, too.

Several good dictionaries are the *American Heritage Dictionary,* the *Funk & Wagnalls Standard Dictionary,* the *Random House Webster's College Dictionary,* and *Merriam-Webster's Collegiate Dictionary.* To have the most current dictionary available at your fingertips (through toolbars), you may want to subscribe to one such as Merriam-Webster at <http://www.m-w.com/>.

Specialized dictionaries concentrate on one functional area. Some business dictionaries are the *Dictionary of Business Terms, The Blackwell Encyclopedic Dictionary of Management Information Systems, The Blackwell Encyclopedic Dictionary of*

Accounting, The Blackwell Encyclopedic Dictionary of Business Ethics, The Blackwell Encyclopedic Dictionary of Finance, the *Dictionary of Taxation,* the *Dictionary of International Business Terms,* the *Concise Dictionary of Business Management,* and the *Dictionary of Marketing and Advertising.* There are also dictionaries of acronyms, initialisms, and abbreviations. Two of these are the *Acronyms, Initialisms, and Abbreviations Dictionary* and the *Abbreviations Dictionary.*

Additional Statistical Sources. Today's businesses rely heavily on statistical information. Not only is this information helpful in the day-to-day business operations, but it also is helpful in planning future products, expansions, and strategies. Some of this information can be found in the publications previously mentioned, especially the government publications. More is available online and can be seen long before it is printed. Even more is available from the various public and private sources described in Figure 18–3.

In order to facilitate the collection and retrieval of statistical data for industry, the U.S. government developed a classification system called the Standard Industrial Classification (SIC) code. In the 1930s, this system used a four-digit code for all manufacturing and nonmanufacturing industries.

In 1997, the U.S. government introduced a new industrial classification system—the North American Industry Classification System (NAICS)—to replace the SIC code. The new system is more flexible than the old one and accounts for changes in the global economy by allowing the United States, Mexico, and Canada to compare economic and financial statistics better. It has also been expanded to include new sectors such as the information sector; the health care and social assistance sector; and the professional, scientific, and technical services sector. The United States and Canada began using this system in 1997, and Mexico in 1998. The first NAICS-based statistics were issued in 1999.

Some of the basic comprehensive publications include the *Statistical Abstract of the United States* and *Standard & Poor's Statistical Service.* These sources are a starting point when you are not familiar with more specialized sources. They include historical data on American industry, commerce, labor, and agriculture; industry data by SIC/NAICS codes; and numerous indexes such as producer price indexes, housing indexes, and stock price indexes. Additionally, the *Statistical Abstract of the United States* contains an extremely useful guide to sources of statistics.

If you are not certain where to find statistics, you may find various guides useful. The *American Statistics Index* is an index to statistics published by all government agencies. It identifies the agency, describes the statistics, and provides access by category. The *Encyclopedia of Business Information Sources* provides a list of information sources along with names of basic statistical sources. The *Statistical Reference Index* publishes statistics from sources other than the government, such as trade and professional associations. These three directories will help direct you to specialized statistics when you need them.

Business Information Services. Business services are private organizations that supply a variety of information to business practitioners, especially investors. Libraries also subscribe to their publications, giving business researchers ready access to yet another source of valuable, timely data.

Mergent, Inc., one of the best-known of such organizations, publishes a weekly *Manual* in each of five business areas: industrials, over-the-counter (OTC) industrials, international banks and finance, municipals, and governments. These reports primarily summarize financial data and operating facts on all major American companies, providing information that an investor needs to evaluate the investment potential of individual securities or of fields as a whole. *Corporation Records,* published by Standard & Poor's Corporation, presents similar information in loose-leaf form. Both Mergent and Standard & Poor's provide a variety of related services, including *Moody's Investors' Advisory Service* and *Value Line Investment Survey.*

- Statistical information is available both online and in printed form.

- A new classification system enables users to compare economic and financial statistics better.

- Basic publications provide broad coverage and source listings for more detailed statistics.

- Guides help you locate sources.

- Private business services collect and publish data. Many such reports are available in public and university libraries.

Figure 18–3

List of Resources by Research Question. Sources with Web addresses provided are available to the general public.

How do I find business news and trends?

ABI Inform Complete on ProQuest

Business & Company Resource Center

Business & Industry Database (includes articles from over 900 trade publications)

Business Source Premier

Factiva (includes Dow Jones and Reuters Newswires and *The Wall Street Journal,* plus more than 8,000 other sources from around the world)

LexisNexis Academic, News and Business sections

Wilson OmniFile Full Text Mega

How do I find information about companies?

The Annual Reports Library (<http://www.zpub.com/sf/arl/>)

Business & Company Resource Center

Business Source Premier

Companies' own websites

D&B's (Dunn & Bradstreet's) *International Million Dollar Database*

D&B's *Million Dollar Database*

Factiva

Hoover's Online

LexisNexis Academic, Business section

Marketline (basic information about 10,000 global companies, including the United States)

Mergent Online (information about 11,000 U.S. and 17,000 international companies)

SEC Filings and Forms (EDGAR) (includes 10-K reports and annual reports)

Standard & Poor's Net Advantage

Thomson Research (Disclosure provides information about 12,000 U.S. companies; Worldscope covers both U.S. and international company filings)

Value Line Research Center

How do I find information about particular industries?

Business Insight

Frost & Sullivan

Global Market Information Database

ICON Group International (see Industry Reports, Country Reports, and Culture Statistics)

IBISWorld

MarketLine

MarketResearch.com Academic

MergentOnline, Industry Reports

Plunkett Research Online

Standard & Poor's Net Advantage, Industries section

How do I find biographical and contact information for business people?

American Business Directory (<http://library.dialog.com/bluesheets/html/bl0531.html>)

Biographical Dictionary of American Business Leaders

Biography Reference Bank

D&B's (Dunn & Bradstreet's) *Million Dollar Database*

LexisNexis Academic, Reference/Biographical Information section

Standard & Poor's Net Advantage (see Register of Executives)

Who's Who in Finance and Business (includes Biography Resource Center)

How do I find information provided by the US government?

Business.gov (government rules and regulations, research, resources)

Fedstats (<http://www.fedstats.gov/>)

STAT-USA (includes State of the Nation Library)

U.S. Bureau of Labor Statistics (<http://www.bls.gov>; comprehensive employment and economic data, including *Monthly Labor Review* and *Occupational Outlook Handbook*)

U.S. Census Bureau (<http://www.census.gov>; links to *Statistical Abstract of the United States*)

U.S. Government Printing Office (<http://www.gpoaccess.gov>; comprehensive site for U.S. government publications)

U.S. Small Business Administration (<http://www.sba.gov/>)

How do I find out about other countries and international trade?

Economists Intelligence Unit—ISI Emerging Markets

Europa World Yearbooks

Global Market Information Database

SourceOECD (from the Organisation for Economic Cooperation and Development)

STAT-USA/Internet (<http://www.stat-usa.gov>)

U.S. Library of Congress, Country Studies (<http://lcweb2.loc.gov/frd/cs/cshome.html>)

U.S. State Department information (<http://www.state.gov>)

The World Factbook (<http://www.cia.gov/cia/publications/factbook/>)

WDI Online (the World Bank's World Development Indicators)

Yahoo!'s country links (<http://dir.yahoo.com/Regional/Countries/>)

How do I find information about cities?

American FactFinder (<http://factfinder.census.gov/home/saff/main.html?_lang=en>)

Cities' own websites

Country and City Data Books (<http://fisher.lib.virginia.edu/collections/stats/ccdb/>)

Sourcebook America (CD-ROM)

Cities of the World (4-volume reference book)

Source: Compiled with the assistance of Business Reference Librarians Wahib Nasrallah, University of Cincinnati, and Patrick Sullivan and Michael Perkins, San Diego State University.

Another organization whose publications are especially helpful to business researchers is The Gale Group, Inc. Gale provides several business services, including publications featuring forecasts and market data by country, product, and company. Its online Business and Company Resource Center is particularly useful. This database provides access to hundreds of thousands of company records, allowing users to search by company name, ticker symbol, and SIC and NAICS codes. It provides links to the full text of news and magazine articles, company profiles, investment reports, and even legal actions and suits. Users can print the information as well as email it to others.

Figure 18–3 lists additional helpful resources, such as *Hoover's Online* (see Figure 18–4) and *Factiva.* Many can be accessed through your school library's website.

International Sources. In today's global business environment, we often need information outside our borders. Many of the sources we have discussed have counterparts with international information. *Principal International Businesses* lists basic information on major companies located around the world. *Major Companies of Europe* and *Japan Company Handbook* are two sources providing facts on companies in their respective areas. The *International Encyclopedia of the Social Sciences* covers all important areas of social science, including biographies of acclaimed persons in these areas. General and specialized dictionaries are available, too. The *International Business Dictionary and References* includes commonly used business terms in several languages. You will even be able to find trade names in the *International Brands and Their Companies,* published by The Gale Group. For bibliographies and abstracts, one good source is the *Foreign Commerce Handbook.* Even statistical information is available in sources such as the *Index to International Statistics, Statistical Yearbook,* and online at the United Nations Department of Economic and Social Affairs Statistical Division (<http://unstats.un.org/unsd/>). Additionally, the U.S. Bureau of Labor Statistics at <http://www.bls.gov/bls/other.htm> provides links to many countries' statistical portals. With the help of translation tools (see Chapter 15 and the textbook website), you can get information you want directly. In addition, libraries usually contain many references for information on international marketing, exporting, tax, and trade.

• Statistical information for the international business environment is available in a wide range of documents.

Using Indirect Methods

Sometimes you may not know what resource will provide you the information you need. In these instances, prepare a list of key terms related to your topic. Then use these key terms to search for information using more general online catalogs, database search engines, or the Internet. These more general resources can guide you to specific sources on your topic. Once you find a specific source, keep a full bibliographic record to cite in your paper or project (i.e., names, dates, volume, issue, and page numbers).

Your acquisition of secondary materials must be methodical and thorough. You should not depend on the material that is readily at hand. You may need to use interlibrary loan services, for example, or gather company documents. Be sure you thoroughly check each source, taking time to review its table of contents, its index, and the endnotes or footnotes related to the pages you are researching. This will help you assess the reliability of the information as well as find additional resources.

The Online Catalog. Today most libraries use electronic catalogs to list their holdings, providing numerous ways to locate sources. As you can see from the main menu screen of one system in Figure 18–5, you can locate sources by the standard Keyword, Title, Author, and Subject options as well as a few other options. Additionally, this menu gives you tips on how to use the catalog. Becoming familiar with these tips is highly recommended, especially for the systems you access frequently. By using effective and efficient searching techniques, you will reap many rewards.

Two options you need to understand clearly are Keyword and Subject. When you select the Keyword option, the system will ask you to enter search terms and phrases. It will then search for only those exact words in several of each record's fields, missing all those records using slightly different wording (See Figures 18–6 and 18–7). However, when you select Subject, the system will ask you to enter the Library of Congress subject heading. While you must know the exact heading, sometimes it will cross-reference headings such as suggesting you *See Intercultural Communication* when you enter *cross-cultural communication.* A Subject search will find all those holdings on the subject, including those with different wording such as *intercultural communication, international communication, global communication,* and *diversity.* If you ran multiple searches under the Keyword option using these terms, you would still miss those titles without the keywords, such as Robert Axtell's book *Dos and Taboos*

- When you cannot find secondary materials directly, try the indirect approach. Start by preparing a bibliography of needed sources.

- Gather all available publications. Check each systematically for the information you need.

- Be sure to assess each source.

- A library's online catalog lists its holdings.

- Electronic catalogs give many search options.

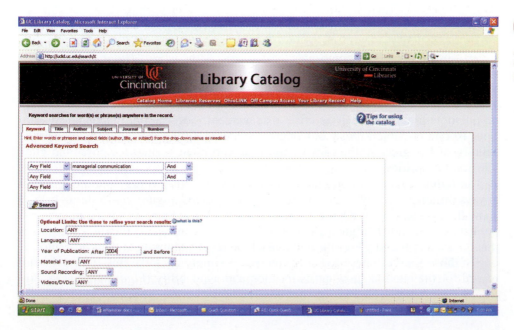

Figure 18–5

A Keyword Search in an Online Catalog for Books Published after 2004

Figure 18–6

Online Search Results for
a Keyword Search

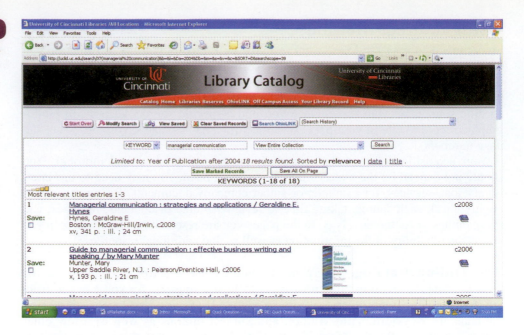

Figure 18–7

The Full Record for the
Top Hit (Shows Location,
Call Number, Availability)

around the World. With a Subject search, you might even find a management book with a chapter on intercultural communication; however, the book's emphasis might be on something else, such as crisis management, negotiation, or conflict resolution. To find possible Library of Congress subject headings for your topic, visit the Library of Congress Authorities webpage at <http://authorities.loc.gov> and click "Search Authorities."

The online catalog never gets tired. If you key in the words accurately, it will always produce a complete and accurate list of sources. Figures 18–5 through 18–9 show the progression of a keyword search for books on managerial communication published after 2004. Figure 18–5 is the initial screen, while Figure 18–6 shows that the system found 18 results and ranked the results in terms of their relevance. If one of those sources interested you, you would simply click the link to find the full record for the citation showing its location and availability (Figure 18–7). As Figure 18–7 shows, you have several options, including saving the search. If the sources are not quite what you're looking for, you could use some of the suggested subject

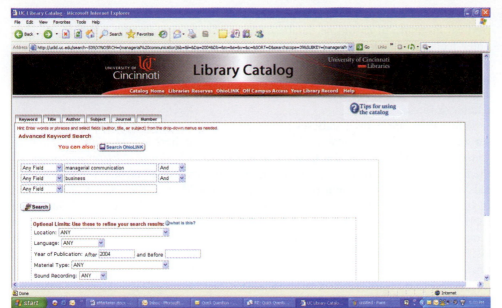

Figure 18–8

Illustration of "Modify Search" Options

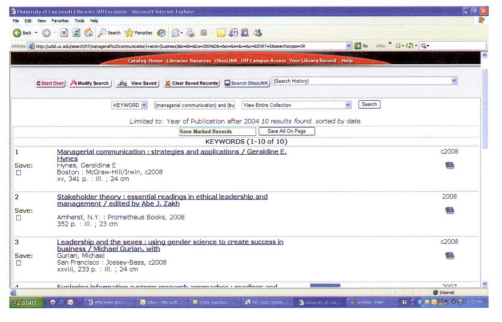

Figure 18–9

Results of the Modified Search

headings to conduct a new search or modify your current search. In the example shown in Figure 18–8, the researcher modified the search by adding a new search term with the operator "and." The results (shown in Figure 18–9) are focused a bit more narrowly because every entry had to have been categorized under both "managerial communication" and "business."

The online catalog is a useful source of information about your library's holdings. Learning how to use it effectively will save you time and will help your searches be fast and accurate.

Online Databases. The online catalog helps you identify books and other holdings in your library. To identify articles published in newspapers, magazines, or journals, you will need to consult an index, either a general one or one that specializes in the field you are researching. Regularly updated indexes are available both online and in the reference section of most libraries.

● To identify articles for your list of prospective sources, consult an index.

- Computer databases hold much of the information recorded in print and accessed through indexes.

- Knowing which online databases to use helps business researchers find the kind of information they need.

- Skilled use of Boolean logic operators—AND, OR, and NOT—helps you retrieve the kind of information needed.

If you are like most business researchers today, you will start your search for periodical literature in an online database. As the sophistication and capacity of computer technology have improved, much of the information that was once routinely recorded in print form and accessed through directories, encyclopedias, and indexes is now stored electronically in computer files. These files, known as *databases,* are accessed through the use of search strategies. However, one first needs to identify which databases to use.

While there are many databases produced by private and government information services, some of those most useful to business researchers are *ABI/Inform, Factiva, LexisNexis Academic,* and the *Business and Industry Database. ABI/Inform* is one of the most complete databases, providing access to hundreds of business research journals as well as important industry trade publications. Most of the articles are included in full text or with lengthy summaries. It allows basic, guided, and natural language searching. *Factiva,* on the other hand, provides access to current business, general, and international news, including access to various editions of *The Wall Street Journal.* It also includes current information on U.S. public companies and industries. Similarly, *LexisNexis* offers access to current business and international articles, providing them in full text (see Figure 18–10). Additionally, it includes legal and reference information. Finally, the *Business and Industry Database* covers over 1,000 trade publications, emphasizing facts, figures, and key events. Over 60 percent of its contents are full text, and the remaining include key figures and facts.

Once researchers know where to begin, their search skills become critical. A good command of Boolean logic combined with the knowledge of how to implement it in the databases (or Internet search engines) used will help researchers extract the information they need quickly and accurately. Boolean logic uses three primary operators: AND, OR, and NOT. If search results yield more citations than you need, the results can be limited. Similar to the online catalog, most databases in the guided or advanced mode allow users to limit the search by article or publication type as well as by date, but the use of Boolean logic operators allows users

Figure 18–10

Illustration of *LexisNexis* Search Results

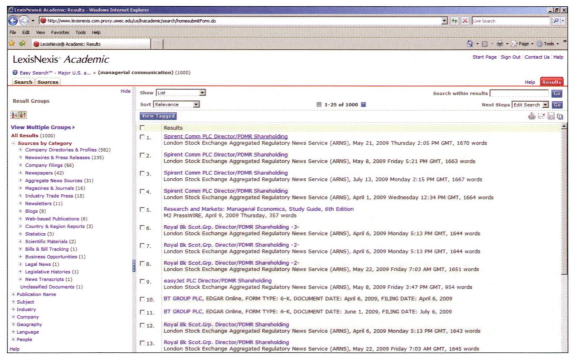

to focus the subject matter more tightly, eliminating citations that are unrelated or tangential to the problem being discussed.

The operator AND is a narrowing term. It instructs the computer to find citations with both terms. The operator NOT is another narrowing term, instructing the computer to eliminate citations with a particular term. It should be used as a last resort because it can eliminate potentially good sources. For example, if one were searching for articles on venture capital, using the NOT term in an attempt to eliminate DotCom companies might eliminate good articles where DotCom was mentioned as an aside or even an article that compared DotCom companies to other funded companies. If a search results in few citations, the OR operator can be used to expand the search by adding variations or synonyms to the basic search term. A search for articles on DotComs AND accountants might add accounting OR comptroller OR controller to expand its results.

If you have difficulty thinking of terms to broaden your search, look at the keywords or descriptors of the items that have already been identified. Often these will give you ideas for additional terms to use. If the search still comes up short, you need to check for spelling errors or variations. Becoming skilled at using Boolean logic will help you get the information you need when you need it.

The Internet. The Internet is a network of networks. It operates in a structure originally funded by the National Science Foundation. However, no one organization owns or runs this globally connected network. Its users work together to develop standards, which are always changing. The network provides a wide variety of resources, including many useful to business. Since no one is officially in charge, finding information on the Internet can be difficult. Nevertheless, this network of loosely organized computer systems does provide some search and retrieval tools.

- A wide variety of business sources is available through the Internet.

These tools can search for files as well as text on various topics. They can search both titles and the documents themselves. Since the Internet is a rapidly growing medium for publishing, the browsers and major portals incorporate links to search tools. Most of the links currently are to individual search engines such as Google, bing, Hotbot, MSN Search, and Yahoo!. Some of these engines compile their indexes using human input, some use software robots, and some use a combination. Google, whose simple, clean screens you see in Figures 18–11 through 18–15, provides users with much more than the ability to search Web pages. From the primary search page, users can search images, groups, directories, and news as well as link to advanced search and translation tools. In Figure 18–11, you may notice that the terms *venture capital women* are entered without the Boolean operator AND. Google automatically ANDs all terms, freeing the user from having to add the operator each time a search is conducted. By hitting enter (or clicking the Google Search button), you execute the search. Notice the result in Figure 18–12: 2,290,000 links found in .12 of a second.

- Using online individual search tools will help you find files and text.

Figure 18–11

Illustration of an Individual Web Search Engine—Google
Source: Copyright © Google, Inc., reprinted with permission.

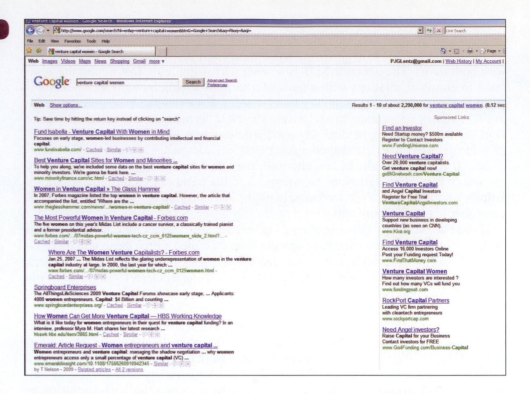

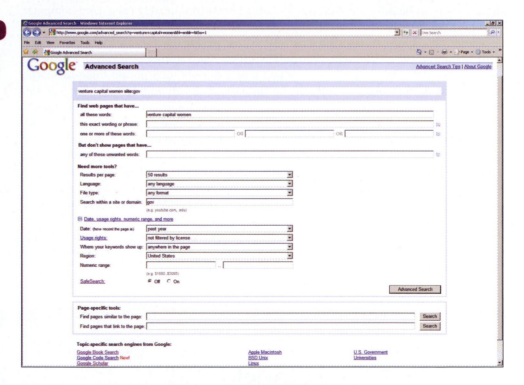

To limit this search, you could use the advanced search tool shown in Figure 18–13. Notice how the first search line (**all**) uses a built-in AND operator, and the third line (**at least one**) uses a built-in OR operator. Additionally, the advanced search allows its user to limit by language, English in this case, and by type of site, .gov here. When this search was run, its results were those shown in Figure 18–14: 4,250 links found in .89 of a second. To further limit the number of links, the user could click on the link *Similar* at the end of any result. It would return the screen you see in Figure 18–15, showing 27 links related to the nwbc.gov site.

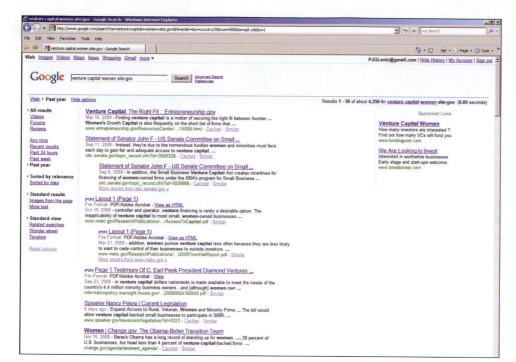

Figure 18–14

An Illustration of Results of an Advanced Search
Source: Copyright © Google, Inc., reprinted with permission.

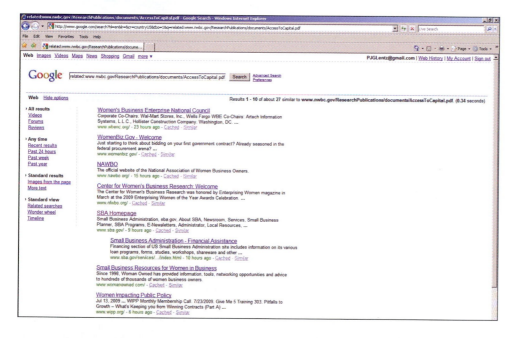

Figure 18–15

An Illustration of Results of a Similar Pages Search
Source: Copyright © Google, Inc., reprinted with permission.

These are only a few of the features of Google. By thoroughly learning the special techniques and features of the search engines you use most frequently, you will find that they can help you immensely in finding the information you need.

As search engines evolve to meet the changing needs of the Internet's content and its users, new forms of these tools have emerged as well. Metasearch tools allow searchers to enter the search terms once, running the search simultaneously with several individual search engines and compiling a combined results page. Examples of these include Dogpile, Kartoo, Mamma, Metacrawler, and Search.com. You will find links to these and other search tools on the textbook website. Figures 18–16 and 18–17 illustrate how Dogpile searches various search engines for the phrase *cross-cultural communication* and then combines the results and presents them in an easy-to-view form.

● Metasearch tools help one use several individual tools more easily.

CHAPTER 18   Business Research Methods

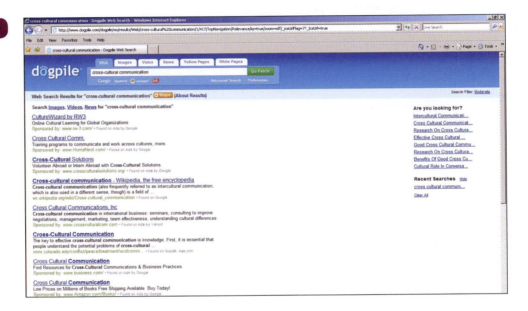

- Specialized search
  engines run efficient
  searches on clearly
  identified subject-related
  sites.

- User-defined agents help
  personalize information
  needs.

- Users must evaluate
  the results carefully
  for both accuracy and
  completeness.

Another type of search tool that has emerged is the specialized search engine. Examples of some of these tools are Yahoo!: People Search for finding people, Deja.com for searching newsgroups, Edgar for finding corporate information, FindLaw for gathering legal information, and Mediafinder for finding print items. There are specialty engines for finding information in finance, music, wireless, medicine, and more. These sites are sometimes referred to as the "invisible web" or "deep web."

Another form of gathering information from the Web is through use of personal agents. These agents allow users to define the kind of information they want to gather. The information gathered can be ready and waiting when users access their personal website, such as at my.yahoo.com, or it can be delivered by email or in the form of "push technology," broadcast directly to the connected user's computer screen. You are using push technology if you have news/traffic/weather updates sent to you.

While these tools assist users in finding helpful Web documents, it is crucial to remember that the tools are limited. You must evaluate the source of the information critically. Also, you must recognize that not all of the documents published on the Web are indexed and that no search tool covers the entire Web. Skill in using the tools plays a role, but judgment in evaluating the accuracy and completeness of the search plays an even more significant role.

Doing More Efficient Repeat Searching through Favorites

Most of the newest versions of today's browsers support tabs, enabling fast and efficient repeat searching. In the background screenshot below, you can see that separate tabs were opened in Internet Explorer 8 to search cross-cultural communication in three different search engines— Alta Vista, Dogpile, and Mamma. It also shows that adding the complete group of tabs to Favorites (called bookmarking in other browsers) can be done in one click. The dialog box shows naming a folder, *Cross-Cultural Searches,* for the collection of tabs. Once they are saved there, you can repeatedly open all tabs in the folder, as in the sample Favorite Sites list below, to run all the searches simultaneously by simply clicking the folder's arrow.

Any search that you need to do repeatedly can be set up this way once and opened whenever you need to review the most recent results.

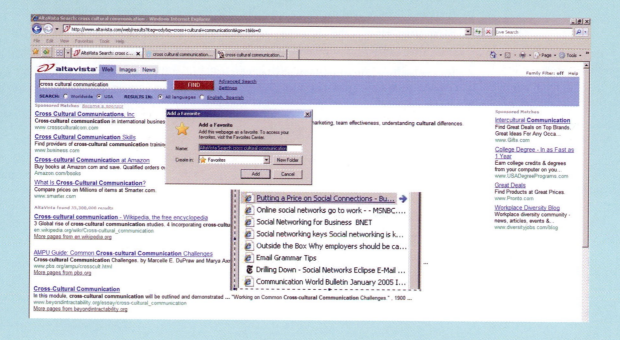

Evaluating Websites

Once you have located information sources, whether print or electronic, you need to evaluate them. Most print sources include items such as author, title of publication, facts of publication, and date in a standard form; however, websites have not yet established a standard form. Additionally, the unmonitored electronic media have introduced many other factors one would want to consider in evaluating the credibility of the source as well as the reliability of the content. For example, most users of search engines do not understand the extent or type of bias introduced in the order in which search engines present their results; they often rely on one exclusively to find the most relevant sites when even the best of them only index an estimated 16 percent of the Internet content.

One solution might be to limit one's use of information only to sites accessed through links from a trustworthy site, a site where others have evaluated the links before posting them. However, these sites are clearly not comprehensive and are often late in providing links to new sources. Therefore, developing the skill and habit of evaluating websites critically is probably a better choice. You can hone this skill by

- All sources need careful evaluation; websites need special attention.

- Research shows that many researchers are overconfident in their ability to judge the reliability of websites.

- You can hone your evaluation skills by habitually asking about the purpose, qualifications, validity, and structure of websites.

getting into the habit of looking at the purpose, qualifications, validity, and structure of the websites one uses.

- **Purpose.** Why was the information provided? To explain? To inform? To persuade? To sell? To share? What are the provider's biases? Who is the intended audience? What point of view does the site take? Could it possibly be ironic, or a satire or parody?

- **Qualifications.** What are the credentials of the information provider? What is the nature of any sponsorship? Is contact information provided? Is it accurate? Is it complete—name, email address, street address, and phone? Is the information well written, clear, and organized?

- **Validity.** Where else can the information provided be found? Is the information the original source? Has the information been synthesized or abstracted accurately and in correct context? Is the information timely? When was it created? When was it posted? Has the site already been validated? Who links to it? (On Google, enter link:*url* to find links.) How long has the site existed? Is it updated regularly? Do the links work? Are they well organized? Are they annotated? Has the site received any ratings or reviews? Is information cited accurately? Do the sources appear credible?

- **Structure.** How is the site organized, designed, and formatted? Does its structure provide a particular emphasis? Does it appeal to its intended audience?

By critically evaluating the websites you use, you will be developing a skill that will help you effectively filter the vast amount of data you encounter.

PRIMARY RESEARCH

● Primary research in business consists of six main methods.

When you cannot find the information you need in secondary sources, you must get it firsthand. That is, you must use primary research. Businesses tend to use six main methods:

1. A search through company records.
2. Experimentation.
3. Observation.
4. Survey.
5. Focus group.
6. Interviews.

Choosing Your Research Strategy

The types of primary research you use will depend on the types of data you need to generate or gather to complete your study. Business researchers work with data that require quantitative research strategies, qualitative research strategies, or mixed-methods strategies (research with both quantitative and qualitative components).

Quantitative Strategies. Quantitative researchers generally begin by constructing a hypothesis to test or developing a very specific research question to answer. They then use primary research methods that generate numeric data such as experimentation, questionnaires, reviews of company data, and surveys. They apply statistical tests to numeric data to see whether the data support or refute their hypothesis or answer their question and also to determine how generalizable or applicable their findings might be to a larger population.

Qualitative Strategies. Qualitative researchers take a more interpretive approach to research. They begin with a more general question about what they want to learn and then study natural phenomena to gather insights into the phenomena or even to learn to ask different questions. Accordingly, they are likely to use research tools that generate verbal data such as reviews of company records, personal interviews, focus groups, and direct observation. Qualitative research does not enable statistical analysis or the application of the findings to larger populations; rather, it enables one to interpret what the data mean at a more localized level.

Neither strategy is superior to the other. Their appropriateness in any research setting is determined by the researcher's goals. And given the complex nature of many business problems, you may often find yourself mixing these approaches. Whatever methods will best tell you what you want to find out are the ones to use.

Searching through Company Records

Since many of today's business problems involve various phases of company operations, a company's internal records—production data, sales records, marketing information, accounting records, and the like—are frequently an excellent source of firsthand information.

- Company records are an excellent source of firsthand information.

There are no standard procedures for finding and gathering information from company records. Recordkeeping systems vary widely from company to company. However, you are well advised to keep the following standards in mind as you conduct your investigation. First, as in any other type of research, you must have a clear idea of the information you need. Undefined, open-ended investigations are not appreciated—nor are they particularly productive. Second, you must clearly understand the ground rules under which you are allowed to review materials. Matters of confidentiality and access should be resolved before you start. And third, if you are not intimately familiar with a company's records or how to access them, you must cooperate with someone who is. The complexity and sensitivity of such materials require that they be reviewed in their proper context.

- Make sure you (1) have a clear idea of the information you need, (2) understand the terms of access and confidentiality, and (3) cooperate with company personnel.

Conducting an Experiment

The experiment is a very useful technique in business research. Originally developed in the sciences, the experiment is an orderly form of testing. In general, it is a form of research in which you systematically manipulate one factor of a problem while holding all the others constant. You measure quantitatively or qualitatively any changes resulting from your manipulations. Then you apply your findings to the problem.

- Experimentation manipulates one factor and holds others constant.

For example, suppose you are conducting research to determine whether a new package design will lead to more sales. You might start by selecting two test cities, taking care that they are as alike as possible on all the characteristics that might affect the problem. Then you would secure information on sales in the two cities for a specified time period before the experiment. Next, for a second specified time period, you would use the new package design in one of the cities and continue to use the old package in the other. During that period, you would keep careful sales records and check to make sure that advertising, economic conditions, competition, and other factors that might have some effect on the experiment remain unchanged. Thus, when the experimentation period is over, you can attribute any differences you found between the sales of the two cities to the change in package design.

Each experiment should be designed to fit the individual requirements of the problem. Nonetheless, a few basic designs underlie most experiments. Becoming familiar with two of the most common designs—the before–after and the controlled before–after—will give you a framework for understanding and applying this primary research technique.

- Design each experiment to fit the problem.

The Before–After Design. The simplest experimental design is the before–after design. In this design, illustrated in Figure 18–18, you select a test group of subjects, measure the variable in which you are interested, and then introduce the experimental factor. After a specified time period, during which the experimental factor has presumably had its effect, you again measure the variable in which you are interested. If there are any differences between the first and second measurements, it is likely that the experimental factor is a cause.

- The before–after design is the simplest. You use just one test group.

Figure 18–18

The Before–After
Experimental Design

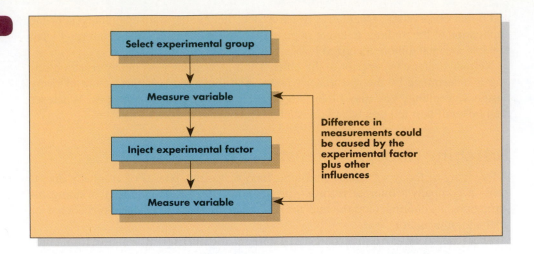

Consider the following application. Assume you are conducting research for a retail store to determine the effect of point-of-sale advertising. Your first step is to select a product for the experiment, Gillette razor blades. Second, you record sales of Gillette blades for one week, using no point-of-sale advertising. Then you introduce the experimental variable: the Gillette point-of-sale display. For the next week you again record sales of Gillette blades; and at the end of that week, you compare the results for the two weeks. Any increase in sales would presumably be explained by the introduction of the display. Thus, if 500 packages of Gillette blades were sold in the first week and 600 were sold in the second week, you would conclude that the 100 additional sales can be attributed to point-of-sale advertising.

You can probably recognize the major shortcoming of the design. It is simply not logical to assume that the experimental factor explains the entire difference in sales between the first week and the second. The sales of Gillette razor blades could have changed for a number of other reasons: changes in the weather, holiday or other seasonal influences on business activity, other advertising, and so on. At best, you have determined only that point-of-sale advertising could influence sales.

The Controlled Before–After Design. To account for influences other than the experimental factors, you may use designs more complex than the before–after design. These designs attempt to measure the other influences by including some means of control. The simplest of these designs is the controlled before–after design.

In the controlled before–after design, you select not one group, but two: the experimental group and the control group. Before introducing the experimental factor, you measure in each group the variable to be tested. Then you introduce the experimental factor into the experimental group only.

When the period allotted for the experiment is over, you again measure in each group the variable being tested. Any difference between the first and second measurements in the experimental group can be explained by two causes: the experimental factor and other influences. But the difference between the first and second measurements in the control group can be explained only by other influences, for this group was not subjected to the experimental factor. Thus, comparing the "afters" of the two groups will give you a measure of the influence of the experimental factor, as diagrammed in Figure 18–19.

In a controlled before–after experiment designed to test point-of-sale advertising, you might select Gillette razor blades and Schick razor blades and record the sales of both brands for one week. Next you introduce point-of-sale displays for Gillette only and you record sales for both Gillette and Schick for a second week. At the end of the second week, you compare the results for the two brands. Whatever difference you find in Gillette sales and Schick sales will be a fair measure of

- The changes recorded in a before–after experiment may not be attributable to the experimental factor alone.

- In the controlled before–after experiment, you use two identical test groups. You introduce the experimental factor into one group, then compare the two groups. You can attribute any difference between the two to the experimental factor.

Figure 18–19

The Controlled Before–After Experimental Design

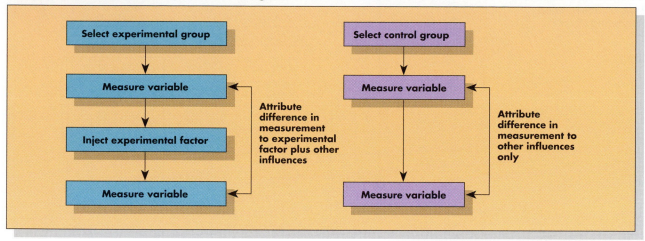

the experimental factor, independent of the changes that other influences may have brought about.

For example, without point-of-sales displays in the control group, if 400 packages of Schick blades are sold the first week and 450 packages are sold the second week, the increase of 50 packages (12.5 percent) can be attributed to influences other than the experimental factor, the point-of-sale display. If 500 packages of Gillette blades are sold the first week and 600 are sold the second week, the increase of 100 can be attributed to both the point-of-sale display and other influences. To distinguish between the two, you note that other influences accounted for the 12.5 percent increase in the sales of Schick blades. Because of the experimental control, you attribute 12.5 percent of the increase in Gillette sales to other influences as well. An increase of 12.5 percent on a base of 500 sales is 63 sales, indicating that 63 of the 100 additional Gillette sales are the result of other influences. However, the sale of 37 additional packages of Gillette blades can be attributed to point-of-sale advertising.

Using the Observation Technique

Like the experiment, observation is a technique perfected in the sciences that is also useful in business research. Simply stated, observation is seeing with a purpose. It consists of watching the events involved in a problem and systematically recording what is seen. In observation, you do not manipulate the details of what you observe; you take note of situations exactly as you find them.

- Research by observation involves watching phenomena and recording what is seen.

Note that observation as an independent research technique is different from the observation you use in recording the effects of variables introduced into a test situation. In the latter case, observation is a step in the experiment, not an end in itself. The two methods, therefore, should not be confused.

- This form of observation does not involve experimentation.

To see how observation works as a business technique, consider this situation. You work for a fast-food chain, such as McDonald's, that wants to check the quality and consistency of some menu items throughout the chain. By hiring observers, sometimes called mystery shoppers, you can gather information on the temperature, freshness, and speed of delivery of various menu items. This method may reveal important information that other data collection methods cannot.

Like all primary research techniques, observation must be designed to fit the requirements of the problem being considered. However, the planning stage generally requires two steps. First, you construct a recording form; second, you design a systematic procedure for observing and recording the information of interest.

- Observation requires a systematic procedure for observing and recording.

Figure 18–20

Excerpt from a Common Type of Observation Recording Form

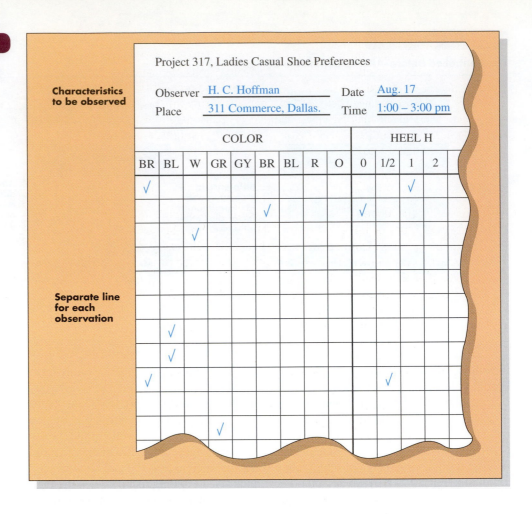

Project 317, Ladies Casual Shoe Preferences

Characteristics to be observed

Observer   H. C. Hoffman   Date   Aug. 17
Place   311 Commerce, Dallas.   Time   1:00 – 3:00 pm

Separate line for each observation

| COLOR | | | | | | | | | HEEL H | | | |
BR	BL	W	GR	GY	BR	BL	R	O	0	1/2	1	2
√											√	
				√					√			
		√										
	√											
	√											
√											√	
			√									

- The recording form should enable you to record details quickly and accurately.

The recording form may be any tabular arrangement that permits quick and easy recording of that information. Though observation forms are hardly standardized, one commonly used arrangement (see Figure 18–20) provides a separate line for each observation. Headings at the top of the page mark the columns in which the observer will place the appropriate mark. The recording form identifies the characteristics that are to be observed and requires the recording of such potentially important details as the date, time, and place of the observation and the name of the observer.

"We sent you on a fact-finding mission and all you found were two facts?"

Source: © 2000 Benita Epstein. Reprinted with permission.

The observation procedure may be any system that ensures the collection of complete and representative information. But every effective observation procedure includes a clear focus, well-defined steps, and provisions for ensuring the quality of the information collected. For example, an observation procedure for determining the courtesy of employees toward customers when answering the telephone would include a detailed schedule for making calls, detailed instructions on what to ask, and provisions for dealing with different responses the observer might encounter. In short, the procedure would leave no major question unanswered.

• An effective observation procedure ensures the collection of complete and representative information.

Collecting Information by Survey

The premise of the survey as a method of primary research is simple: You can best acquire certain types of information by asking questions. Such information includes personal data, opinions, evaluations, and other important material. It also includes information necessary to plan for an experiment or an observation or to supplement or interpret the data that result.

• You can best acquire certain information by asking questions.

Once you have decided to use the survey for your research, you have to make decisions about a number of matters. The first is the matter of format. The questions can range from spontaneous inquiries to carefully structured interrogations. The next is the matter of delivery. The questions can be posed in a personal interview, asked over the telephone, or presented in printed or electronic form.

• Decide which survey format and delivery will be most effective in developing the information you need.

But the most important is the matter of whom to survey. Except for situations in which a small number of people are involved in the problem under study, you cannot reach all the people involved. Thus, you have to select a sample of respondents who represent the group as a whole as accurately as possible. There are several ways to select that sample, as you will see.

• Also decide whom to interview. If the subject group is large, select a sample.

Sampling as a Basis. Sampling theory forms the basis for most research by survey, though it has any number of other applications as well. Buyers of grain, for example, judge the quality of a multi-ton shipment by examining a few pounds. Quality-control supervisors spot-check a small percentage of products ready for distribution to determine whether production standards are being met. Auditors for large corporations sample transactions when examining the books. Sampling is generally used for economy and practicality. However, for a sample to be representative of the whole group, it must be designed properly.

• Survey research is based on sampling.

Two important aspects to consider in sample design are controlling for sampling error and bias. Sampling error results when the sample is not representative of the whole group. While all samples have some degree of sampling error, you can reduce the error through techniques used to construct representative samples. These techniques fall into two groups: probability and nonprobability sampling.

• Good samples are reliable, valid, and controlled for sampling error.

Probability Sampling Techniques. Probability samples are based on chance selection procedures. Every element in the population has a known nonzero probability of selection.[1] These techniques include simple random sampling, stratified random sampling, systematic sampling, and area or cluster sampling.

Random Sampling. Random sampling is the technique assumed in the general law of sampling. By definition, it is the sampling technique that gives every member of the group under study an equal chance of being included. To assure equal chances, you must first identify every member of the group and then, using a list or some other convenient format, record all the identifications. Next, through some chance method, you select the members of your sample.

• In random sampling, every item in the subject group has an equal chance of being selected.

For example, if you are studying the job attitudes of 200 employees and determine that 25 interviews will give you the information you need, you might put the names of

---

[1] William G. Zikmund, *Business Research Methods,* 7th ed. (Mason, OH: South-Western, 2003) 279, print.

Survey Tools Help Writers Lay Out, Analyze, and Report Results of Questionnaires

Survey tools, both software and Web-based tools, help you design professional-looking questionnaires as well as compile and analyze the data collected. Software programs help with construction and layout of questionnaires and allow you to convert the questionnaires to html format for publishing on the Web easily. Web-based programs help you create, distribute, and manage data collection for online questionnaires.

Special data entry screens assist you in selecting the types of questions and desired layout. They then arrange the questionnaire automatically while giving you the freedom to move the questions to change the ordering and arrangement if desired. The tools also let you create open-ended questions. All of these questions can be saved in a library for reuse. Some of the tools even include libraries of surveys that can be adapted for one's particular use.

As shown, one program, SurveyMonkey.com, creates graphics that help you see the results clearly and accurately as the questionnaires are being submitted.

Businesses can use these tools in a variety of applications, including training program evaluations, employee feedback on policies and procedures, longitudinal studies of ongoing practices such as network advertising revenues, opinion surveys of customers and potential customers, and feedback on customer satisfaction.

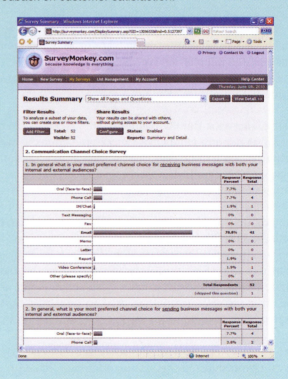

each worker in a container, mix them thoroughly, and draw out 25. Since each of the 200 workers has an equal chance of being selected, your sample will be random and can be presumed to be representative.

Stratified Random Sampling. Stratified random sampling subdivides the group under study and makes random selections within each subgroup. The size of each subgroup is usually proportionate to that subgroup's percentage of the whole. If a subgroup is too small to yield meaningful findings, however, you may have to select a disproportionately large sample. Of course, when the study calls for statistics on the group as a whole, the actual proportion of such a subgroup must be restored.

- In stratified random sampling, the group is divided into subgroups and the sample is randomly selected from each subgroup.

Assume, for example, that you are attempting to determine the curriculum needs of 5,000 undergraduates at a certain college and that you have decided to survey 20 percent of the enrollment, or 1,000 students. To construct a sample for this problem, first divide the enrollment list by academic concentration: business, liberal arts, nursing, engineering, and so forth. Then draw a random sample from each of these groups, making sure that the number you select is proportionate to that group's percentage of the total undergraduate enrollment. Thus, if 30 percent of the students are majoring in business, you will randomly select 300 business majors for your sample; if 40 percent of the students are liberal arts majors, you will randomly select 400 liberal arts majors for your sample; and so on.

Systematic Sampling. Systematic sampling, though not random in the strictest sense, is random for all practical purposes. It is the technique of taking selections at constant intervals (every *n*th unit) from a list of the items under study. The interval used is based, as you might expect, on the size of the list and the size of the desired sample. For example, if you want a 10 percent sample of a list of 10,000, you might select every 10th item on the list.

- In systematic sampling, the items are selected from the subject group at constant intervals.

However, your sample would not really be random. By virtue of their designated place on the original list, items do not have an equal chance of being selected. To correct that problem, you might use an equal-chance method to determine what *n* to use. Thus, if you selected the number 7 randomly, you would draw the numbers 7, 17, 27, and so on to 9,997 to make up your sample. Or, if you wanted to draw every 10th item, you might first scramble the list and then select from the revised list numbers 10, 20, 30, and so on up to 10,000 and make up your sample that way.

- Select the interval randomly or scramble the order of the subject group if you want your systematic sample to be random.

Area or Cluster Sampling. In area sampling, the items for a sample are drawn in stages. This sampling technique is appropriate when the area to be studied is large and can be broken down into progressively smaller components. For example, if you want to draw an area sample for a certain city, you may use census data to divide the city into homogeneous districts. Using an equal-chance method, you then select a given number of districts to include in the next stage of your sample. Next you divide each of the selected districts into subdistricts—city blocks, for example. Continuing the process, you randomly select a given number of these blocks and subdivide each of them into households. Finally, using random sampling once more, you select the households that will constitute the sample you will use in your research.

- For an area or cluster sample, draw items from the subject group in stages. Select randomly at each stage.

Area or cluster sampling is not limited to geographic division, however. It is adaptable to any number of applications. For example, it is an appropriate technique to use in a survey of the employees in a given industry. An approach that you may take in this situation is to randomly select a given number of companies from a list of all the companies in the industry. Then, using organization units and selecting randomly at each level, you break down each of these companies into divisions, departments, sections, and so on until you finally identify the workers you will survey.

Nonprobability Sampling Techniques. Nonprobability samples are based on an unknown probability of any one of a population being chosen. These techniques include convenience sampling, quota sampling, and referral sampling.[2]

- Convenience samples are chosen for their convenience, their ease and economy of reaching subjects, and their appropriateness.

Convenience Sampling. A convenience sample is one whose members are convenient and economical to reach. When professors use their students as subjects for their research, they are using a convenience sample. Researchers generally use this sample to reach a large number quickly and economically. This kind of sampling is best used for exploratory research.

A form of convenience sampling is *judgment* or *expert* sampling. This technique relies on the judgment of the researcher to identify appropriate members of the sample. Illustrating this technique is the common practice of predicting the outcome of an election, based on the results in a bellwether district.

- Setting quotas ensures that the sample reflects the whole. Choose items randomly within each quota.

Quota Sampling. Quota sampling is another nonrandom technique. Also known as *controlled sampling,* it is used whenever the proportionate makeup of the universe under study is available. The technique requires that you refer to the composition of the universe in designing your sample, selecting items so that your sample has the same characteristics in the same proportion as that universe. Specifically, it requires that you set quotas for each characteristic that you want to consider in your research problem. Within those quotas, however, you will select individual items randomly.

Let us say that you want to survey a college student body of 4,000 using a 10 percent sample. As Figure 18–21 illustrates, you have a number of alternatives for determining the makeup of your sample, depending on the focus of your research. Keep in

Figure 18–21

Example of Quota Sample

	Number in Universe	Percent of Total	Number to Be Interviewed
Total student enrollment	4,000	100	400
Sex			
Men students	2,400	60	240
Women students	1,600	40	160
Fraternity, sorority membership			
Members	1,000	25	100
Nonmembers	3,000	75	300
Marital status			
Married students	400	10	40
Single students	3,600	90	360
Class rank			
Freshmen	1,600	40	160
Sophomores	1,000	25	100
Juniors	800	20	80
Seniors	400	10	40
Graduates	200	5	20

[2] Zikmund 279.

mind, though, that no matter what characteristic you select, the quotas the individual segments represent must total 100 percent and the number of items in the sample must total 400. Keep in mind also that within these quotas you will use an equal-chance method to select the individual members of your sample.

Referral Sampling. Referral samples are those whose members are identified by others from a random sample. This technique is used to locate members when the population is small or hard to reach. For example, you might want to survey rolle bolle players. To get a sample large enough to make the study worthwhile, you could ask those from your town to give you the names of other players. Perhaps you are trying to survey the users of project management software. You could survey a user's group and ask those members for names of other users. You might even post your announcement on a newsgroup or listserv; users of the system would send you the names for your sample.

- Referral samples are used for small or hard-to-reach groups.

Constructing the Questionnaire.

Most orderly interrogation follows a definite plan of inquiry. This plan is usually worked out in a published (print or electronic) form, called the *questionnaire*. The questionnaire is simply an orderly arrangement of the questions, with appropriate spaces provided for the answers. But simple as the finished questionnaire may appear to be, it is the subject of careful planning. You should plan carefully so that the results are *reliable;* a test of a questionnaire's reliability is its repeatability with similar results. You also want your questionnaire to be *valid,* measuring what it is supposed to measure. It is, in a sense, the outline of the analysis of the problem. In addition, it must observe certain rules. These rules sometimes vary with the problem. The more general and by far the more important ones follow.

- Construct a questionnaire carefully so that the results it provides are both reliable and valid.

Avoid Leading Questions. A leading question is one that in some way influences the answer. For example, the question "Is Dove your favorite bath soap?" leads the respondent to favor Dove. Some people who would say "yes" would name another brand if they were asked, "What is your favorite brand of bath soap?"

- Avoid leading questions (questions that influence the answer).

Make the Questions Easy to Understand. Questions not clearly understood by all respondents lead to error. Unfortunately, it is difficult to determine in advance just what respondents will not understand. As will be mentioned later, the best means of detecting such questions in advance is to test the questions before using them. But you can be on the alert for a few general sources of confusion.

One source of confusion is vagueness of expression, which is illustrated by the ridiculous question "How do you bank?" Who other than its author knows what the question means? Another source is using words respondents do not understand, as in the question "Do you read your house organ regularly?" The words *house organ* have a specialized, not widely known meaning, and *regularly* means different things to different people. Combining two questions in one is yet another source of confusion. For example, "Why did you buy a Ford?" actually asks two questions: "What do you like about Fords?" and "What don't you like about the other automobiles?"

- Word the questions so that all the respondents understand them.

- Vagueness of expression, difficult words, and two questions in one cause misunderstanding.

Avoid Questions That Touch on Personal Prejudices or Pride. For reasons of pride or prejudices, people cannot be expected to answer accurately questions about certain areas of information. These areas include age, income status, morals, and personal habits. How many people, for example, would answer no to the question "Do you brush your teeth daily?" How many people would give their ages correctly? How many solid citizens would admit to fudging a bit on their tax returns? The answers are obvious.

But one may ask, "What if such information is essential to the solution of the problem?" The answer is to use less direct means of inquiry. To ascertain age, for example, investigators could ask for dates of high school graduation, marriage, or the like. From this information, they could approximate age. Or they could approximate

- Avoid questions of a personal nature.

- But if personal questions are necessary, use less direct methods.

age through observation, although this procedure is acceptable only if broad age approximations would be satisfactory. They could ask for such harmless information as occupation, residential area, and standard of living and then use that information as a basis for approximating income. Another possibility is to ask range questions such as "Are you between 18 and 24, 25 and 40, or over 40?" This technique works well with income questions, too. People are generally more willing to answer questions worded by ranges rather than specifics. Admittedly, such techniques are sometimes awkward and difficult. But they can improve on the biased results that direct questioning would obtain.

- Seek factual information whenever possible.

Seek Facts as Much as Possible. Although some studies require opinions, it is far safer to seek facts whenever possible. Human beings simply are not accurate reporters of their opinions. They are often limited in their ability to express themselves. Frequently, they report their opinions erroneously simply because they have never before been conscious of having them.

When opinions are needed, it is usually safer to record facts and then to judge the thoughts behind them. This technique, however, is only as good as the investigators' judgment. But a logical analysis of fact made by trained investigators is preferable to a spur-of-the-moment opinion.

A frequent violation of this rule results from the use of generalizations. Respondents are sometimes asked to generalize an answer from a large number of experiences over time. The question "Which magazines do you read regularly?" is a good illustration. Aside from the confusion caused by the word *regularly* and the fact that the question may tap the respondent's memory, the question forces the respondent to generalize. Would it not be better to phrase it in this way: "What magazines have you read this month?" The question could then be followed by an article-by-article check of the magazines to determine the extent of readership.

- Ask only for information that can be remembered.

Ask Only for Information That Can Be Remembered. Since the memory of all human beings is limited, the questionnaire should ask only for information that the respondents can be expected to remember. To make sure that this is done, you need to know certain fundamentals of memory.

- Memory is determined by three fundamentals: (1) recency,

Recency is the foremost fundamental. People remember insignificant events that occurred within the past few hours. By the next day, they will forget some. A month later they may not remember any. One might well remember, for example, what one ate for lunch on the day of the inquiry, and perhaps one might remember what one ate for lunch a day, or two days, or three days earlier. But one would be unlikely to remember what one ate for lunch a year earlier.

- (2) intensity of stimulus, and

The second fundamental of memory is that significant events may be remembered over long periods. One may long remember the first day of school, the day of one's wedding, an automobile accident, a Christmas Day, and the like. In each of these examples there was an intense stimulus—a requisite for retention in memory.

- (3) association.

A third fundamental of memory is that fairly insignificant facts may be remembered over long time periods through association with something significant. Although one would not normally remember what one ate for lunch a year earlier, for example, one might remember if the date happened to be one's wedding day, Christmas Day, or one's first day at college. Obviously, the memory is stimulated not by the meal itself but by the association of the meal with something more significant.

- Design the form for each recording.

Plan the Physical Layout with Foresight. The overall design of the questionnaire should be planned to facilitate recording, analyzing, and tabulating the answers. Three major considerations are involved in such planning.

- Provide sufficient space.

First, sufficient space should be allowed for recording answers. When practical, a system for checking answers may be set up. Such a system must always provide for all possible answers, including conditional answers. For example, a direct question may provide for three possible answers: Yes _____, No _____, and Don't know _____.

Second, adequate space for identifying and describing the respondent should be provided. In some instances, such information as the age, sex, and income bracket of the respondent is vital to the analysis of the problem and should be recorded. In other instances, little or no identification is necessary.

● Provide adequate identification space.

Third, the best possible sequence of questions should be used. In some instances, starting with a question of high interest value may have psychological advantages. In other instances, it may be best to follow some definite order of progression. Frequently, some questions must precede others because they help explain the others. Whatever the requirements of the individual case may be, however, careful and logical analysis should be used in determining the sequence of questions.

● Arrange the questions in logical order.

Use Scaling When Appropriate. It is sometimes desirable to measure the intensity of the respondents' feelings about something (an idea, a product, a company, and so on). In such cases, some form of scaling is generally useful.

● Provide for scaling when appropriate.

Of the various techniques of scaling, ranking and rating deserve special mention. These are the simpler techniques and, some believe, the more practical. They are less sophisticated than some others,[3] but the more sophisticated techniques are beyond the scope of this book.

The ranking technique consists simply of asking the respondent to rank a number of alternative answers to a question in order of preference (1, 2, 3, and so on). For example, in a survey to determine consumer preferences for toothpaste, the respondent might be asked to rank toothpastes A, B, C, D, and E in order of preference. In this example, the alternatives could be compared on the number of preferences stated for each. This method of ranking and summarizing results is reliable despite its simplicity. More complicated ranking methods (such as the use of paired comparison) and methods of recording results are also available.

● Ranking of responses is one form.

The rating technique graphically sets up a scale showing the complete range of possible attitudes on a matter and assigns number values to the positions on the scale. The respondent must then indicate the position on the scale that indicates his or her attitude on that matter. Typically, the numeral positions are described by words, as the example in Figure 18–22 illustrates.

● Rating is another.

Because the rating technique deals with the subjective rather than the factual, it is sometimes desirable to use more than one question to cover the attitude being measured. Logically, the average of a person's answers to such questions gives a more reliable answer than does any single answer.

Selecting the Manner of Questioning. You can get responses to the questions you need answered in three primary ways: by personal (face-to-face) contact, by telephone, or by mail (print or electronic). You should select the way that in your unique case gives the best sample, the lowest cost, and the best results. By *best sample* we

● Select the way of asking the questions (by personal contact, telephone, or mail) that gives the best sample, the lowest cost, and best results.

Figure 18–22

Illustration of a Rating Question

What is your opinion of current right-to-work legislation?

Strongly oppose	Moderately oppose	Mildly oppose	Neutral	Mildly favor	Moderately favor	Strongly favor
−3	−2	−1	0	1	2	3

---

[3] Equivalent interval techniques (developed by L. L. Thurstone), scalogram analysis (developed by Louis Guttman), and the semantic differential (developed by C. E. Osgood, G. J. Suci, and P. H. Tannenbaum) are more complex techniques.

Figure 18–23

Comparison of Data
Collection Methods

	Personal	Telephone	Online	Mail
Data collection costs	High	Medium	Low	Low
Data collection time required	Medium	Low	Medium	High
Sample size for a given budget	Small	Medium	Large	Large
Data quantity per respondent	High	Medium	Low	Low
Reaches high proportion of public	Yes	Yes	No	Yes
Reaches widely dispersed sample	No	Maybe	Yes	Yes
Reaches special locations	Yes	Maybe	No	No
Interaction with respondents	Yes	Yes	No	No
Degree of interviewer bias	High	Medium	None	None
Severity of nonresponse bias	Low	Low	High	High
Presentation of visual stimuli	Yes	No	Yes	Maybe
Field-worker training required	Yes	Yes	No	No

Source: Pamela L. Alreck and Robert B. Settle, *The Survey Research Handbook,* 3rd ed. (Burr Ridge, IL: McGraw-Hill/Irwin, 2004) 33, print. © The McGraw-Hill Companies. Used by permission.

mean respondents who best represent the group concerned. And *results* are the information you need. As you can see in Figure 18–23, other factors will influence your choice.

- Develop a working plan that covers all the steps and all the problems.

Developing a Working Plan. After selecting the manner of questioning, you should carefully develop a working plan for the survey. As well as you can, you should anticipate and determine how to handle every possible problem. If you are conducting a mail or Web survey, for example, you need to develop an explanatory message that moves the subjects to respond, tells them what to do, and answers all the questions they are likely to ask (see Figure 18–24). If you are conducting a personal or telephone survey, you need to cover this information in instructions to the interviewers. You should develop your working plan before conducting the pilot study discussed in the following section. You should test that plan in the pilot study and revise it based on the knowledge you gain from the pilot study.

Figure 18–24

Illustration of a Cover
Message for an Online
Survey

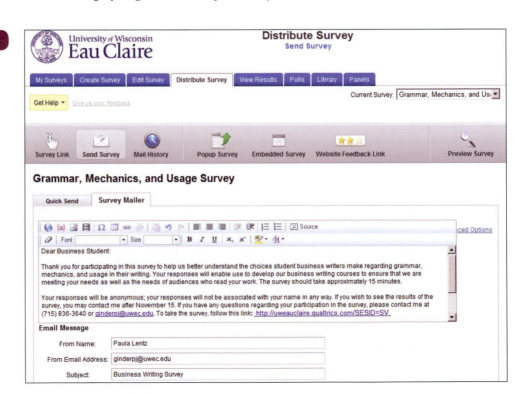

Conducting a Pilot Study. Before doing the survey, it is advisable to conduct a pilot study on your questionnaire and working plan. A pilot study is a small-scale version of the actual survey. Its purpose is to test what you have planned. Based on your experience in the pilot study, you modify your questionnaire and working plan for use in the full-scale survey that follows.

- Test the questionnaire and the working plan. Make any changes needed.

Conducting Focus Groups

The purpose of a focus group is to bring together a group of people to find out their beliefs or attitudes about the topic of a research project. For instance, if you want to find information about how one of your company's products might be improved, you might gather a group of people who currently use your product and have them discuss what they like or don't like about it.

As the moderator of the discussion, you can structure the conversation and ask questions that will elicit useful data from the participants, or you can simply allow participants to voice their ideas. As you may have experienced, when people discuss a topic in a group, they often generate more or new ideas that they may not have done working individually. The focus group can create a sort of brainstorming session of ideas that yield rich data. Of course, as the moderator you also have to make sure that people can freely share their ideas. Some of the tips discussed in Chapters 10 and 13 for encouraging participation in writing projects and meetings may also help you facilitate focus groups. Because of advances in technology, focus groups can be conducted face-to-face, online, or even over the phone.

- Participants in a focus group can generate much useful data.

Conducting Personal Interviews

If you decide that talking with people one-on-one is the best way to gather data to answer your research question, you will likely conduct face-to-face interviews or phone interviews. People may be willing to share their stories and opinions in a personal interview that they might not be comfortable sharing in a larger group.

Preparing for a personal interview is much like preparing for a survey. First, you need to decide whom to interview (your sample). Then you need to construct questions, as you would for a survey. However, the nature of the questions for a face-to-face interview will be a bit different. Many researchers prefer to use closed-ended questions in surveys. Closed-ended questions force the participants into giving only one possible response (e.g., answering a yes/no question, choosing an age range from a list provided by the researcher, or selecting a rating on a scale) and allow for quick data analysis. However, many researchers favor open-ended questions when they construct face-to-face interviews because the conversational nature of the interview setting enables participants to provide detailed, rich, and varied responses. Furthermore, open-ended questions in personal interviews provide the researcher with the opportunity to ask follow-up questions that they would not be able to ask participants taking a written survey.

- Closed-ended questions force the participants to give only one response; open-ended questions allow participants to give a variety of responses.

Whether you conduct a personal interview, convene a focus group, or otherwise gather oral data, you need to decide how you will record the interactions. You cannot rely on your memory. Sometimes, simply taking notes is sufficient. Other times, you may want to record the session so that you can note nonverbal behaviors (e.g., tone, facial expressions, gestures) that influence the interpretation of a participant's response. Then transcribe the notes using a system for coding these nonverbal behaviors in the text of the transcript.

Evaluating and Reporting Data

Gathering information is one step in processing facts for your report. You also need to evaluate it. In the case of secondary research, ask yourself questions about the writer's credibility, including methods of collecting facts and ability to draw inferences from the facts presented. Does the author draw conclusions that can be supported by

- Carefully evaluate the secondary information you find.

● Report statistics from primary research clearly and completely.

As for primary research, this chapter has discussed how to plan and carry out primary data collection properly. Once you have good data to work with, you must interpret them accurately and clearly for your reader (see Chapter 10 for advice on interpreting). If you are unsure of your reader's level of expertise in understanding descriptive statistics such as measures of central tendency and cross-tabulations, present the statistic and tell the reader what it means. In general, you can expect to explain the statistics from univariate, bivariate, and multivariate analyses. In many cases, graphics help tremendously because they clearly show trends and relationships. Statistical programs such as SPSS and SAS help you analyze, report, and graph your data. Finally, you have an ethical responsibility to present your data honestly and completely.

Omitting an error or limitation of the data collection is often viewed as seriously as hiding errors or variations from accepted practices. Of course, any deliberate distortion of the data, whether primary or secondary, is unethical. It is your responsibility to communicate the findings of the report accurately and clearly.

Conducting Ethical Business Research

Many companies, academic institutions, and medical facilities have guidelines for conducting research with human subjects and have institutional review boards (IRBs) that ensure employees comply with the laws and policies that govern research. Be sure that you are familiar with these policies before conducting research.

The main principle behind such policies is that participants in a research study have the right to informed consent. That is, they have the right to know the nature of their participation in the study and any associated risks. In addition, participants' participation must be voluntary, and they also have the right to discontinue their participation at any time during the study. Just because they agreed to participate at one point does not mean they are obligated to finish the project. Furthermore, participants need to know if their participation and data associated with them in the study are confidential (known only to the researcher and participant) or anonymous (known only to the participant).

Because protecting participants' rights can require you to develop a proposal to an IRB, an informed consent letter to the participants, and an informed consent form, be sure you build this process into the planning stage of your project.

SUMMARY BY LEARNING OBJECTIVES

1 Explain the difference between primary and secondary research.

1. Primary research is firsthand research. It can be quantitative, qualitative, or both. You can conduct primary research in six main ways:
   - Looking through company records.
   - Conducting an experiment.
   - Recording observations.
   - Conducting a survey.
   - Conducting a focus group.
   - Conducting interviews.

Secondary research is secondhand research. You conduct secondary research in either a general library (usually public), a special library (usually private), or online.

2. If you need quantitative or factual information, you may be able to go directly to it, using such sources as the following:

- Encyclopedias.
- Biographical directories.
- Almanacs.
- Trade directories.
- Government publications.
- Dictionaries.
- Statistical sources.
- Business information services.

When you cannot go directly to the source, you use indirect methods. You may begin by searching the following sources:

- The online catalog of a library.
- Online databases.
- The Internet.

3. Websites must be critically evaluated to ensure that the information is relevant and reliable. You can hone this skill by looking at the purpose of each site, the qualifications of the information provider, the validity of the content, and the organizational structure and design format.

4. Company records are usually confidential. You must either ask the person responsible for the information for it or gather it yourself from company records.

5. An experiment is an orderly form of testing. It can be designed using the before–after design or the controlled before–after design.

- The simplest is the before–after design. It involves selecting a group of subjects, measuring the variable, introducing the experimental factor, and measuring the variable again. The difference between the two measurements is assumed to be the result of the experimental factor.

- The controlled before–after design involves selecting two groups, measuring the variable in both groups, introducing the experimental factor in one group, and then measuring the variable again in both groups. The second measurement enables you to determine the effect of the experimental factor and of other factors that might have influenced the variable between the two measurements.

6. The observation method may be defined as seeing with a purpose. It consists of watching the events involved in a problem and systematically recording what is seen. The events observed are not manipulated.

7. A sample is a group representative of the whole group. The procedure for selecting the group is called sampling. A good sample is controlled for sampling error. You may use any of a variety of sample designs. Those discussed in this chapter include probability and nonprobability sampling.

- Probability sampling is based on chance selection procedures. Every element in the population has a known nonzero probability of selection. Some of the techniques are described below.

 — Simple random sampling involves chance selection, giving every member of the group under study an equal chance of being selected.

 — Stratified random sampling involves proportionate and random selection from each major subgroup of the group under study.

2 Gather secondary sources using direct and indirect research methods.

3 Evaluate websites for reliability.

4 Describe the procedures for searching through company records.

5 Conduct an experiment for a business problem.

6 Design an observational study for a business problem.

7 Use sampling to conduct a survey.

— Systematic sampling involves taking selections at constant intervals (every fifth one, for example) from a complete list of the group under study.

— Area or cluster sampling involves dividing into parts the area that contains the sample, selecting from these parts randomly, and continuing to subdivide and select until you have your desired sample size.

- Nonprobability sampling is based on an unknown probability of any one of a group being studied. Some of the techniques are described below.

— Convenience sampling involves selecting members that are convenient, easy to reach, and appropriate as judged by the researcher.

— Quota sampling requires that you know the proportions of certain characteristics (sex, age, education, etc.) in the group under study. You then select respondents in the same proportions.

— Referral sampling involves building your sample from other participants' referrals.

8. Construct a questionnaire, develop a working plan, and conduct a pilot test for a survey.

8. The questions you ask should follow a definite plan, usually in the form of a questionnaire. You should construct the questionnaire carefully, ensuring that it is valid and reliable, and the questionnaire should follow these general rules.

- Avoid leading questions.
- Make the questions easy to understand (avoid vagueness, difficult words, technical words).
- Avoid questions that touch on personal prejudices or pride.
- Seek facts as much as possible.
- Ask only for what can be remembered (consider the laws of memory: recency, intensity, and association).
- Plan the layout with foresight (enough space for answers and identifying information, proper sequence of questions).
- Use scaling when appropriate.

You develop a working plan for conducting the questioning—one that covers all the possible problems and clearly explains what to do. It is usually advisable to test the questionnaire and working plan through a pilot study. This enables you to make changes in the questionnaire and improve the working plan before conducting the survey.

9. Explain the purpose of focus groups and personal interviews.

9. Focus groups and personal interviews can be effective ways to gather data when brainstorming or individual stories are important.

10. Analyze and interpret information clearly and completely for your reader.

10. You need to evaluate the facts you gather from secondary research carefully before you include them in your report. Check to make sure they meet the following tests.

- Can the author draw the conclusions from the data presented?
- Are the sources reliable?
- Has the author avoided biased interpretation?
- Are there any gaps in the facts?

You must present the primary information you collect clearly and completely. It is your responsibility to explain statistics the reader may not understand.

11. Explain the ethical considerations for work with human subjects.

11. Researchers must be ethical in their research. Participants must know of any risks the research presents, be able to participate voluntarily, and know whether their data is anonymous or confidential.

1 Suggest a hypothetical research problem that would make good use of a specialized library. Justify your selection. **(LO1, LO2)**

2 What specialized libraries are there in your community? What general libraries? **(LO1, LO2)**

3 Under what general condition are investigators likely to be able to proceed directly to the published source of the information sought? **(LO1, LO2)**

4 Which databases or other sources would be good sources of information for each of the following subjects? **(LO1, LO2)**

   a. Labor–management relations

   b. A certain company's market share

   c. Whether or not a company is being sued

   d. Viewpoints on the effect of deficit financing by governments

   e. The top companies, by sales, in a certain industry

   f. New techniques in interviewing

   g. The job outlook in a certain industry

   h. Recent trends in business-related technology

   i. The potential world market for a certain product

   j. Government regulations for incorporating your business

   k. The qualifications of a new CEO of a company

   l. Promising sites for a new branch of your business

5 Use your critical skills to evaluate websites, identifying those with problems (e.g., false advertising, government misinformation, propaganda, or scam sites). **(LO3)**

6 What is the difference between quantitative and qualitative research? **(LO1)**

7 What advice would you give an investigator who has been assigned a task involving analysis of internal records of several company departments? **(LO4)**

8 Define *experimentation*. What does the technique of experimentation involve? **(LO5)**

9 Explain the significance of keeping constant all factors other than the experimental variable of an experiment. **(LO5)**

10 Give an example of (*a*) a problem that can best be solved through a before–after design and (*b*) a problem that can best be solved through a controlled before–after design. Explain your choices. **(LO5)**

11 Define *observation* as a research technique. **(LO6)**

12 Select an example of a business problem that can be solved best by observation. Explain your choice. **(LO6)**

13 Point out violations of the rules of good questionnaire construction in the following questions. The questions do not come from the same questionnaire. **(LO8)**

   a. How many days on the average do you wear a pair of socks before changing?

   b. (The first question in a survey conducted by Coca-Cola.) Have you ever drunk a Diet Coke?

   c. Do you consider the ideal pay plan to be one based on straight commission or straight salary?

   d. What kind of gasoline did you purchase last time?

   e. How much did you pay for clothing in the past 12 months?

   f. Check the word below that best describes how often you eat dessert with your noon meal.

     Always

     Usually

     Sometimes

     Never

14 Explain the difference between random sampling and convenience sampling. **(LO7)**

15 Develop two business scenarios, one in which a quantitative study would be more appropriate and one in which a qualitative study would be more appropriate. Defend your choices. **(LO9)**

16 Explain the differences between closed-ended and open-ended questions. **(LO9)**

17 When would you use a focus group or personal interview to gather information? What are the advantages and disadvantages of each? **(LO9)**

18 Explain how to evaluate secondary information. **(LO10)**

19 Discuss the writer's responsibility in explaining and reporting data. **(LO10)**

20 What are the basic ethical principles for working with human subjects in business research? **(LO11)**

1 Using your imagination to supply any missing facts you may need, develop a plan for the experiment you would use in the following situations.

a. The Golden Glow Baking Company has for many years manufactured and sold cookies packaged in attractive boxes. It is considering packaging the cookies in recyclable bags and wants to conduct an experiment to determine consumer response to this change.

b. The Miller Brush Company, manufacturers of a line of household goods, has for years sold its products through conventional retail outlets. It now wants to conduct an experiment to test the possibility of selling through catalogs (or home shopping networks or the Web).

c. A national chain of drugstores wants to know whether it would profit by doubling the face value of coupons. It is willing to pay the cost of an experiment in its research for an answer.

d. The True Time Watch Company is considering the use of electronic sales displays ($49.50 each) instead of print displays ($24.50 each) in the 2,500 retail outlets that sell True Time watches. The company will conduct an experiment to determine the relative effects on sales of the two displays.

e. The Marvel Soap Company has developed a new cleaning agent that is unlike current soaps and detergents. The product is well protected by patent. The company wants to determine the optimum price for the new product through experimentation.

f. National Cereals, Inc., wants to determine the effectiveness of advertising to children. Until now, it has been aiming its appeal at parents. The company will support an experiment to learn the answer.

2 Using your imagination to supply any missing facts you may need, develop a plan for research by observation for these problems.

a. A chain of department stores wants to know what causes differences in sales by departments within stores and by stores. Some of this information it hopes to get through research by observation.

b. Your university wants to know the nature and extent of its parking problem.

c. The management of an insurance company wants to determine the efficiency and productivity of its data-entry department.

d. Owners of a shopping center want a study to determine shopping patterns of their customers. Specifically they want to know such things as what parts of town the customers come from, how they travel, how many stores they visit, and so on.

e. The director of your library wants a detailed study of library use (what facilities are used, when, by whom, and so on).

f. The management of a restaurant wants a study of its workers' efficiency in the kitchen.

3 Using your imagination to supply any missing facts you may need, develop a plan for research by survey for these problems.

a. The American Restaurant Association wants information that will give its members a picture of its customers. The information will serve as a guide for a promotional campaign designed to increase restaurant eating. Specifically it will seek such information as who eats out, how often, where they go, how much they spend. Likewise, it will seek to determine who does not eat out and why.

b. The editor of your local daily paper wants a readership study to learn just who reads what in both print and online editions.

c. The National Beef Producers Association wants to determine the current trends in meat consumption. The association wants such information as the amount of meat people consume, whether people have changed their meat consumption habits, and so on.

d. The International Association of Publishers wants a survey of the reading habits of adults in the United States and Canada. It wants such information as who reads what, how much, when, where, and so on. It also wants to gauge reader attitude toward ebooks.

e. Your boss wants to hire an experienced computer webmaster for your company. Because you have not hired anyone in this category in five years, you were asked to survey experienced webmasters using the Web or Usenet groups to gather salary figures.

Physical Presentation of Letters, Memos, and Reports

The appearance of a letter, memo, or report plays a significant role in communicating a message. Attractively presented messages reflect favorably on the writer and the writer's company. They give an impression of competence and care; and they build credibility for the writer. Their attractiveness tells the readers that the writer thinks they are important and deserving of a good-looking document. It reflects on the common courtesy of the writer. On the other hand, sloppy work reflects unfavorably on the writer, the company, and the message itself. Thus, you should want your documents to be attractively displayed.

Currently, the writer has better control over the display in print and portable document format (.pdf) than in email and hypertext markup language (.html). However, as applications migrate to html output and as more browsers and email programs display standardized html similarly, the writer will gain better control over these electronic displays, too. The material presented here will help you present your documents attractively and appropriately in whichever medium you choose.

Today's word processors include automated formatting for a full range of documents and templates that can be customized to serve the precise needs of a business. They can include text, graphics, macros, styles, keyboard assignments, and custom toolbars.

A word of warning, though: Such features as templates and styles that are intended to make your work easier will do so only if you know how to manipulate them. Many writers find these templates and styles helpful, but others become frustrated if they are not familiar enough with the software to tweak the templates and styles to their needs. A word processing software's *Help* menu can help you learn the advanced features. Remember, too, that company styles and preferences will also influence the format of your document.

In fact, learning all you can about your word processing program would be wise. For example, in Word 2007, a new feature called Building Blocks (Insert Ribbon>Quick parts) allows users to select reusable parts to build customized documents quickly. Additionally, you will find a selection of themes that include preselected typefaces and art. Along with layout and media, these are the basic components of document design. Knowing more about these components will help you design a document that conveys your message accurately to your audience.

LAYOUT DECISIONS

Common layout decisions involve grids, spacing, and margins. Grids are the nonprinted horizontal and vertical lines that help you place elements of your document precisely on the page. The examples shown in Figure B–1 illustrate the placement of text on

Layouts Using Different Grids

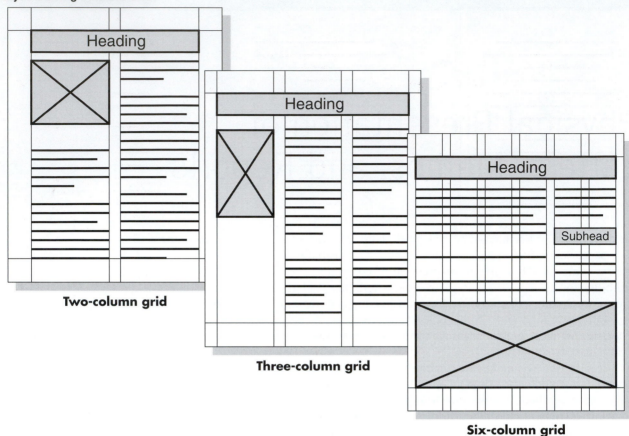

Two-column grid

Three-column grid

Six-column grid

two-, three-, and six-column grids. You can readily see how important it is to plan for this element.

To make your document look its best, you must consider both external and internal spacing. External spacing is the white space—the space some never think about carefully. Just as volume denotes importance in writing, white space denotes importance. Surrounding text or a graphic with white spaces sets it apart, emphasizing it to the reader. Used effectively, white space also has been shown to increase the readability of your documents, giving your readers' eyes a rest. Ideally, white space should be a careful part of the design of your document.

Internal spacing refers to both vertical and horizontal spacing. The spacing between letters on a line is called *kerning*. With word processing programs, you can adjust how close the letters are to each other. These programs also allow you to adjust how close the lines are to each other vertically, called *leading*. Currently, many still refer to spacing in business documents as single or double spacing. However, this is a carryover from the typewriter era when a vertical line space was always ⅙ inch or when six lines equaled an inch. Today's software and hardware allow you to control this aspect of your document much more exactly. Deciding on the best spacing to use depends on the typeface you decide to use. In any case, you need to make a conscious decision about the spacing of the text in your documents.

Another aspect of layout is your margin settings. Ideally, you want your document to look like a framed picture. This arrangement calls for all margins to be equal. However, some businesses use a fixed margin on all documents regardless of their length. Some

Different Forms of Justification

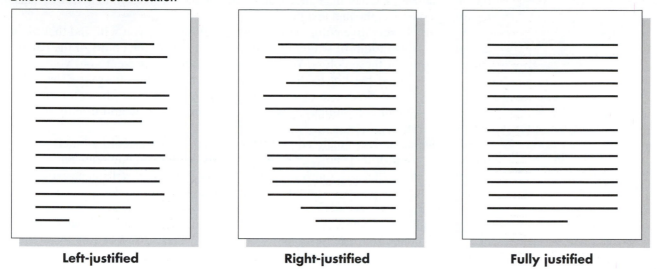

| Left-justified | Right-justified | Fully justified |

do this to line up with design features on their letterhead; others believe it increases productivity. In either case, the side margins will be equal. And with today's word processors you easily make your top and bottom margins equal by telling the program to center the document vertically on the page. Although all margins will not be exactly equal, the page will still have horizontal and vertical balance. And some word processors have "make it fit" experts. With this feature, the writer tells the program the number of pages, allowing it to select such aspects as margins, font size, and spacing to fit the message to the desired space.

Today's programs also have the capability to align your type at the margins or in the center. This is called *justification*. Left justification aligns every line at the left, right justification aligns every line at the right, and full justification aligns every line at both the left and the right (see Figure B–2). Full justification takes the extra spaces between the last word and the right margin and distributes them across the line. This adds extra white spaces across the line, stopping most readers' eyes a bit. Therefore, it is usually best to set a left-justified margin and ignore the resulting ragged right margin. However, if your document's ragged right margin is distracting, you may want to turn on the hyphenation feature. Your program will then hyphenate words at the end of lines, smoothing the raggedness.

CHOICE OF MEDIUM

The media you choose to transmit your documents also communicate. Text and instant messaging and most email today are perceived as informal media. But choosing these media communicates to the reader that you are a user of a particular technology, and its choice may be associated with the nature and quality of your business. Choosing to send your message by fax, especially an Internet-based fax, also may imply your currency with the technology. Also, sending a formatted document, an rtf file, or a pdf document as an attached file both conveys a message and gives you some control over your document's display. By choosing paper as your medium, you will have control over appearance while relinquishing control over delivery to company and mail-delivery systems.

Today, paper is still a common choice of medium. In the United States, standard business paper size is 8½ by 11 inches; international business A4 (210 × 297 mm) results in paper sized slightly narrower than 8½ inches and slightly longer than 11 inches. Occasionally, half-size (5½ × 8½) or executive size (7¼ × 10½) is used for short messages. Other than these standards, you have a variety of choices to make regarding color, weight, and texture.

The most conservative color choice is white. Of course, you will find that there are numerous variations of white. In addition, there are all the colors of the palette and many tints of these colors. You want your paper to represent you, your business, and its brand but not to distract your reader from the message. The color you choose for the first page of your document should also be the color you use for the second and continuing pages. This is the color you would usually use for envelopes, too.

Some businesses even match the color of the paper with the color of their printer ink and the color of their postage meter ink. This, of course, communicates to the reader that the writer or company is detail conscious. Such an image would be desirable for accountants or architects where attention to detail is perceived as a positive trait.

The weight and texture of your paper also communicate. While "cheap" paper may denote control of expenses to one reader, it may denote cost cutting to another. Usually businesses use paper with a weight of 16 to 20 pounds and a rag or cotton content of 25 to 100 percent. The higher the numbers, the higher the quality. And, of course, many readers often associate a high-quality paper with a high-quality product or service.

The choice of medium to use for your documents is important because it, too, sends a message. By being aware of these subtle messages, you will be able to choose the most appropriate medium for your situation.

With the basics taken care of, now we can move on to the specifics for the letter, memo, or report.

FORM OF BUSINESS LETTERS

The layout of a letter (its shape on the page) accounts for a major part of the impression that the appearance of the letter makes. A layout that is too wide, too narrow, too high, too low, or off-center may impress the reader unfavorably. The ideal letter layout is one that has the same shape as the space in which it is formed. It fits that space much as a picture fits a frame. That is, a rectangle drawn around the processed letter has the same shape as the space under the letterhead. The top border of the rectangle is the dateline, the left border is the line beginnings, the right border is the average line length, and the bottom border is the last line of the notations.

As to the format of the layout, any generally recognized one is acceptable. Some people prefer one format or another, and some people even think the format they prefer is the best. Automated formatting allows you to choose your own format preferences. Generally, the most popular formats are block, modified block, and simplified. These are illustrated in Figure B–3. In all formats, single-spacing in paragraphs and double-spacing between paragraphs is the general rule.

Agreement has not been reached on all the practices for setting up the parts of the letter. The following suggestions, however, follow the bulk of authoritative opinion.

Dateline. You should use the conventional date form, with month, day, and year (September 17, 2012). When you are using a word processor's date feature, be sure to select the appropriate one. If you choose to insert a date code, decide whether you want it to record when the document was created (CreateDate), last printed (PrintDate), or last saved (SaveDate). Also, recognize that abbreviated date forms such as 09-17-12 or Sept. 17, '12 are informal and leave unfavorable impressions on some people. Most word processors allow you to set up your preference and will use that preference when you use the date feature.

Standard Letter Formats

Full Block

Letterhead

Vary spacing to lengthen or shorten

April 9, 20–

Vary spacing to lengthen or shorten

Ms. Mary A. Smitherman, President
Smitherman and Sons, Inc.
3107 Western Avenue
New London, CT 04320-4133

Double Space

Dear Ms. Smitherman:

Subject: Your April 14 inquiry about Mr. H.O. Abel

Double Space

Single Space

Double Space

Sincerely,

3 Blank Lines

Calvin C. DeWitte
Secretary-Treasurer

apc

Modified Block, Blocked Paragraphs

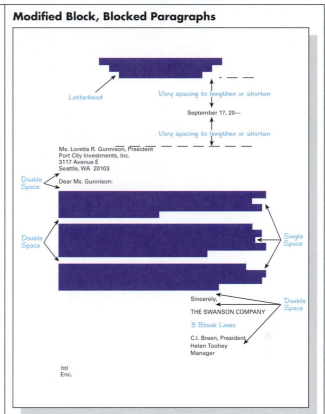

Letterhead

Vary spacing to lengthen or shorten

September 17, 20—

Vary spacing to lengthen or shorten

Ms. Loretta R. Gunnison, President
Port City Investments, Inc.
3117 Avenue E
Seattle, WA 20103

Double Space

Dear Ms. Gunnison:

Double Space

Single Space

Sincerely,

THE SWANSON COMPANY

Double Space

3 Blank Lines

C.I. Breen, President
Helen Toohey
Manager

htl
Enc.

Modified Block, Indented Paragraphs

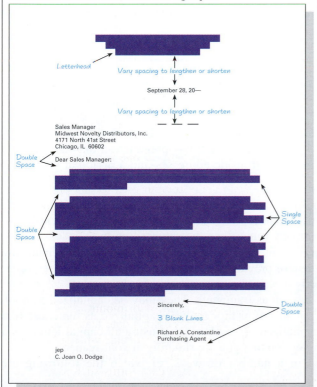

Letterhead

Vary spacing to lengthen or shorten

September 28, 20—

Vary spacing to lengthen or shorten

Sales Manager
Midwest Novelty Distributors, Inc.
4171 North 41st Street
Chicago, IL 60602

Double Space

Dear Sales Manager:

Double Space

Single Space

Sincerely,

Double Space

3 Blank Lines

Richard A. Constantine
Purchasing Agent

jep
C. Joan O. Dodge

Simplified

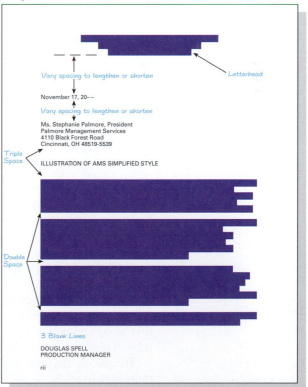

Vary spacing to lengthen or shorten

Letterhead

November 17, 20––

Vary spacing to lengthen or shorten

Ms. Stephanie Palmore, President
Palmore Management Services
4110 Black Forest Road
Cincinnati, OH 48519-5539

Triple Space

ILLUSTRATION OF AMS SIMPLIFIED STYLE

Double Space

3 Blank Lines

DOUGLAS SPELL
PRODUCTION MANAGER

rii

Return Address. In most cases, your return address is printed on the letterhead or filled in on it during automated formatting.

Inside Address. The mailing address, complete with the title of the person being addressed, makes up the inside address. Preferably, form it without abbreviations, except for commonly abbreviated words (*Dr., Mr., Ms.*). In Word, you can use its smart tag feature to quickly and easily enter addresses stored in Outlook.

Attention Line. Some executives prefer to emphasize the company address rather than the individual offices. Thus, they address the letter to the company in the inside address and then use an attention line to direct the letter to a specific officer or department. The attention line is placed two lines below the inside address and two lines above the salutation. When used, the typical form of the attention line is

Attention: Mr. Donovan Price, Vice President

Salutation. The salutation you choose should be based on your familiarity with the reader and on the formality of the situation. As a general rule, remember that if the writer and the reader know each other well, the salutation may be by first name, *Dear Joan*. A salutation by last name, *Dear Mr. Baskin,* is appropriate in most cases.

If you do not know and cannot find out the name of the person to whom you are sending the letter, use a position title. By directing your letter to Director of Human Resources or Public Relations Manager, you are helping your letter reach the appropriate person.

Women's preferences have sharply reduced the use of *Mrs.* and *Miss.* Many writes ask why we distinguish between married and single women when we make no such distinction between married and single men. The logical solution is to use *Ms.* for all women, just as *Mr.* is used for all men. If you know that the woman you are writing has another preference, however, you should adhere to that preference.

Mixed or Open Punctuation. The punctuation following the salutation and the closing is either mixed or open. Mixed punctuation employs a colon after the salutation and a comma after the complimentary close. Open punctuation, on the other hand, uses no punctuation after the salutation and none after the complimentary close. These two forms are used in domestic communication. In international communication, you may see letters with closed punctuation—punctuation distinguished by commas after the lines in the return and inside addresses and a period at the end of the complimentary close.

Subject Line. So that both the sender and the receiver may quickly identify the subject of the correspondence, many offices use the subject line in their letters. The subject line tells what the letter is about. In addition, it contains any specific identifying material that may be helpful: date of previous correspondence, invoice number, order number, and the like. It is usually placed two lines below the salutation.

Subject lines are generally written as fragments. They may be capitalized as book titles (every important word capitalized) or they may be capitalized as sentences (the first word and proper nouns capitalized). Remember that using all capital letters in a subject line may create the impression that you are shouting at your reader.

The block may be headed in a number of ways, of which the following are representative:

Subject: Your July 2nd inquiry about . . .
RE: Please refer to Invoice H-320.

Second Page Heading. When the length of a letter must exceed one page, you should set up the following page or pages for quick identification. Always print such pages on plain paper (no letterhead). These two forms are the most common:

Ms. Helen E. Mann   2   May 7, 2012

Ms. Helen E. Mann
May 7, 2012
Page 2

Most standard templates automatically insert this information—name of addressee, date, and page number—on the second and following pages of your letter.

Closing. By far the most commonly used complimentary close is *Sincerely*. *Sincerely yours* is also used, but in recent years the *yours* has been fading away. *Truly* (with and without the *yours*) is also used, but it also has lost popularity. Such closes as *Cordially* and *Respectfully* are appropriate when their meanings fit the writer–reader relationship. A long-standing friendship, for example, would justify *Cordially;* the writer's respect for the position, prestige, or accomplishments of the reader would justify *Respectfully.*

Signature Block. The printed signature conventionally appears on the fourth line below the closing, beginning directly under the first letter for the block form. Most templates will insert the closing. A short name and title may appear on the same line, separated by a comma. If either the name or title is long, the title appears on the following line, blocked under the name. The writer's signature appears in the space between the closing and the printed signature.

Some people prefer to have the firm name appear in the signature block—especially when the letter continues on a second page without the company letterhead. The conventional form for this arrangement places the firm name in solid capitals and blocked on the second line below the closing phrase. The typed name of the person signing the letter is on the fourth line below the firm name.

Information Notations. In the lower-left corner of the letter may appear abbreviated notations for enclosures, *Enc., Enc.*—3, and so on, and for the initials of the writer and the typist, *WEH:ga*. However, many businesses are dropping these initials since the reader does not need this information, and since most word processors allow businesses to put this information in the document summary. Also, businesses are no longer including filename notations on the letters, since readers do not need them and today's word processors can find files by searching for specific content. Indications of copies prepared for other readers also may be included: *cc: Sharon Garbett, copy to Sharon Garbett.*

Postscripts. Postscripts, commonly referred to as the PS, are placed after any notations. While rarely used in most business letters because they look like afterthoughts, they can be very effective as added punch in sales letters.

Folding. The carelessly folded letter is off to a bad start with the reader. Neat folding will complete the planned effect by (1) making the letter fit snugly in its cover, (2) making the letter easy for the reader to remove, and (3) making the letter appear neat when opened.

The two-fold pattern is the easiest. It fits the standard sheet for the long (Number 10) envelope as well as some other envelope sizes. As shown in Figure B–4, the first fold of the two-fold pattern is from the bottom up, taking a little less than a third of the sheet. The second fold goes from the top down, making exactly the same panel as the bottom segment. (This measurement will leave the recipient a quarter-inch thumbhold for easy unfolding of the letter.) Thus folded, the letter should be slipped into its envelope with the second crease toward the bottom and the center panel at the front of the envelope.

The three-fold pattern is necessary to fit the standard sheet into the commonly used small (Number 6¾) envelope. Its first fold is from the bottom up, with the bottom edge of the sheet riding about a quarter inch under the top edge to allow the thumbhold.

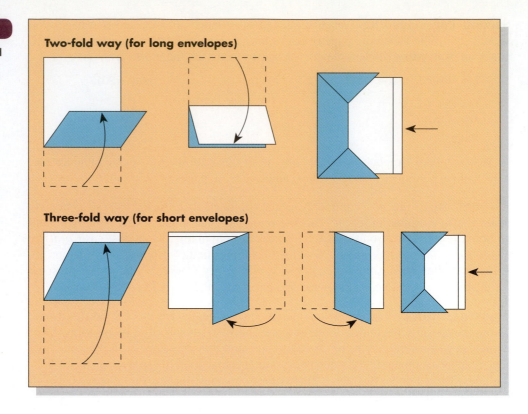

Two-fold way (for long envelopes)

Three-fold way (for short envelopes)

(If the edges are exactly even, they are harder to separate.) The second fold is from the right side of the sheet toward the left, taking a little less than a third of the width. The third fold matches the second: from the left side toward the right, with a panel of exactly the same width. (This fold will leave a quarter-inch thumbhold at the right, for the user's convenience.) So that the letter will appear neat when unfolded, the creases should be neatly parallel with the top and sides, not at angles that produce "dog-ears" and irregular shapes. In the three-fold form, it is especially important for the side panels produced by the second and third folds to be exactly the same width; otherwise, the vertical creases are off-center and tend to throw the whole carefully planned layout off-center.

The three-fold letter is inserted into its cover with the third crease toward the bottom of the envelope and the loose edges toward the stamp end of the envelope. From habit, most recipients of business letters slit envelopes at the top and turn them facedown to extract the letter. The three-fold letter inserted as described thus gives its reader an easy thumbhold at the top of the envelope to pull it out by and a second one at the top of the sheet for easy unfolding of the whole.

Envelope Address. So that optical character recognition (OCR) equipment may be used in sorting mail, the U.S. Postal Service requests that all envelopes be typed as follows (see Figure B–5).

1. Place the address in the scannable area as shown in the white box in Figure B–5. It is best to use a sans serif font in 10 to 12 points.

2. Use a block address format.

3. Single-space.

4. Use all uppercase letters (capitals). While today's OCR equipment can read lowercase, the post office prefers uppercase.

5. Do not use punctuation, except for the hyphen in the nine-digit zip code.

6. Use the two-letter abbreviations for the U.S. states and territories and the Canadian provinces.

Form for Addressing Envelopes Recommended by the U.S. Postal Service, Publication 28

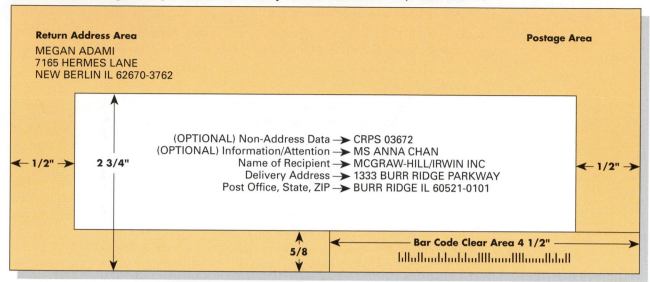

Use other address abbreviations as shown in the most recent edition of the *Post Office Directory* (see www.usps.com). When sending to a foreign country, include only the country name in uppercase on the bottom line.

States and Possessions of the United States

Alabama	AL	Kansas	KS	Northern Mariana	
Alaska	AK	Kentucky	KY	Islands	MP
American Samoa	AS	Louisiana	LA	Ohio	OH
Arizona	AZ	Maine	ME	Oklahoma	OK
Arkansas	AR	Marshall Islands	MH	Oregon	OR
California	CA	Maryland	MD	Palau	PW
Colorado	CO	Massachusetts	MA	Pennsylvania	PA
Connecticut	CT	Michigan	MI	Puerto Rico	PR
Delaware	DE	Minnesota	MN	Rhode Island	RI
District of Columbia	DC	Mississippi	MS	South Carolina	SC
Federated States of		Missouri	MO	South Dakota	SD
Micronesia	FM	Montana	MT	Tennessee	TN
Florida	FL	Nebraska	NE	Texas	TX
Georgia	GA	Nevada	NV	Utah	UT
Guam	GU	New Hampshire	NH	Vermont	VT
Hawaii	HI	New Jersey	NJ	Virginia	VA
Idaho	ID	New Mexico	NM	Virgin Islands	VI
Illinois	IL	New York	NY	Washington	WA
Indiana	IN	North Carolina	NC	West Virginia	WV
Iowa	IA	North Dakota	ND	Wyoming	WY

Canadian Provinces and Territories

Alberta	AB	Newfoundland	NF	Prince Edward Island	PE
British Columbia	BC	Northwest Territories	NT	Quebec	PQ
Manitoba	MB	Nova Scotia	NS	Saskatchewan	SK
New Brunswick	NB	Ontario	ON	Yukon Territory	YT

7. The last line of the mailing address should contain no more than 28 characters. The city should be 13 or fewer characters. Also, there should be one space between city and state; two spaces for the state or province abbreviation; two spaces between the state and zip code; and 10 characters for the zip + 4 code.

8. The return address must be typed in the left corner, beginning on the second line from the top of the envelope and three spaces from the left edge of the envelope.

9. Print any on-arrival instructions (Confidential, Personal) four lines below the return address.

10. Place all notations for the post office (Special Delivery) below the stamp and at least three lines above the mailing address.

FORM OF MEMORANDUMS

Memorandums (memos) have basic components in common, but their form varies widely from organization to organization. The basic components are the heading and body. The heading has four elements: *To, From, Date,* and *Subject.* These elements are arranged in various placements, but all are present.

The body of the memo is usually single-spaced with double-spacing between paragraphs. First-level headings are frequently used in long memos. And notations for typist and enclosures are included just as they are in letters. Chapter 5 provides examples of memo formats.

FORM OF LETTER AND MEMORANDUM REPORTS

Informal business reports may be written in letter or memo format, depending on the audience. The letter report contains the return address or company letterhead, date, inside address, and salutation; it may also contain a subject line. The memo report contains the standard *To, From, Date,* and *Subject* lines.

Beginning with the second page, letter and memo reports must have a header that contains the reader's name, the date, and a page number. Use your word processing software's heading feature. In Word 2007 you can find the heading feature by going to Insert>Header. From here type the text of your header and insert a page number. Because you do not want this information on the first page of your report, also check "Different First Page."

Figure B–6

Levels of Headings.
Use the placement and form of headings to indicate the structure of your report's contents. One way to do so is shown. You can modify your word processor's heading styles to suit your preferences and then easily format your different headings with these styles.

First-level Head

Second-level Head

Third-level Head.

Fourth-level head.

Both letter and memorandum reports may use headings to display the topics covered. The headings are usually displayed in the margins, on separate lines, and in a different style. (see Figure B–6.) Memorandum and letter reports also may differ from ordinary letters and memos by having illustrations (charts, tables), an appendix, and/or a bibliography.

FORM OF FORMAL REPORTS

Like letters, formal reports should be pleasing to the eye. Well-arranged reports give an impression of competence—of work professionally done. Because such an impression can affect the success of a report, you should make good use of the following review of report form.

General Information on Report Presentation

Since your formal reports are likely to be prepared with word processing programs, you will not need to know the general mechanics of manuscript preparation if you use automated formatting, as shown in the Word 2007 template in Figure B–7. However, even if you do not have to format your own reports, you should know enough about report presentation to be sure your work is done right. You cannot be certain that your report is in good form unless you know good form.

Conventional Page Layout. For the typical text page in a report, a conventional layout appears to fit the page as a picture fits a frame (see Figure B–8). This eye-pleasing layout, however, is arranged to fit the page space not covered by the binding of the report. Thus, you must allow an extra half inch or so on the left margins of the pages of a single-sided left-bound report and at the top of the pages of a top-bound report.

Special Page Layouts. Certain text pages may have individual layouts. Pages displaying major titles (first pages of chapters, tables of contents, executive summaries, and the like) conventionally have an extra half inch or so of space at the top. Figure B–9 illustrates that some special pages can be created with templates.

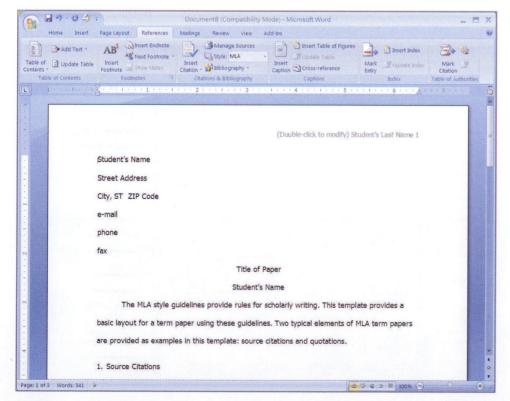

Figure B–7

Illustration of an MLA Report Template for Word 2007

Recommended Page Layouts

Double-spaced Page

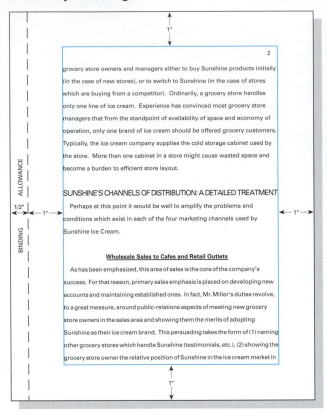

Single-spaced Page

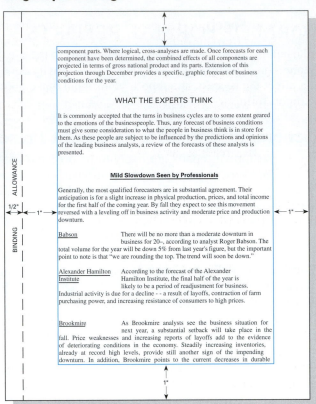

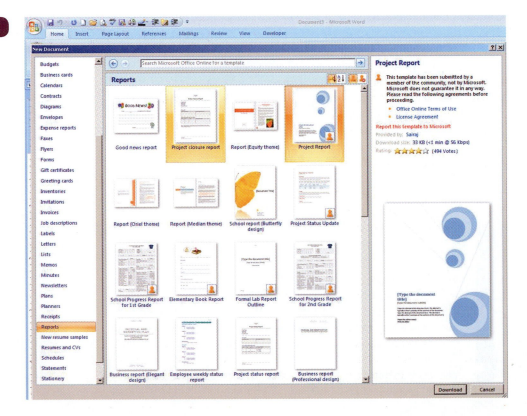

Letters or memos of transmittal and authorization also may have individual layouts. They are arranged in any conventional letter or memos form. In the more formal reports, they may be carefully arranged to have the same general shape as the space in which they appear using the "make-it-fit" feature.

Choice of Spacing. The convention of double-spacing reports is fading. This procedure stems from the old practice of double-spacing to make typed manuscripts more readable for the proofreader and printer. The practice has been carried over into work that is not to be reproduced. The remaining advocates of double-spacing claim that it is easier to read than single-spacing, as the reader is less likely to lose line place.

In recent years, single-spacing has gained in popularity. The general practice is to single-space within paragraphs, double-space between paragraphs, and triple-space above all centered heads. Supporters of single-spacing contend that it saves space and facilitates reading, as it is like the printing that most people are accustomed to reading.

Patterns of Indentation. You should indent the paragraph beginnings of double-spaced typing. On the other hand, you should block single-spaced material because its paragraph headings are clearly marked by the blank lines between paragraphs.

No generally accepted distance of indentation exists. Some sources suggest ½ inch, and others 1" and more. Any decision as to the best distance to use is up to you, though you would do well to follow the practice established in the office, group, or school for which you write the report. Whatever your selection, you should be consistent.

Numbering of Pages. Two systems of numbers are used in numbering the pages of the written report. Small Roman numerals are standard for the front matter of the report. Although these prefatory pages are all counted in the numbering sequence, the numbers generally do not appear on the pages before the table of contents. Arabic numerals are conventional for the main part of the report, normally beginning with the first page of the introduction and continuing through the appendix. See the text website for specific instructions on how to number pages in Word.

Placement of the numbers on the page varies with the binding used for the report. In reports bound at the top of the page, you should center all page numbers at the bottom of the page, two or three lines below the body and usually in a footer.

For left-sided binding, you should place the numbers in the upper-right corner, two or three lines above the top line, usually in the header, and right justified. Exception to this placement is customarily made for special-layout pages that have major titles and an additional amount of space displayed at the top. Such pages may include the first page of the report text; the executive summary; the table of contents; and, in very long and formal works, the first page of each major division or chapter. Numbers for these pages are centered two or three lines below the imaginary line marking the bottom of the layout.

In documents printed back-to-back, page numbers are usually placed at the top of the page even with the outside margin. Not only are today's word processing programs capable of automatically placing page numbers this way if directed, but many printers are also capable of two-sided printing.

Display of Headings. Headings are the titles of the parts of the report. Designed to lead the readers through the report, they must show at a glance the importance of the information they cover.

In showing heading importance by position, you have many choices. If your software and printer make available a variety of typefaces, you can select various progressions of font sizes and styles to fit your needs. Your goal, of course, should be to select forms that show differences in importance at first glance—much as is done in the printing of this book.

You can use any combination of form and placement that clearly shows the relative importance of the heading (Figure B–6 demonstrates one way). The one governing rule to follow in considering form and positions of headings is that no heading may have a higher-ranking form or position than any of the headings of a higher level. But you can use the same form for two successive levels of headings as long as the positions vary. And you can use the same position for two successive levels as long as the forms vary. You also can skip over any of the steps in the progression of form or position.

When you create your headings, use your word processing program's built in automatic styles feature to generate your table of contents. You can also create your own automatic heading formats using your software's styles feature and still automatically generate the table, but if you manually format your text (e.g., select the text and click the "B" icon to make it bold), you will have to manually type the table, which is not efficient. In Word 2007 you can also create a table of contents by marking individual headings that you have formatted in your text and then using the marked headings to generate the table. You will find the feature in References>Table of Contents>Add Text.

Mechanics and Format of the Report Parts

The foregoing notes on physical appearance apply generally to all parts of the report. But as Chapter 11 illustrates, the prefatory sections and appended material of formal reports have special formatting considerations. Below we elaborate on the formatting advice in that chapter.

Title Fly. The title fly contains only the report title. Print the title in the highest-ranking form used in the report, and double-space it if you need more than one line. If your report cover has a window for the title to show through, make sure you place the title in the window.

Title Page. The title page normally contains four main areas of identification. In the typical title page, the first area of identification contains the report title. Preferably, use the highest-ranking form used in the report.

The second area of identification names the individual (or group) for whom the report has been prepared. Precede it with an identifying phrase indicating that individual's role in the report, such as "Prepared for" or "Submitted to." In addition to the recipient's name, include the identification of the recipient by title or role, company, and address, particularly if you and the recipient are from different companies.

The third area of identification names you, the writer of the report. It is also preceded by an identifying phrase—"Prepared by," "Written by," or similar wording describing your role in the report—and it also may identify title or role, company, and address. The fourth and final part of this area of information is the date of presentation or publication. Placement of the four areas of identification on the page should make for an eye-pleasing arrangement. Most word processors will help you align the text vertically on the page.

Letters or Memos of Transmittal and Authorization. As their names imply, the letters or memos of transmittal and authorization are actual letters or memos. You can put the letter or memo of transmittal on company letterhead or in any acceptable form (see the examples on pages 351 and 379). The authorization message should be included in its original form.

Acknowledgments. When you are indebted to the assistance of others, it is fitting that you acknowledge the indebtedness somewhere in the report. If you have only a few people to acknowledge, you may acknowledge them in the introduction of the report or in the letter of transmittal. In the rare event that you need to make numerous acknowledgments, you may construct a special section for this purpose. This section, bearing the simple title "Acknowledgments," has the same layout as any other text page on which a title is displayed.

Table of Contents. The table of contents is the report outline in its polished, finished form. It lists the major report headings with the page numbers on which those headings appear. Although not all reports require a table of contents, one should be a part of any report long enough to make such a guide helpful to the readers. Most word processors are capable of generating a table of contents—complete with page numbers. See the textbook website for a short tutorial on how to create one in Word.

The table of contents is appropriately titled "Contents" or "Table of Contents." The layout of the table of contents is the same as that used for any other report page with a title display. Below the title, set up two columns. One contains the outline headings, generally beginning with the first report part following the table of contents; the other contains the page numbers. You have the option of including or leaving out the outline letters and numbers.

In the table of contents, as in the body of the report, you may vary the form to distinguish different heading levels. But the form variations of the table of contents need not be the same as those used in the text of the report. The highest level of headings is usually distinguished from the other levels, and sometimes typeface differences are used to distinguish second-level headings from lower-level headings. If you use indentation to show the levels of headings, it is acceptable to use plain capitals and lowercase for all levels of headings.

As mentioned in "Display of Headings," if you have used your word processing program's styles feature to create automatic headings, you can automatically generate the table of contents quickly.

Table of Illustrations. The table (list) of illustrations may be either a continuation of the table of contents or a separate table. Such a table lists the graphics presented in the report in much the same way as the table of contents lists the report parts.

In constructing this table, head it with an appropriately descriptive title, such as "Table of Charts and Illustrations," or "List of Tables and Charts," or "Table of Figures." If you place the table of illustrations on a separate page, layout for this page is the same as that for any other text page with a displayed title. And if you place it as a continued part of the table of contents, you should begin it after the last contents entry.

The table consists of two columns, the first for the graphics titles and the second for the pages on which the graphics appear. The look of the table should match the format and layout of the table of contents. Preceding the title of each entry, place that entry's number; and should these numbers be Roman or otherwise require more than one digit, align the digits at the right. If your report contains two or more illustration types (tables, charts, maps, and the like) and you have given each type its own numbering sequence, you should list each type separately.

As with your table of contents, you can use your word processing program's automatic features to create the titles for your illustrations, figures, and charts. If you do so, you can automatically generate a list of figures.

References (or Bibliography). Anytime you use another's idea, you need to give credit to the source. Sometimes business writers interweave this credit into the narrative of their text, and often they use footnotes to convey their source information. But often these sources are listed in a reference or bibliography section at the end of the report. Typically, these sections are organized alphabetically, but they also can be organized by date, subject, or type of source.

As Appendix E illustrates, the format and content of citations vary depending on which citation you use. Among the widely used formats are Chicago, MLA (Modern Language Association), and APA (American Psychological Association). The content for most items on the list of references is similar to that of the footnote. Word 2007's Reference ribbon includes a reference management tool that will help you generate a bibliography in these standard formats—but see Appendix E for cautionary advice about such tools.

General Grading Checklists: Punctuation, Grammar, Number, Spelling, Proofreading, Technique, Strategy, and Formatting

Listed below are general grading symbols and their descriptions. These symbols give you a general idea of how to improve your writing. You will find more detailed information in your text, particularly in Chapter 16.

Punctuation

Symbol	Explanation	Description
APOS	Apostrophe	Use the apostrophe to show the possessive case of nouns and indefinite pronouns.
		Use an apostrophe to mark the place in a contraction where letters are omitted.
Bkts	Brackets	Set off in brackets words that you wish to insert in a quotation.
Cln	Colon	Use the colon to introduce a statement of explanation, an enumeration, or a formal quotation.
		Do not use the colon when the thought of the sentence should continue without interruption. If introducing a list by a colon, the colon should be preceded by a word that explains or identifies the list.
Cma	Comma	
Dsh	Dash	Use the dash to set off an element for emphasis or to show interrupted thought.
Ex	Exclamation mark	Use the exclamation mark at the end of a sentence or exclamatory fragment to show strong emotion.
Hpn	Hyphen	
Ital	Italics	
Parens	Parentheses	
Pd	Period	
Ques	Question mark	Place a question mark at the end of sentences that are direct questions.
QM	Quotation marks	Use quotation marks to enclose the exact words of a speaker or, if the quotation is short, the exact words of a writer.
SC	Semicolon	

Grammar

Symbol	Explanation	Description
AA	Adjective–adverb Confusion	Do not use adjectives for adverbs or adverbs for adjectives. Adjectives modify only nouns and pronouns; and adverbs modify verbs, adjectives, or other adverbs.
Agmt SV	Subject–verb agreement	Nouns and their verbs must agree in number.
AN	Adverbial noun clause	
Awk	Awkward	Avoid awkward writing where word arrangements are unconventional, uneconomical, or simply not the best for quick understanding.
Dng	Dangling modifier	Avoid the use of modifiers that do not logically modify a word in the sentence.
Frag	Sentence fragment	Avoid words used as a sentence that are not a sentence.
Pn	Pronoun	
Prl	Parallelism	Express equal thoughts in parallel grammatical form.
Tns	Tense	

Number

Symbol	Explanation
No	Number

Spelling

Symbol	Explanation	Description
Sp	Spelling	Spell words correctly. Use the dictionary.
Caps	Capitalization	Capitalize all proper names and the beginning words of sentences.

Proofreading

Symbol		Explanation	Description
Align	═══	Align	Line up horizontally or vertically.
Stet	stet	Let original stand	Don't delete.
Close	◡	Close up	Close up space.
Del	℔	Delete	Delete.
Ins	∧	Insert	Insert space, punctuation, text, or graphic.
Keep		Keep together	Keep text and/or graphic together.
LC	lc /	Lowercase	Use lowercase.
Caps	cap ≡	Capitalize	Make all caps.
Mv L	[	Move left	Move left.
Mv R	]	Move right	Move right.
Cntr	] [	Center	Center.
Nl	nl	New line	Start new line.
Run	⌒	Run together	Run text together.
Par	#	Paragraph	Start new paragraph.
Sp O	sp ⬭	Spell out	Spell out.
Trp	tr ⌣	Transpose	Transpose.

Technique

Symbol	Explanation	Description
Adp	Adaptation	Adapt to the one reader. Here your writing is above or below your reader.
Acc	Accuracy	Check for correct information.
Assign	Assignment	Needs to follow assignment.
AV	Active voice	Use active voice.
Blky	Bulky arrangement	Make your paragraphs more inviting by breaking them into shorter units of thought.
Blame	Blaming	Avoid blaming or accusing the reader.
Chop	Choppy writing	Avoid a succession of short sentences that produce an irritating effect.
COH	Coherence	Needs to be easier to follow with clear, logical development.
Copy	Copying	Avoid copying or following examples too closely. Organize around the unique facts of the case.
CTone	Conversational tone	Be natural or less formal in your word choice.
Dis	Discriminatory	Avoid using words that discriminate unnecessarily against sex, age, race, disability, or sexual orientation.
DL	Dull writing	Bring your writing back to life with vivid, concrete words.
Doc	Documentation	Cite source of information.
Emp−	Emphasis too little	Give appropriate emphasis with placement, volume, words, or mechanical means.
Emp+	Emphasis too much	Give appropriate emphasis with placement, volume, words, or mechanical means.
GW	Goodwill	Needs more goodwill.
Intp	Interpretation	Do more than just present facts. Make the data meaningful in terms of the reader's situation.
Jargon	Jargon	Avoid using jargon.
Los	Loose writing	Use words more economically. Write concisely.
Neg	Negative	Try wording more positively.
Ob	Obvious	Include only necessary information or detail.
Ord	Order of presentation	Needs clear, logical order.
Org	Organization	Needs clearer, tighter organization with setup and follow through.
Pomp	Pompous	Use more humble, sincere words.
Pre	Precise	Be more precise or concrete.
RB	Reader benefit	Needs more reader benefit.
Red	Redundant	Avoid unnecessary repetition.
Resale	Resale	Use more resale here.
RS	Rubber-stamp expression	Avoid overused phrases and timeworn words from the past.
Trans	Transition	Avoid abrupt shift of thought here.
Var	Variety	Vary the words and sentence patterns.
WU	Word use	Use words correctly. Misused words call attention to themselves and detract from the writing.
WW	Wrong word	Wrong words refer to meaning one word and using another.
YVP	You-viewpoint	Revise with the reader in mind.

Message Strategy

Symbol	Explanation	Description
O Dir	Directness needed	The opening is too slow in getting to the goal.
O Ind	Indirectness needed	The opening gets to the goal too fast.
O Qual	Quality	The opening could be improved by making it more on subject, logical, or interesting. It should also set up the rest of the message.
C Ex	Excess information	You have included more information than is needed.
C Exp	Explanation	More or better explanation is needed here.
C Id	Identification	Completely identify the situation.
C Inc	Incomplete	You have not covered all the important facts.
E AC	Action close	A drive for action is appropriate in this situation.
E AC S	Action strong	This action drive is too strong.
E AC W	Action weak	This action drive is too weak.
E IT	Individually tailored	Make your close fit the one case.
E OS	Off subject	An off-subject close is best for this case. These words recall unpleasant things in the reader's mind.

Formatting

Symbol	Explanation	Description
Lay	Layout	Use standard or specified format.
T	Type	Select a readable font for size and style.
Media	Media	Use a medium appropriate for the reader and the context.

Special Grading Checklists: Messages and Reports

MESSAGES

The Opening

O Dir *Directness needed.* This opening is too slow in getting to the goal.

O Ind *Indirectness needed.* This opening gets to the goal too fast.

O Qual *Quality.* This opening could be improved by making it more (1) on subject, (2) logical, or (3) interesting.

Coverage

C Ex *Excess information.* You have included more information than is needed.

C Exp *Explanation.* More or better explanation is needed here.

C Id *Identification.* Completely identify the situation.

C Inc *Incomplete.* You have not covered all the important information.

Ending

E AC *Action close.* A drive for action is appropriate in this situation.

E AC S *Action strong.* This action drive is too strong.

E AC W *Action weak.* This action drive is too weak.

E IT *Individually tailored.* Make your close fit the one case.

E OS *Off subject.* An off-subject close is best for this case. These words recall unpleasant things in the reader's mind.

Technique

Adp *Adaptation.* Your words should be adapted to the one reader. Here yours are (1) above or (2) below your reader.

Awk *Awkward word arrangement.*

Bky *Bulky arrangement.* Make your paragraphs more inviting by breaking them into shorter units of thought.

Chop *Choppy writing.* A succession of short sentences produces an irritating effect.

DL *Dull writing.* Bring your writing back to life with vivid, concrete words.

Emp + *Emphasis, too much.*

Emp — *Emphasis, too little.*   Here you have given too much or too little (as marked) emphasis by (1) placement, (2) volume, or (3) words or mechanical means.

Intp *Interpretation.*   Do more than just present facts. In this situation, something more is needed. Make the data meaningful in terms of the reader's situation.

Los *Loose writing.*   Use words more economically. Write concisely.

Ord *Order of presentation.*   This information does not fall into a logical order. The information is mixed up and confusing.

RS *Rubber-stamp expression.*   Timeworn words from the past have no place in modern business writing.

Trans *Transition.*   Abrupt shift of thought here.

Effect

Conv *Conviction.*   This is less convincing than it should be. More fact or a more skillful use of words is needed.

GW *Goodwill.*   The message needs more goodwill. Try to make your words convey friendliness. Here you tend to be too dull and matter-of-fact.

Hur *Hurried treatment.*   Your coverage of the problem appears to be hurried. Thus, it tends to leave an effect of routine or brusque treatment. Conciseness is wanted, of course, but you must not sacrifice your objectives for it.

Log *Logic.*   Is this really logical? Would you do it this way in business?

Neg *Negative effect.*   By word or implication, this part is more negative than it should be.

Pers + *Too persuasive.*   Your words are too high-pressure for this situation.

Pers — *Not persuasive enough.*   More persuasion, by either words or facts, would help your message.

Ton *Tone of the words.*   Your words create a bad impression on the reader. Words work against the success of your message if they talk down, lecture, argue, accuse, and the like.

YVP *You-viewpoint.*   More you-viewpoint wording and adaptation would help the overall effect of your message.

REPORTS

Title

T 1   Complete? The title should tell what the report contains. Use the five Ws and 1 H as a check for completeness (*who, what, where, when, why*—sometimes *how*).

T 2   Too long. This title is longer than it needs to be. Check it for uneconomical wording or unnecessary information.

Transmittal

LT 1   More directness is needed in the opening. The message should present the report right away.

LT 2   Content of the message needs improvement. Comments that help the readers understand or appreciate the report are appropriate.

LT 3   Do not include findings unless the report has no executive summary.

LT 4   A warm statement of your attitude toward the assignment is appropriate— often expected. You either do not make one, or the one you make is weak.

LT 5   A friendlier, more conversational style would improve the transmittal.

Executive Summary

ES 1 *(If the direct order is assigned)* Begin directly—with a statement of findings, conclusion, or recommendation.

ES 2 *(If the indirect order is assigned)* Begin with a brief review of introductory information.

ES 3 The summary of highlights should be in proportion and should include major findings, analyses, and conclusions. Your coverage here is (1) scant or (2) too detailed.

ES 4 Work for a more interesting and concise summary.

Organization—Outline/Table of Contents

O 1 This organization plan is not the best for this problem. The main sections should form a logical solution to the problem.

O 2 The order of the parts of this organizational plan is not logical. The parts should form a step-by-step route to the goal.

O 3 Do not let one major section account for the entire body of the report.

O 4 One-item subdivisions are illogical. You cannot divide an area without coming up with at least two parts.

O 5 These parts overlap. Each part should be independent of the other parts. Although some repetition and relating of parts may be desirable, outright overlap is a sign of bad organization.

O 6 More subparts are needed here. The subparts should cover all the information in the major part.

O 7 This subpart does not fit logically under this major part.

O 8 These parts are not equal in importance. Do not give them equal status in the outline.

O 9 *(If talking headings are assigned.)* These headings do not talk well.

O 10 Coordinate headings should be parallel in grammatical structure.

O 11 This (these) heading(s) is (are) too long.

O 12 Vary the wording of the headings to avoid monotonous repetition.

Introduction

I 1 This introduction does not cover exactly what the readers need to know. Although the readers' needs vary by problem, these topics are usually important: (1) origin of the problem, (2) statement of the problem, (3) methods used in researching the problem, and (4) preview of the presentation.

I 2 Coverage of this part is (1) scant or (2) too detailed.

I 3 Important information has been left out.

I 4 Findings, conclusions, and other items of information are not a part of the introduction.

Coverage

C 1 The coverage here is (1) scant or (2) too detailed.

C 2 More analysis is needed here.

C 3 Here you rely too heavily on a graphic. The text should cover the important information.

C 4 Do not lose sight of the goal of the report. Relate the information to the problem.

C 5 Clearly distinguish between fact and opinion. Label opinion as opinion.

C 6 Your analyses and conclusions need the support of more fact and authoritative opinion.

Writing

W 1 This writing should be better adapted to your readers. It appears to be (1) too heavy or (2) too light for your readers.

W 2 Avoid the overuse of passive voice.

W 3 Work for more conciseness. Try to cut down on words without sacrificing meaning.

W 4 For this report, more formal writing is appropriate. You should write consistently in impersonal (third-person) style.

W 5 A more personal style is appropriate for this report. That is, you should use more personal pronouns (*I*'s, *we*'s, *you*'s).

W 6 The change in thought is abrupt here.

  (1) Between major parts, use introductions, summaries, and conclusions to guide the readers' thinking.

  (2) Use transitional words, phrases, or sentences to relate minor parts.

W 7 Your paragraphing is questionable. Check the paragraphs for unity. Look for topic sentences.

Graphics

GA 1 You have (1) not used enough graphics or (2) used too many graphics.

GA 2 For the information presented, this graphic is (1) too large or (2) too small.

GA 3 This type of graphic is not the best for presenting the information.

GA 4 Place the graphic near the place where its contents are discussed.

GA 5 The text must tell the story, so don't just refer the reader to a figure or table and let it go at that.

GA 6 The appearance of this graphic needs improvement. This may be your best work, but it does not make a good impression on the readers.

GA 7 Refer the readers to the graphics at the times that the readers should look at them.

GA 8 Interpret the patterns in the graphic. Note central tendencies, exceptions, ranges, trends, and such.

GA 9 Refer to the graphics incidentally, in subordinate parts of sentences that comment on their content (for example, ". . . as shown in Figure 5" or "see Figure 5").

Layout and Mechanics

LM 1 The layout of this page is (1) too fat, (2) too skinny, or (3) too low, high, or off-center (as marked).

LM 2 Neat? Smudges and light type detract from the message.

LM 3 Make the margins straighter. The raggedness here offends the eye.

LM 4 The spacing here needs improvement. (1) Too much space here. (2) Not enough space here.

LM 5 Your page numbering is not the best. See the text for specific instructions.

LM 6 This page appears (1) choppy or (2) heavy.

LM 7 Your selection of type placement and style for the headings is not the best.

LM 8 This item or form is not generally acceptable.

Documentation and the Bibliography

When writing reports and other business documents, you will frequently use information from other sources. Because this material is not your own, you may need to acknowledge it. Whether and how you should acknowledge it are the subject of this brief review.

WHEN TO ACKNOWLEDGE

Your decision to acknowledge or not acknowledge a source should be determined mainly on the basis of giving credit where credit is due. If you are quoting verbatim (in the original author's exact words), you must give credit. If you are paraphrasing (using someone else's ideas in your own words), you should give credit unless the material covered is general knowledge.

Today many colleges have academic honesty or academic integrity policies. Businesses, too, have similar ethics policies and codes. Following the policies not only ensures that you get full credit for your own work and develop the thinking and writing skills that will be helpful to you the rest of your life, but it also helps you build an ethical character. This character leads others to trust you, serving you well both professionally and personally.

Plagiarism, presenting another's work as your own, and falsifying data are two unethical practices plaguing schools and businesses alike. These practices range from carefully planned, intentional acts to careless, unintentional acts. However, the results are similar. Presenting another's work as your own steals from the creator—often depriving not only the author of the financial rewards honestly earned but also the whole support staff of editors, artists, designers, and production and distribution workers. Plagiarism is also stealing from classmates who write their own papers, but just as important, a cheater loses the opportunity to develop good writing and thinking skills. Additionally, plagiarism affects your reputation as well as the reputation of those in your class, your school, and those who have graduated from your school. It may also affect your family and friends. Falsifying data is equally malicious, especially when others rely on the information you present to make decisions. Worse yet, if you are successful in passing off falsified or plagiarized work as your own, it sets you up to behave unethically in the future. One writer for *The New York Times* wrote stories creating facts where he had none. After he did it once and fooled his boss and readers, he continued until he was caught. In addition to being fired and publicly humiliated, his actions brought into question the reporting practices and credibility of *The New York Times*.

In your writing tasks, you can eliminate such problems by following these guidelines.

Write Your Own Papers. Do not buy, beg, or borrow papers from others. Not only are instructors adept at spotting plagiarism, they now have powerful search engines

COMMUNICATION MATTERS

Quotation Marks, Citation, Both, or Neither?

For both ethical and complete communication, you should make clear where your words and content come from. To decide whether to use quotation marks, a citation (naming the source of the material), both, or neither, follow these rules of thumb:

- When the content is general knowledge and you use your own words, you need neither quotation marks nor a citation.

  Example: Microsoft is a developer of computer technology.

  You have not borrowed any special words, so you do not need quotation marks. And since anyone would agree with this general claim, you do not need to cite a source.

- When the content is specialized knowledge but you use either your own words or the only words that can be used, you need to cite but do not need quotation marks.

Example: Microsoft was founded in 1975 ("Microsoft at 30").

This is not a generally known fact, so you need a citation, but your words are a common way to state this plain fact, so you do not need quotation marks.

- When you use striking or biased language from a source, whether about a well-known fact or not, you need both a citation and quotation marks.

  Example: Microsoft "was founded upon an ambitious dream" in 1975 ("Microsoft at 30").

  Here, you are using Microsoft's own evocative language, so you need quotation marks—and whenever you have a quote, you need to cite the source.

The chart below summarizes this advice:

You . . .	Use Quotation Marks	Cite the Source	Do Neither
Used a **well-known fact** and **your own or ordinary language**			✓
Used a **special fact** from a source; used **your own language**		✓	
Used **the source's unique wording** (whether for a well-known or special fact)	✓	✓	

and access to large databases of student papers. These databases even contain papers submitted recently. Tweaking these papers to fit your assignment does not get past these tools, which report percentages of similarity to other works. If you are going to go to all this work to copy a paper, you might as well do the work yourself and gain the benefits.

Give Credit to All Ideas That Are Not Your Own. Not only do you need to cite exact quotes, but you also need to cite paraphrased material when the ideas come from someplace else. Changing a few words does not make an idea either original or paraphrased. Also be sure to cite charts, tables, photos, and graphics. Give credit to adapted material as well. When in doubt, cite the source.

Use Discipline and Technological Tools to Manage the Data You Gather. Some unintentional problems arise when writers cannot retrieve the information they know they have collected, leading them to cite inaccurately or falsely. While making the information-gathering phase of research easier, the Internet has made managing the vast amount of information one finds a major task. By disciplining yourself to follow strict organizing practices, you will find retrieving the information easier when you need it. If you have ever used a money management program to manage your bank accounts, you know that it makes gathering tax information and preparing your tax return much easier. Similarly, tools such as EndNote or RefWorks (presented here and in Chapter 18) help tremendously, but only if one uses the tools faithfully and with a good style guide as a reference.

Ask Your Instructor or School's Librarian When You Need Help. Both these people want to help you learn how to document appropriately. They will probably be more approachable if you have shown you have tried to find the answer to your question and if you are asking well before the final hour.

HOW TO ACKNOWLEDGE

You can acknowledge sources by citing them in the text, using one of a number of reference systems. Three of the most commonly used systems are the Chicago (*The Chicago Manual of Style*), MLA (Modern Language Association), and APA (American Psychological Association). Although they are similar, they differ somewhat in format, as you will see in the following pages. Because students tend to be most familiar with MLA format, we will review it in detail.[1] Then we will illustrate the Chicago and APA systems to note primary differences.

After you have selected a system, you must choose a method of acknowledgment. Two methods are commonly used in business: (1) parenthetical references within the text and (2) footnote references. A third method, endnote references, is sometimes used, although it appears to be losing favor. Only the first two are discussed here.

The Parenthetical Citation Method

The parenthetical method of citing sources is widely used in both academia and business. It is called "parenthetical" because it involves putting the author's last name or other identifying information in parentheses immediately following the cited material. This reference is keyed to an alphabetical reference list—variously labeled "Works Cited," "References," or "Bibliography," or given a custom-made title—that appears at the end of the document. Readers thus see a brief reference to your sources as they read your text, and, if and when they are interested in the full reference information, they go to the list of references and use your citation to find that information in the alphabetical list. The following examples in MLA format show how in-text citations and reference-list entries work together. (For a fuller discussion of how to prepare the reference list, see "The Reference List or Bibliography" on pages 640–644.)

A work with one author:

In-text citation: (Matias 47)

If you are citing the whole work, omit the page number. If you are citing more than one work by the same author, provide a short form of the title as well, as in "(Matias, *201* 47)."

Reference-list citation:

Matias, Linda. *201 Knockout Answers to Tough Interview Questions: The Ultimate Guide to Handling the New Competency-based Interview Style.* New York: AMACOM, 2009. Print.

A work with two or three authors or editors:

In-text citation: (Crandall, Parnell, and Spillan 18)

Reference-list citation:

Crandall, William Rick, John A. Parnell, and John E. Spillan. *Crisis Management in the New Strategy Landscape.* Thousand Oaks, CA: Sage, 2010. Print.

---

[1] Examples included here have been adapted to business communication from the *MLA Handbook for Writers of Research Papers*, 7th ed. (New York: MLA, 2009), print; and Diana Hacker, *Documenting Sources: A Hacker Handbooks Supplement, Diana Hacker: Research and Documentation Online*, Bedford/St. Martin's, 2009, Web, 19 July 2009.

A work with more than three authors or editors:

In-text citation: (Zhang et al. 110)

Reference-list citation:

Zhang, Allee M., et al. "Enterprise Networking Websites and Organizational Communication in Australia." *Business Communication Quarterly* 72.1 (2009): 114–119. Print.

A work by a government or corporate author:

In-text citation: (United States 2)

Reference-list citation:

United States. Small Business Administration. *Opening Small Business Opportunities: Federal Government Contracting. U.S. Small Business Administration.* US SBA, n.d. Web. 18 July 2009.

In-text citation: (IBM 7)

Reference-list citation:

IBM. *White Paper: From Reporting to Performance Management—A Roadmap. IBM.* IBM, 14 July 2009. Web. 19 July 2009.

A work with no author identified (and here, with no page numbers provided in the source):

In-text citation: ("Taiwan")

Reference-list citation:

"Taiwan." *World Encyclopedia. Oxford Reference Online Premium.* 2008. Web. 19 July 2009.

If citing more than one work in one parenthetical reference:

In-text citation: (Stolley 354; York and Klassen)

Notice that the authors for the different works are put in alphabetical order, separated by a semicolon (multiple authors for one work stay in their original order).

Reference-list citations:

Stolley, Karl. "Integrating Social Media into Existing Work Environments: The Case of Delicious." *Journal of Business and Technical Communication* 23.3 (2009): 350–371. Print.

York, Emily, and Abbey Klassen. "Getting *Social:* Four Easy Tips." *Advertising Age.* 29 June 2009: 14. Print.

In practice, you may find that it feels more natural to work your sources of information into your sentences rather than naming them in parentheses. For example, rather than write "E-learning has become a multibillion-dollar industry (Jacobs 8)," you might write "According to Jeff Jacobs, e-learning has become a multibillion-dollar industry" (8). Or, if you were citing the whole work rather than a particular page, you would not even need the parenthetical citation. The reader could still find the corresponding entry in the reference list by using the source information in the sentence—in this case, the author's name. Use your sense of good style and readability to decide whether to work the source into the sentence or to name it in parentheses.

Remember that the goal of this, or any, citation method is to enable your readers to identify, verify, and evaluate the sources of your information. At every point in your document, your reader should be able to tell exactly where the information came from. Include citations whenever you believe that the source isn't understood. If you are providing lengthy information from one source, you usually need to cite it only once per paragraph. When you move to a new paragraph, though, you should cite it again, just to confirm for your reader that you are still basing your discussion on that source.

When placing parenthetical references in your text, put them at the end of a sentence or in some other logical break in your text, and put them before any mark of punctuation that occurs there. Here are two examples:

> Palmeri observes that particular organizational contexts "will often both hinder and support the organization's writing goals" (60).

> Collaborative writing is pervasive in the workplace (Couture and Rymer; Ede and Lunsford), and it can be particularly difficult when the collaborators come from different organizational cultures (Spilka).

The Footnote Method

Footnotes are a second means used to acknowledge sources. Two types of footnotes are used in business documents: citation footnotes and discussion footnotes. The emphasis here is on the citation footnote, but the uses of the discussion footnote also will be briefly discussed.

Citation Footnotes. A common way to acknowledge sources is by footnotes; that is, the references are placed at the bottom of the page and are keyed to the text material by superscripts (raised Arabic numbers). The numbering sequence of the superscripts is consecutive—by page, by chapter, or by the whole work. The footnotes are placed inside the page layout, single-spaced, and indented or blocked just as the text is typed.

If your footnotes include the complete facts about the cited sources, then you do not need to include a bibliography unless you believe that your reader would appreciate a list of references as well. Thus, in addition to saving time and trouble for the writer, footnotes can be a convenience to business readers, keeping them from having to flip back and forth from the text to a bibliography as they read. While the latest version of MLA style excludes citation footnotes, we still recommend their use for business readers. Today's word-processing programs feature easy-to-use tools for creating superscripts and placing the footnotes at the bottom of the page.

The following lists show how you would use MLA style to create footnotes for different kinds of sources. The lists give all the possible items in an entry in the order they should appear. The items listed should be used as needed.

Note: Figure E–1 helps you identify what footnote form you need. To see the following examples in bibliographic form, consult the sample "Works Cited" list on pages 642–644.

Print Book (Hard Copy or Accessed Online)

1. *Name of the author, in normal order*. If a source has two or three authors, all are named. If a source has more than three authors, the name of the first author followed by the Latin et al. or its English equivalent "and others" may be used.

2. *Capacity of the author.* Needed only when the person named is actually not the author of the book but an editor, compiler, or the like.

3. *Chapter name.* Necessary only in the rare instances in which the chapter title helps the reader find the source.

4. *Book title.* Usually placed in italics. However, if the font used does not allow the reader to easily discriminate between italics and normal style, use underlining to help the reader see the title more clearly. But be sure to avoid underlining if the document will be posted to the Web so the reader will not confuse it with an active link.

5. *Edition.*

6. *Location of publisher.* If more than one city is listed on the title page, the one listed first should be used. If the population exceeds half a million, the name of the city is sufficient; otherwise, include both the city and the state.

Flowchart for Citing Sources in MLA Style. Start at the top and work your way down to figure out what kind of source you have and which format to use.

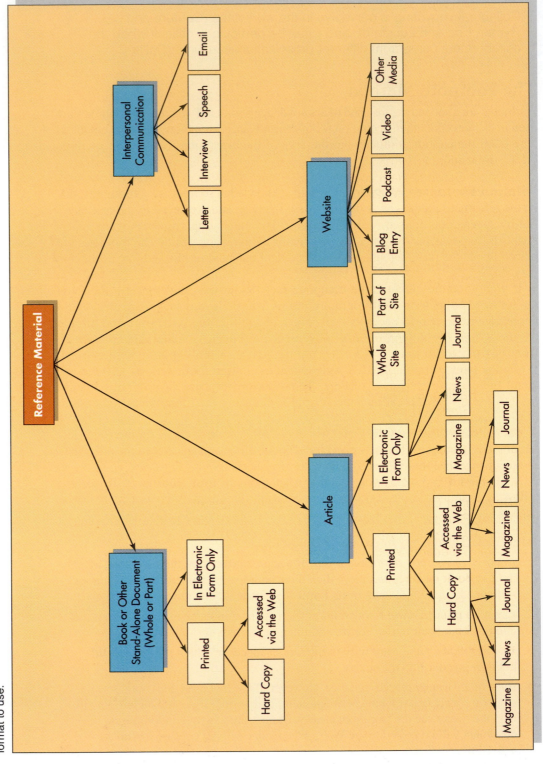

7. *Publishing company.*

8. *Date.* Year of publication. If revised, year of latest revision.

9. *Page or pages.* Specific page or inclusive pages on which the cited material is found.

If citing a hard copy, add

10. *The word "print."*

If citing a print book or document accessed online, add

10. *Title of the website,* italicized.

11. *The word "Web."*

12. *The date accessed.*

The following are examples of book entries:

Book by one to three authors:

[1]Linda Matias, *201 Knockout Answers to Tough Interview Questions: The Ultimate Guide to Handling the New Competency-based Interview Style* (New York: AMACOM, 2009) 47, print.

[1]Gwen Moran and Sue Johnson, *The Complete Idiot's Guide to Business Plans* (New York: Alpha, 2005) 7, *Safari Books Online,* Web, 19 July 2009.

[1]William Rick Crandall, John A. Parnell, and John E. Spillan, *Crisis Management in the New Strategy Landscape* (Thousand Oaks, CA: Sage, 2010) 18, print.

Book by four or more authors:

[1]Hiroyuki Odagiri et al., eds., *Intellectual Property Rights, Development, and Catch Up: An International Comparative Study* (Oxford, UK: Oxford UP, 2010) 421, print.

Edited collection (if citing the whole work):

[1]Julian Barling, E. Kevin Kelloway, and Michael R. Frone, eds., *Handbook of Work Stress* (Thousand Oaks, CA: Sage, 2005), print.

A page or pages from a specific article or chapter in an edited work:

[1]Terry A. Beehr and Sharon Glazer, "Organizational Role Stress," *Handbook of Work Stress,* ed. Julian Barling, E. Kevin Kelloway, and Michael R. Frone (Thousand Oaks, CA: Sage, 2005) 8, print.

[1]Christopher Cumo, "Economics and Trade," *Africa and the Americas: Culture, Politics, and History,* ed. Richard M. Juang and Noelle Morissette (Santa Barbara, CA: ABC-CLIO, 2008) 20, *OhioLink Scholarly & Reference E-Book Collection,* Web, 19 July 2009.

Electronic Book or Document

When citing books or documents (whole works, chapters, or sections) from the Web for which no print publication information is provided, include the first four items as you would for a print book (*author, capacity of the author, chapter name in quote marks, book/document title italicized*) and then provide the following:

5. *Page or pages* (if provided).

6. *Title of the website* (italicized).

7. Site sponsor or publisher. Use "n.p." if not evident.

8. *Date on the document.* Use "n.d." if no date is provided.

9. *The word "Web."*

10. *The date accessed.*

Here are some examples:

[1]IBM, *White Paper: From Reporting to Performance Management—A Roadmap,* 7, *IBM,* IBM, 14 July 2009, Web, 19 July 2009.

[1]United States, Small Business Administration, *Opening Small Business Opportunities: Federal Government Contracting, 2, U.S. Small Business Administration,* US SBA, n. d., Web, 18 July 2009.

[1]"Taiwan," *World Encyclopedia, Oxford Reference Online Premium,* 2008, Web, 19 July 2009.

Print Magazine, Journal, or Newspaper Article (Hard Copy or Accessed Online)

When citing a periodical article for which print publication information exists, include these elements (when available) in this order:

1. *Author name.* If no author is given, the entry may be skipped.
2. *Article title.* Typed within quotation marks.
3. *Periodical title.* Set in italics.
4. *Publication identification.* Complete date for magazines. For newspapers, complete date and edition (such as *Nat'l ed.*) For journals, volume number and issue number, followed by the year in parentheses.
5. *Page or pages* (if applicable).

If using a hard copy, add

6. *The word "print."*

If using a version accessed online, add

6. *Title of database or website* (italicized).
7. *The word "Web."*
8. *The date accessed.*

Examples of magazine, journal, and newspaper entries are shown below:

Print magazine article:

[1]Mike MacPherson, "Entrepreneurial Learning: Secret Ingredients for Business Success," *Training + Development* July 2009: 49, print.

[1]Clint Boulton, "Apps Provide the MySpace Touch," *eWeek* 21 Jan. 2008: 45, *Academic Search Complete,* Web, 19 July 2009.

Print journal article:

[1]Mary Bambacas and Margaret Patrickson, "Interpersonal Communication Skills that Enhance Organisational Commitment," *Journal of Communication Management* 12.1 (2008): 56, print.

[1]Lubomir Stoykov, "Nature and Definitions of Business Communication," *Language in India* 7.2 (2007): 31, *Communication & Mass Media Complete,* Web, 21 July 2009.

[1]Joshua Tusin, rev. of *Writing and Presenting a Business Plan,* by Carolyn A. Boulger, *Business Communication Quarterly* 69.2 (2006): 227, print.

Print newspaper article:

[1]"Corporate News: Corporate Watch," *The Wall Street Journal* 17 July 2009, Eastern ed.: B4, print.

[1]Joann S. Lublin, "Managing Your Career: When Big Résumés Chase Small Jobs," *The Wall Street Journal* 3 Mar. 2009, Eastern ed.: D6, *ProQuest,* Web, 19 July 2009.

When citing a full-text article from a database (rather than an exact visual copy of the article) that does not show where the page breaks are, just cite the full page range, as in the following example.

Full-text article from a database:

"Can Communicators Help Improve Business Performance?," *The Business Communicator* 6.7 (2005/2006): 1-2, *ProQuest,* Web, 21 July 2009.

Online Periodical Articles

When citing a magazine or news article for which no print publication information is provided, include the first three items as you would for a print article (*author, article title in quotation marks, periodical or website title in italics*) and then provide the following:

4. *Publisher or sponsor of the database or website.* If not evident, use "n.p."

5. *Date of publication* (day, month, and year if available). If no date is provided, use "n.d."

6. *The word "Web."*

7. *The date accessed.*

Here are some examples.

Article from an online magazine:

[1]Farhad Manjoo, "Down with Verdana!," *Slate.com,* Washington Post/Newsweek Interactive, 13 July 2009, Web, 19 July 2009.

Article from the companion website for a print magazine:

[1]Bob Diddlebock, "Why Businesses Are Still Giving to the Arts," *TIME,* Time, 30 Apr. 2009, Web, 19 July 2009.

[1]Jennifer Pellet, "An Upside-Down Career Path to the Top," *Chief Executive,* Butler Publishing, 8 Oct. 2008, Web, 19 July 2009.

Article from an online news source:

[1]Jessica Dickler and Steve Hargreaves, "Where the Jobs Are," *CNNMoney.com,* Cable News Network, 13 July 2009, Web, 19 July 2009.

[1]Allan Leinwand, "The Hidden Cost of the Cloud: Bandwith Charges," *Salon.com,* Salon Media Group, 17 July 2009, Web, 19 July 2009.

Article from the companion website for a print newspaper:

[1]"Local Business: Business People and Places," *Cincinnati.com,* The Enquirer, 19 July 2009, Web, 19 July 2009.

When citing an article in a scholarly journal for which there is no print counterpart (that is, the resource exists solely online), format as you would a print article but replace "print" with "Web" and add the date accessed. If there are no page numbers, put "n. pag." (no pagination) in place of the page number or numbers. Here is an example:

Journal article for which there is no print version:

[1]Holly Baumgartner and Jennifer Discher, "Disaster Pedagogy/Building Communities: From Wikis and Websites to Hammers and Nails," *Reflections: A Journal of Writing, Service-Learning, and Community Literacy* 7.2 (2008): n. pag., Web, 19 July 2009.

When citing material from a database that has no print counterpart, use the same form as you would for an online periodical article, as in the example below.

Database material with no print counterpart:

"The Procter & Gamble Company: Overview," *Hoover's Online,* Hoover's, 2009, Web, 21 July 2009.

A Website or Part of a Website

As you may have already noticed, the current MLA citation guidelines for citing electronic sources no longer include URLs (Internet addresses). One reason is that many URLs for the Web either change quickly or are password protected, which means that providing the URL often doesn't really help the reader get to the Web source. Another is that today's Internet search engines make it quite easy to find documented sources without using the URL. If you're used to typing or copying and pasting the extremely long URLs of some online sources into your documents, this will be a welcome change.

If your instructor directs you to include the URLs (web addresses) for your Web sources, though, include them at the end of each entry, in angle brackets, as in the last example below. Otherwise, include just the following items in a citation for a website or other Web-based material:

1. *Author's name* (if available).
2. *Title of the specific page or element in quotation marks* (if applicable).
3. *Title of the site* (italicized).
4. *Sponsor of the site.*
5. *Date of publication or last update* (if no date, use "n.d.").
6. *The word "Web"* (or, if downloaded, the medium, such as "MP3 file").
7. *The date accessed.*

Here are various examples:

A corporate website:

[1]*Ernst & Young,* home page, Ernst & Young Global Limited, n.d., Web, 19 July 2009.

Part of a website:

[1]"Working at Ernst & Young," *Ernst & Young,* Ernst & Young Global Limited, n.d., Web, 19 July 2009.

A part of a website for which the reader requests the URL:

[1]"Working at Ernst & Young," *Ernst & Young,* Ernst & Young Global Limited, n.d., Web, 19 July 2009 <http://www.ey.com/US/en/Careers/Students/Working-at-Ernst—Young/Working-at-Ernst—Young>.

A blog entry:

[1]Linda Hewitt, "13 Most Common Reasons Internal Communications Fail," *Talking Points,* Linda Hewitt, 29 Sept. 2008, Web, 19 July 2009.

An online map:

[1]"Budapest, Hungary," map, *Google Maps,* Google, 19 July 2009, Web, 19 July 2009.

A podcast:

[1]Debbie Davy, "Writing Better RFP Responses," *PCS Podcasts, IEEE Professional Communication Society,* IEEE Professional Communication Society, 9 Oct. 2008, Web, 19 July 2009. (If downloaded, put "MP3 file" instead of "Web.")

Online video:

[1]"Company Picnic," *The Office, Hulu.com,* Hulu, 17 May 2009, Web, 19 July 2009. (If seen on television instead, replace the items following title of the program with the network [e.g., NBC], the call letters for the local station on which the program was viewed [e.g. WNET], the city of the TV station, the date viewed, and the word "televison.")

[1]Best Buy, "The Company as Wiki," *You Tube,* You Tube, 27 Aug. 2008, Web, 19 July 2009.

A public wiki:

[1]"Food & Drinks," *International Students UK Guide,* Wetpaint: Wikis in Education, 25 May 2009, Web, 19 July 2009.

A posting to a listserv:

[1]Alex Rush, "Finding an Internship," The *EDUCAUSE Business Schools and Colleges Constituent Listserv,* EDUCAUSE, 7 Apr. 2009, Web, 19 July 2009.

An online radio program:

[1]Marilyn Geewax, "Minimum Wage Rise: More Money or Fewer Jobs?," *NPR.org,* Natl. Public Radio, 19 July 2009, Web, 19 July 2009. (If down-loaded, put "MP3 file" instead of "Web." If heard live, put "radio" after the date of broadcast and omit "Web" and the access date.)

Interpersonal Communications

Media for interpersonal communication abound in today's business environment. The following examples and those given above should enable you to create an acceptable citation for any type you wish to reference. (Note: Your reader may find it helpful if you include the author's title along with his or her name.)

A letter:

[1]Gregory H. Williams, President, University of Cincinnati, letter to the author, 5 Oct. 2009. TS. (*TS* stands for "typescript.")

An email message:

[1]Betty Johnson, Executive Director, Association for Business Communication, "Portsmouth Convention," message to the author, 15 July 2009, email.

An interview:

[1]Hans Bender, personal interview, 7 Aug. 2008.

A speech or presentation:

[1]Richard Stengel, Acceptance Speech for Honorary Degree, Wittenberg University, Springfield, IL, 16 May 2009. (If there is an actual speech title, include it, in quotation marks after the speaker's name. Add "speech" or "address" at the end of the note unless already obvious.)

[1]Deborah Roebuck, "Building Ethical Leaders from the Inside Out," Association for Business Communication Annual Meeting, Incline Village, NV, Nov. 2008, conference presentation.

The types of entries discussed in the preceding paragraphs are those most likely to be used. Yet many unusual types of resources (conference proceedings, computer programs, advertisements, patents, and others) are likely to come up. When they do, you should classify the source by the form it most closely resembles. Then you should construct the entry that describes the source completely and accurately. Label the item (e.g., *advertisement, abstract*, not italicized) if you think that will help. Because of the enormous variety of media out there, you will frequently need to improvise—to use your best judgment in determining the citation contents.

Subsequent References. Writers used to use the Latin abbreviations *Ibid.* (which means "in the same place") and *Op. cit.* ("in the work cited") to refer back to earlier footnotes. These have largely been replaced by abbreviated forms of the original foot-note entries. Usually the author's last name followed by the relevant page number is adequate for a previously cited work:

[4] Beehr and Glaser 34.

If you happen to have cited two or more works by the same author, simply add a short form of the title after the author's name to distinguish this source from the others:

[4] Beehr and Glaser, "Organization" 34.

Discussion Footnotes. A second type of footnote is the discussion footnote. Through discussion footnotes, the writer strives to explain a part of the text, to amplify the discussion of a certain topic, to make cross-references to other parts of the report, or to add other commentary. The following examples illustrate some possibilities for this footnote type.

¹ See the principle of inflection points on page 72.

Amplification of Discussion and Cross-Reference:

² Lyman Bryson says the same thing: "Every communication is different for every receiver even in the same context. No one can estimate the variation of understanding that there may be among receivers of the same message conveyed in the same vehicle when the receivers are separated in either space or time" (see *Communication of Ideas* 5).

Use such "by the way" notes sparingly; be sure you have a good reason for interrupting the reader's reading with them. When possible, work such material into the text itself, or just omit it.

PRESENTATION OF QUOTED AND PARAPHRASED INFORMATION

You may use data obtained from secondary sources in two ways. You may paraphrase the information (cast it in your own words), or you may use it verbatim (exactly as the original author worded it). In typing paraphrased material, you need not distinguish it from the remainder of the text. Material you use verbatim, however, must be clearly distinguished.

If the quoted passage is short (about 10 lines or less), place it within the text and with quotation marks before and after it. Set off longer quotations from the margins, without quotation marks, as shown in the example below. If the text is double-spaced, you may further distinguish the quoted passage by single-spacing it.

Of those opposing the issue, Logan Wilson makes this penetrating observation:

> It is a curious paradox that academicians display a scientific attitude toward every universe of inquiry except that which comprises their own profession. . . . Lacking precise qualitative criteria, administrators are prone to fall back upon rather crude quantitative measures as a partial substitute. For example, student evaluations of teachers often lack acceptable reliability and validity statistics. And when they are administered is quite illogical. Moreover, most statements on them relate to contextual factors—e.g., office hours, fairness of tests—and not to acquiring knowledge itself. Yet administrators use quantitative scores from these instruments to the minute fraction of a point to assess teaching quality. Multiple measures of teaching performance with an emphasis on student learning would bring a more rational approach to teaching as one dimension of academic responsibility. (201)

These logical, straightforward, and simple arguments of the critics of teacher evaluations appear to be irrefutable.

Frequently, you will find it best to break up or use only fragments of the quoted author's work. Because omissions may distort the meaning of a passage, you must clearly indicate them, using ellipsis points (a series of three periods typed with intervening spaces) where material is left out. If an omission begins before or after the end of a sentence, you must use four periods—one for the final punctuation plus three for the ellipsis points. A passage with such omissions is the following:

> Many companies have undertaken to centralize in the hands of specially trained correspondents the handling of the outgoing email. Usually, centralization has been accomplished by the firm's employment of a correspondence supervisor. . . . The supervisor may guide the work of correspondents . . . , or the company may employ a second technique.

In long quotations it is conventional to show omission of a paragraph or more by a full line of periods, typed with intervening spaces (see page 527, Chapter 16).

THE REFERENCE LIST OR BIBLIOGRAPHY

A bibliography is an orderly list of resources on a particular subject. Usually it provides the full reference information for sources cited in parentheses in the text, as described in the section on parenthetical citation, and is labeled "References" or "List of Works

COMMUNICATION MATTERS

Citation Management Tools: Use with Caution

As Chapter 17 points out, computerized tools for building citation lists (e.g., bibliography, list of works cited) abound. You can find such tools on the Internet, at computer stores, in your own word processing program, and even inside research databases. The top window below shows RefWorks, a widely used online citation-management program, which you may be able to access for free through your school library's website. You can import or create references here and then have RefWorks generate your bibliography from them, as shown. Below that is an illustration of the citation-creation function in *ABI/INFORM*, a ProQuest database. With this function, you can create citations in the desired citation style right from the record you're viewing (in this database, by clicking the "Cite this" link at the bottom of the

record) and then either export the citations to a program like RefWorks or copy and paste them into a document.

But a strong note of caution is in order: Such tools can be limited or misleading, and they can make mistakes. In the RefWorks example, the date of publication is correct only because the writer who entered the information into RefWorks knew to skip the *Pub year* field and enter the full date into the *Pub Date Free Form* field instead; otherwise, the year would have appeared twice in the entry. In the *ABI/INFORM* example, ProQuest's citation creator left off the pages covered by the article and mistakenly abbreviated *July*. But none of these tools is perfect. You will need to carefully check their output against a good citation handbook.

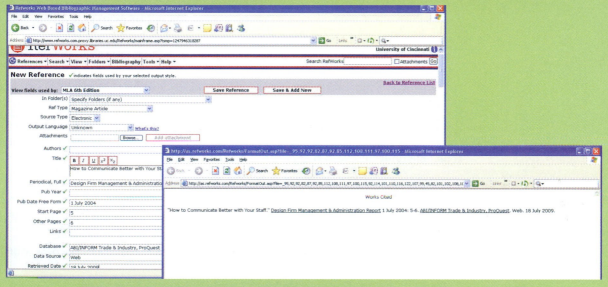

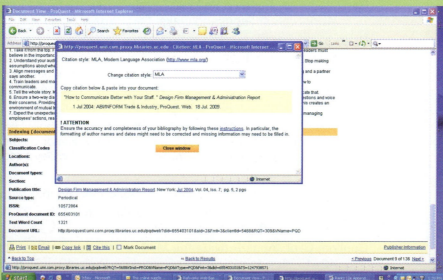

Cited." But sometimes the bibliography is itself the main information product. For example, if someone asked you to compile a list of resources on e-learning, you would prepare your findings in the form of a bibliography, probably preceded by some introductory text. And if someone asked you to provide a brief description with each entry as well, you would prepare what is known as an annotated bibliography. If your bibliography is extensive, you might precede it with a fly page containing the title ("Bibliography" or a custom title such as "List of E-learning Sources"). You could also organize your entries by category, with subheadings (for example, "Books," "Periodicals," and "Internet Resources"). If your document has an appendix, the bibliography follows it.

As with footnotes, variations in bibliographic style are numerous, but in MLA style, the information for a bibliography entry follows the order described in this chapter's section on citation footnotes (pages 633–639). There are significant differences, however, between footnote and bibliography format. The latter uses periods rather than commas between the major components of an entry. Bibliographies also have these distinguishing traits:

1. The author's name is listed in reverse order—surname first—for the purpose of alphabetizing. If an entry has more than one author, however, only the name of the first author is reversed.

2. The entry is generally presented in hanging-indention form. That is, the second and subsequent lines of an entry begin some uniform distance (usually about one-half inch) to the right of the beginning point of the first line. The purpose of this indented pattern is to make the alphabetized first line stand out.

3. The entry gives the inclusive pages of articles, but not for books, and does not refer to any one page or passage.

4. Second and subsequent references to publications of the same author are indicated by a line formed by three hyphens. But this line may be used only if the entire authorship is the same in the consecutive publications. For example, the line could not be used if consecutive entries have one common author but different coauthors.

Below is a bibliography made up of the footnote citation examples presented in this chapter. (The material in brackets at the end of each entry should *not* be included in actual citations; it is included here to identify each type of entry.)

Works Cited

Bambacas, Mary, and Margaret Patrickson. "Interpersonal Communication Skills that Enhance Organisational Commitment." *Journal of Communication Management* 12.1 (2008): 51–72. Print. [Print journal article]

Barling, Julian, E. Kevin Kelloway, and Michael R. Frone, eds. *Handbook of Work Stress.* Thousand Oaks, CA: Sage, 2005. Print. [Print collection]

Baumgartner, Holly, and Jennifer Discher. "Disaster Pedagogy/Building Communities: From Wikis and Websites to Hammers and Nails." *Reflections: A Journal of Writing, Service-Learning, and Community Literacy* 7.2 (2008): n. pag. Web. 19 July 2009. [Article in an online scholarly journal that has no print counterpart]

Beehr, Terry A., and Sharon Glazer. "Organizational Role Stress." *Handbook of Work Stress.* Ed. Julian Barling, E. Kevin Kelloway, and Michael R. Frone. Thousand Oaks, CA: Sage, 2005. 7–34. Print. [Chapter from a print collection]

Bender, Hans. Personal interview. 7 Aug. 2008. [An interview]

Best Buy. "The Company as Wiki." *You Tube.* You Tube, 27 Aug. 2008. Web. 19 July 2009. [An online video]

Boulton, Clint. "Apps Provide the MySpace Touch." *eWeek* 21 Jan. 2008: 42–45. *Academic Search Complete.* Web. 19 July 2009. [Print magazine article accessed via the Web]

"Budapest, Hungary." Map. *Google Maps.* Google, 19 July 2009. Web. 19 July 2009. [An online map]

"Can Communicators Help Improve Business Performance?" *The Business Communicator* 6.7 (2005/2006): 1-2. *ProQuest.* Web. 21 July 2009. [Full-text article from a database]

"Company Picnic." *The Office. Hulu.com.* Hulu, 17 May 2009. Web. 19 July 2009. [An online video]

"Corporate News: Corporate Watch." *The Wall Street Journal* 17 July 2009, Eastern ed.: B4. Print. [Print news article]

Crandall, William Rick, John A. Parnell, and John E. Spillan. *Crisis Management in the New Strategy Landscape.* Thousand Oaks, CA: Sage, 2010. Print. [Print book]

Cumo, Christopher. "Economics and Trade." *Africa and the Americas: Culture, Politics, and History.* Ed. Richard M. Juang and Noelle Morissette. Santa Barbara, CA: ABC-CLIO, 2008. 19–28. *OhioLink Scholarly & Reference E-Book Collection.* Web. 19 July 2009. [Chapter from a print collection accessed online]

Davy, Debbie. "Writing Better RFP Responses." *PCS Podcasts, IEEE Professional Communication Society.* IEEE Professional Communication Society, 9 Oct. 2008. Web [if downloaded, put "MP3 file" instead]. 19 July 2009. [A podcast]

Dickler, Jessica, and Steve Hargreaves. "Where the Jobs Are." *CNNMoney. com.* Cable News Network, 13 July 2009. Web. 19 July 2009. [Article from an online news source]

Diddlebock, Bob. "Why Businesses Are Still Giving to the Arts." *TIME.* Time, 30 Apr. 2009. Web. 19 July 2009. [Article from the companion website for a print magazine]

Ernst & Young. Home page. Ernst & Young Global Limited, n.d. Web. 19 July 2009. [A corporate website]

"Food & Drinks." *International Students UK Guide.* Wetpaint: Wikis in Education, 25 May 2009. Web. 19 July 2009. [A public wiki]

Geewax, Marilyn. "Minimum Wage Rise: More Money or Fewer Jobs?" *NPR.org.* Natl. Public Radio, 19 July 2009. Web. 19 July 2009. [An online radio program]

Hewitt, Linda. "13 Most Common Reasons Internal Communications Fail." *Talking Points.* Linda Hewitt, 29 Sept. 2008. Web. 19 July 2009. [A blog entry]

IBM. *White Paper: From Reporting to Performance Management—A Roadmap. IBM.* IBM, 14 July 2009. Web. 19 July 2009. [Electronic document]

Johnson, Betty. "Portsmouth Convention." Message to the author. 15 July 2009. Email. [An email message]

Leinwand, Allan. "The Hidden Cost of the Cloud: Bandwith Charges." *Salon.com.* Salon Media Group, 17 July 2009. Web. 19 July 2009. [Article from an online news source]

"Local Business: Business People and Places." *Cincinnati.com.* The Enquirer, 19 July 2009. Web. 19 July 2009. [Article from the companion website for a print newspaper]

Lublin, Joann S. "Managing Your Career: When Big Résumés Chase Small Jobs." *The Wall Street Journal* 3 Mar. 2009, Eastern ed.: D6, *ProQuest.* Web. 19 July 2009. [Print news article accessed online]

MacPherson, Mike. "Entrepreneurial Learning: Secret Ingredients for Business Success." *Training + Development* July 2009: 46-51. Print. [Print magazine article]

Manjoo, Farhad. "Down with Verdana!" *Slate.com.* Washington Post/ Newsweek Interactive, 13 July 2009. Web. 19 July 2009. [Article from an online magazine]

Matias, Linda. *201 Knockout Answers to Tough Interview Questions: The Ultimate Guide to Handling the New Competency-based Interview Style.* New York: AMACOM, 2009. Print. [Print book]

Moran, Gwen, and Sue Johnson. *The Complete Idiot's Guide to Business Plans.* New York: Alpha, 2005. *Safari Books Online.* Web. 19 July 2009. [Print book accessed online]

Odagiri, Hiroyuki et al., eds. *Intellectual Property Rights, Development, and Catch Up: An International Comparative Study.* Oxford, UK: Oxford UP, 2010. Print. [Print book, more than three editors]

Pellet, Jennifer. "An Upside-Down Career Path to the Top." *Chief Executive.* Butler Publishing, 8 Oct. 2008. Web. 19 July 2009. [Article from the companion website for a print magazine]

"The Procter & Gamble Company: Overview." *Hoover's Online.* Hoover's, 2009. Web. 21 July 2009. [Material from a database with no print counterpart]

Roebuck, Deborah. "Building Ethical Leaders from the Inside Out." Association for Business Communication Annual Meeting. Incline Village, NV. Nov. 2008. Conference presentation. [A presentation]

Rush, Alex. "Finding an Internship." *The EDUCAUSE Business Schools and Colleges Constituent Listserv.* EDUCAUSE, 7 Apr. 2009. Web. 19 July 2009. [A posting to a listserv]

Stengel, Richard. Acceptance Speech for Honorary Degree. Wittenberg University, Springfield, IL. 16 May 2009. [A speech]

Stoykov, Lubomir. "Nature and Definitions of Business Communication." *Language in India* 7.2 (2007): 2-37. *Communication & Mass Media Complete.* Web. 21 July 2009. [Print journal article accessed via the Web]

"Taiwan." *World Encyclopedia, Oxford Reference Online Premium.* 2008. Web. 19 July 2009. [Article from an electronic reference work]

Tusin, Joshua. Rev. of *Writing and Presenting a Business Plan,* by Carolyn A. Boulger. *Business Communication Quarterly* 69.2 (2006): 226–229. Print. [Print book review]

United States. Small Business Administration. *Opening Small Business Opportunities: Federal Government Contracting. U.S. Small Business Administration.* US SBA, n. d., Web. 18 July 2009. [Electronic document]

"Working at Ernst & Young." *Ernst & Young.* Ernst & Young Global Limited, n.d. Web. 19 July 2009. [Part of a website]

"Working at Ernst & Young." *Ernst & Young.* Ernst & Young Global Limited, n.d. Web. 19 July 2009 <http://www.ey.com/US/en/Careers/Students/ Working-at-Ernst—Young/Working-at-Ernst—Young>. [Part of a website. Provide URL only at reader's request.]

Zimpher, Nancy. Letter to the author. 5 Mar. 2009. TS. [A letter]

DIFFERENCES BETWEEN MLA, CHICAGO, AND APA FORMATS

As noted previously, the Chicago and APA systems differ somewhat from the MLA style presented in preceding pages. The MLA style seems to be the most up to date on popular electronic media, and because it excludes URLs, it has the simplest format for citing online material. The APA favors current scholarly research, especially in the sciences, while the Chicago style gives the most formatting options.

The business field does not have its own citation style. Therefore, you should choose, or even devise, one that will suit your purpose and audience best.

The primary differences among the MLA, Chicago, and APA formats are shown in the following illustrations.

Parenthetical Citation

MLA: (Solomon, Taylor, and Tyler 60)

Chicago: (Solomon, Taylor, and Tyler 2006, 60)

APA: (Solomon, Taylor, & Tyler, 2006, p. 60)

Footnote—Book

MLA:

[1]Amy Solomon, Terry Taylor, and Lori Tyler, *100% Job Search Success* (Clifton Park, NY: Thomson Delmar Learning, 2006) 60, print.

Note: As pointed out on page 633, MLA style no longer includes citation footnotes. Nevertheless, we still recommend their use as a convenience to business readers.

Chicago:

[1]Amy Solomon, Terry Taylor, and Lori Tyler, *100% Job Search Success* (Clifton Park, NY: Thomson Delmar Learning, 2006), 60.

APA:

(Does not use citation footnotes)

Footnote—Periodical:

MLA:

[1]Kathryn Yates, "Internal Communication Effectiveness Enhances Bottom-line Results," *Journal of Organizational Excellence* 25.3 (2006): 71, print.

Chicago:

[1]Kathryn Yates, "Internal Communication Effectiveness Enhances Bottom-line Results," *Journal of Organizational Excellence* 25, no. 3 (2006): 71.

APA:

(Does not use citation footnotes)

Bibliography Entry—Print Book

MLA:

Crandall, William Rick, John A. Parnell, and John E. Spillan. *Crisis Management in the New Strategy Landscape.* Thousand Oaks, CA: Sage, 2010. Print.

Chicago:

Crandall, William Rick, John A. Parnell, and John E. Spillan. *Crisis Management in the New Strategy Landscape.* Thousand Oaks, CA: Sage, 2010.

Note: In Chicago style, the bibliography entries for the footnotes–bibliography citation method differ considerably from those created for the parenthetical citations–reference list style. The entry above is for the former system (used with footnotes). With parenthetical citations, it would look like this:

Crandall, William Rick, John A. Parnell, and John E. Spillan. 2010. *Crisis Management in the New Strategy Landscape.* Thousand Oaks, CA: Sage.

APA:

Crandall, W. R., Parnell, J. A., & Spillan, J. E. (2010). *Crisis management in the new strategy landscape.* Thousand Oaks, CA: Sage.

Bibliography Entry—Print Periodical Article Found Online:

MLA:

Yates, Kathryn. "Internal Communication Effectiveness Enhances Bottom-line Results." *Journal of Organizational Excellence* 25.3 (2006): 71–79. *Business Source Complete.* Web. 21 July 2009.

Chicago:

Yates, Kathryn. "Internal Communication Effectiveness Enhances Bottom-line Results." *Journal of Organizational Excellence* 25, no. 3 (Summer 2006): 71–79. <http://web.ebscohost.com/ehost/pdf?vid=2&hid=9&sid= e0a7c37a-c1ae-4be8-bbd1-b20a60f4cf87%40sessionmgr11>

With the parenthetical citations–reference list method, the Chicago entry would look like this:

Yates, Kathryn. 2006. Internal communication effectiveness enhances bottom-line results. *Journal of Organizational Excellence* 25, no. 3 (Summer): 71–79. <http://web.ebscohost.com/ehost/pdf?vid=2&hid=9&sid= e0a7c37a-c1ae-4be8-bbd1-b20a60f4cf87%40sessionmgr11>

APA:

Yates, K. (2006). Internal communication effectiveness enhances bottom-line results. *Journal of Organizational Excellence,* 25(3), 71–79. Retrieved from <http://proquest.umi.com/pqdweb?did=1044699851&sid=1&Fmt= 2&clientId=5468&RQT=309&VName=PQD>

Note: APA recommends using the Digital Object Identifier (DOI), if possible, when citing all electronic sources. The DOI is a long number that serves as a more stable identifier than a URL. If the source has a DOI, it will be on the electronic record for the source. Your readers can then use this number to find the source on the Internet and/or in research databases. If there is no DOI, provide the stable URL—the one provided by the database—as in the example above.

Bibliography Entry—Online Reference Work:

MLA:

"Taiwan." *World Encyclopedia, Oxford Reference Online Premium.* 2008. Web. 19 July 2009.

Chicago:

World Encyclopedia, Oxford Reference Online Premium. 2008.

Note: In Chicago, in both the footnotes–bibliography and the parenthetical citations–reference list method, the article title ("Taiwan"), the URL for the source, and the date accessed would be provided in the footnote or parenthetical citation, along with the encyclopedia title.

APA:

"Taiwan." (2008). In *World encyclopedia, Oxford reference online premium.* Retrieved from <http://www.oxfordreference.com/views/ SEARCH_RESULTS.html?y=5&q=Taiwan&category=t142&x=10&ssid= 164711131&scope=book&time=0.0230955674432245>

Bibliography Entry—Blog Posting

MLA:

Hewitt, Linda. "13 Most Common Reasons Internal Communications Fail." *Talking Points.* Linda Hewitt, 29 Sept. 2008. Web. 19 July 2009.

Chicago:

(Not usually included in the bibliography. The footnote or parenthetical citation would include the author name, title of posting, title of blog, the date the entry was posted, the URL, and the access date.)

APA:

Hewitt, L. (2008, 29 September). 13 most common reasons internal communications fail [Web log posting]. Retrieved from <http://www .lgh-talking-points.com/>

Whatever system you decide to use, use only one within a document and always be complete, accurate, and consistent.

PHOTO CREDITS

INDEX

Page numbers followed by n refer to footnotes.

649

Woog, Dan, 39
Woolliams, Peter, 498n
Word choice, 24–44
  acronym, 29
  active/passive voice, 32–34
  camouflaged verbs, 34–35
  cliché, 29
  concrete words, 30–32
  familiar words, 27
  gender-neutral language, 37–39
  nondiscriminatory writing, 36–40
  positive effect, 75–77
  precise meanings, 35–36
  sentence structure, 51–54
  short words, 28
  slang, 29
  stereotyping, 40
  technical words, 29–30

Word mechanics. *See* Correctness of communication
Word plurals, 540–541
Word use, 537–538
Works cited, 642–644
WorldCom, 6
Writing process, 88–93
  analyzing/organizing information, 91
  analyzing the audience, 89–90
  drafting, 91–92
  form, channel, format, 91
  gathering information, 90–91
  goals, 89
  planning the message, 88–91
  revising, 92
Wrong way. *See* Contrasting examples
Wrong word, 538
Wycoff, Joyce, 364n

Y

Yate, Martin, 292n
You-viewpoint, 73–75
Yunxia, Zhu, 217

Z

Zatyko, Don, 4
Zemanta, 560
Zhao, Jensen J., 508n
Zikmund, William G., 589n
Zupek, Rachel, 459